The Other Side of Knowledge

The Other Side of Nowhere

JAZZ, IMPROVISATION, AND
COMMUNITIES IN DIALOGUE

EDITED BY DANIEL FISCHLIN
AND AJAY HEBLE

WESLEYAN UNIVERSITY PRESS

Middletown, Connecticut

Published by Wesleyan University Press, Middletown, CT 06459
© 2004 by Wesleyan University Press
All rights reserved
Printed in the United States of America
5 4 3 2 1

"Paracritical Hinge" is reprinted from Mackey, Nathaniel.
Paracritical Hinge: Essays, Talks, Notes. Reprinted by
permission of The University of Wisconsin Press.

Library of Congress Cataloging-in-Publication Data

The other side of nowhere : jazz, improvisation, and communities in
dialogue / edited by Daniel Fischlin and Ajay Heble.— 1st ed.
    p.   cm. — (Music/culture)
Includes bibliographical references (p.   ) and index.
ISBN 0–8195–6681–0 (alk. paper) — ISBN 0–8195–6682–9 (pbk. : alk. paper)
1. Jazz—History and criticism. 2. Improvisation (Music)—History and
criticism. 3. Jazz—Social aspects. I. Fischlin, Daniel. II. Heble, Ajay, 1961–
III. Series.
ML3506.068 2004
781.65—dc22   2003019192

For Martha and Sheila

without whom . . .

Contents

‿

Preface

✦

Since 1994 the Guelph Jazz Festival has been bringing musicians, scholars, critics, and listeners of experimental jazz improvisation together for life-giving weekends of sound and dialogue. This volume encapsulates the spirit of the festival, including as it does the voices of many who have performed at, spoken at, or attended these extraordinary events (I was fortunate enough to have been one of the speakers in 1999). Although it is commonplace to celebrate the dialogic and interdisciplinary implications of jazz improvisation and history, very few books actually "practice what they preach" as well as *The Other Side of Nowhere*. Daniel Fischlin and Ajay Heble have assembled a remarkable group of essays that substantially advance discussion in jazz studies in several dimensions, with particular attention to experimentalism in jazz and the place of women.

For many years there has been scant attention to the legacy of free jazz, or what many authors in this volume prefer to call experimental improvisational music. The hostility toward free jazz expressed by many advocates of jazz neoclassicism—Wynton Marsalis most visibly—created in the 1980s and 1990s a climate in which expressions of African-American aesthetic principles that refused to be confined by tonality or traditional formal structures were regularly demonized as incompetent, not black enough, or overinfluenced by a European concept of avant-garde. No one who reads George Lewis's contribution on Afrological and Eurological perspectives in improvised music after 1950 can maintain this simplistic narrative about jazz experimentalism. Lewis documents the impact of jazz improvisation on the Euro-American and European classical avant-garde and the tendency for classical composers to deny and trivialize the influence of African-American aesthetics on their work. What Lewis calls an "ongoing narrative of dismissal" can be seen in the ways the impact of improvisation on John Cage and many others has been denied or transmogrified by the use of words like "indeterminacy" and "aleatory" in place of the word "improvisation." Rather than view experimentalism in jazz as some kind of concession to the hegemony of Euro-American art music, Lewis illustrates why the relationship of experimental jazz improvisation to classical music is far more complex. The essays by Michael Dessen and Jason Stanyek extend the understanding of experimentalism in jazz by focusing on African diasporic collaborations and their implications for thinking through issues of globalization, interculturalism, transnationalism, and spirituality in contemporary music. These essays illustrate that, far from distancing themselves from issues of relationship to African and African-American tradition and history, contemporary African diasporic intercultural collaborations demonstrate how experimental projects can lead to more expansive understandings of the relationships among history, racial oppression, and community building through music.

If the social construction of the community through music is a major theme in both Dessen's and Stanyek's essays, Sherrie Tucker reminds us that the history of jazz also includes dynamics of exclusion and marginalization. In a music that has prided itself on its universal liberatory possibilities, jazz has been remarkably resistant to the full participation of women, especially as instrumentalists. Through exploring how the category of "women-in-jazz" frequently manages to construct the experience of being "women-out-of jazz," Tucker breaks new ground by thinking of women who improvise as a borderland community in Gloria Anzaldúa's sense: a group without unified core that somehow manages to negotiate multiple modes of insider-/outsiderness. The key theoretical move is recognizing that there are multiple modalities of membership possible in "communities" as complex as the jazz world: not simply members and nonmembers, as Tucker wittily puts it, but "affiliate members, unwelcome members, untenured members, unauthorized members, founding members." If there are various degrees of membership, the task of women has been to negotiate a space of possibility within a larger jazz community that finds all women bands laughable and where women themselves often cringe at being overidentified as a member of their gender, especially when their identities are cross-cut by other dimensions of difference, such as race, sexuality, class, and ethnicity.

The coping mechanisms that women improvisers use to carry on in the face of insulting comments and dismissive attitudes is most poignantly illustrated in Pauline Oliveros's essay, which charts her trajectory as a simultaneous insider/outsider to the many musical scenes that she was a part of from the 1950s to the present. There is no bitterness here, no angry pointing of fingers, no cursing of the patriarchal order of things, but something more devastating: a matter-of-fact description of moments of sexist betrayal (as she calls them—when men reveal their gendered presumptions about the musical creativity of women) and her creative responses to them. From finding communities of sympathetic male and female performers to creating a nonprofit foundation to support her creative and educational endeavors, Oliveros, like most women with a deep commitment to improvisation, exemplifies creative perseverance.

Another theme addressed in this volume is sexuality, a topic often avoided in jazz studies. Julie Smith's exploration of the London-based Feminist Improvising Group (which provided a space of support for women improvisers and celebrated lesbian sexuality) situates this predominantly white and lesbian group within the larger interplay among race, gender, class, and sexuality. The participatory musical processes of improvisation and the liberatory ideals of African-American musical traditions were transformed and adapted to the particular kinds of alienation and oppression facing lesbian women in the 1970s. Unlike many American groups of the same period the FIG made attempts to address both feminist concerns and racial politics; as Smith notes, however, the emphasis on "micropolitics" in the consciousness-raising movement was often at the expense of race, which resulted in an environment that drew few women of African descent. Smith's critical look at the FIG accomplishes both a validation of the community created through the group and a larger analysis of the place of gender and sexuality in larger matrix variables including race, class, and aesthetics.

Although this volume includes essays on both race and gender, for the most part they reside side by side without fully engaging each other (with some notable exceptions, including Tucker's and Gabbard's). This is no criticism of either the individual authors or the editors, but a commentary on the state of the discourse in the field. An actual call and response among perspectives that leads to new analytical understandings of the gendered dimensions of racism and the racial dimensions of gender remains elusive for us all. Krin Gabbard's essay breaks new interpretive ground by pondering the impact of jazz and African-American models of masculinity and sensuality on the development of Marlon Brando's acting style of the 1950s. Brando's brief stint as a drummer, his relationship to Haitian music, and his tendency toward interracial romance, provide Gabbard with biographical details that richly support his larger argument about the interrelationship among bebop aesthetics, black masculinity, and the development of method acting. Indeed, work on masculinity in jazz seems crucial to explaining why the jazz world continues to reproduce itself as a gynophobic environment. Gender also challenges the truthfulness of the modernist aesthetics of jazz:

despite the constant refrain among jazz aficionados that "nothing matters but the music," Gabbard's essay illustrates the historical importance of racialized masculine style in the white male imaginary. It is no wonder that women find they have little symbolic capital no matter how well they play.

Any thematic description of the essays in this volume is bound to fall short, as each essay comprises a constellation of themes. To the themes of free jazz, race, and gender, could be added Mark Anthony Neal's discussion of jazz and hip hop as social improvisation, Michael Jarrett's fine oral history of jazz recording production, Marshall Soules's analysis, via jazz and theater, of "protocols of improvisation," Nathaniel Mackey's boundary-crossing, improvisatory fiction, Dana Reason's deployment of the idea of "navigable structures" in real-time audience and performer interaction, Michael Dessen's discussion of spirituality in the work of Steve Coleman, and Eddie Prévost's interrogation of class and race in "Discourse of a Dysfunctional Drummer." The individual essays begin with an improviser's/ composer's—Michael Snow's—thoughts on the nature of beginnings and finish with John Corbett's meditation on the possibility of conclusive non-endings, providing an open-ended frame that challenges us (as does the anthology's distinctive bibliography of suggested readings) to keep our discussions flowing beyond the boundaries of the text.

What most distinguishes this volume, however, is the plurality of voices included: musicians, novelists, academics (from several disciplines), as well as musician-scholars, a novelist–literary critic, literary theorists–jazz festival producers, and so forth. Indeed, the world of improvisational music seems to encourage the wearing of multiple hats. The variety of voices represented here is not an accident, not artificially constructed by principles of representation, but the fruit of a long history and praxis of bringing musicians and writers together for face-to-face engagement in both words and music at the Guelph Jazz Festival. How sweet it would be if there were more events like it. I hope the American jazz community will raise thunderous applause to the expansive musical vision that resides in Canada—exemplified in the Guelph Jazz Festival's unique colloquy of different voices as represented in this book.

Ingrid Monson
Quincy Jones Professor of African-American Music
Harvard University

Acknowledgments

One of the most powerful arguments to emerge from the essays collected here is that jazz and improvised music have, in their most provocative historical instances, been largely about building purposeful communities of interest and involvement. In editing this book, we have benefited tremendously from the remarkable generosity and commitment of a genuine community of friends, scholars, musicians, students, arts presenters, and civic activists. For many years now, members of this ever-expanding community have been gathering annually under the auspices of the Guelph Jazz Festival colloquium, a unique educational and outreach initiative associated with a festival that has itself sought to showcase the ways in which improvised music can reinvigorate public life with the spirit of dialogue and collaboration. We extend our thanks to members of our colloquium committee—particularly Frederique Arroyas, Ric Knowles, Belinda Leach, Howard Spring, and Jesse Stewart—for their continuing advice and support. Thanks, as well, to Julie Hastings, the Guelph Jazz Festival's executive director, and to Ross Butler, the president of the board of directors, for their fabulous behind-the-scenes work. Our gratitude, too, to all the keynote speakers and panelists who have presented papers at the Guelph Jazz Festival colloquium. Many of those papers appear in revised form in this collection.

Huge thanks also to all the graduate research assistants who have worked so energetically on this project from its very inception. Melisa Brittain, Corina David, Ben Lefebvre, Cory Legassic, Linda Rodenburg, Emily Sanford, and Bart Vautour gave the project extraordinary care through the various stages of its production.

Jesse Stewart's support deserves special mention here. In addition to being a member of the colloquium committee, Jesse worked for us as a graduate research assistant for several semesters. His exemplary scholarship, his knowledge of the music, and his critical acumen enabled him to commit to the project as if it were his own. We extend our heartfelt thanks to him for his extraordinary support.

Our thanks to the Research Development Initiatives program of the Social Sciences and Humanities Research Council of Canada for providing a generous multiyear grant in support of our work. This grant, especially in an era of diminishing support for humanities research, was crucial in enabling us to pay stipends for graduate students and fees for colloquium speakers. We also acknowledge the help we have received from the Centre for Cultural Studies/Centre d'études sur la culture at the University of Guelph; in particular, we thank the Centre's director, Christine Bold, for her vision and commitment. We acknowledge, too, the generous funding received for the colloquium over the years from the Lloyd Carr-Harris Foundation, as well as the support we have consistently received from the College of Arts at the University of Guelph, and from the Macdonald Stewart Art Centre. We specifically thank Alan Shepard and Jacqueline Murray, respectively the director of the School of English and Theatre Studies and the dean of the College of Arts, for contributing so significantly to the unique research and pedagogical atmosphere at the institution in which we both work that has made this sort of book venture possible.

This book has been in the offing for many years. We thank all of our contributors for sticking with us through this long period. Thanks also to the staff at Wesleyan University Press, especially to our editor, Suzanna Tamminen, and to Leonora Gibson. We are also grateful to have received the support of the Music/Culture series editors: George Lipsitz, Susan McClary, and Robert Walser. The anonymous readers who commented on our manuscript offered helpful suggestions. The resulting book is, without doubt, much better than it would have been without their comments.

Thanks to our friends and colleagues who have been a constant source of strength and encouragement during our work on this project. In particular, we acknowledge the support we have received from Adwoa and Fulé Badoe, Gregor Campbell, George Lewis, Judith Nasby, Paul Salmon, Gillian Siddall, Tim Struthers, and Scott Thomson. An earlier (and abridged) version of the introduction to this book was presented at the University of Windsor, through the support of the Department of English and the Social Justice Steering Committee. Special thanks to Darryl Whetter.

Finally, and as always, we thank our amazing families. Everything we do continues to be enriched and sustained by their remarkable love, wisdom, and generosity. Our love and appreciation go to our parents, and to Martha, Damian, Hannah, Zoë, and Esmé, and Sheila, Maya, and Kiran.

The Other Side of Nowhere

DANIEL FISCHLIN AND AJAY HEBLE

The Other Side of Nowhere
Jazz, Improvisation, and
Communities in Dialogue

African-American performance has been a site for the imagination of future possibilities.
—bell hooks

There Are Other Worlds (They Have Not Told You Of)
—Sun Ra

᛫ᴗ

"Somewhere else on the other side of nowhere," muses jazz innovator and Astro-Black philosopher Sun Ra in the 1980 documentary *Sun Ra: A Joyful Noise,* "there's another place." When we chose the title, "The Other Side of Nowhere"—first for the 1998 Guelph Jazz Festival colloquium on improvisation and cultural theory, and later for this book, which emerged out of that colloquium—we took it for granted that the title was our own invention: our metaphor for the alternative sound-world of improvised music making, and perhaps more notably, for the new kinds of social relationships articulated in a music that, while seeming to come out of nowhere, has profoundly gifted us with the capacity to edge beyond the limits of certainty, predictability, and orthodoxy. Little did we know Sun Ra had coined the phrase before us. Moreover, as a referent for the very uncertainty that is itself a form of knowing—something that Ra articulates in his subversive (and witty) notion that "knowledge is laughable when attributed to a human being" (*Sun Ra: A Joyful Noise*)—the "other side of nowhere" challenges easy truisms about the kind of musical knowing that improvisation articulates. Ra emphatically states that his music, so dependent on staging differing forms of improvisation, speaks of "unknown things."

And he links such statements to the more metaphysical notion that it is the unknown one needs to know "in order to survive," a phrase to which we return in relation to the work of improviser William Parker, whose own musical community is predicated on the notion that "in order to survive, we must keep hope alive" (*The Peach Orchard,* liner notes).

Improvisatory practice summons forth that other side of knowing so crucial to Ra's musical theories. These theories cannot be dissociated from the intertwined social theories that Ra espouses in relation to being black in America or from the formation of alternative community structures that link improvised music with the kinds of liberatory cultural practices that also radically resituate history. This liberatory aspect of the rich and varied practices associated with the larger global contexts for musical improvisation generally is the subject of this book. The linkages between improvisation as a social practice within a particular historical lineage that culminates in African-American musickings (especially those grouped, however loosely, under the rubric of the cultural signifier "jazz") and alternative social spaces of engagement and resistance have, with few exceptions, yet to be studied, let alone historicized, to the degree they deserve. "My story," as Ra puts it in *A Joyful Noise,* "is not part of history." Sun Ra is but one example in a rich tradition of jazz improvisers whose musical practices (bound as they are to larger visions of social relations) overwrite, resist, and confound both conventional musical practices and the orthodox social structures those practices reflect. Hence, in this book we have deliberately sought to address a limited number of aspects to a large and complex field of cultural practices incorporated in the notion of improvisation. We recognize that we have not been able to address all forms of global improvisation and all the cultural sites in which improvisation occurs. Moreover, we are well aware that many of these other practices (classical Indian music, for example, in which improvisation plays a crucial role) do not necessarily align themselves with antihegemonic resistance or critical strategies of alternative community building. Neither do all minority communities in which improvisation is practiced necessarily exist in opposition to dominant social structures, nor is all musical improvisation necessarily rooted in alternative communities and activist practices. Nonetheless, with all these qualifications in place and in particular relation to significant (if underrecognized) strains of jazz musickings, we would argue there to be an identifiable and radical form of improvisational practices in which concepts of alternative community formation, social activism, rehistoricization of minority cultures, and critical modes of resistance and dialogue are in evidence and worthy of the kind of attention they get in this book.

In writing about (and editing this collection of essays on) a wide range of improvisatory musical practices, we follow improviser, trombonist, composer, and educator George Lewis's description, from his landmark essay on improvised music after 1950 (joined in this volume by a new essay that revisits the theme). Improvised music, Lewis suggests, is best understood as "a social location inhabited by a considerable number of present-day musicians, coming from diverse cultural backgrounds and musical practices, who have chosen to make improvisation a central part of their musical discourse. Individual improvisers are now able to reference an intercultural establishment of techniques, styles, aesthetic attitudes, antecedents, and networks of cultural and social practice." We are, in this introduction, particularly interested in exploring the complex and varied ways in which improvised music might be understood in relation to what Lewis calls "networks of cultural and social practice." In this regard, the work of African-American pianist and community activist Horace Tapscott provides a compelling example. Tapscott's memoir, *Songs of the Unsung,* discusses the kinds of motivations that led to a series of community-based improvisational groups, in particular, the Pan-Afrikan Peoples Arkestra and the Underground Musicians Association (UGMA):

People got involved with the Arkestra like it was their life's work. They got serious about it. Having a group of people who were trying to preserve, develop, teach, and enlighten was very important. And it was important that the group got together so everyone could speak their minds, and that they put something down on paper, made some kind of sound together, made some kind of point. *So with that kind of musical activity going on inside, it attracted quite a few people, an intense group of people committed to our goal, people with personalities who didn't want to just complain but wanted to find solutions to problems around us, wanted to cut through the shit.* These were the kind of people I wanted to be around. (87; our emphasis)

Tapscott goes on to explain how UGMA's music was "underground," "because the music we played wasn't accepted on top of the ground" and how that underground music, born of the desire to "preserve black music" was thought to be wild, weird, crazy, and ultimately racist: "Because we played and talked about being black, about Africa, about preserving our culture, it scared them. In the early 1960s, no one was talking about these things. So we were called 'those racist cats playing hate music.' Well, I used that phrase because that's the way I saw it. It was called preserving black music by playing it and writing it and taking it to the community. This had nothing to do with hate" (87–88). These passages from one of the most preeminent African-American artists to articulate a musical philosophy in which both improvisation and community making are foregrounded suggest that the politicized aesthetics of improvisatory "wild" musical practices evident in UGMA were profoundly integrated with a unique and energizing communitarian vision. Tapscott's (and his fellow musicians') intensity of commitment and genuine desire to act upon the community and its problems (rather than to offer distanced, disengaged critique) cannot be easily removed from the musical discourses that articulated their intensity and the transgressiveness of their desire to address community needs.

Comments by American trumpeter (and jazz *bricoleur,* as Gene Santoro calls him) Dave Douglas, in relation to *Witness,* a large ensemble recording based on Edward Said's *Representations of the Intellectual* and work by other social activists (the Ruckus Society, Mawal El Saadawi, Eqbal Ahmad, Nahguib Mahfouz, Taslima Nasrin, Pramoedya Ananta Toer, and Ken Saro-Wiwa) speak directly to the relationship among improvised music, social justice, and activist practices that occur in the name of community. Douglas's liner notes explicitly cite Said as "a guiding light for my work on this project." Moreover, he locates the inception of the Witness project with his being "on an Italian train near the Yugoslav border" while reading about the predictable rise of stocks "of American weapons makers during the NATO assault on Yugoslavia" and being aware that "not far away, half a million people were camped in a muddy field without much hope of escaping, or of going home" (*Witness,* liner notes). Douglas's anecdote recalls Charles Mingus's story of playing "Faubus" and "Remember Rockefeller at Attica" in Yugoslavia where "this U.S. Embassy cat came running up and told me not to play songs with titles like that. I told him, 'You know, man, we're from a free country. We're supposed to show people over here how great our country is by telling them we're able to talk about the wrongs and the rights of our country, whereas they're not allowed to.' He wasn't nasty, but he sounded like he forgot he was from America" (*Blues & Politics: Mingus Big Band,* liner notes). Both Douglas and Mingus herald the improviser as a site for locating resistant critiques, iterative consciences that directly address injustice, the meaning of democratic values (often in so-called democratic spaces where those values have been forgotten or lie dormant), and the transcultural importance of these sorts of resistances. As Mingus eloquently (and presciently) put it in talking about where his sense of allegiance lay: "I pledge allegiance to the United States of America. I pledge allegiance to see that someday they will live up to their own promises, to the victims that they call citizens. Not just the black ghettos, but the white ghettos and the Japanese ghettos, the Chinese ghettos, all the ghettos in the world. Oh I pledge allegiance alright—I could pledge a whole lot of allegiance! You think I'm jiving?" (*Blues & Politics: Mingus Big Band,* liner notes).

Elsewhere, Douglas has argued persuasively about the relations among aesthetic experimentation, "community spirit and activism":

The music, just like the culture and the society, has retreated from experimentation quite a bit, retreated into entertainment. And yet I think—and I don't want to over-generalize—that in the American improvised idiom there's been a lot of awareness of other art forms—dance, poetry, and so on—but also of politics/social justice movements and the like. But that awareness has been muted in the way it's been able to speak. Over a period of time it became much harder to make any kind of statement in art itself. While we're seeing things like Ani DiFranco and Steve Earle, and even Springsteen making statements in song, for those of us who are instru-mentalists and dancers and even novelists in the United States it's been harder to make any kind of impact. The resurgence of community spirit and activism in the wake of 9/11 has made that easier to do, in some ways. (Quoted in Santoro, 36)

Douglas asks the pertinent questions: "How do you protest a system that co-opts and marginalizes almost every unique and original thought that confronts it? And how do you stay silent" (*Witness,* liner notes). Impro-vised music and free jazz represent one way out of this nowhere in which co-optation and commodification compromise dissonant critique or what Nathaniel Mackey calls "discrepant engagement." Though largely silent in terms of its broader recognition by mass culture, improvised music locates some of the social energies most articulate in sustaining both its originality and its capacity to remain un–co-opted (though largely still marginalized).[1]

Douglas's interrogative paradox gives rise to the further paradox this book explores: out of the musical form most associated (however incor-rectly) with the virtuosic self engaged in a struggle to be individual over and above anything else comes the musical form that addresses the matter of community in the most compelling of ways. The paradox is profoundly tied to the experience of African-Americans and the music they forged out of their experience in bondage as slaves, where even the possession and playing of drums was prohibited. As Eduardo Galeano tells it in his highly suggestive and radical retelling of the history of the Americas (from below), *Memory of Fire:*

1916: New Orleans

From the slaves comes the freest of all music, jazz, which flies without asking per-mission. Its grandparents are the blacks who sang at their work on their owners' plantations in the southern United States, and its parents are the musicians of black New Orleans brothels. The whorehouse bands play all night without stopping, on balconies that keep them safe above the brawling in the street. *From their improvisa-tions is born the new music.*

With his savings from delivering newspapers, milk, and coal, a short, timid lad has just bought his own trumpet for ten dollars. He blows and the music stretches out, out, greeting the day. Louis Armstrong, like jazz, is the grandson of slaves, and has been raised, like jazz, in the whorehouse. (*Century of the Wind,* 43; our emphasis)

The improvisations of jazz point ahead to a "new music," their emergence from the alternative social formations created by slavery heralding the potential forms of community that the new music's freedom gestures toward. A community of slaves and whores produces the avatar of not only a new music, but also a new cultural formation capable of enunciating the most radical expressions of freedom and memory.

The spirit of group improvisation, so central to New Orleans jazz, has continued to permeate subsequent jazz trends and, in turn, has influenced the emergence of new cultural formations in the face of changing social injustices. A stunning example of precisely this sort of affiliation between the materials of free jazz improvisation and new cultural formations predicated on recuperations of memory in the name of new community alliances occurs with William Parker's In Order to Survive quartet's extraordinary composition "The Peach Orchard," which Parker frames in the following manner:

> . . . The Peach Orchard, draws its inspiration from events that took place on the Navaho land in what is now called New Mexico. The great Navaho chief Manuelito and his people were fighting against being pushed out of their homelands by the United States Army. Out of all the things the Navaho cultivated they loved their peach orchards the most. In the end of this struggle they like all Native Americans lost everything, including their cherished peach orchard which was destroyed. In reading about this I immediately felt a very deep sadness. I can only imagine the sadness they must have felt. It was the beginning of the end. In this composition you can hear the massive blanketing of America by Europe; you can also hear the voice not only of Manuelito, but of Nana, Geronimo, Wovoka, Sitting Bull, Kicking Bird, Kicking Bear, and all of the others. (*The Peach Orchard,* liner notes)

Parker, an African-American playing in an ensemble integrated across both racial and gender boundaries, envisions the music of "The Peach Orchard," radically dissonant and improvisatory as it is, as a way of memorializing the loss of the Navaho, even as it presents its own recuperative historiography in a gesture of solidarity and kinship with that loss. The critique of the "blanketing of America by Europe" and the hearing of the voices of "all the others" is part of a dual project evident with Parker and In Order to Survive. The synergistic reordering of historical time as mysterious past and present takes place: "In this music I hear the history, the mystery and the now." But, at the same time, Parker's liner notes invite listeners to hear the solidary in human experience, as reiterated in the compulsively ascending chordal structure of "The Peach Orchard," which enacts Parker's notion that "the main force in playing this music is having the ability to feel the pain of all who suffer. To feel it as if it were happening to us; not resting until it ceases to be." In this particular example, repetition with all the subtle gradients, digressions, and musical registers that it summons forth in an improvised context, directly materializes the band's capacity for dialogue, its collaborative dissonance giving shape to an enacted form of solidary expression. Dissonant reiterations in this mode articulate George Lewis's notion, expressed in his first essay in this book, that "the African-American improviser, coming from a legacy of slavery and oppression, cannot countenance the erasure of history. The destruction of family and lineage, the rewriting of history and memory in the image of whiteness, is one of the facts with which all people of color must live."[2] Empathic communication across time: a form of historical community made possible in the imaginary space of improvisations played with a direct social purpose—the resistance to human pain and suffering and the imagining of the space of the other who has experienced cataclysmic loss and unspeakable pain. Parker's example speaks across the divide that often separates musical expression from analysis, especially where analysis is couched in terms that avoid addressing the social contexts and purposes of music.

Examples such as Parker's can easily be proliferated from within the ranks of free jazz improvisers. Steve Coleman's Metrics, for instance, in a live recording done with three freestylers (Black Indian, Sub Zero, and Kokayi) entitled *The Way of the Cipher,* iterates in his liner notes that the recording is "a call to our brothers and sisters in the streets with a message of the times." Coleman goes on to associate freestylin' (verbal improvisation) with ancient civilizations that practiced the art of "word in rhythm," suggesting that the improvised music on the recording "represents the journey of our people, it is a record in sound of our pilgrimage. We are united in our desire to bring the message of this pilgrimage to the people using the voice of music" (*The Way of the Cipher,* liner notes).[3] Again, the suggestion is that improvised music archives historical practices and speaks to a community about its past and present, a process that engenders the possibility of solidary relations as mediated by the unified desire of the musicians to "bring the message of this pilgrimage to the people using the voice of music."

Québécois improviser René Lussier, working with a collective of improvising musicians from the "forever surprising Montréal community of musicians" (*Le Trésor de la langue,* liner notes), uses a unique juxtaposition of music and spoken word to reflect on the status of the French language in Québec in the remarkable recording *Le Trésor de la langue.* Using a compositional style based on the alliance of musical pastiche with precise musical transcriptions of random recordings of Québécois speakers, *Le trésor de la langue*'s effect is intensely improvisatory, freely spanning multiple musical styles while reflecting on the precise relationship that exists between spoken and musical expression. The political and community resonances of such a recording are undeniable. The recording brings together an archive of the different forms of French heard in Québec (from the different regional dialects, through to French heavily inflected by English, through to the French spoken in France) while acknowledging that its premise is based on the fact that "the only truly important French speaking community in North America is threatened" (liner notes). The poem "Who remembers?" by Richard Desjardins is foregrounded in the recording, suggesting that "we've killed many people/to assure our own survival./And not all are inscribed/in the ledgers of the Crown./If I have the right to speak French/English/From the depth of my heart/and soul of my being,/Go ask the Iroquois why./But do it quick, while they're still around" (liner notes).

The music of *Le Trésor de la langue* thus speaks not only to the threat posed to extant communities of French speakers in North America but also to the memorialization of other communities, in this case aboriginal, either culturally marginal or on the verge of extinction. Thus, when Lussier states that "it's remarkable what melodies we speak to each other every day!" he does so in the full recognition that representing community in the present does not always do justice to memorializing its links to other communities whose disappearance grounds the here and now. In the case of *Le Trésor de la langue,* improvisatory linguistic and musical contexts animate new possibilities of solidarity as given shape through expression and memory. The vexed relationship of Québécois culture, as a minoritized settler culture in the larger context of North American culture generally, addresses its own relations with the aboriginal cultures it has displaced, suggesting that all forms of representation are profoundly linked and reflective of how memory circulates in the name of community formations.[4] For Lussier and his troupe of musicians, improvisation becomes the site of transgressive intervention into representational patterns that formalize forgetting and thus the aesthetics of disconnection, the politics of exclusion. Remember that in the contexts of Québécois nationalist culture the problem of relations with aboriginal peoples is particularly fraught given that the very arguments used to support Québécois separatism or sovereignty association (with Canada) can be (and have been) used by, for instance, the large Cree population in northern Québec in their attempt to get equitable treatment from settler culture.

Improvisation, in the contexts in which we are discussing it, can provide a powerful form of rebellion against such exclusions, inviting potentially transgressive interventions and giving articulation to fractious or unheard community dissonances. As Davide Ielmini argues in the liner notes to Italian saxophonist Carlo Actis Dato's band's recording *Son para el Che,* the way the improvising musician "intervenes in the disharmonies of the community is crucial."[5] The title of an album like *Son para el Che* (loosely "Song for Che"), clearly gestures toward its revolutionary sympathies, linking its musical contexts, highly improvised as they are, with resistant activity (signified by Che, the Argentine revolutionary who played a key role in the Cuban revolution and in other popular uprisings in Latin America). Perhaps less evident is how the title also invokes Che, a common referent in Latin America for "friend" (derived from an indigenous word for "people") as a trope of community and solidarity. The album's title is clear recognition of how music potentially acts on community and intervenes via its own expression of resistance (Che) and the expressions of solidarity (in this case with "son," an Afro-Cuban musical form) embedded in the improvisatory contexts it chooses. This intervention in the "disharmonies of the community," then, takes the form of a rebellion, "a rebellion that doesn't loosen [the musicians'] ties with their consciences, one that you can interpret in their notes, read between their lines: and you must, because they don't say everything explicitly, nor do they play everything."

Ielmini's comments reiterate Pierre Boulez's notion that "music is in a state of permanent revolution" one in which there are "time-bombs as well as the bombs that explode immediately" (*Orientations*, 71). Boulez is specifically referring to "aspects of a composer's music [that] remain as it were submerged for a time, and only then emerge into the general consciousness." "We cannot therefore claim," Boulez continues, "an absolute knowledge of all aspects of the present even when we accept it *in toto*" (*Orientations*, 71), a recognition that music is revolutionary in its capacity to disrupt the smug notion that the present is an absolute horizon that defines the limits of knowing, musically or otherwise. But improvisation, commonly (and wrongly) thought of as a form of musical difference in which spontaneity is a dominant value (an art of the present), is, as we have seen, crucial to signifying how the space of the present can invoke spontaneity in the name of remembrance, in the name of lost practices and social formations that feed into the creative surge of energies that make the improvisational present. We fully recognize that the bringing together of the various cultural referents used in this paragraph traverses a number of cultural divides and collapses a number of disciplinary spaces in the name of improvisational discourse. Such is the important and dangerous ground we address in this book, especially in relation to the notion of "communities in dialogue."

Whether in articulating a lost sense of connection with a place and a history, or in articulating the rebel energies and commitment with which new communities can be forged from acts of transgressive memory and music making, Lussier's example (like that of Tapscott, Ra, Armstrong, Parker, Douglas, Coleman, and Dato) enacts a powerful counterindication to orthodoxies of expression. These, in the case of black America, for instance, excise certain histories (their own and others such as the Navaho who are "blanketed," to borrow Parker's laconic but pithy expression, by European culture) and their expressive concomitants—the latter being the very place, in both Ra's and Tapscott's broader cultural theories, in which history is sheltered as a radical musical practice that is also a form of alternative narrative contributing to community formation. The story of jazz improvisation (and of so-called free music more generally) cannot be understood without invoking this ability to harbor the very differences suggestive of lost histories, lost practices of communicating through music, and lost practices of building community through the discrepant engagement and play of consonance and dissonance insistently articulated by improvisatory practices.

The other side of nowhere, then, tropes a mysterious horizon beyond which the potential for thinking alternatives—whether musical, social, communitarian, theoretical, and so forth—is activated as a generative principle of seeking out contrarian knowledges, dissonant social practices, and transgressive uncertainties, all in opposition to orthodoxies that limit or circumscribe the limits of human potentiality. The other side is unknowable but there nonetheless; no one can be fully sure what lies on the other side and yet it references a somewhere crucial to the dynamics of improvisatory practice. As Michael Snow persuades us in his improvised essay that opens this volume, for improvisers the other side of nowhere is "where they were the last time they played." Snow's point is that "the other side of nowhere" locates the process and dynamics of free improvisation as definitive: nowhere is where you were last, and the now of playing in the moment is the somewhere you give shape to (only to have that become a nowhere once the moment of playing is over). The idea addresses fundamental tensions in improvisation between the provisional and metaphysical (past) and the certain and material (now), the process of confronting the unknown (a process of generating alternatives as part of creative free play) and the fixity that that process undoes. Again Sun Ra: "It is better to deal with the people who have intuition now . . . you see they don't know what they're doing . . . the ones who do know what they're doing haven't proven anything" *(Sun Ra: A Joyful Noise)*. This comment critiques the extent to which the world as it is has been molded by a restricted, perverse knowing, one shaped by post-Enlightenment, technocratic, and bureaucratic systems of governance, themselves based on exploitation, slavery, militarization, historical amnesia, and the restriction of freedoms in the name of order and progress. This way of knowing (which is to say, way of being in the world) has come at the expense of alternatives to that knowing, which may (at first glance and modulated by Ra's Egyptian mysticism), seem naive and easily dismissed. But the precise point Ra[6] makes here, and one that can not easily be dissociated from his musical and improvisatory practices, is that alternatives *do* exist as part of the social practice of music.

Critic Graham Lock is particularly forthright on this point in his compelling analysis of the crucial role that music has played in articulating alternative visions of human possibility. Focused specifically on the imaginative power expressed in the lifework of three preeminent African-American creative practitioners—Sun Ra, Duke Ellington, and Anthony Braxton—Lock's recent *Blutopia* identifies two major impulses in the music, impulses that, as we argue in this introduction, can enliven our understanding of the new sorts of social relationships summoned forth by improvisatory musical practices: "a utopian impulse, evident in the creation of imagined places . . . and the impulse to remember, to bear witness" (2). Improvisation as remembrance, improvisation as hope and possibility: our point, then, is that musical practices in which improvisation is a defining characteristic *are* social practices, envisionings of possibilities excluded from conventional systems of thought and thus an important locus of resistance to orthodoxies of the imagination (knowing), of relations with others (community), and of relations to the materials of the world around us (instruments). Improvised music takes the materials of existence—knowing, community, and instruments—and reshapes the possible relations they have with each other. Improvisation is the site at which possibility and potential are made real in an exemplary gesture of making. Indeed, Lock's claim that "making the vision real was obviously a central impulse in Sun Ra's work" (40) certainly seems germane in this context. As an exemplary form of ur-performativity, improvisation, in short, symbolizes the recognition that alternatives to orthodox practices are available; this recognition we suggest, is an ideological position that has profound ramifications for thinking about one's relation to the social sphere. Improvisation ramifies that sphere in the most concrete of ways, as a lived, enacted performance of being differently in the world.

The work of Pauline Oliveros—whose own essay in this volume draws on the lived experience of women improvisers to consider the complex ways in which gender inequities have shaped the production and reception of improvised music—provides another pertinent example of how improvisatory performance practices can model different ways of being in the world. Oliveros's vision, articulated through her philosophy and practice of "deep listening," demands an intense form of commitment and responsibility to—as well as interaction with—all that surrounds us: people, environments, nature, the sounds of daily life. In reflecting on her own work, Oliveros has talked specifically about her art in relation to the struggles faced by women. Indeed, one critic, Timothy Taylor, suggests that "it is possible to argue that the entire trajectory of her career has been an attempt to define and then shed the established norms of postwar composition, which she sees as overwhelmingly male" (100). Abandoning these sorts of established compositional norms in favour of a nonexcessive model of performance practice, as well as of what Oliveros herself, in her book *The Roots of the Moment,* calls "the more unpredictable and unknowable possibilities that can be activated by *not* specifying pitches and rhythms" (4; our emphasis), she has sought to revalue spheres of musical experience that have historically and institutionally been undervalued (and, indeed, dismissed) as "feminine."

Moreover, Oliveros's extraordinary reworking of the traditional divide between performers and audiences—her ongoing commitment to democratizing access to performance possibilities by insisting that listeners actively participate in the process of music making—and her attention to the complex ways in which venues and environments necessarily prompt new ways of thinking about what it means to be "in the moment" of a performance situation are all germane in the context of the arguments we're presenting here. Like Oliveros, we argue that improvisation, in its most radical dimensions as both a metaphysics and practice of performance, demands that *every* aspect of those practices be interrogated: from instrumentation to performance space, to relationship with the audience, to traditional techniques and instruments, to conventions around performance practice itself, to the very nature of musical language (volume, pitch, tone, rhythm, timbre, and relations of consonance and dissonance). David Toop, for instance, notes that

for black American improvisers such as Don Cherry and the Art Ensemble of Chicago, and at roughly the same time their European and white American counterparts in AMM, Musica Electronica Viva, Joseph Holbrook, Music Improvisation Company, Nuova Consonanza and the Spontaneous Music Ensemble, a partial move away from the major instruments of jazz and classical music performance was an expression of politics as much as music. From the mid 1960s into the disillusioned 1970s, little instruments and non-instruments (transistor radios, contact microphones amplifying tiny sounds or surface noises extracted from tables, beards, cheese graters, etc.) became symbols of the drive to democratise music, to allow access to unskilled players (including children), to draw sound from instruments rather than subjugate them to systems, open the music up to chance events *and create a sense of collectively organised community* as an attempted break from hard professionalism, particularly the star system that afflicted both jazz groups and classical performers. (133–134; our emphasis)

Democratization, experimentation, and the "sense of collectively organised community" are all at stake in the interrogative, alternative practices that improvisation can potentially enable. Improvisation, by virtue of the interrogative and critical relationships with the practices it (dis)engages, can provide a powerful forum for commentary on the ethics of the "matter" of music, especially since it questions—in its most fully articulated forms—that "matter" with unrelenting curiosity and, in so doing, produces alternatives to the orthodoxies against which it is aligned.[7] The production of these alternatives, as Oliveros's lifework so profoundly illustrates, intensifies and expands what it means to be human in both a musical community and in the larger social sphere in which these alternatives exist. As a provocation to avoid stasis, improvisation is predicated on the exploration of alternative (and alterative) modes of being in community. Alternatives are harbored in spaces of difference that we associate in this book with improvised musical practices, themselves emblems of the potential alternative social arrangements we call communities in dialogue. Encoded in the alternative relations that musical improvisation can summon forth lies the possibility that these alternatives are also, in some profound way, radically alterative of the social sphere to which they are addressed and in which they occur.

John Whiteoak, in his study of Australian improvisatory practices, explicitly associates improvisation in a colonial context with "deviance, irreverence and iconoclasm in 'serious' music-making" (xix), going on to argue that "collectively-improvised jazz style [in Australia] was beginning [in the 1930s] to signify both aesthetic and political radicalism and a recognition (and probably some misunderstanding) of the intensity of expression associated with authentic African-American jazz performance" (xx). Similarly, Denis Levaillant, in his book *Improvisation musicale,* argues that "pour improviser aujourd'hui, ou au moins tenir compte au mieux possible de l'improvisation, il semble donc qu'il faille faire preuve d'imagination sociale" (270) [To improvise today, or at least to account in the best possible way of improvisation, it seems then that one needs to evince a social imagination]. Bernard Lubat, in an interview with Levaillant, argues that improvisation is "le signe d'une crise" (267) [the sign of a crisis] and that "l'improvisation est une forme de clandestinité, de résistance" (267) [improvisation is a form of clandestinity, of resistance]. The American critic Stephen Greenblatt, in a discussion of improvisatory practices in the Renaissance, suggests that "if improvisation is made possible by the subversive perception of another's truth as an ideological construct, that construct must at the same time bear a certain structural resemblance to one's own set of beliefs" (62). These diverse examples of theorizing improvisation from within very different cultural contexts all point to a dominant trope at work in thinking improvisation; namely, its association with transgressive, critical, radical, and aesthetic practices in relation to the communities it engages.

Greenblatt's ideas on improvisation suggest that improvisation cannot be dissociated from the structures with which it dissonantly engages. These ideas have been used to mount the reactionary argument that improvisation as a form of thought or mode of social being lies at the heart of the European conquest of the Americas. In such a view, improvisation, rather than being a social practice to have emerged out of those cultures who most suffered the effects of colonialism (in particular indigenous and African slave populations), in fact originated in settler culture and was the precise tool that allowed for colonial forces to win out over these populations. In linking such an argument with the improvised musickings this book addresses we realize that the very notion of placing an early modern, new historicist critic into the contexts of a book on jazz improvisation may push the limits of the disciplinary structures within which academics and performers traditionally work. We would argue, however, that these ideas are very much in keeping with the contexts that this book seeks to engage, if only to suggest that conquest and colonial discourses have played a significant role in establishing some of the signally important historical conditions and contingencies from which jazz and its improvisational practices have emerged. Literary theorist Tzvetan Todorov, in his book *The Conquest of America,* suggests that the initial contact between Mexican (Aztec) and European (Spanish) cultures was defined by the collision between "ritual discourse," associated with indigenous populations, and improvisatory discourse, associated with Europeans:

the Indians are inadequate in a situation requiring improvisation, and this is precisely the situation of the conquest. [The Indians'] verbal education favors paradigm over syntagm, code over context, conformity-to-order over efficacity-of-the-moment, the past over the present. Now, the Spanish invasion creates a radically new, entirely unprecedented situation, in which the art of improvisation matters more than that of ritual. *It is quite remarkable, in this context, to see Cortés not only constantly practicing the art of adaptation and improvisation, but also being aware of it and claiming it as the very principle of his conduct:* "I shall always take care to add whatever seems to me most fitting, for the great size and diversity of the lands which are discovered each day and the many new secrets which we have learned from these discoveries make it necessary that for new circumstances there be new considerations and decisions." (Todorov, 87; our emphasis)

Greenblatt and Todorov exemplify the ways in which improvisation (as a critical trope) circulates in academic discourse, and their examples point to the pitfalls, dangers, and relevance of interdisciplinary scholarship. We ask, as part of the more general thrust of this introduction, *whose* interests are being served by the use of improvisation in discourse? Or, as Michael Jarrett puts it in his testimonial essay in this volume, "When we write about improvisation, what are we really writing about?"

Todorov's argument, for instance, appropriates the resistant, improvisatory practices that will emerge out of colonization as the very instrument by which colonization takes place. The cultural relativism of this argument is worth noting. But so is the way in which Todorov transposes the situation of conquest. Instead of a confrontation between Montezuma's inept leadership (one based on highly symbolic codes of conduct that have yet to be fully understood) and Cortés's ruthless efficacity (based on the will to power and superior military technologies) we have a confrontation between modes of being based on the ability (or not) to improvise. Regardless of whether or not one agrees with this argument, the point is that improvisation (for Todorov) forms the locus of cultural practices that will (literally) engender the Americas—that the logic of conquest requires the release of improvisational energies that later transmute into the spaces of resistance to dominant ideology discussed throughout this book.

And here is the key to where Todorov gets it wrong: improvisation as a meaningful cultural practice in the Americas depends on that dissonant relation to hegemony. Cortés's actions, from within his own cultural context and in relation to what Cortés understood to be hegemonic power (located in Spain), are never improvisatory so much as they are predictably manipulative and adaptive, dictated by the self-interested goals of the imperial ideology he sought to enforce. And, one wonders, does the way in which Todorov's own academic discourse makes use of improvisation not reflect on a particular set of cultural prejudices and constructions that inflect its usage in this way? In this case, we would argue that Todorov's use of "improvisation" does two things: (1) it reinforces the ways in which colonial discourse operates by abjecting and disempowering difference (in this case the Aztecs or the Mexica); and (2) it also appropriates to itself modes of resistant discourse that one might associate with improvisation in the contemporary historical moment, to perform this abjection and disempowerment. We suggest that this double-edged effect marks some of the difficulties facing interdisciplinary scholarship that seeks to reconcile itself with (or dialogue across) different fields in which wildly variant disciplinary assumptions are at work.

To have been truly improvisatory in the relation to otherness that Cortés initiates, would have required his turning away from the predictable acts of imperial greed and destruction to initiate something quite different—like a peaceful and productive alliance with indigenous cultures in the name of forming a transcultural community based on dialogue and "true" improvisation rather than on the monological deployment of European power. This distinction, barely thinkable as it is given the rhetoric of power and domination that so corrupts discourses of Western encounter, shows that the battle over how to think improvisation is neither inconsequential nor unrelated to larger issues that define one's relation both to a home community and to other communities, whose values, social practices, and cultural formations are differential and difficult to read. Improvisation, in this context, challenges indifference: the smug knowledge that one's own view of the world is self-validating and can be imposed unproblematically on others.

It is instructive to remember that one of the earliest recorded uses of the word "improvisation" in English in 1811 (as stated in the Oxford English Dictionary [OED]) associates it with "the flexibility of Italian and Spanish languages . . . [which] renders these countries distinguished for the talent of improvisation," a referent that points to the long genealogy of Todorov's ideas insofar as they relate to the Spanish conquest. A slightly earlier use of the term "improvisator" (for improviser) occurs in 1795 and explicitly links extemporaneous verbal dexterity with music: "The Italian improvisator never attempts a ballad without striking his mandolino" (OED). Curiously, these early usages of improvisation cognates enact their own ethnic othering in which the consistent association between improvisatory discourse and Latin/Mediterranean cultures are implicitly opposed to Anglo-Saxon culture.

The opposition evident in early usage points to another theme of this book that we wish to highlight: the extraordinary conjunction between improvisational musical practices in jazz and ethnicity and race, especially evident in African-American culture. It is no accident, in other words, that the kinds of associations made by Todorov between imperial culture and improvisation exist; the very genealogy of the word is predicated on cultural assumptions that invoke disparate relations between powers and ethnicities. The importance, then, of improvisational practices that envision (and perform) alternative communities predicated on transgressions against (and critiques of) social formations that continue to enact such disparities, should not be underestimated. It is in this sense that we locate jazz improvisation within a larger field of cultural expression than music alone, if only because jazz improvisational practices challenge assumptions gathered round the term (pace Todorov) as a way of giving form to how communities of difference enter into dialogue with one another.

Amiri Baraka (LeRoi Jones) reminds us that music is the "expression of where we are" at the same time as he envisages a "*Unity Music*. The Black Music which is jazz and blues, religious and secular. Which is New Thing and Rhythm and Blues. The consciousness of social reevaluation and rise, a social spiritualism. A mystical walk up to the street where all the risen live.

Indian-African anti-Western-Western (as geography) Nigger-sharp Black and strong" (*Black Music*, 210–211). Baraka associates black music with re-evaluation and social spiritualism and with the very sorts of community formations embodied in African-American musical forms. But he simultaneously debunks the rhetoric associated with these forms, suggesting "You can say *spiritual*. You can say *Freedom*. But you do not necessarily have to be either one" (210). In so doing, he foregrounds the experience of the music itself over the rhetoric associated with it, suggesting that the very tenuousness of black music's spirit and freedom demands constant scrutiny and reevaluation in order to remain true to its ideals. Here, as with other musicians and creative practitioners that we cite, the language of musical expression and of the theories to which it gives rise inevitably points to notions of spirit, freedom, community, resistance, unity, and so forth—all terms that do not align themselves comfortably with the kinds of academic discourse traditionally associated with music (whether musicological, ethnographical, or theoretical).

Unity music, that resonant and highly suggestive Barakian phrase, articulates the social ideals with which we align our notion of jazz improvisation in relation to dialogical communities. Improvisation—and the alternative forms of being in community it literally and figuratively gives space to—lies on the other side of the "nowhere" that defines a world in which human potential and community are thwarted and curtailed. It's a tricky but important point: the here and now of conventional knowing is nowhere; while the elsewhere that is the "other side" to this "nowhere" finds refuge in musical and social practices where intuition, experimentation, and expressive transgression sustain an alternative, differential space of human being, creativity, and community. Coming out of such a positioning, then, one of the points we and our contributors make in this book is that improvisation is less about original acts of individual self-creation (itself a sort of originary orthodoxy about improvisatory practice) than about an ongoing process of community building, about reinvigorating public life with the spirit of dialogue and difference that improvisatory practices consistently gesture toward, even when at their most extreme they may appear to be doing exactly the opposite. As Anthony Seeger argues in the introduction to a special issue of *Cultural Survival Quarterly* devoted to traditional music in community life, "members of communities around the world use music to create cultural identity and to erase the cultural identity of others, to create unity and to dissolve it" (20). Creation and erasure, unity and dissolution. The very tensions operative in improvisation as a social practice are those that are at stake in the making of community as an ongoing and dynamic interrelational process.

Nothing perhaps could be more exemplary of this fact than the way in which improvised music has effectively been excised from the popular face of music, whether in the classical concert hall (where the most radical form of improvisation may be an extended cadenza carefully thought out by the performer prior to the performance); on the radio where, with few exceptions, the dominance of format-based programming effectively marginalizes the presentation of improvised music (itself predicated on "live" performance); or in the emporia that sell and distribute music to the general public. All are in some way dominated by the business of making pop music (itself based on the very predictability of product that will generate sales, a principle inherently opposed to the largely noncommercial context in which improvised music is created). In such a context, "the other side of nowhere" is also a neat reminder that improvisation doesn't simply come out of nowhere: radical, excessive, and startlingly original as it might sound, improvised music, like all successful acts of music making (and indeed all acts of community building), derives its particularity from the force of context, one that challenges players, listeners and all those caught up in its social field, to reevaluate the "space" (nowhere and elsewhere) in which the conjoined activities of making music and community happen.

This book explores the ways in which discourses on musical improvisation pertain to discourses of community. Through the wide range of contributions from musicians, cultural theorists, composers, creative writers, and so forth (sometimes all in one), we have sought to fill what we feel to be an important gap in literature on the topic of improvisation, itself a surprisingly understudied musical and cultural phenomenon. Not intended as a comprehensive treatment of a vast and complex field, these essays offer more of a starting point for the kind of multiple dialogues and transdisciplinary engagements that we have sought to frame in this book. The book results from a concerted effort in multiple contexts over several years to initiate and sustain a dialogue about the nature and importance of improvisational musical practices in jazz, one that is reflected in the community of sound brought together under the auspices of the Guelph Jazz Festival (in both its colloquium and performance aspects). The volume emerges in large part out of a series of talks, panels, and roundtables (on improvisation and collaboration) presented at the Guelph Jazz Festival colloquia between 1998 and 2001. That some of the papers included here deliberately preserve traces of those occasions is, we think, worth noting, especially since improvised musicking, as Christopher Small points out, is itself profoundly about the different ways in which communities of performers and listeners "pick up the sense of occasion . . . [and] bring it into focus and enhance it" (295).

By bringing together both musicians and academics, we hope that this book (like the jazz festival colloquia that came before it) will broaden our understanding of jazz and creative improvised music in purposeful new ways. We have especially tried to heed George Lewis's salutary call for musicians to intervene in the process of documenting their own work and activity. Lewis's point is that "the organization of concerts, recordings, workshops and other opportunities for direct musical experience, while a fundamental part of the process of helping people to understand new music, must not be pursued to the exclusion of other important activities that directly affect the understanding of music" (107). What is needed, he argues, are "exchanges between improvisors working both inside and out-side the academic system" (107), exchanges that will counter both the insti-tutionally sanctioned assumption that "hearing music is more important than reading about it" (107) and the ethnocentric declarations of musical value that have contributed to the denigration of improvisatory musical practices. A purposeful model for such exchanges, says Lewis, might be found in "the concept of the academic 'conference'" (108). However, "un-like the standard academic conference, which is effectively limited to those within the academic system who can obtain financial support from their in-stitutions, this kind of conference would need to directly support appear-ances by artists outside the academic system" (108). It is our hope that both this book and the colloquia out of which it has emerged can, as per Lewis's vision, trouble "the common division of 'arts' and 'humanities,' [and lead to a recognition] that a fruitful meeting of the two areas places expanded notions of musical creativity before new . . . highly receptive audiences" (108). While we harbor no illusions about the ability of academic knowl-edge–producing elites to capture the range and vitality of improvised music, we have certainly seen how the talks and panel discussions at the Guelph Jazz Festival colloquia have worked to contextualize—and to build an appreciation for—a music that, in other contexts, might seem difficult, challenging, or inaccessible. As with the very planning, programming and publicizing of the music performed at the festival, these attempts to con-textualize the music through conference-style discussions have clearly shaped the way the music gets understood, listened to, and talked about (see Heble, 231).

In many ways, we realize that this book barely hints at a rich and rela-tively underexplored world in which the startling range of musical practices associated with improvisation connects with an equally compelling and de-manding range of social practices associated with improvised music. But at the same time as we recognize the general lack of theoretical attention paid to improvisatory musical practices in jazz (except for general stereotypes about the improviser as an incarnation of self-destructive narcissistic genius), we also seek to avoid simplistic and reductive formulations of what makes improvisation so distinct an element of human expression. As such, we argue (as do many of our contributors) toward an understanding of improvisation as a complex and nonreductive activity that has something important to teach about the ways in which extreme forms of human creative expression (and the experimentation with its multiple alternatives and potentialities) are profoundly tied to much broader social fields in which the forms of production in fact reflect on (and theorize toward) alternative social arrangements activated by the experimental forms of musical production. Moreover, we argue that improvisatory musical practices associated with jazz have an important role to play in enacting the kind of pedagogy of rights that we see as critical to addressing social problems.[8]

Whether in relation to issues of how freedom of expression is to be balanced against responsible expression, to how dialogue is to be sustained in the most impossible of circumstances, to how being human cannot be dissociated from the most basic expressive principles founded in experimentation, dream, unexpected synergies, and communitarian relations, or to how the generative principles of alternative social arrangements are to be found embedded in alternative forms of social practice we associate with free jazz and improvised music generally, improvisation has something important to teach. After all, improvisation is the human practice from which all music derives. Music, as a signifying practice, did not spring fully formed from Mnemosyne's forehead, nor did the range of its formal and expressive modes come into being without an originary history profoundly tied to improvisational practices. Remarkably, those practices remain a surprisingly understudied phenomenon, despite improvisation's crucial role in musical discourse. Moreover, we recognize the ways in which this book's targeting of improvisation as a social space goes against all sorts of orthodoxies and prejudices about improvisational practice, neatly summarized in the following, largely negative, remarks on improvisation made by contemporary French composer Pierre Boulez:

Finally, improvisation is not possible. Even in a baroque ensemble, where the laws were more or less codified, where you had figures instead of chords [figured bass], in other words, where you could place them in a certain position but not in just any way—even in this period improvisation did not produce exclusively masterpieces. People speak of Bach's improvisations, for example. I believe that Bach wrote on the basis of what he had improvised, and that what he wrote was the more interesting of the two. Often, these improvisations are nothing more than pure, sometimes bizarre, samplings of sound that are not at all integrated into the directives of a composition. This results in constant arousal and appeasement, something I find intolerable. . . . The dialectic of form takes precedence over the possible; everybody arouses everybody else; it becomes a kind of public onanism. (Quoted in Attali, 145–146)

Boulez's overheated rhetoric on improvisation localizes many of the energies that we see as being at stake in discourses predicated on improvisational practices: the fear of randomness, the privileging of the logocentric (written) over the phonocentric (aural),[9] the lack of submission to compositional directive, the unachieved mastery that only true composition allows, the arousal of contradictory emotions, the interactivity that produces a public (let alone an *onanistic* public), and sublimated throughout, the erotics of a discourse that plays with the possible (even as Boulez denies that possibility). Clearly, any musical genre that can arouse such resistances from a preeminent and highly respected classical composer/musician (who in many ways is extraordinarily experimental in his own musical practices and who, oddly enough, has even written a piece entitled "Improvisations sur Mallarmé") merits further attention.

It is the purpose of this book to address some of the ways in which improvisation merits our attention. We hope to have produced a space in which key elements of the dialogue we wish to engage have found a home of sorts. Our basic premise, again, is that improvisation has remained a largely unstudied and untheorized phenomenon, especially in terms of its relation to contemporary work in cultural studies. The contributions represented here offer salient points of entry for theorizing a range of issues of cultural concern: power and resistance, the politics of identity formation, intercultural collaboration, gender and music, social mobility, institutional constraints, and, as we suggest in this introduction, human rights, hope, and new networks of social interaction. Indeed, as many of our contributors make clear in their own distinct ways, improvisation is a concept that is central to contemporary debates about the nature (and perhaps even the future) of social understanding.

In his book *Noise: The Political Economy of Music,* Jacques Attali argues that music "is a tremendously privileged site for the analysis and revelation of new forms in our society" (133). Music exists, he tells us, to help us hear the sound of change. "It obliges us to invent categories and new dynamics to regenerate social theory, which today has become crystalized, entrapped, moribund" (4). Following Attali's lead, we'd like to argue that music—specifically, creative improvised music and free jazz—can reinvigorate our understanding of the social function of humanities research within the broader context of how that research plays a role in shaping notions of community and "new forms" of social organization. If, as Dick Hebdige notes, "violations of the authorized codes through which the social world is organized and experienced have considerable power to provoke or disturb" ("Subculture," 130), then musical improvisation, we suggest, offers a rich and provocative—yet little explored—method for assessing the changing conduct and promotion of research in the humanities. Arguing that the social force of improvised music resides, at least in part, in its capacity to disrupt institutionally sanctioned economies of production, to trouble the assumptions (and the expectations of fixity) fostered by dominant systems of knowledge production, this introduction seeks to broaden our understanding of how humanities research might be animated by an analysis of the social impact of process-oriented models of creative practice. To what extent might the move away from goal-oriented methodologies toward an aesthetics (and an ethics) of improvised creative practice foster a commitment to cultural listening, to a widening of the scope of community, to new models of trust and obligation? As a process-oriented model of performance that accents freedom, responsibility, risk-taking, and mutual engagement between both practitioners and listeners, improvisation offers a particularly resonant topic for contemporary cultural debate.

Now in implying such a connection—however tenuous—between improvisation and human rights, we certainly do not mean to offer any easy or uncritical amplification of the assumption that free music should automatically be equated with freedom from oppression. In an important article assessing the political claims often made on behalf of improvisation, Alan Durant points out that some musicians see improvisation as "a human activity which gains value exactly from the fact that it constructs no version of hierarchy or competition, no ensnaring conventions or intrinsically detrimental value judgements." Durant suggests that "this escape from judgement and value has the currently attractive political force of dissent. It is a point of counter-identification against systems of control, hierarchy and subordination" (270). Tempting as it is to situate our understanding of improvisation in the context of the organization of (and resistance to) social relations of power, to argue (as does another critic, Daniel Belgrad) that an aesthetics of spontaneity has "offered a template for expressions of social dissent" (247), it is equally important, as Durant reminds us, to recognize that "no social formations will involve no conventions at all" (270).

What is at stake in Durant's reminder is the fraught relation between improvisation understood as a social practice that critiques and opposes convention and improvisation as a social practice that adheres to its own conventions. Also at stake in his comments are both our understanding of the political force of improvised music (which will always, we suspect, be up for grabs), and, perhaps more suggestively, the very struggle to recognize as legitimate fields of endeavor performance practices that cannot readily be scripted, predicted, or compelled into orthodoxy—even as they produce a range of orthodoxies in terms of their own generic practices. Too often, as institutional histories of college and university programs in music across

North America amply demonstrate, improvisation is dismissed and devalued (by its detractors) for precisely the same reasons that it is said (by its adherents) to exemplify a radical and emancipatory potential. Its alleged lack of governing rules and its radical retreat from orthodox standards of coherence and judgment have, in other words, become a source of both disparagement and celebration. But, for now at least, let's do away with what we call myth number one: the assumption that improvisation involves adherence to neither convention nor protocol, that it tolerates no system of constraint, requires no prior thought, that, in both theory and practice, it's best understood, in the words of one writer, as a kind of "free zone in music where . . . you are responsible only to yourself and to the dictates of your taste" (Chase, 15).[10]

Which brings us to myth number two: the assumption that improvisation is, first and foremost, about unblocking the obstacles that impede access to forms of individual self-expression. Indeed, there is a growing body of work that situates improvisation in the context of such claims about self-definition, self-worth, and self-help. Stephen Nachmanovich, in his *Free Play: Improvisation in Life and Art,* tells us that "spontaneous creation comes from our deepest being and is immaculately and originally ourselves. What we have to express is already with us, *is* us, so the work of creativity is not a matter of making the material come, but of unblocking the obstacles to its natural flow" (10). Similarly, Tom Nunn, in his *Wisdom of the Impulse,* argues that the practice of free improvisation often has as its driving impetus "a search for one's own 'original voice' where specific restrictions of form, style and technique can be dropped, leaving space for the deeper, more intuitive personality to express itself" (131). What troubles us about both of these positions is that in their haste to promulgate arguments about improvisation as a life-strategy for expressions of individuality, originality and creativity, they fail to account for the ways in which jazz improvisation and creative improvised music have always (certainly in their most resilient and most provocative historical instances: bebop, free jazz, AACM, Pan Afrikan Peoples Arkestra, Feminist Improvising Group, and so on, all addressed in this book) been about community building (rather than individual self-expression), about fostering new ways of thinking about, and participating in, human relationships.

Indeed, one way to put this might be to say that improvisation, in some profound sense, intensifies humanity, and that it does so, as we have been arguing, by intensifying acts of communication, by demanding that the choices that go into building communities be confronted. This point has been wisely underscored by a number of critics writing about jazz and improvised music. Christopher Small, for example, argues that "developments in jazz . . . at least since the bebop generation, can be seen as a search, not so much for new sounds or new rhythms, as for new kinds of relationship" (303). Writing specifically about improvisation, Small makes the point that to improvise "is to establish a different set of human relationships, a different kind of society" from that established by composed forms of music making (296). Guitarist and improviser Derek Bailey makes a similar claim in his pioneering book on the theory and practice of improvisation: "For most people improvisation is about playing with other people and some of the greatest opportunities provided by free improvisation are in the exploration of relationships between players" (Bailey, 105). Another highly influential improviser and cultural critic, George Lewis, writes, "Viewed historically . . . the primary reason why jazz has continued to provide trenchant models of alternative musical thinking is that musicians of every era in the music managed, on their own, to create community-based alternatives to segregated or otherwise exclusionary institutions" (83).

Similarly, we would argue that jazz has always been about animating civic space with the spirit of dialogue and collaboration, and that the innovative working models of improvisation and collaboration developed by its creative practitioners have helped to promote a dynamic exchange of cultural forms, and to develop new, socially responsive forms of community building across national, cultural, and artistic boundaries. Both improvisation and collaboration, in short, involve shared responsibility for participation in community life, an ability to negotiate differences, and a willingness to accept the challenges of risk and contingency. Rather than asking how improvisation can unblock obstacles to individual creativity, wouldn't it be more productive to assess how improvisation might be understood to provide new models for dialogue, new opportunities to envision purposeful communities of involvement?

Hebdige puts it nicely in a recent essay: improvisation, he says, "calls into question the myths of individual agency and innovation-in-isolation on which the dominant Western understandings of artistic production are founded" ("Even Unto Death," 337). At the dawn of the twenty-first century, as the relentless privatization of services under "free trade" regimes continues apace, and as institutional measures designed to maximize profit attest to the impoverishment—indeed, the erosion—of public life, putting critical pressure on notions of individualism can, we argue, help articulate the importance of collaborative cultural endeavors in the development of a creative, civic-minded public sphere. Now, while improvisation is hardly a surefire corrective for the malaise of individualism, it does foster, as Ingrid Monson has noted, "the interactive shaping of social networks and communities that accompany musical participation" (2). And this fostering, especially in an era of declining civic engagement in which the very possibilities for hope, imagination, dialogue, and cultural listening are repeatedly being enfeebled, is no small feat.

So what, then, might support for and recognition of improvisation as a valuable model mean for the humanities? As a framework for social practice, what potential does improvisation have for revolutionizing our understanding of the efficacy (as well as the limits) of the kinds of research and teaching that animate work in the humanities? How might it change the way we teach, the way we go about doing research? How might it, in effect, reinvigorate our entire sense of intellectual purpose?

We agree with George Lewis that it is important to rethink our understanding of the division between the arts and the humanities, and to recognize the extent to which improvised music making offers a resonant model for the marriage of theory and practice, for envisioning complex levels of interaction between academic work and broader community-based commitments. In his book *The Culture of Spontaneity,* Daniel Belgrad touches on a related set of matters when he discusses the loss of the public intellectual in today's culture. He argues, in fact, that there has been "a shift in the definition of the intellectual as a social type. Public intellectuals no longer defined themselves as 'intellectuals,' choosing instead the roles of artists, poets, and musicians" (6). The history of jazz and creative improvised music provides no shortage of examples of artists who have exemplified this shift: Muhal Richard Abrams, John Coltrane, Bill Dixon, Billie Holiday, Abbey Lincoln, Amina Claudine Myers, Pauline Oliveros, Sun Ra, Max Roach, Archie Shepp, and Horace Tapscott certainly come immediately to mind.

What all of these artists have demonstrated is that innovative forms of musical expression can contribute to the formulation of new models for civic life by being sources of empowerment, education, and community building. And it's perhaps no surprise that Malcolm X, in his address at the founding rally of the Organization of Afro-American Unity (in June 1964), made an explicit analogy between the black musician's ability to improvise musically and the development of new social and political forms that, in Malcolm's own words, would help "create a new society and make some heaven right here on this earth" for African-American people (64). "I've seen it happen," said Malcolm in that address. "I've seen black musicians when they'd be jamming. . . . that black musician, he picks up his horn and starts blowing some sounds that he never thought of before. He improvises, he creates" (63). His argument was that black people could likewise do the same thing as the black musician, "if given intellectual independence." He tells us that the black person "can come up with a philosophy that nobody has heard of yet. He [*sic*] can invent a society, a social system, an economic system, a political system, that is different from anything that exists or has ever existed anywhere on this earth. He will improvise. . . . And this is what you and I want" (64).

As these words attest, improvisation, for Malcolm, is unabashedly tied to a language of hope, liberation, and genuine human possibility, to the envisioning of what, after the fashion of Sun Ra, we might call "another place," a more just place, that's "on the other side of nowhere." Heard in this context, improvised musicking (to borrow Small's inventive and important coinage) is a powerful instance of what Cornel West, in his book *Keeping Faith*, has called the need to forge "a sense of possible social momentum and motion for a temporal people with few spatial options" (xii–xiv). Nathaniel Mackey, too, is forthright in his insistence that "black linguistic and musical practices that accent variance, variability" (266) need to be understood in the context of black mobility. Enlarging on Amiri Baraka's well-known argument, "Swing—From Verb to Noun," on white appropriation of black music, Mackey explains that "'from verb to noun' means, on the aesthetic level, a less dynamic, less improvisatory, less blues-inflected music, and, on the political level, a containment of black mobility, a containment of the economic and social advances that might accrue to black artistic innovation" (266).

By contrast, the "privileging of the verb," Mackey argues, "the movement from noun to verb, linguistically accentuates action among a people whose ability to act is curtailed by racist constraint" (268). Mackey's comments encourage us to recognize the important role that improvisation has played in African-American struggles for mobility and social momentum. In this context, to cite just one prominent example, the rising cacophony of horns in John Coltrane's 1965 collective improvisation *Ascension* (and the upward momentum, the social and spiritual uplift, implied by both the music and the title) can be heard as a sonic approximation of the spirit of movement (and the related language of hope) that has historically animated the narratives and struggles of African-Americans: "the theme," as John Szwed puts it in his biography of Ra, "of travel, of journey, of exodus, of escape which dominates African-American narratives: of people who could fly back to Africa, travel in the spirit, visit or be visited by the dead; of chariots and trains to heaven, the Underground Railroad, Marcus Garvey's steamship line" (Szwed, 134).[11]

Much has been written about Coltrane, so we shall not belabor the point here. We do suggest, however, that the complex nature of Coltrane's relationship to questions of civic engagement continues to command our respectful attention. The trajectory of his career itself—with its relentless spirit of innovation—exemplifies the trope of movement that is so central to African-American creative practice. Think too about the way in which he would radically revitalize, by improvising upon, a popular tune such as "My Favorite Things." While it's true that other jazz musicians had recorded standard materials well before Coltrane's various renditions of "My Favorite Things," this example merits our consideration here because Coltrane's changing interpretations of the tune serve as a microcosm for the spirit of movement that characterizes his career. Indeed, Coltrane's improvisations would become so extreme that, in later versions of the tune, such as the hourlong rendition on *Live in Japan* (1966), the original would scarcely be recognizable. There's something extraordinary too about the level of group interplay and dialogue both in the classic Coltrane quartet and in later ventures such as "Ascension." Consider, for example, the heightened level of interaction between Coltrane and drummer Elvin Jones in so many of the quartet's recordings, and consider also the social and musical implications of Coltrane's decision to augment the classic quartet by adding a second drummer. And if you listen to Coltrane's improvised solo near the beginning of "Ascension" (Edition 2), what you hear as Coltrane roams across a two-octave range, exploring both upper- and lower-register sonorities, is a musician searching not only for new sonic possibilities, but also, we think, for hope, for new networks of social interaction, and—if we bear in mind that just two years earlier, Coltrane had recorded the mournful "Alabama," a piece in memory of the black schoolchildren killed by a bomb planted by white supremacists at the 16th Street Baptist Church in Birmingham—for justice.

During that same solo in "Ascension," there's an oft-cited moment where Coltrane plays a succession of repeated phrases in both the highest and the lowest registers of his horn, as if he is having a kind of dialogue with himself (Jost, 94; Lewis Porter, 228). Now if genuine dialogue, as Brazilian educator Paulo Freire contends, cannot exist without hope (*Oppressed*, 80), then Coltrane's gesture here, his attempt to explore the full timbral possibilities of his instrument, may have something important—perhaps something profound—to tell us about participation in a world of human responsibility. We believe that it is the task of humanities scholars to "unveil opportunities for hope, no matter what the obstacles may be" (the phrase is Freire's; *Hope,* 9); consequently, our challenge ahead, as we seek to advance the struggle for a more inclusive repertoire of valued knowledges, may well be predicated on our ability to recognize the ethical implications of performance practices that, like Coltrane's, celebrate forms of dialogue and diversity. As George Lipsitz writes, "During times of economic decline and social disintegration, it is tempting for people to blame their

problems on others, and to seek succor and certainty from racist and nationalist myths. But the desire to seek certainty and stability by depicting
the world solely as one story told from one point of view is more dangerous than ever before" (132). For Lipsitz, as, we think, for Mackey, West, and
others, the hope resides in cultural expressions of mobility, in the "ability to
adapt, to switch codes, and to see things from more than one perspective"
(132). Implicit, then, in Coltrane's dialogic improvisation (and in Pharoah
Sanders's use of multiphonics on the same recording) is a profound response to the deadening certainties of fixed ways of knowing the world.
What Coltrane seems intuitively to recognize is that failure to explore the
full resources of his instrument would be tantamount to abandoning possible resources for hope.

Today, Coltrane's legacy is registered in the work of many contemporary
musicians (witness, for example, the numerous high-profile events held recently in honor of his seventy-fifth birthday), but it resounds most powerfully and most creatively, we suspect, not in the explicit tributes (which tend,
at least for the most part, to be insufficiently alive to the spirit of movement
that animates Coltrane's oeuvre), but rather in performance practices that
accent creative investigation, openness, and improvisation as part of an ongoing process of inquiry. Indeed, recent years have witnessed the emergence
of a new generation of artists who, while indirectly touching on Trane's
monumental body of work, have enlivened our understanding of the social
and ethical possibilities of sound. In this context, we would like to return to
the work of bassist William Parker. Describing the work of his large ensemble, The Little Huey Creative Music Orchestra, Parker, in his liner notes for
Sunrise in the Tone World (1997), is explicit in aligning the expanded repertoire of possibilities opened up by improvised music making with a desire
for hope. The Little Huey Creative Music Orchestra, he writes, is dedicated
"to all those who are told not to dream. We exist for those who have had the
flame of hope put out in their lives. All those torn apart by war, poverty,
madness, loneliness and hate." He continues: "One of my ideas is for the
music to eventually evolve to the point of limitless possibility. Where each
player would have complete freedom to go wherever he or she wanted to in
the music. Freedom to use any sound or color to create something beautiful.
I am asked many times is the music we play composed or improvised. I am
not really concerned with this question, for me improvisation is a form of
composition. Everytime we improvise we are spontaneously composing. I
am more concerned with restoring life, with keeping the fire of human compassion burning. The fire of flowers as well as the fire of revolution."

Like Coltrane's "Ascension," Parker's improvised musicking offers the
opportunity to hear the world anew, to sound the hope of another possible

future. Indeed, many of Parker's writings—in addition to scripting highly resonant liner notes for many of his recordings, Parker is also a published poet and award-winning playwright—are unapologetic in their insistence that we make precisely this connection between music and the search for other ways of being in the world. In a world inflected by legacies of injustice, inequality, and massive human suffering, music, Parker insists, can—however modestly and however provisionally—provide us with new models of trust, new cultures of obligation. "In order to survive," he writes in the liner notes to his 1998 recording *The Peach Orchard,* "we must keep hope alive," the suggestion being that hope is an absolute necessity in the face of the degradations that beset us. Music's role in this context, Parker tells us, is "to incite political, social, and spiritual revolution, to awaken us from our sleep and never let us forget our obligations as human beings, to light the fire of human compassion" (quoted in "William Parker—In Order to Survive"). And in an embattled cultural terrain in which the expressive modalities of black culture have repeatedly had to struggle against processes of reduction and commodification—processes that, as Paul Gilroy has noted, have first and foremost had the effect of turning black music into "forms in which it could be frozen and sold" (25)—improvised musicking can make particularly salient interventions.

We have deliberately been invoking Christopher Small's term, "musicking," to accent the performative dimension of improvising: Small's point, indeed, is that music is not simply a thing, but rather an activity. Alluding to Small's notion of musicking, Samuel Floyd Jr., in *The Power of Black Music,* argues that "aesthetic deliberation about African-American music requires a perceptual and conceptual shift from the idea of music as an object to music as an event, from music as written—as a frozen, sonic ideal—to music as making," and suggests that "such a shift, in turn, mandates recognition of the viability and validity of the community from which the music springs" (232). The force of improvised musicking, then, emerges, at least in part, out of the ways in which new understandings of collectivity are articulated through sound. And this is, we think, what William Parker's music so astonishingly demonstrates. The expressive power of the Little Huey Creative Music Orchestra certainly recalls the spirit and sweep of Coltrane's "Ascension," but it also, as the authors of the current edition of *The Penguin Guide to Jazz* suggest, has strong affinities with Lawrence "Butch" Morris's contemporary large-scale experiments in conduction, or "conducted improvisation" (1168).[12] Now Parker's approach to sound, even in smaller, more intimate settings, has always been orchestral, always been rooted in dialogic and collective sensibilities. With the Little Huey Creative Music Orchestra, the swing, the power, and the deep processional logic (again, note the emphasis on movement) of this freewheeling, gloriously cacophonous large ensemble extend the expressive possibilities heard on Parker's solo and small-group outings.

The ensemble's performance practices, as Parker's language of hope and humanity should remind us, ought themselves to be heard as attempts to imagine, perhaps even to articulate, what bell hooks, in the epigraph we quoted at the outset, calls "future possibilities" for African-American people, or what Sun Ra, in the other epigraph, refers to as "Other Worlds (They Have Not Told You Of)." In these contexts, the use of extended techniques, the formidable textural inventiveness, the pooling of resources, and the shared musical gestures sound the possibility of other ways of being in the world. And the ongoing dialogue between the propulsive low-end ostinatos and the soaring horn and vocal melodies in the title track from *Sunrise in the Tone World,* while reminding us of the shifting registers of sound in Coltrane's "Ascension," opens our ears to an understanding of the ways in which collective improvisation can encourage shared responsibility for participation in community life and for the negotiation of differences. The music itself offers an extraordinary statement of human connectedness. Indeed, the spirit of cooperation and adjustment that has energized Parker's musicking seems especially pertinent at a historical and institutional moment when the excesses of privatization and individualism threaten to put the hopes and dreams of aggrieved peoples at risk of being abandoned.[13]

Improvisation in the rich contexts of Parker's collectives asks that we consider what it means to be "in the moment," with choices to be made that are mediated by the variegated contexts that feed into that moment. Improvisation disrupts space and time, resituating them in the play of context and choice that emerge as the improviser's response to the questions "Who are you?" "What do you do?" "What can you make of this moment?" These are the most fundamental of questions that invoke the individual's relational, contingent responsibility to his or her own agency as mediated by the relational contexts that define the moments in which such questions are asked. Improvisations remind us that these moments are omnipresent and beg the further question of how one formulates and sustains a response that accounts for how one is in the world. Improvisation invokes an ethics of the now, poising its practitioners and its listeners in the provisional space of the "now/here" that always remains to be made. In its most radical manifestations, improvisation invokes the limits of expression (such as there are limits), suggesting that beyond the nowhere of expressive limitations lies an other side that improvisational practices consistently seek to attain.

As an always contingent, potentially nonmonologic form of expression, improvisation suggests that human agency cannot be contained by form, while nonetheless producing the context in which agency is required to formalize itself in the moment of improvisation. This inability to be contained, a trope for supraexpressive expression that defines the mystery of human community and being embedded in improvisatory and free jazz practices, is the radical power to which improvisation gives voice. The "other side" that we have been using as a trope for improvisatory practices distinguishes itself from the nowhere of totalizing forms (even those that seek to limit and define improvisation), from repeated aesthetic gestures that become cliché (though these may themselves form part of an improviser's vocabulary), and from music as a nonrelational, de-ideologized commodity in an aesthetic and commercial economy (though improvised music may well reference musical commodification even as it gestures to its own ability to subvert commodification). As a provocation to avoid stasis—itself a form of ethical reneging and disavowal because it suggests a passive disengagement with the world—improvisation intensifies and expands our humanity as a communication of community.

We have studiously avoided defining either improvisation or community in any one way throughout this introduction because to do so would be to limit the very kinds of potential that both invite. Both exceed definition because both are polymorphous and polysemic. Both are contradictory to expectations of form even as both are most defined by their capacity to reinvent or to comment on already established forms. American singer and songwriter Paul Simon's bon mot that "improvisation is too good to leave to chance" (*International Herald Tribune*, 12 October 1990) ironically suggests that the rhetoric of chance (and therefore spontaneity) is best set aside when it comes to improvisation. This we must not forget comes from a musician whose own lyric style is singularly nonimprovisational, rooted in strophic song patterns, even as so-called breakthrough albums, using traditional South African and Brazilian musicians, compulsively stage Simon's commodification of improvisation bound by the format of the three-minute pop song.[14] The paradox (and anxiety) of a chance that can't be left to chance neatly encapsulates how improvisation voids definitional modes of knowing through its polymorphous ability to be both chance and nonchance simultaneously.

Improvisation (in theory and practice) challenges all musical orthodoxies, all musical taxonomies, even its own.[15] As a fundamental site for the confrontation with choices made in a social context, improvisation cannot but engage, animate, and critique the social contexts it speaks to. There are no limits to what an improvisation can or cannot be. It can encompass random noise, noise not always generated by musicians moreover, and it can simultaneously retain an organizational dimension. A good example of the latter is indicated in Gunther Schuller's comments on how he organized the unwritten wishes of Charles Mingus with regard to how to complete his large-scale composition *Epitaph,* the score of which does not provide "for an overall ending" (liner notes; 38): "keeping in mind Mingus' love for spontaneous collective improvisations, I instructed the orchestra on the day of our world premiere performance to collectively improvise the finale of Epitaph in the following three stages: 1) in a slowed-down 3/4, improvise freely, building upwards from the low register; 2) at the peak on cue hit a gigantic *ff* chord, taken from "Osmotin" (and indicated to the musicians), and thence work your way down to your lowest register; and, 3) everybody center in on a low-register F, sustained and brought to a final climax with the aid of percussion, timpani, and tam-tam" (liner notes; 38). The end result is anything but an improvisation in the sense that the piece has a clearly anticipated structure to which the musicians adhere, while nonetheless retaining improvisatory qualities.

Another example of the problem of improvisation as an expression of the tension between spontaneous musical events borne of a particular context predicated on multiple factors and clearly demarcated organizational patterns that produce the structures in which improvisation is enabled occurs in African drumming, itself a crucial source for the rhythmic grammar of jazz. John Miller Chernoff argues that "without tight organization, the improvisations [of West African drummers] become meaningless, and the ensemble cannot continue because the supporting drummers will lose their precision and sense of involvement" (122). Moreover, "precise and impressive control of improvisational style distinguishes excellence in African musical idioms, and the worst mistake in such a context is not participatory restraint but random expression" (122). Thus improvisations necessarily invoke the problem of the relationship of the improvisation to the structure in which it occurs. And that relational problem has profound implications for alternative models of community. The latter must address the exigencies of balancing necessary social organization (to achieve certain ends like social justice, equitable sharing of resources, education and care of its citizens, and so forth) against the freedoms of critique, dissonance, discrepant engagement, and so forth that invigorate and sustain the capacity of an organization to deal with difference.[16]

Improvisation, as a theoretical concept, precisely locates this dialectic and musical improvisation (in all its myriad forms) presents a largely unstudied mapping of the multiple possibilities for resolving the paradox embedded in the trope of organized freedom. Chernoff's book, *African Rhythm and African Sensibility,* consistently remarks on the ways in which West African (and specifically Ghanaian tribal) improvised musical structures reflect on the larger concerns of how best to enact community: "Beyond the innovations with which African musicians refine and sophisticate their traditional rhythms, therefore, African music is improvised in the sense that a musician's responsibility extends from the music itself into the movement of its social setting" (67). Interestingly, Chernoff characterizes social setting as a dynamic space in "movement" that is commented upon and shaped by the movement of musical improvisation. Thus, for the African musician, "the music is important only in respect to the overall success of a social occasion. . . . In an African musical event, everyone present plays a part, and from a musician's standpoint, making music is never simply a matter of creating fresh improvisations but a matter of expressing the sense of an occasion, the appropriateness at that moment of the part the music is contributing to the rest" (67). Chernoff talks of the "reciprocal responsibility" (67) that marks the site of improvised performances in African music (between, for instance, a drummer who is not playing well and the dancers who comment on that play by modifying their steps to reflect the drummer's failings or who help the drummer along by simplifying what they are doing). Thus, in one of the key locations out of which the genealogy of jazz improvisation has emerged (African music), a remarkable musical sensibility that blends improvisational practices and the reciprocal relations of community is foundational.[17]

Chernoff's point is reiterated in the context of the history of Australian improvisation described by John Whiteoak. Whiteoak argues toward improvisation as "social gesture" "influenced by social context" (xix). We reiterate that this relationship has barely received the attention it deserves in the wide variety of contexts to which it is directly relevant. Moreover, the stereotypical rhetoric used in relation to improvisational practices in jazz typically fails to address the sustained paradox of how expressive freedoms operate within set structures. Further, that same rhetoric largely disregards how the structure-freedom paradox, in fact, comments on issues of community formation and organization that are consistently present in (and invoked by) improvised music. Examples abound of improvising musicians seeking out new communities of sound that reflect as much on the genealogy of their musical improvisations as they do on the communitarian ideals they seek to achieve through musical means. African-American pianist Randy Weston, for instance, achieved the historic distinction of bringing together for the first time nine master musicians in the West African tradition of Gnawa, an event captured on the recording *The Splendid Master Gnawa Musicians of Morocco* (also discussed at some length in Jason Stanyek's essay later in this book): "never in the history of their culture [had] there ever been 9 hag'houges (guinbres) together with

2 percussionists" (liner notes; 8). One of these musicians, M'Alem Ahmed Boussou, noted that "Randy Weston's music is related to Gnawa music, by virtue of its African roots; the Exodus of Black people during the age of slavery transported Gnawa ritual both to America and to the North African Maghreb" (liner notes; 8). The music captured on the recording thus denotes more than a unique musical collaboration, referencing instead the recuperative possibilities that the music enacts as it forges new communities in spite of the diasporic forces that have displaced it from its source. This capacity to generate community in spite of difference also marks the kind of relationship that musical improvisation can bring to bear on community formation generally. And like the paradox of organized freedom, the trope of communities of difference also names the kinds of energies that improvisational practices can exemplify.

Even the rhetoric of excess that we have been using vis-à-vis improvisation can be contraindicated by an improvisation's minimalist gestures: an improviser's sparsest gestures (as Pauline Oliveros's work so extraordinarily demonstrates) can be as meaningful as his or her most excessive. Similarly, the notion that improvisation somehow is defined by a form of serial nonrepetition, a deviation from orthodox musical practices in which repeatability is a key musical principle, is unsatisfactory. Improvisations to which we have referred throughout this introduction (like "Ascension" and "The Peach Orchard") involve significant formal repetitions even as they develop a lexicon within the repetitions of dissonant practice and discrepant engagement with those repeated structures, a practice found, to cite but one instance, in the African rhythmic patternings that have had such a profound influence on jazz and creative improvised music. Improvisation in such a context is an adaptive (non)organizing principle of human agency that is both provisional and potential, both contingently mediated and startlingly experimental, both an evocation of the possible and the doable, and an articulation of the unthought and the unexpected. As an expression of multiple adaptive forms that have these qualities, improvisation has much to tell us about the way in which communities based on such forms are politically and materially pertinent to envisioning alternative ways of knowing and being in the world.

"Music," Parker writes, "will save the day. Music must save the day" (*Sound Journal,* 2). If Parker is right in suggesting that music has a vital role to play in struggles for social justice and human rights, then part of what is at stake in such a claim is an ethics of the very matter of music. Improvisation, in short, demands that we ask rigorous questions about what matters in music. For many of its most prominent and most innovative practitioners, what matters is precisely the opportunities, the possibilities, the structures of hope and momentum, that arise out of collective interaction. Indeed, there is something genuinely extraordinary about improvised musicking. Think about it: a group of people who may never have met, who, in many cases, know very little, if anything, about one another, can create inspired, energetic, moving, and hugely compelling music. And they can do this on the spot with no explicit prearranged musical direction. What makes it work?

Well, musicians and improvisers have often been rightly critical of the attempt by academics to impose neat and conclusive frameworks of understanding both on their lived experience and on their complex histories of creative practice; our thoughts here are thus offered not as final or authoritative answers, but as prompts for continuing inquiry. What, then, makes it work? Some critics have suggested that the immediacy of face-to-face interaction in improvised musicking is key to its disruptive force. Gilroy, for example, posits that in real-time performance, "immediacy and proximity reemerge as ethically charged features of social interaction" (24). And Belgrad too, in *The Culture of Spontaneity,* speaks of the "importance, to a democratic society, of face-to-face, human contact" (12). When it works (and, of course, we must be honest about this: it *doesn't* always work), improvised musicking celebrates human contact by reinvigorating our understanding of the possibilities of social interaction. Central to this understanding is a commitment to listen to the voices of those around us, and, moreover, to be able to do so with trust, humility, generosity, and a genuine spirit of openness. "Improvisation," as Ingrid Monson argues, "*is* an apt metaphor for more flexible social thinking, but we'd better keep a basic music lesson in mind: you've got to listen to the whole band if you ever expect to say something" (215). Or, to quote from Article 29 in the Universal Declaration of Human Rights (1948), "Everyone has duties to the *community* in which alone the free and full development of . . . personality is possible" (Ishay 412).

The contributions to this volume make clear that humanities scholars have much to learn from performance practices that accent conversational energy and inventive flexibility, from art forms that disrupt orthodox standards of coherence, judgment, and value with a spirit of exploration and restless innovation. If it is the case, as Sander Gilman notes in a recent collection of essays reflecting on the present state of (and future possibilities for) the humanities, that humanities research and teaching have for too long operated on the flawed assumption that knowledge is a fixed and permanent commodity (36), then the most absorbing testimony to improvisation's disruptive potential may well reside in the spirit of movement and social momentum powerfully exemplified in the history and practice of

African-American musicking that has so shaped the form and content of improvisational and free jazz. What we can learn from the relationships articulated and envisioned through these acts of musicking is precisely that we mustn't allow our thinking to settle into an orthodoxy, that in the ongoing search for new categories of momentum and new forms of community resides the hope that will sustain and empower us in our efforts to edge toward another possible future, a more just place, on the other side of nowhere.

Notes

1. Danny Goldberg, CEO and co-owner of the independent music company Artemis, argues that "despite enormous efforts at consolidation, 'independents' still have 15–20 percent market share in the music business. Reactionaries, knaves, and fools show up at indie companies as regularly as big ones, but independence does provide a more fertile environment for longer-term thinking and edgy creativity" (*Nation,* 7–14 January 2002, 24). The percentage of indie output devoted to creative improvised music and free jazz is unknown and Goldberg's figures suggest that the site of production for independent music is perhaps less compromised by the kinds of market forces that see world production of various media filtered through ten megacorporations (including AT&T, AOL/Time Warner, Liberty Media Production, Viacom, Walt Disney, Sony, Bertelsmann, Vivendi Universal, General Electric, and News Corporation). One also assumes that the appetite for what independent music companies produce coincides with their survival and the fact that they have sustained the kind of market share they have.

2. George Lipsitz provides further relevant contexts for understanding the significance of Parker's work in relation to the more general cultural sphere in which it is created and disseminated: "In appreciating the importance of African-American jazz and blues to music all over the world, we cannot ignore the history of U.S. imperialism or the monopolistic domination by U.S. firms over global networks of commerce and communication. Coercion as well as creativity underwrites the worldwide dissemination of this music.... The history of displacement, dislocation, and dispossession that gave rise to jazz and blues goes a long way toward explaining their enduring relevance to national and international cultural questions" (180). We note the ways in which many of our essayists address this issue, Eddie Prévost's comments on the commodification of hip hop and rap and Mark Anthony Neal's argument about social improvisation in the music of black youth providing a particularly productive interchange that has direct bearing on Lipsitz's observations.

3. We would note that verbal (poetic) improvisation, frequently linked to music, is to be found in a wide variety of cultural contexts. Alexis Díaz-Pimienta's important book on *repentismo,* a form of public poetic improvisation often involving music found in a large number of Spanish-speaking cultures, is an important addition to the growing literature on this aspect of improvisatory practice. It is worth noting that Díaz-Pimienta's work clearly places *repentismo* in the contexts of its relevance to a wider social sphere. See his comments, especially 117, 169.

4. Lipsitz contextualizes the demographic and historical problems facing Québécois culture: "they are also only six million people surrounded by more than two hundred million English speakers. To determine their own destiny they have to overcome the legacies of French domination over Québec, British and U.S. domination over Canada, and federal Canadian domination over Québec and other provinces with significant numbers of Francophone citizens" (147).

5. We note that Dato's recording implicitly references in its title the Afro-Cuban

forms and cultural contexts that make *son* an important form of Latin American music (insofar as those contexts are interculturally transposed to Dato's avant-garde, "postmodern" improvisations). According to Anthony Seeger, "Call-and-response forms, improvisation, and broad community participation in making music have all been identified as having African origins. Certainly these performance processes appear in traditions bearing other obvious African influences. But not all examples of these features should be unquestionably traced to African influences, as they also appear in European and Amerindian traditions" (*The Garland Handbook of Latin American Music*, 74). Olavo Alén Rodríguez notes that the *son*, "because of its influence on dance music and its projection into practically all social and functional spheres of musical activity in the country, has been the most important musical genre in Cuba" (*The Garland Handbook of Latin American Music*, 123). In Alejo Carpentier's study of Cuban music he explicitly notes how *son* relies on improvisation as a key aspect of its formal structure: "Furthermore, the *son*, in its maturity, came to us with a definite form: a *largo* and a *montuno*. The *largo* was the initial recitative, the exposition of the ballad, anciently rooted and Santiago-based, in a deliberate time, sung by one voice. . . . Enter the nervous reaction of the percussion and then the voices came in, all together, establishing in the *montuno* the old call-and-response form. . . . With a minute acceleration of the tempo, the variations could be endlessly improvised within a general rhythmic framework. The instruments embroidered, designing 'filigrees,' subdividing the basic notes, working in tandem with the growing excitement of the dancers, who, in turn, made their steps more intricate" (230–231). All of these comments point to how thoroughly improvisation, community expression and dialogue, and the memorialization of community forms and histories that the music explicitly invokes, are imbricated. Improvisation in such a context is definitively not nonreferential but an important expression of the sedimented experiences it conjures forth. We would also note that improvisation in all its forms and guises does *not* necessarily depend on a dissonant relation to harmony: improvisational practices vary across a wide spectrum of relations with hegemony. In this book we concern ourselves with those practices that we align with improvisation as a critical, resistant mode of expression.

6. See, for example, AACM-member and trumpeter Wadada Leo Smith's comments that link improvisation to "faculties of rightreasoning":

> improvisation is an art form used by creative musicians to deliver an expression or musical thought at the very instant that their idea is conceived. the improvisor must have an ability to instantaneously organize sound, silence and rhythm with the whole of his or her creative intelligence. his total life experience is drawn from, including his faculties of rightreasoning and the make-up of his psychological and physiological existence. all of these factors determine what is actually being expressed at that moment of conception and creation. thus, at each instant, the improvisor's creation includes the entire spectrum of space and cycle of time (past, present and future). (319)

Smith's radical linkage of improvisatory practices with "rightreasoning" resists arguments that posit music's general nonreferentiality, with improvised music (in this sort of an argument) being an exacerbated form of abstraction that does not reflect on political, social, and material realities. See also Eric Porter's evaluation of Smith's take on improvisation in relation to Anthony Braxton's work:

> Like Wadada Leo Smith, Braxton argues for focusing on improvisation as an expression of world creativity and a vehicle in bringing about social transformation. . . . Improvisation is thus a philosophical enterprise and a central ritualistic and aesthetic element of a global musical culture that has been marginalized by the West. (277)

For more on Smith's ideas on improvisation see Porter, 263–268.

7. We fully recognize that not all improvisatory practices are necessarily ideologically dissonant or transgressive, let alone collectivist or community-oriented. A key paradox in any understanding of improvisatory practices involves the relations between the solo (often virtuoso) performer who leads the improvisation and the collectivism out of which an improvisation potentially arises and to which it addresses itself. Ralph Ellison's comments, however idealized, on the Oklahoma City jazzmen who influenced him, point to the ways in which improvisation as a social practice actually negotiates and mediates between individualist and collectivist forms of musical expression and reception.

> [The] driving motivation [of jazzmen from Oklahoma City] was neither money nor fame, but the will to achieve the most eloquent expression of idea-emotions through the technical mastery of their instruments (which, incidentally, some of them were as a priest to a cross) and to give and take, the subtle rhythmical shaping and blending of idea, tone and imagination demanded of group improvisation. *The delicate balance struck between strong individual personality and the group during those early jam sessions was a marvel of social organization.* (Ellison, 5–6; our emphasis)

Robert G. O'Mealley notes how Ellison's seminal notion of the jazz artist is as a "leader of community, or of, as Ellison repeatedly says, *communal* rites. Beyond the question of role modeling, the jazz artist leads a ritual celebration of the American slave's will to self-assertion and freedom against a world of violent denials. As such, jazz comprises an audacious lifting of the personal, and, indeed, of the group's (including, Ellison would say, the national) voice: the un-Europeanized equivalent in music to black storytelling sessions" (Ellison, xix). In light of these remarks, Ellison clearly understands improvisatory practices as transgressive narratives that affirm African-American culture in the face of colonization and slavery. Improvisation provides an alternative social organization that responds to both historical contingency and community needs, framing a creative merging of collectivist and individualist possibilities expressive of crucial qualities of that community.

8. Levaillant argues that "la pratique même de l'improvisation est une pédagogie" (276; the practice of improvisation is itself a pedagogy) and extends this argument to suggest that "l'improvisation joue un rôle d'échangeur culturel" (278; improvisation plays a role as an exchanger of culture).

9. The Dutch improvisational collective known as the ICP Orchestra (Instant Composers Pool), famous for its large-ensemble spontaneous improvisations and led by Misha Mengelberg and Han Bennink, neatly spoofs the preoccupation with written form in the lead-off cut from their recording *Oh, My Dog,* entitled "Write down *Exactly.*"

10. Contrast Paul Berliner's apt reminder that "the popular definitions of improvisation that emphasize only its spontaneous, intuitive nature—characterizing it as the 'making of something out of nothing'—are astonishingly incomplete. This simplistic understanding of improvisation," he argues, "belies the discipline and experience on which improvisers depend, and it obscures the actual practices and processes that engage them. Improvisation depends, in fact, on thinkers having absorbed a broad base of musical knowledge, including myriad conventions that contribute to formulating ideas logically, cogently, and expressively" (492).

11. See also Lawrence Levine's argument in *Black Culture and Black Consciousness:* "The emphasis upon movement in black song reflected the currents that helped to shape Afro-American history in the United States after emancipation" (262). Indeed, "the images of movement that informed so many black songs not only mirrored what was taking place but helped to encourage and perpetuate it—helped to make movement an enduring part of black reality" (264).

12. Morris's vision of "conduction" is documented in his ten-CD recording, *Testament: A Conduction Collection* (New Worlds/Countercurrents 1995).

13. See Lipsitz: "The atrophy of the nation state and the concomitant rise of private enclaves of power and privilege answerable to no one leave little room for collective, coordinated, public struggles for power and resources" (152).

14. For a more complete discussion of Simon's intercultural borrowings and their effects, see Lipsitz's comments in *Dangerous Crossroads*, especially 56–60. Much work remains to be done on the ways in which improvisation has been commodified as a social and musical practice, especially in relation to intercultural borrowings and appropriations.

15. We note that the attempt to marginalize and confine improvisation to a fairly narrow bandwidth of musical practices (in theory and in practice) may well be an indicator of its transgressive potential and significance.

16. See also Zygmunt Bauman's argument about the tension between security and freedom that is played out in attempts to articulate models of community. "There is a price to be paid for the privilege of 'being in a community,'" writes Bauman. "The price is paid in the currency of freedom, variously called 'autonomy,' 'right to self-assertion,' 'right to be yourself.' Whatever you choose, you gain some and lose some. Missing community means missing security; gaining community, if it happens, would soon mean missing freedom. Security and freedom are two equally precious and coveted values which could be better or worse balanced, but hardly ever fully reconciled and without friction" (4–5).

17. Not all people who experience African music agree with this position, a good example being Banning Eyre's argument that in learning Malian guitar styles from Djelimady Tounkara, "I found I preferred the music *stripped* of its context . . . my core interest as a musician was the *sound* of the music, and, more often than not, the context, rather than enhancing and deepening my appreciation, obscured it with sideshows" (48). Eyre has trouble conceiving of Djelimady's music as referential within an active, ongoing social context of establishing and commenting on relations to and within a community. Nonetheless, his book as a whole offers proof of the exact opposite of what he argues, the bulk of it being given over to social, nonmusicological observations about the place of music in Malian culture.

Works Cited

Attali, Jacques. *Noise: The Political Economy of Music.* Translated by Brian Massumi. Minneapolis: University of Minnesota Press, 1996.

Bailey, Derek. *Improvisation: Its Nature and Practice in Music.* New York: Da Capo, 1992.

Baraka, Amiri Imamu (LeRoi Jones). *Black Music.* New York: Da Capo, 1998.

Bauman, Zygmunt. *Community: Seeking Safety in an Insecure World.* Cambridge: Polity, 2001.

Belgrad, Daniel. *The Culture of Spontaneity: Improvisation and the Arts in Postwar America.* Chicago: University of Chicago Press, 1998.

Berliner, Paul. *Thinking in Jazz: The Infinite Art of Improvisation.* Chicago: University of Chicago Press, 1994.

Boulez, Pierre. *Orientations: Collected Writings.* Edited by Jean-Jacques Nattiez. Translated by Martin Cooper. Cambridge, Mass.: Harvard University Press, 1986.

Carpentier, Alejo. *Music in Cuba.* Edited by Timothy Brennan. Translated by Alan West-Duran. Minneapolis: University of Minnesota Press, 2001.

Chase, Mildred Portney. *Improvisation: Music from the Inside Out.* Berkeley, Calif.: Creative Arts Book Company, 1988.

Chernoff, John Miller. *African Rhythm and African Sensibility: Aesthetics and Social Action in African Musical Idioms*. Chicago: University of Chicago Press, 1979.

Coleman, Steve, and Metrics. *The Way of the Cipher*. RCA, 1995.

Coltrane, John. *Live in Japan*. Impulse!, 1991.

———. *The Major Works of John Coltrane*. Impulse!, 1992.

Cook, Richard, and Brian Morton. *The Penguin Guide to Jazz on CD*. 5th ed. London: Penguin, 2000.

Dato, Carlo Actis. *Son Para el Che*. SPLASC(H), 1999.

Díaz-Pimienta, Alexis. *Teoría de la improvisación: Primeras páginas para el estudio del repentismo*. Havana: Ediciones Unión, 2001.

Douglas, Dave. *Witness*. BMG, 2000.

Durant, Alan. "Improvisation in the Political Economy of Music." In *Music and the Politics of Culture*, edited by Christopher Norris, 252–282. New York: St. Martin's Press, 1989.

Ellison, Ralph. *Living With Music: Ralph Ellison's Jazz Writings*. Edited by Robert G. O'Mealley. New York: Random House, 2002.

Eyre, Banning. *In Griot Time: An American Guitarist in Mali*. Philadelphia: Temple University Press, 2000.

Floyd, Samuel A., Jr. *The Power of Black Music: Interpreting History from Africa to the United States*. New York: Oxford University Press, 1995.

Freire, Paulo. *Pedagogy of Hope: Reliving Pedagogy of the Oppressed*. Translated by Robert Barr. New York: Continuum, 1994.

———. *Pedagogy of the Oppressed*. Translated by Myra Bergman Ramos. New York: Continuum, 1989.

Galeano, Eduardo. *Memory of Fire*, Vol. 3, *Century of the Wind*. Translated by Cedric Belfrage. New York: Pantheon, 1988.

Gilman, Sander L. *Fortunes of the Humanities: Thoughts for After the Year 2000*. Stanford: Stanford University Press, 2000.

Gilroy, Paul. "'. . . to be real': The Dissident Forms of Black Expressive Culture." In *Let's Get It On: The Politics of Black Performance*, edited by Catherine Ugwu, 12–33. Seattle: Bay Press, 1995.

Greenblatt, Stephen J. "Improvisation and Power." In *Literature and Society*, edited by Edward W. Said, 57–99. Baltimore: Johns Hopkins University Press, 1980.

Hebdige, Dick. "Even Unto Death: Improvisation, Edging, and Enframement." *Critical Inquiry* 27 (Winter 2001): 333–353.

———. "Subculture: The Meaning of Style." In *The Subcultures Reader*, edited by Ken Gelder and Sarah Thornton, 130–142. London: Routledge, 1997.

Heble, Ajay. *Landing on the Wrong Note: Jazz, Dissonance, and Critical Practice*. New York: Routledge, 2000.

hooks, bell. "Performance Practice as a Site of Opposition." In *Let's Get It On: The Politics of Black Performance*, edited by Catherine Ugwu, 210–221. Seattle: Bay Press, 1995.

ICP Orchestra. *Oh, My Dog*. BVHAAST, 2001.

Ishay, Michelene, ed. *The Human Rights Reader: Major Political Essays, Speeches, and Documents from the Bible to the Present*. New York, Routledge, 1997.

Jost, Ekkehard. *Free Jazz*. New York: Da Capo, 1981.

Levaillant, Denis. *L'Improvisation musicale: Essai sur la puissance du jeu*. Paris: J.-C. Lattès, 1981.

Levine, Lawrence. *Black Culture and Black Consciousness: Afro-American Folk Thought From Slavery to Freedom*. New York: Oxford University Press, 1977.

Lewis, George E. "Teaching Improvised Music: An Ethnographic Memoir." In *Arcana: Musicians on Music*, edited by John Zorn, 78–109. New York: Granary Books, 2000.

Lipsitz, George. *Dangerous Crossroads: Popular Music, Postmodernism and the Poetics of Place*. London: Verso, 1997.

Lock, Graham. *Blutopia: Visions of the Future and Revisions of the Past in the Work of Sun Ra, Duke Ellington, and Anthony Braxton*. Durham: Duke University Press, 1999.

Lussier, René. *Le Trésor de la langue*. Ambiances magnétiques, 1989.

Mackey, Nathaniel. *Discrepant Engagement: Dissonance, Cross-Culturality, and Experimental Writing*. Cambridge: Cambridge University Press, 1993.

Malcolm X. "The Founding Rally of the OAAU." *By Any Means Necessary*. New York: Pathfinder, 1992.

Mingus Big Band. *Blues & Politics*. Dreyfus, 1999.

Mingus, Charles. *Epitaph*. Columbia, 1990.

Monson, Ingrid. *Saying Something: Jazz Improvisation and Interaction*. Chicago: University of Chicago Press, 1996.

Morris, Lawrence Butch. *Testament: A Conduction Collection*. New World/Countercurrents, 1995.

Nachmanovitch, Stephen. *Free Play: Improvisation in Life and Art*. New York: J. P. Tarcher/Putnam, 1990.

Nunn, Thomas. *Wisdom of the Impulse: On The Nature of Musical Free Improvisation*. San Francisco: self-published, 1998.

Oliveros, Pauline. *The Roots of the Moment*. New York: Drogue, 1998.

Olsen, Dale A., and Daniel E. Sheehy. *The Garland Handbook of Latin American Music*. New York: Garland, 2000.

Parker, William. *Sound Journal*. New York: Centering Music, 1998.

Parker, William, and In Order to Survive. *The Peach Orchard*. AUM Fidelity, 1998.

Parker, William, and the Little Huey Creative Music Orchestra. *Sunrise in the Tone World*. AUM Fidelity, 1997.

Porter, Eric. *What Is this Thing Called Jazz? African American Musicians As Artists, Critics, and Activists*. Berkeley: University of California Press, 2002.

Porter, Lewis. *John Coltrane: His Life and Music*. Ann Arbor: University of Michigan Press, 1998.

Ra, Sun. *Lanquidity*. Evidence, 2000.

Santoro, Gene. "Jazzing Politics." *The Nation*, 17 December 2001, pp. 30–37.

Seeger, Anthony. "Traditional Music in Community Life: Aspects of Performance, Recordings, and Preservation." *Cultural Survival Quarterly* 20, no. 4 (Winter 1997): 20–22.

Small, Christopher. *Music of the Common Tongue: Survival and Celebration in African American Music* (1987). Hanover: Wesleyan University Press, 1998.

Smith, Leo. "Creative Music and the AACM." In *Keeping Time: Readings in Jazz History*, edited by Robert Walser, 315–323. New York: Oxford University Press, 1999.

Sun Ra: A Joyful Noise. Directed by Robert Mugge. Performed by Sun Ra and his Arkestra. Rhapsody Films, 1993.

Szwed, John. *Space is the Place: The Lives and Times of Sun Ra*. New York: Pantheon, 1997.

"Take This Media . . . Please!" *The Nation*, 7–14 January 2002, pp. 22–36.

Tapscott, Horace. *Songs of the Unsung: The Musical and Social Journey of Horace Tapscott*. Edited by Steven Isoardi. Durham: Duke University Press, 2001.

Taylor, Timothy. *Global Pop: World Music, World Markets*. New York: Routledge, 1997.

Todorov, Tzvetan. *The Conquest of America: The Question of the Other*. Norman: University of Oklahoma Press, 1999.

Toop, David. *Ocean of Sound: Aether Talk, Ambient Sound and Imaginary Worlds.* New York: Serpent's Tail, 1995.

West, Cornel. *Keeping Faith: Philosophy and Race in America.* New York: Routledge, 1993.

Weston, Randy. *The Splendid Master Gnawa Musicians of Morocco and Randy Weston.* Verve, 1994.

Whiteoak, John. *Playing Ad Lib: Improvisatory Music in Australia, 1836–1970.* Sydney: Currency, 1999.

"William Parker—In Order to Survive." *Jazz Improv* website. <http://jazzimprov.com/r-pkr-w1.htm>. February 1, 2002.

PART ONE

PERFORMERS IMPROVISE

MICHAEL SNOW

A Composition on Improvisation

OK, I'll start at the beginning, what alternatives are there? 1. Don't start at all. 2. Start but since this is writing (i.e., a form of composition) it, this, can be rearranged; hence, I could (later) put the phrase "OK, I'll start at the beginning."

Skipping the middle for the moment (but is that possible? in a text?) I'd like to go directly to the issue of "endings."

An event (temporal by definition) ends when it stops. Well, of course it's not that simple. I'll define pertinent events, later, soon in fact.

In this composition I'll probably use: "I have decided that this is the last sentence in this text." We'll see.

This is a solo, recorded. However.

Previous to "OK, I'll start at the beginning" was the intention: to think and to write (silent, about sound.)

Sound events. Those events where the context and paraphernalia employed indicate that they are involved in directing the spectators' attention primarily to sounds, to sounds produced "for them."

The sounds are produced for those who produce them, as well.

To return to "the middle": in his 1977 well-titled book, *Mozart* (Frankfurt am Main: Suhrkamp), Wolfgang Hildesdeimer wrote and I quote:

Contemporaries report that when he was playing the piano, especially when improvising, he became that other human being they would have liked him to be in his daily life. His expression changed; he seemed to become serene. . . . These must have been the moments (often hours) when he reveled in blissful self-forgetfulness, when he severed his connection with the outside world; here he was the unadorned Mozart, who needed no intermediary in order to communicate—no singers, no instrumentalists or fellow musicians, and no bothersome score, either. Here, and perhaps only here, he achieved true pleasure in his own genius; here he transcended himself, becoming the absolute Mozart. (279)

We'll let that "he became the other human being they would have liked him to be in his daily life" pass, although the implications are pretty interesting.

What's reported on was solo playing. If we listen to a playing of some Mozart solo piano pieces we hear something resembling his improvising.

Ensemble Mozartean improvisation, then, seems possible but unlikely.

Free ensemble improvisation is possible today because improvising musicians exist in the huge aesthetic area opened up by modern "classical" music: Schoenberg, Ives, Varèse, Cage, Xenakis, and many others, and Futurist, Dada, and Fluxus sound experiments. Equally important are recordings, gifts of examples of non-Western musics' attitudes to musical sound and the "color" emphasis given to their music by the great blues and jazz stylists. For example, consider the incredible range of tonal, attack and other qualities in the music of these great trumpet players: Louis Armstrong, Bix Beiderbecke, Bubber Miley, Rex Stewart, Roy Eldridge, Dizzy Gillespie, and Miles Davis. Trumpet!

In jazz improvisation some of the most thrilling moments involve a brilliant player's ways of getting from chorus to chorus, transforming the cadences called for in the harmonic structure of the theme, or, in a blues, not necessarily resolving the ending of each twelve-bar episode.

Following the player's inventions *in relation to the theme* was one of the things that was exciting in jazz playing of all styles.

I often pleasurably asked myself in the sixties "where the hell is he?" while listening to a great improviser such as Sonny Rollins.

Bebop's unprecedented themes and especially the solos of Charlie Parker, Dizzy Gillespie, Miles Davis, and Bud Powell during the fifties, took improvisation further and further away from the boundaries of chorus length, bar lines and "running the changes" (arpeggiating the basic chords of a "piece" using "extended" chords or substitute harmony).

And in the bebop rhythm section, piano, bass, and drums had more independence than in previous styles.

These developments are the main starting area for what became complete independence of parts as an ensemble agreement.

Saying of "free improvisation" that it was impossible, Charles Mingus explained that "you have to start with *something*."

I can easily understand the rage that audiences felt at Ornette Coleman when, in his early days, he sat in with blues-jazz bands and didn't play "choruses." "Where the hell is he?" was infuriating to some.

But, he was intuitively operating in the independence that musicians had been granted by bebop's "advances."

The "modal" playing of Miles Davis and John Coltrane was another step.

When I started to try to play "free," not starting with a tune or playing the blues was mysterious. I *did* ask myself: "Where will it come from?"

But the more one intuitively plays "anything" but also listens critically, the more certain musical areas reveal themselves as interesting and "personal." Try this, try that.

This is one of the ways that composers compose.

Mingus was right in a sense: "free" players *do* start with something; it's where they were the last time they played. The other side of nowhere.

I started out playing "Traditional," New Orleans, Dixieland Jazz. Of all the styles of jazz, its somewhat free counterpoint is the closest to the ensemble music (which probably isn't "jazz") I've been involved in for the last thirty years.

Though I loved Duke Ellington's, Jelly Roll Morton's, and Thelonious Monk's music, I was always more interested in the improvisation part of jazz than the compositional.

In 1960 I led a quartet (Alf Jones, trombone; Terry Forester, bass; Larry Dubin, drums; me, piano) that played blues in whole-tone scales. First partially free for me.

Between '62 and '72 I lived in New York and right from the beginning I fell in with a fast crowd: Cecil Taylor, Albert Ayler, Roswell Rudd, Milford Graves, and many others. I mostly listened, didn't play with any of them because I couldn't.

They were inspiring. Despite the greatness of much of the music I heard then, I early objected to the continued use of "tunes" to open and close "free" or "freer" solo improvisation just like all previous jazz.

I dreamed of a group that would organically find its own music together, by playing it, without the bookends of prior composed themes. This dream was realized with the formation of the CCMC in 1974.

In my free-playing life in Toronto, however, the CCMC was preceded by the Artists Jazz Band.

I'd been playing piano professionally for about fifteen years when some visual artists who were friends of mine, bought instruments and started to play. Gord Rayner (drums), Robert Marble (tenor sax), Nobua Kubota (alto sax), Graham Coughtry (trombone), and others started the AJB in 1960. At first I was, to say the least, skeptical, but they soon changed my tune! Having meager technical or harmonic knowledge ("none" might be better) they "just played" passionate, astonishing music. Their music *was* an extension of their conversation, the stoned ecstatic peak of many great parties at Gord Rayner's Spadina Ave. studio. They showed that you don't have to know "how to play" in any conventional sense to make interesting music. A pre-punk lesson.

London's Nihilist Spasm Band is a related phenomenon, great home-made music. The AJB's models were from jazz whereas the Spasm bands were more rock-related. Amplification.

The original members of the CCMC had arrived at spontaneous playing from many different backgrounds. It was rich: Casey Sokol is a thoroughly schooled classical pianist; Al Mattes had been a folk guitarist, had a degree in psychology and studied electronic music with David Rosenboom at York University; Larry Dubin, a great drummer, came, like me, from jazz; and Nobi Kubota from the AJB.

We all agreed on having as many different sound sources as possible. From the beginnings, we had a wide range of percussion instruments, a huge collection of toys and self-invented instruments. We had synthesizers (from Buclas to "crackle boxes"), Kubota used prerecorded tapes in the music. We used two grand pianos plus two Fender Rhodes electrics so a piece could have four pianos or be all electronic or all rhythm. Everybody played any instrument in addition to their primary one. I regularly played acoustic and electric piano, trumpet, flugelhorn, some self-invented trumpet mouthpiece instruments, guitar, and any other thing that seemed right.

We often referred/refer to what we did as "spontaneous ensemble composition."

The rediscovery of "improvisation" in music is one of the most important aesthetic events of the last hundred years. It will influence, for example, all electronic art.

"Improvising," as for Mozart, means playing the music that you want to hear at that particular time and place on that particular instrument.

Those "particulars" will be partly the source of the music. Another source will be the continuity of real-time extensions of previously made discoveries.

For the past few years I have not been consciously influenced by other music except the music of those I play with.

Currently, the CCMC is Paul Dutton (sound singing), John Oswald (alto sax), me, and frequent fabulous guests, mostly Torontonians.

The reason that Dutton and Oswald are interesting is that they play *their* music. When I play *my* music with *theirs*, it becomes *ours*.

Resemblances are inescapable and quotation, though dangerous, permissible. I wanted, whenever I played, to play my own music. I've convinced myself that when I play now, the music is by me. I even believe that whenever I play, I play some things that I've never heard before.

The heat of present-tense discovering, the raw energy of priority, is one of the strong pleasures for the player of and the listener to, improvised music.

Note. I'm composing this text using a Stanford "Uni-ball" pen, "fine," an acoustic, manually played instrument, as it were.

Later (now?) it will be a digital recording.
There won't be a coda. This will just end, soon . . .

But first:

Of course, everyone "improvises." Conversation is the most common form. All the mental states that one experiences in conversation are *somewhat* applicable to musical improvisation. Often, mostly, one just speaks, hears what one has to say and goes on from there, one is not conscious of thinking, one acts. Sometimes, one's mind will be preparing a reply while listening to someone else's statement. This preparation can only be a tendency toward a certain sense, it may be mentally heard in words but will become "phrased" and understandable when one speaks it. Sometimes one knows a lot about the subject at hand and basically "plays-back" what one knows.

But of course these categories are subject to mutations from one to the other in practice and are inextricable from pleasure, dismay, anger, puzzlement, sadness, astonishment, etc. Aren't they?

To play new music, the first state (of nonthought action) is the best. One is then in what cannot-swiftly-enough, be called the "present," more firmly than in almost any other activity, except making love.

But since one proceeds into the future with the accumulation of what has been learned, it is inevitable that one will repeat oneself. A certain amount of this is comfortable but it is important to modify personal clichés when they seem to be appearing.

Playing music *isn't* "conversation" though. So much of what happens that's moving, happens simultaneously, in group improvisation.

This text *isn't* "conversation" either.

Some of the most miraculous events in group improvisation are the endings. Everything is just charging along and, snap! It stops! And *everyone* is surprised. And it wasn't some cliché resolution, but a hitherto not encountered, new, ending!

PAULINE OLIVEROS

Harmonic Anatomy
Women in Improvisation

In this universe—and perhaps many others—life forms, matter and energy are constantly interacting to promote flow or movement from one moment to the next. This is improvisation.

In music, theater, dance, and the visual arts, improvisation includes acting from inner intelligence and/or impulse without premeditation from the whole field of available possibilities, as well as acting with vocabulary within more prescribed forms.

My early musical education did not include improvisation or any reference to the word. When I was sixteen, however, an inner improvisation of sounds and music exploded in my mind as I listened to unprompted musical forms taking shape. I heard great whooshing orchestral textures mixing with white noise, pops, whistles and other odd sounds that I would identify later as electronic. I announced that I wanted to be a composer.

By age seventeen I had begun to engage in jazz improvisation on my accordion with standard tunes such as "Body and Soul," "Deep Purple," "Stardust," and so forth. I was studying with Bill Hughes, an extraordinary improviser on the accordion who played with Houston jazz groups. I had entered the world of professional music as a soloist, playing standard tunes and improvising over the chord progressions.

Persisting in my desire to be a composer, I would sit at the piano keyboard searching for the notes running through my mind. I realize now that I was slowly learning to improvise as I fished around the piano keyboard. I learned laboriously to write these notes down.

I was nineteen when I wrote my first piano piece but I found that the keyboard was extremely limiting. Ten years later I discovered what I wanted to express in the electronic sounds of my first tape pieces.

It had not consciously occurred to me that women were not included in the musical canon that I learned as a performer. Perhaps this was because women had taught me from early childhood. My mother and my grandmother taught me to read notes but didn't discourage me from playing by ear if I did try it. I do remember striving hard to learn to read music. I was trained to be a performer of other people's music.

My mother, Edith Gutierrez, and grandmother, Pauline V. Gribbin, were dedicated to their piano teaching. Lessons often began early in the morning before school and continued in the afternoon and evening. On Sundays they played duets and two piano pieces together, with me as a fascinated listener. Edith would practice by herself for hours. I picked up their dedication and devotion early on and tried hard to learn to play as they did on my instrument of choice: the accordion.

Edith tells me that she was unaware of the word "improvisation," although she began to improvise while playing piano for dance classes in the 1940s. She called it "filling in." My grandmother had learned to play strictly by the notes. However, her husband, my grandfather John M. Gribbin, played only by ear and was always improvising pieces, called "compositions." My grandmother wrote the pieces down for him.

From an early age I attended numerous concerts of the Houston Symphony and Opera, endless recitals by soloists and chamber groups. I was excited to hear among the many touring artists Stan Kenton, Spike Jones, and the Israel Philharmonic orchestra with Leonard Bernstein conducting.

I listened to the radio every week for years to the New York Philharmonic, the NBC orchestra with Toscanini conducting, the Metropolitan Opera, Grand Ole Opry, Bob Wills and the Texas Playboys. Shows with sound effects, like "I Love A Mystery" and "Fibber McGee and Molly" fascinated me. Music on the radio had a very large influence on me. We owned a wire recorder in the forties, which I used to record myself and music from the radio. I tried to write down what I recorded or to imitate the style on my accordion.

I was thoroughly grounded in many styles of Western music. Exposure to world music came much later. This was the 1940s.

Edith came home one day when I was about thirteen years old and played some "compositions" she had done for a modern dance class at the YWCA. These pieces were oddly dissonant and rhythmical. I also began to notice her "fill-ins" when she played the piano at home. There was still no mention of "improvisation." Little did I know the profound effect that her cue would have on me. I loved the pieces and still do. Her creativity had jumped out at me.

Gender Challenges

I joined the band in junior high school. Since accordions had no place in the band I was introduced to the tuba by the female band director. She would be my last female music teacher. Senior high school was a different story. There were already twelve male sousaphone players. The male band director handed me a French horn to learn to play. Later, when I became serious about studying, the first sexist remark came from a male horn teacher. "Why do you want to be a horn player—you will only get married and have children." Feelings of betrayal welled up inside. My anger made me feel wary and circumspect with male teachers. There was no recourse for me; I was powerless in the student-teacher relationship to express my feelings directly. I quickly abandoned lessons with that teacher but continued my determination to play.

My first composition class at the University of Houston in 1951 included several women with a male teacher. The teacher seemed respectful of everyone, both male and female. I wrote my first pieces in this class, which were performed along with those of my classmates. So far my experiences were relatively positive as a woman interested in composition, although the music models presented by the teacher did not help me. Those models were all by men, even though there were women in the class, including me.

In 1952 I went on from Houston to San Francisco searching for a composition teacher, reaffirming to myself that I was certain that I wanted to be a composer, true to what I was hearing inwardly. It was in San Francisco that I met with gender issues from prospective composition teachers—as I had with the horn teacher in Houston—mostly in the form of doubtful remarks about women and composition. To those teachers women were not candidates for composition lessons.

The composer's workshop at San Francisco State College was populated with men and taught by a man. I joined the workshop. Whenever the instructor considered my music all the twenty or so male students would leave the room. I felt this concerted exodus as another kind of betrayal. However, lack of peer support did not deter me from writing my music. I was determined. This lack of support continued until one day Terry Riley, Loren Rush, and Stuart Dempster were staying and listening to what I was doing. We began to share our musical interests and became lifelong friends.

The mentor I finally found—Robert Erickson—never made sexist remarks and treated me no differently than he did his other students. I met

Erickson at a Composer's Workshop concert at San Francisco State College in 1954. We admired each other's compositions after that program. His attitude of respect for my work drew me to make an appointment for my first lesson. I left this first lesson elated. I discovered that Loren was studying with Erickson too. Eventually Terry took lessons as well. We shared our enthusiasm for the excellence of his teaching. In addition to supporting our compositional efforts Erickson often invited us to his home for familylike occasions. I felt accepted for who I was at the time, even though I was the only woman involved in this circle.

Erickson encouraged all of us to improvise. His prompting was of course totally unusual for a person of his academic training in music. He encouraged me to improvise my way through pieces I was composing. His prompting was encouraging and validating, and it reinforced my way of working.

My first group improvisations were with Terry Riley and Loren Rush in 1957. There were no models; there were no scenes for improvisation as there are today. Gathering three composers of concert music to improvise together was unprecedented.

Terry had to compose a five-minute film score. He didn't have time to write it so we went to Radio KPFA in Berkeley where Loren was working and recorded several five-minute improvisations for Terry to use for the film soundtrack. Terry selected a track and used it very successfully. We were so interested in the results that we decided to meet again and improvise for fun.

We found that it was best to improvise first and talk about it afterward. If we discussed what we were going to do the improvisation seemed to fall flat. Improvising without discussion seemed to give us an exciting edge and arena for discovery, as the world of possibilities remained open.

After my initial improvisations with Terry Riley and Loren Rush, I began to improvise in a similar way with Ramon Sender Barayon, who was also a student of Erickson. Morton Subotnik joined us in 1960 and we performed many concerts together under the auspices of our San Francisco Tape Music Center. We always included a group acoustic improvisation in our home concerts and tours of tape music.

My early composition was gestural rather than formal. I wrote what I heard. As a composer, I was not interested in the textbook forms presented to me in classes; rather, I was interested in sounds, in the interplay and sensual nature of sounds that ran through my mind. Later when I began to work with tape music I found a friendly medium for my musical inclinations and concerns. I could sculpt sound in this medium through improvisation. I improvised almost all of my early electronic music, gleefully avoiding tedious cutting and splicing of tape. Gradually, improvisation, the combinations of tape techniques, electronic sound generation, processing, and acoustic instruments became a solid and continuing part of my music making.

By the end of the sixties, my experience with improvisation was almost exclusively solo or with groups of men. My position was unique. I held my own with male musicians, though sometimes I felt discomfort. Even though I was included in the groups that I worked with, I felt an invisible barrier. As I had noticed early in life, males bond strongly around music and technology and leave women out of their conversations and performances.

Values

Values often emphasized by male musicians and their critics include technique, intelligence, structure, precision, concept, drive and so forth. For example:

Blessed with a seemingly effortless technique, a wittily deconstructive approach to his instrument(s), and a generous intelligence, he never produces work that is less than thoughtful or other than exuberant.

. . . draws from a heady bank of extended techniques that both amplify and personalize the range of his horn.

. . . a genuine original, a percussionist whose combination of hyperactivity, arhythmical structure and intense precision have played a crucial role in the European free aesthetic. *Penguin Guide To Jazz*

On the other hand, critical remarks in reviews about women improvisers go toward qualities of sound, spirit, and feeling. The language softens to emphasize different values:

Ms. Ibarra deftly maneuvered from delicate brushwork to crashing rim shots as the ensemble alternated between soft harmonies and sharp dissonance. Even the cushioned mallets could not dull her insistent inchoate rhythmic patterns.
David Yaffe, *New York Times*

Ingrid Jensen is mindful of the tradition in that she swings, plays real pretty AND with fire, but realizes that you don't live up to "the tradition" by playing it safe.
Mark Keresman, *Jazz Review.com*

Claire Daly's lips blow sweetly and the jazz comes forth sweet and low! She is a great talent that is hard to define. Her expertise on the baritone saxophone is truly remarkable and without peer, and to be sure, listen to "Swing Low" and discover how well this lady knows her jazz techniques and blends them with her own intimate, personal visions! Claire Daly gives a sensual performance of harmonic phrasing, and the power of that jazz sophistication is evident.
Lee Prosser, *Jazz Review.com*

The reviewers' language emphasizes other values at stake in women's performance. The distinction between the qualifiers in the language used to review the women is striking. There is reference to Claire Daly's skill, but it is doubtful the male reviewer would write that "Gerry Mulligan's lips blow sweetly" (even if they do) or speak of his "intimate personal visions and sensual performance." Both sets of values are present in the improvisations of men and women. Yet gender construction sets them apart.

What about the women?

It was not until 1969—the threshold of the emerging women's movement of the seventies—that I explored improvisation with other women. I organized the Women's Ensemble in San Diego. The ensemble featured Betty and Shirley Wong (voice), Lin Barron (cello), Bonnie Barnett (voice), Joan George (bass clarinet) and the late poet Lynn Lonidier (cello). I realized then that women needed opportunities to express their inner voices. No one in the university environment was going to recognize this need or do anything about it, so I set about inviting the women to work with me. (I was teaching in the music department at the University of California, San Diego, during those years.)

The group met at my house in Leucadia, California, every week for two years exploring nonverbal time together, mind/body exercises, dreams, journal writing and reading, and improvisation through my Sonic Meditations. The Women's Ensemble was an important step for me in experiencing the energy of working with women in improvisation informed by the concerns that we shared with one another. Occasionally, we performed concerts as well. We were creating a kind of meditational improvisation based in the layering of sounds. We recorded Music for Expo 70 that was featured in the Pepsi Pavilion in Expo 70 in Osaka.

I was making a transition in my own work with the Women's Ensemble. Working with women gave me a kind of permission to be myself that had been covered or more hidden in the mostly male musical environment I inhabited, where as a woman I had to prove myself more intensely. Coping with competitive males at times was daunting. There was no blueprint for me either.

Improvising with women brings about a feeling of kinship, collaboration and cooperative listening. The music is about inclusion rather than exclusion. There is less emphasis on technical mastery and more concern for sounds weaving into shared textures. I feel that I have been heard and included in consciousness as a collaborator rather than regarded as an intrusive competitor.

I resigned from my position at the University of California, San Diego, in 1981, to pursue a freelance career of composition and improvisation in the Northeast. I started my own nonprofit organization—Pauline Oliveros Foundation—that became the platform for my own creative and educational ideas and concepts. I was on my own and worked mostly as a soloist performing my own music or collaborating with choreographers.

Through the 1980s I continued to develop my freelance work as a soloist and with the Deep Listening Band together with my old friend Stuart Dempster. I concentrated on the development of my electronic processing: the Expanded Instrument System (EIS). EIS grew out of my way of performing my electronic music such as "Bye Bye Butterfly" and "I of IV." I wanted to apply the processing technique to acoustic sounds. EIS is used as an improvisation environment by me as a soloist and the Deep Listening Band. EIS continues to evolve assisted in the 1980s by Panaiotis and continued to the present by David Gamper. In the meantime I enjoyed my growing consciousness of other women appearing as composers and improvisers.

In 1996 after meeting violinist India Cook at the John Coltrane Church in San Francisco I invited her and a vocalist friend of hers, Karolyn Van Putten, to improvise with me. After a couple of sessions at home we performed as a trio together in Berkeley at Bean Benders (formerly a popular venue for improvising musicians in the Bay Area organized by Dan Plonsey). We were invited to come back to Bean Benders the next month, have played together every fall since and produced a recording in 2000: *Live at the Meridian* on Sparkling Beatnik.

Improvising with India and Karolyn was immediately arresting. I felt their responsiveness as uncanny and musically very rewarding. The Circle Trio with India Cooke and Karolyn Van Putten was the second all-woman group organized by me. I was delighted that more women were available to play together with me. The experience reminded me that I missed the Women's Group from San Diego, which had dispersed because of graduations and changes.

Also in 1996, Dana Reason (pianist) and Philip Gelb (shakuhachi) invited me to join their improvising duo for a concert in San Francisco at Radio Valencia, an alternative venue for musicians. I was delighted with their skillful, creative performing and listening. We performed again soon with saxophonist John Raskin of the Rova Saxophone Quartet as our guest at the Center for New Music and Audio Technology (CNMAT) in Berkeley and were recorded by David Wessel. The recording was released on Sparkling Beatnik as *The Space Between*. We continue to perform under that name and released another CD performed and recorded at CNMAT with guest artist Barre Phillips on bass. Our delight is negotiating the space between our three different tunings: accordion in just intonation, piano in equal temperament, and shakuhachi in its unique tuning.

In 1999 drummer Susie Ibarra invited me to perform with her at Tonic in New York, an important venue for new music on the Lower East Side. I suggested the addition of Monique Buzzarté (trombone), Rosi Hertlein (violin/voice), and Kristin Norderval (voice) to form The New Circle Five. We return to Tonic every year to perform and released *Dreaming Wide Awake* on the Deep Listening label June 2003.

Notably, the nineties included more improvisation with women than ever before in my career. Encouraging as this may seem, improvisation groups in the various "scenes" that exist throughout the Western world still seem to consist exclusively of men unless there is a singer or a token woman included. This is true of most genres in Western music. This situation is clearly expressed in the makeup of most concert programs, festivals and touring groups now at the beginning of the twenty-first century. A casual look at newspapers, magazines, internet sites, and media reports will verify this statement.

If a music group consisting exclusively of women turns up (and one *does* from time to time), it may be viewed as an oddity and taken less seriously by audiences, presenters and critics than a male group. Otherwise female groups would sustain themselves and proliferate as readily as male groups do and receive more critical attention. Nonetheless, we can now note exceptions: New Music America in the 1980s, the Guelph Jazz Festival in Canada, and the London Musician's Collective in the United Kingdom. There are a few others and these examples will, it is hoped, proliferate.

Improvisational music, as well as composition, appears to remain the province of men. Perhaps in a field that is already difficult for men, women don't see any future for themselves as improvisers or composers. Women see few if any role models or mentors, few performance opportunities in the field, and relatively no financial support to launch or sustain a career. The socialization of women continues to reinforce the role for them of spectators, supporters, and administrators where men hold forth as participants in the art.

Harmonic Anatomies

Following are introductions to some of the women musicians whom I know through our experience of improvising together. Their feelings and thoughts about improvising may shed more light on the issues of gender, language, and the crucial nature of improvisation as a process for dialogue across communities.

Anne Bourne is a professional cellist, composer, and improviser based in Toronto. I first improvised with Anne over distance between Toronto and New York on a Picture-Tel connection with the Deep Listening Band. (Picture-Tel is a video monitor with a camera mounted on top. The system can be connected to an ISDN telephone line for distance communication with remote locations.) Anne has extraordinary tone and can carry an ensemble with her voice and rhythms as well as with lovely melodic lines on her cello. Anne burst out of her reticence to be heard through an emotional reaction:

Fred Stone used to lead his band like Miles Davis, calling out rhythms and lines midstream. I used to get mad and freeze every time he'd tell me to "take a solo," so he once reversed the strategy and whispered in my ear "Whatever you do, don't take a solo." This made me mad enough to play, and became the beginning of a long phase of making music out of anger.

Anne Bourne

Tapping into emotional energy seemed to open the portals for Anne to express her music. I recall how my own anger spurred me to continue playing horn. This is no less true of men. However, the expression "cool" tempers how men play. To be "cool" is to be technically competent. A flash of technique by an instrumentalist is "cool." An outburst of emotion is definitely "not cool." Fred called out "rhythms and lines" to the band, but Anne could not respond to this language. Fred's psychological twist turned Anne on to a more accessible way for her to improvise.

Monique Buzzarté is a professional trombone player based in New York. Her admirers describe her playing her "butter trombone." Her beautiful tone spreads through an ensemble with great ease and connection.

I have sometimes felt as if I was reaching far into the future or far into the past, time traveling while performing. This is especially true of several short improvisations on conch. I let go of myself and open to other experiences, and they happen to me, through me, as if I in the Monique-body am a channel for the expression of something else much bigger than myself. I don't know how explicit I want to be here, but certainly they are the strongest experiences I've ever had performing. Great power for healing and great responsibility for others are carried in these sounds.

Monique Buzzarté

Monique seems to have a natural propensity for a state of consciousness that opens a large space of spirit. The feeling of being a channel for something bigger than oneself is common to practitioners of healing. Her sense of the power of sounds coming through this mode of consciousness and responsibility for others is an important aspect of healing practice and an important function of music.

India Cooke was introduced as "the world's best kept secret" at one of our concerts in San Francisco. India explains that she is a classically trained violinist, that "playing classical music is challenging." She crossed over to playing jazz: "I found that challenging too. However the most challenging music to perform is free improvisation." Playing with India is like taking the A Train to heaven.

> I exercise the resources available to me. That is, I channel psychic energy, not exclusively musical energy. . . . Then I put together harmonies and melodies and rhythms and whatever comes out as a result of this combination is the musical statement.
>
> India Cooke

India's reference to "channeling" may mean something similar to Monique's "channel." Definitely there is an opening of consciousness implied that infuses India's music and affects other players and the audience; a space of spirit that is wider than ordinary consciousness in daily life.

Susie Ibarra plays the drum set like no other; she plays the space as well as the drums, drumming the air with precision and fluidic confidence. Based in New York, Susie has established herself in improvised music as a top professional supporting and transporting other players.

> I always improvised when I was young. I used to always answer a question with a question. I often felt that there was never only one straight answer to a question.
>
> Susie Ibarra

Susie's metaphor of the question seems to be the root of her way of improvising, especially that there was always more than one straight answer to a question. Hers is an attitude of discovery and freedom to seek alternatives through the analogy of conversation, where rhythms are constantly in flux.

Frances Marie Uitti (professional cellist and improviser based in Amsterdam) is noted for her use of two and three bows simultaneously. Her ecstatic playing transports you immediately.

> I've always enjoyed improvising more than reading music. I feel that improvising is more natural for me than reading music. When I was a child I would much rather play by ear than read. My father played violin and would play my pieces for me. Once my father found out I was copying him rather than reading, he stopped playing for me and I had to learn to read through many a tear. I studied classical music and stopped improvising until I went to Rome in the late seventies and started group improvisation. With vocalist Michiko Hirayama and trombonist John Carlo Schiaffini. Then I started improvising solo again. It was easier for me to push myself into different corners by myself than in a group.
>
> Frances Marie Uitti

Frances expresses a common experience for musicians. Playing by ear is discouraged over the ability to read. The two ways could just as easily be integrated from a fairly early age. Frances found her way out of her classical training to her own music. Her solo work seems to come from a very deep inner place that eschews the diversion of performing with others. She seems to need the quiet of her own "corner" to get to her own inner voice even though she negotiates group improvisations beautifully.

Kristin Norderval is a professional lyric soprano, composer, and improviser. She is classically trained and is based in Norway and in New York. Kristin can hold her own with an orchestra or an industrial soundscape. Her beautiful lyric soprano can sail through any atmosphere and also blend as an instrumentalist in a group.

Really interesting acoustics usually bring up spontaneous vocal improvisations for me. I'm unable to resist diving into a beautiful acoustic pool; it's so delightful to explore the caverns, corral and cut of the stone of the space. I've been recording on-site improvisations in various places for the last four years. The sites give me their own input and offer rhythms, pitches and timbres that I wouldn't come up with on my own. Likewise, when I then process portions of those recordings electronically, the material itself calls for responses from me. The acoustic properties of the sites or the objects that I work with might provide drones, or microtones, or modalities, but the processing might provide different harmonic or rhythmic structures, so there is a merging of various styles that happens automatically. Also, although I'm a classically trained singer, when I'm working over unusual sound landscapes I may borrow from other singing traditions, or imitate sounds that I wouldn't use in a classical context. Some friends hearing my music have described it as urban-tribal.

Kristin Norderval

Kristin's interest in acoustics shows that she is listening. She is responsive to spaces and indeed dialogues with the site. Her consciousness of environment informs her work. She is aware on many levels at once and from the site at hand she draws vocal flexibility, her memory of styles, and her imaginative interplay with all of these elements.

Dr. Jackie Pickett plays acoustic bass and is equally at home with both oral and written traditions of music performance. Classically trained with a DMA (Doctor of Musical Arts) from the University of Wisconsin–Madison, Jackie plays all genres as a freelance professional and devotes herself to teaching inner-city kids. Playing with Jackie is an uplifting experience. Her techniques carry her anywhere on the musical map.

When the group enters an "out of body" space, it is like you can actually look "up/down/over/under/across" and see the group playing . . . locking in. There is a similar sensation in cycling up a hill with the proper "spin" in the pedal.

Jackie Pickett

"Out of the body" from "in the body" to a state of global consciousness that provides for a witnesslike overview of the performing. Again, there is an acute awareness of the state of mind and body sensations.

Dana Reason plays the piano, composes, and improvises. She thinks deeply about improvisation and has completed a dissertation for her Ph.D.

in improvised music at the University of California, San Diego. Dana explores the coloristic possibilities of the piano on the keyboard and inside the piano with daring and intensity. Her intricate patterns weave an ensemble together sometimes as a percussionist, sometimes as a sound artist, sometimes as a keyboard player.

I was always playing things by ear and really didn't want to read music for a while. I liked making things up, although I thought I was composing not improvising. I didn't really know the term "improvisation." I liked putting the television on and turning down the volume to "make the soundtrack." I also liked putting on the radio and playing along with the songs. I used to try and fool my parents into thinking I was practicing by improvising in the style of Bach, Beethoven, or whatever.

Dana Reason

Dana found her way to her music by improvising even though she had no word for it. I wonder how often her parents were fooled by her attempts to imitate the style of Bach or Beethoven? As for most women—my mother and me, included—self-teaching and "playing by ear" brought about the ability to improvise music directly.

There is something about improvising with women that is like coming home. Almost a tribal feeling compels us to find the musical way to understanding and carries the listeners inside. Our bodies merge with the vibrational complexity of a deep ocean. Improvising with women, the undulating movement between chaos and form is strong and challenging; finally, understanding is expressed lovingly, with respect. This I have experienced improvising with both men and women. However the resonance of harmonic anatomy can move me to the bone marrow.

Anne Bourne

The unique values, understanding, and expression each woman brings to our improvisations helps me to understand my own evolution as an improviser in a continually expanding collaborative process and language. That process includes sharing space/time, sharing states of consciousness and body consciousness, elevating the sensuous nature of sound onto a par with technical mastery in making the music. This process is of the body, in the body, and out of the body. The vocabulary of the language includes sounds as well as pitches; the syntax comes through inner and outer dialogue with self, space, and others through weaving and sharing in the moment; the forms arise and shape themselves from the energy of the body. Breath, sensations, and consciousness through listening and tuning to the presence of others—this is "harmonic anatomy."

Musically speaking, it is a very large language that is constantly growing for me. Sometimes it is the gift of playing pure music that seems to be falling right out of the sky. Sometimes it is a gift of communication between people, like a common language that breaks all barriers. Sometimes in life experiences it is the deciding action that can help keep the motion moving and constant. Sometimes it is a saving grace in situations. And sometimes it is a random small act that can make you laugh deep inside at life's absurdities. Sometimes it is an act of love.

Susie Ibarra

Approaches to improvisation vary and evolve with new groupings of performers and dialogues across musical communities. All could benefit greatly from the integration of new feelings, energies, and ideas that come from the language women are developing through improvisation.

My improvisations are primarily tonally coloring an environment/emotion and/or gestural. I don't think about limitations, I think about possibilities, of using my instrument to realize inner hearing.

Monique Buzzarté

Gender Questions

Equality for women in music does not yet exist as we enter the twenty-first century. There will be no equity until all musical organizations, all music educators from street level through institutions of higher education, all professional musicians, all producers, publishers, agents, managers, critics, audiences, and anyone associated with music recognize the need for all people, regardless of gender or ethnicity, to be included in musical activities of all kinds.

Gender can not really be separated from other issues surrounding the production of music such as racism, sexism, or class. One only needs to open many of the current magazines that discuss improvised music to note the use of an essentialized language to describe women improvisers, the reduction of women to their physical descriptions, the lack of experimental and cutting-edge women performers included in reviews, articles and books or the relative exclusion of many women from the handful of festivals that present improvised music. Really, the list can go on. I can only think of a few of the recent books on improvisation that include specific women artists, or include their experiences and voices. There is a lot of work to be done, there are hundreds of women improvisers yet we tend to present or write about only a small number of women, the majority of which tend to be very well established musicians. While this is a positive step, we need to include the growing contributions of the younger generations of women improvisers.

Dana Reason

Dana's dissertation on women improvisers will surely give exposure to many new voices and bring many more issues to the surface for resolution.

Almost all of the professional work that I've done that involves improvisation has been with women, and virtually all of those situations have been both welcoming and inspiring. I haven't worked with very many men professionally in this way. That in itself is a gender issue—it seems integration of groups is hard to come by.

Kristin Norderval

Integration of musical groups as well as other kinds of groups is a major issue in the world everywhere. Women—no less than men—need invitations to perform, financial reward and validation for their creativity.

Because of my social and institutional training I have done pretty well in this business. However, I as a black woman and other black women can hold ourselves back because of our preconceived beliefs of what we think other people think of what we should be or who we should or might be. My experience in the performing arts in jazz as well as classical is that the dominant male culture has a tendency to stereotype women in a curious light. If we are not singers we are not always taken seriously. Playing hot and heavy could be considered a gender-wise personal dysfunction.

India Cooke

Because of my sexual orientation men sensed that they could be my friend but not my lover. Perhaps not participating in a stereotypical relationship was a relief for my male friends. If you play your part in a stereotypical role you lose your original voice. India doesn't do that and neither do I.

I am anticonformist, I am rebellious and I refuse to accept what I do not believe true. I do not want to be captive of only one repertory.

Cathy Berberian

Singers have played a leading role in the development of improvised music even though their contributions do tend to be minimized in various ways through stereotyping and disparagement of the value of their musicianship: "Can't keep time," "doesn't sing what's written," and so forth. The great blues women really led the way for the horn players in jazz improvisation with their expressive phrasing and melodic invention. In concert music, Cathy Berberian taught Luciano Berio the sounds that he fashioned into a composition for her. Her own composing and improvising is much less known than the work of her famous husband.

Improvisation allows me to communicate with others in an honest and direct way. Improvisation teaches me about the importance of being ready to play exactly who, where, and what I am about at that moment. When you improvise, you can't stop time and say "now wait a minute, I wasn't ready for that"; you must be ready for the unexpected and I think that is very much a part of how one thrives in life.

Dana Reason

So what if equality in music is achieved in this century? What difference could it make to you? If you are a father or brother, how would you feel if your daughter or sister was excluded from participating in the creation or performance of music? Would you support such exclusion knowing that participation in the creation of music is a profoundly gratifying process that can lead to mind-expanding development?

Lots of people talk about how art reflects life. But if jazz is art, how can it reflect life if there are only men playing it?   Susie Ibarra

The growing improvisation movement around the world is reaching across boundaries. The difference between composed and improvised music—not often well understood by musicians and music educators who have practiced the classical canon—is changing.

Improvisation draws from a vast amount of experiences . . . the past, present, and future . . . instantaneously. The improviser is at once the composer, player, and interpreter—it is truly a liberating experience that occurs in the moment, a moment born from the totality of all we are. Written music provides an authority (the composer writes . . . and you shall play) relationship between creator and the creation.
                                                                                Jackie Pickett

The difference between composition and improvisation is drawn succinctly by Jackie's statement: liberation. Liberation from the box that can be formed by overemphasis on training and technique and a lack of respect for the nature of sound. Improvisation can bridge differences and open new musical pathways.

It is vital for each of us to tap into our own creativity, to consider ourselves as creators, and not simply re-creators of other people's creativity.
                                                                        Monique Buzzarté

It is crucial that all be encouraged to explore their own creative potential. Playing other people's music is a service that can be rewarding as a regenerative experience for the performer as well as the audience.

Improvising allows for responding in the moment instead of "preparing" for something in a future moment. The more I improvise, the more I'm able to bring the spirit of improvisation to notated music as well—I try to sing it in the moment as if I was making it up on the spot, and not as if I know already what will come next.
                                                                        Kristin Norderval

Improvised music comes more from the intuitive body and composed music more from the intellect, which has the greater connection to writing. Women may feel more comfortable with the language of the body as a way of composition although there is really no separation. We need our intuitive bodies to write music and our intellect to improvise music.

Improvising differs from performing written music because, when reading, or even after memorizing a long piece, when you try to internalize and personalize the piece to become authentic expression, you are still taking on, at a physiological level, a preconceived pattern generated from another's soul and body.

One of the benefits of a score is that it can distract you from self-consciousness. Improvising seems to come from a deeper unconscious part of myself and springs forth unexpected. There are times when the structure and limits of my own personal patterns seem to disintegrate to allow a loud arrival of musical and sensual material previously unknown to myself. Improvising allows me a deeper relationship with the other performers. This is especially apparent when accompanying dance.

Without the grid of a preconceived score between you, one can be open to any new impulse that may emerge from one of you. I merge with a fellow performer and follow their soul walk on an instinctual level. Improvising performers are often surprised, when going beyond craft we find ourselves making choices that lead to simultaneous musical arrival. I am often surprised that being true to myself and singing authentically is exactly the thing that co-creates the strongest and most moving musical event.

The truest voice for myself is the one allowed to be a "composer" in the immediate experience of time and sensation. Being an improvising composer is being a sonic architect to sound lines of geometry allowing for relationship between the invisible and the unknown qualities of life.   Anne Bourne

Anne's unique statement about the composer/improviser dualism twists one's perspective or habitual thought patterns—as a good improvisation can do—to open new pathways of thought: the problem-solving or creative part of the brain/body. For mental and spiritual human development it is important to get beyond the habit of learning patterns to engage in problem-solving activity.

I remember William Parker talking to me about composition and spontaneous composition. I also feel that improvisation is composition in the moment. These two are written and oral languages that although dealing with a common basis of music, can produce very different things.   Susie Ibarra

I myself was neither supported nor prevented from participating in creative music (composing/improvising). I found my way to creative music through listening to sounds in my imagination and taking a cue from my mother's compositions. I practiced my instrument faithfully every day; however, my true interest was to create my own music.

I come out of a solo and chamber music background, where listening is crucial. I use improvisation as a compositional tool—that's my path. One has to study written music until it comes out of you and becomes yours. What I like about improvisation is that I surprise myself with sounds and musical ideas that would never happen otherwise. That's the big pleasure for me: to have a new idea. The longer I go on with improvisation the more important it is for me.   Frances Marie Uitti

Improvisation is an essential tool for my work as a performer and composer. For me improvisation is a way of life and life is an improvisation. Each day brings new challenges. Each moment has infinite possibilities or choices unless one is committed to some binding schedule or limiting design. However, the moment always offers choices even if you are committed to going to work or to a class or to catching a plane. Flux forces us to improvise. Flexibility helps us to cope with the changes that we encounter whether in daily life or in music.

I find improvising offers me far more musical challenges than playing notated music. Being able to play anything and any time in any way, the basics of the improvisational palette, demands a far greater level of preparation from me than anything else I've ever done musically.

Monique Buzzarté

Improvising truly in the moment can be a breathtaking musical challenge that gives enormously to the performer and consequently to the audience. The gift is the expression of the human spirit carried in the music that emerges momentarily and synergistically with all consciousness. Such a shared experience can be empowering to all involved and is the basis for growth and change.

Let one improviser's words provide the needed summation:

Music improvisation is a powerful resource of transformation in the moment. It is a divining tool, a centering technique, and a celebration outlet. It is a direct line for the expression of our inner forces, spirituality, and emotions. It is an indicator of both personal and universal disturbance or beauty, the blooming and expression of the psyche. In the purifying flame of the moment, the gift of music that comes through our voices and hands, speaks to us directly from our own souls. In listening and responding, pulsing with the beat of my own heart, and the rhythms of the world, singing from the source, channeling unselfconsciously, comes the elixir, the equilibrium, and the expression of my own sanctuary. It is an activity that I return to, over and over, as a vehicle for connection of my Spirit with the Great Mystery and Cosmic Creator. As an improviser, I am thankful to be a listener and a player in the direct flow of the Universe.

LaDonna Smith

For a major part of my career I was without peer relationships with women. It is gratifying to find them now by using music as the bridge to dialogues with diverse musical communities of men and women. Improvisation is a portal for creative women musicians to communicate with others and express themselves musically in this century. All people need an egalitarian atmosphere for all means of creating music, whether it is composed or improvised. The power of music used in this way can bring about beneficial changes: equality, collaboration, and cooperation.

OUTTAKES

Until recently an unrecognized, unvalidated practice in the world of formal musical institutions, improvisation has a broad spectrum of styles and concerns as practiced by a wide variety of musicians throughout the world.

Both improvisation and composition are prescribed studies for music in the public schools according to "Goals 2000," a published report from the White House. Many music teachers have no idea how to approach improvisation or composition in teaching music in the schools.

In art music or concert music during the twentieth century the concept of indeterminacy introduced by John Cage began to tap the creativity of performers. Works that did not prescribe notes meant that the performer had to decide what notes were played.

In music, tempering improvisation by training or programming limits possibilities, and formal shapes and styles arise through recognized vocabulary and codifications; for example, classical Indian music with its ragas and talas, or traditional jazz with melodies, chord progressions, and beat.

Musicians trained to play notes as written by composers often improvise by accident through lapse of memory or technical problems and find their own notes for continuity in a performance. Sometimes such accidents are even more interesting than what was written and sometimes the continuity—though wrong according to the score—is not even noticed by the audience.

Women with Whom I Have Improvised in the 1990s:

Susan Alcorn (pedal steel guitar, composer/improviser; Houston, Texas). Susan has extended the instrument to a new genre of music. She performs her own music and adapts other music for the pedal steel guitar.

Abbie Conant (trombone player, composer/improviser; Trossingen, Germany). Professor of trombone and elegant performer with formidable power. Abbie has singular command of her instrument and voice.

Tuliva Donna Cumberbach (professional vocalist/improviser, New York). Extraordinary clarity of voice.

Ellen Fullman (Seattle, Washington; currently in Berlin as DAAD [Deutscher Akademischer Austauschdienst/German Academic Exchange Service] fellow). Ellen has created her own instrument: eighty-five feet long, horizontal strings that sing like an orchestra, brass band, organ, and so forth; it can be played by several players simultaneously. She constructed and developed her Long String Instrument from a single string to multiple strings (160 strings), tuned it, learned to play it, composed for it, taught others to play it, and also improvises with it.

Rosi Hertlein (Brooklyn, New York). Rosi blends her voice and violin to create new timbres. Classically trained in Germany, Rosi has successfully crossed over into free improvisation and performs with Howard Johnson, Joe McPhee, Baikida Carroll, and many others.

Brenda Hutchinson (composer/improviser; San Francisco, California). Brenda sends her voice into a nine-foot tube in between the harmonic resonances to elicit magical sounds modulating in the space between her throat and the tube. Her audio-engineering background also informs her work.

Anne LeBaron (composer/improviser; Los Angeles, California). Anne is now teaching at California Institute for the Arts. She adeptly transforms her concert harp sounds and expertly includes a variety of world harps in her improvisations.

Jeanne Lee In Memoriam. Vocalist with great heart.

Leaf Miller (Saugerties, New York) plays djembe and percussion with a passion. She and her partner, Lorraine DeMarest, maintain Women Who Drum and every summer bring two hundred women together in upstate New York to improvise and study a diverse range of world rhythms and techniques from master women teachers.

Dierdre Murray (New York, New York) plays cello and composes. She is at home with all forms of improvisation.

Maggie Payne (composer/improviser; Berkeley, California). Maggie transforms her flute with mysterious inviting timbres and rhythms of breath. Her years of audio engineering and electronic music deeply inform her flute playing and vice versa.

Julie Lyon Rose (Accord, New York). With her voice that comes from her dancer and avian sensibilities, an instrument that morphs from flutelike to violinlike to otherworldly. Her body disciplines shape timbre and tonality.

Margrit Schenker (Zurich, Switzerland) is a composer/improviser and educator. She studied improvisation with Irène Schweizer and me. She courageously crossed the border between those educated as performers to become a recognized composer in Switzerland. She has created a one-woman show that she has performed throughout Switzerland.

Helen Thorington (Staten Island, New York) is a writer and sound artist who has created a cyberspace venue for improvisation and sound art at http://www.turbulence.org. Her site has hosted several distance improvisations with Brenda Hutchinson, Maggie Payne, myself with Helen, Shelly Hersch, and others.

Karolyn van Putten (Oakland, California) wraps her voice around the group and is a ventriloquist. Her voice, like a chameleon, appears to my left, to the right, at a distance, and sometimes it seems to emerge from my instrument or out of nowhere.

Gayle Young (composer/improviser/installation artist; Toronto, Ontario). Gayle plays sound sculptures and mallet instruments tuned in just intonation.

The Moment of Empowerment

There are so many ways in which people, particularly women, feel the sense of little or no power in their lives. This may be the result of childhood, marriage, or just their own inner voices telling them they do not have the right to do or be this or that. I have discovered a new way to walk through the dense entanglement of vines that appear to bind me to a previous way of thinking. This tool is the gift of being in the moment—or improvisation.

As a girl growing up in Mississippi I was taught that children are to be seen and not heard. This taught me early on not to have a voice. This training continued as I was traumatized in school, for not being like everyone else. I was slower physically and did not wear the latest styles, and did not know how to socialize very well. I had this ever present thought that no one would ever want to hear anything I had to say. One of the things I loved to do was sing. Even that was a source of pain. I participated in a small Southern Baptist Church and was constantly taunted by a group of boys and even the person who led the choir. He had given me a name that he thought was fitting for me: Gorilla. First, he would say, "you look like a monkey and sound like one too," and then he would just laugh and laugh. As an adolescent these ideas took root in my being like a kudzu vine, unwilling to let my true being come forth.

From that path I entered marriage and chose what was familiar to me. A person who had to control me, and tell me that I could not do anything right, and for sure the voicing of my opinions was not honored. I entered the deep wells of depression, constantly wanting and wishing for some waters of renewal.

Years passed and I continued to exist. I was not living. I was maintaining. I had survived only by medication and psychotherapy. If I had a dollar for every time the therapist told me, "You have choices," I would be a millionaire. It took me close to eight years to know that I really did have choices. Then I began to make some better choices for my life. I chose to get out of my marriage, and began a journey of discovery and exploration of new ideas and new ways.

I stumbled into a community of arts, and then into a smaller community of improvisational musicians. My spirit felt like a feather floating in the wind, instead of one confined and pressured to be something it was not. It did not take me long to realize that even though I could not "read music" the community not only allowed me to have a voice, they actually encouraged and celebrated it. Amazing, the joy and new life that rose up in me like a geyser, springing up from the very core of the earth. The old shackles of having to be a certain way have slowly fallen off, and the new wings of being in the moment as I am, without judgment, either internally or externally, at last allow me flight.

As the gift of improvisation enters into society, and the life of women, I believe that paradigms will shift. Those who have never experienced power in their being, can know and discover this, and have a voice to speak for themselves without hesitation or reserve. So, the next time you hand a woman a rattle, a drum, tambourine or just invite her to make a sound, remember that you are enabling her to make choices and changes in her life by learning to be in the moment. To be *who* she really is, instead of *what* someone else has demanded that she be. May the spirit of freedom embraced by the art of improvisation change the world from one that confines to one that offers choices.

DANA REASON

"Navigable Structures and Transforming Mirrors"
Improvisation and Interactivity

By encouraging audiences to share actively in a creative process, improvisation explicitly problematizes forms of musical reception based in culturally rooted assumptions about audience passivity. For audiences and improvisers alike, the journey of improvised music is not predetermined, but rather responsive in real time to the immediate performance situation. While all music engages listeners with some degree of interactivity, in improvisation such an interactivity is an essential structural component, one not merely relegated to the more passive recognition of affect or pattern. The dialogic and interactive aspect of this kind of musical encounter challenges traditional roles, including those adapted from European classical music performance practices, where performers are often framed as transmitters and audiences as receivers. Thus, the interactive nature of musical improvisation encourages both musicians and audiences to rethink traditional expectations about the expression *and* the reception of musical meaning.

The Canadian artist David Rokeby, producer of interactive intermedia installations since the early 1980s, has also written on the subject of interactivity from his own experience as an art-maker. Rokeby's work explores notions of subjectivity, control, and intuition. His signature interactive work, the *Very Nervous System,* has been continuously updated since the completion of the original version in 1982. The piece uses a video camera to follow the audience's movements in a large space. A computer then interprets this information, controlling synthesizers and samplers to create in real time electronic music that accompanies or responds to audience gestures. The end result is a collaboration between the viewers and Rokeby's system. Here, the "viewer" is also the cocreator, emphasizing the blurring of traditional roles between listener and performer that is part of the nature of improvisation itself. Moreover, Rokeby's work privileges the intuitive body as the prime site of the improvisatory gesture: "Computers are supposed to be logical, so I wanted my piece to be intuitive. The computer tends to remove you from your body, so I wanted my piece to engage the body, strongly. My piece takes place in physical space, on a human scale: this is in direct contrast to the computer's activity, which takes place on the tiny playing field of the integrated circuit," ("Very Nervous System").

Rokeby's notions of "navigable structures" and "transforming mirrors" ("Transforming," 133) suggest useful models not only for articulating the nature of the interactive relationship among artists, spectators, and computer media installations, but also for understanding the creative and interactive processes of musical improvisation. In particular, I draw upon these models in exploring a multicultural tradition of improvisation that has been articulated in the United States, Europe, Canada, and Asia from the 1960s to the present. Often called improvised music, creative music, free improvisation, or free jazz, this complex of traditions is articulated by a diverse group of musicians, including Cecil Taylor, Ornette Coleman, Archie Shepp, Albert Ayler, John Coltrane, John Tchicai, Muhal Richard Abrams, and the Association of the Advancement of Creative Musicians, Irène Schweizer, Ikue Mori, Joëlle Léandre, Marilyn Crispell, Jin Hi Kim, Alvin Curran, AMM, Pauline Oliveros, Derek Bailey, and Evan Parker, among others.

Navigable Structures

Rokeby's metaphor of "navigation" constructs the musical experience as a mutable, inclusive environment where individual input can be accommodated and welcomed in the most literal sense. Aiming to underline the interactive potential of technology in art making—that is, the ability of technology to "reflect the consequences of our actions or decisions back to us" (133)—Rokeby ascribes to the artist the role of structuring "the space with a sort of architecture that provides a method of navigation" (138). The "navigable structure," therefore, is a "real, virtual, or conceptual articulation of a space" in which the interactor/viewer is situated so as to be able to adopt "a variety of roles . . . and experience a variety of conflicting perspectives on the event" (139).

Thus, for an improviser, a navigable structure is a method of interpretation that helps to promote connections between ideas, a concept that in turn suggests a collective, communitarian dynamic in musical decision-making. Indeed, many accounts of improvised music suggest that the power of change is collectively articulated, incorporating either a fluctuating or shared leadership and featuring continuous reconstruction of multiple perspectives. For instance, George E. Lewis remarks upon the notion of shared responsibility in his description of one method used by members of the Association for the Advancement of Creative Musicians (AACM) to structure their performances in the mid-1970s: "Organizing the entire concert in advance in broad outline, but leaving the details to the improvisers to structure and glue together as they wished, demanded that improvisers assume personal and collective responsibility for the real-time articulation of form" ("Singing," 73).

The group dynamic may push the improviser to relinquish control over the shape of the piece, adding pieces to a puzzle in which no one "owns" a finalized version. Rokeby, however, not only underlines the interactor's responsibility for the course of the artistic event—"through a series of decisions, the interactor moves into a specific position for which he or she is, in sense, accountable" ("Transforming," 139)—more importantly, he stretches the category of the interactor to include all corporeal presences in the space of the performance.

Live Performance

Jon Panish notes that "jazz is part of a cultural tradition in which live performance is central to the creation of music" (79). His discussion of jazz also highlights the cultural conditions of improvised music, generally, in that the musical significations and meanings of improvisation are best understood during a live setting. Unlike musics invested in providing the listener with a completed version of a musical text or score in performance, improvisation provides an opportunity to engage with an expansive musical environment during the performance, wherein the nature of the text is open and subject to the energy or "vibe" of the audience. In many cases, this vibe is powerful enough to affect and direct many of the parameters of an improvisation, such as how long to play a particular phrase or motif and whether to play loud or soft, fast or slow. In such an environment, sources of meaning cannot be limited exclusively to sonic morphologies such as the order of notes, orchestration, timbre, and the like; meaning is also located in the ways in which improvisers situate their bodies, change their facial expressions, and use their voices to accompany notes, gestures, silences, or phrases.

For Panish, the live performance also assists listeners by providing additional information through which they can decode musical, social, and political meanings embedded in the sounds themselves. Even the space in which the sounds are presented can suggest a political or cultural context for the music. For instance, at a festival of contemporary classical and improvised music I attended in Europe, the presenters tended to direct music that included improvisation to more informal spaces such as loud cafés, while contemporary classical performances were presented in traditional concert hall spaces, thereby sending the message that only some works are worthy of the consideration appropriate to "high" art.

Panish's observation that "jazz musicians learned to play first by listening to other players and imitating their sounds, and second by interacting with and responding to the audience" (80) can be applied to a more generalized conception of improvised music as well, insofar as it implies that the interface between performer and audience itself creates a grammar that crucially influences the navigation of the music. For example, bassist Joëlle Léandre declares that "when you play spontaneous music, the audience participates with you and is in the same boat with you." This dual participation occurs because "there is a tension with what the musicians and audience speak about. We are all in the moment and we are talking about us, the audience is a mirror and they are deeply with us. We talk about life, death, drama, passion, joy and who and what we are" (telephone interview).

Part of the influence exercised by audience members can involve the degree of familiarity they have with the navigable terrain. For example, it may be possible to recognize that the pianist Cecil Taylor tends to use clusters, to play melodies in octaves, or to play rather rapidly using the entire keyboard. As a listener, however, I do not know beforehand if he will use those gestures in a particular performance, and if he does, I cannot be sure of how he will choose to display the materials. An audience member who is familiar with the many possible timbral, harmonic, gestural, structural, and technical strategies available to any improviser at any time may notice various sonic identities, tendencies, and styles. At the same time, these tendencies need not be adopted as the only method of structuring or navigating an improvisation.

Diversity (And Its Discontents)

For Lewis, improvised music is "a social location inhabited by a considerable number of present-day musicians, coming from diverse cultural backgrounds and musical practices, who have chosen to make improvisation a central part of their musical discourse. Individual improvisors are now able to reference an intercultural establishment of techniques, styles, aesthetic attitudes, antecedents, and networks of cultural and social practice" ("Improvised," 110). At the same time, as my earlier thumbnail sketch of the field indicates, there is no overarching training structure or school that prepares people to become improvisers; rather, improvisation depends on a diversity of training and cultural practices thriving among multiple, diverse musical backgrounds and communities—not least because its very substance exemplifies multiplicity.

Henry A. Giroux's observation concerning the field of cultural studies seems apt as a description of improvised music as well: in both fields one has "the opportunity to rethink the relationship between the issue of difference as it is constituted within subjectivities and between social groups. This rethinking suggests understanding more clearly how questions of subjectivity can be taken up so as not to erase the possibility for individual and social agency. As such, subjectivities are seen as contradictory and multiple, produced rather than given, and are both taken up and received within particular social and historical circumstances" (165). Similarly, the structure of improvisation itself—as a field and as a product—necessarily reflects the infinite variability of attitudes, experiences, personal styles, and histories among both improvisers and audience members. In this regard, the flexible, multiply mediated nature of navigable structures makes it possible for individuals to perform with many kinds of musicians, encouraging exchanges, dialogues, and collaborations between different groups of musicians from various parts of the world with relatively little group preparation. The concept of navigation, by problematizing any centrally codified project of improvisation, encourages multiple readings of improvised potentialities, locating and decoding such structures in order to understand and appreciate the kinds of exchanges that take place as new community formations occur.

Of course, an individual may choose to stay with familiar people, materials, and patterns, but this choice in turn can limit the degree to which improvisation allows the opportunity to take chances and move into new territories. Let us view a navigable structure as an environment in which both the audience and improvisers can discover active spaces. In theory, the greater the diversity that can be brought to these spaces, the more challenging and potentially rewarding the creation of the music can be. At the same time, just as meeting people for the first time can be awkward and unsatisfying, new collaborations pose enormous risks as well. John Corbett discusses the nature of risk-taking as part of the improvising work experience: "the performer does not *know* for certain what will be played going into the performance, since the music is by definition undefined; the risk of failure, or complete collapse, is everywhere present" (222). Part of the risk, for both the critic Christopher Small and the pianist Misha Mengelberg, lies in the constantly changing and unpredictable nature of group improvisation.

For Mengelberg, improvising with as little as only one other player dramatically affects the musical environment: "You have, of course, all your expectations and plans destroyed the moment you play with other people" (quoted in Corbett, 236). Thus, as longtime AMM associate Eddie Prévost notes, "improvisation is fragile. Its transience leads to a vast number of evolutionary prospects. The meta-musician has to be undaunted by traditional practices and the seductive power of peer-approval. If the musician fails to accept these challenges and remains trapped in a perception of himself, then he no longer improvises" (81).

What, then, drives an improviser to accept the challenge? Small uses the motif of the journey to make a point about both unpredictability and musical value: "We may not know how long the trip is going to be, or even necessarily where we are going. It may be that we shall not enter any new territory at all, or even if we do, that it will prove just a dismal swamp that no one will wish to revisit, but every now and then we obtain glimpses of glittering new lands, are dazzled by the sight of beauty and meaning which is all the more astonishing for being unexpected" (176). Ultimately, individual musicians are challenged to re-create themselves for each improvisational occasion, allowing for the pleasure of surprise, reawakening, and evolution.

Problematizing the "Work"

The status of the musical work as a reproducible document, including those musics that do not come from the West, that incorporate oral traditions, or that otherwise make little reference to notation, hovers in the background of Western audiences' expectations of music. Philosopher Lydia Goehr points to the historical validation of the concept of musical work as "not just any group of sounds, but [as] a complex structure of sounds related in some important way to a composer, a score, and a given class of performances" (20). For Goehr, this notion prepares musical creations for permanent display in what she calls an "imaginary museum." What Goehr calls the "work-concept" implies that a closed score somehow guarantees its listeners a desirable predictability. Improvisation challenges this concept of a musical work; more important, it questions the very notion of a complete, predictable musical product. While there are many improvised pieces that refer to scores, improvisers generally have plenty of room to add their own understanding of the score and what it may signify to them. The significance of the score in improvised music often serves more as a point of departure than as a set of fixed ideas to which one addresses rigidly. Hence, it is possible for two different improvisers to work with a specific "score" and produce significantly different outcomes.

This important difference between improvised music and music created in deference to the "work-concept" affects those audiences who may be accustomed to receiving a musical product created prior to performance. As a result, adherence to a written score as the locus of musical authenticity and value may well impede appreciation or comprehension of an improvised music that, as Panish observes of jazz, "emphasizes improvisation—invention during the act of performance—over either composition or reproducing a written score" (79). For Goehr, the notion of the separation of the artist from the work is central to the concept of the autonomous work itself. E. T. A. Hoffmann's account, as quoted by Goehr, is paradigmatic: "The genuine artist lives only for the work, which he understands as the composer understood it and which he now performs. He does not make his personality count in any way. All his thoughts and actions are directed towards bringing into being all the wonderful, enchanting pictures and impressions the composer sealed in his work with magical power" (1).

Bassist and composer Gavin Bryars has advanced a similar notion: "Distancing yourself from what you are doing. Now that becomes impossible in improvisation. If I write a piece I don't even have to be there when it is played. They are conceptions. I'm more interested in conception than reality. Because I can conceive of things that don't have any tangible reality. But if I'm playing them, if I'm there at the same time, then that's real. It's not a conception" (quoted in Bailey, 115). In contrast, the paradigm that many improvisers embrace does not advocate a rupture between the art and the artist but rather an inescapable integration of them. With improvisation, it is not possible to claim that the music was not yours to begin with: you are held responsible for a perceived failure or triumph—by you and by the audience. In this regard, Goehr challenges both Hoffmann and Bryars in asserting that "works cannot, in any straightforward sense, be physical, mental or ideal objects. They do not exist as concrete, physical objects; they do not exist as private ideas existing in the mind of a composer, a performer, or a listener; neither do they exist in the eternally existing world of ideal, uncreated forms" (2–3). Rather, works are contingent structures, acting in concert with the richness of human experience and the dynamics of history and culture.

Thus, I align myself with Goehr in maintaining that the personality and life experience of the individual performing, composing, or improvising is revealed by the particular repertoire that individual chooses to perform, the music he or she composes or the way he or she improvises. Individual creative choices in an improvising context constantly reassert the interconnectedness of life and artistic expression. Finally, the notion of improvisatory "work" itself—as product, process, and value—plays an important role in musical reception dynamics. While the act of improvising explicitly involves "work," the nature of work in improvisation, as I understand it, is not to create a finished product but rather to treat work itself as a process through which improvisations are worked out, worked over, or worked on, but *never* finished in the traditional sense in Western culture of "achieving closure." Rather, improvisation problematizes the notion of reproducing a work "only for the standard" that is to be mastered and reproduced (Attali, 101). For example, a recording of a live improvised music concert can only serve as a documentation of that event: it cannot be repeated as such by other improvising groups much less by the original performance group itself, even if there might be pressure in some instances to model one's performance practices after improvisations that have been captured by recording.

Even if, as Attali suggests, the concert itself becomes a reproducible object via the process of recording and distribution (Attali, 101), a recorded improvisation is evidence, not a prescription to be followed. If the documented music proves interesting or extraordinary to some, it can serve as a guide or model for what happened to the "work" during that particular performance, with those particular individuals, at that specific time and place. Here, the nature of improvisation includes an engagement with work as a process of community by which identities are revealed, displaced, and questioned.

Improvisation, Personality, and Authority

Unlike those forms of music in which formal devices make it possible to use technical facility to camouflage a musician's emotional, psychological, physical, and spiritual subjectivities, improvisation allows performers to reveal themselves, to share their embodied experiences. If the relationship between life and music is, as I and others in this book posit, an intimate one, then the improviser exposes the flux of relational creation within the materiality of his or her own existential context, located specifically in space and time. How improvisers play inevitably interacts with how they live, even for those improvisers who approach music as a self-referential musical practice that has no relationship to musicians or to the world in which they live.

Besides providing a portrait of the individual personality, improvisation can also reveal the social and political tendencies of the musician or, as Ingrid Monson points out, "the aesthetic centrality of linking sound to an ethos, cultural identity, and communities of participation" (186). For example, violinist Malcolm Goldstein conceives of "the natural sounding of the world (including people) . . . discovering and focusing in the moment of the sound coming forth," as working in conjunction with "the root of my spirituality/politics" (36–37). For Goldstein, as for many others, the improvised performance presents an opportunity to disrupt structures that for the most part function to discourage people from speaking about important political, social, and personal issues.

What listeners of an improvisation can be assured of is that both they and the musicians are most likely hearing the specific inflections of the improvisation for the first time. In particular, first-time listeners to improvised music are often moved to reevaluate their conception of musical practice. To the extent that improvised music seems perplexing, perhaps because of the newness of the sounds, extended techniques, or the different approaches to musical organization, novitiates even find themselves asking whether or not the sounds they are hearing are really music at all. Soon, however, curious listeners might find themselves challenging, via a few simple queries, the corporate-conditioned distribution arrangements that affect the production and reception of music: where do I find this music on radio or television? Why is this music not advertised in local record stores, newspapers, and billboards? In an age where most media are controlled by a few multinational corporations, listeners often struggle to find a music that redefines or even abandons the typical surfeit of love, hate, revenge songs active on commercial radio. Musics that explore other methods of self-identification, that are in dialogue with philosophical, metaphorical, psychological, ontological, and abstract states of being, may provide alternative listening experiences that speak to new ways by which people can assert agency for organizing and redefining their lives within the larger contexts of local and global communities.

In this sense, can the creation and performance of real-time music pose a threat to the investment by certain worlds of music production and performance in particular notions of interpretation, reproduction, and authority? If one important effect of improvised music is to problematize conditioned listener assumptions and responses, must we not ask ourselves if new forms of cultural expression threaten us and, if so, why? Do we immediately become judgmental and dismissive of a music that seems initially to challenge our orthodox musical beliefs and values?

Particularly when the audience member is trained in another field, he or she may feel an unwelcome challenge via improvised music, especially as almost everyone feels crucially and personally connected to music generally, a connection in which notions of cultural competence are often at stake. Most listeners are exposed to many styles of music, but when they come across unfamiliar music the tendency is to compare it to more familiar forms. At times, listeners may dismiss unfamiliar musical languages rather than accept an alternative definition of what music can sound like.

It may even seem at times as though the listener is being attacked on some level because of the unfamiliarity she or he has with this type of improvised cultural production. Saxophonist and composer Roscoe Mitchell deals with this very issue during the live recording of his piece "Nonaah," recorded at the Willisau Festival in Switzerland in 1977. Mitchell had been asked at the last minute to replace a scheduled concert by Anthony Braxton, who was unable to make the performance. The recording documents a three-way conversation among Mitchell, those who supported his music on that occasion, and those who disliked his performance. Mitchell begins by extracting a single fragment from "Nonaah," playing it over and over again with subtle variations. As heard on the recording, the very vocal restlessness and even hostility among some in the audience is palpable, yet Mitchell retains a commitment to the repeated phrase. Within the first four minutes of the 22-minute piece, the audience starts responding with a complex combination of applause, talking, whistles, and catcalls.

Mitchell remarks in the liner notes to the recording that this concert posed a real challenge for him, given his decision to keep playing what he had set out to perform that day regardless of the audience response. Rather than pleading for quiet, Mitchell directly addresses the issue of maintaining a respectful dialogue between performer and audience through his insistence on playing the same phrase over and over again. In his words, "I went out there and got this tension thing. It was a battle. I had to make the noise and whatever was going on with the audience was part of the piece. The music couldn't move till they respected me, until they realized that I wasn't going anywhere, and if someone was going it would have had to be them" (1). Here, Mitchell clearly recognizes that some people in the audience were not ready to hear his material, and that although this was a festival of new improvised music, certain forms of music were nonetheless to be received less approvingly.

Although Mitchell mentions that he wanted the audience to respect him, what he was really displaying was his seriousness and commitment to the integrity of the improvised music he practices, creates, and believes in. Given the fact that much of the music played at this time in European festivals of "new jazz" or "free improvisation" could be characterized as intense, dense "energy music," Mitchell's music represented another way of thinking that grew out of Chicago's AACM, where other improvisational methodologies, such as the use of space, a large dynamic range, extended techniques, and the use of poetry or performance art elements, were perhaps less consonant with audience expectations. But for Mitchell, this music—more spacious, less frenetic—also needed to be heard. Eventually, the audience calmed down (approximately seven minutes into the piece) and a newfound respect for what he was playing seemed to emerge. The music could at last move to other musical ideas.

Transforming Mirrors

Creative improvisers see each performance as an opportunity for breaking through previous technical or musical limitations, perhaps gaining new insights into themselves through interactions with others. One of the ways improvisers learn about themselves is through a dynamic that Rokeby calls the "transforming mirror." For Rokeby, though "all interactive works reflect interactors back to themselves, in many works the idea of the mirror is explicitly invoked" ("Transforming," 145). As an example, Rokeby mentions video artist Ed Tannenbaum's "Recollections," in which the viewer's body image is represented as a video projection. By the author's own description, "Recollections" is

an interactive video installation that invites the participant to move in front of a large video projection screen. As the person moves, his or her image is recorded by a video camera and passed on to a computer with special image processing capabilities. The person's silhouette or outline is extracted, assigned a color based on the instant that it was recorded, and projected onto the screen. Over time the images build up, creating a painting based on the movement. Since people are always doing new things with the exhibit, the images never repeat. (Tannenbaum)

According to Rokeby, the representation of the viewer on the screen by Tannenbaum "follows the movements of the interactor like a mirror image or shadow, transformed by the potentials with which the artist has endowed the space" (145). Similarly, the potential of multiple dialogues among improvisers acts as a type of transforming mirror where an idea advanced by one player may not lead to the projected musical results but may in its reception be transformed beyond recognition. This interactive community dynamic of mirroring and transformation reflects a social discourse put into practice through musical interaction, calling into question how both improvisers and listeners perceive themselves and the world around them.

A recent recording of the trio Les Diaboliques, featuring Maggie Nicols, Irène Schweizer, and Joëlle Léandre—*Canaille 91*—displays a variety of means and paths through which the music is transformed as materials are magnified, alluded to, varied upon, or discarded. The musicians respond to each other with bodily gestures, tap dancing, or the use of the voice without textual reference. An analysis of the music itself reveals some of the transformations, but ultimately it is the attitude or intention behind each transformation that gives a fuller understanding of the change. The relationship that each of the improvisers has to the musical materials is also transformed, as the players stand ready to respond with contrasts or complementary material depending upon what specific musical statements signify to each musician.

A transforming mirror emerges whenever a reaction, be it negative or positive, happens in relation to any musical experience, not just an improvised one. The cultural implications of transforming mirrors pose new questions concerning both familiar and unfamiliar territories, experiences, situations, and stimuli that challenge the collective sense of what music is and how musical culture is constituted. How do we react as listeners to new organizations of sounds? What is our response when we hear a traditional instrument like the piano being played differently, as for instance, by plucking its strings? Does being intelligent and knowledgeable in other disciplines prepare listeners with insights for improvised musical contexts?

The following example would be one way in which enacting interdisciplinary connections reproduces as well as produces patterns of response at both the musical and the personal level of the improvisers and audience. I recently had the experience of bringing improvised music and dance to a group of individuals who had rarely been exposed to the possibilities improvisation offers. A presentation/lecture at a leadership conference for health professionals in Los Angeles provided an occasion for me, dancer Paula Josa Jones, and her dance-work company to introduce some of the strategies she uses with both dancers and musicians. One strategy that Jones deploys is what she calls mirroring. In mirroring two dancers are to do exactly as the other one does. Jones then had the audience try this out. There was a lot of nervous laughter as people moved their bodies, with the one directive on their mind: to mirror their partner. The moves themselves were to be improvised. Using movement as a way of demonstrating how varied improvisation can be, and how people can creatively interact with one another, enabled the audience members to reexamine how they themselves are empowered as agents in the development of new strategies in their own lives and work.

Conclusion

Navigable structures and transforming mirrors illuminate, for both audiences and improvisers, some of the elements that may inform, direct, or structure an improvisation. Improvisation encourages both improvisers and audiences to discover alternative ways of hearing, receiving, responding, and thinking. Acting in concert, improvisers and audiences deploy the interactive technologies of improvisation to establish the potential of alternative creative identities, new relational structures that reconfigure community. No doubt, there is an important role that the tools of cultural studies can play in developing discourses that explain what improvisers and audiences do. To that end, I trust that this essay has prepared the ground for a further understanding of how improvisational interactivity addresses the social practices through which community is given shape and form.

Works Cited

Attali, Jacques. *Noise: The Political Economy of Music.* Trans. Brian Massumi. Minneapolis: University of Minnesota Press, 1985.

Bailey, Derek. *Improvisation: Its Nature and Practice in Music.* New York: Da Capo, 1992.

Corbett, John. "Writing Around Free Improvisation." In *Jazz Among the Discourses,* edited by Krin Gabbard, 217–40. Durham: Duke University Press, 1995.

Giroux, Henry A. *Border Crossings: Cultural Workers and the Politics of Education.* New York: Routledge, 1992.

Goehr, Lydia. *The Imaginary Museum of Musical Works.* Oxford: Clarendon, 1992.

Goldstein, Malcolm. *Sounding the Full Circle.* Sheffield, Vt.: M. Goldstein, 1988.

Léandre, Joëlle. Telephone interview. 3 June 2000.

Lewis, George E. "Improvised Music after 1950: Afrological and Eurological Perspectives." *Black Music Research Journal* 16, no. 1 (1996): 91–125.

——. "Singing Omar's Song: A (Re)construction of Great Black Music." *Lenox Avenue* 4 (1998): 69–92.

Mitchell, Roscoe. "Nonaah." *Nonaah.* LP. Nessa Records, 1977.

Monson, Ingrid. *Saying Something: Jazz, Improvisation and Interaction.* Chicago: University of Chicago Press, 1996.

Panish, Jon. *The Color of Jazz: Race and Representation in Postwar American Culture.* Jackson: University Press of Mississippi, 1997.

Prévost, Edwin. *No Sound is Innocent.* Essex: Copula, 1995.

Rokeby, David. "Very Nervous System." *Wired Magazine* 3.03 (1995) <http://www.wired.com/wired/archive/3.03/rokeby.html>. 3 May 2001.

——. "Transforming Mirrors: Subjectivity and Control in Interactive Media." *Critical Issues in Electronic Media.* edited by Simon Penny, 133–157. Albany: State University of New York Press, 1995.

Schweizer, Irène. "Avanti Popolo," By Irène Schweizer, Joëlle Léandre, and Maggie Nicols. CD. *Canaille 91,* 1991.

Small, Christopher. *Music, Society, Education.* London: John Calder, 1977.

Tannenbaum, Ed. "Ed Tannenbaum." <http://www.et-arts.com/>. 8 May 2001.

PART TWO

BETWEEN AND ACROSS CULTURES

JASON STANYEK

Transmissions of an Interculture
Pan-African Jazz and Intercultural Improvisation[1]

This brings us back to what we have seen is an important aspect of African musicking:
the musician regards himself as responsible, not just for the sounds that he makes,
but for the whole social progress of the event, for its success as a human encounter.
The musician as he improvises responds not only to the inner necessities of the
sound world he is creating but also to the dynamics of the human situation as it
develops around him. It is his task to create not just a single set of sound perspectives
which are to be contemplated and enjoyed by listeners, but a multiplicity of opportunities
for participation along a number of different perspectives.
—Christopher Small

You can be in unison without being in unison.
—Ornette Coleman

مٍ

At the end of his autobiography *Three Kilos of Coffee,* the Cameroonian
saxophonist, composer, and Pan-Africanist Manu Dibango underscores
the complexity of locating a generalized African identity. In the midst of his
inimitable musings—on the emergence of Paris as the capital of African
music in the early 1980s, on the narrow constructs and stereotypes that are
used to label African musicians, on how unique African identities disappear
under the stern mandates of authenticity—he makes the following statement: "African music was and remains a music of encounters; in this lies its
attractive power" (129). I read this comment as Dibango's artful way of
providing a definition for something that would seem to elude any fixed
definition, as his way of saying that African music gains its identity not
through immutable characteristics and labels that effectively put a strangle-
hold on "those who want to create by keeping their differences" (125) but
through its magnetic pull, its tendency to promote embodied interaction
and dialogue between people with disparate personal and cultural histories.

The present essay is very much about encounters in the African music world and the importance face-to-face intercultural contact has played (and continues to play) in forging links between diasporic and continental Africans. I take a look at what I call "musical Pan-Africanism," a mode of intercultural encounter that has become, since the late 1940s, increasingly prevalent in the world of African music and, in particular, in the jazz world of the United States. Indeed, the growing number of intercultural collaborations taking place between musicians of African descent adds a certain resonance to Dibango's statement and also points to the more general fact that in the past fifty years a highly reflexive form of interculturalism has emerged as an important new framework for both organizing musical performance and analyzing cultural production.

I have labeled these collaborations "Pan-African" because the resonance of the term points to the important correlation to be made between the interethnic and international alliances that have characterized the African diaspora and the musical encounters that have become widespread in the African world during the last fifty years. On a conceptual level at least, these encounters are premised upon a kind of unity that has been "torn asunder" (to borrow a phrase from W. E. B. Du Bois) and, as such, involve negotiating the terrain between similarity and difference, between the universal and the particular. Furthermore, as Joseph E. Harris writes, Pan-African collaborations are enacted in the space between the national and supranational:[2]

The dynamics of black nationalism in the African world during the last generation has transformed the meaning of identity in Africa and the diaspora. Whereas the diaspora of the slave trade era was essentially "stateless," relying primarily on an Africa remembered, the post-independence diaspora promotes a consciousness of new nations, sometimes with new names and ideologies that challenge the older diaspora to make choices between conflicting interests not only within the diaspora community, but also between it and particular African countries. (17–18)

In this paper I start from the simple idea that the collaboration that took place between the bebop trumpeter, composer, and bandleader Dizzy Gillespie and the great Cuban *conguero* and composer Chano Pozo in the late 1940s not only activated a distinct lineage of Pan-African music making but can also be seen as one of the germinal moments in the history of intercultural music making of the second half of the twentieth century. What Gillespie and Pozo did was to set a number of precedents for future Pan-African collaborations in jazz: an emphasis on co-composition with a simultaneous affirmation of improvisation;[3] the insertion of nonjazz repertoires into jazz; the accommodation of instruments not typically found in jazz ensembles; the use of non-English and multilingual texts; the highlighting of African spirituality. But perhaps most important were (1) their ability to juxtapose different histories without sacrificing identity and (2) their reflexive use of notions of cultural difference as a basis for collaboration.

I advance the notion that a highly dialogic brand of improvisation is at the center of Pan-African music making. The tendency to use improvisation not just as a means of generating sonic structures but also as a constitutive tactic in the creation of spaces for intercultural communication was (and still is) a core part of a sensibility that helped diasporic Africans sonically activate and come to grips with the massively complex life they have faced in the diaspora. Indeed, Derek Bailey has written that improvisation is "an essential force in sustaining life. Without it nothing survives" (140). Improvisation is one element in a constellation of tools that contributed to the creation of a Pan-African tradition of musical and social cooperation that extends back to the earliest days of the diaspora and through to the jazz world of the past fifty years. In this regard, the collaboration between Gillespie and Pozo is a kind of fulcrum: on the one hand it relates back to the improvisational Pan-African music making of the preabolition diaspora; on the other, it sparked a remarkable series of post–World War II pancultural encounters, all of which utilize improvisation as a kind of linking device (Charlie Parker's recordings with Machito and his Afro-Cubans, Art Blakey's collaborative percussion records of the 1950s and early 1960s, Babatunde Olatunji's work with Max Roach and Randy Weston in the early 1960s, the collaborations between Dollar Brand (Abdullah Ibrahim) and Archie Shepp, the World Saxophone Quartet and African Drums, the Art Ensemble of Chicago with the Amabutho Male Chorus of Soweto, Randy Weston and the master Gnawa musicians of Morocco, Steve Coleman and AfroCuba de Matanzas, David Murray and Positive Black Soul).[4]

The purpose of this essay is not to provide a detailed and comprehensive history of the Gillespie/Pozo collaboration or of Pan-African music making in general, although such projects are sorely needed if any kind of larger understanding is to be reached regarding how and why interculturalism emerged in the years immediately following World War II as a significant rubric for organizing and thinking about musical production. Rather, I am concerned with providing the basic outlines of a broad conceptual framework that might be used to start thinking about the history of Pan-African music making while, at the same time, providing some room to allow for the substantial variations that characterize the history of these collaborations. I also hope that what follows will be taken as a small step toward tracing the formative role Pan-African music making has had in the production of what has become a global discourse on intercultural collaboration.[5]

I should emphasize that the tentative observations I make in this essay pertain to music making that involves face-to-face contact. I am not directly concerned with questions surrounding musical influence and borrowing, the global dissemination of musics or the general incidence of what has been termed by many observers "hybrid musics" (although these are certainly concomitant phenomena). What is important here is the contact between people.[6] Indeed, the face-to-face, embodied collaborations that I call attention to here might be better labeled "intercorporeal" (to use Patrice Pavis's term) in order to distinguish them from instances of cross-cultural borrowing where the primary interaction is with disembodied pieces of information (Pavis, 15). In the late 1940s, for example, John Cage's incorporation of Eastern philosophy into his music might best be seen as an instance of cross-cultural influence, while Gillespie's work with Pozo could be more appropriately viewed as a face-to-face collaboration that took place within the interculture of the African diaspora.

I take at face value what J. Lorand Matory has referred to as the "live dialogue between Africa and the Americas," the "living web of links" that has always connected the diaspora with the African homeland (36). Matory's position is that if we are to give a thorough historical account of the African diaspora, we need to remember that for the past four hundred years there has been an ongoing and persistent conversation between people of African descent in the Americas and Africa:

When Africa is regarded as part of the cultural and the political history of the African diaspora, it is usually recognized only as an origin—as a "past" to the African American "present," as a source of "survival" in the Americas, as the "roots" of African American branches and leaves, or, at the most dialectical, as a concept conjured up by New World blacks as a trope of racial unity. Yet in truth, the cultures of both Africa and the Americas have shaped each other in a live dialogue that continued beyond the end of the slave trade. (36)

I am guided by a belief that the history and content of this dialogue needs to be moved to the center of any discussion of collaborations that take place between musicians of African descent. In this sense, I veer slightly from the premises of Norman Weinstein's pathbreaking *A Night in Tunisia: Imaginings of Africa in Jazz.* Whereas Weinstein focuses principally on how American jazz musicians have envisioned a kind of metaphoric Africa in their compositions and on how these musicians have used the discourse of Afrocentricity as a generating idea for the creation of their music, I suggest that the most powerful form of this process of imagining has been the ability of African and African diasporic musicians to *work together.* There is a very real difference between music that evokes Africa and music made via an improvisatory process of face-to-face collaboration that involves individuals from various locations in the African world. Weinstein deals with this difference but only insofar as it relates to his larger project of examining how conceptions of Africa have been invoked in the history of jazz. For example, Chano Pozo, a truly central figure in the history of musical Pan-Africanism, garners only a single, elliptical reference in Weinstein's book and this comes in the chapter on George Russell. (And, interestingly, Weinstein makes it sound as if Russell was the sole composer of the seminal composition "Cubana Be/Cubana Bop," a work that would have been inconceivable without Pozo's input [73–74].)[7] For me, the most profound thing that Pan-African jazz has offered the world is not to be found in its evocations of Africa. Rather, it has been the ability of musicians to use Pan-Africanism as a basis for constructing a collaborative space in which they make direct contact with each other and communicate and create in spite of extreme differences of musical style and despite profound linguistic, historical, and cultural disjunctures.

Envisioning Pan-African music making as a part of a larger and continuing dialogue between continental and diasporic Africans has led me to make the following, intersecting observations: (1) Pan-Africanism can be seen as an organizational strategy that musicians of African heritage use to engender an embodied, pluralogical framework for music making within which disparate, and often contradictory, musical ideas can coexist. (2) Pan-Africanism has a performative aspect; it is a mode of listening, a kind of auditory comportment that directs the "gaze" of the ear. (And it is in the *act* of listening to others, not simply in sounds themselves, that differences are marked and negotiated and communities are constructed.) (3) Pan-African creativity is reliant upon a form of group improvisation that presupposes the presence and responsible interaction of people with diverse personal and cultural narratives. (4) Pan-Africanism helps musicians create links between cultural and social movements; indeed, the difference between the cultural and the political is oftentimes blurred in these collaborations. (5) Pan-African collaborations in music can be viewed as part of a historical continuum of interethnic communication and collaboration that goes back to the earliest days of the diaspora. (6) The hybrid soundscapes that oftentimes arise out of Pan-African collaborations are not simply a by-product of the superimposition of diverse musical and social histories; they are also a function of the central place that heterogeneity occupies in African and African diasporic musical practices.

Finally, I'd like to point out that I have chosen, quite consciously, to provide a rather affirmative reading of the musical and sociopolitical potentials of Pan-African jazz. My main purpose here is not to present a forgetting of the "other history" of inter-African communication and relations (that is, the interethnic violence that continues to occupy an all too prominent place in the African world). For example, I could have chosen to devote more space to stories such as this one about an African American male researcher

who worked in Tanzania during the early 1970s. A chain reaction of stirred-up emotions resulted in his being beaten up by an enraged crowd in a back street of Dar es Salaam for speaking Kiswahili with an American accent. The street mob, entrenched in a racist world view, completely misunderstood the American's intent. Identifying him as a 'black man,' they discovered with abhorrence that he was 'speaking like a white man.' (Kubik, 319).

It seems crucial to me instead to bracket off, for the moment, the powerful lessons about human cooperation that are also a key part of the history of Pan-Africanism. An inspiration for me has been Robin D. G. Kelley's recent *Freedom Dreams* in which he gives a beautiful exegesis of the emancipatory potential of the black radical tradition's collective social movements, those "incubators of new knowledge" (8) whose very existence "enable participants to imagine something different, to realize that things need not always be this way" (9). I hope that what follows highlights those moments in the history of Pan-Africanism when its participants have imagined, and offered up to the world, anticipatory epistemologies for collective action and human betterment.

Intercultural Music, Improvisation, and Collective Learning

A sax player once advised [Lonnie] Hillyer: "When you're playing play by all of them. Play by all of them because you learn from them all."
—Paul Berliner

The Pan-African collaborations that I am concerned with in this essay are a subset of a much broader phenomenon of reflexive interculturalism in music that emerged in the United States in the years immediately following World War II. I say "reflexive" to distinguish this recent self-conscious, intentional brand of intercultural collaboration from the more happenstance type of intercultural contact that has, to a some degree, always characterized the music making of this world. The widespread, reflexive use of taxonomies of cultural difference by musicians, concert promoters, the recording industry, grant agencies, and universities to organize musical performance and collaboration, however, is evidence of a recent and profound shift in the production, dissemination, and reception of music.[8]

Music scholarship has, in general, not kept apace of this massive epistemological shift. For example, there are virtually no acknowledgments on the part of ethnomusicologists of the enormous literature in intercultural communication, or of the long tradition that both theater and performance studies have of addressing intercultural issues. Certainly, ethnomusciology has a vital tradition of reflexive ethnography that values the critical examination of encounters between researchers and their "informants." And most ethnomusicologists are highly cognizant that the "field" is an embodied space that is produced by the very intercorporeal relations that take place within it. As the ethnomusicologist Kay Shelemay has written: "Most of us are well aware that we do not study a disembodied concept called 'culture' or a place called the 'field,' but rather encounter a stream of individuals to whom we are subsequently linked in new ways" (Shelemay, 201). But while ethnomusicologists are quite adept at self-reflexively analyzing the intercultural encounters that are the basis for their own scholarship, they have generally not paid much attention to the discourse of institutionalized intercultural creativity that emerged in full force after World War II.

To be sure, the word "intercultural" is often utilized by music scholars (although it is often used interchangeably with "cross-cultural," "transcultural," and so forth); however, there have been, to date, very few extended meditations on intercultural creativity in music. There are exceptions: Louise Meintjes's pioneering article on Paul Simon's *Graceland,* Veit Erlmann's *Music, Modernity, and the Global Imagination,* and sections of Timothy Taylor's *Global Pop,* and George Lipsitz's *Dangerous Crossroads* all stand out as exemplary models of how musical interculturalism might be theorized.[9]

Almost ten years after its publication, Mark Slobin's monograph *Subcultural Sounds: Micromusics of the West* (and in particular its chapter, "Interpolating the Interculture") still remains the most thoughtful study of how interculturality is used as a framework for organizing, activating, and understanding musical collaborations of the face-to-face (or, as Slobin says, the "mouth to ear") variety (Slobin, 68). There is not enough space here to deal with the full implications of Slobin's insights but I would like to point out that one of the principal strengths of his analysis is that he does not conceive of the "intercultural" as a monolithic category; he recognizes that there are a variety of "interculturalisms" out there.

Indeed, Slobin envisions three broad types of intercultures: *industrial interculture,* which is "the creature of commodified music system . . . a large-scale superculture, where whole societies act the role of subcultures" and where "homogeneity of the product" coexists with a striking "diversity of reception" (61–62); *diasporic interculture,* which "emerges from the linkages that subcultures set up across national boundaries"(64); and *affinity interculture,* which describes "a global, political, highly musical network" in which "direct contact" happens between musicians of disparate cultural backgrounds who share an affinity for a particular musical discourse (68).

Because so many of the most visible intercultural projects are of the "industrial" variety Slobin's theorization of affinity and diasporic intercultures helps to remind us that interculturalism can be more than just a projection of First World corporate fantasy, more than just imperial cultures dreaming themselves as beneficent and universal.

Of course, industrial, affinity, and diasporic intercultures can and often do overlap; we could not hope to place Pan-African collaborations exclusively into one of these three categories.[10] A pan-cultural collaboration such as Archie Shepp's with the South African pianist Abdullah Ibrahim is diasporic but, because of Ibrahim's deep knowledge of the jazz traditions of the United States, it could be seen as an "affinity" collaboration as well. And there are only a handful of examples of Pan-African jazz (or, for that matter, any other commercially available music) that are not in some way or other touched by the transnational music industry (although it needs to be said that very few Pan-African collaborations in jazz are given the exposure and the corporate support accorded to a collaboration involving musicians such as Ry Cooder or Peter Gabriel).

Musicians who engage in Pan-African music making more often than not emphasize diasporic connection as a primary grounding element of the collaborative process. As such, this mode of intercultural collaboration is very much about mending and (re)acquaintance, about the lingering effects of the residues of history, about investigating unexplored historical connections through the act of making music. Yet, in the context of the Pan-African music world, pronouncements of diasporic identity are usually cut with a keen awareness of cultural difference and the limits of overarching, generalized notions of shared history, of roots, of common origin. In other words, recognition of divergent cultural histories does not preclude interaction based on diasporic unity. In this sense, "intercultural" collaborations in the African-diasporic world might appropriately be seen as simultaneously inter- and intracultural.

One of the distinguishing intracultural features of Pan-African music making is its reliance on improvisation to activate the links between subcultures in the diaspora.[11] But it is not just improvisation as such that distinguishes African-diasporic collaborations from others. For any number of reasons (expediency, the dictates of temporary relationships) improvisation is used as a sound-generating strategy in a great many intercultural collaborations. As with interculturalism, improvisation needs to be thought of in the plural (improvisations not improvisation) and we need to make a distinction, as George Lewis does, between improvisation that welcomes "agency, social necessity, personality and difference as aspects of 'sound' . . . from work that 'incorporates' or 'uses' improvisation" ("Too Many," 37).

In numerous intercultural encounters improvisation is used, but as a sonic generative device, not as a constitutive one. For example, Paul Simon "incorporated" the improvisations of Los Lobos for the song "All around the World; or, the Myth of Fingerprints" on *Graceland* but the interpersonal dimension of the improvisatory encounter was not central to Simon's shaping of the final product, as Los Lobos members, Cesar Rosas and Louis Perez, outline:

So we got into the studio, there were no songs. After a while we started feeling like idiots: "when is he going to show us the song?" . . . We expected him to have a song ready for us to interpret when we met him in Los Angeles, but he said, "you guys just play," and we said "Play what?" We just worked up a bunch of stuff that he eventually got a song out of, and that was it. . . . We felt a little detached from the finished piece; we didn't have any real involvement in it. (Quoted in Feld and Keil, 244)

As a collective mode of black diasporic consciousness, improvisation has much to do with "real involvement" and also with the attachment musicians have both to the process of collaborative music making and to the heterogeneous results of that process. There is an avowal of improvisation as a critical and dialogic act that, at its heart, is interpersonal and communal. In the context of Pan-African jazz, improvisers take account of both the expected and unexpected collisions that invariably occur when musicians come together to engender a collective space. In such a space, there is a ceding of complete control over the final "product" in exchange for certain advantages that interpersonal and intercultural contact create (shared problem solving, a broader sonic palette, more expansive connections to performance and distribution networks, friendship, and so forth). Improvisation, in this sense, becomes not simply a spontaneous action, but an empathetic, hermeneutic *interaction* that is constituted upon a recognition of the powerful synergy and responsibility that arises when humans with multiple perspectives come together to make music.

Indeed, as Paul Berliner says, definitions of improvisation that focus only on spontaneity and the ex nihilo act are "astonishingly incomplete. Improvisation depends, in fact on thinkers having absorbed a broad base of musical knowledge, including myriad conventions that contribute to formulating these ideas logically, cogently, and expressively" (492). This point cannot be overemphasized. Yet, moving too far from notions of simultaneity, shared context, and the conterminousness of embodied interaction can serve to dissolve the potent role improvisation plays in the construction of nondeferred communal relationships, and neutralize the possibility of using improvisation as a strategy for developing a cohabited space for embodied collective learning.

The idea of learning is crucial to encounters that are constituted on cultural difference. This is especially true in the Pan-African context, where such encounters involve an attempt to create a complex, nonreductive unity out of a diversity of approaches. In an interview with Vijay Iyer, Steve Coleman put it quite succinctly:

> By learning with others you can get instant feedback from other creative minds (each bringing to the table different experiences and insights) *during* the learning process. This enables a kind of collective experience that can be drawn upon when internalizing information the first time. Individual learning does not have this advantage (although it does have its own advantages, but you can always learn on an individual level. You have to reach out and interact with others to learn collectively). (Quoted in Iyer; emphasis in original)

Here Coleman emphasizes simultaneity ("instant" and *"during* the learning process") while also recognizing that the acknowledgment of personal and cultural difference is of constitutive importance in the music-making process ("each bringing to the table different experiences and insights"). The question of collective learning is not incidental to Pan-African improvisation;. rather, the idea that the highly divergent narratives of individuals can be used to engender communal interaction is deeply embedded in the improvisatory process itself. In this context musicians use an open understanding of simultaneous (inter)action to actualize an environment in which exposure to new ideas, and adaptation, speculation, and transformation are paramount. As George Lewis has said, "the development of the improviser in improvised music is regarded as encompassing not only the formation of individual musical personality but the harmonization of one's musical personality with social environments, both actual and possible" ("Improvised," 110–111). In Pan-African improvisatory contexts musicians use their unique personal and cultural histories to construct a heterogeneous present laden with heterogeneous futures. In this sense, the collective learning that plays such a major role in Pan-African collaboration has at its core an anticipatory belief in the power of human interaction.

Indeed, if culture is, as Edwin Hutchins has written, "an adaptive process that accumulates partial solutions to frequently encountered problems," (354) then the highly improvisatory Pan-African collaborations undertaken by continental and diasporic Africans might be seen as intercultural solutions to the problems engendered within what Sidney J. Lemelle and Robin D. G. Kelley have referred to as the "critical matrix of forced labor, European hegemony and racial capitalism" (8). Before I look at Pan-African improvisation in the preabolition diaspora, I would like to make some general points regarding the issue of interethnic cooperation within the critical matrix spoken of by Lemelle and Kelley.

Pan-Africanism, Diaspora, and Interethnic Alliances

It should be axiomatic that, both in our musical and our human, everyday-life improvisations, we interact with our environment, navigating through time, place, and situation, both creating and discovering form.
—George Lewis

Pan-Africanism is a complicated phenomenon, and its history has its own breaks and disjunctures. In looking at the various manifestations of a Pan-African sensibility one is struck by the astounding diversity of strategies, voices, viewpoints, and interventions that have been formulated to foster links within the African world. So, while it is possible to speak, in a general way, about Pan-Africanism as "the acceptance of a oneness of all African people and a commitment to the betterment of all people of African descent," (Walters, 48) it also needs to be stressed that there have been substantial ideological divergences within the Pan-African movement itself. These divergences reflect the varied experiences Africans have had in the diaspora and in precolonial, colonial and neocolonial Africa.

There has been considerable debate as to whether the cultural, religious, ethnic, and linguistic rifts that separate people of African origin are significant enough to invalidate any claim for basing political and cultural movements around notions of race and a shared history of oppression. Kwame Anthony Appiah, for instance, suggests that the assumptions underpinning Pan-African thought are "a bogus basis for solidarity": "Whatever Africans share, we do not have a common traditional culture, common languages, a common religious or conceptual vocabulary . . . we do not even belong to a common race; and since this is so, unanimism is not entitled to what is, in my view, its fundamental presupposition" (26).

On the flip side of Appiah's argument is Afrocentric ideology, which, in its most extreme form, posits a generalized Africa as a monolithic and stable source for all manifestations of African culture. Stressing an authentic, timeless African homeland, Afrocentrism draws what amounts to an innate and an unproblematized (and untroubled) connection between people of African heritage. If taken to an extreme, Afrocentricity can serve to render invisible the extreme differences that need to be addressed if Pan-African unity is to function.[12]

This essentialist position crops up fairly often in writings describing Pan-African music making. Here are two fairly blatant examples. The first comes from the liner notes to a recording of a collaboration between the American jazz pianist Hank Jones and a group of Malian musicians led by Cheik-Tidane Seck:

Concerning Hank Jones, it was much more than a return to the spring in the twilight of the life of a great artist; it was a reunion, declined in simple mode between relations who, to be truthful, had never really left each other. They had simply been waiting for the storm to pass over before beginning to embrace their Mandingo cousins. (Ndiaye, 6)

Or this review from the magazine *The Beat* of American expatriate saxophonist David Murray's record *Fo Deuk Revue*, a collaboration he undertook with musicians from Senegal:

It has a flow so natural that it seems like a conversation across a backyard fence between residents from the same cultural neighborhood, if not family, rather than the intercontinental exchange that it is in purely geographic terms. (Sakolsky, 55)[13]

Given the above quotations it's not hard to see why someone like Appiah would suggest that such sentiments erase history and neutralize difference and that coalitions built upon these romantic notions could not hope to be emancipatory. Generally, however, Pan-African musicians are highly cognizant of the very real differences that separate African peoples and are able, both musically and theoretically, to articulate the extremes of universalism and particularism that are present in any intercultural alliance (and I would add here, in all fairness, that Hank Jones and David Murray's records document exceptionally rich encounters).

For instance, David Murray—whose records *Fo Deuk Revue, Creole,* and those he made with the World Saxophone Quartet and African drums[14] are among the most searching inquiries into Pan-African musical identity—has spoken about his group Fo deuk Revue, comprising musicians from Senegal and the United States, and the difficult questions raised by the process of making music as an African-American in Africa. Indeed, the very name of the group is a question: *fo deuk* is the Wolof phrase meaning "Where do you come from?" This basic question becomes an injunction against simplistic notions of African unity, implying, as it does, that there is no easy answer to the question of origins. Murray declares: "This group, which has certain elements of all my previous bands, is also a political statement about how I perceive the world, how I see myself as a person of African descent relating to people who live in Africa and about the difficulty and problems that exist for Africans all over the planet" (Liner notes). Murray is careful here not to make a direct equivalence between all people of African descent. The group represents, as he says, the act of "relating" that takes place between continental and diasporic Africans who share common problems but who are not identical because of these problems. Murray is clear that commonalities do not automatically engender equivalence. In an interview, he once said that "you can't find your African roots, even Alex Haley proved you can't find your roots" (Interview). Placed in this light the question "fo deuk?" becomes a driving force for collaboration, a call to explore connections without reifying those connections, an appeal for complex interaction, not simple answers.

So, while one can deny the existence of a unified, transcendent "Africanness," it is not possible to deny that Pan-Africanism, as a strategy for linking diverse people for a common cause, has functioned and continues to function in powerful ways in the African diaspora and on the African continent. We need to account for the possibility of a nonessentialist Pan-Africanism, one that recognizes the plurality of forms that African and African diasporic cultures have taken while at the same time acknowledging that race continues to matter and that racial alliances are still necessary. As Randy Weston once said, "the real Africa is simply one place, with a diversity of many kinds of people doing things so many different ways (quoted in Kean, 37).

Nor does the antiessentialist position acknowledge the powerful role that Pan-Africanism still plays in the formation of social movements and in the creation of cultural forms. In other words, the solidarity that those of African heritage feel might not be based simply on the mere fact of white hegemony, but, perhaps more crucially, on the history of collaborative resistance against that hegemony. Pan-African links have buttressed a struggle that, for the past five hundred years, has been a powerful antidote to racial oppression. To insinuate that these links are founded upon "a bogus basis for solidarity," as Appiah does, serves as a dismissal of the varied, and sometimes profound, attempts made by people of African descent to forge proleptic pan-cultural alliances across national and ethnic boundaries. As I mentioned at the beginning of this essay, it would be far-fetched to suggest that all instances of Pan-African contact deserve celebration (one need not look further than the horrendous violence that still plagues interethnic relations on the African continent). It would be equally far-fetched, however, not to acknowledge that Pan-African alliances have, at times, managed to offer a positive vision of communication and collaboration across deep human divides. The history of Pan-Africanism is, undeniably, a part of the social reality of continental and diasporic Africans and they can access, in an affirmative and creative way, the power of this history. The live dialogue that Matory speaks of is part of the African past as well as the African present.

In other words, I am suggesting that every time a Pan-African collaboration happens, musicians are activating the history of the live dialogue even as they are contributing to it. Or, to put it more simply: the history of Pan-Africanism can and does inspire musicians to form coalitions and to create music.[15] I think it needs to be stressed that the unpacking of the complex phenomenon of musical Pan-Africanism does not depend on the correctness or sanctity of certain theoretical positions; rather, what becomes central is how African and African diasporic musicians use notions of a common history, whether musical, racial, institutional, or ideational to instigate communication and to construct communities.

For example, Olodum, the Brazilian *bloco afro* (black carnival organization) and *grupo cultural* (cultural organization) has engaged in Pan-African collaborations with jazz musicians Wayne Shorter and Herbie Hancock and with the Jamaican reggae star Jimmy Cliff [16] and has, very much like the AACM in Chicago or Katherine Dunham's Performing Arts Training Center in East Saint Louis, used Pan-African ideology as a basis for radical interventions in the black community of Bahia: they sponsor seminars and conferences on social and political issues; they publish a news journal; they run a school for underprivileged children. As João Jorge Santos Rodrigues (Olodum's director of culture) and Nelson Mendes (Olodum's adviser to the Department of International Relations) have said, they are engaged in a process of "reafricanizing" Brazil. And central to this project is Pan-Africanism, especially the lusophone writings of Amilcar Cabral, Samora Machel, and Agostinho Neto. Olodum's Pan-Africanism is not naive, it is not shrouded in romantic rhetoric:

We were never able to focus on only one part of Africa. We were unable to locate the mythical Africa we had imagined. We are from different places, and therefore we absorbed the ideas of Kwame Nkrumah, Sekouh Toure, Amilcar Cabral, Agostinho Neto, Samora Machel, Cheikh Anta Diop, and Franz Fanon. We tried to take these ideas out of the classroom and lecture halls and share them with people who had been harassed by the police many times. (Rodrigues and Mendes)[17]

In putting communication and the construction of communities at the center we move away from a notion of diaspora as dispersal plain and simple to a view that recognizes the intimate connection between diaspora and dialogue. A continuing conversation with or about the homeland is a core component of all diasporas. And, obviously, Pan-Africanism is intimately connected with diaspora. In this sense I am suggesting a subtle shift of focus, from giving priority to the hybrid forms produced by what Stuart Hall has called the "diaspora aesthetic" (31) to acknowledging, as Pnina Werbner does, that "the current fashion with cultural hybridity masks an elusive paradox. Hybridity is celebrated as powerfully interruptive and yet theorized as commonplace and pervasive" (1). I am driven here by a conviction that Pan-African music making has something "powerfully interruptive" and emancipatory about it, but that its transgressive qualities do not simply reside in the hybrid soundscapes produced through diasporic encounters; they rest also, and perhaps most fundamentally, in the highly particular processes of intersubjective engagement that undergirds Pan-African music making. Much recent scholarship has emphasized hybridity without dealing frontally with the human relationships that produce hybrid forms. In this regard, the dialogic improvisatory processes used by musicians in Pan-African encounters might be suggestive to scholars seeking theoretical tools for dealing with performance traditions within African-diasporic culture.

In *The Black Atlantic,* a seminal text on the African diaspora, and one that highlights the hybrid cultural forms of the Black Atlantic world, Paul Gilroy evokes a powerful guiding metaphor for his project of moving beyond "national and nationalistic perspectives" (7): "the image of the ship—a living, micro-cultural, micro-political system in motion" (4), a microsystem of "linguistic and political hybridity" (12). For him ships represent the antithesis of fixed, rooted identities, purified essences, and simple origins.[18] There is certainly something evocative about his use of the ship as a representation for the movement of people, material objects, and ideas within the interstices of the Black Atlantic. Here I would like to provide a gloss on his ship theme and present an image that for me powerfully symbolizes the "live dialogue" of the African diaspora. Here I'm talking about "shipmates."

In their classic monograph, *The Birth of African-American Culture: An Anthropological Perspective,*[19] Sidney W. Mintz and Richard Price call attention to the remarkable ethnic, linguistic, and cultural diversity of slave communities in the Americas and ask a simple but provocative question about "how such heterogeneous aggregates of men and women could compose a social order for themselves, within the boundaries of maneuver defined by the masters' monopoly of power" (40). Their answer is, essentially, a basic one: "through certain simple but significant *cooperative* efforts" (43; emphasis in original). For Mintz and Price, the true origins of Afro-American culture can be found in the community and institution-building projects that "the slaves undertook to inform their condition with coherence, meaning, and some measure of autonomy" (41).

We can locate a wide spectrum of what amount to interethnic forms of cooperation during the slave period. On the one hand we have large-scale endeavors such as the construction of the fully autonomous, multiethnic, maroon societies that sprang up throughout the Americas: *cimarronnes, cumbes, palenques, quilombos* (Nascimento, 138–142). Or, to cite another example, the slave revolt of 1822 led by Denmark Vessey in Charleston, South Carolina for which Vessey, in the hope of "maximizing cooperation," chose lieutenants from several African ethnic groups (Johnson, 7). On the other hand, we have the smaller-scale, but no less important, projects of "establishing friendships, evolving kin groups, constituting domestic units, perfecting life crisis solutions (the social patterning to handle birth, illness and death), establishing religious groups, and solving the problems of servility (by dissimulation, malingering, etc.)" (Mintz and Price, 40). And, finally, according to Mintz and Price, the most "striking example" of the early social bonds that the slaves fostered were the ones that developed between the shipmates who sailed together in the holds of the slave ships on their way to the Americas, bonds that "in widely scattered parts of Afro-America . . . became a major principle of social organization and continued for decades or even centuries to shape ongoing social relations" (43).

I call attention to the importance of the shipmate bond to emphasize that cooperation suffused with an ethic of care was indeed the most basic and earliest strategy for survival that enslaved Africans had. But it is not the cooperation as such that is so astonishing; it's the fact that this cooperation developed under such extreme conditions. Not only did enslaved Africans have to deal with the dehumanizing, brutal conditions of forced labor; simultaneously, they had to negotiate new relationships and alliances across ethnic, linguistic, and cultural divides. As Mintz and Price write,

> [The context of slavery and] the initial cultural heterogeneity of the enslaved produced among them a general openness to ideas and usages from other cultural traditions, a special tolerance (within the West African context) of cultural differences. We would suggest that this acceptance of cultural differences combined with the stress on personal style to produce in early Afro-American cultures a fundamental dynamism, an expectation of cultural change as an integral feature of these systems. (26)

It needs to be pointed out that this "general openness" toward divergent worldviews developed in societies in which many Europeans had the luxury of choosing cultural homogeneity (Mintz and Price, 8). This initial, fundamental difference between European and African experiences in the Americas can be seen as a possible explanation (or if nothing else, a poignant metaphor) for the fact that African diasporic musical practice has been a particularly fertile ground not only for the development of hybrid forms but also for the enactment of intercultural collaborations.

Pan-African Improvisation in the Pre-Abolition Diaspora

> Within the society we did the same thing we did with the music. First we learned the proper way and then we improvised on that. It seemed the natural thing to do because the style or mode of life among black folks went the same way as the music.
> —Dizzy Gillespie

Pan-African music making inevitably took place in the diverse communities that sprang up on plantations and in the free and fugitive communities of the diaspora. The ethnic, linguistic, cultural, and religious diversity of the slaves must have extended to the realm of the musical, and the political alliances I briefly mentioned above must have had their musical correlates. For the most part, what these were like can only be the subject of conjecture. I suggest that the Pan-African collaborations in jazz I call attention to here have historical precedents that resulted from the intermixing of diverse ethnicities in the "critical matrix" mentioned by Lemelle and Kelley. There is a parallel to be drawn between the early interethnic musical experiences of enslaved Africans in the Americas and the collaborations that developed in the second half of the twentieth century.

In his article "African Music in Seventeenth-Century Jamaica: Cultural Transit and Transitions," Richard Cullen Rath provides a meticulous analysis of Pan-African music making that took place on a plantation in southern Jamaica in 1688. As source material he uses transcriptions of the melodies, phonetic renderings of the song texts, drawings and ethnographic commentary made at the time by Hans Sloane (a member of the British Royal Society) and a French musician whom we know only as Baptiste. Rath makes a strong case for the multiethnic origin of the three songs preserved by Sloane and Baptiste: "Angolans and Koromantis did not simply retain their African cultures intact; a process of interchange and experimentation was taking place in the music. . . . The ways in which these negotiations were carried out were ethnically identifiable in 1688" (725). One of the strengths of Rath's analysis is that it places human contact at the center of the various processes of intermixing that were transforming African musics in the diaspora. Accounts of the rise of musical forms in the Americas all too often foreground the interchange of musical materials without showing that these materials were transformed by humans in performance (that is, music is usually the subject, not the object of analysis).[20] Rath also highlights what Sally and Richard Price have referred to as creolization "in the inter-African, not Europeanized sense" (285), the process of intercultural exchange between Africans that produced the varied African cultures in the diaspora. The creation of localized Pan-African musics happened through embodied *interactions* undertaken by Africans, through intercultural processes of communication and negotiation, not just through cross-cultural processes of borrowing and influence.

In Rath's account, a unique African culture in the Americas arises when Africans with different traditions, cultures, histories are in dialogue, exchanging, experimenting, negotiating, working together, to synergetically create new musical forms. For instance, his analysis of "Angola," one of the songs transcribed by Sloane and Baptiste, leads Rath to see it as "a mixture of two discrete styles, with a Kwa—probably Akan—musician playing the harp and singing in the upper register while an Angolan played the lute in the lower register. . . . The two primary musicians positioned their identities in a way that allowed them to negotiate a whole that was new from parts that were not" (Rath, 724).

I don't think it would be far-fetched to speculate that these "ethnically identifiable," "inter-African" negotiations happened all over the Americas throughout the entire period of slavery. For instance, in 1653 Richard Ligon, an Englishman in Barbados, wrote: "The Negres . . . are fetch'd from severall parts of *Africa,* who speake severall languages, and by that means, one of them understands not another. . . . When any of them die, they dig a grave, and at evening they bury him, clapping and wringing their hands, and making a dolefull sound with their voyces" (Epstein, 63–64). A century later in Newport, Rhode Island, an observer of music making during "'Lection Day," a holiday commemorated by African-Americans in New England from 1750–1850, gave this description: "Every voice in its highest key, in all the various languages of Africa, mixed with broken and ludicrous English, filled the air" (Southern, 53).

From what we know of African and African-diasporic musical practice during the slave period we would have to assume that improvisation was a fundamental tactic in these early Pan-African exchanges and that the "attractive power" of African improvisation would have served to unite diverse communities throughout the diaspora. Descriptions of African music making, from the earliest accounts of Europeans in Africa to the narratives describing music making in the diaspora, almost invariably draw attention to extempore and impromptu singing, and to the fact that music making was often "left to the fancy of the performer" (Southern, 14).[21] Here, for example, Eileen Southern recounts the Englishman Nicolas Cresswell's experience at a Sunday evening Negro Ball in Maryland in 1774: "The singing at Cresswell's 'Negro Ball' reflects the African propensity for musical improvisation. The singers vied with one another in poking fun at their masters—a practice reported again and again by chroniclers—making up their verses as they sang and each trying to outdo the previous singer" (48). In this example, improvisation is more than just a strategy for producing sound and sonic structure; it is a critical and oppositional form of social action through which a collective voice emerges. Each individual is permitted to retain his or her own distinct personality even as the group unifies to rally against the hegemony of the slave masters.

The important point here is that the intercultural improvisations undertaken by Africans in the Americas can be seen as collective responses to shared conditions, arising from the proximate relationships that developed under the brutal conditions of slavery. Lawrence Levine suggests as much when he writes that African-American "spirituals both during and after slavery were the product of an improvisational communal consciousness"

(29). And Peter H. Wood has called attention to the important role musical improvisation played in the "complex process of culture building" that "strangers from different regions" of Africa undertook in the Americas: "A musical tradition that stressed improvisation provided a welcome hearth where the sharing process could begin" (85–86). A particular kind of improvisation that stressed community building and communal interaction was a common denominator that would have enabled the exchange of ideas, musical and otherwise, creating solidarity between Africans who had not much in common. Africans in the New World, with their separate languages, distinct musical utterances, divergent histories, had a core aesthetic that while not monolithic, still provided some kind of ground upon which negotiation could occur.

The possibility that improvisation provided the bridge (or, in Wood's phrase, the "welcome hearth") that enabled diverse Africans to collaborate with one another cannot be stressed enough. For if, as I have suggested, group improvisation is about paying attention to others and creating a unity out of an unsuppressed diversity, then improvisation must have played a critical role in fostering a Pan-African understanding. It must have served as a strategy for survival, as a critical forum for learning and trying out new ideas, for creating solutions to a range of problems, and as a communal space for expressing an anticipatory concern for the future.

I do not believe that it is off the mark to suggest that the Pan-African collaborations of the late twentieth century hearken back to these initial encounters between ethnically diverse groups of Africans during the period of slavery. The taxonomies of these intercultural collaborations have, in some ways, changed: the intercultural encounter now makes a more complex braid with national, international, and transnational formations. And although we cannot discount the possibility that enslaved Africans had a degree of agency in choosing their collaborators, the prototypical Pan-African collaborations that began on the slave ships must have been more circumstantial than not. Finally (and this almost goes without saying), there were no institutions or institutional arrangements to promote interculturalism: no record companies, no grant programs, no festivals, no concert venues, no university departments, that could have helped musicians as they sought out potential collaborators and contexts for collaboration.

Nonetheless, in many ways the core of Pan-African music making seems to have remained remarkably constant. Just as the earliest collaborations in the Americas can be viewed as cooperative actions taken within the context of the slave system, recent Pan-African music making can be seen as a collective response to the monumental social, political, economic, and cultural changes that have marked life in the Pan-African world in the past fifty years. And the preabolition and the post–World War II collaborations have in common the use of improvisation as a mode of ethical creativity that opens up a space in which the accommodation of diverse outlooks, perspectives, styles, ontologies, and sounds can be performed. Indeed, it is in those early encounters that we find the antecedents of the first full flowering of a highly particular diasporic consciousness. In music, this consciousness would come to be fully articulated in the fifty-year history of Pan-African music making that begins with Dizzy Gillespie and Chano Pozo.

Cubana Be/Cubana Bop: Pozo, Gillespie and Pan-African Jazz

[Pozo] showed the way towards new and unlimited possibilities.
Jazz will never go back to how it was before.
—Marshall Stearns

On the morning of 19 October 1947, Dizzy Gillespie's orchestra was on a bus making its way from Ithaca, New York to Boston's Symphony Hall. Somewhere on the road Chano Pozo began chanting what George Russell later described as "Nañigo, this Cuban music that was like black mysticism" (Gillespie and Fraser, 324). Using just his voice and the seat in front of him as a drum, Pozo injected a vital part of his own personal and cultural history into the otherwise mundane and tedious world of the tour bus. We don't know what happened after Pozo began singing but it's highly likely that a jam session took place.[22] We do know that by the time they had reached their destination Pozo, Russell, and Gillespie had found a way to incorporate Pozo's chant into the "Afro-Cuban Suite," a work that had been premiered less than a month earlier at Carnegie Hall. The terminus of the ride from Ithaca was the performance of a radical new version of the "Suite" (Pujol, 114).

If there was an encounter of "attractive power" that could be seen as the possible originary moment of post–World War II face-to-face Pan-African music making this might well be it, if for no other reason than because we have access to physical traces that the collaboration left behind: the December 1947 studio recording of "Cubana Be/Cubana Bop" (the two sections of the "Afro-Cuban Suite") and the live recording of the "Suite" from the Salle Pleyel (Paris) concert of February 1948. These recordings provide tangible evidence that something extraordinary was taking place between Pozo and Gillespie (and his band) and that during the latter part of 1947 an intercorporeal form of musical Pan-Africanism was beginning to emerge in the jazz world of the United States.

But it's not just the sonic residues of the encounter that are important; the collaboration among Pozo, Russell, and Gillespie left behind other traces as well. In particular it offered up an example of a flexible mode of intercultural communication that had at its core the embracing of multiple ideas regarding the production of music (both composition and improvisation functioned heavily in the creative process) and that presented a paradigm for cooperation that acknowledged individual and cultural difference as a potential source for experimental creativity. As Paul Berliner has written:

collective interplay can lead players beyond the bonds of their initial plans and even cause them to invent new musical forms that subsequently serve as vehicles for the group's improvisations. Such practices, reminiscent of the genesis of tunes in solo invention reveal the perpetual interplay between formerly composed ideas and those conceived in performance. It is this dynamic reciprocity that characterizes improvisation as both an individual and a collective music-making process. (386)

It is important to note that the collaboration that took place on the bus going from Ithaca to Boston did not come out of nowhere. In New York City in the 1930s and the early 1940s there was a remarkable confluence of creative, political, and intellectual activity that set the ground for collaborations between musicians of African descent in the jazz world. For example, the singer, writer, actor, and political activist Paul Robeson, whom Gillespie described as his hero (Gillespie and Fraser, 498), was looking toward Africa as both the root and as a continuing source for African-American creative activity.[23] In 1934, Robeson wrote: "in my music, my plays, my films I want to carry always this central idea: to be African" (91). And the dancer, choreographer, anthropologist, and political activist Katherine Dunham was creating a body of work (based on her numerous field trips throughout the African world), that represented an enormous catalogue of diasporic movement and that constituted a persuasive call for Pan-African creativity.[24]

Particularly important to Gillespie's own career was Asadata Dafora, a dancer, choreographer, and musician, and a native of Sierra Leone, who relocated to New York in 1929 and who in 1934 unveiled the dance-drama *Kykunkor,* which exclusively used musicians from Africa, and included African dancers and a number of dancers who were New Yorkers (Franko, 487).[25] Mark Franko has said that *Kykunkor* presented what amounted to "a redefinition of dance modernism in tune with Pan-Africanism" (490). In Gillespie's autobiography he mentions that in the 1940s at the African Academy of Arts and Research, he and Charlie Parker provided music for a piece by Dafora.[26] And, not incidentally, Gillespie also mentions that at the African Academy, he and Parker played concerts with African and Cuban drummers: "Just me, Bird, and Max Roach, with African drummers and

Cuban drummers; no bass, nothing else" (290).[27] Gillespie claims that through these concerts he and Charlie Parker "found the connections between Afro-Cuban and African music and discovered the identity of our music with theirs" (290).

The person who was most directly responsible for the Gillespie/Pozo collaboration was Mario Bauzá, the great Cuban trumpet player, composer, and bandleader. Bauzá is a towering figure in the history of Latin jazz and one of the primary instigators of a distinct phase in the history of Pan-African collaborations. In many senses, he laid the tracks for Dizzy Gillespie to become the first spokesman for intercultural collaborations within the jazz world. Bauzá came to New York City from Cuba in 1930, at the height of *afrocubanismo,* a cultural movement that utilized Cuba's African heritage as a counter against the hegemony of the Machado regime.[28] From 1932 to 1936 he was the musical director of Chick Webb's orchestra during which time he hired Ella Fitzgerald. Later, as a member of Cab Calloway's group he was the one who convinced Calloway to give Dizzy Gillespie a job. In 1940 he cofounded the big band "Machito and his Afro-Cubans"; this group was to have a profound effect on the history of Latin music in the United States. And, in 1943 Bauzá composed "Tanga," a piece generally considered to be the first work of Afro-Cuban jazz.

Most important for our purposes here is that Bauzá was instrumental in bringing Pozo from Cuba to New York City. Pozo probably arrived during January 1947 and Bauzá introduced him to Gillespie sometime that spring.[29] According to Gillespie, it was Bauzá who propositioned him: "I got the guy for you if you want the real stuff" (Shipton, 1999). It's not hard to see why Bauzá thought that Pozo was the real stuff: not only was Pozo one of the most prominent composers and choreographers in Cuba from the late 1930s until the time he migrated; he was also a member of the Abakuás secret society, which has its origins in a South Nigerian cult of the Efik people of Calabar (Jahn, 69–70). Pozo also brought with him the repertoire from the Afro-Cuban religion Santería. At the time of his arrival in the United States this repertoire had not really been heard in New York City.

Even though Pozo was only to live another two years (he was shot to death in Harlem on 2 December 1948), he played an enormous role in transforming the sound of Dizzy Gillespie's music and, I would suggest, helped put Gillespie on the road to being a "world statesman" of jazz. Together with Gil Fuller they wrote the classic "Manteca" and, as I related above, Pozo (along with Gillespie and George Russell) was a prime force behind the composition of "Cubana Be/Cubana Bop," which features him leading Gillespie's band in a call and response introduction drawn directly from the chant repertoire of Santería.[30]

Taken as a whole "Cubana Be/Cubana Bop" is one of the most remarkable pieces of the bebop era if for no other reason than its brash accommodation of two highly distinct musical worlds. Perhaps the most astounding moment is the opening of "Cubana Bop," which begins with Pozo softly accompanying his singing with a roll on the conga drum. He intones, in Lucumí, the Yoruba dialect of Cuba, a prayer for the orisha[31] Ochun:

> Iya modupe foba e
> Iya fodupe foba e o
> Obanla adofa ago agolona
> Iya modupe foba iyalode[32]

Pozo's invocation of the Yoruba orishas reaches spatially and spiritually across the diaspora. Not only was the 1947 recording of "Cubana Bop" possibly the first time that the music of Santería was commercially available in the United States;[33] it also set a precedent for using the orishas as a kind of linking device for African-diasporic musical practice. For example, the opening of "Message From Kenya," the first recorded collaboration between Art Blakey and the Puerto Rican American percussionist Sabu Martinez from 1953, features Martinez, in slightly garbled Lucumí, singing the identical phrase Pozo used to start "Cubana Bop": "Iya modupe foba e." (Whether Martinez learned this directly from Pozo, from the Gillespie recording, or from someone else aquainted with the music of Santería can only be a source of conjecture.) Martinez's own *Palo Congo* of 1957, a stunning Pan-Latin collaboration between Martinez and a number of Cuban musicians (including the great Arsenio Rodriguez), includes "Aggo Elegua" and "Billumba-Palo Congo," both drawn from Afro-Cuban religious traditions and which further emphasized the African roots of Cuban and Puerto Rican musics. The song "Shango" from Olatunji's 1959 record *Drums of Passion* has Olatunji and the great African-American percussionist Chief Bey[34] singing, in call and response, an invocation to the orisha Shango. (In 1997 Bey, with his group Ile Omo Olofi, made a beautiful record, *Children of the House of God*, which mixes Yoruba orisha music with Afro-American spirituals.) *Transmissions of the Metaphysics of a Culture*, the record Steve Coleman and the Mystic Rhythm Society made with AfroCuba de Matanzas in 1996, could also be put on this list.[35] For an example outside of the jazz world of the United States I could point to "Reggae Odoyá" a song that came out of a collaboration between Olodum and the Jamaican reggae star Jimmy Cliff. ("Odoyá" is the call used to summon the orisha Yemanjá, another deity within the Yoruba pantheon, who figures prominently in the Afro-Brazilian religion of Candomblé.) The "heterogeneous idolatries"[36] that Alexander Crummel said Africa was the victim of have been put to good use in musical Pan-Africanism (Crummel, quoted in Gerard, 40).

There is no doubt that the collaboration between Gillespie and Pozo was founded upon a complex notion of a common African heritage. Gillespie's autobiography *to Be, or not . . . to Bop* is strewn with anecdotes and reminiscences that emphasize this. For instance, there is a famous line that Gillespie attributes to Pozo. Here is Gillespie's phonetic rendition: "Deehee no peek pani, me no peek Angli, bo peek African" (318). But it is also clear that the connections between them were not sufficient to do away with all differences. For example, in a testament to how revolutionary Pozo's presence must have seemed in the late 1940s, Al McKibbon, Gillespie's bass player at the time of these collaborations, makes the astonishing remark that "to hear a drum played by hand was new to me" (Gillespie and Fraser, 320).[37] Gillespie himself commented at great length on these disjunctures, especially those pertaining to rhythm.

When Chano came, he really opened things up. There are things that he played—he died in 1948—that I'm just beginning to understand now. Chano wasn't a writer, but stone African. He knew rhythm—rhythm from Africa. He sang a chant that was authentic on "Cubana Be" and "Cubana Bop" that was call-and-response between himself and the guys in the band. There are things he would play and sing at the same time on that, and I could never figure out where the first beat was. The downbeat, one! We really had a mutual way of working together after I learned how he heard the rhythm and could signal him to put him in the right time with the band because *his beat and our beat were different.* (321; my emphasis)

Here is an instance of what I mentioned above: the radical role that listening plays in the construction of intercultural communities. Gillespie and Pozo's Pan-Africanism is not simply ideological. Neither is it just a pretext for getting musicians into the same space. Gillespie and Pozo *perform* a Pan-Africanism that has at its center an understanding that plurality does not necessarily rupture universality; that Afrocentricity does not, as a matter of course, eradicate the highly particular manifestations of African culture that have sprung up throughout the Pan-African world. As the above quote from Gillespie makes clear, there was an enormous amount of "working together" between Gillespie and Pozo; through the use of both collective improvisation and collaborative composition they were in dialogue, teaching, learning, experimenting, and transforming the way music was heard and performed in the late 1940s.

It's important to note that a number of observers have commented negatively about the musical results of the Gillespie/Pozo collaboration. For instance, John Storm Roberts, who is in some ways sympathetic to Pozo's work with Gillespie, comments that the musical results of their collaboration were "inchoate and sometimes awkward" (76). He also insinuates that the weaknesses of their recordings derive from their differences: "Gillespie was a leader in a revolutionary style whose innovations had a strong harmonic element; Pozo was a *típico* traditionalist." He goes on to say that neither Gillespie or Pozo "had time to bridge the gap" between their divergent knowledges (77). In his *Bebop: The Music and Its Players,* Thomas Owens says that despite the presence of a new kind of groove for the opening theme of "Manteca" (straight eighth notes instead of the swing eighth notes of 1940s jazz), "Gillespie's irrepressible interest in moving harmonies surfaces in the bridge, suggesting that the embrace of the Cuban idiom is not complete." He goes on to claim that in the improvisation section "Gillespie and the full band continue in the bebop mood, using swing eighths in spite of Pozo's continuing even eighths, until the final *a* section of the theme returns. Complete assimilation of Afro-Cuban rhythms and improvisation on a harmonic ostinato was still a few years away for the beboppers in 1947" (21).[38]

What Owens says is true: there are two different rhythmic sensibilities operating simultaneously in the improvisation section of "Manteca." Moreover, this rhythmic divergence can be found in a fair amount of the music Pozo made with Gillespie's band. Different senses of groove developed in different parts of the diaspora; you can hear this on any number of Pan-African recordings. One astute reviewer called attention to the "problematic" rhythmic and stylistic divergences on Steve Coleman's recording with AfroCuba de Mantanzas: "Hip hop rhythms problematically push ahead of the beat or land squarely on it, whereas all the other rhythms here pull behind or anticipate it in a much more rounded fashion. Coleman's alto sax playing doesn't interact with the Cuban players so much as it intersects perpendicularly from overhead" (Holtje, 51).[39]

These kinds of evaluations reveal the aesthetic of homogeneity that colors traditional notions of musical coherence. Gillespie and Pozo did not perform in a kind of musical melting pot as such; what they did do was to communicate and create music out of a dialogue that took place across very real cultural, linguistic, and musical divides. The most compelling musical evidence we have of this is the duet between the two of them on the version of "Afro-Cuban Suite" from the February 1948 Pleyel concert—which, interestingly enough, marks one of the first times bebop was heard live in France. This duet, which Gillespie refers to as a *montuno* (Gillespie and Fraser, 323), was cut short on the original version of the tune—the studio recording of "Cubana Be" from 1947.[40] The version from the Pleyel concert lasts only a minute but it offers a forceful reminder of the ingenuity it took to allow such divergent musical and personal identities to coexist. Here Pozo and Gillespie are in dialogue, using improvisation not just to generate sound, but also to create a space that allows for a simultaneity of action, where embodied collective learning happens through a process of listening to both African unity and Pan-African difference.

This minute-long encounter, the concentrated alluvium of eight or so months of close collaboration, can also be seen as the first in a long line of Pan-African duets in the jazz world: the call and response vocals of Abbey Lincoln[41] and Babatunde Olatunji on "All Africa" from Max Roach's *Freedom Now Suite;* Abdullah Ibrahim and Archie Shepp on their album *Duets;* David Murray and Gérard Lockel on "Guadeloupe after Dark" from *Creole;* M'alem Abdellah Boulkhair el-Gourd and Alex Blake on "Introduction to Haghouge and String Bass" from Randy Weston's live recording *Spirit! The Power of Music.* And this tradition of intercultural duets in jazz that starts with Gillespie and Pozo's montuno could also be extended back in time, back to earlier days in the diaspora, back to the Angolan and Kwa musicians jamming on a plantation in southern Jamaica in 1688.

"Multiplicity of Approaches (The Afrikan Way of Knowing)"[42]

One of the principal injunctions of Pan-African music making is precisely its ability to allow multiple perspectives, discourses, and identities to exist simultaneously. This coexistence is in contradistinction to intercultural collaborations that seek to "iron out" discontinuities and attempt to present a coherent, homogeneous soundscape despite the real differences that the collaborators bring to the table. For example, in her article on Paul Simon's *Graceland* record, Louise Meintjes points to the kind of homogenizing logic that underlies Simon's song "You Can Call Me Al." This sort of appraisal could be applied to a large number of intercultural collaborations:

In order to appeal more strongly to *Graceland's* international audience, the *kwela* pennywhistle on "You Can Call Me Al" is "cleaned up." Its pitch is more exact and its tone production purer than that of the 1950s counterpart; there are fewer glissandos; there is more precision in beat alignment, and the timbre is not as "windy." . . . Furthermore, the instrument, played originally by Black street youths, is played on *Graceland* by an exiled White South African. (Meintjes, 44)

Graceland is one of the quintessential examples of a collaboration coming out of what Slobin refers to as the "industrial interculture" and this type of encounter usually seeks to use the "universal language" of music to transcend cultural differences. On the other hand, in Pan-African collaborations there is a tendency not to efface difference but to embrace it through an enactment of a highly complex notion of unity, one that goes beyond mere homology. This seems to me to be true whether one listens to Steve Coleman with AfroCuba de Matanzas or the World Saxophone Quartet with African Drums or Wayne Shorter with Milton Nascimento.[43] One of the most vivid examples of this complex notion of unity, or as the

Ornette Coleman quote that began this essay implies, "being in unison without being in unison," can be heard on "Chalabati" a piece that comes from the recording *The Splendid Master Gnawa Musicians of Morocco,* a collaboration between the pianist Randy Weston and a group of eleven master musicians *(m'alems)* of the Gnawa people of Morocco.[44] The Gnawa, originally from sub-Saharan West Africa, were brought as slaves to Morocco beginning in the sixteenth century and are thus representatives of a diaspora internal to the African continent. Weston's contribution to "Chalabati," a song about the enslavement of the Gnawa and their plea to Allah to help them, is striking for a couple of reasons. First, the mere presence of the piano in an ensemble of *guimbris* and *krkabas* is not typical and could be read as a kind of ironic postcolonial retort to European hegemony. Indeed, Weston's conception of the piano is unique, a reminder of the complex origins of cultural artifacts (and, not incidentally, the fact that intercultural collaborations involve not only people and ideas, but material objects as well):

I approach the piano as an African instrument. I really do. Because inside the piano is a harp. The harp is one of the oldest instruments coming out of ancient Egypt and Ethiopia. So Africa is already inside the piano. To get the real touch of the piano, the only thing that is great for the hands is ivory. Now you have plastic on the pianos today, but only the ivory has that wonderful freedom on your hands. So you go to the ivory, you gotta deal with the elephant. The spirit of Africa is already in the instrument. So I approach it as an African instrument.

The piano also brings along with it a tuning system that does not correspond with the intonational conceptions of the Gnawa. The "out of-tuneness" between Weston's piano and the *guimbris* of the Gnawa musicians is instantly discernable, and provides a compelling sonic analogue to a kind of intercultural communication that does not sublate difference. This intonational disjuncture can be read as the sonic product of a diverse encounter. As we've seen in the Simon example, it's important to remember that interculturality does not necessarily presuppose the preservation of difference. Heterogeneity cannot be ascribed simply to the layering of multiple discourses or to the presence of culturally diverse actors and their disparate worldviews. In the case of the Weston/Gnawa collaboration difference is enacted through what Antonio Baldassarre calls "creative remembrance," (Baldassarre, 17) an improvisatory consciousness, an interactive form of memory that characterizes music making in Gnawa communities. An evaluation of Weston's contribution to Chalabati could stress that his piano is out of tune with the *guimbris;* it could point out that, with regard to melodic, harmonic, and rhythmic directionality, Weston makes no attempt at mimesis. Yet, there is communication between the Master Gnawa musicians and Weston: they just don't flatten out the complex "relation-ships—interpersonal and transpersonal—that emerge during a [gnawa] ceremony" (Baldassarre, 12).

The question arises here as to where this propensity for the allowance of difference, found in so many Pan-African collaborations, comes from. I suggest that the hybrid soundscapes of Pan-African music making are not simply by-products of the superimposition of diverse musical and social histories but are also a function of the central place that heterogeneity oc-cupies in African and African-diasporic musical practices.

For instance, in the Weston example the tuning disjuncture could be seen as falling squarely within the bounds of a particular West African musical practice. In his article, "Vibrato Octaves: Tunings and Modes of the Mande Balo and Kora," Roderic Knight illumines the highly individual nature of the tuning practices of the Mande. He says that "*balo* tuning is an individual affair . . . no two instruments are quite alike." He continues: "And yet . . . if *balo* players from widely-flung areas converge on a large event they usually can and *do* play together" (13). The result of this mixing is what Knight re-fers to as "vibrato octaves": the "*differences*—not inaccuracies—in octaves, in unisons, in other intervals, between instruments" (43).[45]

There have been a number of observers who have sought those elusive "retentions" of some essential African practice in the musics of the dias-pora; obviously, by evoking Mande's musical practice in a discussion of Randy Weston and the Gnawa, I am doing something similar. I believe, however, that any empirical analysis of African-based musical practices, whether rumba or jazz, samba or mbalax, will reveal a pervasive tendency toward the incorporation of heterogeneous sonic elements. With respect to the dimension of timbre, Olly Wilson has referred to "the heterogene-ous sound ideal," which he sees as one of the "core of underlying concep-tions that define African and African-American music."[46] He defines this ideal as "a common approach to music-making in which a kaleidoscopic range of dramatically contrasting qualities of sound (timbre) is sought after in both vocal and instrumental music. The desirable musical sound texture is one that contains a combination of diverse timbres" ("Heteroge-neous," 329). I wholeheartedly agree with Wilson and suggest that his no-tion of "the heterogeneous sound ideal" is applicable not only to timbre but to other musical parameters and modes of musical interaction as well. For example, the predilection in African and African diasporic practices for polyrhythm, call and response forms, and, as I mentioned above, intona-tional variability can all be read as manifestations of a general conception that privileges sonic heterogeneity over sonic homogeneity. Wilson him-self, in his discussion of the polyrhythmic approach to the organization of rhythm in black musics, uses words such as "contrast," "clash," "disagreement," and "ambiguity" to describe the relationship between the rhythmic layers that make up a polyrhythmic texture ("Heterogeneous," 328).

In essence, I'm claiming, tautologically perhaps, that within the musical structures of African musics there already exists a framework that allows for Pan-African expression. Heterogeneity is, thus, not something located only in the "pan" but also in the African itself. And here, I'd like to take this discussion of heterogeneity one step further: from the soundscapes of African musics to the realm of the individual agents who create these soundscapes. Indeed, as George Lewis says, "notions of personhood are transmitted via sounds, and sounds become signs for deeper levels of meaning beyond pitches and intervals" ("Improvised," 117). Or, as Dizzy Gillespie wrote when discussing bebop's relationship to social change, "the music proclaimed our identity" (291).

In other words, the heterogeneous sound ideal can be seen as extending out from the sonic to the personal and, by extension, to the interpersonal. The ambiguities, disagreements, clashes, and contrasts that Wilson writes of are not simply sonic configurations; they are the by-products of intercorporeal processes that allow for the personal narratives of all participants to be taken into account. The remarkable thing about African music making (and this goes for Pan-African practice as well) is that out of an utter, unsuppressed diversity of musical and cultural materials some kind of unity is formed.

Such, in a nutshell, is what John Miller Chernoff writes about in his magisterial *African Rhythm and African Sensibility*. One of the principal characteristics of the "African musical sensibility" that he so persuasively documents is "a tendency toward situating multiple conflicting and opposing forces into a process of mediated and balanced communication" (162). What is important, he doesn't describe a process that eradicates difference but one that "situates" the members of a community within a dialogic space, which, in turn, gives the community its integrity:

Africans rely on music to build a context for community action, and analogously, many aspects of their community life reflect their musical sensibility. Knowing what we do about artistic realization in African musical events, we should be better able to appreciate the way that, in Africa, the power of community comes from the dramatic coordination and even ritualized opposition of distinct personalities. (161–162)

Central to the aesthetic conception of most intercultural collaborations is the "coordination of distinct personalities," not the "opposition of distinct personalities." Pan-African music making, insofar as it has some relation to the framework Chernoff describes, would seem to offer up a truly powerful paradigm for intercultural collaboration and cooperation that takes account of both coordination and opposition. The history of Pan-African collaborations from the late 1940s to the present day seems to support this. Certainly Pan-African encounters do appear, on the whole, to place a greater emphasis on the coexistence and maintenance of diverse sonic and personal identities than do the more prevalent and commercially available "industrial intercultural collaborations," which tend to iron out difference to create what might be thought of as neutered hybrids. The important point is that while the sonic differences between these two forms of intercultural collaboration may seem simply aesthetic to some, they are really indicators of vastly different conceptions regarding the construction of community. Indeed, bell hooks has written that "aesthetics . . . is more than a philosophy or theory of art and beauty; it is a way of inhabiting space, a particular location, a way of looking and becoming" (65). (Her evocation of "space" is particularly relevant here because interculturalism is, in many respects, intimately bound up with geography.) In the end, the difference between Pan-African collaborations and other intercultural encounters rests upon the fact that there very well may be what Steve Coleman has called "An Afrikan Way of Knowing" whose aesthetic dimension revolves around the simultaneous mobilization of a "multiplicity of approaches" that in turn leads to the construction of communicative spaces in which divergent identities can be performed and articulated.

Improvisation is a key mode of interaction in the performance and articulation of divergent identities in the African aesthetic space, and the collaborations that I have somewhat fleetingly called attention to in this essay rely on this improvisational aesthetic to a great degree. In Pan-African collaborations, where interpersonal difference extends out to the intercultural, a critical, dialogic, responsible, and experimental brand of improvisation that stresses group interaction becomes an indispensable tool for engendering empathetic creativity. Steve Coleman's "multiplicity of approaches" is, in this context, an epistemology that can be used to take advantage of the heterogeneous responses that musicians with disparate backgrounds will have when placed in proximate relationships. To be sure, improvisation is only one of the "approaches" used by Pan-African musicians. Yet, it represents perhaps the most powerful strategy for activating an embodied understanding of how the worldviews of individuals intertwine with broader cultural and historical frameworks and how this intertwining can be used in musical perfromance. As George Lewis has said, "in performances of improvised music, the possibility of internalizing alternative value systems is implicit from the start. The focus of musical discourse suddenly shifts from the individual, autonomous creator to the collective creator, to the individual as a part of global humanity" ("Interacting," 102).

Conclusion

There is a music that has the quality to preserve life.
—Ornette Coleman

I don't find it at all surprising that the post–World War II fascination with intercultural collaboration, as a reflexive organizational and creative strategy, emerged full-blown in the revolutionary context of bebop. As Ingrid Monson has written, "the heterogeneity of musical elements found in jazz improvisation is deeply related to the heterogeneity of African-American cultural experiences" (*Saying*, 130). I have tried to show that there is an intimate link between the social and cultural experiences of Africans in the Americas and the development of a heterogeneous intercultural space within which dialogic forms of musical interaction, such as improvisation, can take place. It needs to be emphasized that this link does not simply exist as a parable for the connection between art and life or as an instantiation of the analogic relationship between sound and society. There is more to it than that.

One of the most amazing things about bebop was its ability to allow various kinds of identities to exist simultaneously without collapsing them away from their distinctiveness, without their becoming identical. Bebop musicians activated and, in many senses, refined, a way of constructing performance in which musical materials and the processes for creating those materials became inextricably and dialogically linked to personal and communal identities. The communal aspects of bebop made a powerful and persuasive challenge to the notion that "only individuals compose" (Meyer, 107) without renouncing either individuality or the intersubjective noise that inevitably arises in any encounter that engages agents with highly distinctive and, sometimes, contradictory worldviews.

The intercultural collaborations that began to happen in the late 1940s simply amplified modes of interaction already present in bebop and that can be seen as central to African and African-diasporic aesthetics. In this sense, improvisation, the most important of these modes, should not be seen principally as a way of producing sonic structures. Nor should it be seen as "the art of the individual, the role of the single performer taking precedence over the collective effort" (Stewart, 22). Instead improvisation, especially as manifested within the discourse of bebop, needs to be understood as a kind of space in which diverse participants are able to enact multiple viewpoints through understanding, a giving over of control, trust. Improvisation has as its concomitant heterogeneity and together they become a kind of moral imperative; it is this, perhaps, that allows for the strong connection between musical Pan-Africanism and social movements and, perhaps, brings us back to the shipmate theme I high-lighted earlier in this essay.

Paul Robeson once wrote of a "fresh spiritual, humanitarian principle" that African culture could offer this barbarous world. The principle he spoke of, "human friendship and service to the community," might sound quaint and perhaps a little bit naive in relation to the level of barbarism attained by humans in the twentieth century (quoted in Stuckey, "I Want," 23–24). Yet, maybe he hit the nail right on the head. The way the epistemological framework of Pan-Africanism has induced community building on a local level is indeed powerful, and is suggestive of a liberatory model for human interaction and the formation of communities that relies on the very notion of preserving heterogeneity within unified spaces for social and cultural action. Musical Pan-Africanism can be seen as providing a paradigm for the building of local forms of resistance and communication that, simultaneously, have global relevance.

At its best, intercultural improvisation can help activate an anticipatory process of striving for the heterogeneous futures that a humanist such as Paul Robeson hoped for in the face of an utterly inhumane world. In the context of Pan-African music, improvisation allows diverse performers to bridge local knowledges within a heterogeneous global space. I would, however, hesitate to suggest that heterogeneity as manifested in intercultural improvisation is the miracle salve that's going to help us correct the ills that Robeson evokes. It's not. But as Theodor Adorno once said, "as the heterogeneous collides with its limit it exceeds itself" (5). What musical Pan-Africanism offers, through a direct acknowledgment and acceptance of the pluralogical nature of individuals and cultures, is an exceeding of the limits of heterogeneity. This does not, in any sense, imply a transcendence of difference, which is so often seen as the prime mandate to be fulfilled by intercultural encounters. Transcendence, in and of itself, is not the revolutionary thing about interculturalism. Instead, what intercultural encounters can offer is a model for engaging with those things that separate us: the structures of dominance and the systems of representation that produce distinct histories, specific knowledges, and divergent belief systems. In fact, transcendence can be seen as the very limit with which heterogeneity must engage. Musical Pan-Africanism is not the only form of intercultural music making that has gone face-to-face with this issue. It does, however, have a long and successful history of balancing heterogeneity on the one hand, and the transcendence of that very heterogeneity on the other.

The discourse of interculturalism does have the potential to activate community and communication. It is not, however, equal to these. Nor, as I related above, is hybridity, one of the principal concomitants of interculturalism, always "powerfully interruptive." Interculturalism needs to be seen for what it is: an organizational strategy built upon categories of difference. Yet, at the same time, it needs to be stressed that not all forms of intercultural music making are alike. Interculturalism is not always liberatory although in certain configurations it can be. Musicians from Africa and the African diaspora have hit upon a mode of intercultural relating that provides a convincing example of how intercultural relationships can point toward something transcendent while still retaining a firm grip on the socially and historically constructed processes that contribute to the production of human difference.

Notes

1. The first part of the title, "Transmissions of an Interculture," is a refashioning of the title of Steve Coleman and AfroCuba de Mantanzas's recording, *The Sign and the Seal: Transmissions of the Metaphysics of a Culture,* one of the pivotal Pan-African collaborations of the 1990s. I follow Gary Weaver in distinguishing the word "intercultural" from "cross-cultural": "Cross-cultural communication involves comparing and contrasting cultures while *intercultural* communication includes the actual interaction of people from various cultures" (Weaver 5).

2. See Ingrid Monson's article "Art Blakey's African Diaspora" for a poignant analysis of the connections between the nation-building projects taking place in Africa in the 1950s and Pan-African music making, principally the collaborations undertaken by Art Blakey.

3. The issue of co-composition is, perhaps, not so clear. Max Salazar ("Manteca Story") has written an article that examines the possibility that perhaps Pozo was not given proper credit for his role in the composition of "Manteca." Appropriation, a theme so common to so many intercultural collaborations, might therefore have been an issue during the incipient phase of reflexive intercultural music making in the post–World War II jazz community of the United States.

4. See the Discography for a fuller list of these encounters.

5. In this regard I think that further inquiries into how intercultural collaboration came to be a common, reflexive strategy for organizing musical performance will reveal that African and African diasporic musicians have played a role analogous in importance to that played by African-American musicians in the development of the popular musics of the United States.

6. The development of an intercorporeal form of musical Pan-Africanism in the years around World War II was, in many senses, a function of changing immigration and migration patterns that led to, in particular, the increased presence of Puerto Ricans and Cubans of African descent in New York City. More recently, immigration to the United States from Africa has played a role in the further development of Pan-African jazz.

7. See Gillespie (324) for Russell's account of Pozo's contribution to the collaboration.

8. During the past twenty-five years especially there has been a sharp increase in the number of intercultural collaborations in the music world. These collaborations are organized and facilitated by highly specific institutions that devote large parts of their energies to arranging, documenting, and marketing intercultural music: festivals (Music Bridges Around the World, WOMAD); workshops (the Creative

Music Studio); magazines (*Rhythm Music*); grant programs (the Ford Foundation's ten-year-long initiative "Internationalizing New Work in the Performing Arts"), academic departments (Center for Intercultural Performance at the University of California, Los Angeles); and record companies (Axiom, ECM, Real World, Water Lily Acoustics).

9. Max Peter Baumann's recent (2001) essay "Festivals, Musical Actors and Mental Constructs in the Process of Globalization" could also be included on this list.

10. The difficulty of applying rigid classificatory schemes to intercultural collaboration is illustrated by the recent work of the Chinese American pianist Jon Jang. His Pan Asian Arkestra also involves African-Americans, which perhaps reveals that for Jang the appellation "Asian" has a significance that goes beyond narrow racial categorizations. Music such as Jang's points to categories beyond the three given by Slobin: collaborations in which musicians emphasize a common past of racial or ethnic oppression and discrimination; alliances that are built upon notions of a shared colonial history and shared colonial languages; coalitions that engender a collaborative space by threading together notions of a common musical, spiritual, and social past.

11. I should be clear here that I am not contending that all forms of improvisation in the African world are identical. I do believe, however, that most African and African-derived improvisative processes do have a common basis. I elucidate this point later in the essay.

12. While Molefi Kete Asante is generally taken to be the key proponent of Afrocentricity it is important to recognize that his position is a bit more subtle than the one I outlined above insofar as it does not proclaim a "universal" African culture or history but stresses the importance of moving beyond the universalizing tendencies of Eurocentric ideology. For instance at the beginning of his book *The Afrocentric Idea* he writes:

> My work has increasingly constituted a radical critique of the Eurocentric ideology that masquerades as a universal view in the fields of intercultural communication, rhetoric, philosophy, linguistics, psychology, education, anthropology, and history. Yet, the critique is radical only in the sense that it suggests a turnabout, an alternative perspective on phenomena. It is about taking the globe and turning it over so that we see all the possibilities of a world where Africa, for example, is subject and not object. Such a posture is necessary and rewarding for both Africans and Europeans. The inability to "see" from several angles is perhaps one of the common weaknesses of provincial scholarship. (1)

Indeed, Asante makes a distinction between what he calls Africanity (which "broadcasts identity and being" through general notions about "the customs, traditions, and traits of people of Africa and the diaspora") and Afrocentricity (which for him "seeks agency and action"). He writes about the possibility of developing a "nexus between Africanity and Afrocentricity" (Asante, 19). Pan-African music making very often takes place within this nexus.

13. The tropes of the "distant cousins" and the "backyard fence" seem to have something of a history in the study of the relationships between African and African diasporic musical practices. See, for example, Alan Lomax's liner notes to the album *Root of the Blues* (1977), where he writes: "This pair of work hollers—one that I recorded in the Mississippi penitentiary in the sixties and the other that David Sapir recorded in a rice field in Senegal about the same time—sounds like a conversation between second cousins over a backyard fence."

14. The World Saxophone Quartet has made two records with African Drums: *Metamorphosis* (1991) and *Four Now* (1996). Their collaborators on these two records were the Senegalese percussionists/composers Mar Gueye and Mor Thiam

and the African-American percussionist/composer Chief Bey (see note 34 below for more information on Bey). On "Selim Sivad: A Tribute to Miles Davis" (1998) they team up with Chief Bey, and three other percussionists: the Ghanaian Okyerema Asante, the Congolese Titos Sompa and the African-American Jack DeJohnette. The World Saxophone Quartet has also made "M'Bizo," a record on which they collaborate with a diverse pool of musicians drawn from a number of different ethnic groups in South Africa. The record, dedicated to the memory of South African bass player Johnny Dyani (an expatriate musician who left South Africa with Chris McGregor's group Blue Notes in 1964) takes as one of its themes "the South African diaspora, the creativity of the artists roaming around the world and their dissatisfaction and their nostalgia for their homeland" (Aronson). Murray's record *Creole* (1998) was made in collaboration with guitarist Gérard Lockel and other musicians from Guadeloupe.

15. It's interesting to note here that a number of Pan-African musicians have commented on the role their families played in teaching them about Pan-Africanism. For instance, Taj Mahal has said: "My father became a strong follower of Marcus Garvey and the back-to-Africa movement . . . so as a child and a young man I always had a positive image of Africa" (qtd. in Eyre, 22). And Randy Weston has said much the same: "My father was totally into Africa. He was a great follower of Marcus Garvey. And he always told me about the greatness of African civilization. When I would go to school and got the reverse, or I'd go to the movies and Africa was always a place to be ashamed of. My dad kept many books on Africa. He told me many stories about Africa. So my dad really set the stage as far as that's concerned" (Weston).

16. Olodum collaborated with Hancock and Shorter on the songs "The Seven Powers" and "Gwagwa O De" from the album *Ritual Beating System* (1992). Cliff appears with Olodum on the song "Reggae Odoyá," which can be found on Olodum's records *Da Atlântida Bahia* (1994) and *The Best of Olodum* (1997).

17. In another passage in the same article Rodrigues and Mendes point even more specifically to how important Pan-African knowledge was to the formation of black consciousness in Salvador:

In the Liberdade and Engenho Velho neighborhoods [of Salvador, Bahia], black consciousness grew fervently. Books of African literature in Portuguese circulated from hand to hand like rare coins. The ideas of Amilcar Cabral, Samora Machel, and Augostinho Neto, and the role of organizations such as the MPLA (Movimento Popular de Libertação de Angola); PAIGC (Partido Africano da Independência da Guinéa e Cabo Verde); and FRELIMO (Frente de Libertação de Moçambique) were very important.

18. In his *Slave Culture: Nationalist Theory and the Foundations of Black America,* Sterling Stuckey also describes the slave ship as a site for the creation of Pan-African unity: "As such, slave ships were the first real incubator of slave unity across cultural lines, cruelly revealing irreducible links from one ethnic group to the other, fostering resistance thousands of miles before the shores of the new land appeared on the horizon—before there was mention of natural rights in North America" (3).

19. *The Birth of African Culture: An Anthropological Perspective* is a reprint, with slight modification, of "An Anthropological Approach to the Afro-American Past," originally published in 1976. The reprint contains a short but intriguing preface that places the original monograph within the contentious debate it provoked after its publication. Also relevant is Richard and Sally Price's book, *Maroon Culture: Cultural Vitality in the African Diaspora,* which, again, takes up many of the issues raised in the original monograph. Particularly useful as a rebuttal to some of their more forceful critics (including John Thornton) is the long footnote on 330–332.

20. Here is an example: "Wherever the Africans were taken, the music went with them, merging to a degree with the white man's culture, but never losing its distinctive qualities" (Epstein, 16).

21. For such accounts see, especially, Epstein, Levine, and Southern.

22. In his autobiography Gillespie gives an account of what these tour bus music-making sessions were like: "On the bus, [Pozo would] give me a drum, Al McKibbon a drum, and he'd take a drum. Another guy would have a cowbell, and he'd give everybody a rhythm. We'd see how all the rhythms tied into one another, and everybody was playing something different. We'd be on the road in a bus, riding down the road, and we'd sing and play all down the highway. He'd teach some of those Cuban chants and things like that. That's how I learned to play the congas" (Gillespie and Fraser, 319).

23. Robeson also demonstrated what was, according to Sterling Stuckey, "such intense reciprocity between cultural and political nationalisms that the two were rendered virtually indistinguishable ("I Want," 28–29). In the early 1960s this kind of "reciprocity" became incredibly important in the creation of revolutionary political works of musical Pan-Africanism such as Max Roach's *Freedom Now Suite*, Randy Weston's *Uhuru Africa* and in the community-building projects of the Nigerian percussionist Babatunde Olatunji in Harlem, and the Association for the Advancement of Creative Musicians in Chicago.

24. Dunham was also responsible for bringing a number of important African and African diasporic musicians to the United States including the Cubans Francisco Aguabella and Julito Collazo and, in the late 1960s, the great Senegalese percussionist singer and composer, Mor Thiam, a musician who, principally through his work with the World Saxophone Quartet, would become a prime participant in the Pan-African music world of the 1990s. To understand further the importance Dunham played in the creation of an Afro-diasporic consciousness in the United States, see the article, "The Yoruba Orisha Tradition Comes to New York City" in which Marta Moreno Vega writes:

> All of the leading performers who have been instrumental in the promulgation of the Orisha tradition were part of the cultural aesthetic movement nurtured by Katherine Dunham. Before they became major performing artists in the Latino community, Mongo Santamaria, Tito Puente, Celia Cruz, Perez Prado, Julito Collazo, and Francisco Aguabella all exchanged information and ideas in the nurturing environment Dunham established. The interrelationship of the cultural experiences of the African American and African Latino communities dates to the mid-thirties, and the music of Tito Puente, Celia Cruz with La Sonora Matancera, and Celina would educate New York audiences in the songs and celebratory messages and practices of the Orisha tradition of Cuba. (205–206 n.2)

25. See Franko (485–491) and Gerard (57–58) for information on Dafora's life.

26. Dafora was also, along with Marshall Stearns, responsible for introducing West African music to Randy Weston, the great Brooklyn-born pianist and Pan-Africanist (Weinstein, 109).

27. According to Jordi Pujol, the performance with Dafora took place on 7 May 1947 at the Hotel Diplomat in New York and was called "African Interlude." In a piece called "Bombastic Bebop," Gillespie and Parker teamed with six percussionists: Billy Alvarez (bongos), Pepé Beké (quinto), Diego Iborra, Eladio González and Rafael Mora (conga drums) and Max Roach (drums) (Pujol, 113). Clearly, this performace could be seen as a direct predecessor to Art Blakey's Pan-African "drum records" of the 1950s and 1960s.

28. See Robin Moore's *Nationalizing Blackness: Afrocubanismo and Artistic*

Revolution in Havana, 1920–1940 for information on the cultural milieu Mario Bauza left when he immigrated to the United States.

29. Most of the information on Pozo in this paper is drawn from Jordi Pujol's extensive liner notes to the three-CD set *Chano Pozo: El tambor de Cuba* and Max Salazar's three-part series on Pozo's life that appeared in *Latin Beat Magazine* (April–June 1993). Pujol and Salazar seem to be in disagreement regarding when Pozo actually arrived in the United States. Salazar gives the arrival date as May 1946. In his convincing account Pujol provides a detailed analysis of available evidence and suggests that Pozo probably didn't arrive until January 1947. I have accepted Pujol's account in this essay.

30. In this regard Russell's description of Pozo's chant on the bus ride from Ithaca to Boston as "Nañigo, this Cuban music that was like black mysticism" is probably incorrect (Gillespie, 324). The recorded versions of Pozo's chant come from the repertoire of Santería.

31. In the context of Santería, orishas are Yoruba deities, "divine ancestors, immaterial in form, who control some aspect of nature and some domain of human activity" (Myers, 1669).

32. After the prayer for Ochun, Pozo leads the group in a call and response section whose origin and language I have not been able to identify (it is possible that some of the words he uses are of Bantu derivation). Pozo then introduces a steady rhythm and sings, again in Lucumí, a prayer for the orisha Chango (which mentions the orisha Iroko):

> Ure ure kore Iroko
> Iroko lo ki ki
> Ure ure kore Iroko
> Iroko lo ki ki
> Ibankoro lo laroye
> Laroye alanami

The texts of the prayer for Ochun and the song for Chango are virtually untranslatable; each word has layers upon layers of meaning. Out of respect to the tradition of Santería and to my sources I have refrained from making an attempt at translation. I'd like to thank Regino Jimenez and Mark Lamson for providing the transcriptions of the Lucumí texts from "Cubana Bop."

33. In her article "The Yoruba Orisha Tradition Comes to New York City" Marta Moreno Vega suggests that Tito Puente's record *Top Percussion* (1957) which he made in collaboration with the Cuban musicians Mongo Santamaria, Francis Aguabella, and Julito Collazo and the Puerto Rican-American Willie Bobo, and which incorporated Yoruba chants was the first commercial recording of Santería music available in New York City. It's interesting to note that Pozo's recording with Gillespie was released a decade before Puente's recording.

34. Chief Bey (James Hawthorne Bey) is one of the truly important and enigmatic figures in the history of Pan-African music-making. He has taken part in a number of the crucial collaborations over the past forty years including Babatunde Olatunji's *Drums of Passion* (1959), Art Blakey's *The African Beat* (1962) and the three records he made with the World Saxophone Quartet in the 1990s (given in note 14 above). Even though Bey was born in Yasmeen, South Carolina (sometime around 1915) he is often listed as being Senegalese (see, for example, the liner notes to Blakey's *African Beat* and *Four Now* by the World Saxophone Quartet), Yoruba (see the review of Bey's record *Ile Omo Olofi* in the May 1998 issue of *Jazz Times*), or African (Szwed, 218). These confusions underscore the complex issue of

assigning identity in the African diaspora and give added depth to Murray's question "Where do you come from?" I thank Craig Harris and Sherry Scott for information on Bey's life.

35. Coleman has pointed out that the common bond on *The Sign and the Seal* was the African idea of expressing the universe through sound and that the underlying concept connecting his group and the AfroCuba de Matanzas involved "the process of expressing forces of nature in their rhythmic-tonal configurations" (Coleman; liner notes).

36. There is, perhaps, an analogy to be drawn between the "heterogeneous idolatries" of some African religions and African musical practice. John Chernoff, for example, writes: "There is a clear parallel, certainly, between the aesthetic conception of multiple rhythms in music and the religious conception of multiple forces in the world" (156). Another parallel might also be drawn between heterogeneous religious conceptions and the pronounced ability Africans in the Americas had for dealing with ethnic difference and, also, their marked proclivity for creating syncretic forms.

37. Like Al McKibbon, Weston was introduced to the hand drum through Pozo's collaboration with Gillespie: "Dizzy brought back the drum. . . . The hand drum was outlawed here, which is one reason why I think we put the drums into pianos and trumpets and trombones and the English language. Hearing Chano Pozo with Dizzy Gillespie's Orchestra turned me around, and I've been working with hand drums ever since. Chano was Cuban, but you could hear pure Africa in his drum sound. It was a marriage, a complete circle" (qtd. in Panken, 23).

38. Not all observers, however, have been so critical. See, for example, Gary Giddens's extended analysis of "Manteca" which begins by referring to it as "one of the most important records ever made in the United States" (288).

39. On this issue of coherence I could also point to this evaluation of David Murray's *Fo Deuk Revue:* "*Fo Deuk* is an intriguing and vibrant rhythmic to and fro. But though it delivers satisfying music in several styles, the sharp internal contrasts at times create a tension that restricts a more organic blend" (Palmer, 35). Or this review of Maleem Mahmoud Ghania's collaboration with Pharoah Sanders: "At times, Sanders sounds out of place, struggling to incorporate his most explosive, emotional outpourings without disrupting the trance-inducing rhythms established by Ghania's insistent guimbri. Then you wonder, 'Why is this man screaming?'" (42). There is also the famous *Life Magazine* spread on bebop from 1948 with a caption underneath a photograph of Pozo that reads, in part, "Shouting incoherently, drummer goes into bop transport." ("Life Goes to a Party," 141).

40. On the recording of the "Afro-Cuban Suite" from the Carnegie Hall concert of 29 September 1947, Gillespie and Pozo are joined by Lorenzo Salín on bongos.

41. One of the threads I did not take up in this essay is the complex role women have played in the history of Pan-African jazz. I have already called attention to Katherine Duncan and Abbey Lincoln, both of whom made enormous contributions to this history. There is also the trombonist, composer, and arranger Melba Liston who worked extensively with Randy Weston until her death in 1999. In the 1970s, Liston moved to Jamaica where she taught at the University of the West Indies and the Jamaica Institute of Music. More recently, the Afro-Brazilian dancer and musician Rosangela Silvestre has made vital contributions to Steve Coleman and AfroCuba de Matanzas's *The Sign and the Seal* and the tours undertaken to promote that record.

On the subject of African-American women and black nationalism, Robin D. G. Kelley has recently written: "Here lay the crux of the problem: The relative invisibility of black women in these radical freedom dreams is less a matter of deliberate exclusion than *conception,* or the way in which the interests and experiences of black people are treated. . . . The ostensibly gender-neutral conception of the black community (nothing is really gender neutral), presumes that freedom for black people as a whole will result in freedom for black women (Kelley, 136–137). I hope to take up this issue in relation to Pan-African jazz in a future essay.

42. Again, the title of this section comes from Steve Coleman. His piece "Multiplicity of Approaches (The Afrikan Way Of Knowing)" appears on his album *Def Trance Beat* (Modalities of Rhythm), released in 1995.

43. Shorter and Nascimento collaborated on *Native Dancer* in 1975.

44. Another collaboration between the Gnawa and a jazz musician can be found on *The Trance of Seven Colors* (1994), a record saxophonist Pharoah Sanders made with the Gnawa master musician Maleem Mahmoud Ghania. Particularly evocative is their interaction on "La Allah Dayim Moulenah."

45. John F. Szwed's description of improvisatory communal music making in Sun Ra's band points to another example of this kind of practice: "Tones. Not notes. Every C note had to be sounded differently from every other C, with a distinct timbre and volume" (Szwed, 112).

46. Wilson has also dealt with the general characteristics of African musical practice in "Significance" and "Black Music."

A Selected Discography of
Pan-African Collaborations in Jazz (1947–2001)

Art Ensemble of Chicago with Amabutho. *Art Ensemble of (Chicago) Soweto*. DIW, 1990.

Art Ensemble of Soweto [Art Ensemble of Chicago with Amabutho Male Chorus of Soweto]. *America-South Africa*. DIW, 1992.

Bahia Black (Featuring Herbie Hancock and Wayne Shorter with Olodum). *Ritual Beating System*. WEA/Axiom, 1992.

Blakey, Art. "Message from Kenya." Included on Horace Silver. *Horace Silver Trio*. Blue Note, 1989. (Originally released 1953.)

Blakey, Art. *Orgy in Rhythm*. Vols. 1 and 2. Blue Note, 1997. (Originally released 1957.)

Blakey, Art. *The Drum Suite*. Sony/Columbia, 1998. (Originally released 1957.)

Blakey *Holiday for Skins*. Vols. 1 and 2. Blue Note, 1958.

Blakey, Art, and the Afro-Drum Ensemble. *The African Beat*. Blue Note, 2000. (Originally released 1962).

Brand, Dollar (Abdullah Ibrahim), and Archie Shepp. *Duet*. Denon, 1978.

Carter, John. *Dance Of The Love Ghosts*. Rykodisc, 1994. (Originally released 1986.)

Coleman, Steve. *The Sign and the Seal: Transmissions of the Metaphysics of a Culture*. BMG, 1996.

Ghania, Maleem Mahmoud, with Pharoah Sanders. *The Trance of Seven Colors*. Axiom, 1994.

Gillespie, Dizzy. *The Complete RCA Victor Recordings, 1937–1949*. BMG/RCA, 1995.

Gillespie, Dizzy. *The Legendary Dizzy Gillespie*. Vogue: DP 18, 1973. (Contains recordings from the Salle Pleyel concert, recorded in Paris on 28 February 1948.)

Jones, Hank, and Cheick-Tidane Seck. *Sarala: Hank Jones Meets Cheick-Tidane Seck and the Mandinkas*. Universal/Verve, 1996.

Lateef, Yusef. *In Nigeria*. YAL Records, 1983.

Machito and His Afro-Cuban Orchestra with Charlie Parker. "Okiedoke" and "Mango Mangue." *The Original Mambo Kings*. Verve, 1993. ("Mango Mangue" and "Okiedoke" originally recorded 1948 and 1949, respectively.)

Murray, David. *Fo Deuk Revue*. Justin Time, 1997.

Murray, David. *Creole*. Justin Time, 1998.

Pozo, Chano. *El tambor de Cuba*. Tumbao, 2001. (Three-CD set contains collaborations from the late 1940s with James Moody and Art Blakey, and Dizzy Gillespie. Includes three versions of Cubana-Be/Cubana-Bop [Afro-Cuban Suite].)

Roach, Max. *We Insist! Freedom Now Suite*. Candid, 1960.

Sanders, Pharoah. *Message From Home*. Universal/Verve, 1996.

Shorter, Wayne, and Milton Nascimento. *Native Dancer*. Sony/Columbia, 1974.

Weston, Randy. *Uhuru Afrika, Freedom Africa*. Roulette, 1960.

Weston, Randy. *The Splendid Master Gnawa Musicians of Morocco*. Universal/Verve, 1992.

Weston Randy, African Rhythm Quartet and the Gnawa Master Musicians of Morocco. *Spirit! The Power of Music*. Universal/Verve, 2000.

World Saxophone Quartet and African Drums. *Metamorphosis*. Nonesuch, 1991.

World Saxophone Quartet with African Drums. *Four Now*. Justin Time, 1996.

World Saxophone Quartet. *M'Bizo*. Justin Time, 1999.

Works Cited

Adorno, Theodor W. *Negative Dialectics*. Translated by E. B. Ashton. New York: Continuum, 1983.

Andrews, John. Review of "The Trance of the Seven Colors." *Down Beat* 62, no. 3 (April 1995): 42.

Appiah, Anthony. *In My Father's House: Africa in the Philosophy of Culture*. New York: Oxford University Press, 1992.

Aronson, David. Liner notes to audio recording *M'Bizo* by the World Saxophone Quartet. Justin Time Records (Just 123–2), 1999.

Asante, Molefi Kete. *The Afrocentric Idea*. Revised and expanded edition. Philadelphia: Temple University Press, 1998.

Bailey, Derek. *Improvisation: Its Nature and Practice in Music*. New York: Da Capo, 1993.

Baldassarre, Antonio. Liner notes to *The Masters of Guimbri: The Red and Green Suites (Gnawa Leila Volume IV)*. Al Sur Records (ALCD 147), 1995.

Baumann, Max Peter. "Festivals, Musical Actors and Mental Constructs in the Process of Globalization." *World of Music* 43, nos. 2–3 (2001): 9–29.

Berliner, Paul. *Thinking in Jazz: The Infinite Art of Improvisation*. Chicago: University of Chicago Press, 1994.

Chernoff, John. *African Rhythm and African Sensibility: Aesthetics and Social Action in African Musical Idioms*. Chicago: University of Chicago Press, 1979.

Coleman, Steve. Liner notes to audio recording *The Sign and the Seal: Transmissions of the Metaphysics of a Culture*, by Steve Coleman and the Mystic Rhythm Society in collaboration with AfroCuba de Matanzas. BMG Music (74321–40727–2), 1996.

Dibango, Manu (in collaboration with Danielle Rouard). *Three Kilos of Coffee: An Autobiography*. Translated by Beth G. Raps. Chicago: University of Chicago Press, 1994.

Epstein, Dena. *Sinful Tunes and Spirituals: Black Folk Music to the Civil War*. Urbana: University of Illinois Press, 1977.

Erlmann, Veit. *Music, Modernity, and the Global Imagination: South Africa and the West*. New York: Oxford University Press, 1999.

Eyre, Banning. "Taj Mahal and Toumani Diabate: An American Bluesman and a Malian Griot Record a Historic Collaboration." *Rhythm Music* (August 1999): 22–24.

Feld, Stephen, and Charles Keil. *Music Grooves: Essays and Dialogues.* Chicago: University of Chicago Press, 1994.

Franko, Mark. "Nation, Class, and Ethnicities in Modern Dance of the 1930s." *Theatre Journal* 49, no. 4 (1997): 475–491.

Gerard, Charles D. *Jazz in Black and White: Race, Culture, and Identity in the Jazz Community.* Westport, Conn.: Praeger, 1998.

Giddens, Gary. *Visions of Jazz: The First Century.* New York: Oxford University Press, 1998.

Gillespie, Dizzy, and Al Fraser. *to Be, or not . . . to Bop.* New York: Doubleday, 1979.

Gilroy, Paul. *The Black Atlantic: Modernity and Double Consciousness.* Cambridge, Mass.: Harvard University Press, 1993.

Hall, Stuart. "Cultural Identity and Diaspora." In *Diaspora and Visual Culture: Representing Africans and Jews,* edited by Nicholas Mirsoeff, 21–33. London: Routledge, 2000.

Harris, Joseph. "The Dynamics of the Global African Diaspora." In *The African Diaspora,* edited by Álusine Jalloh and Stephen E. Maizlish, 7–21. College Station: Texas A&M University Press, 1996.

Holtje, Steve. Review of *The Sign and the Seal: Transmissions of the Metaphysics of a Culture,* by Steve Coleman and the Mystic Rhythm Society with AfroCuba de Matanzas. *Rhythm Music* (June 1997): 51.

hooks, bell. "An Aesthetic of Blackness—Strange and Oppositional." *Lenox Avenue: A Journal of Interartisic Inquiry* 1(1995): 65–72.

Hutchins, Edwin. *Cognition in the Wild.* Cambridge, Mass.: MIT Press, 1995.

Iyer, Vijay. "Steve Coleman, M-Base, and Music Collectivism." <http://www.cnmat.berkeley.edu/~vijay/mbase4.html>. 17 August 2001.

Jahn, Janheinz. *Muntu: African Culture and the Western World.* New York: Grove Weidenfeld, 1990.

Johnson, Sterling. *Black Globalism: The International Politics of a Non-state Nation.* Aldershot: Ashgate, 1998.

Kean, Kirby. "Randy Weston: Learning From the Elders." *Rhythm Music* 4, no. 3 (1995): 36–40.

Kelley, Robin D. G. *Freedom Dreams: The Black Radical Imagination.* Boston: Beacon, 2002.

Knight, Roderic. "Vibrato Octaves: Tunings and Modes of the Mande Balo and Kora." *Progress Reports in Ethnomusicology* 3, no. 4 (1991):1–49.

Kubik, Gerhard. "Documentation in the Field. Scientific Strategies and the Psychology of Culture Contact." In *Music in the Dialogue of Cultures: Traditional Music and Cultural Policy,* edited by Max Peter Baumann, 318–335. Wilhelmshave: Florian Noetzel, 1991.

Lemelle, Sidney J., and Robin D. G. Kelley. "Imagining Home: Pan-Africanism Revisited." In *Imagining Home: Class, Culture, and Nationalism in the African Diaspora,* edited by Sidney J. Lemelle and Robin D. G. Kelley, 1–16. London: Verso, 1994.

Levine, Lawrence. *Black Culture and Black Consciousness: Afro-American Folk Thought from Slavery to Freedom.* New York: Oxford University Press, 1977.

Lewis, George E. "Improvised Music after 1950: Afrological and Eurological Perspectives." *Black Music Research Journal* 16, no. 1 (1996): 91–122.

———. "Interacting with Latter Day Musical Automata." *Contemporary Music Review* 18, no. 3 (1999): 99–112.

———. "Too Many Notes: Computers, Complexity and Culture in *Voyager.*" *Leonardo Music Journal* 10 (2000): 33–39.

"Life Goes to a Party." *Life Magazine* 25, no. 15 (11 October 1948): 138–142.

Lipsitz, George. *Dangerous Crossroads: Popular Music, Postmodernism, and the Poetics of Place*. New York: Verso, 1994.

Litweiler, John. *Ornette Coleman: A Harmolodic Life*. New York : W. Morrow, 1992.

Matory, J. Lorand. "Afro-Atlantic Culture: On the Live Dialogue Between Africa and the Americas." In *Africana: The Encyclopedia of the African and African American Experience*, edited by Kwame Anthony Appiah and Henry Louis Gates, 36–44. New York: Basic Civitas, 1999.

Meintjes, Louise. "Paul Simon's *Graceland*, South Africa and the Mediation of Musical Meaning." *Ethnomusicology* 34, no. 1 (1990): 37–73.

Mintz, Sidney W., and Richard Price. *The Birth of African-American Culture: An Anthropological Perspective*. Boston: Beacon, 1992.

Meyer, Leonard B. *Style and Music: Theory, History, and Ideology*. Philadelphia: University of Pennsylvania Press, 1989.

Monson, Ingrid. "Art Blakey's African Diaspora." In *The African Diaspora: A Musical Perspective*, edited by Ingrid Monson, 329–352. New York: Garland Publishing, 2000.

———. *Saying Something: Jazz Improvisation and Interaction*. Chicago: University of Chicago Press, 1996.

Moore, Robin. *Nationalizing Blackness: Afrocubanismo and Artistic Revolution in Havana, 1920–1940*. Pittsburgh: University of Pittsburgh Press, 1997.

Murray, David. Interview with Steve Bachall (3 November 1995). <http://www.eyeneer.com/Jazz/Murray/index.html>. 7 August 2000.

———. Liner notes to audio recording *Fo deuk Revue*, by David Murray and Fo deuk Revue. Justin Time Records (Just 94–2), 1997.

Myers, Aaron. "Santería." *Africana: The Encyclopedia of the African and African American Experience*, edited by Kwame Anthony Appiah and Henry Louis Gates, 1669–1671. New York: Basic Civitas, 1999.

Nascimento, Abdias Do, and Elisa Larkin Nascimento. *Africans in Brazil: A Pan-African Perspective*. Trenton: Africa World Press, 1992.

Ndiaye, Macodou. "A Family Reunion." Liner notes to audio recording *Sarala: Hank Jones Meets Cheick-Tidane Seck and the Mandinkas*. Verve: (314 528 783–2), 1995.

Oulette, Dan. "Steve Coleman's Jazz Outreach." *Down Beat* 63, no. 10 (October 1996): 28–32.

Owens, Thomas. *Bebop: The Music and Its Players*. New York: Oxford University Press, 1995.

Palmer, Don. "David Murray: Afro-Caribbean Connections." *Rhythm Music* 8, no. 4 (April 1999): 34–35.

Panken, Ted. "African Soul." *Down Beat* 65, no. 10 (October 1998): 20–25.

Pavis, Patrice. *The Intercultural Performance Reader*. London: Routledge. 1996.

Price, Sally, and Richard Price. *Maroon Arts: Cultural Vitality in the African Diaspora*. Boston: Beacon, 1999.

Pujol, Jordi. Liner notes to audio recording *Chano Pozo: El Tambor de Cuba*. Tumbao Cuban Classics (TCD 305), 2002.

Rath, Richard Cullen. "African Music in Seventeenth Century Jamaica: Cultural Transit and Transition." *William and Mary Quarterly*, 3d ser., 50, no. 4 (1993): 700–720.

Roberts, John Storm. *Latin Jazz: The First of the Fusions, 1880s to Today*. New York: Schirmer, 1999.

Robeson, Paul. *Paul Robeson Speaks: Writings, Speeches, Interviews, 1918–1974*. Edited by Philip S. Foner. New York: Brunner/Mazel, 1978.

Rodrigues, João Jorge S., and Nelson Mendes. "Olodum's History Legacy and Mission." (13 February 1996). <http://www.e-net.com.br/olodum/report.html>. 22 February 1999.

Sakolsky, Ron. "David Murray: Fo Deuk Revue." Review of *Fo Deuk Revue,* by David Murray. *The Beat* 17, no. 2 (1998): 54–56.

Salazar, Max. "Chano Pozo." *Latin Beat Magazine* 3, no. 3 (1993): 6–10.

———. "Chano Pozo." *Latin Beat Magazine* 3, no. 4 (1993): 22–24.

———. "Chano Pozo." *Latin Beat Magazine* 3, no. 5 (1993): 16–18.

———. "The Manteca Story." *Latin Beat Magazine* 9, no. 8 (1999): 24–26.

Shelemay, Kay. "The Ethnomusicologist, Ethnographic Method, and the Transmission of Tradition." In *Shadows in the Field: New Perspectives for Fieldwork in Ethnomusicology,* edited by Gregory F. Barz and Timothy J. Cooley, 189–204. New York: Oxford University Press, 1997.

Shipton, Alyn. *Groovin' High: The Life of Dizzy Gillespie.* New York: Oxford University Press, 1999.

Slobin, Mark. *Subcultural Sounds: Micromusics of the West.* Hanover: Wesleyan University Press, 1993.

Southern, Eileen. *The Music of Black Americans: A History.* 3d ed. New York: Norton, 1997.

Stewart, Zan. "The Spirit of Collaboration: Melba Liston and Randy Weston." *Down Beat* 62.2 (1995): 22–24.

Stuckey, Sterling. *"I Want to Be African": Paul Robeson and the Ends of Nationalist Theory and Practice, 1919–1945.* Los Angeles: Center for Afro American Studies, 1976.

———. *Slave Culture: Nationalist Theory and the Foundations of Black America.* New York: Oxford University Press, 1987.

Szwed, John F. *Space is the Place: The Lives and Times of Sun Ra.* New York: Pantheon, 1997.

Taylor, Timothy. *Global Pop: World Music, World Markets.* New York: Routledge, 1997.

Vega, Marta Moreno. "The Cuban Orisha Tradition Comes to New York City." *African American Review* 29, no. 2 (1995): 201–206.

Walters, Ronald W. *Pan-Africanism in the African Diaspora: An Analysis of Modern Afrocentric Political Movements.* Detroit: Wayne State University Press, 1993.

Weaver, Gary. "Culture and Communication." *Readings in Intercultural Relations,* 2d ed., edited by Gary R Weaver, 1–7. Needham Heights, Mass.: Simon and Schuster, 1998.

Weinstein, Norman C. *A Night in Tunisia: Imaginings of Africa in Jazz.* New York: Limelight Editions, 1993.

Werbner, Pnina. "Introduction: The Dialectics of Cultural Hybridity." In *Debating Cultural Hybridity: Multi-Cultural Identities and the Politics of Anti-Racism,* edited by Pnina Werbner and Tariq Modood, 1–26. London: Zed Books, 1997.

Weston, Randy. "Standing on the Shoulders of His Ancestors: Randy Weston's Journey From Brooklyn to Africa and Beyond." Interview with Sean Barlow. <http://www.afropop.org:85/weston.html>. 21 February 1999.

Wilson, Olly. "Black Music as an Art Form." *Black Music Research Journal* 3, no. 1 (1983): 1–22.

———. "The Heterogeneous Sound Ideal in African American Music." In *New Perspectives in Music: Essays in Honor of Eileen Southern,* edited by Josephine Wright (with Samuel A. Floyd), 327–338. Detroit Monographs in Musicology/Studies in Music, No. 11. Warren, Mich.: Harmonie Park, 1992.

———. "The Significance of the Relationship Between Afro-American Music and West African Music." *Black Perspectives in Music* 2, no. 1 (1974): 3–22.

Wood, Peter H. "Strange New Land: 1619–1776." In *To Make Our World Anew: A History of African Americans*. Edited by Robin D. G. Kelley and Earl Lewis, 53–102. Oxford: Oxford University Press, 2000.

GEORGE E. LEWIS

Improvised Music after 1950
Afrological and Eurological Perspectives[1]

Since the early 1950s controversy over the nature and function of improvisation in musical expression has occupied considerable attention among improvisers, composers, performers, and theorists active in that sociomusical art world that has constructed itself in terms of an assumed high-culture bond between selected sectors of the European and American musical landscapes. Prior to 1950 the work of many composers operating in this art world tended to be completely notated, using a well-known, European-derived system. After 1950 composers began to experiment with open forms and with more personally expressive systems of notation. Moreover, these composers began to designate salient aspects of a composition as performer-supplied rather than composer-specified, thereby renewing an interest in the generation of musical structure in real time as a formal aspect of a composed work.

After a gap of nearly one hundred and fifty years, during which real-time generation of musical structure had been nearly eliminated from the musical activity of this Western or "pan-European" tradition, the postwar putative heirs to this tradition have promulgated renewed investigation of real-time forms of musicality, including a direct confrontation with the role of improvisation. This ongoing reappraisal of improvisation may be due in no small measure to musical and social events taking place in quite a different sector of the overall musical landscape. In particular, the anointing, since the early 1950s, of various forms of "jazz," the African-American musical constellation most commonly associated with the exploration of improvisation in both Europe and America, as a form of "art" has in all likelihood been a salient stimulating factor in this reevaluation of the possibilities of improvisation.

Already active in the 1940s, a group of radical young black American improvisers, for the most part lacking access to economic and political resources often taken for granted in high-culture musical circles, nonetheless posed potent challenges to Western notions of structure, form, communication, and expression. These improvisers, while cognizant of Western musical tradition, located and centered their modes of musical expression within a stream emanating largely from African and African-American cultural and social history. The international influence and dissemination of their music, dubbed "bebop," as well as the strong influences coming from later forms of "jazz," has resulted in the emergence of new sites for transnational, transcultural improvisative musical activity.

In particular, a strong circumstantial case can be made for the proposition that the emergence of these new, vigorous, and highly influential improvisative forms provided an impetus for musical workers in other traditions, particularly European and American composers active in the construction of a transnational European-based tradition, to come to grips with some of the implications of musical improvisation. This confrontation, however, took place amid an ongoing narrative of dismissal, on the part of many of these composers, of the tenets of African-American improvisative forms.

Moreover, texts documenting the musical products of the American version of the move to incorporate real-time music making into composition often present this activity as a part of "American music since 1945," a construct invariably theorized as emanating almost exclusively from a generally venerated stream of European cultural, social, and intellectual history—the "Western tradition." In such texts, an attempted erasure or denial of the impact of African-American forms on the real-time work of European and Euro-American composers is commonly asserted.

This denial itself, however, drew the outlines of a space where improvisation as a theoretical construct could clearly be viewed as a site not only for music-theoretical contention but for social and cultural competition between musicians representing improvisative and compositional modes of musical discourse. The theoretical and practical positions taken with regard to improvisation in this post-1950 Euro-American tradition exhibit broad areas of both confluence and contrast with those emerging from musical art worlds strongly influenced by African-American improvisative musics.

This essay attempts to historically and philosophically deconstruct aspects of the musical belief systems that ground African-American and European (including European-American) real-time music making, analyzing the articulation and resolution of both musical and what were once called "extramusical" issues. This analysis adopts as critical tools two complementary connotative adjectives, "Afrological" and "Eurological." These terms refer metaphorically to musical belief systems and behavior that, in my view, exemplify particular kinds of musical "logic." At the same time, these terms are intended to historicize the particularity of perspective characteristic of two systems that have evolved in such divergent cultural environments.

Improvisative musical utterance, like any music, may be interpreted with reference to historical and cultural contexts. The history of sanctions, segregation, and slavery, imposed upon African-Americans by the dominant white American culture, has undoubtedly influenced the evolution of a sociomusical belief system that differs in critical respects from that which has emerged from the dominant culture itself. Commentary on improvisation since 1950 has often concentrated on several key issues, the articulation of which differs markedly according to the cultural background of the commentators—even when two informants, each grounded in a different system of belief, are ostensibly discussing the same music.

Thus, my construction of "Afrological" and "Eurological" systems of improvisative musicality refers to social and cultural location and is theorized here as historically emergent rather than ethnically essential, thereby accounting for the reality of transcultural and transracial communication among improvisers. For example, African-American music, like any music, can be performed by a person of any "race" without losing its character as historically Afrological, just as a performance of Hindustani vocal music by Terry Riley does not transform the raga into a Eurological music form. My constructions make no attempt to delineate ethnicity or race, although they are designed to ensure that the reality of the ethnic or racial component of a historically emergent sociomusical group must be faced squarely and honestly.

In developing a hermeneutics of improvisative music, the study of two major American postwar real-time traditions is key. These traditions are exemplified by the two towering figures of 1950s American experimental musics: Charlie "Bird" Parker and John Cage. The work of these two crucial music makers has had important implications not only within their respective traditions but intertraditionally as well. The compositions of both artists are widely influential, but I would submit that it is their real-time work that has had the widest impact upon world musical culture. The musics made by these two artists, and by their successors, may be seen as exemplifying two very different conceptions of real-time music making. These differences encompass not only music but areas once thought of as "extramusical," including race and ethnicity, class, and social and political philosophy.

Bird

In the musical domain, improvisation is neither a style of music nor a body of musical techniques. Structure, meaning, and context in musical improvisation arise from the domain-specific analysis, generation, manipulation, and transformation of sonic symbols. Jazz, a largely improvisative musical form, has long been explicitly and fundamentally concerned with these and other structural issues. For African-American improvisers, however, sonic symbolism is often constructed with a view toward social instrumentality as well as form. New improvisative and compositional styles are often identified with ideals of race advancement and, more important, as resistive ripostes to perceived opposition to black social expression and economic advancement by the dominant white American culture.

Ebullient, incisive, and transgressive, the so-called bebop movement brought this theme of resistance to international attention. Influencing musicality worldwide, the movement posed both implicit and explicit challenges to Western notions of structure, form, and expression. In the United States, the challenge of bop, as exemplified by the work of Charlie "Bird" Parker, Dizzy Gillespie, Thelonious Monk, Bud Powell, and Kenny "Klook" Clarke, obliged the dominant European-American culture to come to grips, if not to terms, with Afrological aesthetics.

Bop improvisers, like earlier generations of jazz improvisers, used "heads," or precomposed melodic material, as starting points for a piece. Bop heads, however, as Gridley points out, "resembled little or nothing that the average listener had heard before" (165). In a further abstraction, bebop improvisers felt no obligation to use the melodic material of the "head" as material for improvisational transformation. Instead, the underlying harmonic sequence, usually subjected to extensive reworking by the improvisers, became the basis for improvisation. Often this harmonic material was appropriated from the popular show tunes of the day, linking this music with earlier jazz styles. The musicians often "signified on" the tunes, replacing the melodic line with another, then naming the new piece in an ironic signifying riff on Tin Pan Alley as well as upon the dominant culture that produced it.

Bebop raised the stakes in the game of cultural thrust and parry to a new level of intensity, providing models of both individual and collective creativity that were adopted and extended during later periods in improvised music. The outlines of this model are well described by Walton, who characterizes bebop as requiring "concentrated listening, allowing an expansion of self through identification with the symbolic communication of the performer" (95). Moreover, through extensive improvisation, each performance of a given bebop "piece" could become unique, different in many respects from the last. Even in many strains of Afrological improvisative practice today, the generative and interactional aspects of how the roles of both improviser and listener are constructed carry distinct traces of the attitudes promulgated by bebop improvisers.

Bebop's challenge to the dominant culture was not limited to musical concerns; in fact, bebop musicians challenged traditional notions of intra- and extramusicality. The composer and improviser Anthony Braxton comments that "bebop had to do with understanding the realness of black people's actual position in America" (124). Frank Kofsky (270–271) quotes Langston Hughes's blues signifying on bebop's origins in "the police beating Negroes' heads . . . that old club says, 'BOP! BOP! . . . BE-BOP!' . . . That's where Be-Bop came from, beaten right out of some Negro's head into them horns."

In *Blues People,* Amiri Baraka (then LeRoi Jones) asserts that bebop "had more than an accidental implication of social upheaval associated with it" (188). For the bebop musicians this upheaval had a great deal to do with the assertion of self-determination with regard to their role as musical artists. While jazz has always existed in the interstices between Western definitions of concert music and entertainment, between the commercial and the experimental, challenging the assigned role of the jazz musician as entertainer created new possibilities for the construction of an African-American improvisative musicality that could define itself as explicitly experimental.

This radical redefinition was viewed as a direct challenge, by extension, to the entire social order as it applied to blacks in 1940s apartheid America: "The young Negro musician of the forties began to realize that merely by being a Negro in America, one *was* a nonconformist" (Jones, 188). Indeed, the musicians were often called "crazy"—an appellation often assigned to oppositional forces, either by the dominant order itself or by members of an oppressed group who, however onerous their present situation, are fearful of the consequences of change.

Cage

In his essay exploring improvisation, the theorist Carl Dahlhaus provides us with five defining characteristics of a musical work that, in his view, must be present for the work to be considered a composition. These characteristics are interconnected in a kind of logically daisy-chained sentence, which I shall present in exploded form.

According to Dahlhaus, a composition is, first, an individually complete structure in itself ("ein in sich geschlossenes, individuelles Gebilde").

Second, this structure must be fully worked-out ("ausgearbeitet"). Third and fourth, it is fixed in written form ("schriftlich fixiert") in order to be performed ("um aufgeführt zu werden"). Finally, what is worked-out and notated must constitute the essential part of the aesthetic object that is constituted in the consciousness of the listener[2] (Dahlhaus, 10–11).

That these five characteristics identify the very notion of composition as European in nature is asserted by Dahlhaus at several points. The dialectic between composition and notation, according to Dahlhaus, is critical to the notion of composition itself. Compositions that are worked-out without being notated, in Dahlhaus's view, are neither compositions nor improvisations (21). Dahlhaus, however, does not present his own view about just what such a hybrid might be called or how, given his definitional stance, the nature of such music might be accounted for theoretically.

Recognizing that his definition excludes much non-European music, Dahlhaus consoles the reader with the thought that some things simply are what they are: "A historian who hesitates to describe a piece of non-European music as composition gives, by so doing, no understanding that he values it any the less"[3] (22). In any event, given the explicitly particularist nature of Dahlhaus's theory, characterizing it as prototypically Eurological should present no great analytical obstacles.

The work of John Cage presents an explicit challenge to this fixed notion of composition. Like Bird, the activity of Cage and his associates, such as Christian Wolff, David Tudor, Morton Feldman, and Earle Brown, had profound and wide-ranging influence not only in the musical, literary, and visual domains but socially and culturally as well. The musical and theoretical work of these composers can be credited with radically reconstructing Eurological composition; the trenchancy of this reconstruction involved in large measure the resurrection of Eurological modes of real-time musical discourse, often approaching an explicitly improvisative sensibility.

Along with his associates, Cage was responsible for the entrance into musical history of the term "indeterminacy." Cage's essay on indeterminacy from *Silence* presents examples of "indeterminate" elements in European music from the last two centuries, from Karlheinz Stockhausen's *Klavierstuck XI* to J. S. Bach's *Art of the Fugue*. According to Cage, Bach's nonspecification of timbre and amplitude characteristics identifies these elements not as absent but simply as nondetermined but necessary material, to be realized by a performer. The construction as indeterminate of nonspecified elements in the Bach work allows "the possibility of a unique overtone structure and decibel range for each performance" (35). The performer's function in this case is "comparable to that of someone filling in color where outlines are given" (35).

Later descriptions of indeterminacy, such as that advanced by Elliott Schwartz and Daniel Godfrey in their survey text on "music since 1945," define a musical factor as indeterminate "if it is dictated by chance and operates without any links to other factors" (92). Cage's own initial definition of indeterminacy, however, did not necessarily include the use of chance as a salient factor. In *Silence,* Cage provides several methods, unranked as to preference, by which the performer may realize the indeterminate aspects of the *Art of the Fugue:* "feeling his way, following the dictates of his ego . . . following his taste . . . employing some operation exterior to his mind: tables of random numbers . . . or chance operations, identifying there with no matter what eventuality" (35).

Another of Cage's lasting contributions to both compositional and improvisative method is the radical use of these "chance operations." The 1951 *Music of Changes* was composed by Cage using the ancient Chinese oracular method known as the *I Ching* (Book of Changes) to generate musical material within parameters chosen by the composer. The object of the use of the *I Ching,* as described by the composer himself in explaining his compositional process for the *Music of Changes,* is the creation of "a musical composition the continuity of which is free of individual taste and memory (psychology) and also of the literature and 'traditions' of the art" (59). In this regard, Cage consistently maintains that "sounds are to come into their own, rather than being exploited to express sentiments or ideas of order" (69).

Cage, though perhaps not the first to promulgate the concept of the experimental in music, did provide, in his important manifesto *Silence,* several working definitions for the term "experimental music." The composer has written that "an experimental action is one the outcome of which is not foreseen" and is "necessarily unique" (39). Cage's notion of spontaneity and uniqueness was informed by his studies of Zen and in particular by his attendance at Daisetz Suzuki's early 1950s lectures on that subject in New York City (Revill, 108–110).

That this view of music would have social implications was fully recognized by Cage himself. Indeed, Cage's social and philosophical views form a prominent part of the literature about him. In the Kostelanetz interviews from 1987, Cage explicitly addresses his own essential anarchism at several points (266). Connecting his view of sound to his anarchism, the composer expresses his need for "a music in which not only are sounds just sounds but in which people are just people, not subject, that is, to laws established by any one of them, even if he is 'the composer' or 'the conductor.' . . . Freedom of movement is basic to both this art and this society" (257).

Cage's notion of social instrumentality, however, does not connect this very American notion of freedom—perhaps reminiscent of the frontier myth—to any kind of struggle that might be required in order to obtain it. The composer denies the utility of protest, maintaining that "my notion of how to proceed in a society to bring change is not to protest the thing that is evil, but rather to let it die its own death. . . . Protests about these things, contrary to what has been said, will give it the kind of life that a fire is given when you fan it, and that it would be best to ignore it, put your attention elsewhere, take actions of another kind of positive nature" (Kostelanetz, 265–266).

In terms of social location, composers such as Cage and Feldman located their work as an integral part of a sociomusical art world that explicitly bonded with the intellectual and musical traditions of Europe. The members of this art world, while critiquing aspects of contemporary European culture, were explicitly concerned with continuing to develop this "Western" tradition on the American continent. The composer's "History of Experimental Music in the United States" (Cage, 67–75) identifies as relevant to his concerns both European and American composers and artists, including the European Dada movement, composers such as Debussy and Varèse, and later European experimentalists such as Pierre Boulez, Karlheinz Stockhausen, Luigi Nono, and Luciano Berio. Among the American composers that Cage mentions as being part of America's "rich history" of music are Leo Ornstein, Dane Rudhyar, Lou Harrison, Harry Partch, and Virgil Thomson.

Though these and other composers do earn criticism, the only indigenous music that receives sharp denunciation from Cage is the African-American music that he frequently refers to as "hot jazz." Criticizing the expression of Henry Cowell's interest in this and other American indigenous traditions, Cage appropriates the then current conventional wisdom about the opposition between "jazz" music and "serious" music: "Jazz per se derives from serious music. And when serious music derives from it, the situation becomes rather silly" (Cage, 72).

We may regard as more rhetorical device than historical fact Cage's brief account of the origins of jazz. In any event, despite such declarations as "the world is one world now" (75) or "when I think of a good future it certainly has music in it but it doesn't have one kind . . . it has all kinds" (Kostelanetz, 257), it is clear that Cage has drawn very specific boundaries, not only as to which musics are relevant to his own musicality but as to which musics suit his own taste. The Cageian tendency is to confront this contradiction through the use of terms that essentially exnominate (see below) or disguise his likes and dislikes as such: "some music . . . which would not be useful to me at all might be very useful to someone else" (Kostelanetz, 257).

The composer does, however, make allowance for the fact that others may draw different boundaries: "I can get along perfectly well without any jazz at all; and yet I notice that many, many people have a great need for it. Who am I to say that their need is pointless?" (Kostelanetz, 257). This basic reference to freedom of choice, however, can hardly be extrapolated to argue that Cage is characterizing himself as possessing a culturally diverse musical sensibility. Rather, the composer is reaffirming a relatively mundane truism concerning the diversity of personal taste, while simultaneously making clear that, for him, a "need for jazz" would indeed be pointless.

Exnomination

Despite Cage's disavowal of jazz, however, the historical timeline shows that Cage's radical emphasis upon spontaneity and uniqueness (not generally found in either American or European music before Cage) arrives some eight to ten years after the innovations of bebop. And it is certain that bebop, a native American music with a strong base in New York City, was well known to what has come to be known as the "New York School" of artists and musicians of which Cage and Feldman were part. In the case of visual artists from that social circle, such as Jackson Pollock and Franz Kline, the connection with jazz has been remarked upon in a number of essays (see Mandeles, 139).

The composer Anthony Braxton's pithy statement concerning the disavowal of Afrological forms by the art world that nurtured Cage's work advances the essential issue directly: "Both aleatory and indeterminism are words which have been coined . . . to bypass the word improvisation and as such the influence of nonwhite sensibility" (366). Why improvisation and non-white sensibility would be perceived by anyone as objects to be avoided can usefully be theorized with respect to racialized power relations.

Commentators such as the media critic John Fiske, the cultural theorist George Lipsitz, and the legal scholar Cheryl I. Harris have identified "whiteness" as an important cultural construct in American society. For Harris and Lipsitz, whiteness is a historically emergent phenomenon; for Lipsitz, whiteness appears in large measure "because of realities created by slavery and segregation, immigration restriction and Indian policy, by conquest and colonialism" (Lipsitz, 370).

Both Lipsitz and Harris have recourse to economic terms in describing the role of whiteness. Harris traces the evolution of the construction of whiteness as a form of legally constituted property, while Lipsitz refers to a "possessive investment in whiteness." Quoting legal theorist Kimberle

Crenshaw, Harris (1759) utilizes the language of investment in referring to the "actual stake in racism" that the previously Balkanized European ethnics developed, through the legal and social privileges that attend their classification as "white."

For Fiske, whiteness is "not an essential racial category that contains a set of fixed meanings, but a strategic deployment of power. . . . The space of whiteness contains a limited but varied set of normalizing positions from which that which is not white can be made into the abnormal; by such means whiteness constitutes itself as a universal set of norms by which to make sense of the world" (42). Fiske identifies "exnomination" as a primary characteristic of whiteness as power: "Exnomination is the means by which whiteness avoids being named and thus keeps itself out of the field of interrogation and therefore off the agenda for change. . . . One practice of exnomination is the avoidance of self-recognition and self-definition. Defining, for whites, is a process that is always directed outward upon multiple 'others' but never inward upon the definer" (42).

It is my contention that, circumstantially at least, bebop's combination of spontaneity, structural radicalism, and uniqueness, antedating by several years the reappearance of improvisation in Eurological music, posed a challenge to that music which needed to be answered in some way. All too often, the space of whiteness provided a convenient platform for a racialized denial of the trenchancy of this challenge, while providing an arena for the articulation of an implicit sensibility which I have termed "Eurological."

The anthropologist and improviser Georgina Born presents the circumstantial case:

Some of the main elements of experimental music practice—improvisation, live group work, the empirical use of small, commercial electronics in performance—were pioneered in the jazz and rock of the 1950s and 1960s. Moreover, the politics of experimental music are similar to those of the advanced black jazz of the '60s. Its musical collectivism, for example, was prefigured by the Chicago black musicians' cooperative, the Association for the Advancement of Creative Musicians (AACM), which became a model for later progressive, cooperative music organizations. The fact that these influences often remain unacknowledged and subterranean, even within experimental music, signals their status as deriving from an "other" culture and the reluctance of the postmodern sphere of legitimate music to admit its indebtedness to the "other." (Born, 351 n.29)

The sociologist Howard Becker, using an example from jazz, identifies an explicit aesthetic system as being useful to an art world by conditioning competition and justifying access to resources:

It ties participants' activities to the tradition of the art, justifying their demands for the resources and advantages ordinarily available to people who produce that kind of art. To be specific, if I can argue cogently that jazz merits as serious consideration on aesthetic grounds as other forms of art music, then I can compete, as a jazz player, for grants and fellowships from the National Endowment for the Arts and faculty positions in music schools, perform in the same halls as symphony orchestras, and require the same attention to the nuances of my work as the most serious classical composer. (132–133)

In a transnational, transcultural musical environment where exchanges of musical information are increasingly commonplace, ethnicized or racialized grounds for classification of musical discourse, though not explicitly named, nevertheless become disclosed. Advocates of particular aesthetic systems are rarely as explicit as Becker would have it about class and race grounding, often preferring to couch support of certain musical forms and disavowal of others in "objective" terms. Despite Baraka's contention that bebop was the African-American musical form that obliged the larger society to confront Afrological aesthetics in creative black music itself as "art" (Jones 190), the fact that both Bird and Cage expressed an experimental bent in describing their respective creative processes has not, so far, induced the authors of music history texts concerned with "American music since 1945" to classify the output of these two composers according to their relationship with the experimental.

Instead, texts appropriating the term "experimental music" construct this classification as denoting a particular group of postwar music makers who come almost exclusively from either European or European-American heritage. Michael Nyman's important book *Experimental Music* is representative. This text, like most others, presents this group of composers as the intellectual heirs to what is vernacularly known as the "classical" or "Western" tradition, even when this tradition is subjected to critique through its inheritors' music.

Coded qualifiers to the word "music"—such as "experimental," "new," "art," "concert," "serious," "avant-garde," and "contemporary"—are used in these texts to delineate a racialized location of this tradition within the space of whiteness; either erasure or (brief) inclusion of Afrological music can then be framed as responsible chronicling and "objective" taxonomy. The passing reference to the Art Ensemble of Chicago in the Schwartz and Godfrey text on *Music Since 1945*, for example, was necessary "because their music was as much 'serious' or avant-garde music as jazz" (202). The quote demonstrates the role assumed by whiteness in defining the Art Ensemble as not quite so "other" as some of the others.

The improviser-theorists Malcolm Goldstein and Derek Bailey both discuss the decline and eventual near-disappearance in the nineteenth century of improvisative development in European music. Both authors refer to a gap of about 150 years in the European intellectual history of improvisation, from the late eighteenth to the mid-twentieth century. As with a number of texts dealing with Eurological improvised music, however, the composer and theorist David Cope feels obliged to mention that despite an apparent gap in the improvisational record, improvisation has indeed been part of European musical history.

In particular, two long-dead musical practices, the use of figured bass and the performance of cadenzas, are invoked by Cope (127) to assure the reader that improvisation has had a long tradition in European music. The third major stream within European improvisation, the small yet persistent French school of organ improvisers, is not mentioned in the Cope text. Bailey (29), writing about improvisation in various world-musical traditions, identifies this group as representing practically the only improvisative activity in European music from the end of the eighteenth century to the mid-twentieth.

In any event, survivals or retentions of improvisative traditions in present-day Eurological improvisation have only begun to be identified and researched. Information about those survivals that have been found would, so far, appear insufficiently well documented or disseminated to provide a historical or cultural basis for the reemergence of improvisation in Eurological music in the mid-1950s. In this light, Cope's cautious claim that "the circumstances under which more recent improvisation developed are less clear. . . . Interest in this century may be rooted in jazz" (127) may be viewed as an excellent illustration of Born's remark about the reluctance of commentators on Eurological music to admit indebtedness to "the other."

Exemplifying the sort of exnomination of whiteness that Fiske and Born identify, the Cope text rigorously avoids extended, serious treatment of major figures in postwar Afrological improvisation, while devoting considerable attention to something called "contemporary" improvisation. Improvisers of worldwide stature—such as Parker, Coltrane, Taylor, and Coleman—are (at best) mentioned in passing, while pages are devoted to the work of relatively obscure individuals whose written descriptions of their improvisations far outpace in quantity their audio documentation.

The reader is encouraged to assume that this kind of "contemporary" improvisation, despite the fact that a number of its proponents "are or were actively involved in jazz" (Cope, 127), must have developed sui generis—perhaps in a sort of parthenogenesis. According to Cope, the likeliest origin of this sort of improvisation lay, not in any kind of musical miscegenation with jazz, but in "classical" performers' "inability to realize correctly the complexities of recent music; the composer, perhaps out of frustration, perhaps because the result was the same or better, chose to allow a certain freedom in performance" (127).

Eurological modernist music criticism, while erasing the practitioners of Afrological improvised music from postwar histories of "contemporary" music, has nonetheless felt obliged to present a series of ongoing critiques of its construction of "jazz." Such critiques may represent an attempt to create what social scientists Somers and Gibson term an "epistemological other." According to Somers and Gibson (38), social groups often perform such constructions "to consolidate a cohesive self-identity and collective project."

The construction of the epistemological other may be viewed as the contrapositive aspect of the construction of whiteness, particularly when coded appeals to racial and ethnic solidarity are involved. John Cage's critique of jazz—well presented in his 1966 interview with the jazz critic Michael Zwerin—is of relatively little value as music criticism but may serve us well here as a textbook example of the power relationships that Fiske has recognized. In response to Zwerin's query about his thoughts on jazz, Cage replies, "I don't think about jazz, but I love to talk, so by all means, come on up" (161).

To this African-American observer, situated in the 1990s, the interview should perhaps have ended there. From a 1960s perspective, however, we are in the presence of power, as two white males prepare to discuss "the trouble with black people" without, in the declining days of American high media apartheid, having to worry about a response. Even on a subject to which he freely admitted his lack of attention, Cage's opinion was apparently deemed sufficiently authoritative, by the structures of media power that decide such things, for the interview to continue and, finally, to be published and reprinted.

The colloquy between Cage and Zwerin, like Schwartz and Godfrey's reference to the Art Ensemble, displays whiteness in its defining role. Zwerin, though supposedly taking the side of jazz, ends up agreeing with Cage that jazz could use some work. The work of black artists is defined by whiteness as the primitive (yet improving) work of children: "But jazz is still young, and still evolving"; jazz could benefit from serious study of "our" models; already, it has started to explore areas "suggested by Ives"; "jazz is getting freer" through the use of tone-rows, and "getting away from the time dependence—inferring it rather than clobbering you with it all the time"; and so on (162–164).

In this wide-ranging, blunderbuss attack on black musical culture, both Zwerin's assigning Cage to the role of aesthetic arbiter and the acceptance and performance of this role by Cage serve to present whiteness as a normalizing position from which others are judged. At the same time, the "arguments" presented by both men against Afrological forms are framed in ostensibly "objective" musical terms, thereby exnominating their basis in notions of whiteness. Moreover, the process of erasure or gatekeeping with regard to media access by alternative voices—particularly black voices—ensured that neither a more worthy adversary nor a more wide-ranging set of topics (such as a contrapositive critique of Eurological forms) would be presented. Witness Coltrane's laconic but pregnant comment to Kofsky concerning media criticism: "I don't make the phrases" (quoted in Kofsky, 225).

Clearly jazz must have been a powerful force in postwar improvisative music, as so many fledgling Eurological improvisers needed to distance themselves from it in one way or another. In this regard, the ongoing Eurological critique of jazz may be seen as part of a collective project of reconstruction of a Eurological real-time musical discipline. This reconstruction may well have required the creation of an "other"—through reaction, however negative, to existing models of improvisative musicality.

Indeed, the avoidance of jazz, and its recasting in the form of an epistemological other, has served explicitly as a defining pattern that animated many projects in the formation and exploration of a particularly Eurological improvisative sensibility. For example, in 1955 the European composer Lukas Foss organized a group devoted to "nonjazz" group improvisation (Schwartz and Godfrey, 63). In addition, a number of the early postwar European and Euro-American experimenters working in Eurological forms had, in fact, been jazz musicians. The British improvisers who formed the free improvisation group AMM describe in detail their need to break away from the "very emulative style of American jazz" that they had been performing (Childs and Hobbs, 34). The American composer Larry Austin, relating his experiences with group improvisation in the early 1960s, describes his group as having "consciously ruled out any overt jazz expression" (quoted in Childs and Hobbs, 30–31). Apparently, according to Austin's account, this attempt on the part of his improvising group to erase jazz from their bodies was not entirely successful; Foss still detected traces of jazz, or Afrological, sensibilities in the group's work.

Despite this rather powerful circumstantial evidence, however, most survey texts dealing with this period in Eurological music are unfailingly solicitous in disabusing the reader of any nascent notion that jazz could have had any impact on the development of either "contemporary" improvisation or indeterminacy. These texts, despite the apparent concern of their authors with creating separate tables at the restaurant for indeterminacy and improvisation, nonetheless typically discuss both of these musical activities in the same chapter—thus effectively associating them.

Paul Berliner's encyclopedic study of the creative process among jazz musicians discusses the use of harmonic sequences or "progressions" as a basis for improvisation. The author asserts that improvisers liken a harmonic sequence or "progression" to "a road map for charting the precise melodic course of a rendition" (Berliner, 71)—remarkably similar to Cage's already cited notion of a performer's function with regard to indeterminate scores as "filling in color where outlines are given." Thus, a strong case could be made for the contention that, just as chance operations can constitute one method for realizing performer indeterminacy, performer indeterminacy may be one method of realizing an improvisation. In this view, despite Cope's cautious statement that "one major precursor of musical indeterminacy may be improvisation" (Cope, 124), indeterminacy could well be not a successor to improvisation but a subset of it.

Spontaneity

Spontaneity is an important value for improvisers working in both Eurological and Afrological forms, though the definition of spontaneity certainly differs according to tradition. Following Cage, Schwartz and Godfrey affirm that the result of a musical experience created through indeterminate means is meant to be "immediate, spontaneous, and unique: a ritual celebration, not a fixed art object bounded by predetermined relationships or notational straitjackets" (92).

Notions of uniqueness and the unforeseen, however, are hardly unique to Eurological indeterminacy. Saxophonist Steve Lacy observed that "you have all your years of preparation and all your sensibilities and your prepared means but it is a leap into the unknown" (quoted in Bailey 57). Many commentators have identified the uniqueness of an improvisation as a highly prized goal among African-American improvisers. Berliner (268) quotes the trumpeter Doc Cheatham, whose work straddles the pre- and postwar eras, to the effect that Armstrong and others of comparable creative ability would "play fifteen or thirty different choruses, and they would never play the same thing. . . . Every time they'd play a tune, the solo would be different." A similar sentiment was expressed with Coltrane's amazement at how Gillespie could play the introduction to "I Can't Get Started" differently every time (Berliner, 269).

Despite the statements of these and other highly experienced improvisers who have gone on record with their experiences of uniqueness and discovery, a number of composers and theorists working in Eurological music have asserted a quite different view of the same music. The cognitive psychologist John Sloboda (141) maintains that jazz improvisers use "a model which is, in most cases, externally supplied by the culture." Lukas Foss has asserted that in improvisation, "one plays what one already knows" (quoted in Cope, 127).

This viewpoint, which has attained the status of conventional wisdom in some circles, is similar to Schwartz and Godfrey's claim that "Cage's indeterminacy should be distinguished from improvisation, in that the latter is directed to a known end" (92). Cage's own statement that "improvisation is generally playing what you know" leads naturally to his opinion that improvisation "doesn't lead you into a new experience" (quoted in Kostelanetz, 223).

The cognitive psychologist Philip Johnson-Laird has termed one version of this conventional wisdom as the "motif" theory. According to Johnson-Laird's construction of this theory, jazz improvisers are wont to use a set of memorized motifs, which are "strung together one after the other to form an improvisation" (Johnson-Laird, 292). The scientist's own metaphor of improvisation, involving an approach to the analysis of bebop solos based in theories of generative grammars, likens improvisation to speech. This perceived similarity to speech leads Johnson-Laird to question the validity of the motif theory: "Discourse would be intolerably difficult if it consisted solely in stringing together remarks that one had committed to memory. It is this sort of stilted jumble of phrases that one is forced to produce in a foreign language where one's only guide is indeed a book of 'licks,' i.e., a phrase book" (293).

Johnson-Laird goes on to ask: "Why can we be confident that the 'motif' theory is wrong? . . . First somebody has to invent the motifs. If a musician is the first to play a particular motif, then he or she cannot merely be regurgitating it from memory." Johnson-Laird adduces two other reasons for the doubtful validity of this theory: "an analysis of corpora of the musician's improvisation yields many phrases that occur only once. Third, the labour of committing to memory a sufficient number of motifs to guarantee the improvisation of complete solos is altogether too large to be practical" (293).

The motif theory, in both its scientific and its vernacular versions, denies the possibility of achieving creative agency and experiential spontaneity through improvisative musicality. For example, Dahlhaus (10), commenting on improvisation from the standpoint of a variant of this theory, finds a contradiction in the notion that an improvisation is "on the one hand pieced together from formulae and on the other hand experienced as spontaneous."[4] The motif theory, with its overemphasis upon the role of memory in Afrological improvisation, has often been used by commentators, ususally influenced by the work of John Cage, to define improvisation in terms of a pure spontaneity, unmediated by memory. The composer and theorist Larry Solomon (226), for example, has defined the "fundamental ideal" of improvisation as "the discovery and invention of original music spontaneously, while performing it, without preconceived formulation, scoring, or content."

Buried within this Eurological definition of improvisation is a notion of spontaneity that excludes history or memory. In this regard, "real" improvisation is often described in terms of eliminating reference to "known" styles. Among the styles that are already "known," "jazz" is the most often cited in the literature on the subject—perhaps by reason of its role as epistemological other. According to composer Harold Budd, for instance, "Jazz, after all, has a noble tradition. Everybody knows what it is" (quoted in Childs and Hobbs, 53). In posing the question about how far "originality" may be carried in creating "truly improvised" music, Solomon asks: "Would this also exclude reproducing a known style of music, such as jazz?" (226). The inescapable conclusion from a Eurological standpoint is that jazz, whose character is "known," cannot be truly spontaneous or original. Moreover, jazz's supposed dependence upon memorized motifs prevents it from exemplifying "true" improvisation—despite its practitioners' experience of it.

Bailey theorizes about the interface with "known" styles in improvisation with his distinction between "idiomatic" and "nonidiomatic" forms of improvisation. This mode of theorizing, however, allows "true" improvisation to take place in both, while avoiding fixed definitions of spontaneity based on historical or cultural reference: "Idiomatic improvisation . . . is mainly concerned with the expression of an idiom—such as jazz, flamenco or baroque—and takes its identity and motivation from that idiom. Nonidiomatic improvisation has other concerns and is most usually found in so-called 'free' improvisation and, while it can be highly stylised, is not usually tied to representing an idiomatic identity" (xi–xii).

From the Eurological perspective, allowing chance to enter the performance becomes an important method of avoiding "known" models of improvisation. Solomon feels that improvisation "relies on the performer's control and intuition but also includes chance as a pathway to exploration and discovery" (227). Schwartz and Godfrey refer to "whims, wills—and accidents" as contributing to a sense of unpredictability (414). Berio theorizes jazz improvisation as "a continuous correction of little errors, a continuous adjusting of sights relative to a target that, by its very nature, is never perfectly clear and defined" (84).

As with any music, close listening and analysis of improvised music requires attention to information at different laminar depths. Thus, each of the numerous released recordings of, say, Coltrane's "Giant Steps," regarded at the level of individual passages, is the result of careful preparation—"ausgearbeitet." At the same time, each improvisation, taken as a whole, maintains its character as unique and spontaneous.

The Eurological notion of pure spontaneity in improvisation fails to account for this temporally multilaminar aspect of an improvisation. By fixing upon the surface level of immediate spontaneity, unsullied by reference to the past or foreshadowing of the future, the reduction of the notion of improvisative spontaneity to the present moment insists on ephemerality. In its extreme form this notion requires that an improvisation be done once and never heard in any form again. Solomon's insistence that a recorded improvisation, "upon replay, is no longer an improvisation" (226) reduces experienced immediacy on the part of both listeners and improvisers to an infinitely small now, a Euclidean point, excluding both the past and the future.

However, listeners have heard some recorded improvisations literally thousands of times. The performances are learned by heart, yet even after many years, new layers of meaning are spontaneously discovered. While a memorized improvisation is, taken note by note, utterly predictable, these recorded versions often seem to renew themselves when viewed in a more expansive temporal context. Moreover, improvisers are hearing their music at the same time as any potential listener; in this sense, the experiences of improviser and listener are similar. Returning to Walton's identification of the role of empathy in listening to improvisations, it seems clear that the listener also improvises, posing alternative paths, experiencing immediacy as part of the listening experience.

The elimination of memory and history from music, emblematic of the Cageian project, may be seen as a response to postwar conditions. Seen in historical terms, the decline of improvisation in European music in the nineteenth and early twentieth centuries would seem to preclude any identification of exclusively or even primarily European antecedents for Eurological improvised music. In such an atmosphere, the postwar modernist emphasis of musicians such as Cage on "the present," deemphasizing memory and history, would appear to be a natural response to the impossibility of discovering such antecedents on the part of those for whom the preservation of European purity of musical reference would be a prime concern.

This response to historical conditions, moreover, may be viewed not only in terms of the more usually theorized postwar modernist desire to be made new through "negation of the principles of the previous tradition" (Born, 40) but, again, with respect to the quintessentially American myth of the frontier, where that which lies before us must take precedence over "the past." On the other hand, the African-American improviser, coming from a legacy of slavery and oppression, cannot countenance the erasure of history. The destruction of family and lineage, the rewriting of history and memory in the image of whiteness, is one of the facts with which all people of color must live. It is unsurprising, therefore, that from an ex-slave's point of view an insistence on being free from memory might be regarded with some suspicion—as either a form of denial or of disinformation.

Improvised Music

The classically trained pianist Mildred Portney Chase has written of the value of improvisation for composers, performers, and students of music—particularly children. For performers of notated music (for whom "most of the music we study comes from another time and place" [95]) improvisation can provide "moments of inspiration similar to those experienced by the greatest composers—even if the comparison ends there" (93). Alternatively, improvisation can aid in helping a composer to open "channels of his musical stream of consciousness . . . being utterly permissive, he may open at the deepest levels those passages to the musical persona that are buried underneath all that he consciously knows" (90).

For Chase, although she questions the historical composer-performer axis typical of Eurological music, her book (in chapters titled "To the Composer," "To the Pianist," and so on) frames improvisation as something done by performers and composers—not exactly a combination of the two, but something similar. This framework does not seem to leave room for the musical role of "improviser"; indeed, there is no chapter titled "To the Improviser."

In fact, a field termed "improvised music" has arisen and come to some prominence in the period since 1970. I would identify improvised music as a social location inhabited by a considerable number of present-day musicians, coming from diverse cultural backgrounds and musical practices, who have chosen to make improvisation a central part of their musical discourse. Individual improvisers are now able to reference an intercultural establishment of techniques, styles, aesthetic attitudes, antecedents, and networks of cultural and social practice.

Media reports, scholarly essays, and other literature about such musicians have tended to coalesce around "improvised music," a posteriori, as a catchall term for a variety of musical forms. Bailey has written perhaps the most perceptive essays on the topic of what improvised music is—to him— and how it has evolved. Working as an improviser in the field of improvised music emphasizes not only form and technique but individual life choices as well as cultural, ethnic, and personal location. In performances of improvised music, the possibility of internalizing alternative value systems is implicit from the start. The focus of musical discourse suddenly shifts from the individual, autonomous creator to the collective—the individual as a part of global humanity.

In order to distinguish improvised music as a field from Eurological work "incorporating" or "using" improvisation, or featuring "indeterminacy" or aleatoric practices, the simplistically racialized taxonomies found in texts such as the Nyman and Cope works must be abandoned. A more nuanced view of improvised music might identify as more salient differentiating characteristics its welcoming of agency, social necessity, personality, and difference, as well as its strong relationship to popular and folk cultures.

In my own view, the development of the improviser in improvised music is regarded as encompassing not only the formation of individual musical personality but the harmonization of one's musical personality with social environments, both actual and possible. This emphasis on personal narrative is a clear sign of the strong influence of the Afrological on improvised music.

One important model in the area of improvised music is the sort of "open" improvisation practiced by members of the Association for the Advancement of Creative Musicians (AACM), the African-American musicians' collective widely recognized for the variety of innovative musical ideas promulgated by its membership since its inception in 1965 on Chicago's nearly all-black South Side. Along with the important St. Louis–based Black Artists Group, including improvisers such as saxophonists Hamiet Bluiett, Oliver Lake, and Julius Hemphill, the AACM improvisers were clearly Afrological in perspective as a group, yet influenced individually by a wide range of non-Afrological musics.

The AACM's improviser-composers include pianist Muhal Richard Abrams (a founding member of the organization); saxophonist Fred Anderson; multi-instrumentalist Douglas Ewart; the Art Ensemble of Chicago; saxophonists Anthony Braxton, Henry Threadgill, and Edward Wilkerson; drummer Kahil El-Zabar; pianist Amina Claudine Myers; violinist Leroy Jenkins; trumpeter Wadada Leo Smith; and the trombonist-author. Other frequent collaborators have included the pianist Anthony Davis, saxophonist David Murray, and flutist James Newton.

The "AACM model" stresses a composer-improviser orientation and the importance of asserting the agency, identity, and survival of the African-American artist: "The Black creative artists must survive and persevere in spite of the oppressive forces which prevent Black people from reaching the goals attained by other Americans. We must continue to add copiously to an already vast reservoir of artistic richness handed down through the ages.

Black artists must control and be paid for what they produce, as well as own and control the means of distribution" (Abrams and Jackson 72).

Another important and very different model of "improvised music" is practiced by the European "free" improvisers, such as contrabassist Joëlle Léandre; guitarist and theorist Derek Bailey; bassist Barry Guy; pianists Misha Mengelberg, Alexander von Schlippenbach, and Irène Schweizer; percussionist Paul Lytton; vocalists Maggie Nicols and Phil Minton; multi-instrumentalist and composer Lindsay Cooper; and saxophonists Peter Brötzmann and Evan Parker. Reflecting their diverse backgrounds, these musicians often blend personal narrative reminiscent of an Afrological perspective with sonic imagery characteristic of European forms spanning several centuries.

The European form places great emphasis on the social necessity for the role of improviser. Bailey (142) is very clear on this point: "Improvisation has no need of argument and justification. It exists because it meets the creative appetite that is a natural part of being a performing musician and because it invites complete involvement, to a degree otherwise unobtainable, in the act of music-making." In this regard it becomes entirely probable that the direct use of the term "improvised music" in the sense that I am using it here began among this group of European improvisers. The term was adopted, I believe, not to distinguish it from jazz in the sense of critique but to better reflect the European improvisers' sense of having created a native model of improvisation, however influenced by Afrological forms.

Bailey, like other European improvisers, makes no attempt to deny the Afrological influence upon his own work. Bailey's critique of jazz, therefore, far from adopting the premises of Cage in critiquing its improvisers, is actually a critique of the art world surrounding jazz, with its tendency toward canonization and toward what is perceived by many as its capitulation to the influence of corporate power in the form of a rather limp neoclassicism (Bailey, 48). In this sense Bailey's critique finds company in Radano's similarly pointed critique (Radano, *New Musical Figurations*, 269).

A third strain within improvised music is the so-called downtown (New York) school, represented by saxophonist John Zorn; guitarists Fred Frith, Eugene Chadbourne, and Elliott Sharp; vocalist Shelley Hirsch; percussionists David Moss and Ikue Mori; trombonist Jim Staley; harpist Zeena Parkins; and electronic improviser Bob Ostertag, among others. The music of this group is often timbrally and dynamically disjunctive, with rapid and frequent changes of mood and extremes of dynamics, extensive use of timbres reminiscent of rock, and strong interface with popular culture. Again, the emphasis here on personality in improvisation is Afrological in nature;

this group, in my view, has attempted to come to terms with the innovations of Cage in terms of time, spontaneity, and memory, while declining to accept Cage's critique of jazz and improvisation.

Perhaps the most thorough accounts of the AACM's early activity are contained in Radano ("Jazzin' the Classics"; *New Musical Figurations*). Jost, Litweiler, Wilmer, and Corbett also offer useful and informative accounts. Litweiler, Bailey, Dean, and Corbett offer a good deal of information on European post–free jazz improvisers. The East German critic Bert Noglik *(Jazz-Werkstatt; Wege)* has written extensively on these musicians as well, although these German-language works are difficult to locate. As for information on the "downtown" school, this group is much better documented on recordings than in print at the present time; the accompanying discography of improvised music should prove useful. In any event, this brief survey of certain areas within improvised music can hardly be taken as exhaustive.

The extensive and well-documented collaborations among improvisers from these and other cultural locations lead us to a view of improvised music, seen in historical terms, as a transcultural practice. For example, California's large and vibrant Asian-American improvisers' community—which includes pianists Jon Jang and Glenn Horiuchi; saxophonists Russel Baba, Gerald Oshita, and Francis Wong; bassist Mark Izu; storyteller Brenda Wong Aoki; and kotoist Miya Masaoka—has made a point of exploring and researching the musical, cultural, and political links among Afro-American, Euro-American, and Asian-American musical forms (see Jang, 88; and Houn).

In recent years, moreover, the emergence of musicians who do not claim roots in either European or American forms has further served to identify improvised music's transcultural nature. Improvisers such as the Korean percussionist Kim Jin Hi, the Japanese multi-instrumentalist Torikai Ushio, and the South African percussionist Thebe Lipere have become part of the increasing internationalization of improvised music. Their examples emphasize the dangers of essentialist thinking with regard to the connection between music, race, and national origin. The recent biography of the South African pianist Chris McGregor, by Maxine McGregor, is a useful guide to some of these transnational and transcultural issues.

Given the above-mentioned historical antecedents and the associated and concomitant social and cultural themes, we can now identify "improviser" as a functional musical activity role in world-musical society, along with such roles as "composer," "performer," "interpreter," "psychoacoustician," and various flavors of "theorist." In identifying the role of "improviser," the derived notion of improvisation as "real-time composition" is implicitly disavowed. Once this construct is discarded, the notion of the improviser as "performer" in the Eurological sense also comes into question; as in many cases the piece that the improviser is to "perform" is missing.

I do not, however, wish to present these musical activity roles as fixed constructions but as potentials. Creating compositions for improvisers (again, rather than a work that "incorporates" improvisation) is part of many an improviser's personal direction. The work of Roscoe Mitchell, Anthony Braxton, John Zorn, and Misha Mengelberg provide examples of work that retains formal coherence while allowing aspects of the composition to interact with the extended interpretation that improvisers must do—thus reaffirming a role for the personality of the improviser-performers within the work.

Freedom

The advent of various strains of "free" improvisation—including "free" jazz, which emerged in the early 1960s, as well as the European "free" improvisation which emerged in several cultural strata in the 1970s—placed "freedom" back on the musical agenda. In the case of "free" jazz, the tumultuous push for human rights in the United States had clear analogues in the music, as remarked upon by politically active musicians such as Archie Shepp. With regard to the improvisations of musicians such as Vinko Globokar and Cornelius Cardew, where improvisation itself became a symbol for freedom, the events of May 1968 in Paris and other European capitals could be seen as germane[5] (Globokar, 29–30).

As with the theme of spontaneity, notions of freedom and control differ markedly between Eurological and Afrological viewpoints. "Free jazz" was, as one can readily observe from the drummer Arthur Taylor's interviews with Afrological improvisers, quite controversial among jazz musicians. Whatever the viewpoints of the musicians on free jazz itself, the responses of several improvisers on the topic of "freedom" are instructive. In particular, the Eurological discourse concerning "rules" for improvisation is almost entirely absent. Rather, the improvisers seem to agree that freedom in Afrological improvisation is perceived as being possible only through discipline, defined as technical knowledge of music theory and of one's instrument as well as thorough attention to the background, history, and culture of one's music.

Drummer Elvin Jones puts the case succinctly with regard to his own involvement in what some people called "freedom music": "There's no such thing as freedom without some kind of control, at least self-control or self-discipline. . . . Coltrane did a lot of experimenting in that direction

. . . even though it gave an impression of freedom, it was basically a well thought out and highly disciplined piece of work" (quoted in Taylor, 228). The bassist Ron Carter, on the same subject, maintains that "you can play as free as you want, only you should have some kind of background to relate to this freedom. Otherwise you're putting yourself into a corner" (quoted in Taylor, 61).

Another view constructs freedom as always being present through improvisation. The drummer Philly Joe Jones insists that improvisation is itself perfectly free and not in need of any license: "Everybody's been playing free. Every time you play a solo you're free to play what you want to play. That's freedom right there" (quoted in Taylor, 1993 reprint, 48). Echoing this theme, pianist Randy Weston says of "free music," "I don't see how this music is more free than another. I've heard Monk take one note and create unbelievable freedom. Freedom is a natural development" (quoted in Taylor, 27).

Among improvisers from the Eurological standpoint, freedom is sometimes framed in terms of European music's traditional composer-to-performer hierarchy. According to Chase, "improvisation is the free zone in music, where anything is permitted and considered acceptable. You are responsible only to yourself and to the dictates of your taste." Similarly, preparation for improvisation is described in terms of the need to "free ourselves from those negative attitudes that inhibit us" (15).

A much more widespread view that has evolved in Eurological music circles with regard to improvisation is the notion that, to be musically coherent, improvisation cannot be left as "free," but must instead be "controlled" or "structured" in some way. The composer and critic Tom Johnson's characterization of Cage's indeterminacy is typical: "Cage began referring to work indeterminate of its performance because to have called his work 'improvisations' would have implied that the performers were not guided by goals and rules" (207–208). Another reason for asserting this necessity for rules is exemplified in the complaint by Berio that "improvisation presents a problem in that there's no true unanimity of discourse among the participants, only, once in a while, a unity of behavior" (81).

In any event, the most common Eurological method of providing these rules is the construction, by a composer, of autonomous, often culturally ad hoc systems of specified musical behavior options. These systems typically leave certain dimensions intentionally unspecified and presumably available for filling in as desired. Diether De la Motte has outlined a number of rule-specification strategies used by 1960s and 1970s European composers into whose works improvisation has been "included" ("einbezogen"). De la

Motte includes his own comments and critiques about the procedures used. For example, Bernd Alois Zimmermann's *Tempus Loquendi* (1963) for flute solo uses nine phrases already created by the composer. If the soloist wishes, he or she is "encouraged" ("ermuntern") to improvise "personal" versions from the given material (De la Motte, 45).

Sometimes the rules concern not what to play, but what to think. Stockhausen's description of his "intuitive" music, as exemplified by his composition "Aus den sieben Tagen," rejects any notion that his "intuitive music" might be regarded as a pseudonym for improvisation. His justification for distancing his "intuitive" work from improvisation resurrects a version of the motif theory: "One always connects improvisations with the presentation of underlying schemata, formulae, and stylistic elements"[6] (Stockhausen, 123). For Stockhausen, music should come directly from the intuition, manifesting a unity of mood, which he describes in a play on words of the meanings of "einstimmen" (to agree) and "Stimmung" (tuning or mood):

The orientation of the musicians, which I have also called "Einstimmung" [unanimity of mood/tuning], is, however, not an arbitrary or purely negative one—excluding all musical thought in certain directions—rather, it is at any given time concentrated through a text written by me, which provokes the intuition in a completely definite fashion.[7] (Stockhausen, 123–124; my translation)

Even a simple set of these ad hoc formalisms, however, would still require a certain amount of preparation for their performance—presumably reducing their capacity for inducing spontaneity or provoking intuition. Moreover, despite the apparent attempt by many Eurological commentators to differentiate these performer choice systems from Afrological improvisative systems, the systems described by De la Motte in particular often seem reminiscent of the African-American practice of using chord progressions, appropriately named "changes," as musical behavior options systems. Though the Eurological "choice" systems do not necessarily present harmonic sequences, they nonetheless function in analogous ways in promoting, guiding, and conditioning real-time choice, thereby producing "changes" in the content of the music.

In any event, performer choice and "intuition" systems, as promulgated by Stockhausen and other Eurological composers, do indeed turn out to be somewhat different from improvisation in the Afrological sense. These systems seem to take account of the absence of pedagogy in the Eurological music education system with regard to improvisation. At the very least, they are designed to compensate for this lack by mitigating, for the performer, the "terrifying prospect of being free to play whatever comes to mind" (Small, 302), by providing material to supplement or even to supplant the performer's own creative lexicon.

My own view is that in analyzing improvisative musical activity or behavior in structural terms, questions relating to how, when, and why are
critical. On the other hand, the question of whether structure exists in an
improvisation (or, for that matter, in any human activity) often begs the
question in a manner that risks becoming not so much exegetic as pejorative. It should be axiomatic that, both in our musical and in our human,
everyday-life improvisations, we interact with our environment, navigating
through time, place, and situation, both creating and discovering form. On
the face of it, this interactive, form-giving process appears to take root and
flower freely, in many kinds of music, both with and without preexisting
rules and regulations.

Personality

One central aspect of Afrological improvisation is the notion of the importance of personal narrative, of "telling your own story." Berliner's sub-
chapter on this topic identifies this metaphor of the story as underlying the
structural process of many improvisers (Berliner, 201). Erroll Garner encapsulates this viewpoint well: "If you take up an instrument, I don't care
how much you love somebody, how much you would like to pattern yourself after them, you should still give yourself a chance to find out what
you've got and let that out" (quoted in Taylor, 97).

Part of telling your own story is developing your own "sound." An Afrological notion of an improviser's "sound" may be seen as analogous to
the Eurological concept of compositional "style," especially in a musically
semiotic sense. Moreover, for an improviser working in Afrological forms,
"sound," sensibility, personality, and intelligence cannot be separated from
an improviser's phenomenal (as distinct from formal) definition of music.
Notions of personhood are transmitted via sounds, and sounds become
signs for deeper levels of meaning beyond pitches and intervals. The saxophonist Yusef Lateef makes it plain: "The sound of the improvisation
seems to tell us what kind of person is improvising. We feel that we can
hear character or personality in the way the musician improvises" (44).

Crucial to the creation of a personal sound is the development of analytic skill on the part of an improviser. For the beginner, this process almost
always commences with the emulation of other improvisers. Fraser quotes
Gillespie to the effect that an improviser starts by "playing exactly like
somebody else" (141). Such emulation amounts to a version of music analysis for music based in orature and the body. Fraser further maintains that
"the prospective improviser . . . is enculturated into a way of listening and
of regarding the environment. . . . A way of hearing develops, a preferred

musical language, the terms and patterns of which one subconsciously employs to listen to the world" (81).

Interestingly, Cage's critique of jazz also likens it to personal storytelling. Cage's description of jazz seems to liken the music to a ring shout: "The form of jazz suggests too frequently that people are talking—that is, in succession—like in a panel discussion. . . . If I am going to listen to a speech then I would like to hear some words" (quoted in Zwerin, 162). This perceptive comment from a composer who could not, by any stretch of the imagination, be portrayed as possessing any affinity with Afrological musical forms, provides some intersubjective justification for the notion that one of the central aesthetic demands made on Afrological improvisers is that the improviser "tell a story."

In any event, Eurological improvisers have tended to look askance on the admission of personal narrative into improvisative activity. I believe that, for postwar Eurological improvisers, the ideas of Cage have, again, had the greatest impact in this regard: "What I would like to find is an improvisation that is not descriptive of the performer, but is descriptive of what happens, and which is characterized by an absence of intention" (quoted in Kostelanetz, 222). Interviewing the members of AMM, the composer Christopher Hobbs states that one of the joys of listening to the group is that "you can't distinguish who is playing what, and that it is completely unimportant one way—or the other" (Childs and Hobbs, 40). British composer Gavin Bryars, who moved away from improvisation during the 1970s, maintained that "one of the main reasons I am against improvisation now is that in any improvising position the person creating the music is identified with the music. . . . It's like standing a painter next to his picture so that every time you see the painting you see the painter as well and you can't see it without him" (quoted in Bailey, 115).

In some respects the distancing of personal narrative updates the concept of a post-Kantian "autonomous significant structure" identified by Subotnik in her essays on contemporary Eurological music. This autonomy is based on the assumption that "humans can build structures or domains that are complete and meaningful within themselves." Moreover, according to Subotnik, "the recognition of validity in such a structure is not thought to depend on the particular identity, power, habits, or values of those who create or receive the structure in question. Rather, validity is supposed to inhere in the ability of a structure to carry out its own laws with consistency" (266).

Subotnik believes that this ideal of autonomy is a fiction; the popular understanding of Gödel's theorem concerning the impossibility of a logical system's self-description in its own terms would seem to provide some corroboration. In any event, Bryars's painterless painting, as well as the Cageian notion of "sounds as themselves" possessing only frequency, loudness, length, overtone structure, morphology (Cage, 14), divorced from social or cultural implications, would seem to harmonize well with this concept of autonomy.

As with the motif theory of improvisation, even in Eurological music the notion of personal narrative and autonomy has been the subject of debate. Though the members of the innovative improvisation group Musica Electronica Viva (including pianist Alvin Curran, electronic improviser Richard Teitelbaum, trombonist Garrett List, and pianist Frederic Rzewski) have all had close associations with Cage, their ideas about group improvisation—as with other "post-Cage improvisers" such as Malcolm Goldstein—seem to part company with Cage's views. Frederic Rzewski's "Description and Analysis of a Process" maintains that the music of MEV is "based on friendship. This element of friendship is communicated in the music; it cannot be concealed" (Rzewski, 3).

Earlier in this passionate, brilliant, yet somewhat rambling treatise, Rzewski states that "any unfriendly act on the part of some individual threatens the strength of the music we are all trying to create" (3). Malcolm Goldstein is even more direct than Rzewski, maintaining, with Erroll Garner, that the improvisative act demands from the improviser that an answer be created to this important question: "Who are you? How do you think or feel about this moment/ sounding?" (10). Perhaps the most trenchant conception of what improvisation can be is to be found in this testament by Charlie Parker: "Music is your own experience, your thoughts, your wisdom. If you don't live it, it won't come out of your horn" (quoted in Levin and Wilson, 24). The clear implication is that what you do live *does* come out of your horn.

Notes

1. A version of this essay originally appeared in *Black Music Research Journal* 16 (Spring 1996): 91–122. My sincere thanks to Bonnie Wright of Spruce Street Forum in San Diego; to Prof. Jann Pasler, my colleague at the University of California, San Diego; and to Muhal Richard Abrams, all of whom made useful suggestions about the text. Thanks are also due to Isabelle Lytton, for information on the German critic Bert Noglik.

2. "Das Ausgearbeitete and Notierte den essentiellen Teil des ästhetischen Gegenstandes ausmacht, der sich im Bewußtsein des Hörers konstituiert."

3. "Ein Historiker, der zögert, ein Stück außereuropäische Musik als Komposition zu bezeichnen, gibt dadurch keineswegs zu erkennen, daß er es gering schätzt."

4. "Daß sie einerseits aus Formeln zusammengestückt sei and andererseits als spontan empfunden werde."

5. In 1968, a number of European cities experienced student and worker strikes, riots, and other disturbances. These events proved to have a trenchancy of effect

and affect that was at first severely underestimated, both by traditional governmental authority and by the European intellectual establishment of the day. In analyzing the causes of this new militancy, both commentators and participants agreed that the unrest could be viewed as a revolt against various forms of societal repression. The more conservative, technocratically oriented J. J. Servan-Schreiber (21) ascribed the citizen activism to "the confrontation of a particularly rigid social order with an accelerating technological, scientific—and therefore intellectual—transformation."

Perhaps more in tune with the aesthetic and cultural currents of the period, the famous French leader of the May 1968 Nanterre student strikes, Daniel "Danny the Red" Cohn-Bendit, attributed the power of the movement to "an 'uncontrollable' spontaneity" (Bourges, 103).

6. "Da man mit Improvisation immer auch die Vorstellung von zugrunde liegenden Schemata, Formeln, stilistischen Elementen verbindet."

7. "Die 'Orientierung' der Musiker, die ich auch 'Einstimmung' nannte, ist aber nicht eine beliebige oder nur negative—das heißt, alles musikalische Denken in bestimmten Richtungen ausschließende—sondern sie ist jeweils konzentriert durch einen von mir geschriebenen Text, der das Intuitive in ganz bestimmter Weise herausfordert."

A Selected Discography of Improvised Music

Abrams, Muhal Richard, and Roscoe Mitchell. *Duets and Solos.* Black Saint 120133–2. Compact disc.

Anderson, Fred, and Steve McCall. *Vintage Duets.* Okkadisk OD12001. Compact disc.

Art Ensemble of Chicago. *A Jackson in Your House.* Affinity CD AFF752. Compact disc.

Bailey, Derek. *Solo Guitar, Volume 2.* Incas CD11. Compact disc.

Braxton, Anthony, and Evan Parker. *Duo* (London) 1993. Leo LR 193. Compact disc.

Brotzmann, Peter, and Hamid Drake. *The Dried Rat-Dog.* Okkadisk OD12004. Compact disc.

Chadbourne, Eugene. *Strings.* Intakt CD 025. Compact disc.

Curran, Alvin, and the ROVA Saxophone Quartet. *Electric Rags* II. New Albion NA027. Compact disc.

Davis, Anthony. *The Ghost Factory.* Gramavision 18–8807–2. Compact disc.

Ethnic Heritage Ensemble. *Dance With the Ancestors.* Chameleon 61494–2. Compact disc.

Ewart, Douglas. *Bamboo Meditations at Banff.* Arawak AA003. Compact disc.

Goldstein, Malcolm. *Sounding the New Violin.* Nonsequitur/What Next? WN005. Compact disc.

Guy, Barry, and the London Jazz Composers Orchestra. *Theoria.* Intakt CD 024. Compact disc.

Hemphill, Julius. *Big Band.* Elektra/Musician 9–60831–2. Compact disc.

Hirsch, Shelley, and David Weinstein. *Haiku Lingo.* Review Records 139. Compact disc.

Horiuchi, Glenn. *Calling Is It and Now.* Soul Note 121268–2. Compact disc.

Izu, Mark. *Circle Offire.* Asian Improv Records AIR 0009. Compact disc.

Jang, Jon, and the Pan-Asian Arkestra. *Self Defense!* Soul Note 121203–2 Compact disc.

Jenkins, Leroy, and Muhal Richard Abrams. *Lifelong Ambitions.* Black Saint 120033–2. Compact disc.

Lacy, Steve. *Futurities.* Hat ART 6031/6032. Two compact discs.
Léandre, Joëlle, and Carlos Zingaro. *Ecritures.* ADDA 590038. Compact disc.
Lewis, George. *Changing with the times.* New World 80434-2. Compact disc.
Masaoka, Miya. *Compositions.* Asian Improv Records AIR 0010. Compact disc.
Mengelberg, Misha. *The ICP Orchestra performs Monk.* ICP 026. Compact disc.
Mitchell, Roscoe. *Roscoe Mitchell Quartet.* Sackville 2009.
Myers, Amina Claudine. *Salutes Bessie Smith.* Leo LR103. Compact disc.
Newton, James. *Suite for Frida Kahlo.* AudioQuest Musics AQCD1023. Compact disc.
Ostertag, Bob. *Attention span.* RecDec33. Compact disc.
Parker, Evan. *50th anniversary concert.* Leo LIZ 212/213. Compact disc.
Schweitzer, Irene. *Piano solo, volume 1.* Intakt CD 020. Compact disc.
Smith, Wadada Leo. *Kulture jazz.* ECM 1507. Compact disc.
Spontaneous Music Ensemble. *Karyobin.* Chronoscope CPE2001-2. Compact disc.
Staley, Jim. *Don Giovanni.* Einstein 002. Compact disc.
Teitelbaum, Richard. *Concerto grosso.* Hat ART CD 6004. Compact disc.
Threadgill, Henry. *Making a move.* Columbia CK67214. Compact disc.
Wong, Francis. *Ming.* Asian Improv Records AIR 0009. Compact disc.
Zorn, John. *Cobra.* Hat Hut CD 60401/60402. Two compact discs.

References

Abrams, Muhal Richard, and John Shenoy Jackson. Association for the Advancement of Creative Musicians. *Black World* 23, no. 1 (November 1973): 72–74.
Bailey, Derek. *Improvisation: Its Nature and Practice in Music.* London: British Library National Sound Archive, 1992.
Becker, Howard. *Art Worlds.* Berkeley and Los Angeles: University of California Press, 1982.
Berio, Luciano. *Two Interviews.* London: Marion Boyars, 1985.
Berliner, Paul F. *Thinking in Jazz.* Chicago: University of Chicago Press, 1994.
Born, Georgina. *Rationalizing Culture.* Berkeley and Los Angeles: University of California Press, 1995.
Bourges, Hem. *The Student Revolt: The Activists Speak.* Translated by B. R. Brewster. London: Jonathan Cape, 1968.
Braxton, Anthony. *Tri-Axium Writings.* Volume 1. Dartmouth: Synthesis/Frog Peak, 1985.
Cage, John. *Silence: Lectures and Writings.* Middletown, Conn.: Wesleyan University Press, 1961.
Chase, Mildred Portney. *Improvisation: Music from the Inside Out.* Berkeley, Calif.: Creative Arts, 1988.
Childs, Barney, and Christopher Hobbs, eds. "Forum: Improvisation." *Perspectives of New Music* 21 (1982–83): 26–112.
Cope, David. *New Directions in Music.* Madison, Wis.: Brown and Benchmark, 1993.
Corbett, John. *Extended Play: Sounding Off from John Cage to Dr. Funkenstein.* Durham: Duke University Press, 1994.
Dahlhaus, Carl. "Was heisst Improvisation?" In *Improvisation and neue Musik: Acht Kongreßreferate,* edited by Reinhold Brinkmann, 9–23. Mainz: Schott, 1979.
Dean, Roger T. 1992. *New Structures in Jazz and Improvised Music Since 1960.* Philadelphia: Open University Press, 1992.
De la Motte, Diether. "Improvisation in der neuen Musik." In *Improvisation and neue Musik: Acht Kongreßreferate,* edited by Reinhold Brinkmann, 42–54. Mainz: Schott, 1979.

Fiske, John. *Media Matters: Everyday Culture and Political Change*. Minneapolis: University of Minnesota Press, 1994.

Fraser, Wilmot. "Jazzology: A Study of the Tradition in which Jazz Musicians Learn to Improvise." Ph.D. diss., University of Pennsylvania, 1983.

Globokar, Vinko. "Reflexionen über Improvisation." In *Improvisation and neue Musik: Acht Kongreßreferate,* edited by Reinhold Brinkmann, 24–41. Mainz: Schott, 1979.

Goldstein, Malcolm. *Sounding the Full Circle*. Sheffield, Eng.: Goldstein/Frog Peak, 1988.

Gridley, Mark. *Jazz Styles: History and Analysis*. Englewood Cliffs, N.J.: Prentice-Hall, 1994.

Harris, Cheryl I. "Whiteness as Property." *Harvard Law Review* 106, no. 8 (1993): 1707–1791.

Houn, Fred Wei-han. "Asian American Music and Empowerment." *Views on Black American Music* 3 (1985–88): 27–32.

Jang, Jon. "We Don't All Sound Alike." *Views on Black Music* 3 (1985–88): 33–38.

Johnson, Tom. *The Voice of New Music: New York City, 1972–1982*. Eindhoven, The Netherlands: Het Apollohuis, 1989.

Johnson-Laird, Philip N. "Jazz Improvisation—A Theory at the Computational Level." In *Representing Musical Structure,* edited by Peter Howell, Robert West, and Ian Cross, 291–325. London: Academic Press, 1991.

Jones, LeRoi. *Blues People*. New York: William Morrow, 1963.

Jost, Ekkehard. *Free Jazz,* Vienna: Universal Edition, 1975.

Kofsky, Frank. *Black Nationalism and the Revolution in Music*. New York: Pathfinder, 1970.

Kostelanetz, Richard. *Conversing with Cage*. New York: Limelight, 1987.

Lateef, Yusef A. "The Pleasures of Voice in Improvised Music." *Views on Black American Music* 3 (1985–88): 43–47.

Levin, Michael, and John S. Wilson. "No Bop Roots in Jazz: Parker." *Down Beat* 61, no. 2 (1994): 24–24. (Originally published 9 September 1949.)

Lipsitz, George. "The Possessive investment in Whiteness: Racialized Social Democracy and the "White" Problem in American Studies." *American Quarterly* 47, no. 3 (1995): 369–427.

Litweiler, John. *The Freedom Principle: Jazz after 1958*. New York: Da Capo, 1984.

Mandeles, Chad. "Jackson Pollock and Jazz: Structural Parallels." *Arts Magazine* 57 (1981): 139–141.

McGregor, Maxine. *Chris McGregor and the Brotherhood of Breath: My Life with a South African Jazz Pioneer*. Flint, Mich.: Bamberger, 1995.

Noglik, Bert. *Jazz-werkstatt international Musik*. Berlin: Verlag Neue Musik, 1981.

———. *Wege improvisierter Musik*. Berlin: Verlag Neue Musik, 1990.

Nyman, Michael. *Experimental Music: Cage and Beyond*. New York: Schirmer, 1974.

Radano, Ronald M. 1992. "Jazzin' the Classics: The AACM's Challenge to Mainstream Aesthetics." *Black Music Research Journal* 12, no. 1 (1992): 79–95.

———. *New Musical Figurations: Anthony Braxton's Cultural Critique*. Chicago: University of Chicago Press, 1993.

Revill, David. *The Roaring Silence: John Cage, a Life*. New York: Arcade, 1992.

Rzewski, Frederic. *Description and Analysis of a Process*. Unpublished, obtained from the author, 1968.

Schwartz, Elliott, and Daniel Godfrey. *Music Since 1945: Issues, Materials and Literature*. New York: Schirmer, 1993.

Servan-Schreiber, J. J. *The Spirit of May.* New York: McGraw-Hill, 1969.

Sloboda, John A. *The Musical Mind: The Cognitive Psychology of Music.* Oxford: Oxford University Press, 1985.

Small, Christopher. *Music of the Common Tongue.* London: Calder, 1987.

Solomon, Larry. "Improvisation II." *Perspectives of New Music* 24, no. 2 (1985): 224–235.

Somers, Margaret R., and Gloria D. Gibson. "Reclaiming the Epistemological "Other": Narrative and the Social Constitution of Identity." In *Social Theory and the Politics of Identity,* edited by Craig Calhoun, 37–99. Cambridge; Blackwell, 1994.

Stockhausen, Karlheinz. *Texte zur Musik, 1963–1970.* Cologne: Verlag M. DuMont Schauberg, 1971.

Subotnik, Rose Rosengard. *Developing Variations: Style and Identity in Western Music.* Minneapolis: University of Minnesota Press, 1991.

Taylor, Arthur. *Notes and Tones: Musician-to-Musician Interviews.* Liège, Belgium: A. Taylor, 1977. Reprint, New York: Da Capo, 1993.

Walton, Ortiz. *Music: Black, White and Blue.* New York: William Morrow, 1972.

Wilmer, Valerie. *As Serious as Your Life: The Story of the New Jazz.* London: Allison and Busby, 1977. Reprint, London: Serpent's Tail, 1992.

Zwerin, Michael. "A Lethal Measurement." In *John Cage: An Anthology,* edited by Richard Kostelanetz, 161–168. New York: Praeger, 1970. Reprint, New York: Da Capo, 1991.

GEORGE E. LEWIS

Afterword to
"Improvised Music after 1950"
The Changing Same

·➔

The editors of the present volume asked me to revisit several issues prompted by the original "Improvised Music after 1950" essay (Chapter 6). This chapter takes a slightly more personal tone in responding to these questions, while suggesting opportunities for further development that interested persons might take up.

To continue where we left off when the article was first written in 1995, pan-European identity politics continues to play a major role in journalistic and historical accounts of improvised and experimental music. More recent texts dealing with experimental music continue to exhibit the dismissive tendencies regarding African-American experimental forms identified in the original essay (see Cameron 1996 and Duckworth 1999),and critics such as David Toop (2001) continue to insist that real freedom in music means freedom from the overweening influence of jazz. The methods used in these and other recent texts to erase African-Americans from histories of experimental music differ not at all from those described in the original essay, so we need not review more cases here.

Even as both uptown and downtown New York musics of the 1980s sought to challenge prevailing wisdom in so many areas, the dominant response of white American experimentalism to a notion of hybridity in experimental forms continues to display fealty to the disapprobation of African-American cultural production, while at the same time appropriating its sounds and methods. Perhaps expressing a vain hope, one downtown-associated critic, with a nod to Adorno's notion of jazz as perennial fashion, opined in quasi-historical tones that with the advent of Wynton Marsalis, "the brittle modernism of the AACM went out of fashion" (Gann, 311).

If similarly pointed critiques of the post-Cage experimentalists exist, they seem buried in the avalanche of hagiographic encomia produced in the area of Cage studies, where challenges to cultural hegemony, or examinations of notions of race or class, are in the shortest conceivable supply. Perhaps this is in part because new music generally appears to many of its proponents to be so endangered and marginalized that critiques seem, following the title of a well-known Cage essay, only to "make matters worse." This dynamic is strikingly similar to the constant demand for "positive" black images: the Essence Awards and so on, and the concomitant proscription on airing dirty laundry. Two notable exceptions to this rule are Frances Dyson's (1992) analysis of the notion of "letting sounds be themselves" and Jonathan Katz's theorizing of "silence" as a "queer" resistance to social conditions of the 1950s (Katz).

The foreword to Michael Nyman's second edition of *Experimental Music* (Nyman 1999) gingerly admits that a new, more comprehensive effort to chronicle new music—which he dubbed "Son of Experimental Music" (daughter?)—"would have to be less ethnocentric": that is, less situated along the "US/UK axis." Nonetheless, the second edition seems firmly planted along that very axis. Ultimately, were he writing the work today, Nyman asserts the paradox that he "would not do it any differently, though it would not be possible not to do it differently" (Nyman, xvii), inadvertently rendering the work (if not the "experimental tradition" itself) something of an ethnic period piece.

A Hard Look at Race: Coming Soon?

The development of a historical notion of "experimental music" that excludes the so-called bebop and free jazz movements, perhaps the most influential experimentalist musics of the latter part of the twentieth century, could be accounted for in terms of the general absence of discourse in American experimentalism related to issues of race and ethnicity, an aspect of this music's intellectual environment that separates it from both post-1960s jazz and from contemporary work in visual art, literature, and dance. Although experimental music seems to provide a vast untapped field of endeavor for cultural studies—especially given its emphasis upon resistance, and upon excavating subaltern and marginalized histories—it can fairly be said that at the time the 1995 essay was first published, few histories had confronted the connection between experimental music, ethnicity, and race in any sustained or serious way. Discussions of race in the contemporary music community tend to fall back on notions of colorblindness, transcendence, and universality very similar to those articulated, not only from within high modernism, but also by the American political right wing (see, for example, Johnson 1979).

Among the few texts that do confront race in experimental music, those written or edited by improvisers stand out, such as Leo Smith's early writings (Smith 1973, Smith 1974) and Anthony Braxton's massive three-volume *Tri-Axium Writings* (1985), which dwarf practically all other composer-produced texts, regardless of presumed genre, not only in sheer volume, but in range of inquiry and trenchancy of insight. What is particularly fascinating about these texts are two shared assumptions: (1) that a new musical order will necessarily involve some degree of code-switching across traditions and genres, and (2) most important, that improvisation itself provides a key to this kind of mobility. This view was shared by Karl Berger and Ingrid Sertso, the founders of the Creative Music Studio (CMS) in Woodstock, New York (Sweet 1996). CMS practices extended the code-switching concept to include musical exchanges across borders of language and musical culture. Miya Masaoka (2000) and John Corbett (2000) have also produced exciting work in this area, as have Georgina Born and David Hesmondhalgh (2000).

"Beyond Category": So What Else Is New?

The phenomenon of code-switching has obliged me to sharpen my focus on the recent (that is, since 1970) history of genre transcendence discourses in experimental music, with particular emphasis on press and critical reception. Between 1975 and 1980, the term "eclectic" is no longer a term of disapprobation; in fact, genre diversity becomes framed as a transgressive cultural and political stance.

For Jacques Attali, it was free jazz that originally "eliminated the distinctions between popular music and learned music, broke down the repetitive hierarchy" (Attali, 140). Later, the first activities of AACM artists in New York City, occurring roughly between 1970 and 1983, played a crucial and very public role in the emergence during this period of now-standard musical and critical discourses of genre mobility and musical hybridity. As AACM trumpeter Lester Bowie asserted, not long after the dawn of post-modernism, "We're free to express ourselves in any so-called idiom, to draw from any source, to deny any limitation. We weren't restricted to bebop, free jazz, Dixieland, theater or poetry. We could put it all together. We could sequence it any way we felt like it. It was entirely up to us" (Beauchamp, 46).

In the ensuing years, a "Downtown II" school, most prominently represented by John Zorn, his associates and spiritual descendants, gradually became distinct, in terms of method, aesthetic and cultural reference, from the pre-1980, post-Cage "Downtown I" musicians whose exploits were extensively chronicled by Nyman and 1970s *Village Voice* critic Tom Johnson. Commentary on Downtown II artists routinely celebrates the diversity of sonic and cultural reference in their work. In 1988 John Rockwell declared that Zorn not only "transcends categories; better, he's made a notable career crashing them together and grinding them to dust" (Rockwell 1988). In this respect Downtown II artists have become the heirs to the image of catholicity ascribed to Cage.

Zorn himself, however, connects this notion of diversity with the AACM, an important influence on his work. In discovering Braxton and the Art Ensemble, Zorn notices that "the guy's [Braxton] got a great head, he's listening to all this different music. It is all connected up" (Gagne, 511). Echoing long-standing AACM premises, Zorn declared that "I want to break all these hierarchies: the idea that classical music is better than jazz, that jazz is better than rock. I don't think that way" (Watrous 1989).

Incidentally or not, Downtown I and Downtown II are generally coded in press accounts as white, and the most recent press accounts have identified Downtown II as something of a successor to Downtown I's much sought-after connection with pan-European high culture. This coding is not only at variance with Downtown II's carefully nurtured image of diversity; it seems to have little basis in either New York City's geography or the flow of musical affinities there. New York–based African-American saxophonist Greg Osby's acerbic observation neatly encapsulates the issue: "I played with all the downtown cats but nobody called *me* a downtown cat (Nai, 16).

Indeed, claims of genre transcendence often feature a complementary Othering of someone else as "genre-bound," with criteria for the identification of genre diversity that shift according to not only (or even primarily) musical direction, but also the race, ethnicity, class position and, quite often, the gender of the artist involved. Thus, in 1982, even such a progressive critic as Rockwell could insist of Anthony Braxton that "however much he may resist categories, Mr. Braxton's background is in jazz, which means an improvisatory tradition" (Rockwell 1982), an evocation in a single sentence of the eugenicist power of the one-drop rule that revokes, rather than celebrates Braxton's mobility.

This evocation of the dominant culture's generally high levels of investment in white positional diversity, with its complementary disinvestment in black positionality, is all too current today. As George Lipsitz notes, "whiteness is everywhere in US culture, but it is very hard to see" (Lipsitz, 1). The framing of Downtown II artists as transcending race as well as genre appears aimed at rendering the deployment of the defining power of whiteness "hard to see," while continually pointing to the color of African-

American artists, effectively reasserting a "possessive investment in whiteness" through a rhetoric of diversity. In this light, curator Thelma Golden's efforts to assert a "post-black" aesthetic (Cotter 2001) represent not so much a new phenomenon as the reassertion of a trope that stretches back to her historical counterpart, 1920s "New Negro" theorist Alain Locke, architect of the Harlem Renaissance. One fervently hopes that history will not render her efforts similarly quixotic.

Post-Dating Indeterminacy

The 1995 essay expresses a certain disappointment with the gap between rhetoric and reality with regard to multiculturalism in postwar American experimental music. At the same time, recent research on the period, aided by the opening of the David Tudor archive at the J. Paul Getty Museum in Los Angeles, intimates that this gap may well have extended to the actual performance of the music itself. Composer and theorist Sean Griffin's work on the Tudor archives has centered on a set of detailed, completely and relatively conventionally notated secondary scores, made by pianist Tudor himself, as realizations of the early indeterminate works of Cage, Morton Feldman, Christian Wolff, and Earle Brown. According to Griffin, the performance of at least one such secondary score has been issued as Tudor's recorded version of Feldman's supposedly indeterminate "Intersection 3" from 1953 (Feldman 1969; Griffin, 15).

While a later analysis by John Holzaepfel opines that it was "the act of piano playing" and "tactile advantage" that played decisive roles in Tudor's realization of "Intersection 3" (Holzaepfel 2002, 171), according to Griffin's music and theoretical analyses, the scores show strong affinities with the style of postwar serialism, reflecting Tudor's training in composition by Stefan Wolpe. The secondary scores constitute a ringing affirmation of the link between these younger composers and the European tradition, reinforcing Anthony Braxton's view that "there was no need for Europe to view the Cage movement as a threat, but rather an expanded arm of western continuance . . . in fact in America the post-Cageian movement has done everything it could to be viewed as European—or 'of Europe'—or 'of white people and Europe exclusively'" (Braxton, 325).

Though Wolff and Brown aimed at provoking performance indeterminacy, and were critical of the secondary-score approach, Tudor actually resisted such on-the-spot decision-making, declaring that he "would not accept a performance that happened by chance, just simply because I happened to read something on the spur of the moment" (Holzaepfel, 196; quoted in Griffin 2001). While contemporary accounts by persons apparently not in the know at the time, such as the poet Frank O'Hara, credited Feldman with "improvisatory collaboration, with its call on musical creativity as well as interpretive understanding" (O'Hara, 26), Griffin's recent, more dispassionate revelations challenge the accepted historical accounts of the early indeterminacy period, indicating that at the very least, the legacy of indeterminacy may need some postdating.

How Far Can "Afrological" and "Eurological" Take Us?

Certainly the metaphors "Afrological" and "Eurological" could be more sufficiently theorized. For instance, my use of these complementary metaphors points up a metonymic dialectic between "composed" and "improvised" ways of producing musical texts that serves to obscure a more fundamental, historically asserted competition between the two most influential musical cultures of the twentieth century: the trans-European and trans-African.

In any event, the reality is that in a transcultural sociomusical environment, each one is a part of the other. Less remarked upon (for the moment) are other actual and potential musicocultural "logics" that must be considered as well. This dynamic strongly militates against simplistic uses of the two metaphors as markers of culturally nationalistic purity; in my usage, "-logical" is not a synonym for "-centric." Thus, I shall leave to others the task of extending the historical and descriptive scope of the two metaphors to encompass earlier eras of music. My primary concern in this essay (and in general) remains the articulation of the complex web of cultural exchange that marks my own era of new music.

In this context, the near-absence of scholarship on African-American experimental improvisers emerging since the death of Coltrane (particularly in the United States) was starting to resemble a yawning black hole. Coltrane, with his strong influences from African-American oral culture, Africa, Asia, and the Islamic world, was certainly one of the most influential precursors of contemporary genre transcendence and multicultural reference discourses in experimental music (see Putschoegl 1993; Benston 2000); yet the significance of Coltrane's work in the context of genre transcendence is rarely remarked upon in Coltrane studies. The question of Coltrane's importance to a postcolonial musical aesthetics that developed in the wake of his work merits further study.

Critical engagement with music after Coltrane opens exciting new avenues of inquiry that promise to challenge essentialized notions of black musical subjectivity, posing new questions about methodological hybridity, expanding networks of sociomusical practice, multicultural reference, and the politics of resources and infrastructure. Recent new studies by Graham Lock (1999), Ajay Heble (2000), and Eric Porter (2001) are breaking new ground, while recapitulating the vitality of earlier works, such as Philippe Carles and Jean-Louis Comolli's important French-language text (still as yet untranslated into English), *Free Jazz/Black Power* ([1971] 2000) or Jost's (1987) and Noglik's (1983 and 1992) surveys of the work of post-1960 European improvisers.

Afrofuturism and Embodiment

Particularly in the digital age, the notion that a particular orientation to the body is somehow essentially constitutive of black expression now serves to recapitulate the containment and policing of the black body generally, while the important question of how the Afrological might be articulated in virtual worlds goes begging. If the contemporary cyberspatial conception of the body obliges us to confront life in a posthuman age, as Hayles (1999) asserts, then the borders of the Afrological body must inevitably become permeable, ingesting and excreting both fluids and data.

Discourses surrounding computer music, as with other areas of computer-based new media (see Lewis 1997 and 2000), assert the same ideologies of color-blindness that were discussed earlier. Accordingly, conceptions of "race in digital space" (the subject of a recent traveling exhibition by that name, curated by Erika Muhammad and documented at <http://cms.mit.edu/race/>) have been theorized to a far lesser extent than gender; Cameron Bailey (1996) and Native Canadian artist/theorist Loretta Todd (1996) provide tantalizing early models for further work. In experimental music, the innovations of Sun Ra asserted a kind of interplanetary Ethiopianism to envision a borderless future.

At the same time, reclamations of Ra as the prototypical Afrofuturist musician tend to take the composer's own pronouncements at face value, while evading questions concerning the politics of the Arkestra (see Eshun 1998). Nonetheless, Ra's creation of a nurturing virtual world for his musicians constituted an important starting point for the efforts of younger experimentalists to confront, in ways that Ra himself rarely attempted, the expansion of networks of sociomusical practice, and the political economy of resources and infrastructure.

"Hey Man, I Just Play": Responding to Conditions

In comparing post-Bird and post-Cage aesthetics of real-time music making, one is confronted with two opposing tropes: (1) the image of the heroic, mystically ego-driven Romantic improviser, imprisoned by his own will; (2) the detached, disengaged, ego-transcending artist who simply lets sounds be themselves. The notion of the ego-driven mystic who is unable to describe his or her own creative process is a staple of conventional cultural wisdom about jazz, and as "Improvised Music after 1950" noted, Cage and his followers, as with canonical composers of contemporary music such as Berio and Stockhausen, often deployed this trope in describing improvisation. Moreover, jazz musicians have themselves used this trope more often than many people realize to ward off potentially offensive questions about their work: "Hey man, I just play."

But if we disconnect improvisation from notions based in European romanticism, then we can recontextualize a classic piece like Alvin Lucier's "Vespers" (Lucier, 1980), in which the performers use echolocation to explore a dark resonant space using a clicking device. Lucier himself commonly presents the performance procedures for this work as constituting the utter antithesis of improvisation. The composer describes one performance in which inexperienced conservatory students used the piece as an occasion for insipid jamming on silly rhythms, certainly out of tune with the piece.

Lucier's view of the efforts of these students as characteristic of improvisation itself, however, is based firmly in that Romantic trope. In the non-Romantic view, "Vespers," with its emphasis on analysis, exploration, discovery, and response to conditions, rather than on ad hoc formalisms or Puritanical rule bases designed to police the creative body, becomes the purest, most utterly human form of improvisation, expressive of its fundamental nature as a human birthright. In that context, discipline is not imposed from without, but truly becomes a cultural and even a spiritual practice, evoked from within.

Finally, the real point of both my original essay and this revisiting was to pose the thesis that the tradition of American experimentalism in music is at a crossroads, facing a stark choice: (1) to grow up and assert its character as multicultural and multiethnic, with a variety of perspectives, histories, traditions, and methods, or (2) to remain an ethnically bound and ultimately limited tradition that appropriates freely, yet furtively, from its presumed Others. I am optimistic enough to advocate the former option.

Works Cited

Attali, Jacques. *Noise: The Political Economy of Music.* Translated by Brian Massumi. With a foreword by Fredric Jameson. Minneapolis: University of Minnesota Press, 1989.
Bailey, Cameron. "Virtual Skin: Articulating Race in Cyberspace." In *Immersed in*

Technology: Art and Virtual Environments, edited by Mary Anne Moser and Douglas MacLeod, 29–49. Cambridge, Mass.: MIT Press, 1996.

Beauchamp, Lincoln T., Jr., ed. Art Ensemble of Chicago: Great Black Music—Ancient to the Future. Chicago: Art Ensemble of Chicago, 1998.

Benston, Kimberly W. Performing Blackness: Enactments of African-American Modernism. New York: Routledge, 2000.

Born, Georgina. Rationalizing Culture: IRCAM, Boulez and the Institutionalization of the Avant-garde. Berkeley and Los Angeles: University of California Press, 1995.

Born, Georgina, and David Hesmondhalgh, eds. Western Music and Its Others: Difference, Representation, and Appropriation in Music. Berkeley: University of California Press, 2000.

Braxton, Anthony. Tri-Axium Writings. Volume 1. Dartmouth: Synthesis/Frog Peak, 1985.

Cameron, Catherine M. Dialectics the Arts: The Rise of Experimentalism in American Music. Westport, Conn.: Praeger, 1996.

Carles, Philippe, and Jean-Louis Comolli. Free Jazz/Black Power. Paris: Gallimard [1971], 2000.

Corbett, John. "Experimental Oriental: New Music and Other Others." In Western Music and Its Others: Difference, Representation, and Appropriation in Music, edited by Georgina Born and David Hesmondhalgh, 163–186. Berkeley and Los Angeles: University of California Press, 2000.

Cotter, Holland. "Beyond Multiculturalism, Freedom?" New York Times, 29 July 2001, 2:1.

Duckworth, William. 20/20: 20 New Sounds of the 20th Century. New York: Schirmer Books, 1999.

Dyson, Frances. "The Ear That Would Hear Sounds in Themselves." In Wireless Imagination: Sound, Radio, and the Avant-Garde, edited by Douglas Kahn and Gregory Whitehead, 373–407. Cambridge, Mass.: MIT Press.

Eshun, Kodwo. More Brilliant Than the Sun: Adventures in Sonic Fiction. London: Quartet Books, 1998.

Feldman, Morton. New Directions In Music 2: Morton Feldman. Columbia/Odyssey MS 6090. 1969.

Gagne, Cole. Soundpieces 2: Interviews with American Composers. Metuchen, N.J.: Scarecrow, 1993.

Gann, Kyle. American Music in the Twentieth Century. New York: Schirmer Books, 1997.

Griffin, Sean. Unpublished Ph.D. Qualifying Examination. University of California, San Diego, 2001.

Hayles, N. Katherine. How We Became Posthuman: Virtual Bodies in Cybernetics, Literature, and Informatics. Chicago: University of Chicago Press, 1999.

Heble, Ajay. Landing on the Wrong Note: Jazz, Dissonance and Critical Practice. New York: Routledge, 2000.

Holzaepfel, John. "David Tudor and the Performance of American Experimental Music, 1950–1959." Ph.D. diss., City University of New York, 1993.

———. "Painting by Numbers; The Intersections of Morton Feldman and David Tudor." In The New York Schools of Music and Visual Arts, edited by Steven Johnson, 159–172. New York and London: Routledge, 2002.

Johnson, Tom. "July 2, 1979: New Music, New York, New Institution." In A Voice for New Music: New York City, 1972–1982, edited by Tom Johnson and Paul Panhuysen, 392–400. . Eindhoven: Het Apollohuis [1979] 1989.

Jost, Ekkehard. Europas Jazz, 1969–80. Frankfurt am Main: Fischer Taschenbuch, 1987.

———. *Jazzmusiker: Materialen zur Soziologie der afro-amerikanischen Musik.* Frankfurt am Main: Verlag Ullstein, 1982.

Katz, Jonathan D. "John Cage's Queer Silence; Or, How to Avoid Making Matters Worse." *GLQ: A Journal of Lesbian And Gay Studies* 5, no. 1 (1999): 231–252.

Lewis, George. "Singing the Alternative Interactivity Blues." *Grantmakers in the Arts* 8, no. 1 (1997): 3–6.

———. "Too Many Notes: Computers, Complexity and Culture in *Voyager.*" *Leonardo Music Journal* 10 (2000): 33–39.

Lipsitz, George. *The Possessive Investment in Whiteness: How White People Profit from Identity Politics.* Philadelphia: Temple University Press, 1998.

Lock, Graham. *Blutopia: Visions of the Future and Revisions of the Past in the Work of Sun Ra, Duke Ellington and Anthony Braxton.* Durham: Duke University Press, 1999.

Lucier, Alvin. *Chambers: Scores by Alvin Lucier, Interviews with the Composer by Douglas Simon.* Middletown: Wesleyan University Press, 1980.

Masaoka, Miya. "Notes from a Trans-Cultural Diary." In *Arcana: Musicians on Music,* edited by John Zorn, 153–166. New York: Granary, 2000.

Nai, Larry. Interview with Greg Osby. *Cadence* (May 2000): 5–16.

Noglik, Bert. *Jazz-Werkstatt International.* Rowohlt: Taschenbuch Verlag, 1983.

———. *Klangspuren: Wege improvisierter Musik.* Frankfurt am Main: Fisher Taschenbuch, 1992.

Nyman, Michael. *Experimental Music: Cage and Beyond.* 2d ed. New York: Schirmer, 1999.

O'Hara, Frank. "New Directions in Music: About the Early Work." In *Morton Feldman Essays,* edited by Walter Zimmermann. Kerpen, Germany: Beginner, 1985.

Porter, Eric. *What is This Thing Called Jazz?* Berkeley and Los Angeles: University of California Press, 2001.

Putschoegl, Gerhard. *John Coltrane und die Afroamerikanische Oraltradition. Jazzforschung 25.* Graz: Akademische Druck und Verlagsanstalt (Adeva), 1993.

Rockwell, John. "As Important as Anyone in His Generation." *New York Times,* 21 February 1988, C:21.

———. "Jazz: Two Braxton Programs." *New York Times,* 23 April 1982, C:23.

Smith, Leo. "American Music." *The Black Perspective in Music* 2, no. 2 (Fall 1974): 111–116.

———. *Notes: 8 pieces. A New World Music—Creative Music.* New Haven: Kiom, 1973.

Sweet, Robert E. *World Music. Music Universe, Music Mind: Revisiting the Creative Music Studio in Woodstock, New York.* Ann Arbor: Arborville Publishing, 1996.

Todd, Loretta. "Aboriginal Narratives in Cyberspace." In *Immersed in Technology: Art and Virtual Environments,* edited by Mary Anne Moser and Douglas MacLeod, 179–194. Cambridge: MIT Press, 1996.

Toop, David. "Music: A Style of No Style That Spurns All Constraints." *New York Times,* 13 May 2001, 2:19.

Watrous, Peter. "John Zorn Takes Over the Town." *New York Times,* 24 February 1989, C:23.

Zorn, John, ed. *Arcana: Musicians on Music.* New York: Granary Books, 2000.

MICHAEL DESSEN

Improvising in a Different Clave
Steve Coleman and Afrocuba de Matanzas

Let me begin by saying that, to some, my notions concerning voice in improvised music may border on the realm of speculation; however, I am suggesting that the door for research is open. To be specific: one researcher, Mr. Walter J. Ong, a University Professor of Humanities and Psychiatry at St. Louis University in Missouri, has said: "In various parts of the world, new methods of analysis have been developed whose conclusions reveal the limitations of the Anglo-American outlook we inherit."

I once asked the late Jo Jones, "What was Lester Young's philosophy concerning improvised music?" He promptly replied, "Lester played his philosophy."
—Yusef Lateef

Like many of the improviser-composers coming out of African-American creative traditions in the late twentieth century, Steve Coleman has been active in a wide range of cultural and musical spaces.[1] While known within the jazz world as a key member of the M-Base collective,[2] Coleman has also collaborated with musicians in Cuba, Senegal, India, Ghana, and Indonesia, worked on computer music at IRCAM,[3] and taught through grassroots community residencies as well as in universities.

In 1996, Coleman took one of his groups, the Mystic Rhythm Society, to Cuba, where they collaborated with AfroCuba de Matanzas. Led since 1957 by Francisco Zamora Chirino, AfroCuba de Matanzas performs a wide range of folkloric music and dance from the main Afrocuban subcultures, including Lucumí[4] (Yoruba), Arará (Dahomey), Abakuá and Bantu (Congo), as well as secular rumba genres. The two groups of musicians and dancers worked together for two weeks, performing at the Havana Jazz Festival and recording a compact disc.

In this essay, I focus on this collaboration in order to develop a number of arguments about innovative forms of contemporary improvised music and cultural practice. The first section situates the Coleman/AfroCuba project within a trajectory of musical experimentation centered on improvisation, spirituality, and intercultural dialogue, suggesting that these linked concerns form an important thread within African-American creative music traditions since the mid-twentieth century. Next, I ground these ideas in a discussion of the specific musical strategies these two groups used, drawing on both interviews and music analysis. In the final section, I explore connections between these musical methodologies and the concerns emerging in contemporary cultural studies; I argue that this kind of intercultural improvised music is itself a form of theorizing about culture.

Following Lateef's passage above, then, this essay centers on the idea of improvised music as a form of philosophizing. In addition, both Lateef's reference to the world of humanistic academic scholarship and his suggestion that "the door for research is open" refer to another kind of dialogue that concerns me here. Although academic scholarship on music has broadened in scope over the past decade, far less attention has been paid to the intercultural modes of experimentalism emerging in contemporary improvised music. Another central claim of this essay, then, is that this project, along with the larger traditions it references, draws on sophisticated approaches to musical improvisation in order to interrogate culture itself, resonating in this way with much of contemporary critical theory.

What, then, is this music saying? I confess to being reluctant to make definitive exegetical claims, not out of piety to poststructuralist theories of subjectivity but rather because, as a musician myself, I am acutely aware of the limitations of writing (especially mine) to encompass the richness of what I hear. Yet being a musician has also taught me the value of communicating across our differences, however imperfect and incomplete this process may be. In this spirit, this essay weaves my own hearings and interpretations with those of participants in the hope of passing through some of Lateef's open doors and expanding the dialogic qualities of this music itself outward into broader communities.

Contexts and Histories: Spirituality, Politics, and Musical Innovation

In his liner notes to the recording of *Sign and the Seal*, Coleman points to the Machito–Charlie Parker recording of "Mango Mangüé" as his first exposure to African-American and Afrocuban traditions "coming together through common roots," explaining that the collaboration with AfroCuba de Matanzas represents his own eventual response to that "initial inspiration." This reference comes as no surprise, as Parker's work with Machito and Mario Bauzá, along with Dizzy Gillespie's collaborations with Chano Pozo (discussed by Jason Stanyek earlier in this book), represented an important step in the developing dialogue between African-American and Afrocuban traditions.

This dialogue predates the 1940s; as John Storm Roberts documents in detail, what Jelly Roll Morton called the "latin tinge" was a central influence on the development of early African-American music.[5] Still, artists emerging in the 1940s such as Gillespie, Pozo, Bauzá and Parker were especially significant in a number of ways. For one, their innovations were part of the broader claim so-called bebop musicians made to be taken more seriously as artists, despite the racially coded conceptions of high and low culture within the United States at the time.[6] Part of this challenge had to do specifically with improvisation. As George Lewis argues, these musicians "created new possibilities for the construction of an African-American improvisative musicality that could define itself as explicitly experimental" ("Improvised," 95). The fact that intercultural experiments such as Gillespie and Pozo's were situated within this larger redefinition of improvisation, art music, and the boundaries of African-American music is extremely important because it distinguishes their work from the hybrid forms and crossover performers from the earlier decades that Roberts describes. Equally crucial was the fact that these collaborations in the 1940s embodied both a pan-African and an internationalist stance that was simultaneously musical and political (a topic that Stanyek also discusses in his essay in this volume, see chapter 5).

These collaborations reverberated in different ways over the following decades. On the one hand, many musicians continued to develop hybrid approaches that integrated African-American, Caribbean, and Brazilian musical traditions, generating a wide range of music now commonly referred to as "latin jazz."[7] At the same time, however, the collaborative work of Gillespie, Bauzá, Pozo, Parker, and others in the 1940s also served as a starting point for a more explicitly experimental trajectory of intercultural improvised music. From the mid-twentieth century to the present, collaboration with musicians from other cultures and/or creative appropriation of non-Western traditions has been central to the work of numerous improvisers, including people like John Coltrane, Randy Weston, Sun Ra, Pharoah Sanders, Yusef Lateef, Don Cherry, Ornette Coleman, the Art Ensemble of Chicago, David Murray, Wadada Leo Smith, Jon Jang, Michele Rosewoman, Jin Hi Kim, Anthony Davis, Susie Ibarra, Steve Coleman, Anthony Brown, Glen Horiuchi, Evan Parker, and Miya Masaoka.

There is no singular approach to improvised music or to intercultural collaboration shared by all of these musicians, in part since they emerged in different time periods and sociomusical networks; these include the "jazz avant-garde" of the late 1950s and the 1960s, the Association for the Advancement of Creative Musicians (AACM), the Asian-American improvisers community, the European improvisers network, the so-called downtown New York improvisers, and M-Base.[8] Despite this diversity, among the diverse modes of experimentalism that have flowered out of the jazz tradition since the mid-twentieth century, a key thread involves experimental improvisation as a basis for intercultural practice.

Spirituality is another central trope in many of these collaborations, and is particularly important in the case of Cuba. Many Cuban musicians themselves such as Chucho Valdés and Gonzalo Rubalcaba have syncretized jazz with Afrocuban genres. Yet foreigners have also sought to integrate more recent developments in jazz with explicitly religious Cuban forms. Michele Rosewoman, leader of the New Yor-Uba ensemble and one of the first North American musicians to integrate post-1950s forms of jazz with Cuban folkloric music, describes how she came to study Cuban music after being "touched by the more spiritual aspects" of the genre early in her career.[9] Such comments must be read within a larger history of discourses, long employed by musicians based in African-American music traditions, through which improvised and collaborative music making is linked with notions of universality, communicating across cultural difference, and spiritual transformation.

Yet this emphasis on spirituality and essence has often taken shape in relation to debates about how African-American music and jazz specifically is—or should be—situated politically. John Coltrane, for example, is one of the more prominent figures who foregrounded questions of spirituality and transcendence in the context of the divisive and politically charged 1960s music world. In his famous interview with Marxist historian Frank Kofsky, Coltrane responds to loaded questions in an oblique way, affirming Kofsky's leftist politics on some level yet unequivocally placing his music and his goals within a larger, spiritual context.[10] This discursive legacy has continued to be relevant for many musicians working within the trajectory of intercultural, experimental improvised music I mentioned above. These include Asian-American improvisors Jon Jang and Francis Wong, who deal with political themes in their music yet simultaneously stress their discomfort with the idea of "political music" because it rarely includes spiritual concerns, a point Wong situates within a larger critique of the "separation of politics and spirituality" in the twentieth century (1997).

Similarly, both Coleman and Chirino dismissed any simple readings that would see their project as a comment upon the political relationship between the United States and Cuba. Coleman insisted that his interest in Cuba was about spiritual traditions and that his goals had nothing to do with the problems between the United States and Cuba, which he referred to as "only obstacles" to what they were trying to accomplish. Similarly, Chirino responded to my mention of politics by saying that "a musician is not a politician . . . he is a musician," and stressed that musicians are important in cultural exchange but ultimately act within their own field.

However, respect for musicians' self-described goals and concerns should not blind us to the ways in which notions of spirituality and universality can obscure the power differentials that are a part of intercultural music making and that are clearly important in the case of a collaboration involving Cuban and North American musicians. Because of the U.S. embargo, Cuban musicians who chose to stay on the island after the 1959 revolution were largely cut off from the substantial commercial opportunities that the United States represented. Although this restriction has slowly begun to change over the last decade, the legalization of the dollar in the mid-1990s and the earlier collapse of the Soviet Union created a complex dual economy in Cuba where the dollar is extremely valued compared to the peso. As a result, Cuban musicians working with North American and European ones are not only able to connect with more international infrastructures and exposure, but to use work abroad to earn dollars that are extremely valuable back home. As Ariana Hernandez-Reguant puts it, "the introduction of market policies [in Cuba] has resulted in social stratification, first and foremost within the music profession, due to its position at the forefront of the encounter with transnational capitalism."[11] Thus, regardless of the sincerity of anyone's spiritual interests, it is not difficult to imagine that many Cubans see their foreign colleagues in terms of access and that they would hesitate to criticize them openly or assert a more leading role in a supposedly collaborative project for fear of losing their gig.

For this reason, I felt it important to ask Chirino about this question of agency, even though most of the tracks on this recording have author credits shared between Coleman and Chirino, and even though I suspected he would be unlikely to say anything negative about Coleman to me. When I mentioned the idea of North American jazz musicians hiring Cubans (especially percussionists) but only using them in superficial ways, Chirino recognized the tendency but emphasized that his work with Coleman was different; in fact, he proudly situated it as a historical advance in comparison to earlier periods. While he praised Chano Pozo, Machito, and the many other Cuban musicians who "invaded the United States" in the

1940s, he claimed that the Cuban percussion in those earlier collaborations was generally used "on a secondary level, like a background accompaniment." He distinguished his project with Coleman by emphasizing that if AfroCuba de Matanzas were to falter even slightly, the entire piece would fall apart, and that they were a "primordial part" of the process, something he felt was "the opposite of the jazz that was played in the United States before, in those years."[12] In contrast, the Coleman/AfroCuba project involved an entire folkloric ensemble of more than ten members performing religious and secular music from their regular repertoire; even more important, as I will discuss in the next section, this project is based less on the idea that one group should "accompany" the other than on group improvisation as a way to facilitate complex layers of multiple narratives, and on compositional and improvisational frameworks not limited to popular song forms. In this respect, this project—unlike most contemporary "latin jazz"—is deeply informed by many of the experiments with more flexible, open-form improvisational structures that took place in the African-American avant-garde of the mid- to late-1960s. A work like Coltrane's *Ascension*, for example, resonates with Coleman's approach here in that both link a radically heterogeneous kind of large-scale group improvisation with the notion of music as a spiritually transformative process.

This association between spirituality and more open-ended approaches to group improvisation can be traced back to even earlier innovations such as the "modal jazz" of the late 1950s and early 1960s. As Ingrid Monson argues, "spiritual ideas of essence, unity and transcendence served as one of several factors shaping the deepening interest of jazz musicians in non-Western religious and musical expressions," an interest that she suggests was "embodied musically in the more open forms generated by modal improvisational thinking" ("Oh Freedom," 157). When I showed Coleman this comment from Monson, he more or less agreed, but extended her argument to include a broader, more mythic context for the kind of music making he is involved in:

Using John Coltrane as one possible example (although the issue is much more complicated than that including hundreds of other musicians) there is definitely a more conscious concern for universal principles of essence and creation being expressed in the music. However what is just as important as what Coltrane and his colleagues accomplished is what they were "trying" to accomplish! What I mean by this is in most creative activity you have the thing realized and the "idea" that is driving what was realized. I am looking at that idea.

Of course Coltrane played with Dizzy during and right after the time when Dizzy was very involved with trying to connect with a certain non-European rhythmic aesthetic with his experiments with Chano Pozo et al. You can also hear this direction in the experimental things that Bird did with the Machito Orchestra. Many musicians were getting inspiration from Caribbean, African, and eventually Asian sources such as India. This was on both a subconscious and conscious level but I think that there is a larger issue here than the mixing of different styles of music and that is what I am getting at. I think what we see happening here is the slow introduction of another level of consciousness and what was happening in music, art, dance, literature, physics etc. is just the manifestation of this among creative people, which is where these things tend to show up first among the human race. This consciousness has a lot to do with the way we are communicating and I think that symbolic communication is at the base of it. ("Email")

While Coleman is fundamentally interested in "the idea" and the transformation of consciousness he feels is at work here, he also relates this rather mythic process to specific musical practices, especially rhythmic ones. With this interdependence of form and content in mind, I turn now to questions of musical process in this particular project.

Strategies and Strata of Intercultural Improvisation

"Universal principles of essence" notwithstanding, all participants commented that the initial encounter between the two ensembles was anything but comfortable. Laila Jenkins, a dancer in Coleman's ensemble, referred to the "ultimate shyness" and "cultural barriers" that the groups faced at the beginning of the project (including, I would add, a language barrier).[13] Both Chirino and former AfroCuba de Matanzas member Ramon Garcia Pérez explained that while they were very familiar with "jazz" and "latin jazz," they recognized immediately that Coleman's musical language was altogether different from theirs. Chirino referred repeatedly to the fact that Coleman's rhythmic practices, involving unusual rhythmic cycles and meters (for example, five, seven, eleven, and so forth), "really sounded strange to us." Similarly, the members of Coleman's group were unfamiliar with Afrocuban folkloric music and, according to Coleman, were speechless upon hearing AfroCuba de Matanzas play at the first rehearsal, in which each group performed for the other something from its standard repertoire (Coleman 2000). After that first experience, many musicians in both groups apparently felt discouraged, with doubts as to whether the project would work at all.

Gradually, though, the groups became more comfortable and developed strategies for working together. The two leaders and some of the key members of each group took more prominent roles than others; yet in the words of Yosvany Terry, a Cuban saxophonist who acted as a translator and bridge between the two ensembles, the fact that it was "something so new which was happening in that moment" meant that developing the pieces was "very collaborative," with musicians in both groups making suggestions and remaining very attentive to what was happening. Attentiveness and careful listening was also stressed by Chirino, who pointed out that because of the strangeness of the experience, his musicians had to "put all five senses" into what they were doing while maintaining a high level of concentration.

Each of the tracks the groups eventually recorded contained a religious or secular piece from the repertoire of AfroCuba de Matanzas. Simultaneously, Coleman's group added another musical layer of rhythmic cycles that, while based on the same smaller-scale rhythmic subdivisions used by AfroCuba de Matanzas, were usually structured in different lengths. As a result, the beginnings of one group's cycle did not frequently line up with those of the other, and a thick fabric of periodic patterns emerged upon which various kinds of soloistic improvisations and call and response passages were layered.

Notation is a gross oversimplification here, but as an example of this technique I include in Figure 1 an approximation of selected rhythmic lines from the piece "The Metamorphosis of Amalia." Throughout this twelve-minute piece, AfroCuba de Matanzas performs a yambú, a style of rumba based on an eight-beat clave pattern (fig. 1). This clave acts as a core around which numerous other rhythmic patterns of the same length are performed by percussionists in the Cuban ensemble. The phrase structure of the vocal call and response *(inspiración y coro)* that Chirino and other members of AfroCuba de Matanzas sing, is also based on phrase lengths of two bars, four bars, eight bars, and so forth.

After a twelve-second introduction by AfroCuba, Coleman's group enters and, for the rest of the piece, simultaneously performs rhythms structured around beat groupings of 4 and a half, 9, 18, and so forth (figs. 2 and 3). Although they are working with the same underlying quarter-note pulse as AfroCuba, the cycles Coleman's group plays create a 9:8 (or 4.5:4 or 18:16) ratio with those of AfroCuba. Like the underlying yambú cycles, those of Coleman's group also exist on both smaller- and larger-scale phrase structures; some exist at the level of nine beats (such as the repeating cowbell pattern in fig. 2) and others only repeat at larger multiples of nine beats (such as the 72-beat line in fig. 3).

As in most of the pieces on the album, these kinds of rhythmic relationships create a thick groove upon which various musical narratives enter into dialogue. This layering of different solos or call-and-response sections is often extremely dense. In another piece entitled "The Seal," for example,

Figure 1

Figure 2

the ensemble begins to increase in intensity just before the four-minute mark, at which point the rapper Kokayi (from Coleman's group) enters with freestyle vocals, alongside a chorus sung by the Cuban vocalists. The groove is augmented here by a repeated rhythmic horn line (Coleman's group), that builds further as Chirino adds soloistic calls between the choruses, and Kokayi is replaced by Coleman improvising on alto sax. By seven minutes in, these added events and the combined ensemble's responses to them—especially from the lead percussionists in each group—have changed the overall feel (as well as pulse speed) considerably from the beginning of the track. This kind of large-scale transformation is an important site for group improvisation and dialogue, as are the interactions between the different soloistic and call-and-response statements themselves on a more middle-ground level and the more microlevel negotiation of the groove going on continually within and between the two groups' rhythm sections.

In terms of how group improvisation and cultural traditions are approached, then, this music doesn't quite fit into Derek Bailey's description of "non-idiomatic" or "free" improvisation as that which lacks a "commitment" to any particular idiom or style (99). As Yosvany Terry put it, "the starting point for working together was what the musicians already knew, because, I think, one can't begin working with something he doesn't know. We have to depart from somewhere." On the other hand, calling this music "idiomatic" would miss the centrality of an experimental sensibility—"departing"—that is about more than simply leaving one's idiom to embrace another. Vijay Iyer, a pianist in Coleman's group,[14] explained that Coleman "didn't go there to try to play [their music] back at them" and that "mastery of Afrocuban music was not the point":

it wasn't Steve's project to try to create this fusion. It was more about creating music from the coexistence of these two pretty distinct traditions that have common roots. So—especially in retrospect it's easier to see—he made a point of keeping the stuff somewhat separate; it wasn't like we were all playing just in the same

Figure 3

clave, grooving off of what those guys were doing. It was a bit more complex than that, and, in my mind, anyway, that was the metaphor for the complex relationship between our history and theirs.

Improvising within these structures thus becomes a way of negotiating those histories and relationships. Whereas Bailey's "non-idiomatic" category links experimental improvisation to an allegedly culture-free space, the model of experimentalism at work here does not seek to avoid cultural traditions so much as to bring them into dialogue and, in doing so, interrogate and transform them. Chirino also emphasized this same idea to me when speaking of the particular *sello* (seal) that AfroCuba has, a term comparable to the idea of an individual or group "sound" so often cited in jazz. In this context, he spoke of the hybrid "Batarumba" genre they invented, as well as their collaborations with symphony orchestras, jazz groups, and a Puerto Rican bomba ensemble, stressing that he was concerned with "looking for new ways, new sounds—because African culture is very rich. It's been studied, many people have unearthed a lot, but there still remains a lot to be discovered."[15]

Yet while speaking of African culture, overall, Chirino also emphasized that his musical work was very much grounded in the traditions specific to the Matanzas region.[16] He took care to differentiate the traditions of Matanzas from those of nearby Havana, and even within the context of Matanzas he emphasized his own group's distinct *sello*. This multileveled concept of tradition—as well as improvisation specifically—as operating on local, regional, national, and diasporic scales was expressed by others as well. Coleman, for example, had this to say about the section roughly seven minutes into the piece I mentioned above, "The Seal":

First I believe that my response to what is happening here and the responses of say the Iyá [largest batá drum] player are basically the same except for some differences of emphasis as follows:
I am moving at what I call a faster "rate of change," meaning I'm basically thinking about parts and responses when I'm improvising but I'm changing the parts and responses more quickly.
I'm thinking on a melodic voice-leading as well as a rhythmic voice-leading level. I'm interacting in a way that is based on ideas of the traditional calls of my own sub-culture and not on the traditional calls in the sub-culture of the players from Matanzas (as is the Iyá player). However, the principles are basically the same as they are derived from the same source (West Africa). (Email)

Many musicians mentioned this broader diasporic level of connection, often describing it in terms of spirituality. Jenkins, for example, contrasted "Westernized" perspectives focused around "entertainment" with the more "African or African diasporic perspective" at work here, one she repeatedly described in terms of spiritual transformation. Terry commented on an even more specific way in which Coleman's musical conception fit well with that of AfroCuba, in that both conceived of music as *fundamentada,* based on something concrete:

The concept of Steve's music is very well-founded. It is founded on something. It is not that concept [of music] that rises out of nothing. So, this is something that happens of course with Cuban culture, and especially with Afrocuban music. That everything . . . has a particular function. Everything is representing an energy, representing a saint, representing an orisha [Yoruban deity], representing something, something specific.[17]

African-American traditions, while connected in complex ways to religious and spiritual functions, are not always so directly and so explicitly religious in function as in the case of AfroCuba, a group who performs music from—and often in—ceremonial contexts. Yet Terry's characterization here comes from the fact that Coleman has pursued his own studies of African culture and ancient civilizations and that, like many other African-American musicians, he has incorporated these directly into his conception of improvisation and compositional form. For example, in the notes to his recent recording *The Sonic Language of Myth,* he describes how the "information" on this recording "is being derived from Kemetic,[18] astrological, astronomical, and metaphysical sources, all of which are symbolized through the use of structures (forms, rhythms, and tones plus intent, emotion, and intuition) that masquerade as composition."

This resonance Terry points to was not lost on the members of Afro-Cuba. Sandy Pérez also suggested that although Coleman's own esoteric studies of African culture and ancient civilizations were somewhat foreign to him, they were nonetheless similar to Pérez's own folkloric tradition in terms of overall approach, therefore acting as an important form of connection. My impression is that this was even more the case with Chirino, whose studies of the ancient history and spiritual traditions of Africa overlap in many ways with Coleman's. The larger point here is that just as spirituality served as a driving force in the development of new modes of experimental and intercultural improvised music after midcentury, the shared idea that music functions in real time to effect spiritual transformation is what creates a basis for collaborative and improvisatory practice.

Another important area that some musicians spoke of in terms of diasporic connections was that of rhythmic sensibility. Coleman described a particular "approach to [rhythmic] space" that he hears in various music of Africa and of the African diaspora, though he was quick to clarify that he was not speaking about all music usually classified as "black." His examples ranged from the music of West Africa or AfroCuba de Matanzas to James Brown and John Coltrane. Pérez also used the term "space" *(espacio)* when describing Coleman's approach to music, stating that this is what distinguished Coleman's project from the jazz he was more familiar with. Pérez felt that this sense of space was similar to the approach to rhythm in the Matanzas region specifically, as compared to that of Havana, and that this resonance was partly what gave him the "confidence" to overcome the other difficulties of working with Coleman's unusual metric structures.

Although such descriptions of rhythmic sensibility are highly subjective, I think they are worth thinking about here for a few reasons. For one, they point to a performative and improvisatory dimension of extreme importance to these musicians; namely, the nuances of rhythmic placement and articulation that make up a musician's (or group's) individual rhythmic "feel." While many factors go into establishing that feel, I think that one of the most important in this context is the use of subtle deviations in placement of rhythms against a regular pulse. Charles Keil has used the term "participatory discrepancies" to suggest that such intentional deviations against a pulse are central to the aesthetics of groove-based music (Keil and Feld, 96–108). This topic has also been explored in quantitative studies by members of the University of California, Berkeley's CNMAT research group on rhythm, including one by pianist Iyer, whose dissertation refers to this technique as " expressive microtiming."[19] Work by both Iyer and Jeff Bilmes suggests that within certain African diasporic musical traditions, musicians develop extremely fine-tuned control over rhythmic deviations from an isochronous pulse, and that these deviations are used in a conscious and expressive way.

Coleman's description of an African-based rhythmic "sensibility" includes not only explicitly groove-based music but also late Coltrane and other so-called free improvisation. In this sense he seems to be speaking about a broader phenomenon than these microtiming studies; at the same time, his comments are also more specific in that he, along with Pérez, seems to be referring less to the practice of microtiming generally than to a particular manifestation of it that he hears in certain players. Still, I think that these scientific studies suggest that the kind of rhythmic "sensibility" Coleman and Pérez are talking about here may indeed be a very real aesthetic resonance between the two groups, and that such studies warn us not to reduce claims like those of Coleman and Pérez to purely subjective imaginings based on racialized notions like "black rhythm." Equally important, the concept of microtiming also points to an important site for improvisation and interaction in this project. The continual negotiations between and within the two ensembles—particularly given the "complex relationship" between them rhythmically—demands a high level of sensitivity to not only macro- but microtiming. Improvisation at this level is more about what Iyer writes of as "a processual notion of communication, as a collective activity that harmonizes individuals," one that contrasts with a "telegraphic model of communication" based on "conveyance of literal, verbal meanings" (1998, 105).

This is not to say that the "telegraphic model" is not also at work in this project; rather, improvisation, agency, and intercultural contact exist not only in the more blatant, soloistic kinds of articulations here, but also on this processual and fine-tuned microlevel of groove. I think that this kind of understanding of improvisation and interaction helps explain, for example, Chirino's reactions to my questions about whether or not he had felt empowered with agency or a sense of his own "voice" in the project *(voz propia)*. Repeatedly, he emphasized his responsibility, as leader of AfroCuba, in maintaining the rhythmic integrity of the groove. He described this role as that of (1) preventing the overall ensemble's groove from falling apart, and (2) simultaneously maintaining AfroCuba's own particular *seal* along the way. Chirino, of course, improvises frequently in this music in the more soloistic and explicit sense of the term as a lead vocalist for AfroCuba. Yet this sensitivity to "expressive microtiming" and emergent models of group interaction is equally central to his conception of agency and music making.

Overall, then, I think we need a multileveled understanding of the role of improvisation in this project. In contrast to models of improvisation based on "freedom" from predetermined musical structures or traditions or on egalitarian social orders, improvisation here is linked closely to collaboration, from the most microlevel of groove to the larger levels where soloistic articulations, contrasting rhythmic cycles, and interrelated but distinct histories continually negotiate a complex coexistence.

Playing Philosophy

Over the last few decades, both academic scholars and improvisers themselves have published work that theorizes the impact of transnational cultural formations on contemporary music practice.[20] Yet a central point in this article is that music making can be another form of theorizing, a type of experimentalism that interrogates not only formal materials but also conceptions of culture.

In this sense, I see some parallels between this kind of music practice and some of the concerns emerging in cultural theory. In his landmark essay "New Ethnicities," for example, Stuart Hall describes a newly emerging (in 1989) cultural politics that "has to do with the awareness of the black experience as a *diaspora* experience," one whose relationship to the past and "to its different 'roots' is profound, but complex" (447). He suggests that "there can . . . be no simple 'return' or 'recovery' of the ancestral past which is not re-experienced through the categories of the present: no base for creative enunciation in a simple reproduction of traditional forms which are not transformed by the technologies and the identities of the present" (448). This kind of complex relationship to the past and to one another—maintaining difference while simultaneously searching for a larger level of common ground—underlies the musical strategies I discussed in the previous section.

Critical to my previous discussions, though, is the question of how such ideas are embodied in actual methods of music making. Countless musicians throughout the world would quickly echo Hall's point about tradition and the "identities of the present." Yet respectfully considering musicians' own views on what music making means to them does not mean taking their interpretations at face value nor ignoring what they actually do. One idea driving this article, then, is that the approach to music and sound evidenced in this project reflects a particularly deliberate and self-conscious investigation (however incomplete and imperfect) into these intercultural questions, as compared to many contemporary "world music" collaborations in the popular sphere. Consider George Lipsitz's critique of David Byrne's *Rei Momo:*

When Byrne sings lyrics that describe love as "a pizza in the rain" and then calls out to "my little wild thing," he has the great Cuban exile singer Celia Cruz answer him in Yoruba as she sings "yen yere cumbe." In traditional Cuban music, Yoruba lyrics resonate with collective memories of slavery and racism, they reinsert distinctly African identity back into collective national culture. But in Byrne's song, Cruz's Yoruba passage signifies only primitivism, exoticism, orientalism; she is an all-purpose "other" summoned up to symbolize Byrne's delight in musical difference on the west side of Manhattan. (60)

In contrast, the Yoruba (and Abakuá) text and music performed by Afro-Cuba de Matanzas is not only something Coleman has studied; it represents the prime reason for his being there in the first place. More important, though, methodology reflects intention. Whereas the multitracking environment of the studio and the musical conventions of "global pop" are adequate tools for Byrne, the kinds of improvisational processes I have been describing as part of this project come out of a more profoundly dialogic sensibility.

Using *Rei Momo* as a foil in this way does risk describing these projects in terms of oversimple "tropes of celebration" and "tropes of anxiety," two interrelated discourses that Steven Feld suggests have been central to how world music is "routed through the public sphere" in the late twentieth century ("Sweet Lullaby"). Yet rather than idealize the Coleman/AfroCuba collaboration as a utopic, transcendent communion, I simply suggest that its methods embody an especially keen attention to the complexities of negotiating cultural identity and difference.

In this way, collaborations like this one might help us move beyond bleak conclusions about the limited possibility for human agency and creativity within musical discourses grounded in global systems of commodification. Consider Veit Erlmann's suggestion that "the key principle of world music" is a Jamesonian sort of "pastiche": "I take pastiche and its central role in the postmodern global culture as an index of the rapid loss of referentiality and, thus, as broadly analogous to Baudrillard's idea of a 'culture of the simulacrum,' or Virilio's 'aesthetic of disappearance'" (482). To my ears, the collaborative models of improvisation in this project embody a different approach to heterogeneity and difference; rather than fall on either side of the "referentiality–post-referentiality" divide that Erlmann implies, they call this binary into question.

In this respect, I am reminded of Monson's more optimistic comment that "riffs, repetition and grooves—as multilayered, stratified, interactive, frames of musical, social and symbolic action—might be helpful in thinking through some of the more challenging issues in contemporary critical thinking" ("Riffs," 32). Yet "riffs, repetition and grooves" paints an extremely broad picture; Byrne's *Rei Momo* certainly riffs, repeats, and grooves as well. My focus here has therefore been on particular ways of riffing, repeating, and grooving, and on how these practices and the larger traditions they reference constitute a deliberate form of theorizing in itself, what Monson calls a "critical resource" (61) for scholars, and what Lateef refers to as "playing philosophy." Specifically, the musical approach to cultural identity and difference here brings to my mind what Hall defines as one of the challenges of contemporary "black cultural politics," which he describes as the act of discovering

how a politics can be constructed which works with and through difference, which is able to build those forms of solidarity and identification which make common struggle and resistance possible but without suppressing the real heterogeneity of interest and identities, and which can effectively draw the political boundary lines without which political contestation is impossible, without fixing those boundaries for eternity. (444)

In this music, the multilayered rhythmic cycles, as well as the broader Afrocentric practices of heterogeneity that these cycles reference and embody, function as a kind of "boundary line" or framework for the negotiation of interrelated histories and identities. At the same time, like Hall's political boundary lines, these musical practices and "extramusical" stances are not fixed, not conceived as static musical styles, but are processes and strategies that can be applied in continually varying circumstances.

The term "politics" in Hall's passage brings us back to the previously cited ideas of Wong and Coltrane, who insisted on larger spiritual contexts for discussing the political dimensions of their work. One of the reasons I think the Coleman/AfroCuba project, as well as the larger creative music traditions it references, has particular relevance for contemporary cultural theorists is that many of these scholars also seem to be trying to carve out a broader notion of politics than the ones they inherited, broader in that its analytical scope moves beyond purely materialist paradigms. This is not to deny the urgent need to combat contemporary crises on concrete activist levels. Yet my point is that both contemporary cultural theorists and creative improvising musicians like these work within other understandings of what constitutes the political, out of a conviction that the challenges we face today also demand a transformation in how we understand ourselves and relate to one another.

Thus, while Erlmann may be right in his assessment of the global popular music he takes as his topic, I think the Coleman/AfroCuba collaboration points toward a different kind of "world music" happening at the margins of contemporary black music. One that is indebted to innovative African-American traditions while simultaneously a part of larger diasporic contexts. One that links sophisticated strategies of improvisation with collaborative, intercultural models in order to "work with and through difference." One whose conception of experimentation is grounded within a larger understanding of music as both spiritually transformative practice and as a form of philosophizing. And one that warrants—to borrow a phrase from improviser Pauline Oliveros—some "deep listening."

Notes

1. Many thanks to the musicians and dancers who spoke with me, all of whom were exceedingly generous with their time and ideas. These include Steve Coleman, Francisco Zamora Chirino, Yosvany Terry, Vijay Iyer, Laila Jenkins, and Ramon Garcia Pérez. Thanks also to the many others who offered important feedback, including Michele Rosewoman, George Lewis, Ingrid Monson, Nancy Guy, Nathaniel Mackey, Wadada Leo Smith, Kazadi Wa Mukuna, J. D. Parran, Jann Pasler, Anthony Davis, George Lipsitz, Bennetta Jules-Rosette, Mariángeles Soto-Díaz, Dana Reason, Jason Stanyek, Anthony Burr, Shahrokh Yadegari, Jason Robinson and Alan Lechusza. Earlier versions of this paper were presented at the 1999 Guelph Jazz Festival Colloquium, the 2000 Conferencia Internacional de Cultura Africana y Afroamericana (Santiago, Cuba), and the 2000 Annual Meeting of the Society for Ethnomusicology.

2. M-Base was a network of musicians that emerged in Brooklyn in the 1980s and included Geri Allen, Robin Eubanks, Kevin Bruce Harris, Graham Haynes, Greg Osby, Marvin "Smitty" Smith, and Cassandra Wilson, among others. For more, see Iyer 1996.

3. IRCAM (Institut de Recherche et Coordonation Acoustique/Musique) is a research institute in Paris founded by Pierre Boulez.

4. Santería is the term most often used outside Cuba to refer to Yoruba-based, syncretic religious practices in the Americas, notably in Cuba and Puerto Rico. The term "santería" was originally derogatory and although this has changed, most Cubans still refer to this religion as Regla de Ocha (The Rule of Orisha) or La Regla Lucumí (Lucumí refers to Yoruban cultural presence in Cuba generally). Also note that the term "folclórico" has a clearer meaning for most Cubans than does its English cognate; for a taxonomy of Afrocuban music by a well-known Cuban musicologist, see León 1991.

5. See Roberts, *Latin Tinge*, 24–99.

6. In a 1949 interview, Charlie Parker is reported to have said "Man, there's no boundary line to art" (Levin and Wilson [1949] 1994).

7. John Storm Roberts recently published one of the first books dedicated exclusively to this subject (1999).

8. This taxonomy in part follows that of Lewis (1996, reprinted in this volume). For more on the late 1950s and 1960s, see also Kofsky 1998, Jost 1974, Litweiler 1990, and Monson 1998; on the AACM, see Kelley 1997, Radano 1993, and the AACM website; on Asian-American jazz and improvised music, see Asai 1997, Jang 1985–88, Masaoka 2000, Wong 1997, as well as the Asianimprov website; on European improvisers, see Jost 1987; on the "downtown" improvisers scene, see Zorn 2000, Litweiler 1990, and Gann 1997; on M-Base, see Iyer 1996 as well as Coleman's M-Base website. Also, on Pan-Africanism see Weinstein 1992 and Lewis 1998, and on "intercultural free improvisation" (specifically Evan Parker), see Stanyek 1999.

9. During the 1990s, many other North American and European musicians have followed Rosewoman's lead by initiating projects that center around religious Afrocuban genres, typically Lucumí (Santería) batá drumming and chant. These include Jane Bunnett (Canada), Nikki Yeoh (UK), Mark Alban Lotz (Netherlands), Kevin Diehl (USA), and Coleman (USA).

10. For more on how discourses of spirituality were utilized by African-American musicians to intervene in the critical discourses surrounding their work, see Porter 2002, chapters 5 and 6, and Monson, "Oh Freedom."

11. Although this quote is from an unpublished conference paper (Hernandez-Reguant 2000), Hernandez-Reguant's forthcoming dissertation (2001) deals in more depth with recent developments in Cuban culture industries.

12. ". . . invadieron a los Estados Unidos"; ". . . en segundo plano, como un acompañamiento atras"; "como parte primordial"; "lo contrario del jazz que se utilizó en los Estados Unidos anteriormente, en esos años." All subsequent comments by Chirino, Iyer, Jenkins, Pérez and Terry are from the interviews cited at the end of this paper, unless otherwise noted. All translations are my own.

13. Although dance is a central aspect of Cuban folkloric traditions, its role in this collaboration is beyond the scope of this article, in part because the only commercially released work from this collaboration was an audio CD.

14. Iyer was not involved with the project in Cuba but did perform this music on subsequent tours.

15. "Buscando nuevas formas, nuevas sonoridades. Porque la cultura Africana es muy rica. Se ha investigado, se ha desenterrado bastante, pero todavía queda mucho por descubrir."

16. Matanzas, a major industrial and port city, is an important cultural center in Cuba, particularly for folkloric traditions.

17. "El concepto de la música de Steve es muy fundamentado. Está fundamentado en algo. No es el concepto aquel que surge sobre la nada. Entonces, eso es una cosa que pasa por supuesto con la cultura Cubana, y la música Afrocubana principalmente. Que todo . . . está en función de algo. Todo está representando una energía, representando un santo, representando a un orisha, a algo, en específico."

18. "Kemetic" refers to the ancient civilization of Kemet. Coleman's ideas here come out of his studies of ancient cultures and their mystical, scientific, and philosophical traditions, including but not limited to those of Africa. While this is a broad and relatively esoteric area, a good starting point is Schwaller De Lubicz (1998).

19. See Jeff Bilmes, Iyer, Wright, and Wessel; Jeff Bilmes; Iyer. Iyer wrote his dissertation on rhythm perception and embodied cognition while simultaneously working as a sideman for Coleman. The notion of the "temporal atom" or "tatum" used in many of these studies comes from Jeff Bilmes, whose earlier thesis utilized a quantitative, computer-based analysis of a performance by Los Muñequitos de Matanzas, another well-known Cuban folkloric ensemble. Researchers at CNMAT—particularly director David Wessel—have also explored these rhythmic concerns in intercultural collaborations using new performance-based computer technologies and improvisation. See the CNMAT website.

20. For some examples of recent academic scholarship, see Taylor; Monson; Lipsitz; Feld; Meintjes; Guilbault; Erlmann; Slobin; Goodwin and Gore; Triaxium Writings (see Braxton 1985), and more recent writings by younger artists like Fred Ho, Miya Masaoka, and Vijay Iyer.

Works Cited

AACM Website. <http://aacmchicago.org/>. 20 July 2000.

Asai, Susan. "Sansei Voices in the Community." In *Musics of Multicultural America,* edited by Kip Lornell and Ann K. Rasmussen, 257–85. New York: Schirmer, 1997.

Asianimprov Website. <http://www.asianimprov.com/>. 20 July 2000.

Bailey, Derek. *Musical Improvisation: Its Nature and Practice in Music.* Englewood Cliffs, N.J.: Prentice-Hall, 1982.

Bilmes, Jeff. "Timing Is of the Essence: Perceptual and Computational Techniques for Representing, Learning, and Reproducing Expressive Timing in Percussive Rhythm." M.A. thesis, Massachusetts Institute of Technology, 1993.

Bilmes, Jeff, Vijay Iyer, Matt Wright, and David Wessel. "A Novel Representation for Rhythmic Structure." 1997. <http://cnmat.CNMAT.Berkeley.EDU/ICMC97/papers-html/Rhythm.html>. June 2001.

Braxton, Anthony. *Tri-Axium Writings.* Volume I. Synthesis Music, 1985.

Chirino, Francisco Zamora. Personal interview. 6 April 2000.

Coleman, Steve. Email to the author. 14 October 1999.

———. Personal communication. 10 May 2000.

———. Personal communication. 1 February 2001.

———. *The Sonic Language of Myth.* BMG, 74321–64123–2, 1999.

Coleman, Steve, with The Mystic Rhythm Society and AfroCuba de Matanzas. *The Sign and the Seal: Transmissions of the Metaphysics of a Culture.* RCAVictor, 74321–40727–2, 1996.

Erlmann, Veit. "The Aesthetics of the Global Imagination." *Public Culture* 8, no. 3 (1996): 467–87.

Feld, Steven. "Pygmy Pop: A Genealogy of Schizophonic Mimesis." *Yearbook for Traditional Music.* 28 (1996): 1–35.

———. Feld, Steven. "A Sweet Lullaby for World Music." *Public Culture* 12, no. 1 (2000): 145–171.

Gann, Kyle. *American Music in the Twentieth Century.* New York: Schirmer, 1997.

Gillespie, Dizzy. *Algo Bueno: Dizzy Gillespie Big Band.* Rec 1946–49. Definitive Records, DR2CD1138. (Reissued 1999).

Goodwin, Andrew, and Joe Gore. "World Beat and the Cultural Imperialism

Debate." In *Sounding Off!: Music as Subversion Resistance Revolution*, edited by Fred Wei-han Ho and Ronald B. Sakolsky, 121–132. New York: Autonomedia, 1995.

Guilbault, Jocelyne. *Zouk: World Music in the West Indies.* Chicago: University of Chicago Press, 1993.

Hall, Stuart. "New Ethnicities." In *Stuart Hall: Critical Dialogues in Cultural Studies*, edited by David Morley and Kuan-Hsing Chen, 441–49. London: Routledge, 1996.

Hernandez-Reguant, Ariana. "The Nostalgia of Buena Vista Social Club: Cuban Music and "World" Marketing." Presented at the International Association for the Study of Popular Music Meeting, Toronto, 2000.

———. "Radio Taino and the Globalization of the Cuban Culture Industries." Ph.D. diss., University of Chicago, 2001.

Ho, Fred Wei-han, and Ronald B. Sakolsky, eds. *Sounding Off! : Music as Subversion Resistance Revolution.* New York: Autonomedia, 1995.

Iyer, Vijay. "Microstructures of Feel, Macrostructures of Sound: Embodied Cognition in West African and African-American Musics." Ph.D. diss., University of California, Berekeley, 1998.

———. *Re-Imagining South Asian Diasporic Culture.* <http://cnmat.CNMAT.Berkeley.EDU/~vijay/reimagining.html>. 1 February 2001.

———. *Steve Coleman, M-Base, and Music Collectivism.* 1996. <http://www.cnmat.berkeley.edu/~vijay/toc.html>. 3 July 2000.

———. Telephone interview. 13 March 2000.

Jang, Jon. "We Don't All Sound Alike." *Views on Black American Music* 3 (1985–88): 33–38.

Jang, Jon, and Wong, Francis. "A Conversation with Jon Jang and Francis Wong (Interviewed by Nic Paget-Clarke)." *In Motion Magazine* (online magazine). 1997. <http://www.inmotionmagazine.com/jjfw1.html>. 18 October 2000.

Jenkins, Laila. Telephone interview. 20 March 2000.

Jost, Ekkehard. *Europas Jazz, 1960–1980.* Frankfurt: Fischer Taschenbuch, 1987.

———. *Free Jazz.* Graz: Universal Edition, 1974.

Keil, Charles, and Steven Feld. *Music Grooves: Essays and Dialogues.* Chicago: University of Chicago Press, 1994.

Kelley, Robin D. G. "Dig They Freedom: Meditations on History and the Black Avant-Garde." *Lenox Avenue* 3 (1997): 13–27.

Kofsky, Frank. *John Coltrane and the Jazz Revolution of the 1960s.* New York: Pathfinder, 1998.

Lateef, Yusef. "The Pleasures of Voice in Improvised Music." *Views on Black American Music* 3 (1985–88): 43–47.

Léon, Argeliers. "Notes toward a Panorama of Popular and Folk Musics." In *Essays on Cuban Music: North American and Cuban Perspectives*, edited by Peter Lamarche Manuel, 1–23. Lanham, Md.: University Press of America, 1991.

Levin, Michael, and John S. Wilson. "No Bop Roots in Jazz." *Downbeat* [1949] 1994: 24–25.

Lewis, George. "Improvised Music after 1950: Afrological and Eurological Perspectives." *Black Music Research Journal* 16, no. 1 (1996): 91–122.

———. "Singing Omar's Song: A (Re)Construction of Great Black Music." *Lenox Avenue* 4 (1998): 69–92.

Lipsitz, George. *Dangerous Crossroads: Popular Music, Postmodernism, and the Poetics of Place.* London: Verso, 1994.

Litweiler, John. *The Freedom Principle: Jazz after 1958.* New York: Da Capo, 1990.

Masaoka, Miya. "Notes from a Trans-Cultural Diary." In *Arcana: Musicians on Music*, edited by John Zorn, 153–166. New York: Granary Books, 2000.

M-Base Website. <http://www.m-base.com>. 20 July 2000.

Meintjes, Louise. "Paul Simon's Graceland, South Africa, and the Mediation of Musical Meaning." *Ethnomusicology* 34, no. 1 (1990): 37.

Monson, Ingrid. "Riffs, Repetitions, and Theories of Globalization." *Ethnomusicology* 43, no. 1 (1999): 31–65.

————. "Oh Freedom: George Russell, John Coltrane and Modal Jazz." In *In the Course of Performance,* edited by Bruno Nettl with Melinda Russell, 149–168. Chicago: University of Chicago Press, 1998.

Parker, Charlie with Machito and his Afrocuban Orchestra. *South of the Border.* Recorded 1949–1952. Verve, Reissue 1995.

Pérez, Ramon Garcia. Telephone interview. 26 June 2000.

Porter, Eric. *What Is This Thing Called Jazz?: African American Musicians as Artists, Critics, and Activists.* Berkeley and Los Angeles: University of California Press, 2002.

Radano, Ronald Michael. *New Musical Figurations : Anthony Braxton's Cultural Critique.* Chicago: University of Chicago Press, 1993.

Roberts, John Storm. *Latin Jazz: The First of the Fusions, 1880s to Today.* New York: Schirmer, 1999.

————. *The Latin Tinge: The Impact of Latin American Music on the United States.* New York: Oxford University Press, 1979.

Rosewoman, Michele. *Harvest.* Enja, 7069, 1993.

————. Telephone interview. 24 July 2000.

Rubalcaba, Gonzalo. *Antiguo.* Somethin' Else, CDP 7243 8 37717 2 1, 1998.

Schwaller De Lubicz, R. A. *The Temple of Man: Apet of the South at Luxor.* Translated by Deborah Lawlor and Robert Lawlor: Inner Traditions International, 1998.

Slobin, Mark. "Micromusics of the West: A Comparative Approach." *Ethnomusicology* 36, no. 1 (1992): 1–87.

Smith, Wadada Leo. *Notes (8 Pieces) / Source a New / World / Music: Creative Music.* 1973.

Stanyek, Jason. "Articulating Intercultural Free Improvisation: Evan Parker's *Synergetics* Project." *Resonance* 7, no. 2 (1999): 44–47.

Taylor, Timothy D. *Global Pop: World Music, World Markets.* New York: Routledge, 1997.

Terry, Yosvany. Telephone interview. 12 March 2000.

Weinstein, Norman. *A Night in Tunisia: Imaginings of Africa in Jazz.* Metuchen, N.J.: Scarecrow, 1992.

Wong, Deborah. "Just Being There: Making Asian American Space in the Recording Industry." In *Musics of Multicultural America,* edited by Kip Lornell and Ann K. Rasmussen, 257–85. New York: Schirmer, 1997.

Zorn, John, ed. *Arcana: Musicians on Music.* New York: Granary Books, 2000.

PART THREE

SOCIAL PRACTICE AND IDENTITY

MARK ANTHONY NEAL

"...A Way Out of No Way"
Jazz, Hip-Hop, and Black Social Improvisation

·⤳

The Black Church remains a dominant public institution for many African-Americans. Although the Black Church's furthering of a unique and autonomous religiosity is evident in its variant forms, such as the black Pentecostal or the African Methodist Episcopal (AME) traditions,[1] its impact has arguably been most pronounced in the secular world. To support such an observation one can invoke the largely undisputed expectation that black religious figures should legitimately embrace the role of public spokesperson or organic public intellectual—the noted antislavery activist the Reverend Henry Highland Garnett, who edited *The Clarion* in Troy, New York, during the 1820s, is but one example. In more recent years, further evidence of the Black Church's influence on the secular world can be gleaned from the example of Martin Luther King Jr., who deftly employed liberal Christian discourses with generous amounts of African-American–based rhetorical strategies to serve the interests of one of the most dramatic social mobilizations of the twentieth century.[2] But the Black Church's social impact can also be discerned in the everyday lives of African-Americans, where the church has provided the physical and psychic space for people to congregate and enjoy the comfort of close community while holding political meetings, having social dances, or merely playing cards. According to Evelyn Brooks Higginbotham, one example of the false dichotomy between the secular world and the Black Church is the way its economically disadvantaged members, "through vernacular discourses of religion ... waged a struggle over cultural authority that ultimately subverted the hegemonic values and aesthetic standards of the traditional Protestantism of the black middle class"(158–159). At the core of this subversion have been efforts to use the Black Church and black religious discourses to enhance diverse concepts of community for African-Americans. Notions of community were firmly embedded in some of the most basic expressive practices of the Black Church, especially in relation to improvisation. Using examples of strategies from various gospel quartets that have been a mainstay of twentieth-century African-American religious expression, Ray Allen suggests that "improvised drive sections allow lead singers to express their own personal feelings of Spirit-induced joy while simultaneously inviting their listeners to share in the experience. Lead singers employ drive sections as their final and most persuasive strategy for achieving social and spiritual union with their listeners" (313).[3] Allen's comments link black musical improvisation and the building and maintenance of black community. For my purposes here, I propose to explore how black popular music, particularly jazz and hip-hop, frames musical improvisation as an important social phenomenon drawing upon various forms of sociality geared toward building and maintaining community.

As early as the antebellum era, African-Americans were using a range of discourses of black spirituality and religiosity to negotiate the existential realities of black life in the United States. Such negotiations were often embodied in creative energies deployed by African-Americans to counteract the impositions of white supremacy, gender oppression, and exploitative labor practices. In song and in prayer this worldview was represented by the notion of "making a way out of no way" and other more contemporary adages such as "tryin' to make a dollar out of 15 cents." As Allen suggests, black expressive practices in the church "aim to transcend, at least temporarily, the temporal and spatial boundaries separating humankind from the almighty" (297). Borrowing Allen's distinctly religious argument, I argue that black communities have employed creative survival tactics or what I refer to as "social improvisation," which allows the use of inadequate and diminishing economic and spatial resources to create some semblance of an autonomous and transcendent relief, if only temporally, from the realities of impoverishment, racism, class hierarchies, and a host of other everyday threats. The creation of "imagined communities" in the rear of municipal surface transit, the use of fire hydrants to cool down during summertime heat, rent parties and church dinners used to raise funds for community members on the verge of eviction, or the cultivation of street corners and project lobbies as incubators of doo-wop and hip-hop, are but a few well-known examples of the practice of "social improvisation."[4]

Within the realm of black expressive culture(s) a worldview based on social improvisation is particularly notable, especially within the tradition of improvisation that informs the jazz aesthetic, rooted and incubated initially within black social spaces. Christopher Small notes that "when a musician improvises, the act of creation is experienced first hand, with the active participation of all those present, listeners as well as performers" (289). Because for many African-Americans the necessity to share restricted spaces was an unavoidable reality, the logic of segregation would suggest the absence of class hierarchy within black communities. On the contrary, however, such hierarchies did exist and musical improvisation in public venues often buttressed efforts to build and maintain community despite the intense stratification that undergirded community relations. Ingrid Monson adds that "by identifying with modernist notions of formal and stylistic rebellion," jazz musicians "provided a link between the social extremes of the African-American community" that collapsed the social and emotional distance between the black middle classes and the black working class and working poor (396). Comparing the lack of improvisation generally present in modern classical forms with the seemingly intrinsic improvisation in some African-American forms, Small suggests that improvisation is inherently connected to African-American traditions because "performers are free to choose within a number of styles and modes . . . the various styles of improvisation will not be separated, but flow instead into and feed one another, producing an interaction of idioms, which is to say, of communities, that is absent in the virtual monoculture" of contemporary classical music (291). This mode of collective cultural expression was powerfully facilitated by racial segregation and the need for people within those spaces to cultivate sites of leisure and psychic recovery such as jazz clubs (less defined along class lines) and churches (intensely defined by class allegiances).

Such dynamics are witnessed in the intimate exchanges that framed the emergence of bebop in the 1940s and the development of a distinct black youth culture in urban spaces where bebop was prominent and accessible. The idea that bebop artists were "anti-assimilationist" social critics was, as Monson argues, "embodied in and visualized through various sonic, visual, linguistic, and ideological markers. Any one of these markers could be taken to stand for a complex non-conformist attitude" (398). Thus, bebop musicians and the music they created were viable social models for the creative survival tactics that black urban youth, particularly impoverished youth, created in the 1940s. The migration process itself was often emblematic of the tensions and struggles that bebop musicians reified in a musical context. Reflecting on his own childhood migration from Arkansas to Detroit, Al Green writes of the experience of "leaving behind everything you've ever known for something you've never seen. Pulling up stakes and striking out to chase the rumor of a better life can only be the desperate act of people who've got nothing left to lose" (Green and Seay, 57). What I am suggesting is that faced with the traumas of dislocation (produced largely by the dynamic of migration) and marginalization (because of the racial, gender, and economic realities of their experiences), black urban youth embraced bebop culture as a mechanism to counter the most egregious features of those experiences, allowing them to create an oppositional, though not an unproblematic, subculture of resistance. It is my contention that such embrasures remain integral to black youth culture today.

It is not my intention to romanticize the struggle of black youth during this era. Roi Ottley, one of the most cited chroniclers of life in Harlem in the 1940s, is straightforward in his assertion that the "products of poverty, overcrowding, ignorance, and lack of adequate health facilities are illness and crime" (157). To buttress his point, Ottley cites the example of Lee Edward Wilkes, who, as a homeless boy living in Harlem, engaged in forms of petty crime and ultimately accidentally killed a white man whom Wilkes and his friends mugged of seventeen cents and his suit (161–163). Rather than a romanticized narrative of resistance, I wish to pursue some theoretical perspectives deriving from the connection between black youth resistance in its variant forms and forms of improvisation in popular music. Bebop and hip-hop, as musical genres, are thoroughly imbricated in the social transformations that marked black communities during the migration periods of the pre– and post–World War II eras and the postindustrial era of the 1970s.

Bebop or Be Dead: The Rhythm(s) and Improvisation of U.S. Black Youth Culture in the 1940s

In the 1940s, black youth were generally regarded as younger representations of commonly held stereotypes of blacks that existed within mainstream culture. Donald Bogle writes that the "pickaninny was the first of the coon types to make its screen debut. It gave the Negro child actor his place in the black pantheon . . . he was a harmless little screwball creation" (16). The images of the "sambo" were initially conveyed through racist illustrations in Helen Bannerman's "classic" *Little Black Sambo,* and "pickaninnies" were integral to the dynamics of early twentieth-century advertising and mainstream popular culture. Despite the presence of these images, notions of a distinct youth culture within the black experience did not emerge until the late 1930s and early 1940s.[5] Indeed, the sambo and pickaninny alternately represented younger versions of Jim Crow, Jezebel, and Zip Coon. Those images were updated and distributed to suit mainstream society's often paradoxical notions of racial difference in efforts to counter African-American achievement and empowerment and serve as valuable commodities within the burgeoning mass culture industries of popular music and literature, film, and museum exhibition.[6] Such efforts to control and curtail the political and social aspirations of the black community were rooted in mainstream reactions to black migration to urban centers and to the emerging optimism that could be discerned in black middle-class notions of "New Negroness."

Coming of age after more than a decade of unprecedented migration into northern cities, the first generation of black youth born in urban centers like Harlem were articulating desires and needs that were often at odds with the "promised land" ideals so central to the lives of their parents. While their parents and others were initially driven by desires for economic opportunity and liberal notions of race relations, the increasingly disaffected and militant generation of black youth that emerged was the direct product of the changing demographics of depression-era urban spaces and the inability of the federal government and black mainstream organizations (like the Urban League and the NAACP) to advance strategies that truly countered economic collapse in black communities. Roi Ottley made the point at the time that "unrest in the adult population is often reflected by the children. Some are hypersensitive to the bitterness and rebellion of their parents, who they feel have received unfair treatment at the hands of white people. In one sense, then, juvenile crime is an inarticulate protest of the most depressed elements" (159). The well-known feud between NAACP director Walter White and NAACP founding member W. E. B. Du Bois, which led to the resignation of the latter as editor of *Crisis* in June 1934, was largely predicated on Du Bois's suggestion that the NAACP lacked a relevant and coherent economic policy to address poverty among blacks in the wake of the depression.[7]

No segment of the black community was more impacted by the failure of black leadership and the state to address impoverishment than black youth. Federal policies that often denied depression-era relief to families with a working male made it increasingly difficult for black male family heads to remain present in their households; as Ottley suggests, "men had lost their self-respect, pride, dignity, and dependence, and with this came loss of authority in the family—which eventually brought about desertion and broken homes" (155). Given the extent to which the black community was invested in the pursuit of a normative patriarchy, at least within the context of the American mainstream, it is not surprising that "able-bodied men, unable to support their families by their own toil," would pursue "petty crime and vice" to achieve some semblance of economic support for their families (155). Black male responses to these conditions are directly correlated to increasing rates of delinquency, neglect, and criminality among black urban youth; more than 3,200 black youth were arrested during the first five years of the 1930s alone (Brandt, 41).

Furthermore, as Nat Brandt argues in his popular history of Harlem during World War II, urban educational policies often actively eroded the value of educating black children by unevenly appropriating federal monies, with the overwhelming amount going to distinctly "white" school districts, despite the fact that depression-era New York may have had the largest population of urban-based youth in any city in the United States (40–41). Many such children became working-age youth as the 1940s progressed and World War II dawned. Eventually an oppositional culture of "street" survival emerged among some black urban youth, in part as a response to the lived experiences of unemployment, police brutality, racism, and poverty. In many ways, the survival strategies within this subculture embraced the same "make a way out of no way" adages, popularized within the Black Church traditions, that had been so integral to the survival of enslaved black communities centuries earlier. In the absence of viable progressive leadership within some urban spaces, this worldview, which I referred to earlier as a mode of social improvisation, embodied the increased radicalization of black youth in ways that were clearly problematic but that represented political resistance, no matter how unsophisticated. Arguably, "Bigger Thomas," the central character of Richard Wright's *Native Son,* could be considered the prototypical example of a disaffected black youth in the 1940s. The book is drawn from Wright's own experiences of witnessing young blacks who challenged Jim Crow segregation in the south and young black boys at the South Side Boys' Club in Chicago during the 1930s. Wright explains that "the Bigger Thomases were the only Negroes I know of who consistently violated the Jim Crow laws of the south and got away with it, at least for a sweet brief spell" (xi).

African-American youth culture has rarely been driven by ideological programs but instead has embraced existing structures that African-American youth perceived as potentially empowering within various social, cultural, and economic constructs—or at least as offering temporal transcendence from the material realities of black youth (Alexander, 104–105). I would suggest that this ability is a structural component of black youth culture. Prior to World War II, African-American youth culture was largely hidden from mainstream culture, subsumed within the parameters of segregated black spaces. The Zoot Suit riots and the explosion of bebop music represented the first real glimpse into African-American youth culture for those beyond the confines of segregated urban spaces. Though bebop was an aesthetic movement driven by the sensibilities of black male musicians, the movement was given its energy and stylistic acumen by

African-American youth who embraced the movement as a form of transcendence/resistance from the everyday drudgery of an impoverished existence. Zoot suits, the lindy-hop, and jive all provided opportunities for African-American youth to be active participants in the subculture that bebop music provided.

Harlem's *Amsterdam-Star News* captured the general tenor of the early 1940s in this way: "Where there was once tolerance and acceptance of a position believed to be gradually changing for the better, now the Negro is showing a 'democratic upsurge of rebellion,' bordering on open hostility" (quoted in Ottley, 306). Ottley, in his study of black life in America published shortly before the Harlem Riot of 1943, writes: "Listen to the way Negroes are talking these days! Gone are the Negroes of the old banjo and singin' roun' the cabin doors . . . Instead black men have become noisy, aggressive, and sometimes defiant" (306). The new energies associated with black expression at the dawn of the United States's involvement in World War II, while largely instigated by the burgeoning militancy of black youth, was also buoyed by general optimism among African-Americans regarding their potential service in the war effort, playing roles in both the war industries and the battlefield (Lewis, 3–24). These sensibilities are captured in the concept of "Double V"—victory abroad and victory at home—victories that were denied the first generation of northern migrants at the close of World War I. The black public's demands for equality, symbolically represented in the planned 1941 march on Washington organized by former African Blood Brotherhood member and president of the Brotherhood of Sleeping Car Porters A. Phillip Randolph, were realized with Franklin D. Roosevelt's signing of Executive Order 8802, which guaranteed fair hiring practices in both wartime industry and government. Despite real gains for African-Americans, as witnessed by Roosevelt's signing of this order, the burgeoning militancy within black youth culture, compounded by natural senses of isolation and alienation among black urban youth, helped create a subculture appropriate to the conditions of urban malaise, dislocation, and social isolation.

Culled from the covert spaces of Minton's Playhouse, Monroe's Uptown, and Small's Paradise—spaces that were ultimately efforts to re-create the covert black publics of the American South—bebop, with its requisite examples of jive, zoot suits, and heroin, attempted to subvert musically and thus counteract the impact of being distanced from familiar people and places. Lewis Gordon sheds some light on the power of social spaces like Minton's and Small's in his assertion that jazz has "a politics all its own. Total strangers can meet, choose a tune, and strike up a performance that seems almost magic. A form of virtue-based democracy emerges. . . . The community, the musical moment, the people assembled, all understand that the music is to be played, and played well. A good jazz performance is a moment of and for communal celebration" (219). The intense rhythmic sounds found within these social spaces became sites that not only incubated oppositional tendencies but provided a safe haven and community for disaffected black youth. The music itself may have been a natural conduit for the alienated sensibilities of black youth given the desires of bebop's core figures to create a musical culture that was distinct from the swing tradition that had come to dominate jazz.

In his book *Blues People*, Amiri Baraka (LeRoi Jones) suggests that "Parker, Monk, and the others seemed to welcome the musical isolation that historical social isolation certainly should have predicated" (191–192). Bebop as a practice and a cultural artifact helped re-create the vitality of the covert social spaces of both the rural south and the urban cities, allowing for the creation of havens or "safe spaces" where "community" could be re-constituted. In her text examining African-American migration narratives, Farah Jasmine Griffin suggests that "safe space" could be found in the "song, oral culture, memory, dreams and spirituality, of African-American migrants during the 20th century" (111). One of the most visceral examples of the power of "safe space" could be discerned in the Creole language of new migrants, jazz musicians, and other fellow travelers. Eric Lott writes: "The shock of relocation was 'handled' by the common language that musicians developed—styles of dress, music, drugs, and speech homologous with the structures of their experience . . . such a common language became a closed hermeneutic that had the undeniable effect of alienating the riff-raff and expressing a sense of felt isolation, all the while affirming a collective purpose" (247). Furthermore, as Small suggests, bebop musicians created a musical language closed off from musicians unfamiliar with bebop sensibilities, adding that "it was as if someone had taken a familiar vocabulary and, by altering the syntax by means of which the relationships between the words were established, had created a new language, tantalizingly similar to the old, but one in which they [the older musicians] were unable to converse" (303).

Perhaps one way to think through these musical strategies and their connection to social practice is to examine the ways in which black youth have cultivated their identity in relation to practices of structured—in the case of organized athletics—and unstructured play. In an examination of Michael Jordan's "aesthetics" on the basketball court, Michael Eric Dyson asserts that there are "three defining characteristics" of Jordan's style of play that are influenced by African-American culture: the "will to spontaneity . . . the way acts of apparently random occurrence are spontaneously and imaginatively employed," the "stylization of the performed self," and the "subversion of perceived limits through the use of edifying deception" (*Reflecting*, 67–68). Dyson further suggests that acts of improvisation, stylized performative gestures, and a willingness to "deceive" and find some visceral pleasure in those acts of deception are integral to some of the strategies that African-Americans, in this case African-American males, employ in an effort to assert themselves into the world, be it Michael Jordan on the stage of the NBA or young black men in the 1940s who posited the street and the dance hall as their stages. For my purposes here, I would argue that the attributes Dyson outlines in his essay could be considered under the rubric of making a "way out of no way"—acts of social improvisation that when employed by black youth during the 1940s were "safe spaces" in their own right. I am particularly interested in Dyson's notions of the stylized performative self and the use of acts of deception and the ways these skills were crucial for the ability of black youth in the era to both survive urban life and at the same time construct and assert their identities. These two sensibilities were deeply imbricated: the practice of "edifying deception" disturbs "widely understood boundaries through mesmerization and alchemy, a subversion of common perceptions of the culturally or physically possible through the creative and deceptive manipulation of appearance" (Dyson, *Reflecting*, 68–69). Dyson's perception is supported by Griffin's notion that "safe spaces" were "'safe time' as well. . . . In these spaces linear notions of time are challenged" (111). It is important to reinforce that these were not "spaces" where black youth articulated clearly defined political intent; until the stirrings of the post–World War II civil rights movement there is little indication that youth worked in concert with each other on the sophisticated level usually expected of political insurgents. I am not arguing that black youth in the 1940s were distinct political agents, but rather suggesting that there were political connotations, if only in the arena of constructing and reconstructing—improvising—viable and meaningful personal and group identities, that can illuminate the ways in which more concrete youth politics (such as those witnessed during the civil rights movement) and less concrete politics (such as those of the "hip-hop" generation) can be better differentiated.

Taking a riff from the cliché that the personal is political, I would suggest that "play" or leisure and the cultivation of spaces to engage in play and leisure can also be political. Claire Alexander makes the point that the actual "form and content" of youth leisure spaces is not so important as the way they are "manipulated by individuals to articulate a self-image which in turn expresses a stance on wider concerns" (120). Historically, most accessible spaces for urban youth, regardless of race, have been urban streets themselves. The history of urban play features examples ranging from games such as "double-dutch," where young girls and boys jump over a pair of jump ropes to improvised and syncopated rhythms to street corner harmonizing and graffiti art. But the actual identities of the participants also informed how much freedom youth and children would be allowed to express themselves. Clearly, given the general demonization of black and Latino males at various historical moments, activities such as "tagging" buildings, street corner harmonizing, and creating hip-hop "ciphers" were not simply interpreted as black youth joyously expressing themselves. Griffin adds that "even migrant-defined 'safe spaces' fall under the authority of the dominant society" but even more so during periods when black youth were generally perceived as undermining that authority; hence Griffin's acknowledgment that "safe spaces may play an important role in assisting migrants to resist dominant constructions of them" (103). Thus, many of the efforts at "play" by black youth in the 1940s also entailed elements of risk.

Robin Kelley's description of black youth disrupting public transportation in the city of Birmingham during this era immediately comes to mind as one example of how "playful" activities were not simply games but efforts for those black youth to have an impact on the everyday functions of a city that helped define segregation in the south.[8] How many of those youth may have perceived themselves in such a context as adults allowing them to become participants in the civil rights movement a decade or more later? Small responds that the exclusive nature of bebop music and the black youth who embraced it inspired a "greater freedom and intimacy among those who could cope with the new twists of language, an intimacy that was not unconnected with the first stirrings of the modern black civil rights movement. . . . The new musical forms and relationships articulated and celebrated new social relationships in which the blacks, free to love one another like brother and sister, at the same time received the respect that was their due" (303). While Small's characterization of these elements is arguably drenched in a sentimentality that betrays the difficult struggles of blacks in the post–World War II period, he is correct in his assertion that the era emboldened black youth to become more compelling actors in the ongoing drama that defines race relations in the United States.

Malcolm X is probably the best example of a post–World War II political icon who was shaped in part by the social resistance of black youth in the 1940s, although he would later repudiate many of the activities of his youth. Historically, Malcolm X's political maturation has been attributed to the influence of the Nation of Islam, initially during his imprisonment, and later as a devoted follower and national spokesperson for Elijah Muhammed. Such an interpretation of Malcolm X's political development erases the obvious childhood influences of his family, particularly his father, a member of Marcus Garvey's United Negro Improvement Association and, more significant, the impact that urban black youth culture of the 1940s had on Malcolm X's subsequent emergence as political spokesperson and human rights activist. As Kelley suggests in his essay on the cultural politics of the 1940s, "whether or not Malcolm acknowledged the political importance of that era on his own thinking . . . his participation in the underground subculture of black working-class youth during the war was not a detour on the road to political consciousness but rather an essential element of his radicalization" (163). While Malcolm X could not acknowledge the reality of his political development, owing in part to the essentialist demands of Nation of Islam instruction, the true legacy of his political incubation within black youth culture was later manifested in his centrality to some black youth cultures in the late 1980s and early 1990s, particularly as represented in some genres of hip-hop.

In this regard, some of the stylistic excesses associated with African-American youth culture were conscious efforts to deconstruct and critique mass-mediated images of African-American youth. Such was the case with the zoot suit, which became the most prominent uniform of black urban militancy within black youth culture. The context of this militancy was a rationing act by the War Production Board in March 1942 that attempted to regulate the excessive use of fabrics that contained cotton by instituting a 26% reduction in the use of those fabrics. The law essentially outlawed zoot suits, which were partly defined by their bright colors, longish jackets, and baggy pants. In his work on the geopolitics that undergirded the Zoot Suit riot of 1943 in Los Angeles, Eduardo Obregon Pagan argues that the "zoot suit became a shorthand in the written and articulated discourse of the politically dominant over hegemonic concerns about public safety and the social relations upon which both 'public' and 'safety' rested" (248). According to Stuart Cosgrove, the strident divisions between American military staff and black and Mexican youth gangs or "Pachucos" that led to the eruption of violence in California in 1943 was predicated on the perception that the "chino shirt and battledress were evidently uniforms of patriotism, whereas wearing a Zoot-suit was a deliberate and public way of flouting the regulations of rationing" (80). According to Mauricio Mazon, "Pachucos" were the Chicano equivalent to the Harlem-based youth described as "Teddy Boys," adding that the "zoot-suiter . . . disrupted the roles assigned to adolescents" (7). Rendered as the "other" within mainstream culture, black youth embraced this site of "otherness" in order to radicalize their identities in ways that would further oppositional perceptions of black youth culture. In other words, if black youth culture was to be identified as "oppositional" or deviant from mainstream culture, black youth would embrace such oppositionality on their own terms via stylistic excesses such as brightly colored zoot suits with wide-brim hats and doo-rags that in and of themselves represented conscious critiques, if not rejections, of mainstream interpretations of black youth. As the fashion magazine *Tailor and Cutter* would observe, the style of zoot suits "consists of making everything bigger and brighter and bolder and louder than anyone has ever attempted" (quoted in Chibnall 61). In this regard black youth became bigger, bolder, louder, and much more visible in an era that was noted for its neglect of them and of their issues.

Ironically, the comment in *Tailor and Cutter* was made in 1948, five years after the Zoot Suit riots and three years after the end of the war. The comment powerfully addresses how aspects of black and Latino youth cultures, demonized when connected to those populations, were being mainstreamed to broader consumers. The comparative move of "bebop" downtown from Harlem to Fifty-second Street in the late 1940s had the same effect of mainstreaming the sounds and rhythms of what was largely an oppositional culture. Monson writes that to the "extent that well-meaning white Americans have confused the most 'transgressive' aspects of African American culture with its true character, they fall into the trap of viewing blackness as an absence. Whether conceived as an absence of morality or of bourgeois pretensions, this view of blackness, paradoxically, buys into the historical legacy of primitivism and its concomitant exoticism of the 'Other'" (398). Oppositional cultural politics were thus relegated to emblems of style, be they the clothes worn by white jazz musicians or their presence in animated shorts such as the *Tom and Jerry* series or Tex Avery's classic *Three Little Pigs*. This commodification of oppositional practices is also a structural component of black youth culture that has, ironically, informed mass culture's uses of black youth culture in the realm of fashion and other forms of popular expression like music, dance, hairstyles, and language, particularly as such expressions are parlayed into mass consumables. In this context, black youth remain the "Other," but this "Other" is now contained and thus reproduced, distributed, and consumed in the open markets where commodities and popular opinions are exchanged, serving both corporate and public policy interests.

Many meanings were attributed to black youth culture in the aftermath of the Harlem, Detroit, and Los Angeles Zoot Suit riots of 1943, some of which simply related the riots to the deviant nature of black youth and, by extension, to African-American culture generally. In many regards, the period represented a complex historical moment in which the militancy that pervaded much of black life manifested itself in youthful and often illicit resistance, artistic innovation, and challenges to Jim Crow America. But the period also highlighted a clear distance between the sensibilities of black youth and a politically mainstream black middle class. As Ralph Ellison notes in his oft-cited analysis of the riots of 1943, "much in Negro life remains a mystery; perhaps the Zoot suit conceals profound political meaning; perhaps the symmetrical frenzy of the Lindy Hop conceals clues to great potential power—if only Negro leaders would solve this riddle" (301). Ellison suggests that mainstream leadership was unable or unwilling to understand or address the increasing stratification within the black community and the reality that this distance would ultimately impede full communal empowerment as black youth were increasingly marginalized politically and socially within public life. Ellison's observations also suggest that the improvised making and remaking of black youth identities represented distinct generational differences in how various elements within the black community negotiated the new cultural, social, and political terrains that migration inaugurated and that post–World War II cultural politics put into greater focus.

"Not Even a Flow No More . . . It's Fluent": Hip-Hop, Freestylin', and Social Flow

As the music starts to fade at the end of his collaboration with De La Soul on the song "The Bizness," Common casually states: "It's not even a flow no more, it's fluent." In her work on the "play" of young black girls, Kyra Gaunt suggests that "play is considered an experience or act that is performed for its own sake, for pleasure and reward known as flow. The rewards for experiencing flow are said to be intrinsic, often marked by imaginative creativity, improvisation, and adventurousness." (148). Here, Common references "flow"—lyrical flow—to acknowledge the very energies of creativity and improvisation that have become a feature of hip-hop culture and music. As Gaunt adds, hip-hop artists "use flow to communicate the feeling of a never ending performance. Flow . . . is not simply about random improvisation, formless and idle" (148). Within this context, I would suggest that the modes of social improvisation engaged by black youth of the 1940s have morphed into a language of improvisation that is openly craved and acknowledged in contemporary hip-hop. I highlight the closing moments of "The Bizness" because Common's comments suggest that not only is lyrical flow not "random;" it is also evidence of a shared fluency that has been elevated to an acceptable "language" of creativity and improvisation that extends from the lyrical performances within hip-hop to the larger social terrains that the artists and their audiences inhabit.

Todd Boyd argues for an explicit connection between jazz improvisation and the practice of freestyling within hip-hop: within jazz, he suggests, "you are required to improvise, to create your own form of expression by using other bits of information as they inspire you . . . in this way jazz and rap are similar. As jazz improvises, rap emphasizes the freestyle, an impromptu lyrical explosion that is defined by its spontaneity" (19). Female Rap artist T-Love describes freestyling as the "ability to rhyme straight from the top of the head, as opposed to rapping lyrics which have been previously written and memorized." She locates the importance of freestyling to the "livelihood of true hiphop music" in its ability to "keep the form alive by encouraging creative competition," its role in defining the distinctions between MCs and rappers, and by aiding the "feat of never letting people forget where hip-hop/rap came from." According to her, the difference between rappers and MCs lies in the latter's ability to improvise successfully as opposed to reciting already mapped-out narratives. T-Love's distinction between the "rapper" and the MC acknowledges some of the tension around the transition of hip-hop from a localized "authentic" live art, one more or less connected to the everyday practices of black youth, to one that is increasingly mediated by global market forces where "authenticity" is stylized to meet the desires and demands of global consumers. T-Love clearly suggests that MCs represent practitioners of an authentic folk art who are "committed to all facets of the music form, not just the ones that earn the duckets (money)" (Cross, 306).

As it relates to the issue of social improvisation, T-Love's comments place into crisis easily decipherable distinctions between a "freestyle" that is risky (and perhaps haphazard and unstructured) and one that is more fully cognizant of the social and physical terrains that it is responsive to (including the inherent dangers of those terrains) while continuing to find value in the instability and risk-taking that improvisation naturally engenders. Boyd resolves this crisis partially in his comments about hip-hop sampling "where preexisting forms of music are incorporated into the contemporary as a way of enhancing the overall project. As with improvisation, the original is useful not as an object of sacred devotion but as a way of motivating contemporary expression . . . the improviser and the sampler are judged on their ability to recontextualize" (10). Boyd's comments recover a concept of improvisation that is critically engaged but still connected to risk-taking. This distinction is important within hip-hop and black youth culture(s) because it endows the purveyors of hip-hop and its organic audiences with a sense of agency often missing in analyses of these populations. Boyd's insights also make T-Love's suggestion that freestyling connects hip-hop to specific local and cultural landscapes more significant because her comment suggests that freestyling may be one of the ways that hip-hop artists and black youth negotiate these landscapes.

Tricia Rose suggests that the broad range of practices within hip-hop culture—namely rapping, graffiti art, break dancing, and DJing/producing—are stylistically interconnected through attention to flow, layering, and ruptures in lines: within hip-hop, "visual, physical, musical, and lyrical lines are set in motion, broken abruptly with sharp angular breaks, yet they sustain motion and energy through fluidity and flow" (38). Rose's comments are useful in theorizing social improvisation in an urban context because they highlight an aesthetic logic that privileges instability and dislocation with some semblance of continuity. According to Rose, the aforementioned attributes of hip-hop culture "create and sustain rhythmic motion, continuity, and circularity via flow; accumulate, reinforce, and embellish this continuity through layering; and manage threats to these narratives by building in ruptures that highlight the continuity as it momentarily challenges it" (38). For Rose, these elements are productive from a theoretical standpoint because they suggest on the "level of style and aesthetics . . . affirmative ways in which profound social dislocation and rupture can be managed and perhaps contested in the cultural arena" (39).

Rose's speculations support my own theories about the relationship between aesthetic choices within some subgenres of hip-hop (most notably "gangsta" rap) and the real challenges and obstacles faced by black youth in urban settings. For some urban youth, these challenges necessitate hustling and the ability to analytically and critically read urban landscapes in ways that produce creative options for survival and forms of social resistance that are improvised and not planned. I am not simply conceiving of resistance in the strict sense of the word, but rather a resistance that is inclusive of the pursuit of pleasure: in other words, a form of resistance predicated on political and existential survival that values pleasure and in fact finds pleasure in resistance. Rose argues as much when she suggests that hip-hop practitioners and audiences are "prepared for rupture, find pleasure in it, in fact, plan on social rupture" (39); furthermore, she implores critics to "imagine these hip-hop principles as a blueprint for social resistance and affirmation" that creates sustaining narratives and accumulates, layers, embellishes, and transforms them (39).

The obstacles that necessitate a social and aesthetic vision that embraces ruptures and disconnections include those posed by the very logic of urban landscapes and the ongoing desire by the state to police those landscapes and the brown and black bodies that inhabit them. In the most simplistic terms, the progenitors of early hip-hop music never knew when the plug would be pulled, most likely by law enforcement officers, from the lamppost where they siphoned off electricity for their informal public "jams." S. Craig Watkins writes that the "creators of hip-hop devoted immense energy to carving out spaces of pleasure and recreation in the face of an eroding urban infrastructure . . . accentuating what analysts claim is one of the central themes in the movement: the struggle over public space, who occupies it, and how its resources are put to use" (67). Houston A. Baker Jr. makes explicit connections to struggles over public space and the surveillance of black bodies in his facetious reading to the 1989 Central Park rape case in which several black youth were accused and convicted of sexually attacking a Wall Street investment banker in the park in an act of "wilding." With tongue firmly in cheek, Baker writes: "Wilding. How ominously uncivil and antipublic it sounds! Yet how commensurate with the site of its invention. Wasn't the idea of the park as urban space precisely to preserve some frisson of 'the wild' for citizens with Wall Street connections? Further, don't the very 'natural' configurations of the park as civil space suggest a controlled 'wildness'?" (46). Baker's sarcastic comments underline the ongoing efforts to contain the energy and movement of black urban populations, particularly black youth. For black youth who are subjected to surveillance and efforts to contain them, their predators are not always clearly defined. As John L. Jackson Jr. observes, "The police always seem to be playing hide-and-seek with the public. One moment it is a silent night, dark, almost dank; the police are ever cloaked and camouflaged, waiting to pounce on any wrongdoer" (179).

The ways in which hip-hop artists meld social improvisation with aesthetic choices are most compellingly captured on a narrative level. No genre has done this more effectively within hip-hop music than "gangsta" or hardcore rap. In particular, I want to focus on a distinct subgenre of gangsta rap; namely, that produced in New York beginning with the release of the Notorious B.I.G.'s *Ready to Die* in 1994. I am primarily interested in mid-1990s East Coast "gangsta" rap because of its fixation with the built environment of postindustrial urban spaces, its emotional proximity to 1950s hard-bop jazz, and, finally, its commercial appeal. The music of Gangstarr featuring Guru and DJ Premier and later that of Notorious B.I.G. (aka "Biggie"), Nas and Jay-Z represented a distinct moment in hip-hop that was a direct response to styles popularized by West Coast–based acts such as NWA (Nigga With an Attitude), Ice Cube, Snoop Doggy Dogg, and producer Dr. Dre (Andre Young). While East Coast "gangsta" rap appropriated elements of its West Coast counterpart, particularly the lurid details of drug dealing and street hustling, it distinguished itself in key ways. On the level of narrative, East Coast hip-hop in the mid-1990s privileged the kind of postindustrial landscape of cities such as New

York and Philadelphia, which is distinct from the postindustrial terrain of Los Angeles and its surrounding communities of Compton, Long Beach, and Watts.

Referencing one aspect of the differences between the two styles of hip-hop, Brian Cross writes that "large park jams were possible, but only under the watchful eye of the city authorities. Public space is different in LA. Cruisin' in a kitted out ride (car) is a popular pastime. Graffiti are more common on the freeways than on public transport" (20). Cross's comments suggest that West Coast hip-hop was less fixated with the built environment than its East Coast counterpart. David Harvey describes the built environment as a "bundle of resources . . . streets and sidewalks, drains and sewer systems, parks and playgrounds" (47). Most important to my concerns, Harvey also notes that the "built environment requires collective management and control, and it is therefore almost certain to be a primary field of struggle between capital and labor over what is good for accumulation and what is good for the people" (47). Harvey's comments partially explain the fixation within most "gangsta" rap (and East Coast "gangsta" rap in particular) with capital accumulation and gaining control of the illicit and illegal sites of that accumulation within a context where "legitimate" capital accumulation has little positive effect on their lived realities.

Second, West Coast hip-hop largely appropriated the mid-1970s funk of Parliament Funkedelic and later groups such as Roger Troutman's Zapp as witnessed in Dr. Dre's "Let Me Ride," which borrows profusely from the music of George Clinton and Parliament and his collaboration with Troutman on the production of Tupac Shakur's "California Love." East Coast producers and artists preferred a more minimalist—some would say cerebral and layered—sound. Producer Pete Rock's rich horn arrangements, drawn from the music of Tom Scott on Pete Rock and CL Smooth's "They Reminisce Over You," is but one example of this. In this regard I am also interested in the East Coast "gangsta" rap of the mid-1990s because of its affinity to hard bop, or what I refer to as East Coast hip-hop's minimalist hard-bop sensibilities. In his book on hard bop, David Rosenthal notes that the genre generally featured "sinuously minor melodies and strong rhythmic patterning" (39). He adds that hard bop was the "basic idiom" of black urban youth in the late 1950s and the early 1960s because it was "expressive. It was sometimes bleak, often tormented, but always cathartic; and it was 'bad' (sinister, menacing) in the sense that James Brown was 'bad'" (63). Rosenthal's comments point to a stripped-down minimalist sound that was also highly expressive of some of the basic sentiments contained in black urban communities, particularly in East Coast cities. Rosenthal also highlights the comments of jazz critics during the hard-bop era who aligned hard bop with "unalloyed hatred," adding that "as the word 'hard' suggests, it gave an opening to darker emotions than he would find in Louis Armstrong or even Charlie Parker" (129). Though it never matched the commercial appeal of artists like Dr. Dre, Snoop Doggy Dogg, and NWA at their peaks, it is nevertheless crucial to theorize around commercially successful texts like East Coast "gangsta" or hardcore rap—even considering the value of T-Love's earlier distinctions between MCs and rappers—as opposed to more esoteric choices because the sheer popularity of the former suggests that these narratives were more influential on urban audiences, who were likely more responsive to these texts.

Like hard bop two generations earlier, East Coast "gangsta" rap narratives featured a brooding introspection that raised critical questions about the existential conditions that necessitated street hustling and drug dealing. For example, Notorious B.I.G.'s (aka "Biggie") "Everyday Struggles" features the chorus "I don't wanna live no more / Sometimes I hear death knockin' at my front do' / I'm living every day like a hustle, another drug to juggle / another day, another struggle."[9] Largely autobiographical, the chorus captures Biggie's anxieties about his life as drug dealer and the urgency in which he lives that life in order to sustain himself—as urgent as impending death. Thus, he hustles and improvises his way through the postindustrial urban landscape in order to ward off a death, both economic and physical, that will surely consume him, regardless, if he stays in the "drug game." Later in the song, Biggie explains his rationale for violence, stating that "Glock nineteen for casket and flower moves / for chumps tryin' to stop my flow." In this particular instance, "flow" is connected to Biggie's activities as a drug runner or, in other words, as a form of social flow. He is specifically involved in the "drug game" because he has a "baby on the way mad bills to pay." For Biggie the drug trade was a logical site to create economic opportunities for himself. Given its illegal and illicit nature the drug trade necessitated those within the "game" to develop the talent to improvise socially in order to remain beyond the radar of law enforcement, rival drug dealers, and antagonistic community members. As Biggie notes in the introduction to "Juicy," "Yeah this album is dedicated to all the teachers that told me I'd never amount to nothin', to all the people that lived above the buildings that I was hustlin' in front of that called the police on me when I was just tryin' to make some money to feed my daughter."[10]

Biggie's narratives about hustling articulate an accessible language that both reflects and influences the contours of social improvisation or social "freestylin'" in the communities where his music is consumed and revered by black youth. In fact, these improvised blueprints are validated by their presence in mass culture, particularly given perceived correlations between Biggie's success in the drug game and his ability to "come up" in the world of hip-hop. Referencing Sudhir Venkatesh's work on black gangs in Chicago, I would suggest that Biggie's narratives and those of others of his ilk put into place narrative maps of social improvisation or flow that, to Venkatesh, would "enable them to reproduce a lifestyle in accordance with their own visions of morality, right, justice, and social order. In other words, their practices helped create the larger contextual structures that (in turn) shaped their experiences" (101). Contrary to T-Love's definition of authentic hip-hop, Biggie articulates a notion of the "authentic" rooted in his ability to provide autobiographical examples of his social flow. Much of Notorious B.I.G.'s debut *Ready to Die* narrated his transition from street-level drug dealer to best-selling hip-hop artist, so that throughout the recording the artist conflates representations of social flow with those of artistic flow, like that embodied in a hip-hop performance. For instance, on the track "Things Done Changed" Biggie raps "If I wasn't in the drug game / I'd probably be knee deep in the crack game."[11] Not just simply metaphors for real-world hustling, Biggie's narratives suggest an intimate relationship between successful social flow and credible lyrical flow—and they suggest a direct correlation between his social improvisation and his lyrical improvisation.

In one example from the track "The What," which features Wu Tang Clan member Method Man, Biggie raps: "Playin' the villain / prepare for this rap killing / Biggie Smalls is the illest / Your style is played out. . . . The thrill is gone, the black Frank White is here to excite. . ."[12] In the lyric, Biggie compares his dexterity as a rap artist to that of murderer or villain, suggesting that his emergence as an elite rapper is like the emergence of a fictional mafioso don. Frank White is the lead character in the film *The King of New York* (1990), directed by Abel Ferrara. In the film the character, played by Christopher Walken, is an incarcerated drug lord who upon his release from prison redistributes the wealth derived from his illicit activities to the poor via the funding of an inner-city hospital. Biggie's distinction that he was a "black Frank White" acknowledges the rapper's obvious racial identity but also suggests a sphere of flow, both capital and social, that is radically different—as radical as general differences in racial identity—from those maintained by mythical and real crime families. In this case, Biggie becomes a Don of the "rap game" largely via his success in the "drug game" and his subsequent ability to capture the visceral details of that success in his rap lyrics. Biggie's assertions that the "thrill is gone" and that he is "here to excite" suggest the ways that his lurid and realistic narratives reinvigorated the previously dormant East Coast hip-hop scene, which prior to the release of *Ready to Die* and Wu Tang's *Enter the Wu Tang (36 Chambers)* was dominated by the Black Nationalist/Afrocentric styles of Public Enemy and KRS-One and the avant-garde styles of De La Soul and A Tribe Called Quest. Given the proximity of the film's plot to Biggie's own circumstances, Biggie returns from his own prison stint as the "king" of New York hip-hop, redistributing his lyrical flow to audiences and consumers impoverished by a lack of "quality" East Coast hip-hop.

Biggie makes another reference to the concept of lyrical flow or freestylin' as a form of social flow and capital in the intro verse of the remix of Craig Mack's "Flava in Your Ear," which also featured cameos by LL Cool J, Busta Rhymes, and Rampage. In the narrative, Biggie provides commentary on rival rap artists, encouraging them to "Disappear, vamoose, you're wack to me / Take them rhymes back to the factory / I see the gimmicks, the wack lyrics / The shit is depressing, pathetic, please forget it. . . . You shoulda been a cop fuck hip-hop / With that freestyle you're bound to get shot."[13] Biggie's comparison of lyricists with "wack freestyles" and law enforcement officers suggests his belief that both pose a threat to his ability to freestyle successfully. Specifically, rappers with "wack freestyles" pose a threat because the marketplace is glutted with various rap artists, many of whom achieve commercial success—MC Hammer and Vanilla Ice come immediately to mind—without necessarily being the most technically proficient artists. Alternatively, the lyric suggests that "wack" lyricists are also targets in their own right because they fail to exhibit the kinds of artistic and social flow that will ensure they adequately improvise their way through a challenging cultural terrain.

Monson suggests there was significant social capital assigned to bebop jazz artists within black social spaces because of their profile as complex nonconformists who challenged the status quo most notably via their abilities as musical improvisers. I use the term *social capital* in this instance to denote the heightened value assigned to various social actors and those in relationships with or in close proximity to those social actors. These social actors are valued because associations with them "provide information and create opportunities and obligations that allow people to achieve their interests" (McCarthy and Hagan 1038). In the case of bebop artists, I would suggest that those who witnessed their performances likely achieved a sense of catharsis and recovery that was largely achieved because of their close proximity to those performers. Some may have also experienced a sense of urgency and crisis associated with the political conditions of African-Americans in the era, conditions that the performers heightened with their theoretical efforts to undermine the social and political status quo via their improvisatory style of performance. As Bill McCarthy and

John Hagan explain, "social capital is both an individual or private asset, as well as a group-level or community good: people use their associations as resources to achieve desired incomes and they profit from the accumulated social capital of their community" (1038). McCarthy's and Hagan's work specifically deals with the kind of criminal social capital that "arises from associations with skilled offenders" with "specialized skills and knowledge about offending" (1038).

However skillful bebop artists were, I am not suggesting that such skills were criminal acts, but rather that a close proximity to bebop artists reinforced the outlaw aura of those most affected by their performances in the underground culture that cultivated bebop. Not surprisingly, contemporary hip-hop artists are also valued for their "criminal" social capital conveyed largely in their music but also in their personal lives as well as more traditional forms of social capital like that that derives from their relative celebrity and significant influence in the recording industry itself. Thus, suggestions by some artists that they are "handling their bizness" acknowledge complex forms of flow related to their success at freestylin' in their music, in their business affairs, and in their personal and professional lives.

Jay Z's "Do It Again (Put Ya Hands Up)" from his project *Volume 3 . . . Life and Times of S. Carter,* featuring Beanie Sigel and Amil, offers some insight into the complex web of social and artistic flow. The project was the last in a trilogy based on the real-life experiences of Shawn Carter, whose primary "stage" persona is Jay Z, though he also uses at times the stage personas Jigga and J-hova, which are accordingly spins on the words "nigga" and "Jehovah." Jay Z's various stage personae, an increasing phenomenon within the hip-hop industry, speak to the ways that he and others negotiate their statuses in the myriad of places and spaces where they exhibit their flow. Jay Z, a former protégé of The Notorious B.I.G. and as the president of Roc-A-Fella Records (a label distributed by Def Jam Recordings Music group) uses narratives fixated on his dual roles as hardcore "gangsta" rapper and as music industry insider. In this regard, Jay Z's social and lyrical flow resembles the "Flows of Capital" that David Harvey first forwarded.

"Do it Again" chronicles the everyday rituals of Jay Z and his associates, specifically Beanie Sigel and female rapper Amil. Sigel opens the track by acknowledging the kind of special favors that they receive from women in clubs, largely because the "Whole squad get it down like this / Whole squad buying rounds of Cris / Whole squad got crowns on their wrist / Whole squad got a pound of twist / Whole squad got a pound to spit / In case a clown want to flip."[14] The exploits that Sigel describes in the club, where he and his cronies buy rounds of expensive champagne like Kristal, wear diamond bracelets, and carry guns just in case they have "beef" with jealous rivals, are largely realized because of the social capital that resonates from Jay Z. Sigel makes such a point later in his verse when he states that women are "in the back bouncin' to 'Jigga What'" in a song from Jay Z's *Volume 2 . . . Hard Knock Life*. The song was originally recorded as "Nigga What, Nigga Who" (Originator 99) but the title and lyrics were changed to "Jigga What, Jigga Who" to allow the recording to achieve the crossover appeal that Jay Z and his label desired. Jay Z's persona "Jigga" directly correlates to the transference of Jay's social flow from black urban enclaves into the sphere of mainstream popular music. In this case, Jay Z improvised and created a new persona to function within an ever-changing media landscape. The final line of Sigel's lyrics draws attention to the connection to his lyrical flow and social flow, stating that "you got your hands up and I ain't even stick ya'll up," which suggests that his lyrical flow is as affecting and provocative as a stickup. The subtext of the song's title "Throw ya hands up" is a reference to the ability of Jay Z's music and presumably Jay Z himself to throw those within his vicinity into a dance-floor frenzy where they throw their hands up in the air.

Later in the song Jay Z acknowledges his own social flow. In response to criticisms that the Roc-A-Fella clique had become too commercial, Jay Z asks, "how the fuck you gonna talk about MCs on our hill / when . . . both arms are chunky the sleeves on chill / any given time 100 Gs in your grill?" In opposition to suggestions that "real" MCs are proficient in lyrical flow or freestylin', Jay Z offers a concept of artistic flow that is instead governed by commercial success as reflected by his diamond-adorned arms and his $100,000 gold teeth. Jay Z responds to critical suggestions that "he's alright, but he's not real" with the quip "Don't talk to me 'bout MCs got skills," suggesting that across the commercial terrain in which hip-hop's current popularity has been realized, record sales and not skill level are the measurements of successful artistic and, of course, social flow. Jay Z explicitly acknowledges his social capital with the comment "Jay Z's that deal with seeds in the field," a reference to the artists signed to the Roc-A-Fella label including Memphis Bleek, Beanie Sigel, Amil, DJ Clue, and Rell. Conceding the quality of some MCs, Jay Z raps "you gotta flow that's cool with me / You gotta lil' dough that cool with me / you gotta little cars little jewelries / but none of ya'll . . . could fool with me." Jay Z's comfort with the skill level and commercial success of others is predicated on his greater commercial success and the realization that his commercial success and consequent social capital also influence the styles that his competitors embrace. Jay Z asserts that he "shipped two million, then I blew to three / Then I skated to four, before I went on tour / I came back and it's plain / Ya'll niggaz ain't rappin' the same / Fuck the flow, ya'll jackin' the slang."

Jay Z's comments imply that his commercial success has forced other rappers to reevaluate the value of traditional artistic flow in a world where social flow and capital conveys much more prestige for commercial artists.

Like the Notorious B.I.G., Jay Z's initial commercial success was garnered because of the street credibility of his autobiographical debut *Reasonable Doubt*, which included narratives about his life as a crack dealer in Brooklyn's Marcy Projects during the early 1990s. Part of Jay Z's appeal has to do with his ability to successfully weld hardcore street narratives with catchy and distinctive musical samples. The one track responsible for the commercial success he now enjoys is "Hard Knock Life (The Ghetto Anthem)," the title track to his third project *Volume 2 . . . Hard Knock Life.* The song brilliantly produced by Mark the 45 King samples the chorus of the "Hard Knock Life" anthem from the musical and movie *Annie.* As Jay Z reflects in an interview, "You live in the Marcy projects . . . and then you see someone on TV—they don't have much, they're an orphan, and then they get to live in a big mansion" (quoted in Harrington, G01). According to the artist, when he first heard the song he thought "whoa, that's amazing—those kids are too strong to let the ghetto life bring them down! That's the emotion of the ghetto, that's how people feel right now: 'instead of treats we get tricked; instead of kisses we get kicked'" (quoted in Harrington G01). Jay Z's use of the *Annie* theme loosely connects his narratives to the kind of struggles faced by youthful underclass formations of the pre–World War II era while reinscribing, albeit in superficial ways, those narratives onto the social terrain where contemporary black youth also confront a "hard knock life." The fact that Jay Z successfully juxtaposed the hardcore narratives of his life with the theme song of a highly successful Broadway production that was itself based on a long-running popular mainstream comic strip speaks volumes about the extent of his popularity and by extension the wide-ranging consumer communities where he exhibits social flow. But Jay Z's social flow is also deeply connected to other variant forms of social improvisation, including those used to buttress his commercial success and others that are both products of that commercial success and the ongoing efforts by others to find crevices within Jay Z's social apparatus to improvise their own forms of social flow.

Jay Z's first full-length release *Reasonable Doubt* was released on Priority Records in 1996. Despite its commercial success, Jay Z was disappointed with the label's promotion and distribution apparatuses. Shortly thereafter he created Roc-A-Fella with Damon Dash and Kareem "Biggs" Burke, the label's name both a reference to the wealth of the Rockefeller family and to the late former New York State governor Nelson Rockefeller, who was the architect of the notorious Rockefeller drug laws that have been singularly responsible for increased incarceration rates in the state of New York (Harrington, G01). Whereas Priority was limited in their promotion, Roc-A-Fella was able to increase Jay Z's record sales and social capital by revolutionizing the promotion process with the deployment of Street Teams. Because of the ways that rap music and rap labels have been systematically denied access to traditional promotional vehicles such as television and radio, many labels—led by Roc-A-Fella—developed alternative strategies to reach their core audiences. Basic Street Team activities include creating a buzz around a release by leaking tracks to local DJs, who then create "mix tapes" that get played in clubs and bought and sold in the underground. Shortly before these albums are released, "ghetto" neighborhoods are plastered with posters by a veritable army of Street Teams. As Damon Dash relates, "If I'm the quarterback, the street team is our front line" (Leland and Samuels, 70). The Street Teams themselves were largely made up of "corps of hungry urban youth looking for a break in the business and a few free CDs" (Leland and Samuels, 70).

Of particular interest is the creation of mix tapes. Increasingly labels will allow "unsigned hype" to record mix tapes to test their appeal to urban listening audiences. In this context artists are evaluated solely on the basis of their lyrical, artistic flow, reflecting T-Love's concept of the *authentic* MC. This style of breaking in an artist suggests that the practitioners and audiences of hip-hop still find value in aesthetics but have realized that the commercial landscape necessitates concepts of artistic flow and improvisation that are deeply imbricated with transnational capitalism. If their social flow is to be recognized outside of the urban enclaves that produced them, then it is in the artists' best interests to make their lyrical flow as accessible as possible. Hence, power relations within the "ghetto" engage a crass materialism that resonates with diverse audiences who are alternately enticed by the human drama of the narratives and by the discreet voyeurism they engage in when consuming "hardcore" narratives.

In the past, record labels have considered mix tapes—which date back to the earliest days of hip-hop culture when "street" DJs and MCs sold cassettes of their live "still in the park" performances—to be a form of music piracy. On a basic artistic level mix tapes serve as primary evidence of a DJ's artistic flow, particularly so given the contemporary erosion of the DJ's prominence as a performer. Whereas the DJ held the most prominent role in the early days of hip-hop culture (hence the elevation of Kool Herc, Afrika Bambaataa, and Grandmaster Flash to iconical status) lyricists have since emerged as the most prominent figures, perhaps with the exception of DJ/producers Dr. Dre, The RZA, DJ Premier, Jay Dee and Pete Rock.

With the increased popularity of hip-hop and with very little attention paid until recently to the how and why of the genre's increased sales, hip-hop recordings became a logical target for bootleggers. In the early 1990s several stellar debut recordings, in particular Brand Nubian's *All For One,* fell victim to bootleggers, who sold bootlegged cassettes for prices substantially lower than those found in the major music chains. Bootlegs could be distinguished by their second- and third-generation copies of the cover art and equally inferior audio reproductions. As the technology has advanced, so has the quality of bootlegs as the development of writable compact disc media and CD burners have allowed for the bootlegging of CDs without any appreciable loss of audio quality. According to the music industry, illegal bootlegging accounts for more than $300 million in losses in the United States alone (Marzulli, Santiago, and Standora, 3). As one law enforcement officer acknowledged, "Bootlegging is more lucrative than selling drugs. . . . When you can make $4,000 a day and a fine costs $250, why not bootleg?" (3). It is the issue of bootlegging that was at the center of Jay Z's 1999 arrest for the stabbing of a fellow record company executive. Lance "Un" Rivera is the CEO of the Undeas label, which is distributed by Atlantic Records and the head of the Epic label's Untertainment imprint.

In December 1999, Jay Z was arrested after purportedly stabbing Rivera at the Kit Kit Klub, where many industry insiders congregated for a party in support of Q-Tip's (formerly of A Tribe Called Quest) debut solo release. At the root of the dispute between the two men was Jay Z's belief that Rivera was responsible for the bootlegging of his *Volume 3 . . . Life and Times of S. Carter.* Nearly three weeks before the official release date of the project with its suggested retail price of $18.97, bootlegged versions were being sold along the strip of Fulton Avenue between Nostrand and New York Avenues in Brooklyn for $5.00 (Marzulli, Santiago, and Standora, 3). Rivera coproduced the track "Dope Man" on the legitimate version of the recording that was released to the public so it is likely that he drew suspicion because he would have had access to the various tracks recorded by Jay Z for the recording. Regardless of whether or not Rivera was behind the bootlegging scheme, the incident highlights the interests of a wide range of actors all attempting to increase social flow and generate social and economic capital. The obvious case is of the bootleggers themselves who generate increased wealth from the relatively inexpensive process of bootlegging CDs. The CDs themselves, even as bootlegs, derive their value from Jay Z's already established social capital. If Rivera was indeed responsible for the bootlegging of Jay Z's recording, it was a logical move for a record executive vying for the same audience that Jay Z attracts. Theoretically, Rivera would not only benefit financially from the sale of the CDs—taking money direct from Jay Z—but also could remove considerable luster from Jay Z's image as a commercially successful artist as those discs bought on the black market would not be included among the official sales. Like Jay Z and his close friend the Notorious B.I.G., Rivera was a former drug dealer who translated his street flow into a successful career promoting and reproducing street culture in the recording industry. Not so ironically, Jay Z's alleged attack on Rivera—the rapper was released on $50,000 bail shortly after the attack and currently awaits trial in the case—helped buttress his own notoriety as a street thug turned rap artist, thereby heightening his commercial appeal (Gamboa, A03).

Conclusion

Though the social spaces that produced bebop and hip-hop and the youth constituencies that embraced these artistic forms in those spaces are radically different, the value of improvisation as an artistic and social concept remains crucial to the ability of black youth and others to survive, on their own terms, in these spaces. The petty criminality of black youth in the 1940s was an attempt to find economic sustenance across a social landscape that, at best, disregarded the needs of black urban populations. Such petty criminality was also embraced by impoverished black youth forty years later in postindustrial urban spaces in cities like New York and Detroit, though the illicit drug economy of those spaces represented a generational advance of the risk associated with such criminality. Whereas both bebop and hip-hop were perceived initially as having little artistic or economic value, the latter has become an integral part of the still evolving global entertainment industry, conveying both celebrity and some real semblance of material wealth to the artists, producers, and industry executives involved in the production and distribution of hip-hop. Ironically it is the lurid details of black youth criminality in the narratives of hip-hop that have been a primary impetus in the commercial appeal of the genre. However problematic some of these narratives are, hip-hop provides powerful evidence of the ability of black youth to use their improvisatory musical practice(s) to also create and improvise opportunities in their social, political, and cultural lives.

Notes

1. The first AME church was founded by Richard Allen in 1896 in the city of Philadelphia.
2. See Michael Eric Dyson's *I May Not Get There* for a more detailed exploration of this aspect of King's political project.
3. According to Allen, "Drive" sections are extended sections of improvised chanting and singing.

4. See my essay, "You Remind Me of Something" in *Soul Babies* for a brief commentary on the "imagined communities," to use Benedict Anderson's term, referenced in the Outkast recording "Rosa Parks" ("ooh, uh, hush that fuss, everybody moves to the back of the bus").

5. Though the narrative of the book is somewhat innocuous, the book's illustrations inspired generations of unflattering depictions of African-Americans in print media and film and television animation.

6. Lee Baker's *From Savage to Negro* examines the ways in which Museum culture and anthropology were intertwined with American race relations in the late nineteenth and early twentieth centuries.

7. See Lewis.

8. See Kelley, 53–75.

9. The Notorious B.I.G., "Everyday Struggles," *Ready to Die* (Bad Boy Entertainment/Arista 73000–2 1994).

10. The Notorious B.I.G., "Juicy," *Ready to Die* (Bad Boy Entertainment/ Arista 73000–2 1994).

11. The Notorious B.I.G. with Method Man, "Things Done Changed," *Ready to Die* (Bad Boy Entertainment/Arista 73000–2 1994).

12. The Notorious B.I.G. with Method Man, "The What," *Ready to Die* (Bad Boy Entertainment/Arista 73000–2 1994).

13. Craig Mack featuring The Notorious B.I.G., Rampage, LL Cool J, and Busta Rhymes, "Flava in Ya Ear," *Bad Boy Greatest Hits, Volume 1* (Bad Boy Entertainment/Arista 73022–2 1998).

14. Jay Z featuring Beanie Sigel and Amil, "Do It Again (Throw Ya Hands Up)," *Volume 3 . . . Life and Times of S. Carter* (Roc-A-Fella Records 314 546 822–2 1999).

Works Cited

Allen, Ray. "Shouting the Church: Narrative and Vocal Improvisation in African-American Gospel Quartet Performance." *Journal of American Folklore* 104 (1991): 295–317.

Alexander, Claire. *The Art of Being Black: The Creation of Black British Youth Identities.* New York: Oxford University Press, 1996.

Baker, Houston A., Jr., *Black Studies, Rap, and the Academy.* Chicago: University of Chicago Press, 1993.

Baker, Lee. *From Savage to Negro: Anthropology and the Construction of Race.* Berkeley and Los Angeles: University of California Press, 1999.

Bogle, Donald. *Toms, Coons, Mulattos, Mammies and Bucks: An Interpretive History of Blacks in American Films.* New York: Continuum Pub Group, 2001.

Boyd, Todd. *Am I Black Enough For You?: Popular Culture From the Hood and Beyond.* Bloomington: Indiana University Press, 1997.

Brandt, Nat. *Harlem at War: The Black Experience in WWII.* Syracuse: Syracuse University Press, 1996.

Chibnall, Steve. "Whistle and Zoot: The Changing Meaning of a Suit of Clothes," *History Workshop Journal* 20 (1985): 56–81.

Cosgrove, Stuart. "The Zoot-Suit and Style Warfare," *History Workshop Journal* 18 (1984): 77–91.

Cross, Brian. *It's Not About a Salary: Rap, Race, Resistance in Los Angeles.* London: Verso, 1993.

Dyson, Michael Eric. *I May Not Get There With You: The True Martin Luther King, Jr.* New York: Free Press, 2000.

———. *Reflecting Black: African-American Cultural Criticism.* Minneapolis: University of Minnesota Press, 1993.

Ellison, Ralph. *Negro Digest* 1, no. 4 (Winter-Spring 1943).

Gamboa, Glenn. "Life Mirrors Music" *New York Newsday*, 14 April 2001, A03.

Gaunt, Kyra. "Translating Double Dutch to Hip Hop: The Musical Vernacular of Black Girls' Play," In *Language, Rhythm and Sound: Black Press Popular Cultures into the Twenty-First Century*, edited by Joseph Adjaye and Adrianne Andrews, 146–163. Pittsburgh: University of Pittsburgh Press, 1998.

Gordon, Lewis. *Her Majesty's Other Children: Sketches of Racism from a Neocolonial Age*. Lanham, Md: Rowman and Littlefield, 1997.

Green, Al, and David Seay. *Take Me to the River*. New York: Harper Entertainment, 2000.

Greenberg, Cheryl. *"Or Does It Explode?": Black Harlem in the Great Depression*. New York: Oxford University Press, 1991.

Griffin, Farah Jasmine. *"Who Set You Flowing?": The African American Migration Narrative*. New York: Oxford University Press, 1995.

Harrington, Richard. "Jay Z's Rhymes of Passion." *Washington Post*, 2 January 2000, G1; G8–9.

Harvey, David. *Consciousness and the Experience: Studies in the History and Theory of Capitalist Urbanization*. Baltimore: Johns Hopkins University Press, 1985.

Higginbotham, Evelyn Brooks. "Rethinking Vernacular Culture: Black Religion and Race Records in the 1920s and 1930s." In *The House That Race Built: Black Americans, U.S. Terrain*, edited by Wahneema Lubiano, 157–176. New York: Vintage Books, 1998.

Jackson, John L., Jr. "The Soles of Black Folk: These Reeboks Were Made for Runnin' (From the White Man)." In *Race Consciousness: African American Studies for the New Century*, edited by Judith Jackson Fossett and Jeffrey A. Tucker, 177–190. New York: New York University Press, 1997.

Jones, LeRoi (Amiri Baraka). *Blues People*. New York: William Morrow, 1963.

Kelley, Robin. *Race Rebels: Culture, Politics, and the Black Working Class*. New York: Free Press, 1994.

Leland, John, and Allison Samuels. "Taking to the Streets," *Newsweek* 132, no. 18 (1998): 70–72.

Lewis, David Levering. *When the Negro Was in Vogue*. New York: Oxford University Press, 1989.

Lott, Eric. "Double V, Double Time: Bebop's Politics of Style," In *Jazz Among the Discourses*, edited by Krin Gabbard. North Carolina: Duke University Press, 1995.

Marzulli, John, Robert Santiago, and Leo Standora, "Cops Think Jay Z Pal Stole His CD," *Daily News* (New York), 5 December 1999.

Mazon, Mauricio. *The Zoot-Suit Riots: The Psychology of Symbolic Annihilation*. Austin: University of Texas Press, 1984.

McCarthy, Bill, and John Hagan. "When Crime Pays: Capital, Competence, and Criminal Success." *Social Forces* 79, no. 3 (2001): 1035–1069.

Monson, Ingrid. "The Problem with White Hipness: Race, Gender and Cultural Conceptions in Jazz Historical Discourse." *Journal of the American Musicological Society* 49, no. 3 (1995): 396–427.

Neal, Mark Anthony. *Soul Babies: Black Popular Culture and the Post-Soul Aesthetic*. New York: Routledge, 2001.

Ottley, Roi. *New World A-Coming (Inside Black America)*. New York: Arno, 1968.

Pagan, Eduardo Obregon. "Los Angeles Geopolitics and the Zoot Suit Riot, 1943," *Social Science History* 24, no. 1 (2000): 223–256.

Rose, Tricia. *Black Noise: Rap Music and Black Culture in Contemporary America*. Hanover: Wesleyan University Press, 1994.

Rosenthal, David. *Hard Bop: Jazz and Black Music, 1955–1965.* New York: Oxford University Press, 1992.

Small, Christopher. *Music of the Common Tongue. Survival and Celebration in Afro-American Music.* Hanover: Wesleyan University Press, 1985.

Venkatesch, Sudhir. "The Social Organization of Street Gang Activity in an Urban Ghetto." *American Journal of Sociology* 103, no. 1 (1997): 82–130.

Watkins, S. Craig. *Representing: Hip Hop Culture and the Production of Black Cinema.* Chicago: University of Chicago Press, 1998.

Wright, Richard. *Native Son.* New York: Harper and Row, 1969.

JULIE DAWN SMITH

Playing like a Girl
The Queer Laughter of the Feminist Improvising Group[1]

Culturally speaking, women have wept a great deal, but once the tears are shed, there will be endless laughter instead. Laughter that breaks out, overflows, a humor no one would expect to find in women—which is nonetheless surely their greatest strength because it's a humor that sees man much further away than he has ever been seen.
—Hélène Cixous

·ᵔ

In Greek mythology there is a story of an old woman named Baubo who, in an effort to help Demeter momentarily forget her grief over the loss of her daughter Persephone, pulled her dress up over her head, exposed her genitals and shouted obscene remarks and dirty jokes.[2] Apparently the distraction worked; accounts of the incident indicate Baubo's indecent gestures and lewd comments caused Demeter to laugh.

Scholars speculate that this obscene spectacle is replicated in a number of terra-cotta statues dated roughly from the fourth century B.C.E. Depicting a collapsed female body that consists of virtually nothing but two orifices, the statues reflect the Greek belief that women possess not one, but two mouths (Carson, "Gender," 72). One mouth is of course the opening to the oral cavity; the other leads to the cavernous depths of the female sex. The anatomical deformity is strangely accentuated by the reversal of the mouths on the figures; that is, the "upper" mouth is situated in the statue's abdomen, the "lower" positioned on the top of her head. As poet and scholar Anne Carson suggests, the representation of Baubo's aural and visual gesture reflects the general confusion surrounding the representation of the female body in a masculinist culture: "This Baubo presents us with one simple chaotic diagram of an outrageously manipulable female identity. The doubling and interchangeability of mouth engenders a creature in whom sex is cancelled out by sound and sound is cancelled out by sex" ("Gender," 76). According to the legend, however, Baubo is in control of the erasure. Her spontaneous and excessive performance strategically utilizes the confusion and mutability associated with the female body in order to disrupt the representation of woman as passive and silent spectacle. Baubo's gesture obscures her upper mouth to make it appear as though her lower mouth is doing all the talking, enacting a strange ventriloquism that throws the voice produced by her vocal folds into the folds of her labia. The shock of Baubo's aural/visual play ruptures the moment of viewing with an unexpected interval—a stutter—that creates a "zone of disruption and destabilization" (Buckley, 60). Laughter and the stutter are sonic twins in this respect, disruptions that linger at the threshold of sense and non-sense. The stutter shatters the silent repetition of the female body, resists fetishization, penetrates the ear with the noise of resistance while it utters profanities that trouble patriarchal space. Perhaps this is why public soundings by women produce a great deal of anxiety: the female body breaks the silent repetition of representation with its stuttering laughter.

Julia Kristeva writes that laughter is a signifying practice, a lifting of inhibitions that is transgressive, transformational, pleasurable, and productive: "Every practice which produces something new (a new device) is a practice of laughter: it obeys laughter's logic and provides the subject of laughter's advantages" (*Revolution,* 225). The practice of laughter destabilizes the boundaries separating the conscious from the unconscious, jumbles the parameters of interior and exterior space, ridicules the isolation of body from mind, and defies the gravitational pull of predictability and repetition. It is a sonic borderline state, a space of psychic excess that generates a "constant calling into question of the psyche and the world" (Kristeva, *Sense,* 19). In other words, laughter is an improvisation.

Baubo's improvisational laugh engenders a sonic and somatic outpouring, an extemporaneous reversal that turns the body inside/out. Her actions exceed specularity; her sounds confound vision and defy anatomical expectations. When Baubo laughs, sound becomes flesh, corporeal play becomes aural display and sexuality is intoned. Baubo's laughter challenges the threshold of intelligibility and normalcy; she utters the limit, the place where the subject is both articulated and annihilated: inside/womb/life merges with outside/abjection/death. Perhaps this is why Demeter doubled over in laughter. She got the joke.

Some might interpret this allegory as a warning: women who improvise in public are in danger of surrendering to the visibility of their sexual difference by making a spectacle of themselves. Was it appropriate for De-meter to laugh given the circumstances? This is a rhetorical question, of course; there is always a risk involved anytime a woman opens her mouth(s). Baubo's action suggests—as does Demeter's (re)action—that if the female body is always already spectacle by virtue of her difference, then making a spectacle of oneself by improvising that difference is a crucial per-formance of agency. As a critical reflection on the social order and a plea-surable "interval of potentiality" (Buckley, 60), the laughter of Baubo and Demeter confounds representation, reconfigures spectacle, regenerates subjectivity, and improvises woman.

In his discussion of Baubo, Maurice Olender identifies three aspects as-sociated with spectacle: gesture, desire, and gaze (89). Where and with whom desire is located is key to interpreting the spectacle, as desire medi-ates the network of power relations that circulate across the positions of spectacle and spectator. It is Baubo's desire to make herself a spectacle that disrupts the one-way gaze of the spectator, a refusal to mirror the "specular logic of the same" that defines the heterosexual voyeur (Moi, 133). In turn Baubo's distraction attracts Demeter—it reminds her of a knowledge that exists in excess of death, forgotten in her moment of grief—and her desire to respond is aroused.

The sonic exchange of desire between Baubo and Demeter underscores the possibility of an insurgent and noisy female improvisation. It points to the pleasure and the power of transgressive sounding, challenges the silence of repetition and questions the anxiety associated with female "noise." Baubo's perverse voice and Demeter's spontaneous laughter are simultane-ously embodied and disembodied: "Sounds that are interstitial, defiant, pe-culiar at times . . . *queer*, in the most musical sense of the term" (Mockus, 53). As one woman exposes her flesh/voice to the other, a flesh/voice is echoed back. The laughter quells the pain of death and the ache of abjection while it celebrates the sharp tongue, the promise of mutability, the flux of sound. This is an antiphonal exchange—an excessive gesture, a queer laugh-ter—that breaks Demeter's silence, reciprocates Baubo's laugh and reso-nates with/in both women. The story of Baubo is an improvisational sounding of body politics that as Mary Russo suggests, transforms the spec-tacle of the female body into active "multivalent, oppositional play" (62).

Fast forward to the 1970s: the legacy of Baubo and Demeter resonates with/in women improvisers, women who choose to make spectacles of themselves by sounding body, sexuality, knowledge, difference, freedom, and experience: "to smash everything, to shatter the framework of institu-tions, to blow up the law, to break up the 'truth' with laughter" (Cixous, "Castration," 258). Beginning in 1977 this revolution was sounded with particular energy in the queer laughter of the Feminist Improvising Group (FIG).

Improvising Freedom

Within the European music community interest in improvisational experimentation had developed more than a decade earlier in the 1960s, piqued by the presence of American expatriate free jazz musicians in Europe, the desire of local improvisers to stretch beyond the structures of idiomatic improvisation toward greater aesthetic freedom, and the disillusionment of improvisers with the growing commodification of music (Bailey, xi–xii; Prévost, 10). Percussionist Eddie Prévost suggests that although for some European improvisers jazz was viewed as a "major artistic and ideological force within the development of a wider-ranging creative improvised music" that continually struggled to "escape the confinement of a white-dominated capitalist culture," it too had begun to solidify "into conventions that became as hard to escape as the unfreedoms of classical or popular musics" (10).

The appeal of freedom in improvisational practices resonated with/in the emerging political climate of the 1960s as improvisers began to discard codified procedures, including those found in jazz improvisation, in favor of experimental practices. These practices were not only concerned with aesthetics but with political, economic, and social matters as well. Irène Schweizer recounts that this politically charged time influenced her decision to stop playing "the changes" and to leave improvisational structures and systems behind: "For me, it was a natural development. We had always played the music of the time. In 1968 a lot of things were happening in Europe. There were student revolutions. Barriers were falling. It seemed natural to want to free yourself" (Hale, 15).

Nathaniel Mackey observes a similar impulse in black music, particularly free jazz, that challenged the dominant culture while striving toward aesthetic, individual, and collective freedom:

During the sixties, assertions were often made to the effect that jazz groups provided glimpses into the future. What was meant by this was that black music—especially that of the sixties, with its heavy emphasis on individual freedom within a collectively improvised context—proposed a model social order, an ideal, even utopic balance between personal impulse and group demands. (34)

The parallel development of free jazz in the United States and free improvisation in Europe speaks of the ability of freely improvised music to cut across aesthetic boundaries of containment and categorization. James Snead describes this common aesthetic impulse:

The extension of "free jazz," starting in the 1960s, into the technical practice of using the "material" qualities of sound—on the horns, for instance, using overtones, harmonics and subtones—became almost mandatory for the serious jazz musician and paralleled a similar movement on the part of European musicians branching out of the classical tradition. (222)

Although the simultaneous development of a congruent sonic aesthetic linked the practices of free jazz and free improvisation together, it has sometimes obscured the fact that the two were distinct (albeit interrelated) practices grounded in different traditions and communities. Joëlle Léandre explains the differences from a European perspective:

> We received free jazz in Europe at the time when Ornette Coleman and all the other players were creating, but free jazz is not free music, free jazz is a Black music too. Free music is, I think, definitely a European music. We have a long history of the music, we have Monteverdi, we have Bartok, we have Stockhausen, it's a long line. . . . I think that this kind of music, free music, is very much a European music, and where different people come from they bring their own ways to it. You know, we have very wonderful jazz musicians in France, but they play the American music, they don't play the European music (laughs) but what I like is all this mixture. (quoted in Vickery, 18)

The suggestion here is that neither free jazz nor free improvisation existed in a vacuum; neither, however, were they completely interchangeable. It is important to recognize that the hybridity and mixing of the practices did not obscure the differences, especially in regard to the intersection of aesthetic freedom with race and class.

For example, in free improvisation—exercised within a predominately white, male improvising community existing on the margins of avant-garde and mainstream music—the move toward aesthetic freedom was a critique of class structures and power networks embedded in European music and society. Renewed interest in improvisation challenges the marginalization of improvisational practices in European art music that culminated in the nineteenth century, by destabilizing the "dominant procedures through which music is made and consumed, especially in challenging established roles for composers, musicians, and audiences" (Durant, 276). Free improvisation questions how music functions in society, especially in relation to power, to become "a point of counter-identification against systems of control, hierarchy and subordination" (Durant, 270).

African-American explorations of freedom in free jazz similarly critiqued the function of music in relation to power, but did so in the context of racial oppression. Free jazz actively critiqued and resisted racial oppression of the dominant culture within a historical continuum that connected black music to the resistance of slavery and traced its musical roots to Africa:

The music itself describes the political position of Blacks in America just as their position dictates their day-to-day life, the instruments they play and the places where their music can be heard. In the case of African-American music, the fact that the creators are the colonised in a colonialist society, has a vital bearing on the way the music has evolved, how it is regarded by the world at large, and the way in which the artists are treated. (Wilmer, *As Serious* 14)

Neither free improvisation nor free jazz, however, extended their critiques to include the aesthetic, economic, or political liberation of women. For the most part, a practice of freedom that resisted gender oppression and oppression on the basis of sexual difference was excluded from the liberatory impulses of male-dominated improvising communities. The opportunity for freedom in relation to sexual difference, gender, and sexuality for women improvisers was strangely absent from the discourses and practices of both free jazz and free improvisation.

Thus, it is difficult to describe accurately just how integral women's contributions to the development of free improvisation and free jazz were in the early days, as women's participation was limited and remains underdocumented. Chronicles of free improvisation and free jazz from a variety of sources—including Derek Bailey's *Improvisation: Its Nature and Practice in Music*,[3] John Litweiler's classic book on free jazz, *The Freedom Principle: Jazz After 1958;* the more recent work of Kevin Whitehead in *New Dutch Swing,* documenting the scene in Holland; as well as John Corbett's provocative article, "Ephemera Underscored: Writing Around Free Improvisation" pay little or no attention to the music's female constituents. Perhaps because improvisationally based music struggled from the beginning for recognition, its practices and documents have not always been liberatory, often reduplicating the marginalization and exclusion women face(d) in more mainstream musical structures and in patriarchal society at large.

The particular challenges encountered by women improvisers due to the effects of gender and sex oppression, including the gendering of women's performances and audiences as feminine and/or lacking, are rarely acknowledged. In *Swing Shift: "All-Girl" Bands of the 1940s,* Sherrie Tucker discusses how "stories of devaluation and absence are woven into the familiar rhythms of the popular history books about the Swing Era" (3). As with the majority of women musicians in a variety of genres throughout history, all-women swing bands were either omitted from historical accounts, treated as novelties, or considered inauthentic because they were assumed to lack ability by virtue of their sexual difference. Angela Davis notes a similar masculinist bias in historical and critical accounts of the blues that fail "to take seriously the efforts of women blues musicians and the female reception of their work. As a consequence, the central part played by women both in the blues and in the history of African-American cultural consciousness is often ignored" (44–45).

In relation to free improvisation Irène Schweizer often acknowledges that although she was the only female instrumentalist on the European scene throughout the 1960s and the early 1970s her contributions are conspicuously absent from historical accounts:

I had been taking part in the FMP festival during its development in the '60s and '70s, being the only woman on every festival. . . . There was a photo exhibition about all the jazz musicians from FMP festivals from 1968 to 1978, and not one single photo of me even though I took part every second year. (Les Diaboliques)

In contrast, Val Wilmer's classic book *As Serious as Your Life*—as one of the first documents of women's experiences in and around the "new jazz" in African-American communities—is an exception to the masculinist rule of exclusion. Wilmer's approach is twofold: she writes of women's experiences as support systems for their male musician partners and of their struggles as players trying to cope with a male-dominated scene. She pays particular attention to the intersections of race and class with gender and sexual difference, unearthing differences in the experiences and attitudes of both white and black women. Although the focus on women is not the core of Wilmer's project, it is extensive enough to paint an accurate, yet somewhat bleak portrait of women's position in relation to men and improvisation. Wilmer reports that many women gave up their own artistic ambitions to support their men. When they did venture out to play in clubs the reception was often lukewarm, and as Wilmer points out, the skepticism that scrutinized and devalued women's playing is summed up in the comment, "You sound good—for a woman!" (204).

By raising the issue of sexual politics in free jazz, Wilmer also unearthed the sexual politics of music criticism. She recounts that after writing these passages on women in her book, male critics criticized her for being insufficiently "feminist." She describes her dilemma:

It was true that I had dwelt on women's supportive role rather than participatory contribution, but as someone pointed out, jazz wasn't exactly a feminist area of endeavor. Many's the time I have wished that I could rewrite that particular part of the book with a more thorough analysis of women's position. It was an intervention, though, and by and large, the response to *As Serious* was positive. (*Mama*, 287–288)

This reflection appears in Wilmer's subsequent book *Mama Said There'd Be Days Like This: My Life in the Jazz World*, a personal history centering on a young girl's passion for jazz that develops into a lifelong commitment to the music. Written from her perspective as a white, lesbian, working-class photojournalist, Wilmer details the complex negotiations required of her to navigate the world of jazz. The result is a superb descriptive journey that moves the reader through a number of seemingly incommensurable communities simultaneously. The exploration of her complex, shifting selves consistently questions white, heterosexual, middle-class notions of identity, community, and music and demonstrates alternative possibilities of community and care. Similar to Minnie Bruce Pratt's "Identity: Skin Blood Heart," Wilmer rewrites herself "in relation to shifting interpersonal and political contexts" that enable her to construct "a notion of community as inherently unstable and contextual, not based on sameness or essential connections, but offering agency instead of passivity" (de Lauretis, 12–13). This is the vision and possibility of community when the struggle toward freedom recognizes the intersections of sexual difference, gender, and sexuality in addition to race and class, as the basis for improvisational practices.

Playing the Personal Is Political

The impetus to gather a group of women improvisers together into a collective was galvanized by the glaring absence of women improvisers en masse in performance situations. At a musician's union meeting in London, vocalist Maggie Nicols expressed to multi-instrumentalist/composer Lindsay Cooper (Nicols) her desire to explore improvisation with other women. Even with the emergence of a burgeoning "women's music" scene, Cooper and Nicols recognized the glaring absence of women improvisers. As Cooper recounts: "We got talking and we agreed that improvisation had become very important and no women were doing it. And suddenly we thought, well, let's do it! Let's get women together and do it ourselves!" (personal interview).

Involvement in the feminist movement coupled with a strong commitment to class politics and lesbian activism encouraged Nicols and Cooper to commingle the personal and the political within an improvisational context. Although both women performed extensively with men, their experience playing with other women was very limited. Nicols wondered out loud what the experience of playing with women would be like:

We recognized that women were being excluded and we wanted to just experience what it was like to play with other women. One of the strongest things for me that came out of the Women's Liberation Movement was the recognition of the connection between the personal and the political. So to say for me that it was a personal thing was also political. I wanted to feel the intimacy musically that I felt with women. You know when you hang out with women, that quality of shared experience. How would that translate artistically? (personal interview)

Already an accomplished player by the late 1970s, Lindsay Cooper continues to look back on her choice to play with other women as a crucial move that gave her confidence in her ability as an artist:

It's hard to admit it but it's only now that I realise there were *years* when I felt intimidated by men and the assumptions concerning their abilities. It's actually fantastically liberating to realise I've been through all of that and recovered. This is not to say that one's internal oppression is the only thing to be faced because men can be difficult to work with, but what working with women has done for me is to give me a much stronger sense of myself as a musician. This means that now when I work with men I feel much more *centred*. (Wilmer, "Half," 4)

It was Nicols's approach to improvisation—an openness to inclusivity inspired by the philosophy and practice of her mentor and friend, drummer John Stevens—that initially shaped the Feminist Improvising Group. Nicols envisioned an open and changing pool of women musicians that would bring a wide range of approaches to improvisation, varied experience to technical facility, and stylistic diversity to spontaneous performances. The initial pool of musicians consisted of Cooper, Nicols, Corine Liensol, Georgie Born, and Cathy Williams. Irène Schweizer and Sally Potter joined the Feminist Improvising Group in the spring of 1978, and Annemarie Roelofs, Frankie Armstrong, Angèle Veltmeijer, and Françoise Dupety participated intermittently to form a variety of combinations of up to eight women improvising together in any given performance.[4]

Nicols arranged the first public performance of an entirely female group of improvisers during a Music for Socialism concert at the *Almost Free* in London (Wilmer, *Mama*, 284). When the leaflet advertising the concert appeared, the name of the group was listed as the Feminist Improvising Group, a name neither Nicols nor Cooper had chosen:

We didn't call ourselves the Feminist Improvising Group. We were going to call ourselves the Women's Improvising Group but the promoters of the Music for Socialism event gave us that name! So we grew into it. We actually took it on board. It was very strange that men gave us the name. (Les Diaboliques)

Nicols's suspicion of the feminist label was well founded as in the early days of the movement feminism was, in the words of Teresa de Lauretis, "anchored to the single axis of gender as sexual difference" (10). Second-wave feminism tended to present a singular, unified view of "woman" that ignored the differences that existed *between* women on the basis of sexuality, race, and class. As Nicols suggests: "I was skeptical in regard to the feminist label. Not that I don't consider myself a feminist, but more because of the association with dogmas" (Meier and Landolt, 17).

The feminist label had the potential to polarize the sexual politics already embedded in improvisation and to stigmatize women improvisers even further. Claiming a space for women in improvised music was contentious enough, but how much more contentious would it be for women to claim a feminist space within improvised music? Still, the term "feminist" had its charm. It was a subversive and powerful moniker that was, as Nicols slyly recounts, eventually adopted by the group: "We took on the challenge and we thought okay, so be it. You want feminism, we'll give you feminism. And we certainly did, scissors and all!" (Les Diaboliques).

Improvising Consciousness

The first performance of FIG was preceded by a sort of consciousness-raising rehearsal/workshop in which the players discussed among themselves their feelings and experiences as women. The discussion was a catalyst for the pastiche of sounds and images that found their way into the improvisation:

I spoke about being a mother, Corine spoke about being treated like a child because of her disability, so already we had a mother-child scenario which we started the gig with. The others spoke of their particular personal/political issues as women—appearance, image, etc. We brought kitchen props. It was a sort of prepared spontaneity that was a very powerful, anarchic, humorous beginning. (Nicols)[5]

On stage the women appeared in drag, engaged in role-playing, performed domestic chores, peeled onions, and sprayed perfume. It was a performance Nicols describes as "absolute anarchy":

The people were shocked, because they felt the power that was emerging from the women. We did not do that on purpose. We didn't even realize ourselves what was happening. We improvised, but we improvised our own lives and our biographies. We parodied our situation, perverted our dependencies and threw everything high into the air. (Meier and Landolt, 17–18)

Throwing everything high into the air was, for the Feminist Improvising Group, the improvisation of a "critical method." To use a common cliché of the early feminist movement, it was a way of making their voices heard. On this level FIG approached improvisation as a practice of self-discovery and a process of collective negotiation, politically motivated practices linked to the consciousness-raising groups of the 1970s that endeavored to express women's lived experiences. Although now debunked as ineffectual and essentialist (a marker of white, middle-class, radical feminism) the prioritization of gender issues in feminist consciousness-raising groups was both productive—

Consciousness-raising groups affirmed the most dramatic insight of the early women's liberation movement: the personal is political. Individual women shared personal experiences with the aim of rendering explicit the underlying politics shaping women's lives. (Davis, 55)

—and exclusionary:

Because of the complicated racial politics of the 1960s, which defined the women's movement as white, and because of its emphasis on personal micropolitics (often seen as a retreat from the macropolitics of race), black women generally found it difficult to identify with the strategy of consciousness-raising. (Davis, 55)

Teresa de Lauretis points to the substantive contributions of women of color and lesbians to consciousness raising that shifted the emphasis away from the narrowness of "personal micropolitics" toward a transformation of feminism as a "pursuit of consciousness and political practice" (5). This approach to consciousness raising required the recognition of and struggle with multiple dimensions of difference, a struggle that moved beyond the notion of writing the self toward a *re*writing of the self: "a process of struggle and interpretation . . . in relation to a new understanding of community, of history, of culture" (de Lauretis, 18). Consciousness-raising groups could create a space for women to unearth knowledge that was subjugated as a result of oppression on the basis of gender and sexual difference. Practicing improvisation as a form of consciousness raising enabled women to experiment with a variety of power-sharing arrangements, to negotiate leadership, and to reimagine a political practice in which women controlled their own artistic destinies by drawing directly from their lived experiences.[6]

Although FIG's members were predominantly white, so too were they lesbian and working-class, thus the intersections of gender with race, class, and sexuality were important aspects of its improvisations. For Nicols a comprehensive knowledge of these intersections has always informed her improvisations:

I see my music in connection to my political attitude. I am a woman and I identify myself with the worker's movement. That is my social background. In addition I have learned about social privileges and recognize I have privileges as a white woman in our society. I think I wanted to cross boundaries in many ways: social, emotional and in music. That is difficult to convey openly to an audience. That's why you have to be committed to the social environment you are a part of. I mean the political environment as well. You need to know what's going on around you, which political discussions are taking place. (Meier and Landolt, 18)

Being aware of the political environment also meant that the straight members of FIG, if uninitiated in the politics of lesbian sexuality, were soon politicized by their lesbian comrades:

I was not so politically involved in Holland—besides making modern music—but I wasn't lesbian and I think that makes a difference. Talking to Lindsay and Maggie helped me a lot in forming my thinking at that time. And of course that is what was happening when we were touring and doing concerts, they were telling me what was happening, or they were talking over things in London. In that case it was much more political than any men's group who were just interested in playing music. (Roelofs)

FIG performances staged numerous parodies that commented on the aesthetic, political, economic, and social position of women on a number of levels. The mother/child scenario staged between Nicols (a white woman) and Liensol (a black woman) in the inaugural FIG performance (described by Nicols above)—"I was an insane mother while Corine behaved like a child"—can be read not only as a parody of the infantilization of a woman with a disability, but as an indictment of the racial politics of the early feminist movement performed as the oppression of a black woman by an authoritative white woman.[7]

FIG also critiqued whiteness in humorous parodies of middle-class domesticity. The incorporation of everyday domestic "found" objects such as vacuum cleaners, brooms, dustpans, pots and pans, and egg slicers—in Lindsay Cooper's words transforming "the sound's of women's work into a work of women's sounds"—highlighted women's work in the private sphere as well as the subordination of working-class women as domestics (Wilmer, *Mama*, 285). Throughout the performances one or more players could be found sweeping the stage, while others gathered in small ensembles to explore the sonic possibilities of household items.

FIG used drag to critique and parody the institution of compulsory heterosexuality that existed in society and in various forms of music as well: "To concentrate while singing [Nicols] usually puts her hands over her broken fly. . . . Sally is "sweet" and "demure" in a well-known hetero love song" (Jankowski). This set the stage for role-playing and interactions between members of the group that challenged heteronormative roles causing one reviewer to comment: "On stage, they often touch each other. A lot of 'acts,' 'fights' and hugs ended up on the stage floor tonight" (Jankowski). By violating taboos of musical propriety and masculinist competition that prohibited musicians from touching one another, FIG more than hinted at the possibility of sensuous and sexual relationships between women. The integration of lesbian sexuality into the improvisational text enabled the Feminist Improvising Group to ask, "what gets *lost* when [a woman] and her music are studied in the 'company of men,' and what is recuperated when [a woman] joins 'the company of women?'" (Mockus, 52).

Following this trajectory Irène Schweizer continues to question the assumptions that constructed the world of jazz and improvised music as heterosexual:

Why are so few jazz musicians gay? This question has never been asked. The jazz musician has a totally different image. He has to act macho: to read the notes with one eye and to peek around in the audience for nice women. With improvised music the consciousness of musicians has changed a little bit. There are some emancipated men: George Lewis, Maarten Altena, Lol Coxhill, but gay musicians? Even if they were gay, they wouldn't be showing it. With some exceptions like Cecil Taylor, but there are not many. (Meier and Landolt, 17)

The decentering of heterosexual interactions that are assumed to exist in and around musical performances and a refusal to "pass" as straight opened possibilities for the improvisation of female sexuality. In effect FIG queered space of improvisational practice. As Nicols explains, "We are not lesbians [on the music scene] by chance. That has something to do with autonomy. . . . The lesbians were pioneers and had to be lesbian" (Meier and Landolt, 18).

Improvising Antiphony

Improvisation served as a site for the negotiation of individuality and collectivity through the multiplicitous interactions of improviser to improviser, improviser to audience, as well as audiences to one another. FIG performances improvised self and community as a feminist consciousness "attained through practices of political and personal displacement across boundaries between sociosexual identities and communities, between bodies and discourses" (de Lauretis, 18). Part of FIG's political and aesthetic program was to institute opportunities for antiphonal exchange between performers and audiences by consciously dismantling the divisions that separated them, a power-sharing tactic that extended well beyond the stage. For FIG member Sally Potter, breaking down the division between the audience and the performer was a political strategy that emerged from an awareness of feminist and class politics:

Both the specialness ascribed to individual performers and the performer/audience divide itself are seen as unhealthy symptoms of a class divided society, the performer taking an honorary position of power. The strategy then becomes to break down the divide and emphasize participation as a way of saying anyone can do it. (291)

The idea that "anyone can do it" was often unpalatable to improvisers and audience members who valued the display of technical virtuosity as the marker of improvisational competence above all else. Improvising percussionist Eddie Prévost cautions against the tendency he calls "technological elitism," insisting that improvisation requires "dexterity of all kinds (social as well as technical)" (5). For Nicols the ability to integrate dexterity of all kinds into improvisation requires a skill she calls "social virtuosity":

For me social virtuosity—social skills really—is part of [what it takes] to communicate with an audience and with other musicians. It also involves the social skills used to live your life. How you are in the community and those sorts of things. Being able to have that kind of creative spontaneity in every aspect of your life. (telephone interview)

For Irène Schweizer, reading technical virtuosity through social virtuosity provided an opportunity to redefine improvisation and (re)invent standards:

It is very important that we all got the chance to play together. But there are also problems: Which musicians are you going to invite? Which are the standards you demand? Technical brilliance? Professionalism? Enthusiasm? Invention? Imagination? I would prefer a mixture of all. That's an important gain of FIG. It defined new standards. Until then these were defined by men. (Meier and Landolt, 18)

In part, inventing new standards meant dispensing with the notion that "men are destined to be the keepers of the musical flame." Val Wilmer describes this reinvention as "moving from total immersion in the lives of men who structured the music" toward an awareness of the "prejudices" women have internalized about their own abilities in an effort "to support women's right to an equal share of the bandstand" (Wilmer, "Half," 4).

Nicols remembers that FIG's challenge to "technological elitism" and fixed notions of "musical competency" was often dismissed by male musicians: "Whether it was the jazz community that said to Irene and me, 'you and Irene are really great but everybody else is crap' or the more progressive rock 'Henry Cow' people [who] would like what Lindsay and Georgie were doing and all that. So, divide and rule." Schweizer came up against similar sentiments:

Some people asked me: "Why do you play with those women? They can't play and they're no good and you don't have to do that. Why do you play with those women?" It was always difficult for me to explain why, because for me it was just important to play like this in a group of women and to support them.

For Roelofs, the lack of support from men was disheartening but also suspect:

We were eight people, some of whom were good players and some of whom weren't so experienced but were politically very right and in terms of improvising picked up nice things. [FIG] was more like a sort of workshop where people of all different kinds of levels attended. That could certainly be heard but, I don't know, maybe we could have hoped for more support from the men's side. [They could have said] well, just keep on going. But mostly the men said it's no good. I definitely think it's not only the musical level they were talking about. I think it was felt as a threat for a lot of men to just see so many women on stage.

Nicols, Schweizer, and Roelofs agree that the criticism received from men (often communicated indirectly) was frequently imbalanced and rarely constructive:

The critics were never medium, it was always high calling our work very interesting stuff or it was absolutely low, the deepest saying, how can a festival have these women? . . . I think Lindsay and Maggie would certainly agree that the feeling we sometimes felt when the critics were criticizing us was very denigrating. They would say, these *women*, not these musicians, these *women*, argh, eight women on stage, oh god what's happening, get some men out there! (Roelofs)

One incident that stands out in the minds of all of the FIG members I interviewed was their performance at the Total Music Meeting in Berlin in 1979 and the response of the well-known avant-garde musician Alexander von Schlippenbach. Nicols describes what happened as she remembers it:

He came up to us before the gig and he was kissing our hands. Now, we did a phenomenal gig there. I mean it was phenomenal. It was mad, it was anarchic. It was a mixture of grace and clumsiness—the audience loved it. Then we found out from [the organizer's partner] that Alex had gone to him and complained about us being there, saying that he could have found loads of men that would have played a lot better, that we couldn't play our instruments. I mean this included Irene and Annemarie and Lindsay and myself! And it was the hypocrisy of that. [Later] Lindsay and I went to a women's festival in the same place and we went into the gents toilets and wrote graffiti all over the gents toilets: "Watch out Alex von Schlippenbach, we've got our scissors ready." You know, we graffitied the gents toilets [laughs]. And it was only just recently that I started speaking to him again because I thought I've got to let it go. He probably doesn't even realize this.

The extent to which readings of FIG performances were effected by gender and sexual difference is difficult to assess or dissect. Was there a masculinist musical gaze/ear operative here? Did the disavowed gender anxiety—related to the spectacle of so many unsupervised and unpredictable women on the stage—(re)surface in the accusations of technical incompetence, lack of speed, and fluency? Guitarist Eugene Chadbourne, who also played at the 1979 Total Music Meeting, speculates that gendered style as well as sexual difference factored into the critical assessment of FIG's performances, although these were not the sole criteria:

My impression at the time was that the cool, in-crowd clique at the Total Music Meeting in Berlin wasn't into anything that was outside of what they were doing. . . . This was my main experience with FIG because the festival went on over four nights and I think each group played three or four times. I was playing with the Japanese trumpeter Toshinori Kondo and our music was not well liked by either this in-crowd of older players or the audience. The lack of support for FIG must obviously extend beyond the boundaries of that group into the entire area of women musicians. . . . I am sure the lack of men on stage made some men feel excluded. Then I guess the next step is they listen to the music or watch what is going on with an attitude, like let's see them prove themselves.[8]

At the most fundamental level, male improvisers regularly excluded women from their groups, and even if the exclusion was inadvertent, it was also blatant. This meant that the mere presence of FIG as an exclusively female group stirred controversy in the improvising community. The extreme reactions to FIG performances raised questions about the level of anxiety attached to the "exclusion" of men from FIG, the general lack of support for women improvisers, the heteronormative reading of improvisation, and the severity of critical response. The spectacle of women improvising without men tended to overshadow the improvisations themselves and obscure how the performances were received:

It's amazing the number of men that were saying, "Why are there no men?" And yet nobody had ever dreamed to think of asking why there were men only [in groups]. They'd say, well, there are just no women around. There's a kind of weird, twisted logic whereby men think it's not deliberate, we haven't deliberately excluded women. And that's even more insidious because they just haven't thought about it. At least we thought about it. (Nicols, personal interview)

FIG demonstrated that free improvisation was not free of masculinist tendencies, heterosexual expectations, or immune to gender anxieties. Although not all practices in improvisation reinforced the normative performance of gender, sexual difference, and sexuality it is clear that the position and participation of queer and straight women in the development and deployment of improvisational practices and codes was, and to a great extent still is, tentative at best.

Nor was FIG immune to criticisms from feminist audiences purportedly supportive of "women's music."[9] The dogmatic feminist gaze that criticized FIG for being too virtuosic and abstract—interpreted as macho posturing and elitism—at times plagued them. Val Wilmer recalls one of several frustrating incidents when the collective was performing at Drill Hall in London as part of a newly organized Women's Festival:

The Drill Hall concert left many women at a loss. It was a freewheeling, improvised piece, played by forthright musicians who obviously knew their instruments. But the "free music" idiom was unknown to most of the audience, and the unease and uncertainty were expressed about whether, being so "inaccessible," theirs was an elitist concept. It was bitterly frustrating for the musicians involved to be rejected in this way. Most of them had a history of struggle against male refusal to allow them a place on the bandstand. Now, having shown that not only could they play their instruments but were equipped to handle the most demanding of concepts, they were under attack from the quarter where they most needed friends. (*Mama*, 285)

There were, of course, many favorable reactions to FIG improvisations by both women and men that attended the concerts. FIG was able to introduce feminist politics to a largely uninitiated group of men as well as introduce free improvisation to a largely uninitiated group of women. Nicols cites FIG as an influence on the improvisational group "Alterations," while Cooper recalls reactions from a woman artist working in another medium: "I remember one gig FIG did and a friend of mine that I was working on a film with said: 'I don't know what on earth you're doing but I like it.' And I thought well, that really is all you need to say."

Overall, the Feminist Improvising Group did play in a number of women's festivals—the Stockholm Women's Music Festival, the Copenhagen International Women's Music Festival—and to a majority of all-women audiences:

Women, who did come because we were women, trusted us because we were women, and through that started listening to the music. I know that because of that experience a lot of women went on to listen to the whole spectrum of improvised music, not just women's music. So in a way we were ambassadors for the music as well. And I love the way—I'm being ironic here—women are not seen as an important audience. (Nicols, personal interview)

In these performances FIG applied their skills of social and technical virtuosity, improvising issues particular to women from complex sociopolitical, economic, and aesthetic perspectives: "By treating improvisation not as an isolated artifact but as something springing directly from women's experience, the musicians drew women into their music who might not otherwise be concerned with the concept of free improvisation" (Wilmer, "Feminist").

The opportunity to play for women audiences became an opportunity to reconfigure the relationship between spectacle and spectator apart from the typical scenario of masculine desire that constructed improvised music as heterosexual, positioned women musicians as spectacles for the masculine gaze and/or assumed that women on and off the bandstand were either wives, girlfriends, or groupies. Instead, improvising on their own terms was a chance for women to foreground *their* bodies and *their* sounds for the pleasure of other women. If women in the audience were not particularly fluent in deciphering the codes of free improvisation, their fluency with the all-too-familiar tropes of the female body and women's precarious position to sound and spectacle was indeed proficient. FIG's improvisations were attuned to the facility of the audience to play with and against the political codes of race, gender, sexuality, and class as well as their facility to play with the aesthetic codes of improvisation. For FIG playing was a sonic negotiation of eroticism, resistance, liberation, joy, pleasure, power, and agency, a mulitlayered call and response between individual improvisers and a community of listeners.

FIG was instrumental in encouraging listeners/interpreters to negotiate the work from a queer perspective, opening a space for the listener who responds to the laughter of women with her own improvised laughter. In other words, the spectacle of the Feminist Improvising Group was a queer sounding that demanded queer listening, an antiphonal and erotic playing by ear that heard pleasure and desire in the strange resonances and sonic exchanges of women's embodied, lived experience. There is a moment during a FIG performance recorded live at the Stockholm Women's Music Festival, in which the audience spontaneously responds to the screams, wails, and instrumental flurries of the players on stage with their own shrieks and ululations. The players pay attention to this response and reciprocate with/in a cacophony of sound: the flesh/voice of Baubo echoed in Demeter's laugh. The pleasure and pain heard in the disruptive stutters of Baubo and Demeter are heard again in the performances of the Feminist Improvising Group. The insurgent, noisy, female spectacle performed in ancient Greece is (re)played in the queer laughter of women improvisers, the improvised laughter of queer women.

Notes

1. See Young and Poynton.
2. For a comprehensive discussion of Baubo that includes the dating and significance of the statues attributed to this story, see Olender, "Aspects of Baubo" and accompanying plates.
3. A number of women I interviewed were bewildered by Bailey's omission of women improvisers from this project.
4. Instrumentation was as follows: Lindsay Cooper (bassoon, oboe, soprano sax); Maggie Nicols (voice, piano); Corine Liensol (trumpet); Georgie Born (bass, cello); Cathy Williams (voice); Irène Schweizer (piano); Sally Potter (voice, alto sax); Annemarie Roelofs (trombone, violin); Frankie Armstrong (voice); Angele Veltmeijer (flute, tenor, soprano and alto sax); Francoise Dupety (guitar).
5. The source of this excerpt is an informal written correspondence with Nicols that was not part of the formal interviews: used with permission.
6. Thanks to Becki Ross for this insight and for providing a perspective on the heterosexism and racism that pervaded many consciousness-raising groups of the time.
7. The scenario described to me by Nicols also appears in Meier and Landolt: "I was a mother and on stage there was a gap between me as a mother and as a performer. Corine was in a peculiar situation, she wanted to work on her music—she had played the piano and the violin since she was four years old—but she lost the function of her arm in a car accident. So she started to play the trumpet. She changed so much and threw everything she knew about composed music overboard. In addition she went through constant pain. . . . All of this was raw material for our show" (18).
8. Elsewhere in the interview Chadbourne refers to the prevailing FMP style as "old-school macho."
9. See Tucker for a discussion of the differences between the political and aesthetic attitudes of women who played in the "all-girl" swing bands of the 1940s and second-wave feminists who discovered their music in the late 1970s.

Works Cited

Bailey, Derek. *Improvisation: Its Nature and Practice in Music*. New York: Da Capo Press, 1992.
Buckley, Sandra L. "An Aesthetic of the Stutter." In *Cassandra: Voices From the Inside*, edited by Freda Guttman, 58–61. Montreal: Oboro, 1998.
Carson, Anne. "The Gender of Sound." In *Cassandra: Voices From the Inside*, edited by Freda Guttman, 62–81. Montreal: Oboro, 1998. Originally printed in *Glass, Irony and God*. New York: New Directions, 1995.

———. "Putting Her in Her Place: Woman, Dirt, and Desire." In *Before Sexuality: Construction of Erotic Experience in the Ancient Greek World*, edited by David M. Halperin, John J. Winkler, and Froma I. Zeitlin, 135–169. New Jersey: Princeton University Press, 1990.

Chadbourne, Eugene. Email interview. 1 November 1999.

Chenard, Marc. "FMP and Beyond: A Conversation with Irène Schweizer." *Coda* (October–November 1998): 11–13.

Cixous, Hélène. "Castration or Decapitation?" In *Out There: Marginalization and Contemporary Cultures*, edited by Russell Ferguson, Martha Gever, Trinh T. Minh-ha, and Cornel West, 345–356. The New Museum of Contemporary Art and MIT Press, 1990.

———. "Laugh of the Medusa." In *New French Feminisms*, edited by Elaine Marks and Isabelle de Courtivron, 245–264. Translated by Keith Cohen and Paula Cohen. Amherst: University of Massachsetts Press, 1980.

Cooper, Lindsay. Personal interview. 5 August 1999.

Corbett, John. "Ephemera Underscored: Writing Around Free Improvisation." In *Jazz Among the Discourses*, edited by Krin Gabbard, 217–240. Durham: Duke University Press, 1995.

Davis, Angela. *Blues Legacies and Black Feminism*. New York: Pantheon Books, 1998.

de Lauretis, Teresa. "Eccentric Subjects: Feminist Theory and Historical Consciousness." *Feminist Studies* 16, no. 1 (1990): 115–151.

Durant, Alan. "Improvisation in the Political Economy of Music." In *Music and the Politics of Culture*, edited by Christopher Norris, 252–282. London: Lawrence and Wishart, 1989.

Hale, James. "Irène Schweizer: Many and One Direction." *Coda* 276 (November–December 1997): 14–15.

Jankowski, Angely Thomas. "FIG: Feminist Improvising Group." N. pag. Zurich: N.p., 9 March 1979.

Kristeva, Julia. *The Sense and Non-sense of Revolt: The Powers and Limits of Psychoanalysis*. Translated by Jeanine Herman. New York: Columbia University Press, 2000.

———. *Revolution in Poetic Language*. Translated by Margaret Waller. New York: Columbia University Press, 1984.

Les Diaboliques. Personal interview. 5 November 1999.

Litweiler, John. *The Freedom Principle: Jazz After 1958*. New York: William Morrow, 1984.

Mackey, Nathaniel. *Discrepant Engagement: Dissonance, Cross-Culturality, and Experimental Writing*. New York: Cambridge University Press, 1993.

Meier, Rosmarie, and Patrick Landolt. Interview with Maggie Nicols and Irène Schweizer. "Wir Sind Nicht Zufallig Lesben. Das Hat Mit Autonomie Zu Tun." Translated by Suzanna Desinger and Berndt Desinger. 17–18 October 1986.

Mockus, Martha. "Lesbian Skin and Musical Fascination." In *Audible Traces: Gender, Identity, and Music*, edited by Elaine Barkin and Lydia Hamessley, 50–69. Zurich: Carciofoli, 1999.

Moi, Toril. *Sexual Textual Politics: Feminist Literary Theory*. New York: Routledge, 1988.

Nicols Maggie. Personal interview. 4 November 1999.

———. Telephone interview. 4 March 2000.

Olender, Maurice. "Aspects of Baubo: Ancient Texts and Contexts." In *Before Sexuality: Construction of Erotic Experience in the Ancient Greek World*, edited by David M. Halperin, John J. Winkler, and Froma I. Zeitlin, 83–113. New Jersey: Princeton University Press, 1990.

Potter, Sally. "On Shows." In *Framing Feminism,* edited by Rozsika Parker and Griselda Pollock, 290–292. London: Pandora, 1987.

Poynton, Cate. "Talking Like a Girl." In *Musics and Feminisms,* edited by Cate Poynton and Sally Macarthur, 119–127. Sydney: Australian Music Centre, 1999.

Prévost, Eddie. *No Sound Is Innocent.* Essex: Copula, 1995.

Roelofs, Annemarie. Personal interview. 11 August 1999.

Russo, Mary. *The Female Grotesque: Risk, Excess and Modernity.* New York: Routledge, 1994.

Schweizer, Irène. Personal interview. 5 November 1999.

Snead, James. "Repetition as a Figure of Black Culture." In *Out There: Marginalization and Contemporary Cultures,* edited by Russell Ferguson, et al., 213–230. The New Museum of Contemporary Art and MIT Press, 1990.

Tucker, Sherrie. *Swing Shift: "All-Girl" Bands of the 1940s.* Durham: Duke University Press, 2000.

Vickery, Steve. "Joëlle Léandre: Music Actuelle." *Coda* 243 (May–June 1992): 16–19.

Whitehead, Kevin. *New Dutch Swing: jazz+classical music+absurdism.* New York: Billboard Books, 1998.

Wilmer, Val. *As Serious As Your Life: The Story of the New Jazz.* Westport, Conn.: Lawrence Hill, 1980.

———. "Feminist Improvisers at Music for Socialism Festival." N.p. (1978?): n.pag.

———. "Half the Bandstand." *City Limits* (30 April–6 May 1982): 4.

———. *Mama Said There'd Be Days Like This: My Life in the Jazz World.* London: The Women's Press, 1989.

Young, Iris Marion. *Throwing Like a Girl and Other Essays in Feminist Philosophy and Social Theory.* Bloomington: Indiana University Press, 1990.

SHERRIE TUCKER

Bordering on Community
Improvising Women
Improvising Women-in-Jazz

Like many people who love jazz, I count among my most meaningful social connections those formed through engaging others in jazz soundscapes: physical spaces for listening, playing, moving, and learning, and even cyberspaces.[1] For a feminist research geek, these community meeting places include jazz theoretical and historical spaces as well, and every imaginable space specializing in the transmission of jazz knowledge. These include living rooms where aging women saxophonists and trumpet players retell jazz histories that include them, parking lots where pristine vinyl is swapped from trunks of unkempt cars, and hushed climate-controlled archives where *Down Beat, Music Dial,* and the *Chicago Defender* are stored. All of these spaces of jazz sounds, cultural contexts, varied meanings, stories, and histories have surprised me again and again with their potential for fostering profound social relations that warrant the term *community* as much as anything else in my experience.

But wait. I have not exhausted my inventory of jazz communities. To return to those living rooms of aging women musicians, for a moment, let me clarify that jazz community, as narrated by women who played instruments associated with men, teems with contradictions. Stories of jazz community, for such women, usually also include stories of exclusion and marginalization from jazz community. Or women may tell of great camaraderie they experienced on some levels in their jazz communities, then add that they were not asked to be on the records of the men with whom they worked and jammed. For women who only played in all-female bands when it was their only option, even the best "girl band" experiences were mixed blessings. If such all-female bands were not taken seriously, as they so often weren't, women musicians are often more interested in narrating their memories of jazz community in terms of emphasizing the fleeting moments when they were able to play with famous men. It is tempting to romanticize all-woman bands as women's jazz communities, but important to note that for women musicians, these organizations were often exploitative, and represented lack of access to the most valued spheres of the industry. Even today, such gendering of jazz jobs is so common to appear simply normal, except to the women who aspire to the same challenges and opportunities as their male colleagues. Take, for example, the Lincoln Center Jazz Orchestra, which, as Lara Pelligrinelli has brought to the fore, has never hired a woman or held an audition.[2]

In response to these patterns, we find another set of jazz communities, sex-specific, with antisexist intentions: the women's jazz festivals, women-in-jazz panels, women-in-jazz presentations, talks, books, films, and concerts. These, too, have fostered incredibly meaningful social relationships for me and for many other people, yet have probably irritated as many women musicians as they have helped. The need for a separate category is a reminder that even jazz communities have been unable to guarantee respite from the mundane or unpleasant sorts of human relations that we find in society at large. Even the most experimental varieties of jazz, while they may transform how we hear and think and play and conceive relationships, do so not by transcending culture and history, but by signifying within constellations of historically situated meaning. As such, jazz communities are not immune to reproducing hierarchical social meanings of their times and places through musical narratives, divisions of labor, and distribution of prestige, even as they may strive for the new. As Robin Kelley reminds us in his race and gender analysis of 1940s zoot suit culture, "the creation of an alternative culture can simultaneously challenge *and* reinforce existing power relations."[3] Women's jazz events enable me to do my work, even as they remind me that I am not supposed to be a record collector, jazz fan, or jazz researcher, any more than women of the 1940s were supposed to improvise on brass instruments, go on the road with big bands, or be included in jazz history.

Therefore, I am going to resist the temptation to write nostalgically or romantically about jazz community, even though I love jazz and attest to its social importance in my own life. Rather, I wish to examine seriously a kind of romance and nostalgia for "jazz community" that I find rather seductive but I also want to punch in the nose. I aim to think critically about seduction, a difficult task, and one seldom advocated by the lyrics of jazz standards. Yet I am driven by an urgent longing for alternate takes on one set of jazz communities that I—as a member of various research, listening, and writing communities—have found particularly seductive. I'm talking about that sometimes voluntary, sometimes reluctant, set of imagined jazz communities that we may awkwardly call "women-in-jazz."

I emphasize awkwardness, not out of sheer pessimism, but because I suggest that it is precisely through highlighting the poor match (of the women-in-jazz framework with the women who play jazz) that we may find new ways of thinking about jazz communities. Indeed, the noisy illogic of women-in-jazz as a category uniting all women who play jazz, the "wrong notes" of it all, as Ajay Heble might say, may be useful in theorizing the potential of experimental improvisation to trouble gender and other social constructions programmed to appear fixed and natural.[4] I separate the term "women-in-jazz" from the players it seeks to contain, in order to suggest that the power of women-in-jazz is that it marks a place just on the edge of jazz where women have persisted as cultural producers despite differences among them, and despite a centurylong gendered history bent on excluding them.

Women-in-jazz is a shoe that doesn't fit. Improvising women are the jazz musicians who sometimes wear it, only to kick it off behind the bass drum, or to stand tall in its six–inch heel and play screech trumpet "with balls." The power of women-in-jazz is not its ability to celebrate the contributions of women musicians, patiently jamming without reward, but rather its role as the bane of women-on-the-edge-of-jazz, who, often irritated by being tracked into devalued or hidden or tired musical spaces, have improvised, and continue to improvise, within and against this long and winding margin in all kinds of creative ways—often in ways designed to obliterate it. The ways improvising women have improvised women-in-jazz may, in fact, prove theoretically useful in deconstructing nostalgic notions of jazz community that obscure others who jam outside:

I did not pick this lifestyle because I am a woman-in-jazz. At the same time, I feel deeply supportive of other women in jazz because I know the shit they go through. I think there's a way of feeling supportive of each other, while at the same time feeling resentful when you only get called for the women-calls.[5]

The same conclusion is expressed in more theoretical terms by Trinh T. Minh-ha, feminist theorist, filmmaker, and composer: "In a way, a feminist always has at least two gestures at the same time: that of pointing insistently to difference, and that of unsettling every definition of woman arrived at. As a Zen saying goes, 'Never take the finger pointing to the moon for the moon itself.'" (186).

Improvising Communities versus Unison Unities

If one is an improvising woman, how does one balance annoyance with women-in-jazz as a limiting and nonsensical professional trap, with gender-based mutual support based on common experiences with other women who play jazz? These other improvising women may or may not share anything with you other than the fact that they are often tracked into women-in-jazz gigs and otherwise slip the mind of jazz job central. Yet, if women play jazz no differently than men, it follows that some women will appreciate each other's musical ideas, just as jazz players of any sex sometimes do and sometimes don't share musical interests. And isn't mutual support also a kind of community? It does seem hasty to throw out the possibility of jazz community that is conscious of women's particular experiences of gender constructions.

Feminist theorists have grappled with trying to find frameworks for talking about women in ways that argue that women are neither exactly the same as men, nor polar opposites. If women are the same, the argument goes, then why do women often have different experiences? Are women trombonists less recorded than their male colleagues, for example, because they aren't living up to their potentials? If women are polar opposites to men, does that mean that women have essential natures that give them different callings in life (men are from trumpet, women are from flute)? Does that mean that all women are the same, across culture, race, class, sexuality, and history?[6] Can improvising women shed some light on how to negotiate these tricky changes? Are there models in jazz community-formation history that would address these dilemmas? Conversely, do the struggles of improvising women (who may or may not be feminists) and feminist theorists (who may or may not be musicians) provide a welcome entry for examining critically the mainstream fantasies about jazz community?

Jazz discourse is a curious mix of romance about modernist geniuses who appear to have no communities and nostalgic communities for whom playing jazz seems to achieve historical and social and political transcendence. In each case, politics and power disappear from jazz history. Critical historical research and musicians' own accounts of their lives can, and often do, unearth evidence to the contrary. Modernist geniuses usually turn out to have families, friends, neighbors, and/or collaborators—they did not achieve greatness alone—and nostalgic communities, on closer inspection, often turn out to be much more complex than popularly imagined. Yet these myths, the isolated jazz genius who is understood by no one until discovered by the record-collecting hipsters, and the harmonious jazz community of days-gone-by, continue to dominate the construction of popular jazz meaning. While both are deserving of critical scrutiny, it is the latter that I wish to revisit at the moment.

Nostalgia for lost community, the old "back when we were all together," holds great appeal for many people, including many feminist historians seeking to reclaim histories in which women escape the isolation and tedium of gender-proscribed lives. Indeed, the fantasy of going on the road with an "all-girl" band, despite knowledge of exploitation and hardship, holds at least one obvious advantage to that inspirational road trip taken by Thelma and Louise. Many a fantasy of jazz community is constructed as liberating for all involved. Yet, it is also important to remember that totalizing visions of the past nearly always mask power and dissent, are wisely constructed as romantic by those who benefit by them, and alienate those lacking subject positions within that imagined unity. Nostalgia for lost jazz community is not, I might add, the exclusive realm of feminist historians researching all-woman bands. Nor, interestingly enough, is it particular to people of either sex who long for musical communities that practiced aesthetic forms that privileged unison, harmony, and precise section work.

Examples of such nostalgia include notions of jazz as a color-blind liberal community where race never mattered and everyone got along—a fantasy that may assuage white liberal guilt, but erases the complexity of the social geography of lopsided integration (instances where white people could enter black clubs, but not the other way around, and so forth). The nostalgia for jazz as an always oppositional community is another fiercely guarded ideal, even though countless jazz musicians have wanted their music to be commercially successful—and certainly, improvement of material conditions of African-Americans has historically not been antithetical to black cultural politics. Another is the idea that jazz consumption is somehow a way for people with power and privilege to achieve, through subcultural soundtracks, a sense of community with people different than themselves, who are imagined as intuitive, wise, sexual (what Ingrid Monson calls the "problem of white hipness"). And there is the resurgence of popular collective jazz identity, recently produced through a mass-mediated series of romantic narratives about remarkable individuals—almost invariably U.S. American and male, usually poor, and often black, routinely unique, natural geniuses—who transcend humble backgrounds by creating very special music that makes America feel good, and makes the rest of the world feel good about America. Obviously, these are romantic fantasies that I find dangerous and in need of critical examination.

As the last example demonstrates, the isolated individual represented by the modernist jazz genius is scarcely an alternative to the pitfalls of nostalgic community. What other kinds of jazz communities are imaginable and who imagines them? Is there a kind of jazz community-formation that avoids exclusionary politics that plague other group identity projects? If not, whose bodies and desires are unimaginable enough that they may mark the outer limits of these jazz utopian visions? Do models for social transformation exist in those edges of jazz, and, if so, might improvising women's familiarity with those edges provide such models? Can jazz musicians jam new social relations? Or does even the most startlingly new manifestation of the sound of surprise signify within discursive limits? Can free improvisation exist in an unfree world? Can improvising communities improvise new kinds of communities?

This barrage of questions, musical, social, and political, is meant to bust open the definitions of community and women, to suggest that it is not the simple sing-along versions of such terms that makes them useful, but the tensions and differences that fill and exceed each. "All definitions are devices," wrote Trinh Minh-ha in her film *Naked Spaces*. It is not any sense of natural or complete meanings behind "community" or "woman" that interests me, but the way that these forms are used, played, improvised upon and against, constructed and reconstructed through collective play. It is not with pessimism, therefore, but with hope for transformation through improvisation, that I seek other ways to think of differences among women, jazz communities, and women in jazz communities.

It makes no more sense socially, historically, or politically, than it does musically, to imagine jazz community as Mr. Rogers's Neighborhood. Communities don't naturally pop out of their front doors each morning singing and waving; they are forged through affinity, practice, and labor. In terms of inclusion and exclusion, they run the gamut. Community-formation includes unbelonging, as well as belonging; complicated by variety within these seemingly cut-and-dried opposites. Belonging may be reluctant, or by default (they won't let me in over there so I will belong here) or it may be elective. Unbelonging includes resistance, refusal, and exclusion, as well as lack of interest.

Community-belonging, like national belonging, is defined both by who is in and who is out, designated by lines that are sometimes fuzzy, sometimes deadly sharp, and usually contested. It is, in fact, often more difficult for communities whose group identities are formed through its members' exclusions from other communities to recognize their own outsiders, exclusions, and margins, than it is for communities who define themselves through proclaiming insider status and exclusive membership. Communities, like health clubs and long distance plans, have a maddening array of ever-changing membership policies all operating at once, some more broadly beneficial than others. Because communities are social, and societies are complex, it should not be surprising to find not only members and non-members, but affiliate members, unwelcome members, untenured members, unauthorized members, founding members, former members, aspiring members, rebellious members, substitute members, partial members, missing members, members in dispute, members in love, members who leave, and members who would rather belong somewhere else. Like nations, communities often have not only borders, but borderlands, so usefully theorized by Gloria Anzaldúa, where terms like "inside" and "outside" are far too simple. Like Anzaldúa's "new *mestiza*," people in the borderlands cope by functioning "in a pluralistic mode"; they learn to "sustain contradictions," to transform "ambivalence into something else." Neither inside nor outside, people on the borderlands juggle nonmembership and multiple membership at the same time.[7]

For many jazzwomen, "jazz community" has meant jamming in the margins of the margins (to elaborate on Krin Gabbard's expression), sometimes in women-in-jazz communities (ranging from "all-girl" bands to women's jazz festivals) with varying degrees of reluctance and enthusiasm. For jazzwomen, to improvise has often meant to trouble gender (consciously or not, intentionally or not, willingly or not). Women who see themselves as challenging musical structures are sometimes heard primarily as challenging people's expectations for what women sound like, what women do, what jazz musicians look like, what is the gender of jazz.[8] Collaboration in jazz, for many jazzwomen, has often meant collaboration with the very discourses that exclude them from other jazz communities. "I don't approve of most club owners I've met," confided one female musician, "but I'm forced to collaborate with them, in a sense."[9] Rather than total inclusion or total exclusion, it may be that improvising women historically border on many jazz communities, including those that have been labeled women-in-jazz.

How might a critical investigation of the concept of jazz community as a network of contested social formations with borderlands as well as nuclei, yield possible theories and practices of community formation that are porous, flexible, strategic and liberatory, as opposed to ideas about belonging and unbelonging that are conservative, comfy, and entrenched? For me, this entails examining edginess, as well as collectivity; limitations, as well as possibilities of jazz as a site of community-formation, improvisation, and collaboration. Such new approaches may be found through theorizing the ways that women horn players, drummers, and/or record collectors may imagine themselves as active community members (perhaps without full membership privileges), yet find themselves unimaginable and unrepresentable at many community functions. Except, of course, at those aforementioned, awkwardly labeled, often well intentioned, still necessary functions called "women-in-jazz."

Dreams of Community, Politics of Difference

Ajay Heble and Gillian Siddall have written incisively about the awkwardness of women-in-jazz as an antisexist jazz strategy.[10] In 1997, the Guelph Jazz Festival took as its theme "Women in Jazz." This move was not predicated on any illusions that women-as-women play nicely together or play a special brand of jazz. Rather, the festival crafted its theme as a conscious way of making connections between the historical struggles of women jazz musicians, and of contemporary underrepresentation and marginalization of women jazz musicians (Heble, 7).

As someone who was, at that moment, quite passionately involved in working on a dissertation and book about all-woman bands during the 1940s, this sounded like my kind of jazz community and I eagerly flew three thousand miles to participate, and subsequently heard a fantastic range of challenging and stimulating concerts and papers. In fact, the range of approaches was so striking, I remember thinking afterward that this festival had achieved perhaps the best thing that could be achieved at a women-in-jazz festival: it rendered the term "women-in-jazz" utterly meaningless, as meaningless as the term "jazz" itself. As I later learned, however, from reading Heble and Siddall's account in *Landing on the Wrong Note*, there had been a good deal of behind-the-scenes resistance to the whole idea of focusing on "Women in Jazz." It seemed that a community that supported experimental music did not automatically and unanimously support a political focus on women as a marginalized group of that community; nor did female players necessarily identify as "women-in-jazz." For some women musicians, being one of two or three women instrumentalists invited to a supposedly gender-free jazz festival felt inclusive, whereas being invited to a woman-in-jazz festival felt marginalizing, even though the intention was to have an event where women musicians were at the center of the agenda for a change, and to come to terms with a historical legacy that is, like most historical legacies, not gender-free.

Yet, the responses of women musicians who did not wish to be lumped into the women-in-jazz framework are very familiar to me; both from my interviews with women musicians who played in all-woman bands during the 1920s, 1930s and 1940s, and from my own experiences as a jazz disc jockey, jazz journalist, and jazz academic. In my old radio days, I once worked very hard to target myself for a particular radio station that played jazz. I studied the format, learned the sonic parameters of the various day parts, observed the dose and tone and level of background information provided by the regular announcers, and auditioned: "We really like your tape," I was told, "but we already have a woman." Not only did this leave me with the feeling that I did not belong in the jazz radio community, it left me feeling resentful of the only other woman disc jockey I knew of who played jazz on the air. This experience did not, oddly enough, leave me feeling skeptical of women's jazz communities in the past, but, rather, hungrier than ever for models of jazz practice where women were prominent.

In an article entitled "The Ideal of Community and the Politics of Difference," Iris Marion Young wrote:

> The ideal of community privileges unity over difference, immediacy over mediation, sympathy over recognition of the limits of one's understanding of others from their point of view. Community is an understandable dream, expressing a desire for selves that are transparent to one another, relationships of mutual identification, social closeness and comfort. The dream is understandable, but politically problematic. (300–301)

The problem, continued Young, is that "those motivated by" the dream of community "will tend to suppress differences among themselves or implicitly to exclude from their political groups persons with whom they do not identify." As an alternative, she suggests a "politics of difference," a framework for social and political interaction in which sameness is not the measure for collective potential (300–301).

It was, in fact, a dream of community, not a politics of difference, that drew me to research all-woman bands. Yet my dream of recovering lost communities of marginalized women who had banded together and played jazz (even though society told them not to) often proved far too simple. Imagine my surprise to meet women musicians who preferred not to play in all-woman bands; or women who said, "I don't think of myself as a woman, I think of myself as a jazz musician" (a very common statement for women jazz musicians, both of the past and the present). Or women who flat-out told me that other women musicians were not serious; that men played better; that the all-woman bands were terrible except for the one she played in.

As a feminist historian, it took me some time to understand these complications. I am not the only woman researcher who, amid the second-wave women's movement, longed for examples of sisterhood, of women working together across differences of race, class, sexuality, and so forth, harmonious yet diverse communities of women, such as we were seeking, struggling for, but not always able to create in our women's studies classes, organizing efforts, activist communities, and so forth. Along the way, in fact, I met many other women who were researching women-in-jazz with similar romantic fantasies about what we would find out about women's jazz communities. When we interviewed women musicians, our romantic notions were often challenged with other versions of women jazz musicians' explanations of roles of women in jazz history.

"I want to tell you the difference between working with men and working with women, one special difference," said trumpet player Jane Sager, who had played with both women's and men's bands in the 1930s and 1940s. I quote at length the example she offered, and invite you to imagine (and giggle if you wish) at my astonishment:

The two trumpet players that sat on either side of me, the first man and the third man, would argue about the four forty tune-up "A." And one would say to the other one, "You're sharp" and the other one would say, "No, you're flat." And then they'd turn to me and say, "Janie, what are we? Come on, tell us. Settle this." And I'd say, "I will not. You go and hit that four forty bar and figure it out yourselves." And they got so angry about this that one night they went out in the alley and they hit each other; they had a powing job. And they came back. We went on the air and we went on for the night for the job. And you would never know a thing had happened. They played perfectly. And they acted like gentlemen. Everything was great. Now, if they had been girls and they'd had a big to-do about something . . . ! The girls were so emotional. This is what used to get me. To me it was a job and you did it. Anything outside couldn't interfere. And the girls would let it interfere. And they'd play badly, or they'd start to cry, or do some darn thing like that. And, of course, I never could see that. Maybe it was because I grew up with all boys when I was a kid back there in Wisconsin. But that's the big difference. (personal interview)

Elsewhere in the interview, Sager spoke highly of women musicians whom she admired, and even spoke out critically that they haven't received credit for their talents. A romantic take on women-in-jazz and all-woman bands might miss her negotiation with the category women-in-jazz; her refusal to occupy the subject position of representative forgotten jazz woman when it was dumped on her, and to make use of it at other times when she could exercise some control. The category, both in her career and in our interview, compelled her to reject women-in-jazz as an identity if she wanted to be accepted as part of the larger jazz community, but it also compelled her to find work in that category at times, and it was also clear that she found meaningful spaces of community-formation as well as critical spaces of unbelonging, in both men's and women's bands. Hanging on to a romantic longing for unity would prevent us from seeing the many ways that differently positioned women who play jazz have historically negotiated women-in-jazz as a category.

In my research of all-woman bands during World War II alone, I found a stunning array of negotiations, both performative and rhetorical, that women musicians engaged when laboring both in and out of the women-in-jazz categories of their day.[11] Women's bands, like men's bands, were mostly segregated on one side of the color line or the other. Women musicians negotiated women-in-jazz in various ways, in part because social constructions of gender, race, ethnicity, and class made different normative definitions of womanhood available to different women.

Yet even on either side of the black/white color line, there was great variety in performance strategies of gender and jazz. On the white side, all-woman bands negotiated women-in-jazz in different ways that ranged from visual sex-spectacle emphasizing titillation of white women playing hot music popularly associated by white audiences with sexual licentiousness (Ina Ray Hutton's "Blonde Bombshell" image) to the girl-next-door performance of patriotic young women playing American jazz and swing very well for the troops (Ada Leonard's "All-American" Girls, Sharon Rogers All-Girl Orchestra, and so forth), to the upper-class "accomplished" feminine difference expressed both in emphasis on musical styles associated with European whiteness, so-called high culture, and femininity, and by costumes hailing Victorian angels of the hearth (Phil Spitalny's "Hour of Charm").

Gender performances on the black side ranged from schoolgirl images that emphasized black education and improved conditions of African-American women (the Prairie View Co-eds, the International Sweethearts of Rhythm, and Swinging Rays of Rhythm); to the international theme that linked African-Americans with nonwhite people around the globe (the International Sweethearts of Rhythm); to an emphasis on styles of playing associated with masculinity and deemphasis on looking and sounding "pretty" (the Darlings of Rhythm come to mind, though there were many bands on either side of the color line that engaged this strategy at least some of the time). I have recently written an article entitled "Improvising Womanhood, or a Conundrum is a Woman: Race, Gender, and Representation in Black Women's Jazz, 1920–1950," in which I explore how some African-American women jazz musicians drew from the respectability politics of the Black Clubwomen's Movement to counter stereotypes and claim a dignified presence as black women and as jazz musicians.[12] Again we arrive at the question: if there is so much variety to how women jazz musicians have coped with women-in-jazz as a category, and if it is so complex and often a nuisance, how does one justify ever focusing on women jazz musicians as a group? How might we improve conditions for, and increase knowledge about female players that does not lump them together and separate them from the category jazz?

Rock scholar Norma Coates analyzed similar tensions when she wrote that the label, "women-in-rock," rather than elevating female rockers, "delineates hegemonic space. 'Rock' is separate from 'women.' 'Women' are only related to 'rock' by being allowed 'in'. The 'in' of 'women in rock' has a contingent feel about it, an aura of something that will never be complete never fully integrated with the whole" (Coates, 61). Yet Coates winds up advocating a new use of "women-in-rock" with a self-conscious critical edge, a use that would deploy such catchy and bombastic ironic style that women rock fans would take to calling themselves "women-in-rock," along with established female rock stars, journalists, and disc jockeys. Used so broadly and aggressively, it would no longer signify a history of rock without women. This, obviously, has not yet occurred.

Likewise, Heble and Siddall speculate on the subversive potential of the phrase "women in jazz," by suggesting that the term "is unsettling because it threatens to expose that naturalized conception of jazz as male and to call attention to the social and institutional inequalities that continue to militate against women's access to performance and recording opportunities, media exposure, and influential management positions in the music industry" (160–161).

I agree that the term "women-in-jazz," like "women-in-rock" (as well as women-in-history, women-in-literature, women-in-business, the list goes on), holds this threat, to the extent that it contains it; the trick is to find a way to liberate the contents. This is the crux of my longing for alternate takes on women-in-jazz. Without a critical spin, "women-in-jazz" most threatens to unsettle women who identify and work as jazz musicians. If taken uncritically and unself-consciously, the term threatens *not* to expose these naturalized equations of men and jazz; in fact, in very powerful ways it constructs women who accept this category as women-out-of-jazz. The women-in-jazz designation has been around, after all, in some form or another, throughout the history of jazz. Sometimes it has taken the form of "all-girl" bands, sometimes feminized instrument choices, sounds, techniques, venues, and genres; the gender codes have changed from time to time, but marginalization remains. Despite the variety of intentions involved, women-in-jazz, in all its phases, is often experienced as the bane of women jazz musicians. Women instrumentalists who wish to maximize their jazz opportunities are compelled to reject "women-in-jazz" if, like Jane Sager, they want to be seen and heard as inside, not outside, the community of jazz musicians. This marginalization, after all, is not just an accident of omission, but has often been actively produced, sometimes in jazz practice, but most definitely in jazz discourse, or the dominant ways that jazz has been represented, and in the normative definitions of gender and labor in the societies in which jazz discourse has circulated.

As a quick and dirty example, I shall now regale you with an excerpt from a longer poem that is not at all atypical of the trivializing and humorous approach to women jazz musicians in *Down Beat* magazine of the 1930s and 1940s. The author of "To Hubbys [*sic*] of Wives Who Horns and Saxes Blow," is listed as Kay "Sugar Puss" Weber. Weber, Dan Morganstern reminds me, was a well-known big band vocalist who sang with Tommy Dorsey. Apparently, she was also one of the few women who wrote for *Down Beat*, mostly as a columnist, but at least once, in the summer of 1937, as a poet. A couple of stanzas, to set the tone:

> Tell me something, little woman,
> You, who horns and saxes blow
> Are you wed, or are you single
> Tell me what's your status quo?[13]

After trivializing women musicians through diminutive address, and inquiring after their marital status, the poem then goes on to quiz the "hubby" of such a woman about the effect of his wife's career on his masculinity. What does he do while his wife is off playing her trombone? Does he "keep the home fires burning / Stew the beef and broil the mutton?" Does he babysit? And when she goes on the road with the band, does he travel on the bus, or does he "go home to mother?"

At one point, Weber cheerfully quips that her poem is "written all in jest," but that doesn't change the fact that it rhetorically supports, and is typical of, press notices that constructed all-woman bands as freak shows, novelties, and jokes in a women-in-jazz context of the time period. One could argue that Weber's poem also calls critical attention to a double standard, using role reversal to deconstruct gender divisions of labor. But even if the poem functions to call attention to the unacknowledged loneliness and labor of "our bandsmen's wives," it does so at the expense of satirizing women musicians and all-woman bands as unnatural, ridiculous, and damaging to men's manliness. Its sympathies remain within the traditional division of jazz and swing labor.

Yet, Kay Weber, the poem's author, as a vocalist with the Glenn Miller and Tommy Dorsey bands, was a woman-in-swing (which, for *Down Beat* of the 1930s was a woman-in-jazz). Presumably, she did not keep the home fires burning, either. Like the women "who horns and saxes blow," she worked late hours and traveled on the road. Because the press about female band singers is heavy on the personal gossip, one of the few things we can read about Weber's career is that she was romantically involved with co-vocalist Bob Eberly when she sang with the Dorsey brothers in the 1930s, and that she eventually married Bob Crosby trombonist Ward Silloway. Is she in the same "jazz community" as the women instrumentalists of her day? All of the bands she mentions in her poem are white women's bands, again, consistent with *Down Beat's* treatment of women jazz musicians and all-woman bands. Are the white band women in the same "jazz community" as the women of color who were excluded from their organizations? Were the women in Phil Spitalny's Hour of Charm in the same jazz community as the women in the Harlem Playgirls, who were not written about in *Down Beat,* yet whose repertoire seems to have been closer to what the magazine saw as real jazz? Is there any wonder that women who play jazz have, for many different reasons, historically found women-in-jazz a messy and unforgiving label? Simply to reject it, however, is hardly to undo its damage. What is an improvising woman to do?

As I sat at my computer, trying to think through the conundrums of women-in-jazz for improvising women, I found myself longing for, well, other people with whom to bounce around some ideas about women-in-jazz. Well, okay, I'll admit it, I longed for a women-in-jazz community. I didn't long for a community that would agree with everything I said, but a community that would struggle with me over hard questions that matter. So I did what people in search of community do in this day and age: I logged on. My first stop was Jeanette Lambert's site, <Jazzgrrls@topica.com>, where I posted a request for feedback, ending with the following questions:

Is belonging to a jazz community important to you? Do you consider yourself a member of a jazz community? What is your jazz community? Do you belong to more than one jazz community? Do you feel excluded from one or more jazz communities? Is belonging to a women-in-jazz community important to you? Do you consider yourself a member of one? Do you form community when you are playing? talking with musicians? listening with friends? going to meetings? chatting online? Do some jazz/improvised music traditions foster community more than others? I'm thinking very flexibly about "community"—could be a band, this list, jazz history, a venue, musicians you 'flow' with, an organization. . . . you name it! Many thanks, in advance.[14]

I received an immediate selection of varied and fascinating responses, many from cynical and practical perspectives. Several women told me flat out that the only time they have a jazz community is when they get the gig, but that they were overlooked when others were hiring. Many stressed that community was formed while playing, but that opportunities to play were dependent on networks from which they were often excluded. Much of what the jazzgrrls respondents wrote about was not musical form or aesthetics, but labor issues. It is significant that the vast percentage of respondents asked me not to quote them by name. Most women spoke of holding marginal positions in communities of players. One woman explained that while she belonged "loosely" to a jazz community, "I have no mentor. I do not feel supported. I often play badly when I play with them." Women spoke of feeling tested when they played, of having their work constantly devalued. "It's like if a guy plays a quarter note, it's worth more," wrote one saxophonist.

Several women spoke of groups of women jazz musicians they had formed or joined that attempted to address labor issues, not as a means of separating women musicians into women-in-jazz, but as a means of trying to support one another as they sought careers in jazz. One respondent situated this in the "tradition in the jazz community to pass on knowledge and find ways of giving back to the community," rather than as a special "women's" tradition. Another respondent described "a network of female jazz musicians" that she had been attending for ten years. "We primarily get together once a month to talk—each person gets time to talk about whatever problems/successes they've been having then they get feedback from the group. We also have jam sessions from time to time. The group was formed because these musicians felt they needed their own community to respond to their unique needs, as well as a way to network since we often are excluded from the old-boy jazz network. We do hire each other for gigs/recording sessions etc. and refer each other for work." After this woman's posting, several women sent emails expressing envy for this woman's group. Many respondents described as desirable those women-in-jazz communities that did not involve working and playing as women-in-jazz, but that did provide behind-the-scenes support for women who saw themselves as struggling for acceptance in jazz period; as a way of gaining the information, resources, and connections necessary for leaving behind the jobs labeled women-in-jazz.

Some women felt that developments sometimes regarded as negative for musicians seemed to benefit women in jazz. Two women spoke positively about the trend away from working cohesive bands and toward pickup groups, as improving their chances of being called to play. One woman pointed out that "being a musician isn't really like belonging to a club," but more like moving in and out of a network of subsets, some friendlier than others. Jazz community, for her, meant "feeling a part of a larger group," and counted it as "important to anyone's development as a player." Jazz community, for her, included all those players who influenced her musical development, whether or not she ever had personal contact with them.

By and large, the women who responded to my posting did not feel united with other women jazz musicians in any kind of automatic or natural way; yet they all participated on a list-serve for women jazz musicians, and chose to answer my posting about women's jazz communities. Their approaches to women's community and jazz community were not dreamy delusions of sameness, but practical notes from the trenches and borders of many communities.

Contradictions abounded, even in this small sample of women jazz musicians who belong to a single list-serve. Though most felt that more experimental forms of playing were more open to all kinds of difference, including gender, some musicians noted that, as women, they were often tracked into less adventuresome musical practices. One player of Latin jazz said she longed for a community that would nourish her "need to expand," which involved experimentation. She found that the other Latin jazz players she knew tended to be purists, and "put her down" for veering from tradition. As a Latina New Yorker, this criticism felt particularly personal, and she wished she could find a community that could support her and her music.

Another musician stressed that she felt more acceptance in bebop and swing than in the "outside and exploratory" jazz she wished to play, and that in the circles of the jazz community in which she loosely operated, "dangerous harmonic terrain" was the prestigious turf of young white men. These comments are a reminder that gender is rarely, if ever, just about organization of meaning, but about organization of power. The gender of sound may signify differently across the time, but the tendency for sounds associated with masculinity to be more highly valued than those that signify femininity is relatively predictable. "Free jazz," like other musical practices, may be feminized in periods when it holds less prestige, and masculinized when it holds more prestige. Some women felt that working in all-woman settings was similar to working as the only women in an otherwise all-male group, in that the attention is called to her sex rather than to her musicianship. One women wrote that for this reason, she sought a balance between women and men in a collective of jazz composers that she founded.

Some musicians felt that new technologies were conducive to new and exciting forms of jazz community in which women could participate more fully. "Oddly enough, I have found a jazz community through MP3.com," wrote one musician, who had been forming community through "writing to musicians whose music I like who also have sites there, asking if they'd listen to my music." This musician had already collaborated with a number of other musicians internationally that she had met online. "Because it's becoming cheaper and easier to make clean recordings digitally, musicians will be able to record themselves, mix, and even distribute their work without as much need for the intervention of third parties." She felt that MP3 facilitated making connections that were based primarily on music. "In a sense, I feel women fit into this community very easily because it's a do-it-yourself arena. You don't have to wait for anyone's permission to be accepted into a clique or awarded a recording contract.

Baritone saxophonist Claire Daly, one of the few musicians who agreed to be quoted by name, walked an interesting line in discussing these issues with me. "Like all jazz musicians," she said, "you go to where the work is. If you are a woman and you play jazz, then an all-female band is one of the places where you fit the requirements. At the same time, because it is 'women-in-jazz,' it gets dismissed." She made an interesting point by stressing that the experience can be musically wonderful, "if the focus is on the music," or it can be terrible, just like any other kind of job. But it doesn't get taken seriously because it is seen as "women-in-jazz" (personal interview).

Daly's distinction between being a woman who plays jazz and women-in-jazz intrigued me, as she seemed to see the latter as a kind of format. This made me think of other feminized, devalued formats in jazz marketing, like smooth jazz, or what used to be called "dinner jazz" on the old KJAZ FM, San Francisco. Dinner jazz signified a kind of domesticated jazz mix associated with the kinds of upscale mainstream audiences that salespeople can more easily sell to advertisers than those lint-encrusted hipsters, or retirement-aged working-class black people, or whoever the ad agencies, rating services, and market researchers imagine as the audience for the real McCoy.

Daly also suggested that some genres might be more "open minded" and inclusive than others, that "freer music will often include a more mixed group of people playing it." While not wanting to make a staunch generalization, she said that for herself, the playing and listening experience of avant-garde jazz was more conducive to openness and inclusiveness than bebop and swing. Describing herself as "into the out" in the 1970s, she said that this music was more open in terms of destination. In other words, not only note choice, chord structures, and form, were freer, but ideas of "where you're going" were freer. "You get in the car and you go and hopefully you find some exciting places. You're not there to prove you can make the changes. Certain styles, at their worst, can be like a sport." The kind of ensemble playing she valued seemed to resonate with Iris Marion Young's "politics of difference." Success was not measured in sameness. The music journey she described was enabled and energized by internal differences, rather than policed by community-as-unity.

Yet, many improvising women will tell you that free jazz, in social practice, has not exactly been known for its gender equity. In 1997, The Women's Avant Fest was held in Chicago, by composers Maura Bosch and Kitty Brazelton. Brazelton, as well as composer, flutist, and performance artist Janice Misurell-Mitchell, both of whom performed at the festival, told me that they felt that the avant-garde field was more open to women in classical music than in jazz. According to Brazelton, "the 'downtown' experimental jazz world is extremely male-dominated, as well as instrumentally dominated (which seems to lead to a sort of gender segregation)." In fact, the festival strategically cut across genre in order to create an environment where the gendering of the genres would not work against the performers, and included performers who used voice, text, and performance art, all areas in which women have found more acceptance than in playing jazz on band instruments. Deconstucting genre was one of the musical projects already for Brazelton and Bosch in their composition. Brazelton felt that this festival strategy "led to the excitement of looking at a cross-section of innovative musics on the basis of gender, which seemed like a very new way to look."

While these tactics of the Women's Avant Fest certainly offer some additional ways to think through the issues faced by improvising women, I cannot help worrying about what it means to combine jazz and classical histories. Can "genre busting" avoid the danger of subsuming very different histories of improvisation, so usefully theorized by George Lewis? For Lewis, "'Afrological' and 'Eurological' systems of improvisative musicality" are "historically emergent rather than ethnically essential" (93). These different approaches are not genetically dependent on who plays them, but are connected to the social histories of players who developed these systems. Not only aesthetic differences are at stake here, but different notions of history, memory, and artistic expression—notions meaningful to many players, women as well as men. According to Lewis, Afrological improvisation sees itself as social and as engaging histories of struggle, whereas Eurological improvisation wishes to transcend history, to see itself as more abstract.[15]

Yet certainly Women's Avant Fest made interesting tactical use of one form of improvisation that has been somewhat friendlier to women, in order to "create a festival for cutting-edge women's music in all genres," where "the only criteria for inclusion were artistic merit, originality and leadership."[16] This approach to conceiving improvising women as a group is inspiring in its encouragement of an encounter of musical women that are assumed to play differently and to push the envelope. It invites collective and community-formation that values difference.

Janice Misurell-Mitchell also offers an approach to improvising gender that seems especially valuable to rethinking how women musicians may improvise women-in-jazz. Noting that more women musicians "still play the traditional instruments—piano, flute, so you can't easily compete in terms of instrumental power," Misurell-Mitchell opts to play the flute and sing in ways that explicitly challenge and signify upon traditional notions of instruments and gender. "A composer/flutist speaking here, and I'll tell you that I work quite hard to avoid the pretty in flute music, unless I'm forced to in performance or am being ironic. Further, I use extended techniques, distortion, amplification, and recently a lot of vocal work in my flute sound. I've added text in a number of ways—singing and playing, speaking and playing (sprechstimme), multiphonics, key clicks, air rushes—things which distort and give power and mystery to the sound. These elements also move the sound away from gender, or if gender is present, the implications are intended (for example, I use parts of Ginsberg's *Howl* and say the word 'Moloch' in an angry tone into the flutes, partriarchy intended)."

By commenting on gender, and working against assumptions of the gender norms of people and instruments and genres and labor, Misurell-Mitchell might be said to "trouble gender," in the Judith Butler sense, by showing the constructedness of gender, and confronting the audience with its own gendered expectations of flute and women. Indeed, she performs gender musically in a way that calls attention to its social coding and to the fact that it may be reconstructed. In addition, her "not pretty" approach to flute might be said to ring with the "noise of Festival and Freedom," in the Jacques Attali sense of disorganizing the sounds of power and "creat[ing] the conditions for a major discontinuity extending far beyond its field." Attali does not use "noise" in a disparaging or derogatory way. On the contrary, to equate Misurell-Mitchell's music with Attali's noise, is to praise it for what Attali hoped "may be the essential element in a strategy for the emergence of a truly new society" (133). Misurell-Mitchell's approach could be theorized as "Gender Noise," in a way of performing sonic noise that makes gender noisy at the same time.

In her afterword to Attali's *Noise,* Susan McClary noted that this theory may be particularly useful for "people who managed not to be silenced by the institutional framework, who are dedicated to injecting back into music the noise of the body, of the visual, of emotions, and of gender" (157). For McClary, women who play drums would be an example of the "culturally noisy." Might improvising women improvising women-in-jazz on the borders of jazz be among those "culturally noisy" musicians who are well positioned to create sonic noise that battles for social change? Might working conditions of women who play jazz best be improved, not by dreams of same-sex unity, but by the willingness of musicians and theorists, whose interests and practices are so inclined (I won't assume this includes all women jazz musicians or all feminist theorists!), to engage in practices of troubling gender through noise bent on disorder and new order (in that order)? I'm going to close by moving out from these varied responses to some varied suggestions for alternate takes on women-in-jazz.

Alternate Takes on Women-in-Jazz

Take One: Conceptualize women-in-jazz as a border community, not as a community with a unified core, but as a community on the edge, that has, as its closest thing to common experience, scattered patterns of unbelonging, partial belonging, loose connections, and guerilla tactics. Use this conceptual space as a way for thinking about other kinds of community-formation theory and practice, in jazz and otherwise.

Take Two: Replace the term women-in-jazz with "improvising women." Roll it around in your head until "improvising women" or "improvising woman" is a verb, like Trinh Minh-ha's "writing woman" (28). Instead of thinking of an "improvising woman," as a musician with a female sex–assigned body or a musician who identifies as a woman (and who may or may not have anything in common with other "improvising women"), focus on musical practices of "improvising woman," or ways of playing that challenge social structures of music and social structures of gender simultaneously. To think of "woman" as a set of changes that can be improvised upon exposes the flexibility, variability, and historicity of the category "woman": it does not reduce all women to essentialist expectations of common female culture; nor does it restrict them to roles constructed within their historical cultural contexts.

Take Two (B-Side): That said, understand that while "improvising woman" is, for some musicians, a project worthy of their creative energies, many "improvising women" are tired of having to "improvise woman" every time they play. "Improvising woman" means challenging dominant notions of "what is a woman" and "what is a jazz musician." Think of "improvising woman" as a working condition of "improvising women" and that it is an extra and extremely difficult set of changes in itself. Do you call attention to your difference and attempt to signify upon it? Do you strive for musical language and community in which meanings of gender are reworked? Or do you refuse to think about gender, and do what you love with chops that may very well be attained within structures that marginalize people like you? While it is fascinating to explore how meanings of gender, race, class, sexuality, and so forth, are struggled over in women's jazz performances (especially in experimental music that seems particularly well suited to taking apart prior assumptions), realize that "improvising woman" can cost hard-won footholds in slippery terrain. Remain interested in how various performance tactics affect working conditions of women who improvise.

Take Three: Give up the term "women-in-jazz" altogether. Next time I write a book on all-woman big bands, for example, I may simply call it, *The Swing Era,* or just *Jazz.* A book on women musicians in the 1960s and 1970s, suggests my editor, could simply be called *Five Lives in the Post-Bop Business* (I may write this yet). Or maybe it is better to take Norma Coates's tack and reclaim the term women-in-jazz, use it as often as possible, especially in cases where women are not present. Apologize for not being able to find them. I'm sorry, I read the book you recommended about jazz and I must have missed the women-in-jazz. Use it as a weapon against tokenizing exceptional women. Yes, I saw the paragraph on Mary Lou Williams. But what were the women-in-jazz categories of the day and how did women who played jazz negotiate them? I couldn't find the sections about how much they were paid and who profited from their labor. Can you recommend a more thorough source? Make it an uncomfortable observation. I couldn't help noticing that this documentary sees woman-in-jazz as primarily prostitutes, unbearable wives, and irresponsible or doting mothers. May I see your verifiable evidence?

Take Four: Reclaim the term women-in-jazz, but only in ways that make it do some interesting work. In my old radio days, for instance, I could have said, "Good afternoon, this is Sherrie Tucker, woman radio announcer, filling in for Bob Parlocha, man radio announcer." Wait, why limit ourselves to one industry? I could enter a classroom with, "Good morning, I am Sherrie Tucker, woman assistant professor of American Studies." Call attention to gender and sex, in other words, but in ways that call attention to the absurdity of naturalized definitions.

A couple of years ago, while teaching women's studies classes at a small-ish, delightful liberal arts college, I inherited a course from the 1970s that was still on the books as "The Female Experience." "Hello, class," I used to say when I walked in the room. "Is anyone having a female experience?" It seemed important to use that course title to help students to see how gender construction affected their expectations that women's studies classes were places where they would feel something, rather than learn something or have to read or analyze anything. Laughing at the course title helped students to think critically about their expectations that in this class, we would experience female-ness if we were female, and, if not, we would be voyeurs to the mysteries of females having female experiences among other females. It was a real problem, but laughing at the title helped us to reach the second half of the semester having convinced nearly everyone that women's studies was an academic program, with a vast array of theories, methods, histories, cultures, gender constructions, controversies, and issues. Historicizing that course title helped us to make that leap.

What can we do to support women who play jazz without approaching women-in-jazz as though it was "the female experience"? Maybe we should approach "woman-in-jazz" as a kind of job that women who play jazz don't simply experience, or naturally thrive in, but that must be analyzed, historicized, and deconstructed by theorists and musicians. And that women musicians analyze, historicize, and deconstruct even as they decide whether or not to accept such work, or how to work against it in performance. A conundrum on which improvising women improvise.

As such, women-in-jazz may prove useful as a conceptual tool for theorizing other kinds of communities that do not wish to sacrifice vital differences in the interest of unity. Many social movements are striving for similar leaps. Experimental music collectives may have important knowledge to share about how to achieve group identity with room for difference. Read theorists who are working on this problem, such as Chela Sandoval's conception of "differential consciousness" or a theory and practice of developing affinity through difference, a theory and method she attributes to feminists of color on the borders of both the white-dominated women's liberation movement, and as well as male-dominated liberation movements of people of color such as black power and La Raza, and leftist political organizing dominated by white men.[17] Compare these ideas with improvised music sites where difference is valued in collective exploration. And when you think you've found such practices, ask how its borders were drawn, how they are traversed, and what they protect. Then take a listen to those who jam outside.

Notes

1. I presented an earlier version of this article as a keynote presentation at the Guelph Jazz Festival, 6 September 2001. I thank Ajay Heble for the opportunity to develop the ideas generated by the theme of the festival, as well as the comments shared by festival participants. I also thank complex women-in-jazz communities that have been very helpful to me in thinking through the limitations as well as the possibilities of women-in-jazz as a framework: (1) the musicians from 1940s "all-girl" bands whose versions of jazz history so productively shook my assumptions about jazz and about women's history; (2) the other researchers who share my interests in these women and their careers; and (3) the contemporary jazz musicians who jammed with me on these ideas in cyberspace, a dialogue largely facilitated by a women-in-jazz community—the <Jazzgrrls@topica.com> list-serve started by Jeanette Lambert.

2. See Pelligrinelli and Hentoff.

3. Kelley, 88.

4. See Ajay Heble for the usefulness of "out-of-tuneness" in critical theory and

practice. I also sample, in this paragraph, the notion of gender as something that is produced through performance and that may be troubled through performance as well, from Judith Butler, and the concept of noise as a way of disordering power to create new orders, from Jacques Attali. I shall return to these concepts and their potential relationships at the end of this piece.

5. Claire Daly (baritone saxophonist), telephone interview, 27 August 2001.

6. For a lucid introduction to the sameness/difference debates in feminist theory, see Scott.

7. Anzaldúa 379. This is not to say that musicians on the edge of what counts as jazz can be equated in all ways with Latina lesbian feminists in the borderlands between Mexico and the United States. While some "new Mestizas" may indeed also be jazz musicians, what I mean here is that Anzaldúa's theorizing of borderlands is helpful for thinking about how people have negotiated spaces between inside and outside in relation to nation and community building.

8. As Robert Walser demonstrates in his analysis of glam metal, to trouble gender does not necessarily mean to transform social hierarchies of sex and power.

9. This female jazz musician preferred to remain anonymous. Email correspondence with the author, 23 August 2001.

10. Ajay Heble with Gillian Siddall, "Nice Work if You Can Get It," in Heble, 141–165.

11. Sherrie Tucker, *Swing Shift: "All-Girl" Bands of the 1940s*. Durham: Duke University Press, 2000.

12. Sherrie Tucker, "Improvising Womanhood, or a Conundrum is a Woman: Race, Gender, and Representation in Black Women's Jazz." In *Black Culture and Everyday Life*, edited by Craig Watkins (forthcoming).

13. Kay "Sugar Puss" Weber, "To Hubbys [*sic*] of Wives Who Horns and Saxes Blow." *Down Beat* (August 1937).

14. Sherrie Tucker, posting <jazzgrrls@topica.com>, 23 August 2001.

15. George Lewis, "Improvised Music After 1950: Afrological and Eurological Perspectives." *Black Music Research Journal* 16, no. 1 (Spring 1996): 93. A revised and updated version of this article is included in the present anthology.

16. Maura Bosch and Kitty Brazelton, Women's Avant Fest, Mission Statement, <http://www.womensavantfest.org/mission.html>. I look forward to Ursel Schlicht's analysis of experimental music as a beneficiary of women's exclusion from more traditional career paths in jazz, in her manuscript, "It's Gotta Be Music First" (forthcoming).

17. Sandoval, 1–24.

Works Cited

Anzaldúa, Gloria. "La conciencia de la mestiza: Towards a New Consciousness." In *Haciendo Caras: Making Face, Making Soul,* 377–389. San Francisco: Aunt Lute, 1990.

Attali, Jacques. *Noise: The Political Economy of Music*. Minneapolis: University of Minnesota Press, 1992.

Butler, Judith. *Gender Trouble: Feminism and the Subversion of Identity*. New York: Routledge, 1990.

Coates, Norma. "(R)evolution Now: Rock and the political Potential of Gender." In *Sexing the Groove: Popular Music and Gender,* edited by Sheila Whiteley, 50–64. London; Routledge, 1997.

Heble, Ajay. *Landing on the Wrong Note: Jazz, Dissonance, and Critical Practice*. New York: Routledge, 2000.

Hentoff, Nat. "Testosterone Is Not An Instrument." *Jazz Times* (June 2001): 166.

Kelley, Robin D. G. "'We Are Not What We Seem': Rethinking Black Working-Class Opposition in the Jim Crow South." *Journal of American History* 80, no. 1 (1993): 75–112.

Lewis, George. "Improvised Music After 1950: Afrological and Eurological Perspectives." *Black Music Research Journal* 16, no. 1 (1986): 91–122.

Minh-ha, Trinh T. *Framer Framed*. New York: Routledge, 1992.

———. *Woman, Native, Other: Writing Postcoloniality and Feminism*. Bloomington: Indiana University Press, 1989.

Monson, Ingrid. "The Problem with White Hipness: Race, Gender, and Cultural Conceptions in Jazz Historical Discourse." *Journal of the American Musicological Society* 48, no. 3 (1995): 396–422.

Pelligrinelli, Lara. "Dig Boy Dig." *Village Voice* (November 2000): 8–14.

Sandoval, Chela. "U.S. Third World Feminism: The Theory and Method of Oppositional Consciousness in the Postmodern World." *Genders* 10 (1991): 1–24.

Scott, Joan W. "Deconstructing Equality-Versus-Difference; Or, the Uses of Poststructuralist Theory for Feminism." In *Conflicts in Feminism*, edited by Marianne Hirsch and Evelyn Fox Keller, 134–148. New York, Routledge, 1990.

Walser, Robert. "Forging Masculinity: Heavy Metal Sounds and Images of Gender." In *Running with the Devil: Power, Gender, and Madness in Heavy Metal Music*, 108–136. Hanover: Wesleyan University Press, 1993.

Weber, Kay "Sugar Puss." "To Hubbys [*sic*] of Wives Who Horns and Saxes Blow." *Down Beat* (4 August 1937).

Young, Iris Marion. "The Ideal of Community and the Politics of Difference." In *Feminism/Postmodernism*, edited by Linda J. Nicholson, 300–323. New York: Routledge, 1990.

MARSHALL SOULES

Improvising Character

Jazz, the Actor, and Protocols of Improvisation

> There is a cruel contradiction implicit in the art form itself. For true jazz is an art of individual assertion within and against the group. Each true jazz moment (as distinct from the uninspired commercial performance) springs from a contest in which each artist challenges all the rest, each solo flight, or improvisation, represents (like the successive canvases of a painter) a definition of his identity: as individual, as member of the collectivity and as link in the chain of tradition. Thus, because jazz finds its very life in an endless improvisation upon traditional materials, the jazzman must lose his identity even as he finds it.
> —Ralph Ellison

.⌐

Ralph Ellison, who wrote extensively on jazz as both critic and writer of fiction, affirms the importance of character in any formulation of the "true jazz moment." The complex negotiation of identity within a performance context—whether the art be music, acting, writing, or the performance of self in everyday life—pits individual freedoms against the constraints and opportunities of society. Jacques Attali claims that music is "an affirmation that society is possible. . . . Its order simulates the social order, and its dissonances express marginalities" (29). Ellison's curious choice of the word "cruel" to describe the apparent contradiction of losing one's identity in the moment of finding it may seem overdramatic to some. However, as an echo of Artaud's famous articulation of the "theatre of cruelty"—with the actor as a martyr burning at the stake and signaling through the flames—Ellison's "cruel contradiction" suggests something of the commitment, courage, and risk-taking required of the dedicated jazz musician or stage actor. Derrida reminds us that the theatre of cruelty is marked by its "affirmation"of an "implacable necessity" (232). Cruelty in this sense connotes a matrix of character traits and registers the difficulty of authentic self-less performance.

In the following, I trace some of the lines of intersection between improvised music and improvised acting as performative practices. Both tend to characterize themselves as variations within a broader range of performance—music and acting—and both are often marked by a spirit of subversion to conventions of orderliness and control, whether of the score/script or director/conductor. I also suggest that an inherent paradox animates improvisation in a manner similar to Ellison's cruel contradiction: both improvising musicians and actors must lose their identities even as they find them, but they do so within a framework of productive constraints—the protocols of improvisation. In a seeming paradox that threatens to erase the traces of identity, improvisation thrives when the performance of character is given latitude of expression within the framework of the ensemble. Michael Chekhov, renowned Russian actor and teacher, confirms the legitimacy of this approach for the actor:

Every role offers an actor the opportunity to improvise, to collaborate and truly co-create with the author and director. This suggestion, of course, does not imply improvising new lines or substituting business for that outlined by the director. On the contrary. The given lines and the business are the firm bases upon which the actor must and can develop his improvisations. *How* he speaks the lines and *how* he fulfills the business are the open gates to a vast field of improvisation. The "hows" of his lines and business are the *ways* in which he can express himself freely. (36)

For Chekhov—echoing Ellison's cruel necessity—actors "must" develop their improvisations within the constraints of both character and the given "lines and business."

Ajay Heble's *Landing on the Wrong Note* reviews how the discourse on jazz and its cultural signification is not only evolving and somewhat unstable in the current critical climate; it also resonates with self-professed dissonance in which "timbral innovation, playful improvisation, altered harmonies, and wrong notes" (28) operate as a kind of "sonic symbolism" (a term borrowed from George Lewis) marking both a critical practice and an approach to cultural stratagems of power and representation. Similarly, in her discussion of modal jazz in the work of George Russell, John Coltrane, and Miles Davis, Ingrid Monson positions her discourse at a figurative crossroads of cultural analysis, reflective, expansive, open to possibility in a dialogic style I use as one of my models here: "Music truly served as a crossroads through which this wide range of social discussions were brought into dialogue. The musical changes that came to be associated with modal jazz—fewer chords, greater freedom in melodic and harmonic choices during improvisation, and more open forms over which to improvise—opened the door to a more international dialogue in the musical community" (163). In the dialogic spirit recommended by both Heble and

Monson, I shall explore the cultural and aesthetic crossroads where jazz and the theatrical character intersect through their respective "protocols of improvisation": those voluntary guidelines used by performers (among them musicians, writers, actors) to ground the play of creativity within a matrix of constraints. By interrogating in close juxtaposition the nature of improvised music and acting, we gain insight into the nature of improvisation itself—though it would be imprudent to suggest an essential definition suitable for all performance situations—and learn something about the dialogic construction of character.

Protocols—"long-established codes" determining "precedence and precisely correct procedure"—may at first seem antithetical to popular notions of improvised creativity. However, interdisciplinary research into the nature of improvisation shows that it typically occurs either within, or in close relation to, voluntary constraints. Jeff Pressing, for example, writes: "To achieve maximal fluency and coherence, improvisers, when they are not performing free (or 'absolute') improvisation, use a referent, a set of cognitive, perceptual, or emotional structures (constraints) that guide and aid in the production of musical materials" (52). In turn, Attali writes extensively about the "codes" found in the production of music: "rules of arrangement and laws of succession" that provide "precise operationality" (25). Protocols are strategies or agreements that "glue" events together (after the Greek *protókollon*, a first leaf glued to the front of a manuscript and containing notes as to its contents). These guidelines, whether explicitly stated or implicitly embodied in the mode of expression, ground the play of improvisation in performance situations and, in Pressing's analysis, signify expertise.

Even in a piece as radically improvisational as Ornette Coleman's *Free Jazz*, a few protocols were required: "Not only is the improvisation almost total, it is frequently collective, involving all eight men inventing at once. And there were no preconceptions as to themes, chord patterns or chorus lengths. *The guide for each soloist was a brief ensemble part which introduces him and which gave him an area of musical pitch.* Otherwise he had only feelings and imagination—his own and those of his accompanists—to guide him" (Williams; my emphasis).

Martin Williams, in his liner notes, describes the recording as a "kind of polyphonic accompaniment based on pitch, melodic direction, an emotional complement." For Coleman, the guidelines embodied a different emphasis, one more attuned to the needs of the players: "The most important thing . . . was for us to play together, all at the same time, without getting in each other's way, and also to have enough room for each player to *ad lib* alone—and to follow this idea for the duration of the album. When the soloist played something that suggested a musical idea or direction to me, I played that behind him in my style. He continued his own way in his solo, of course." Improvisation for performance—both in jazz music and otherwise—is thus not typified by unrestrained freedom, though it does provide unique expressive opportunities for individual performers within the ensemble.

Coleman's emphasis alerts us to the importance of character in the improvisational transaction, and how character is inextricably entwined with the relationship of the individual to the collective. In many ways, the centrality of character to jazz and acting (and, by extension, to the relationship of the individual to society) justifies Robin Balliger's argument for "music and noise as social forces, fully involved in the 'dialogic process' of social life and as such, an important site of control—and resistance" (13). A network of analogies informs improvised music, transformational acting, and the notion of the improvised character in a "culture of spontaneity" (Belgrad). We are often called upon to improvise our characters within a matrix of social codes, and there is much to learn about how and why we do this from a study of improvisation as a performative practice across a variety of disciplines. In another tip of the hat to Artaud's holy actor, Michael Chekhov insists that the "actor who has not felt the pure joy of transforming himself on the stage with each new part can scarcely know the real, creative meaning of improvisation" (36).

Performance at the Crossroads of Culture

Any writing that purports to explore intercultural and interdisciplinary correspondences immediately treads on highly contested ground regarding questions of authority, authenticity, subjectivity, and appropriation. In *The Predicament of Culture,* James Clifford argues that contemporary societies have become "too systematically interconnected to permit easy isolation of separate or independently functioning systems": everywhere we see individuals and groups who "improvise local performance from (re)collected pasts, drawing on foreign media, symbols and languages" (15). Clifford and others refer to these intercultural formations as "creolized"[1] in reference to the heterogeneous and layered cultures of, for example, the Caribbean. In Clifford's predicament, there is a complex interplay of value, influence, and adjustment that resists easy reconciliation and that puts the ethnographer in the position of performing in relation to the performance of the culture under study.

Dwight Conquergood responds to this predicament by charting out five attitudes (or strategies) for approaching the ethnography of performance, four of which he believes are morally compromised. Carlson nicely summarizes Conquergood's schema:

> The suspect stances were that of the custodian, the enthusiast, the skeptic, and the curator. The custodian collects examples of performance, interested only in acquisition or exploitation. The skeptic, like many traditional ethnographers, stands aloof from and superior to the performance being studied. The enthusiast goes to the opposite extreme, seeking an easy identity in quick generalizations. The curator takes a tourist's stance, seeking exoticism or spectacle. Against all four of these, Conquergood champions the fifth stance, a "dialogical" performance, which aims to "bring together different voices, world views, value systems, and beliefs so that they can have a conversation with one another." The result sought is an open-ended performance, resisting conclusions and seeking to keep interrogation open. (Carlson, 31)

While the reader will certainly find traces of the custodian, the enthusiast, the skeptic, and the curator in what follows, it is in the spirit of dialogical performance that the present study of improvisation is offered. Despite differences of culture, ethnicity, and gender, many individuals find themselves to be "'out of tune' with orthodox habits of coherence and judgment" and struggle "to achieve control over the ways in which their identities have been constructed, framed, and interpreted" (Heble, 9), even by an audience. The work of Brazilian director Augusto Boal is animated by his goal of making us aware of the "cop in the head," the oppressive imaginal character who seeks to keep us in line.

The Improvised Self: Scrambling the Codes

There is no such thing as a human nature independent of culture," Geertz writes, meaning by culture not primarily "complexes of concrete behavior patterns—customs, usages, traditions, habit clusters"—but rather "a set of control mechanisms—plans, recipes, rules, instructions . . .—for the governing of behavior." Self-fashioning is in effect the Renaissance version of these control mechanisms, the cultural system of meanings that creates specific individuals by governing the passage from abstract potential to concrete historical embodiment.
—Greenblatt, 3–4

In her discussion of George Russell's theory of tonal organization, Monson describes the influence of the Russian mystical philosopher Georges Gurdjieff, subject of Peter Brook's film *Meetings with Remarkable Men*. With Russell and Coltrane as exemplary figures, Monson attempts to give substance to the argument that "improvisation has often been taken as a metaphor for freedom both musical and social" (149). Gurdjieff's conception of character was evidently suggestive for Russell and continues to be a subject of great interest in psychological circles. Gurdjieff used the symbol of the enneagram—a nine-pointed figure inscribed within a circle—to map the human psyche according to Pythagorean notions of harmonious musical scales (Bennett). Each of the nine points on the symbol represents a different character archetype within the individual psyche, and each character type operates in relation to other types depending on an individual's temperamental proclivities and life experience. In effect, Gurdjieff believed that we all carry the potential for many characters within ourselves: each of us is an ensemble. We adopt a repertoire of character traits to adjust to changing circumstance, and this liberation of character from fixity may have been what attracted Russell to Gurdjieff's teaching.

Arriving at a working definition of the self—especially one that accommodates the exigencies of improvisation and contemporary theories of character—is difficult. Baumeister provides a lucid overview of "how the self became a problem," arguing that our notions of identity have become progressively destabilized: "In the absence of consensual, unimpeachable guidelines (values) that are adequate for making the choices that define the self, these guidelines are presumed to exist hidden within the self" (173). "Self-presentation," or "the extent to which the self is inextricably linked with how it is perceived by other persons" (174) is of growing interest to psychologists, who now seem prepared to substantiate Goffman's insights of the late 1950s about the presentation of self within the frames of culture.

One theory of the self seeks to introduce greater spontaneity and multiplicity into the formulation. John Beahrs, a psychoanalyst working largely with hypnosis and trance states, argues: "We may indeed be true multiple personalities in a far more literal sense than the way the term is defined in the psychiatric nomenclature" (3). Using the term "simultaneous co-consciousness" to describe his notion of self, Beahrs likens the self to a symphony orchestra in which individual musicians (the unconscious) synergistically create a sound under the direction of the conductor (the conscious) who, while in charge, is largely silent during performances. Because this model suggests that the conductor directs the orchestra, a better analogy for illustrating "simultaneous co-consciousness" would be the example of a free jazz ensemble.

Psychologists Hermans, Kempen, and van Loon articulate an ingenious argument derived from Bakhtin's narrative theories. They claim that the self is "dialogical" because people arrive at an understanding of the self and the world by telling and listening to stories. The self, as "dialogical narrator," is "social, with the other not outside but in the self-structure, resulting in a multiplicity of dialogically interacting selves" (23). The authors cite Bakhtin's argument that dialogue "not only represents a literary genre and possible conceptualization of personality, but also the very essence of personality" (28), while defining the self as a "dynamic multiplicity of relatively autonomous *I* positions in an imaginal landscape" (28). They complicate Beahrs's analogy of the self as symphony orchestra by suggesting that the conductor (the *I*) is nomadic: "The *I* has the possibility to move, as in space, and from one position to the other" and "has the capacity to imaginatively endow each position with a voice so that dialogical relations between positions can be established. The voices function like interacting characters in a story" (28).

In *Anti-Oedipus,* Deleuze and Guattari advocate one of the more radical models of the improvising self by deconstructing the "restrictive codes of Oedipus" and the tyrannical suppositions of psychoanalysis in general. In their place, they substitute "schizoanalysis," a method that shifts its attention from the neurotic—"the one on whom the Oedipal imprints take" (xxi)—to the psychotic, the one who is "incapable of being oedipalized": "It might be said that the schizophrenic passes from one code to the other, that he deliberately *scrambles all the codes,* by quickly shifting from one to the other" (15). The work of the Open Theatre on transformations and of Grotowski with the holy actor have many parallels with Deleuze and Guattari's mythopoetic schizophrenic, not the least of which are the goals of penetration and fluidity.

In his introduction to *Anti-Oedipus,* Mark Seem claims that such an analysis is intended to kindle "forces that escape coding, scramble the codes, and flee in all directions" (xxi). Estrangement is the rule. Deleuze and Guattari's politics seek to "de-normalize and de-individualize through a multiplicity of new, collective arrangements against power" (xxi). Ultimately, "singularity and collectivity are no longer at odds with each other"—a formulation that seems to address Ellison's "cruel contradiction." What happens when we position the improvising character within the open-ended constraints of jazz or acting? As we shall see, the doubling of performative consciousness is both a requisite of performance in general, and a site marked by the pan-cultural archetype of the trickster.

The Protocols of Jazz Improvisation

The problem of the self is compounded in this case by the difficulty of defining jazz improvisation as an initial paradigm of comparison. Derek Bailey notes the contingent nature of musical improvisation and its subsequent resistance to analysis: "Any attempt to describe improvisation must be . . . a misrepresentation, for there is something central to the spirit of voluntary improvisation which is opposed to the aims and contradicts the idea of documentation" (ix). His approach, then, and along with the one taken by Paul Berliner in *Thinking in Jazz,* is to explore improvisation through its practice: "For there is no general or widely held theory of improvisation and I would have thought it self-evident that improvisation has no existence outside of its practice" (x). For Bailey, musical improvisation is either "idiomatic" (such as jazz, flamenco, or baroque) or "nonidiomatic," "most usually found in so-called 'free' improvisation and, while it can be highly stylized, is not usually tied to representing an idiomatic identity" (xi–xii). As I shall note below, the idea of idiomatic improvisation resonates deeply with the related notion of the vernacular in identifying both the character of the performer and the nature of the performance. Bailey's interrogation of musicians to find out what they do—the practice of practice—attempts to skirt some of the problems of theorizing improvisation in a method similar to Berliner: "close observation and description of the full range of musical activities that occupied active members of a community known for its expertise in improvisation" (4). While the approach taken here attempts to synthesize a diversity of observations and ideas about improvisation as a mode of performance, it does so with the understanding that any theory is less than useful if not confirmed—or at least entertained—by the practice of experts.

While many cultural threads weave together to tell the story of improvisation, African cultures and styles of music claim pride of place when the central focus is jazz and its related musics. While the characteristics of African musical aesthetics may seem a far cry from improvisation for the Western stage, underlying principles of social organization and style have many commonalities including, it will be suggested, the dynamics and neurophysiology of play.

In *African Rhythm and African Sensibility,* musicologist John Miller Chernoff studies the musical aesthetics and social practices surrounding the performance of music in West Africa, chiefly in Ghana. One of his overarching discoveries is the importance of organizing principles in improvisation: "Those who have pressed us to recognize the achievements of extemporaneous improvisation have often underemphasized the importance of organization to the critical aesthetic sense" (122). Chernoff describes how the apparently spontaneous and improvisatory music is performed within a set of codes, some related to the aesthetics of performance, some related to social contingencies. Reciprocity and restraint complement energy and expressivity in framing the performance of music:

A drum in an African ensemble derives its power and becomes meaningful not only as it cuts and focuses the other drums *but also as it is cut and called into focus by them.* Rhythmic dialogues are reciprocal, and in a way that might seem paradoxical to a Westerner, a good drummer restrains himself from emphasizing his rhythm *in order that he may be heard better* . . . [a] rhythm is interesting in terms of its potential to be affected by other rhythms. (60; emphasis in original)

In this telling, the style of improvisation seems directly related to the social purposes of the music: "Improvisation for the master drummer . . . lies not so much in the genesis of new rhythms as in the organization and form given to the already existing rhythms, and a musician's *style* of organizing his playing will indicate the way he approaches from his own mind the responsibility of his role toward making the occasion a success" (82). Style, according to Chernoff and his sources, is "another word for the perception of relationships, a dynamic aesthetic attitude which focuses the music on the occasion" (82). More than just guidelines, protocols retrieve traditions and recuperate them into present practice; they imply a cultural repository of aesthetic taste; and they signify an attitude toward social responsibility and engagement. All, I would suggest, apply equally to the challenges facing an improvising actor on the Western stage. Anthropologist Victor Turner uses the term "normative communitas" to describe times when "individuals come together and devise rules for themselves" (*Anthropology*, 44). As a demonstration of normative communitas, improvisation uses protocols to create conditions that allow individual voices a place for spontaneous expression in a communal setting. With a similar intention of creating an ensemble of players in a social organization respecting individual voices and contributions, Joseph Chaikin—one of the founders of the Open Theatre—calls normative communitas a "voluntary discipline." The discipline is necessary in its relation to notions of character: "Because of the way things are in this country, we often act out of a dictate that has nothing to do with ourselves. We must not take that into our work, for, if we do, we won't be able to recognize our own impulses" (80). That the discipline is voluntary marks the practice as being noncoercive, not conceived for purposes of power and control, and thus culturally subversive in its contrast to any authoritarian cultural regime. Because the discipline is voluntary, individuals are encouraged to take a high degree of personal responsibility for their involvement.

One might say, then, that improvisation for performance involves a voluntary discipline when individuals come together to devise rules for their play in an open-ended arrangement allowing individual expression within the ensemble of players. Referring to the model of African musical improvisation, Chernoff elaborates: "The musical form is open rather than rigid, set up so it affords a focus for the expression of individuality that subtly distinguishes an occasion within the context of tradition" (126). Normative communitas—and improvisation—seeks to strike a balance between the human needs for individual expression and social integration. Here we encounter another of the seeming paradoxes implied by the term protocols of improvisation: the importance of tradition to the uniqueness of individual spontaneous expression.

Signifyin(g) in the Vernacular

In his vernacular theory of the blues, Houston Baker situates the African-American idiomatic music at the railway junction, the place where road crosses tracks:

> The railway juncture is marked by transience. Its inhabitants are always travelers—a multifarious assembly in transit. The "X" of the crossing roadbeds signals the multi-directionality of the juncture and is simply a single instance in a boundless net-work. . . . Polymorphous and multidirectional, scene of arrivals and departures, place betwixt and between (ever *entre les deux*), the juncture is the way-station of the blues. (7)

Baker's conceit suggests that the blues musician provides "expressive equivalence for the juncture's ceaseless flux" and thus the blues performer may be considered a "translator" (and simultaneously suggesting an important correlation with the Greek understanding of the actor as translator). Baker refers to John Felstiner's argument that translation preserves something of value, as in the giving of a gift, by "keeping it in motion" (206). The blues musician, working in the vernacular—*of the slave, native or inhabitant of a particular country or locality*—translates experience at a particular cross-roads that is also a node in a network of cultural relations. The crossroads marks both a particular instance of local expression—the vernacular—and a point with no fixed address, something of a cultural universal ruled by archetypes and protocols.

The Yoruba trickster Eshu-Elegbara claims the crossroads as his special domain; analogously, the hippocampus in the limbic system has been characterized as a neurophysiological crossroads where sensation is translated into cognition. As both Gates and Turner suggest, the archetype of the trickster at the crossroads may be a figure for the hardwiring of the brain concerned with spontaneous appropriation.

The importance of continuity and cultural influence remain central to an understanding of improvisation. Paul Berliner quotes Wynton Marsalis: "Jazz is not just, 'Well, man, this is what I feel like playing.' It's a very structured thing that comes down from a tradition and requires a lot of thought and study" (63). The protocols of improvisation derived from the knowledge and study of the tradition provide a context for the greater freedom of spontaneous invention. Berliner comments that "despite stylistic changes over time, jazz retains the continuity of certain underlying practices and values associated with improvisation, learning, and transmission. These factors of continuity, moreover, rest at the very core of the tradition, contributing to its integrity as a music system" (14). In his description of Henry Minton's club as a "retreat" where a "collectivity . . . could find continuity and meaningful expression," Ellison contends that the jam session was the jazz musician's "true academy." The jam or "cutting session" was a "contest of improvisational skill and physical endurance between two or more musicians. . . . It is here that he learns tradition, group techniques and style. . . . All this through achieving that subtle identification between his instrument and his deepest drives which will allow him to express his own unique ideas and his own unique voice. He must achieve, in short, his self-determined identity" (208–209).

What does improvisation as a musical practice involve, and how does this practice lend itself to appropriation or mimesis by other types of performance such as acting? One significant point of intersection grows out of the previously discussed notions of continuity and tradition: the idea of referencing previous expressions. In literary studies, this use of allusions can take the form of troping—a kind of linguistic play—or intertextuality, when one text participates in a "dialogue" with a previous text. In jazz, the use of allusions, echoes, or references is often called "riffing." Albert Murray elaborates in *Stomping the Blues:*

> When they are effective, riffs always seem as spontaneous as if they were improvised in the heat of the performance. So much so that riffing is sometimes regarded as being synonymous with improvisation. But such is not always the case by any means. Not only are riffs as much a part of some arrangements and orchestrations as the lead melody, but many consist of nothing more than stock phrases, quotations from some familiar melody, or even clichés that just happen to be popular at the moment. . . . [I]mprovisation includes spontaneous appropriation (or inspired allusion, which sometimes is a form of signifying) no less than on-the-spot invention. (96)

Murray also notes that the efficacy of the creative process "lies not in the originality of the phrase . . . but in the way it is used in a frame of reference" (96), an idea that essentially repeats what Keith Johnstone claims for originality in improvised acting: the more obvious one is, the more original one appears (87). What distinguishes the jazz musician adept at improvisation is "idiomatic orientation." The "character" of the jazz musician is revealed by the "voice" of the instrument; idiomatic orientation is the relation of that voice to the other instruments and to the tradition, and can be seen as a variation on the idea of the vernacular.[2]

In the theater, actors are given their lines by the writer or director, but they must also contribute physical actions and voice. Since Stanislavsky first articulated his "Method of Physical Actions," the gestures and voicings of the actor have been considered as important as the emotional motivation of character. Following Stanislavsky, Michael Chekhov advises: "While incorporating your character on the stage you use your emotions, voice and your mobile body. These constitute the 'building material' from which the higher self, the real artist in you, creates a character for the stage" (87). Chekhov associates the voice of the actor with both character and "atmosphere": "See that all your movements, the timbre of your voice and the lines you speak are in full harmony with the atmosphere you have chosen" (134). As Murray claims for jazz improvisations, the "voice" of the instrument reveals not only the character of the musician, but contributes to the all-important atmosphere of the performance and its allusions to the tradition within which it is played.

In *The Signifying Monkey*, Henry Louis Gates Jr. explores a related notion of improvisation in which the performer "repeats and revises" musical figures, styles, and instrumental voices. Gates associates this activity with the African-American practice of "Signifyin(g)—playing with linguistic figures to parody or pastiche a rival" (46).[3] Gates notes how this process of "Signifyin(g)," of repetition and revision, has become a staple of jazz improvisation:

Improvisation, of course, so fundamental to the very idea of jazz, is "nothing more" than repetition and revision. In this sort of revision, again where meaning is fixed, it is the realignment of the signifier that is the signal trait of expressive genius. The more mundane the fixed text ("April in Paris" by Charlie Parker, "My Favorite Things" by John Coltrane), the more dramatic is the Signifyin(g) revision. It is this principle of repetition and difference, this practice of intertextuality, which has been so crucial to the black vernacular forms of Signifyin(g), jazz—and even its antecedents, the blues, the spirituals, and ragtime. (63–64)

For Gates, the repetition and revision of the improvising jazz musician has its counterpart in the intertextual networking of the cultural critic: both trade on indeterminacies resurrected from the tradition; both act as translators hoping to preserve the gift of culture. The same might be said of actors who give their unique interpretation of a given stage character. In "The Idea of the Actor," Niall Slater argues that acting is dialogic performance: the concept of "actor" did not exist on the Athenian stage until audiences were able to compare the same dramatic role by different performers. One performance entered into a dialogue with all previous performances of the same role. "Only in the fourth century . . . are plays the repeatable texts we think of today, because a social context for a reperformance has at last been created. The actors through their skills and their assertion of their individuality are a key force in that transformation" (394).

It is no coincidence that Gates associates this Signifyin(g) practice with the trickster archetype and with the practice of cultural and literary criticism:

Signifyin(g) in jazz performances and in the play of black language games is a mode of formal revision, it depends for its effects on troping, it is often characterized by pastiche, and, most crucially, it turns on repetition of formal structures and their differences. . . . [T]he Signifying Monkey, he who dwells at the margins of discourse, ever punning, ever troping, ever embodying the ambiguities of language, is our trope for repetition and revision. (52)

In Gates's complex mythopoetics, the literary critic and the improvising jazz musician are equally engaged in acts of translation and dialogic networking, much like Slater's dialogic actor. By tracing the path of the Yoruba trickster Eshu-Elegbara to his multiple New World incarnations as Exú, Papa Legba, and the Signifying Monkey among others, and by associating the act of literary criticism with musical improvisation through the conceit of Signifyin(g), Gates plots an intersection of performative activities that include "individuality, satire, parody, irony, magic, indeterminacy, open-endedness, ambiguity, sexuality, chance, uncertainty, disruption and reconciliation, betrayal and loyalty, closure and disclosure, encasement and rapture" (6). Without the frame of tradition, these activities would cease to resonate their *différance*. Animating these often contradictory activities is the spirit of play.

Play and Cognition

One of the great practitioners of theatrical improvisation in the twentieth century, Jacques Copeau, associated the "essence of the dramatic personality" with "the child who, in sheer bodily delight, jumps and shouts for joy on a spring morning: that is where to find the origin of exultation" (5). Copeau looked to the energy and attitude of children—their ability to play—for the origins of the impulse to improvise, and thus to be a source of inspiration for actors (and musicians): "The habit of improvisation will give back to the actor the suppleness, the elasticity, the true spontaneous life of the word and the gesture, the true feeling of the movement, the true contact with the public, the inspiration, the fire and daring of the jester" (153). Frost and Yarrow, among others, identify Copeau and his followers as central figures in the resurgence of interest in improvisation in the twentieth century. Copeau's training techniques and orientation to spontaneity would ultimately find expression in the vogue of stand-up comedy, the Second City phenomenon, and improvisational troupes such as Theatre Machine (founded with Keith Johnstone as director in 1967).

It may need to be clarified that Copeau promoted "the *art* of improvisation and the *illusion* of spontaneity" (155; my emphasis) in his actors, seeking to define a "pre-established form which is inspirational" (158). Apart from repeating the idea that improvisation occurs within a matrix of constraints, Copeau draws our attention to the self-reflexive awareness required of performance. Marvin Carlson notes that "all performance involves a consciousness of doubleness, through which the actual execution of an action is placed in mental comparison with a potential, an ideal, or a remembered original model of that action. Normally this comparison is made by an observer of the action. . . . Performance is always performance *for* someone, some audience that recognizes and validates it as performance even when that audience is the self" (5–6; emphasis in original). Similarly, in his discussion of masks and improvisation, Sears Eldredge discusses the importance of "dual consciousness" for the improvising actor, a formulation wherein the performer is both participant and observer simultaneously: "What is important is the *inscribing* and *imprinting* of mental and emotional forms onto the actor's 'other' consciousness through physicality" (37).

Eldredge suggests that "acknowledging the cast of characters within" (34) is closely allied with both dual consciousness and the transformative power of masks in improvisational acting. This double consciousness is highly involving cognitively and involves translating—inscribing and imprinting—what can be formulated in consciousness onto the "undisciplined" realms of the unconsciousness. In many respects, the double consciousness required of performance is a rehearsal for character development.[4]

For improvising actors and musicians alike, and indeed for many playful children as well, performance often involves notions of decorum and suitability: what is acceptable by the audience, what goes too far. Similarly, performers may need to be aware of how far they can go in terms of their own dignity and safety. This focus on "performative-consciousness" (Schechner) draws attention to the need to keep the open-ended structures of improvisation safe for the performers or players. Richard Schechner comments: "Because performances are usually subjunctive, liminal, dangerous, and duplicitous they are often hedged in with conventions and frames: ways of making the places, the participants, and the events somewhat safe. In these relatively safe make-believe precincts, actions can be carried to extremes, even for fun" (xiv).[5] Influenced by Grotowski's reading of Artaud—that the image of actors "signaling through the flames" embodies the "whole problem of spontaneity and discipline"—Schechner concludes that "both spontaneity and discipline are *risks* for the performer" (57).

Schechner's description of performative consciousness is influenced by the work of anthropologist Victor Turner who conceived of play as a *liminal* or boundary-crossing experience. Synthesizing the research of van Gennep, Huizinga, Caillois, and others, Turner argues that, in play, we combine what we have at hand (that is, the indicative function) with what could be (the subjunctive, or provisional function) (*From Ritual*, 28). For example, we might take a stick or a pencil and play *as if* it were a sword. We make paper airplanes. We drum on our desks. We are *bricoleurs* who assemble the materials at hand into something new and heterogenous, often on the fly.[6] As did the Surrealists, we make radical juxtapositions to shock the unconscious into awareness. In so doing, we participate in an activity that is highly engaging cognitively as we are integrating analytical (indicative) and associative (subjunctive) mental processes.

In his essay "Body, Brain and Culture," Turner draws on the work of various neurophysiologists to speculate that "at the neurobiological level play might have something to do with the sensitization of neural structures of an interface type, like the limbic system at the core of the brain" (*Anthropology*, 167). Edward Hall reaches a similar conclusion: "Seated in the old mammalian brain, improvisation is a process originating in play in mammals. . . . With these new types of animals, a new brain evolved, a horseshoe shaped structure called the limbic system. . . . The limbic system is the center of emotions, parenting, social organization and play. And *play* is the device which permits all mammals to have fun, but gives them the means of mastering the skills needed for survival" (224). Turner gives this playful function a distributed location in the limbic system, at the intersection of energy-expending (ergotropic) and energy-conserving (trophotropic) processes within the nervous system. Turner cites the research of d'Aquili and Laughlin, which suggests that

when either the ergotropic or trophotropic system is hyperstimulated, there results a "spillover" into the opposite system after "three stages of tuning," often by "driving behaviors" employed to facilitate ritual trance. . . . In particular, they postulate that the rhythmic activity of ritual, aided by sonic, visual, photic, and other kinds of "driving," may lead in time to simultaneous maximal stimulation of both systems, causing ritual participants to experience what the authors call "positive, ineffable affect." (165)

In effect, repetitive "driving" behaviors, whether sustained by meditation, ritual, or music, may create a state of satori or ecstasy.[7]

Turner, however, does not rest here. He notes that d'Aquili and Laughlin are absolutely silent on the question of play, which he sees as a kind of neurophysiological free agent, sampling, revising, re-creating: "play does not fit in anywhere in particular; it is transient and is recalcitrant to localization, to placement, to fixation—a joker in the neuro-anthropological act" (167). Play is, for Turner, "a liminal or liminoid mode, essentially interstitial, betwixt-and-between all standard taxonomic modes, essentially 'elusive.' . . . Like many Trickster figures in myths . . . play can deceive, betray, beguile, delude" (168). The alignment between Turner's formulation of the trickster as an archetype embodying the spirit of play and Gates' association of the trickster with Signifyin(g) is striking.

More recent neurophysiological research seems to confirm Turner's insights. Candace Pert's discovery of widespread peptide receptors throughout the body conclusively blurs previous distinctions between cognition and emotion, as well as existing notions of where they occur in the body. As reported by Fritjof Capra in the *The Web of Life,* peptides are the equivalent of "molecular messengers" which interconnect nervous, immune, and endocrine systems into "one single network" (282). Pert's research on peptides—short chains of amino acids—identifies them as the biochemical instantiation of emotions translated in the limbic system into cognition about those emotions. In a unique convergence of terminology, James Austin suggests in *Zen and the Brain* (1999) that the hippocampal formation lies at an "obvious crossroads in the limbic system" where it provides a "single association matrix" that marks the "conjunction between an event, its occurrence in time, its place in space, and the lively coloration it receives from its emotionalized limbic correlates" (182–183). The limbic system, a crossroads of human anatomy, translates sensation and emotion into cognition through the widely distributed agency of peptides.

Is it possible, then, that the archetype of the trickster embodies, as Turner suggests, a deep intuitive understanding of how the human mind translates feeling into action on the fly, how it grapples with paradox, how it reconciles the one with the many? If so, then neurophysiologists may be close to identifying how and where play and improvisation occur in the body, thus providing insight into the origins of the mythopoetics of the crossroads, the trickster archetype, and the dynamics of improvisation. Cognition—and its relationship to emotion and action—introduces protocols into all improvisational transactions, from play to music, acting, writing, and negotiating character. In their introduction to improvisation in drama, Frost and Yarrow claim that improvisation is a "paradigm for the way humans reflect (or create) what happens," a kind of "creative organization" for how we "respond to and give shape to our world" (2). The following section will review how theater practitioners accommodate the protocols of improvisation in actor training and performance.

Improvisation and Acting

Improvisation is fundamental to all drama. All performance uses the body of the actor, giving space and form to an idea, situation, character or text in the moment of creation. It does not matter that the play has been rehearsed for a month, with every move, every nuance of speech learned and practiced. In the act of performance the actor becomes an improviser.
—Anthony Frost and Ralph Yarrow

Through the notion of protocols and the performing self, we can begin to explore some of the common ground occupied by jazz and acting improvisation. It can be argued, for example, that both modes of performance thrive when individual expressive freedom is framed by organizing principles, though these principles will differ in kind. There is the common perception that both are subversive of culturally valorized art forms, deserving only marginalized or fringe status.

Frost and Yarrow point out that while improvisation has deep roots in the dramatic practices of the world, there has been a resurgence of interest in the European and North American contexts in the twentieth century, during which it developed in close juxtaposition to jazz. While jazz may have taken little notice of dramatic improvisation, there are countless examples of theater practitioners inspired by the organization, expressive goals, and discipline of the jazz ensemble. Most important, however, is the unifying notion of the improvised character: both jazz and improv acting are procedural systems that challenge restricting constructions of character; both seek to open up character to greater expressive potential, wider freedoms and responsibilities. Improvised jazz and acting both refashion character to provide alternate models of human aspiration and interaction.

While it is not the place here to survey the history of improvisation in acting from the Dionysian *rhapsodein,* through the popular commedia dell'arte of the Italian late Middle Ages, or the complex self-fashioning of the Elizabethan theater of Marlowe and Shakespeare, it is appropriate to trace briefly some of the major instantiations of acting improvisation in the last century. Frost and Yarrow investigate the history of acting improvisation in the twentieth century along three intersecting trajectories or contexts: (1) as an element of actor training and character development in the tradition of Stanislavsky and the American Method (what they call the "traditional" theater); (2) as a practice associated with the "alternative" nonrealist drama; and (3) in the "paratheatrical" context typified by Grotowski's later experiments, the work of Augusto Boal, and other activities that seek to involve the audience more directly in the making of the performance. There is so much intersection of influence, however, that such a scheme of organization serves only rudimentary purposes of clarification. As the authors suggest, "improvisation is not just a style or acting technique; it is a dynamic principle operating in many different spheres; an independent and transformative way of being and doing" (13). As a method of "creative organization" (2), however, the related questions of character and authenticity are central to acting improvisation in all contexts.

For those working in the mode of naturalism, the well-made play, and the actor preparation techniques inspired by Stanislavsky, improvisation has traditionally been considered a rehearsal technique for exploring depth of character, a repertoire of physical actions suitable to the character, and elements of the subtext. The technique of emotional memory, for example, allows the actor to invest the character with deeply felt feelings in a reasonably consistent way in performance after performance. The "magic as-if" exercises—another stock-in-trade of method acting derived from Stanislavsky—require the actor to enter imaginatively into the psychology and physical actions of the character. (Stanislavsky conceived of the rehearsal process as first developing a "score of the part" derived from the actor's creative imagination. Ultimately, the individual scores are brought together into a single "score of the performance," essentially the matrix of constraints within which the ensemble has agreed to improvise.) Both techniques require the actor to improvise the character into existence in the moment of performance through a variation of spontaneous appropriation, or riffing. While the degree of improvisation in the performance is often at the discretion of the director and subject to the discipline of the actors, improvisation in traditional drama animates character and promotes the illusion of spontaneity and presence. The work of Jacques Copeau and his disciples—Joan Littlewood, John Cassavettes, Ariane Mnouchkine, Mike Leigh, Caryl Churchill, and Mike Figgis—illustrates dramatic improvisation in this context.

This kind of improvisation tends to assume a concept of character as the locus of "deterministic forces" (Frost and Yarrow, 14), which for many theater critics is the hallmark of dramatic naturalism and realism. In his attempt to establish a solid theoretical ground for naturalism in the theater, Strindberg broached this question in his "Author's Preface to *Miss Julie*" and subsequently complicated any rigid conceptions of character entertained by students of modern drama:

The term *character* has come to mean many things over the course of time. Originally, it must have meant the dominant trait in the soul-complex and was confused with temperament. Later it became the middle-class expression for the automaton, one whose disposition was fixed once and for all or had adapted himself to a particular role in life. In a word, someone who had stopped growing was called a character.

In *Miss Julie*, Strindberg sets about to define the modern dramatic character as "more vacillating and disintegrating than their predecessors, a mixture of old and new" (859). His "souls (characters) are conglomerates of past and present cultural phases, bits from books and newspapers, scraps of humanity, pieces torn from fine clothes and become rags, patched together as is the human soul" (859). This conception is reflected in a dialogue where "characters' minds function irregularly, as they do in real-life conversation, where no topic of discussion is exhausted entirely and one mind by chance finds a cog in another mind in which to engage" (861–862). Strindberg allows the dialogue to wander, "presenting material in the opening scenes that is later taken up, reworked, repeated, expanded, and developed, like the theme in a musical composition" (862). Finally, Strindberg suggests that the actors might take their inspiration from the Italian commedia del'arte, which requires that actors improvise portions of their own dialogue, "although in accordance with the author's intentions" (863).

A more contemporary version of the improvised character is found in the work of Sam Shepard. Read together, Shepard's introductory notes on the music and to the actors in *Angel City* sum up the conjunction of music, acting, and character that I have taken as my theme. The "Note on the Music" suggests that the character Sax remain "cut off from the other characters . . . even when he appears on stage" (61). His music is meant to contribute a dominant mood of "lyrical loneliness" (61) in the style of Lester Young, though with occasional explosions of Charlie Parker and Ornette Coleman. Significantly, the "musician should be free to explore his own sound within the general jazz structure" (61) and is given license to "heighten or color the action" (61) at places not indicated by the script.

The "Note to the Actors" is often cited by critics to make the point that Shepard's conception of character is consistent with the principles of acting transformations, with their goal of subverting the conventions of coherent motivation characteristic of realism:

Instead of the idea of a "whole character" with logical motives behind his behavior . . . [the actor] should consider instead a fractured whole with bits and pieces of character flying off the central theme. In other words, more in terms of collage construction or jazz improvisation. (61–62)

Shepard clarifies that he is not describing one actor playing multiple roles ("doubling up") but an actor combining "many different underlying elements and connecting them through his intuition and senses to make a kind of music or painting in space" (62). What at first appears to be an overtly expressionistic notion of character retains some basis, if not in realism, then at least in reality. Shepard explains, "If there needs to be a 'motivation' for some of the abrupt changes . . . they can be taken as full-blown manifestations of a passing thought or fantasy, having as much significance or 'meaning' as they do in our ordinary lives" (62).

In their various ways and with many variations of approach, both Strindberg and Shepard explore the limits of dramatic realism and both, in part, belong equally to what might be called the antirealist tradition of Western drama. This "anti-tradition," according to Frost and Yarrow,

rests on a more radical acknowledgement of the fragmentation of nineteenth-century notions of a consistent personality. The comic and satiric vein, often allied to improvisation, challenges assumptions about stable social personality and "bourgeois" respectability; taken to extremes, it undercuts political, religious and philosophical myths about the coherence of individual identity and its consonance within a system of stratified order and significance. (14–15)

With *Miss Julie,* Strindberg attempts to "destabilize" Ibsen's coherent, if complex, treatment of characters such as Nora Helmer (*A Doll's House*), or Hedda Gabler. Jarry's satiric portrait of the authoritarian personality in *Ubu Roi,* and Pirandello's philosophical deconstruction of presence and identity in *Six Characters in Search of an Author* or *Tonight We Improvise* continued to subvert the idea of the overdetermined character. In different ways, both Beckett and Brecht challenged assumptions about the construction of character; for one, the existential underpinnings of the absurd character is sustained by play, temporary, in-the-moment stratagems used to confirm a tenuous hold on identity; for the other, empathy in the plight of the character is "alienated" from the audience by various distancing effects, including a repertoire of acting techniques designed to remind the audience that they are watching acting (the demonstration of an event, attitude, or character trait) and not reality. Brecht was concerned that sustained audience empathy with the plight of the character would promote catharsis rather than motivate social change.

In these examples taken from the antirealist tradition, the playwrights promote the illusion of spontaneous improvisation on the stage, even though the words and actions of the characters are carefully scripted. Though their means may vary considerably, the illusion of spontaneity *Signifies* (à la Gates) on the assumptions audiences tend to make about the construction and nature of character, substituting instead destabilized, fragmentary, collaged, and musically inspired alternatives. In his essay "Just be your self," Philip Auslander reviews the problematic construction of the actor's self, tracing the intersecting analyses derived from literary theory (including Derrida's deconstruction of the "metaphysics of presence") against the theories developed by Stanislavsky, Brecht, Grotowski, and others. Auslander asserts that, while "all theorize the actor's self differently, all posit the self as an autonomous foundation for acting" (30). Using Derrida's critique of the performance of presence (28), Auslander concludes that "the actorly self is, in fact, produced by the performance it supposedly grounds" (30). Performance precedes presence, and clearly usurps essence.

In the Western dramatic tradition, there has evolved a conviction that the work of the actor should provide a model for inspired human interaction. Peter Brook's term, "the holy theatre," describes performance that aspires to "a reality deeper than the fullest form of everyday life" (*Empty Space,* 40). In his analysis of catharsis in the holy theater of Artaud, Copeau, Brook, and others, Auslander writes: "Divorced from reality yet reflecting it, communal theatre carries artists and audience together to a level of universal emotional response then returns them to quotidian reality with a keener sense of the psychic structures shared by all people" (19). In contrast to Aristotle's view that the "new balance achieved through catharsis" contributes to the "emotional equilibrium" of the responsible citizen, Copeau and Brook "imply that the balance achieved is a fresh understanding of the individual's relationship to the collective" (19). At the heart of this cathartic effect lies the ability of the spectacle (in the way envisioned by Artaud) to accomplish this in "much the way music does—through abstract theatrical elements (rhythm, sound, archetypal imagery) rather than through mimesis" (21). Auslander's distinction between spectacle and mimesis—or between presentation and representation—brings forward Aristotle's original definition of catharsis in the *Politics* (VIII:7): individuals, Aristotle claimed, are "possessed" by strong emotions, but "when they have made use of the melodies which fill the soul with orgiastic feeling, they are brought back by these sacred melodies to a normal condition as if they had been medically treated and undergone a catharsis" (quoted in Auslander, 14). This distinction between the representation of character and the presentation of "the individual's relationship to the collective"—undertaken in the context of musical ways of knowing and feeling—is of central importance when considering the question of improvisation in drama. Such an analysis also serves to pry drama away from the traditional venues and invigorate a contemporary interest in performance—the rebirth of the medieval *jongleur* (Attali, 14 and 141).

At the heart of the holy theater is the notion that the actor, in clearing away obstacles to being fully present in a role, is in effect charting a course for individual human behavior. The extreme articulation of that concept is Artaud's oracular "actors should be like martyrs burnt alive, still signaling to us from their stakes" (13). In Jerzy Grotowski's view, such a claim contains "the whole problem of spontaneity and discipline, the *conjunction of opposites* which gives birth to the total act" (125).

Grotowski's famous concept of the *via negativa* describes how the actor does not seek to build up a character but rather to eliminate obstacles that prevent the actor from being less than fully present. In the following description of the holy actor, Grotowski reveals the impulse to challenge the illusions and limitations of personality so central to his (and those of Brook and Chaikin, among others) actor-training techniques: "If the actor, by setting himself a challenge publicly challenges others, and through excess, profanation and outrageous sacrilege reveals himself by casting off his everyday mask, he makes it possible for the spectator to undertake a similar process of self-penetration. If he does not exhibit his body, but annihilates it, burns it, frees it from every resistance to any psychic impulse, then he does not sell his body but sacrifices it" (34). He goes on to distinguish the technique of elimination used by the holy actor from the accumulation of skills by the "courtesan actor" (35). For Grotowski, the holy actor, something of a trickster, provides a model for ideal humanity. As noted earlier, Grotowski's formulation of the holy actor resonates deeply with Ellison's notion of the cruel contradiction facing the jazz improviser.

The actor Ryszard Cieslak characterized Grotowski's negative way as a "score": as with the banks of a river, the actor's spontaneous and authentic energies are given direction, force, and relevance. In Grotowski's "poor theatre," spontaneity must be given form by "external discipline": "the more we become absorbed in what is hidden inside us, in the excess, in the exposure, in the self-penetration, the more rigid must be the external discipline" (39). He compares this style of acting with a sculptor "who takes away what is concealing the form" to reveal contours of the self that were formally only felt as vague outlines. On this point, Grotowski found himself in agreement with Artaud's appreciation of Balinese theater, wherein "spontaneity and discipline, far from weakening each other, mutually reinforce themselves" (121). Grotowski felt that Stanislavsky did not understand this principle, as he allowed "natural impulses to dominate"; neither was it understood by Brecht, "who gave too much emphasis to the construction of a role" (121).

While their ends may differ, Peter Brook shared many of Grotowski's notions of the actor's relation to a character. Brook writes that "preparing a character is the opposite of building—it is demolishing, removing brick by brick everything in the actor's muscles, ideas and inhibitions that stands between him and his part" (*Shifting Point,* 7–8). Similarly, Brook affirms the importance of what Grotowski terms the "conjunction of opposites": "As soon as a performance begins, the actor steps into the structure of the *mise-en-scène:* he too [like a runner] becomes completely involved, he improvises within the established guidelines and . . . enters the unpredictable" (8). For Brook, preparation is not meant to "establish form"; the "exact shape" only comes into being "at the hottest moment, when the act itself takes place" (8).

To illustrate how improvisation can establish a dialogue with an audience that does not speak the same language as the actors, Brook relates how he and a troupe of thirty actors traveling through northern Africa performed fragmentary improvisations when they reached a town. In one place, they used a pair of dusty boots sitting in the middle of a carpet as a starting point: "One person after another came in and did various improvisations with them, on a really shared premise: that first of all there was the empty carpet—there was nothing—then a concrete object. . . . Through the boots a relationship was established with the audience, so that what developed was shared in a common language" (*Shifting Point*, 115). This anecdote illustrates what Nettl, in the context of musical improvisation, calls a "point of departure": "Improvisers always have a point of departure, something they use to improvise upon. There are many types, extending from themes, tunes, and chord sequences to forms, from a vocabulary of techniques to a vocabulary of motifs and longer materials, from what is easy or 'natural' for the hand to what is intellectually complex" (16). What this reveals about Brook's orientation to the theater is, first of all, a search for the essential elements that constitute the theatrical experience, and that can serve as points of departure. Second, as a practitioner of the holy theater—in which "theatre becomes life in a more concentrated form" (*Shifting Point*, 114)—he is drawn toward community and away from the isolated individual.

This emphasis on forging a community of interaction was explored in the work of Chaikin's Open Theatre, founded in 1963. The aesthetic intention of the Open Theatre was, according to Chaikin, "to bring about a kind of theatre immediacy—a presence, being present, in the theatre. To explore those powers which the live theatre possesses" (Blumenthal, 15). He explored "alternate understandings of character" and attempted to find "new ways to enter stage roles using somatic and musical methods" (17). Informing these explorations of the relation between the actor and the character is a perception akin to Reich's notion of "armoring," of the essential nature in retreat behind an "individual neurotic superstructure"[8] (5). Chaikin describes such an understanding as follows: "We have to shake off the sophistication of our time, by which we close ourselves up and to become vulnerable again. . . . We've closed off a great deal of our total human response" (quoted in Martin, 121). Both Chaikin and Brook were suspicious of the Method actor's freedom to improvise on the "gestures of everyday life" because, as Brook writes, "the actor is not drawing on any deep creativity. He is reaching inside himself for an alphabet that is also fossilized" (*Empty Space*, 112).

Improvisation exercises are fundamental to the kind of actor training advocated by both Brook and Chaikin. Brook, for example, writes: "Those who work in improvisation have the chance to see with frightening clarity how rapidly the boundaries of so-called freedom are reached" (*Shifting Point*, 112). The aim of improvisation exercises in rehearsal is to bring the actor up against personal barriers and is thus a form of boundary-crossing activity. One such improvisation exercise adapted from Nola Chilton by Chaikin was a "sound and movement" technique in which the shape of a sound is passed back and forth across the room. Emotions come to be embodied in action and sound, making what is normally invisible, visible (Martin, 121–122; Blumenthal, 96). The actors are thus encouraged to become vulnerable to difficult emotions.

Other improvisation exercises used by the Open Theatre included the chord, conductor exercises, and jamming. Blumenthal cites the following description of an actor's jam:

One actor comes in and moves in contemplation of a theme, traveling with the rhythms, going through and out of the phrasing, sometimes using just the gesture, sometimes reducing the whole thing to pure sound. . . . Then another comes in and together they give way and open up on the theme. During the jamming, if the performers let it, the theme moves into associations, a combination of free and structured form. (76)

Throughout the Open Theatre workshops, music and musical analogies were used to explore, among other things, the nonlinguistic dimensions of sound, "thought-music"—"the fleeting, often contrapuntal interplay of feelings and ideas" (Blumenthal, 97)—and musical prototypes for dramatic structures. To underscore the pervasive musical analogy, Blumenthal quotes Chaikin's statement that the theater "exists not just to make a mirror of life, but to represent a kind of realm just as certainly as music is a realm" (47).

In its earlier workshops, the Open Theatre made extensive use of improvisation exercises developed by Viola Spolin, who brought forward the teachings of Neva Boyd and inspired a whole generation of acting improvisers: among them Paul Sills, Bernie Sahlins, and Andre Alexander of Second City fame. Underlying Spolin's theory of improvisation is a principle similar to Grotowski's "conjunction of opposites" in which spontaneity is given form by external discipline. In *Improvisation for the Theatre,* she emphasizes that games, and theater games in particular, require the mutual acceptance by all performers of the rules. Once the rules are accepted, games encourage participants to improvise solutions to the problem posed by the game: "The energy released to solve the problem, being restricted by the rules of the game and bound by group decision, creates an explosion—or spontaneity—and as is the nature of explosions, everything is torn apart, rearranged, unblocked. The ear alerts the feet, and the eye throws the ball" (6). The Reichean principle that character fixation and emotional trauma are *embodied* as armoring underscores Spolin's understanding of the efficacy of improvisation exercises. The explosion of spontaneity, prepared for by the acceptance of rules, transpires through the body at a bio-energetic level. In her discussion of "physicalization," she contends that the "physical is known, and through it we may find our way to the unknown, the intuitive" (7). As there are often few props, costumes, or set pieces in improvisational theater, the actor is required to project a stage reality having depth, texture, and substance through the physicalization of ideational forms. This act of translation characterizes improvisation across the arts.

Eugenio Barba, founder of the Odin Teatret and one of Grotowski's most influential assistants, approaches the training of actors in a related yet distinct way. While working with Grotowski on the cross-cultural Theatre of Sources Project—which "explored the connections between ritual and ceremonial practices in different cultures" (Watson, 133)—Barba became fascinated with Eastern performance techniques, especially regarding the question of the performer's presence. Through his "theatre anthropology," Barba conceived of two features of Oriental forms contributing to commanding stage presence: "the use of learned body techniques designed to break the performer's automatic daily responses, and the codification of principles which dictate the use of energy during performance" (133). The intentional physical distortions of *kathakali* or precarious balance of Noh for instance rely on learned technique and patterns of behavior distinct from daily behavior. For Barba, this "extra-daily technique" contributes to actor presence "since it establishes a pre-expressive mode in which the actor's energies are engaged prior to personal expression" (134). Like Grotowski's score, these extra-daily techniques function as a productive constraint on performance, not to limit expressivity but to open it up to new dimensions and energies through physical means. For the performers of the Odin Teatret, "training is improvisation structured by the application of principles" (135).

At the Open Theatre, the transformations that evolved from the improvisation exercises inspired by Spolin, Chilton, Brook, and Grotowski brought the actors (and, it is hoped, their audiences) up against the boundaries of unconscious behavior. Megan Terry, widely acknowledged as instrumental in the early development of transformations, joined the Open Theatre as a writer in 1963. The concept of transformations grew out of a desire to move away from the usual dramatic focus where "one person gets to show three or four aspects of the personality, while all the other people have supporting roles and usually are stereotypes" (245). The egalitarian impulse behind the transformation exercises traded on the audience's familiarity with the stories and editing techniques of films, radio, and television. Terry believes that a playwright "can speak to people in a new kind of shorthand, by the use of dramatic clues. It's like Gestalt psychology—connect the dots, the incomplete completes itself" (246). There is no need to supply subjective motivations for characters because audience members will do that of their own accord. Transformations are a way of "playing with the elements of theatre" (46), using jump cuts, dissolves, and fades, creating comedy from quickly changing situations. She cites stand-up comics, impressionists, cartoons, and Gertrude Stein as other influences. The essence of the transformation is to eliminate transitions: "When people try to show the transition, they fall into a morass. Transitions should be as pure and quick as those of a child playing—with total commitment each time" (247).

The difference between method actors and transformational actors in Terry's view is an ability to "drop" a character quickly. "Our actors were trained to that. It takes Actors Studio actors half an hour to drop it" (246). One exercise used to promote acting responsiveness and flexibility is the "transformation of styles": "You take the same dialogue and do it as Molière, as Shakespeare, as *The Days of Our Lives* [a TV soap opera], as Noel Coward, as Tennessee Williams" (246). The actor involved in transformations is riffing like the jazz musician, a channel for a dialogic mix of cultural voices unencumbered by reifications of personality or place.

The transformational exercises of the Open Theatre and other companies in the 1960s reflected a deep interest in the therapeutic value of improvisation. J. L. Moreno's psychodrama, first developed in Vienna in 1923—besides inspiring theater practitioners—continues to inform family reconstruction therapies (pioneered by Satir and Minuchin in their separate spheres), as well as other approaches to psychotherapy promoted by Jung, Maslow, and Rogers. Moreno borrowed from the Greek paradigm in which a character experiences a degree of catharsis through some form of enactment wherein issues of choice, receptivity, responsibility, and identity are of central concern. Psychodrama allows participants to discover their character armoring (Reich) and their attachment to the attributions of others (Laing). The work of the Wooster Group, Mabou Mines, Laurie Anderson, Spalding Gray, Karen Finley, and of risk-taking stand-up comics from Robin Williams to Richard Pryor all owe a debt of influence to Moreno's use of drama, play, and improvisation as a way of opening up the self to greater freedom and possibility.

Frost and Yarrow offer the term *disponibilité* (derived from Lecoq) to suggest a range of meanings reflecting the therapeutic possibilities of improvised drama:

Availability—openness—readiness—acceptance: the precondition of creativity. It implies not resisting, but flowing *with* the world and the self. . . . The performer is without armour, but not without weapons: such as wit, agility, mobility, and inventiveness. . . . *Disponibilité* is the state of "armed neutrality" from which all movements are equally possible. (151–152)

Through the agency of *disponibilité*—"the power to *dispose* of oneself and one's activity" (153)—one is ready to discover what Hakim Bey has called the "temporary autonomous zone" (153). Ruled by the spirit of festival rather than revolution, the TAZ requires us to become nomadic—ready to move on, to relinquish attachments and preconceptions, to enter a state of temporary neutrality. There may, in fact, be a cruel contradiction in our discovery of the improvised character: as we perform ourselves into a sense of authenticity—of authoring ourselves in our own voices—our performance erases the traces of our individuality within the ensemble of humanity.

Notes

1. Fred Wei-han Ho argues for an alternate spelling—"kreolization"—to distinguish it from the "creolization" of Herskovitz "pertaining to the intermixing in the Caribbean." Kreolization, a concept promoted by Dorothy Désir-Davis, emphasizes "cultural and social cross-fertilization, a process that leads to the formation of entirely new identities and cultures," some of which may be appropriated into "the dominant identity and culture, but politicized and deracinated" (143 n.3).

2. That character can be identified or located by voice may be approached profitably in terms of Mikhail Bakhtin's notions of dialogism, multivocality, and heteroglossia. Marvin Carlson suggests that the "creative tension between repetition and innovation" implied by Bakhtin's dialogic model "is deeply involved in modern views of performance" (58).

3. Gates coins the neologism "Signifyin(g)" to distinguish it from the semiotic "signifying." Signifyin(g)—"to engage in certain rhetorical games" (48), to repeat with revisions—refers to an African-American vernacular tradition of rhetorical troping.

> Whereas signification depends for order and coherence on the exclusion of unconscious associations which any given word yields at any given time, Signification luxuriates in the inclusion of the free play of these associative rhetorical and semantic relations. Jacques Lacan calls these vertically suspended associations "a whole articulation of relevant contexts," by which he means all of the associations that a signifier carries from other contexts, which must be deleted, ignored, or censored "for this signifier to line up with a signified to produce a specific meaning." Everything that must be excluded for meaning to remain coherent and linear comes to bear in the process of Signifyin(g). . . . Signifyin(g), in Lacan's sense, is the Other of discourse.(50)

4. Keith Johnstone cites a number of descriptions by actors of their sensation of split consciousness while acting; for example, Fanny Kemble: "'The curious part of acting, to me, is the sort of double process which the mind carries on at once, the combined operation of one's faculties, so to speak, in diametrically opposite directions'" (151). Johnstone claims that this bifurcated consciousness is typical of trance states, that the actor is, in effect, possessed.

5. Schechner elaborates on this idea that improvisation for performance occurs within frames by positing an "axiom of frames" for the theater: "the looser an outer frame [performance space, dramatic conventions, text, director], the tighter the inner [the "free" space allotted to the improvising performer], and conversely, the looser the inner, the more important the outer" (*Performance Theory*, 14).

6. In his essay "Structure, Sign and Play in the Discourse of the Human Sciences," Derrida reports: "The *bricoleur*, says Lévi-Strauss, is someone who uses 'the means at hand,' that is, the instruments he finds at his disposition around him, those which are already there, which had not been especially conceived with an eye to the operation for which they are to be used and to which one tries by trial and error to adapt them, not hesitating to change them whenever it appears necessary, or to try several of them at once, even if their form and their origin are heterogeneous" (*Writing and Difference*, 285).

7. Johnstone claims that Western culture is hostile to trance states: "We distrust

spontaneity, and try to replace it by reason: the mask was driven out of the theatre in the same way that improvisation was driven out of music" (149). Because the association of trance and improvisation is relatively foreign to the Western ethic of artistic control, Johnstone resorts to such sources as Maya Deren's trance experiences in Haiti and Jane Belo's descriptions of Indonesian trance possessions to make his point that acting improvisation has many affinities with trance states.

8. Reich writes: "In the conflict between instinct and morals, ego, and outer world, the organism is forced to *armour* itself against the instinct as well as the outer world. This armouring of the organism results inevitably in a limitation of the total ability to live. . . . This armour is the chief reason for the loneliness of so many people in the midst of collective living" (4). Reich develops this concept of armouring to account for personality differences: "What makes people individually different is . . . essentially their individual neurotic superstructure" (5).

Works Cited

Artaud, Antonin. *The Theatre and its Double.* Translated by Mary Richards. New York: Grove, 1958.

Attali, Jacques. *Noise: The Political Economy of Music.* Translated by Brian Massumi. Minneapolis, Minn.: University of Minnesota Press, 1977.

Auslander, Philip. *From Acting to Performance: Essays in Modernism and Postmodernism.* London: Routledge, 1997.

Austin, James. *Zen and the Brain: Toward an Understanding of Meditation and Consciousness.* Cambridge, Mass.: MIT Press, 1999.

Babcock, Barbara. "'A Tolerated Margin of Mess': The Trickster and His Tales Reconsidered." In *Critical Essays on Native American Literature,* edited by Andrew Wiget, 153–185. Boston: G. K. Hall, 1985.

Baker, Houston, Jr. *Blues, Ideology, and Afro-American Literature: A Vernacular Theory.* Chicago: University of Chicago Press, 1984.

Bailey, Derek. *Improvisation: Its Nature and Practice in Music.* New York: Da Capo, 1992.

Bakhtin, Mikhail. "Discourse Typology in Prose." In *Readings in Russian Poetics: Formalist and Structuralist Views,* edited by L. Matejka and K. Pomorska, 176–195. Cambridge, Mass.: MIT Press, 1971.

Balliger, Robin. "Sounds of Resistance." In *Sounding Off!: Music as Subversion/Resistance/Revolution,* edited by Ron Sakolsky and Fred Wei-han Ho, 13–26. Brooklyn, N.Y.: Autonomedia, 1995.

Baumeister, Roy. "How the Self Became a Problem: A Psychological Review of Historical Research." *Journal of Personality and Social Psychology* 52, no. 1 (1987): 163–176.

Beahrs, John O. *Unity and Multiplicity: Multilevel Consciousness of Self in Hypnosis, Psychiatric Disorder and Mental Health.* New York: Brunner/Mazel, 1982.

Belgrad, Daniel. *The Culture of Spontaneity: Improvisation and the Arts in Postwar America.* Chicago: University of Chicago Press, 1998.

Bennett, J. G. *Enneagram Studies.* York Beach, Maine: Samuel Weiser, 1983.

Berliner, Paul. *Thinking in Jazz: The Infinite Art of Improvisation.* Chicago: University of Chicago Press, 1994.

Bey, Hakim. *T.A.Z.: The Temporary Autonomous Zone, Ontological Anarchy, Poetic Terrorism.* Brooklyn, N.Y.: Automedia, 1991.

Blumenthal, Eileen. *Joseph Chaikin: Exploring the Boundaries of Theatre.* Cambridge: Cambridge University Press, 1984.

Boal, Augusto. "The Cop in the Head: Three Hypotheses." *Drama Review* 34 (Fall 1990): 35–42.

——. *Theatre of the Oppressed*. Translated by Charles A. McBride and Maria-Odilia Leal McBride. New York: Theatre Communications Group, 1985.

Brook, Peter. *The Empty Space*. New York: Atheneum, 1987.

——. *The Shifting Point*. New York: Harper and Row, 1987.

Capra, Fritjof. *The Web of Life; A New Scientific Understanding of Living Systems.* New York: Doubleday, 1997.

Carlson, Marvin. *Performance: A Critical Introduction*. London: Routledge, 1996.

Chaikin, Joseph. *The Presence of the Actor*. 1972. New York: Theater Communications Group, 1991.

Chekhov, Michael. *To the Actor: On the Technique of Acting*. 1953. Translated by Andrei Malaev-Babel. London: Routledge, 2002.

Chernoff, John Miller. *African Rhythm and African Sensibility: Aesthetics and Social Action in African Musical Idioms.* Chicago: University of Chicago Press, 1979.

Clifford, James. *The Predicament of Culture: Twentieth-Century Ethnography, Literature, and Art.* Cambridge, Mass.: Harvard University Press, 1988.

Coleman, Ornette. *Free Jazz: A Collective Improvisation*. Liner notes by Martin Williams. Atlantic SD 1364, 1961.

Copeau, Jacques. *Copeau: Texts on Theatre*. Edited and translated by John Rudlin and Norman H. Paul. London: Routledge, 1990.

Deleuze, Gilles, and Félix Guattari. *Anti-Oedipus (Capitalism and Schizophrenia)*. Translated by R. Hurley, M. Seem, and H. Lane. New York: Viking, 1977.

Derrida, Jacques. *Writing and Difference*. Translated by Alan Bass. Chicago: University of Chicago Press, 1978.

Eldredge, Sears. *Mask Improvisation for Training and Performance: The Compelling Image.* Evanston, Ill: Northwestern University Press, 1996.

Ellison, Ralph. *Shadow and Act*. New York: Random House, 1964.

Frost, Anthony, and Ralph Yarrow. *Improvisation in Drama*. London: MacMillan, 1990.

Gates, Henry Louis, Jr. *The Signifying Monkey: A Theory of African-American Literary Criticism*. New York: Oxford University Press, 1988.

Goffman, Erving. *The Presentation of Self in Everyday Life*. Garden City, N.Y.: Doubleday Anchor, 1959.

Greenblatt, Stephen. *Renaissance Self-Fashioning: From More to Shakespeare*. Chicago: University of Chicago Press, 1980.

Grotowski, Jerzy. *Towards a Poor Theatre*. Various translators. New York: Simon and Schuster, 1968.

Hall, Edward. "Improvisation as an Acquired, Multilevel Process." *Ethnomusicology* 36, no. 2 (1992): 223–235.

Heble, Ajay. *Landing on the Wrong Note: Jazz, Dissonance, and Critical Practice*. New York: Routledge, 2000.

Hermans, Hubert, H. J. G. Kempen, and R. van Loon. "The Dialogical Self: Beyond Individualism and Rationalism." *American Psychologist* 47, no. 1 (January 1992): 23–33.

Ho, Fred Wei-han. "'Jazz,' Kreolization and Revolutionary Music for the 21st Century." In *Sounding Off!: Music as Subversion/Resistance/Revolution,* edited by Ron Sakolsky and Fred Wei-han Ho, 133–143. Brooklyn, N.Y.: Autonomedia, 1995.

Hyde, Lewis. *Trickster Makes This World: Mischief, Myth, and Art*. New York: Farrar, Straus and Giroux, 1998.

Johnstone, Keith. *Impro: Improvisation and the Theatre*. 1981. London: Methuen, 1990.

Kerouac, Jack. "Essentials of Spontaneous Prose." *Evergreen Review* 2 (Summer 1958): 72–73.

Martin, Jacqueline. *Voice in Modern Theatre.* London: Routledge, 1991.

Monson, Ingrid. "Russell, Coltrane, and Modal Jazz." In *In the Course of Performance: Studies in the World of Musical Improvisation,* edited by Bruno Nettl with Melinda Russell, 149–168. Chicago: University of Chicago Press, 1998.

Murray, Albert. *Stomping the Blues.* New York: Da Capo, 1976.

Nettl, Bruno. "An Art Neglected in Scholarship." In *In the Course of Performance: Studies in the World of Musical Improvisation,* edited by Bruno Nettl with Melinda Russell, 1–23. Chicago: University of Chicago Press, 1998.

Pressing, Jeff. "Psychological Constraints on Improvisational Expertise and Communication." In *In the Course of Performance: Studies in the World of Musical Improvisation,* edited by Bruno Nettl with Melinda Russell, 47–67. Chicago: University of Chicago Press, 1998.

Reich, Wilhelm. *The Sexual Revolution: Toward a Self-Governing Character Structure.* Revised ed. Translated by T. P. Wolfe. New York: Farrar, Straus and Giroux, 1969.

Schechner, Richard. *Performance Theory.* Revised ed. New York: Routledge, 1988.

Seem, Mark. Introduction to *Anti-Oedipus (Capitalism and Schizophrenia),* edited by Gilles Deleuze and Félix Guattari. Translated by R. Hurley, M. Seem, and H. Lane. New York: Viking, 1977.

Shepard, Sam. "Note to the Actors. *Angel City.*" In *Fool For Love and Other Plays.* New York: Bantam, 1984.

Slater, Niall. "The Idea of the Actor." In *Nothing to Do with Dionysis? Athenian Drama in Its Social Context,* edited by John J. Winkler and Froma I. Zeitlin, 385–395. Princeton: Princeton University Press, 1990.

Spolin, Viola. *Improvisation for the Theatre.* Chicago: University of Chicago Press, 1963.

Strindberg, August. "Author's Preface to *Miss Julie.*" In *Modern Drama: Selected Plays from 1879 to the Present,* edited by Walter Levy. Upper Saddle River, N.J.: Prentice-Hall, 1999.

Terry, Megan. Interview. In *In Their Own Words: Contemporary American Playwrights,* by David Savran, 240–256. New York: Theatre Communications Group, 1988.

Thompson, Robert Farris. *Flash of the Spirit: African and Afro-American Art and Philosophy.* New York: Vintage, 1984.

Turner, Victor. *The Anthropology of Performance.* New York: PAJ, 1986.

———. *From Ritual to Theatre: The Human Seriousness of Play.* New York: PAJ, 1982.

Watson, Ian. "Eastern and Western Influences on Performer Training at Eugenio Barba's Odin Teatret." In *Acting (Re)Considered: Theories and Practices,* edited by Phillip Zarrilli, 129–136. London: Routledge, 1995.

Williams, Martin. Liner Notes to *Free Jazz: A Collective Improvisation.* The Ornette Colemen Double Quartet. Atlantic SD 1364, 1961.

KRIN GABBARD

Improvisation and Imitation
Marlon Brando as Jazz Actor

·⁓

What is jazz improvisation when there is no music? More specifically, what happens when a nonmusical art form is profoundly influenced by the practice of jazz improvisation? This essay grows out of an attempt to find a place where, like single-cell organisms under a microscope, jazz and another art form can be observed exchanging genetic material. At the outset this search was complicated by the vagaries of jazz history, with its unending debates about what is and is not the real jazz, its constantly shifting appeals to its constantly shifting audience base, and the highly personal "misreadings" of jazz by painters, poets, filmmakers, choreographers, and photographers.[1] After all, "jazz" paintings can include the flat geometry of line and color in Mondrian's *Broadway Boogie Woogie* (1943), as well as the playfully perverse representation of Willie "The Lion" Smith at the piano in Bearden's *Lion Takes Off* (1981). In fact, if we consider only the artists' intentions, the two paintings are very similar, both representing the improvisations of premodern jazz pianists.

In this essay, however, I am more interested in works where the jazz influence enters on multiple levels, not all of them explicitly acknowledged by artists and audiences. The American cinema is, in the words of Robert B. Ray, "massively overdetermined," and a great deal of important scholarship in the last several decades has taught us how to read the "political unconscious" of filmmakers and their audiences.[2] I have chosen to concentrate on a film from the early 1950s when jazz improvisation had an especially significant appeal for American artists and intellectuals. Although not every aspect of it is appealing, the performance of the young Marlon Brando in *A Streetcar Named Desire* embodies, on several levels, what we might call an aesthetic of jazz improvisation.

Where Jazz and Hollywood Intersect

The story of jazz overlaps at several points with the development of the Hollywood cinema. Both art forms are uniquely American, and both began to develop and mature dramatically after 1900. According to Mary Carbine, black jazz artists were improvising in orchestra pits during the screening of presound films in African-American neighborhoods in Chicago in the 1920s (28–29). African-American participation at some point in the production and exhibition of the first feature films was, of course, an anomaly. As with most American institutions at the beginning of the twentieth century, blacks were excluded from virtually all aspects of the film industry, with the notable exception of a handful of independent filmmakers, such as Oscar Micheaux, who worked outside the mainstream film industry. The omnipresence of white actors in blackface in D. W. Griffith's *Birth of a Nation* (1914) is the most striking example of Hollywood's long history of relying upon myths about African-Americans to forge fundamental narratives and ideologies while harshly limiting the actual presence of black actors, directors, writers, and technicians.[3]

The radically different racial orientations of jazz and cinema did not, however, prevent either from being considered low culture during the early decades of the century. The guardians of America's moral, sexual, and religious health launched similar attacks on both. The two art forms became somewhat more sedate in the 1930s with the rise of superego forces, specifically the Production Code, which made movies safe for children, and the success of white swing bands, which made jazz safe for Middle Americans.[4] In the 1950s, new bugbears appeared to make jazz and film seem less disreputable. Rock and roll replaced jazz just as television replaced movies as the explanation for the corruption of America's youth and the lowering of standards of taste. Coincidentally, as Bernard Gendron has argued, claims that jazz and Hollywood films could be "art" first surfaced at about this time in the late 1940s and early 1950s. By the 1980s, after several decades of experimentation, both jazz and cinema fell back into periods of what might be called "recuperation": while some welcomed a return to more classical, more accessible models, others believed that the exhilarating evolution of vital art forms had stopped. At any rate, by the 1990s both jazz and film had begun to acquire the status of elite entertainment. At New York's Lincoln Center, a ticket to a jazz concert cost as much as a ticket to an opera or a ballet. Across the street, at the Lincoln Plaza Cinemas, moviegoers could purchase gourmet food and espresso in the lobby while Baroque music played in the auditoriums before each screening.

At least a few critics have speculated about the specific ways in which jazz has actually influenced the movies. Stanley Crouch has made a provocative claim for the centrality of Afrocentric practices in American culture, pointing to the call and response dialogue that African-American preachers improvised with their congregations and that eventually became the basis for the interaction between blues singers and their audiences and between the brass and reed sections in arrangements played by black jazz orchestras in the 1920s and 1930s. Crouch argues that Hollywood's shot-reverse shot editing is also an appropriation of call and response (82).

Crouch has almost certainly exaggerated the actual impact of African-American practices on an industry that was much more invested in white mythologies of blackness. Clear evidence of the influence of jazz improvisation in Hollywood is also minimal, especially in the industry's "prestige" products where a small army of producers and technicians oversees each step in a film's deliberate progress to the big screen. Nevertheless, there may have been a substantial—if highly mediated—exchange between jazz improvisation and film in the 1950s.[5] Both jazz and the Method acting that made its way into American cinema at this time were part of a modernist mix that also included a romance with psychoanalysis, new forms of racial imitation, the development of postwar masculinities, and a fascination with improvisation. *A Streetcar Named Desire* had a revolutionary jazz-inflected score by Alex North;[6] it was based on the play by Tennessee Williams, who was obsessed with masculine performance; and it was directed by Elia Kazan, who was obsessed with psychoanalysis. All of these strains came together in an aesthetic of jazz improvisation that resonates most powerfully in the performance of the youthful Brando.

Mythologies of the Unconscious

Among the many myths and assertions that circulate in jazz writing, three are especially useful for identifying an improvisatory aesthetic in Brando's performance. Later on I shall take up the myths that jazz gives whites safe access to a fascinating but proscribed Otherness and that jazz as an improvised art music can only be performed by disciplined artists. First, however, I would like to explore the myth that improvising jazz artists dig into their unconscious minds and bypass more conventional modes of intellection. Various versions of this myth have circulated since the beginnings of jazz history when the predominantly African-American musicians were considered too primitive to be playing a music mediated by intellect. The idea that "primitive" people are instinctual rather than thoughtful goes back at least to the fifth century B.C.E. when Herodotus wrote that the Persians, for whom the Greeks coined the term "barbarian," would only make important decisions when they were drunk (I:133).

The trope of the improvising jazz artist as the unthinking explorer of the unconscious is still very much with us. As Will Straw has pointed out, "strength and mastery independent of knowledges" have long been an admired aspect of a musician's stance (8). Certainly, the legend of Louis Armstrong is based more on his muscularity and joie de vivre than on his thoughtful artistry. But there is also a more spiritual side to the myth in which the jazz artist, in the heat of improvisatory creation, achieves a semireligious state of transcendence. In James Baldwin's 1965 story "Sonny's Blues," the pianist brother of the narrator behaves like a mystic, "wrapped up in some cloud, some fire, some vision all his own" (129). The eponymous hero of Rafi Zabor's novel *The Bear Comes Home* (1997), a saxophone-playing Kodiak with more intelligence and musical talent than most humans, at one point plays with such ecstatic abandon that he is "plucked out of existence like a cheap suit" (454). (In the cinema, the intuitive jazz musician is seldom allowed such transcendence. Consider the Charlie Parker of Clint Eastwood's *Bird* (1988), whose mysterious ways are simply inscrutable or even pathological. Or consider the self-destructive saxophonist played by Dexter Gordon in *Round Midnight* (1986), who needs a sensitive French aficionado to ascertain and then fulfill his needs.)

Specific connections between jazz artists and the unconscious mind appeared for the first time in the late 1940s and early 1950s, a heady time for psychoanalysis. John Burnham has shown how a new optimism in the psychiatric and psychoanalytic professions was driven to a large extent by their substantial success in integrating shell-shocked veterans of World War II back into American life. Psychoanalytic concepts of repression and the family romance soon entered popular discourse, and visiting a psychotherapist gained in cachet what it lost in stigma. The fascination with psychoanalysis was especially prominent in the arts, where surrealism and other avant-garde movements had already made the unconscious an essential player in the creative process. The links between jazz and the unconscious were explicit in a number of articles appearing in psychoanalytic journals in the 1950s. Miles D. Miller, for example, wrote in 1958 that jazz can be used "as a sublimated means of releasing tension associated with repressed hostile and aggressive impulses" (235). More specifically, Miller associated the sounds of the jazz trombone with "anal expulsive components" that bring delight to audiences who would surely find such sounds objectionable in other situations (237).[7]

The Method acting that enjoyed a vogue in the late 1940s and 1950s was also promoted in terms of what is ordinarily repressed and ignored. Actors sought to build their performances around "affective memory," a term coined to describe pockets of the mind, often unconscious, in which emotional reactions to specific events are stored. Like patients in therapy working through repressed moments in the past, Method actors looked back to incidents in their own lives to find the emotional key to constructing a character. Although many of the central ideas in this discipline had already been introduced by Konstantin Stanislavsky at the Moscow State Theatre in the 1920s, a uniquely American version developed at the same time that intellectuals were especially fascinated by psychoanalysis. In fact, the Actors' Studio, the home of the Method in postwar New York, has been conceptualized as a therapeutic institution with its leader Lee Strasberg playing the role of psychoanalyst and his actors the role of analysands (Naremore, 197). With the help of elaborate exercises, frequently built around improvisation, actors sought to "unblock" themselves and connect with their inner selves in hopes of bringing authenticity and immediacy to their performances.

Some jazz artists engaged in elaborate exercises of their own at the same time that Method acting was gaining in popularity. Although not every jazz artist was seeking to unlock emotional resources through experiments in improvisation, many who fancied the new jazz believed that the musicians were voyaging inward. Bebop solos were conceived as journeys into the emotional turmoil of the musician's unconscious. The pianist Lennie Tristano sought to create an improvised music without key signature that suggested automatic writing, a practice among the surrealists inspired by Freud. The notion that improvising jazz artists rely primarily on emotion and the unconscious is, of course, a gross oversimplification of the process. And as James Naremore has observed, the performances of most actors trained in the Method seldom differ from those with more conventional backgrounds. The specific achievements of the enterprise, he argues, are "difficult to assess" (198). My point is that a new fascination with psychoanalysis popularized discourses of the unconscious and emotional memory that were then recruited to describe both Method acting and jazz improvisation in the years after World War II.

Stanley Kowalski's Cold Plate Supper

Marlon Brando has been known as an improviser throughout his career. One of his more sensational moments was the tearful speech he seemed to make up on the spot as his character grieved over the corpse of his wife in Last Tango in Paris (1973).[8] Brando's most famous piece of apparently improvised business, however, involves Eva Marie Saint's glove in *On the Waterfront* (1954). The scene is regularly cited as the locus classicus of Brando's improvisatory style in particular and of Method acting in general (Naremore, 193–212). While strolling through a playground with Edie Doyle (Eva Marie Saint), Terry Malloy (Brando) picks up the white glove that Edie seems to have dropped by accident. While sitting on a child's swing, Terry absent-mindedly toys with the glove, eventually putting it on his own hand. Brando actually improvised with the glove after Saint accidentally dropped it during a rehearsal while director Kazan was present. At the director's urging, the business was preserved when the scene was actually shot (Schickel, 91). How much Brando subsequently improvised while the cameras were rolling is open to debate. Indeed, the amount of improvisatory leeway available to an actor—even to one as original as Brando—is extremely limited, especially within the highly conventionalized strategies for achieving "realistic" effects in mainstream cinema. Nevertheless, the variety of gestures that Brando explores with the glove, seemingly without artifice, convinced many that he was letting his unconscious do the work for him and that he was drawing on training that was heavily inflected by psychology.

For my purposes, however, an even more telling scene takes place in *Streetcar* when Brando ranges through a fascinating variety of stage business. Early in the film, Stanley's wife Stella (Kim Hunter) serves him a "cold plate" supper so that she and her recently arrived sister Blanche (Vivien Leigh) can go out to dinner at Galatoire's for Chatauqua Night. Stanley loudly questions Stella about Blanche, fully aware that she is just around the corner in the bathtub. He is especially concerned about a family inheritance that he suspects Blanche has squandered on clothes instead of splitting with Stella who must, according to Stanley's understanding of the Napoleonic Code, share it with her husband. While eating his supper, Stanley explores the clothes and jewelry in Blanche's trunk, recently deposited in the dining room.

As with the glove in *On the Waterfront*, Brando is doing much more than reading lines and responding to Kim Hunter in the scene. You can see Brando doing what actors are told to do when they eat: bite small and chew big. You can also see him using the food as a prop and refusing to meet Hunter's gaze. All of these actions present a man for whom appetite is all. Stanley is clearly disappointed by his meager supper, but he is also hungry for information about Blanche, who has profoundly raised his suspicions as well as his sexual curiosity. Like a jazz artist playing changes on a familiar tune, Brando continually finds ways to develop his character as he eats, interacts with Stella, and inspects each of the items in Blanche's trunk. Yet even today, it all seems fresh and "in the moment." The seeming naturalness of his acting in these scenes has made "Marlon Brando synonymous with Stanley Kowalski in world theatre" (Kolin, 24). One critic even says he heard a passerby at the filming of a 1983 television version of *A Streetcar Named Desire* ask, "Who's playing Marlon Brando?" (Card, 98).

As is often the case with a Hollywood film, we do not know how many takes Brando needed to create effects that seem so appropriate to his character. Nor do we know exactly how much credit must go to the director Elia Kazan, to the playwright Tennessee Williams, or to Oscar Saul, who is credited with "adapting" Williams's play. I would only point out Kazan came to cinema from the theater and was more likely to block and direct his actors in a "stagey" fashion. And other actors who have played the part of Stanley Kowalski have scarcely made the part their own as did Brando. To the extent that film is a collaborative art, the other participants appear to have stepped back and let Brando make the most of his solo space.

Within the Racial Matrix

According to the second jazz myth that is relevant to Brando and *Streetcar*, the white musician can gain privileged access to Otherness through the music of African-Americans. Michael Rogin has written that whites have historically benefitted not only from the surplus value of African-American labor; they have also exploited the "surplus symbolic value" of blacks in much of American entertainment. This is as true of the white minstrel men in the nineteenth century who sought to imitate the language, music, and humor of black men as it is of the numerous white pop singers today whose every gesture and vocal inflection shows the influence of black American entertainers. Given this long history of exploitation, specific cases of white males borrowing from black jazz artists can be described with varying degrees of censure. At one extreme, whites have taken to jazz in ways that are consistent with Fred Pfeil's characterization of rock music in the 1970s: "rock authenticity means . . . not just freedom from commerce and opposition to all straight authority . . . but being a free agent with ready access to the resources of femininity and Blackness yet with no obligations to either women or Blacks" (79). The same was often true in the 1940s and early 1950s, when jazz was still the music of youthful revolt and many of the tropes of what was to become rock authenticity, including an aloof pose on the bandstand and the refusal to play the tepid pop music preferred by the uninitiated, were being developed in the discourses of jazz. Bebop in particular offered white hipsters a stance of defiance that linked artistic integrity, a thorough renunciation of bourgeois convention, and contempt for the institutions of white culture. At any moment, of course, the white artist could turn away from this counterculture and comfortably return to the bosom of Middle America. With very few exceptions, the black artist had nowhere else to go but down.

In contrast to this critique of the escape clause in the white artist's investment in black culture, LeRoi Jones (Amiri Baraka) in *Blues People* takes a stance reminiscent of Ralph Ellison when he speaks generously about white artists such as Bix Beiderbecke who made a commitment to jazz in the 1920s: "The entrance of the white man into jazz at this level of sincerity and emotional legitimacy did at least bring him, by implication, much closer to the Negro" (151). Beiderbecke approached the music of African-Americans at one or two removes, learning his craft almost exclusively from white recording artists such as the Original Dixieland Jazz Band (ODJB) and the New Orleans Rhythm Kings (NORK) before he had direct experience of black music. But for the many white artists whose performance styles were rooted in black culture, racial appropriation need not be cast as an absolute evil. Other discursive strategies are available. While Baraka has suggested that white jazz artists helped break down the gap between black and white, Eric Lott has employed the phrase "Love and Theft" to describe the ambivalence of whites toward blacks that informed minstrelsy, and David Meltzer has coined the term "permissible racism" to characterize the uncritical adulation of black artists qua black artists by white jazz fans (4).

Brando, permissibly or not, can be regarded as another member of the white bourgeoisie whose racial and gender borrowings can on some levels be traced to jazz and the improvisations of black artists. In spite of the ethnic ring to his last name as well as the working-class demeanor he convincingly affected in many of his early roles, Brando grew up in comfortable middle-class surroundings first in Omaha, Nebraska, and later in the Illinois towns of Evanston and Libertyville. As in the case of Bix Beiderbecke, Brando's parents sent him to military school when his behavior disappointed them. But Brando's parents were not the staid burghers who raised Beiderbecke. Both were notorious for their public drunkenness and freely engaged in extramarital affairs. Brando's older sister was already in New York studying dramatic art when Brando arrived there a few years later. Unlike Beiderbecke, Brando did not have to break dramatically with his family when he embraced the bohemian life of the actor. Or when he became interested in jazz.

Peter Manso, perhaps the most diligent of the actor's biographers, reports that Brando listened to jazz when he was growing up, to Louis Armstrong, Jimmy Rushing, and Bessie Smith as well as to Goodman and the Dorseys (43). We also know that Brando had a fascination with dark-skinned women, and that he joined Katherine Dunham's School of Dance in the late 1940s, where sixty-five percent of the students were black. There he met Henri "Papa" Augustine, a revered Haitian drum teacher who gave Brando lessons on congas and bongos and introduced him to black culture. Among many anecdotes about Brando's attraction to African-Americans, Manso recounts a story about a party given by Norman Mailer for the Hollywood elite at which Brando spent the entire evening speaking with the bartender, the only black person in the house (285).

Brando once wanted to be a jazz drummer. As late as the Broadway production of *Streetcar* in 1947, he was still keeping a jazz drummer's trap set backstage along with his bongos and barbells. In high school, Brando briefly led a few bands of his own at the same time that he was tormenting his school band director by playing Gene Krupa riffs in the middle of Sousa marches. The Krupa connection is revealing. After starring with the Benny Goodman band in the mid-thirties, the white drummer broke away to form his own band in 1938. Krupa was arrested on a widely reported drug charge in 1943 and forced out of the music business for several months. For many, the drummer's dangerous romance with proscribed substances only increased his glamour. Even before Krupa's arrest, however, his band had a certain subversive appeal. In 1941, the new "girl singer" in Krupa's orchestra was Anita O'Day, who projected a more sexually experienced persona than did most of the demure white women who sang with the big bands. O'Day raised many eyebrows when she refused to wear the prom dresses common among girl singers, choosing instead to wear a blazer like the men in the band. Also in 1941, Krupa hired the black trumpeter Roy Eldridge and prominently featured his improvised solos *and* his singing. The band had a hit with "Let Me Off Uptown" in which Eldridge sang with O'Day. The interracial romance implied in the couple's double entendres was especially daring for 1941. The patter begins with O'Day asking Eldridge if he has been "uptown" and concludes with her urging him, "Well, blow, Roy, blow!" The veiled invitation to interracial oral sex was not lost on the hipsters in the audience. The gender and racial titillation in which Krupa's band specialized may have been as important for the young Brando as Krupa's drumming.

In films such as *Hollywood Hotel* (1938), *Ball of Fire* (1941), *Beat the Band* (1947), and *The Glenn Miller Story* (1954), Krupa can be observed flamboyantly performing his sexuality and masculinity, surely as part of an attempt to re-create what he found most fascinating about black men and their music. Anyone who has watched the revered African-American drummer Jo Jones in a film such as *Jammin' the Blues* (1944) has witnessed an artist who seems, by contrast, to inhabit his exuberance without affectation. I would speculate that Krupa saw and heard sexual power in the improvisations of black drummers like Jones and created his own style of bringing it to the surface in hopes of projecting that same power. At some point in his early life, Brando may have been using Krupa as a transitional object in his appropriation of black masculinity, just as Beiderbecke first discovered black music through the white artists of the ODJB and NORK. Identifying a parallel phenomenon, Eric Lott has written that imitators of Elvis Presley play out their fascination with black male sexuality safely at one remove by trying to inhabit the body of Presley as he appeared in the 1950s, "as though such performance were a sort of second-order blackface, in which, blackface having for the most part disappeared, the figure of Elvis himself is now the apparently still necessary signifier of white ventures into black culture—a signifier to be adopted bodily if one is to have success in achieving the intimacy with 'blackness' that is crucial to the adequate reproduction of Presley's show" ("All the King's Men," 205).

In 1969, Brando attended a meeting to raise money for the Poor People's March on Washington, sponsored by the Southern Christian Leadership Conference in the wake of the assassination of Martin Luther King Jr. The meeting was attended by other Hollywood celebrities, including Barbra Streisand, Harry Belafonte, Natalie Wood, and Jean Seberg, who brought along the man to whom she was married at the time, the French novelist Romain Gary. In his autobiographical novel, *White Dog,* Gary contemptuously describes the behavior of Brando at the event. After stressing the need for a steering committee to continue the work of raising money for the poor, Brando asked for volunteers. In a crowd of approximately three hundred, thirty hands went up: "He glares at the audience and at the thirty raised hands. He braces himself, balances his shoulders in that famous half-roll, then the chin goes up. He is acting. Or rather overacting, for the sudden violence in his voice and the tightening of his facial muscles and of the jaws bears no relation whatsoever to the situation." According to Gary, Brando then said, "those who didn't raise their hands, get the hell out of here!" (172).

As of this writing no scholarly book narrates the long history of how white Americans have played out their conflicted fascination with black Americans. Lott has contributed the background for such a study by writing a history of blackface minstrelsy in the nineteenth century. Among many valuable observations in *Love and Theft,* Lott points out that, although minstrelsy allowed whites to indulge their contempt and even hatred for blacks, it also invited white people in the early nineteenth century, especially working-class males, to regard black men as sexual role models. Minstrel men constantly played up the hypersexuality, spontaneity, and phallic power of black men. Although his major focus is the nineteenth century, Lott also shows continuity between minstrelsy and more contemporary practices. He points out, for example, that adolescent boys today base a great deal of their behavior on their perceptions of African-American males. Lott observes that "this dynamic, persisting into adulthood, is so much a part of most American white men's equipment for living that they remain entirely unaware of their participation in it" (*Love*, 53). For the white minstrel man, "to put on the cultural forms of 'blackness' was to engage in a complex affair of manly mimicry. . . . To wear or even enjoy blackface was literally, for a time, to become black, to inherit the cool, virility, humility, abandon, or *gaité de coeur* that were the prime components of white ideologies of black manhood" (52).

The dark side of what Lott describes is especially apparent in *Birth of a Nation*, with its white actors playing former slaves in sexual pursuit of white women. Although the film vividly inscribes the racist myth that black-on-white rape is always imminent if African-American males are not carefully policed, the film unintentionally dramatizes the fantasy among white men that inhabiting a black body allows them to unleash their sexual desires. In this sense, the institution of lynching, which almost invariably included the castration of black victims, represents the white man's attempt to repress his own sexual longings by projecting them into the African-American male, who is then destroyed for allegedly acting on these desires. As Lott notes, the celebration of the black penis in minstrelsy was "obsessively reversed in white lynching rituals" (9).

Not far from working-class white men, who took their multiple, contradictory pleasures at the minstrel show, stood the abolitionists, church workers, and many other well-intentioned white people of the middle classes with their own sets of complex beliefs about African-Americans. Some members of these groups may have regarded African-Americans as inferior and thus in need of religious instruction. They may also have regarded African-Americans as closer to the spirit and the *gaité de coeur* that Lott mentions. After so many centuries of enforced racial hierarchy in the United States, few whites have been able to look past racist constructions and regard African-Americans as individual human beings.

By the first decades of the twentieth century white connoisseurs of black music were developing their own ambivalent attitudes toward negritude. The filmmaker Dudley Murphy cast Duke Ellington in *Black and Tan* (1929), consistently portraying him as a serious composer and a principled bandleader. In the same film, however, Murphy unleashed the black comedians Edgar Connor and Alec Lovejoy as illiterate, shiftless piano-movers, very much in the minstrel tradition. Murphy's fascination with black culture led him to prize the dignity of Ellington as much as the tomfoolery of

Connor and Lovejoy (Gabbard, *Jammin'*, 160–167). Consider also the "Moldy Figs" who waged war with the proponents of modern jazz in the 1940s, insisting that the premodern jazz of New Orleans was the "true" jazz because it was the music of primitive, "folk" artists.[9]

More recently, Lee Atwater helped elect George Bush in 1988 by terrifying white Americans with the story of Willie Horton, the sinister-looking African-American who assaulted a white couple in their home while he was on "furlough" from a Massachusetts prison. Hardly the first politician to use white America's fear of black male sexuality to win votes, Atwater took the practice to new lengths in a national election, even bragging that he would make Horton the running mate of Democratic presidential nominee Michael Dukakis, then the governor of Massachusetts. In spite of a large early lead in the poles, Dukakis eventually lost the election to Bush, thanks in no small part to the racist advertisements created by Atwater. But as his biographer John Brady has reported, even while running the Bush campaign, Atwater was an avid fan of Chicago blues and once seized the opportunity to play his Fender Telecaster on stage with B. B. King. A few years later, when he was dying from a brain tumor, Atwater asked African-Americans to forgive him for using a presidential campaign to foment racial fears. Atwater's affection for the sensuality of black blues seems to have co-existed with a loathing that allowed him to make race-baiting a crucial element in the presidential election of 1988. We can also speculate on the repressed anxieties about black bodies within even the most enthusiastic believer in the virtue or the artistic achievement of black Americans.

The Miles Davis Connection

Although it would be unfair to diagnose Marlon Brando's advocacy of African-American causes as part of a neurotic fascination with the sexuality of black men and women, there is no question that his attitudes, like those of most white Americans, changed dramatically with the times. Brando's desire to study dance with Katherine Dunham in the 1940s is part of the same cultural history as his angry insistence that wealthy celebrities join his steering committee at the meeting in the 1960s on which Romain Gary reported. In the early 1950s Brando's negrophilia inflected his stunning performance as Stanley Kowalski. In researching a forthcoming biography of Miles Davis, John Szwed learned that Brando was consciously imitating the trumpeter's voice when he performed in *A Streetcar Named Desire* (Szwed, personal communication). In his 1989 autobiography Davis admits to physically abusing virtually every woman with whom he had a sexual relationship. It is doubtful that Brando was aware of this aspect of

Miles Davis's character, although as Robin D. G. Kelley has argued, both Davis's seductive music as well as his violent misogyny can be understood as part of a "pimp aesthetic": "listening for the pimp in Miles ought to make us aware of the pleasures of cool as well as the dark side of romance. We get nostalgic for the old romantic Miles, for that feeling of being in love, but who understands this better than the mack, that despicable character we find so compelling and attractive?" (7). Brando may have sensed this character in Davis as early as 1950 and brought it into his portrayal of Stanley Kowalski, who beats and romances his wife with the same intensity.

The Brando/Davis connection can also be traced to Brando's brief encounter in 1965 with Frances Taylor Davis, Miles Davis's second wife. Frances was in Hollywood, having left her husband a few days earlier because of his escalating drug abuse. She ended up at a party for Bob Dylan where Brando was in attendance with Pat Quinn, an actress with whom he was in the middle of an on-again, off-again love affair. According to Manso, when Brando became angry that Dylan was paying so much attention to Quinn, he began an intense conversation with Frances Davis. Finding Brando a sympathetic listener, Frances eventually went home with him but was upset when the actor sat her down in front of a pornographic movie in his bedroom. Otherwise he paid her little attention (Manso, 619). Brando may also have imitated Davis's notorious practice of leaving the stage while other musicians soloed during his club appearances. Rod Steiger bitterly complained about Brando's behavior during the crucial scene between the two men in the back of a taxi in *On the Waterfront*. Steiger says that he sat patiently and reacted in character while the camera was on Brando. But when the camera was turned toward Steiger for his speeches, Brando left the set (Manso, 365).

In the film of *A Streetcar Named Desire*, Brando's Stanley is prone to preening, sudden violence, and childlike vulnerability, all of them part of white America's construction of the black male behavior, especially in the first half of the twentieth century. When he first appeared in *Streetcar* on the New York stage in 1947, costume designer Lucinda Ballard effectively created the vogue for tight jeans by making crucial decisions about how to dress Brando. Ballard kept seven pairs of Levi's in a washing machine for twenty-four hours, then fitted them to Brando's wet body, pinning them tight. Brando's friend Carlo Fiore told a biographer that Brando liked the tight jeans because they made it look as if he had "a perpetual hard-on"; the critic George Jean Nathan went so far as to call *Streetcar* "The Glands Menagerie" (Kolin, 28). Ballard also made sure that Brando's u-shirt fit like a second skin. Steven Cohan has convincingly described Brando's "gender masquerade" in the section of his *Masked Men* called "Why Boys Are Not

Men" (241–252). As the photos in Cohan's book indicate, Brando was more than willing to display much more of a well-muscled physique than audiences were accustomed to seeing. At least some portion of this display surely grew out of Brando's observations of black dancers and athletes.

The menace and sensuality in the persona of someone like Miles Davis appealed to Brando as did fantasies of how black men treat their women. When Stanley attacks Stella in *Streetcar,* the worst violence is offscreen, but he appears to be striking her with his fist. At the beginning of the twenty-first century, when spousal abuse of women is increasingly regarded as criminal and immoral, we may lose sight of how differently Americans felt about wife-beating in the years after World War II. Especially because women had so recently been active in the workforce and had proved themselves capable of doing "a man's job," some men, white as well as black, felt justified in using violence to restore the prewar gender hierarchy. Then as now, many white men have regarded black men as more assertive, more capable of controlling their women through violence. Stanley's wild attack on Stella must be understood at least in part in this context. But Brando's Stanley is also capable of childlike contrition. After his famous tearful cry of "Stella! STEL-LA!," Brando falls to his knees in front of his wife. The way he buries his head in Hunter's stomach has led Ann Douglas to suggest, "It's not just sex he wants, but birth, in reverse" (E24).[10] Some portion of Brando's performance in this scene may be rooted in the hoary fantasy of the childlike black man fixated on a mother that was the creation, most famously, of Al Jolson. With or without the burnt cork, blackface impersonation gave white men license to act out much that was forbidden to them, including hypersexuality, the mistreatment of women without reprisal, and the pathos of the child—all of them extremely prominent in Brando's gender performance.

After Blackface

Blackface disappeared from the American screen around 1952, at the same time that Brando was appearing on screens everywhere as Stanley Kowalski, exactly the kind of white working-class male who was both actor and audience at the minstrel shows of the nineteenth century. After a century of prominence on American stages, blackface moved comfortably into American movies, most memorably with the "black" characters played by whites in *Birth of a Nation* as well as in the person of Jolson. In addition to his stunning arrival in *The Jazz Singer* (1927) as the first singing movie star, Jolson wore blackface in several subsequent films, including *Big Boy* (1930), in which he starred as an African-American jockey, a part he had created for the stage in 1925 (Goldman, 136). In the same year as *Big Boy*, Charles Correll and Freeman Gosden blacked up to reprise their radio roles as Amos 'n' Andy in *Check and Double Check* (1930). A partial list of white stars who have also appeared under cork would include Eddie Cantor in *Whoopee!* (1930), Fred Astaire in *Swing Time* (1939), Mickey Rooney and Judy Garland in *Babes in Arms* (1939), and Bing Crosby in *Dixie* (1943). Larry Parks blacked up to play Jolson in two extremely successful biopics, *The Jolson Story* (1946) and *Jolson Sings Again* (1949). In 1951, Doris Day did a blackface imitation of Jolson in *I'll See You in My Dreams*, a film that also starred Danny Thomas and was directed by Michael Curtiz for Warner Bros. In 1952, however, when Warners celebrated the twenty-fifth anniversary of *The Jazz Singer* by remaking it with Danny Thomas as star and Curtiz as director, there was no blackface performance.

Blackface should have been inevitable in a remake of *The Jazz Singer*, especially as the same studio, star, and director had been involved with a film that *did* include blackface just one year earlier. Although I have found no evidence of a decision-making process at Warner Bros. that resulted in a ban on blackface, it is possible that groups such as the NAACP learned of the film in the early stages and convinced studio executives that the practice was offensive. It is also likely that the men at Warners decided on their own that times had changed and that blackface had become too provocative to be part of mainstream entertainment. After Keefe Brasselle blacked up to play Eddie Cantor in the 1953 biopic, and Joan Crawford appeared under a light coat of dusky body paint in MGM's *Torch Song*, also in 1953, no films with blacked-up actors appeared again until *Black Like Me* (1964), which took the practice in an entirely different direction. As John Szwed has suggested, the disappearance of blackface "marks the detachment of culture from race and the almost full absorption of a black tradition into white culture" ("Race," 27). Significant portions of the black tradition that white Americans accepted involved a fascination with improvisation and a nuanced, even polymorphous masculinity.

By the late 1940s, when Brando was coming of age as an actor, the African-American traditions had become, in Szwed's phrase, so "absorbed" that Brando could partake of a variety of models when he performed his gender. Consider the lyricism and vulnerability that accompanied the assertiveness in the solos of Miles Davis, or the pathos in many of the saxophone solos of Ben Webster and Charlie Parker, of whom Brando was surely aware. Brando was in some ways the nonmusical counterpart of Chet Baker, a white trumpeter who played in the style of the young Miles Davis and flourished in the early 1950s. Baker, the photogenic ephebe turned weathered junkie in Bruce Weber's 1988 documentary *Let's Get Lost*,

has been associated with the polymorphous, postwar masculinities represented by film stars such as Brando, James Dean, and Montgomery Clift.
In *From Here to Eternity* (1953), Clift projected a gentle/tough masculinity,
explicitly connected to a postphallic trumpet/bugle at the same time that
both Brando and Chet Baker were at the peak of their early fame.[11]

Feathers in the Air

Brando's performances in films such as *A Streetcar Named Desire* were
striking primarily because he refused the conventional poses of male stars
from the classical cinema such as Wayne, Gable, and Bogart. His fascination with black male sexuality may be partially responsible for his softer,
more sensual masculinity as well as for behavior more typical of children
and adolescents than of grown-up men. The incident with Eva Marie
Saint's glove was not just a bravura piece of improvisation (if indeed it was
by the time the film was shot); it also allowed Brando to reveal a feminine
side, by putting on the clothing of a woman, as well as an innocent, childlike quality, by sitting on the swing. In *Streetcar* when he inspects the items
in Blanche's trunk, he is once again unafraid to handle female garments. He
also sulks like a child, paraphrases the Napoleonic Code in the language of
a schoolboy, and plays the boys' game of keep-away whenever Stella tries to
grab back whatever Stanley has unceremoniously plucked from the trunk.
Brando was in touch with a generation of jazz artists, both black and white,
who acted out their gender in more subtle ways. The ability of Miles Davis
to project vulnerability and even to "cry" with his trumpet became as essential to his gender presentation as his "manly" fascination with boxing and
expensive sports cars.

We can also see the influence of the jazz improviser when Stanley man-
handles Blanche's possessions. Toward the end of the scene, when white
feathers drift away from her stole, Brando tries to pick them out of the air
with the purposeful purposelessness of a child. Once again he has ingeni-
ously found a way to react "in character" outside of any scripted directions.
In this context, the myth of the jazz improviser as divinely inspired primitive or bold explorer of the unconscious should be placed alongside the
equally powerful myth of jazz soloists as disciplined artists in full control of
their craft. As Naremore points out, Brando the actor was forging a new
level of artifice in order to camouflage artifice. Slipping on Eva Marie
Saint's glove or eating his cold plate supper, Brando seems so loose and at
ease that everyone else around him seems stiff and awkward. This is especially the case with Karl Malden, who plays Mitch in *Streetcar*; he is meant
to be stiff and awkward, but Brando makes him seem even more so. We see

a virtuoso performance by an actor who knows his craft exceedingly well, and who can convince us that he is making it up as he goes along, not relying on tricks.

Improvisation as Discipline

And at least according to some jazz scholars, it is craft and not tricks on which the improvising jazz musician relies. Although jazz musicians, like Method actors, have been constructed as more in touch with their unconscious minds than the rest of us, it is not at all accurate to say that jazz musicians simply dig into their ids during a solo. In fact, Barry Kernfeld has compared the improvising jazz musician to the oral poet, the singer of tales studied by Milman Parry and Albert Lord. Parry and Lord carefully analyzed the performances of preliterate poets in Muslim Serbia in the 1930s in order to explain Homer's method of composition 2600 years earlier. An oral poet like Homer could go on for days seeming to make up new stories in perfect dactyllic hexameter because he had committed to memory a huge reservoir of formulas and epithets and in some cases entire lines of verse that could always be inserted into a new line: "wine-dark sea," "rosy-fingered dawn," and so on. Similarly, in Kernfeld's argument, accomplished jazz artists have large bodies of music under their fingers and can insert favorite motifs, bits of scales learned in practicing, and fragments of familiar melodies into a performance. They also have different strategies for deploying this material or "running the changes" so that each improvised performance will be different from what they played in the past. This model of improvisation is a long way from the one in which jazz artists simply get in touch with their inner selves.[12]

The improvising jazzman has also internalized a series of musical and physical gestures that connote masculinity. In *Jammin' at the Margins* I have argued that jazz artists can learn a set of masculine codes and then signify on them in a variety of ways (138–159). Dizzy Gillespie, for example, could assert himself with fast, loud solos in the upper register whenever he wished. But when young trumpet turks challenged him in solo duels, he often responded to their lightning-fast assaults on the upper register with short, quiet, often humorous phrases, thus setting himself apart from the pretensions of the challenger and winning a laugh in the process. Affecting a look of well-earned insouciance, Gillespie would signify on the challenger as well as on his own role as the patriarch of the jazz trumpet. Miles Davis surely developed the most flamboyant revision of the trumpet as masculine signifier by seeming to reject conventional virtuosity, preferring instead to strive for emotional expression.[13]

The best jazz improvisers do more than simply construct a gendered persona. They also know how to build a solo with structure and logic. Jazz Schenkerians have developed carpal tunnel syndrome transcribing recorded solos in order to demonstrate the structural elegance of a jazz musician's improvisations. In a book about Charlie Parker, for example, Henry Martin takes the different versions of the same song that Parker recorded in a single recording session and then shows how Parker was effectively presenting a more rigorously logical composition in each successive version of the tune. By using the methods of Schenker, Martin gives us a Parker who has more in common with Johannes Brahms than with Ornette Coleman.

And yet, to the uninitiated, jazz musicians seem to be making all of it up as they go along. The accomplished improviser has also learned the codes that connote freshness, looseness, and a feeling of spontaneity. When Marlon Brando as Stanley Kowalski picks feathers out of the air in *A Streetcar Named Desire,* he too is dipping into a large reservoir of formulas and gestures acquired through years of training and practicing. But he makes it all seem as if it's coming to him out of the air along with the feathers. In a film such as *Streetcar,* Brando is at the nexus of several discrete discourses directly related to jazz. And like the virtuoso male jazz improviser, he is entirely in control as he performs his masculinity.

Notes

1. Following Harold Bloom, I use the term "misreading" nonjudgmentally. According to Bloom, all artists misread predecessor artists in order to create their own works of art. Among several books in which Bloom has developed this idea, see *The Anxiety of Influence* and *A Map of Misreading.*

2. In *The Political Unconscious,* Fredric Jameson applies the term to literary works. Film scholars have found a wide variety of approaches to applying the psychoanalytically inflected ideological criticism of literary theorists such as Jameson to the American cinema. See, for example, the collections edited by Grant, James and Berg, and Collins, Radner, and Collins, as well as the books by Williams, Rogin, and Gabbard.

3. For thorough explorations of the racial logics driving *Birth of a Nation* and much of early American cinema, see Williams, *Playing the Race Card,* 96–135, and Rogin, *Blackface, White Noise,* 73–156.

4. For an excellent account of the American film industry before and immediately after the imposition of extensive censorship, see Doherty. For the domestication of jazz during the Swing Era, see Erenberg.

5. A few years later, filmmakers such as John Cassavetes and Robert Altman would acknowledge the influence of jazz and encourage their actors to improvise. For Cassavetes, see Carney. For Altman, see Gabbard, "Kansas City Dreamin'."

6. North was an extremely successful and versatile writer of music for American films. Although he successfully integrated a certain jazz feel into the soundtrack for *Streetcar,* he made little use of jazz during the rest of his career, always writing in a style that was appropriate to his projects. His best-known films include *Viva*

Zapata! (1952), *The Rose Tattoo* (1955), *The Rainmaker* (1956), *Spartacus* (1960), *Cleopatra* (1963), *Who's Afraid of Virginia Woolf?* (1966), *Bite the Bullet* (1975), *Under the Volcano* (1984), *Prizzi's Honor* (1985), and *The Dead* (1987).

7. Also see the essays by Margolis and Esman.

8. Surprisingly, Brando has said that his work on *Last Tango* was "a violation of my innermost self" (Naremore, 196).

9. For the best account of the discourses among jazz writers of the 1940s, see Gendron. For a broader account of the fascination with "the primitive," see Torgovnick.

10. Although eventually rejected, a cigar was often in the mouth of Brando's Kowalski during rehearsals of the original stage version of *Streetcar*. In describing Stanley's sexuality, Elia Kazan wrote, "he sucks on a cigar all day because he can't suck on a teat" (Kolin, 28). The choice of words is revealing. By writing "teat" rather than "tit," Kazan refers to the infantile qualities of Stanley rather than to the oral pleasures of a sexually mature adult.

11. I have used the terms "phallic" and "postphallic" to describe the styles of jazz trumpeters in *Jammin' at the Margins* (138–159).

12. The model of jazz improvisation that informs this essay might be called "classic jazz improvisation" and should be distinguished from the perilous improvisatory adventures at the outer reaches of free jazz that is admirably analyzed by John Corbett in "Ephemera Underscored."

13. For an excellent account of Davis's "mistakes" in performance, see Walser.

Works Cited

Baldwin, James. "Sonny's Blues." In *Hot and Cool: Jazz Short Stories*, edited by Marcela Breton, 112–129. London: Bloomsbury, 1991.

Baraka, Amiri (as LeRoi Jones). *Blues People: Negro Music in White America*. New York: Morrow, 1963.

Bloom, Harold. *The Anxiety of Influence: A Theory of Poetry*. New York: Oxford University Press, 1973.

———. *A Map of Misreading*. New York: Oxford University Press, 1975.

Brady, John. *Bad Boy: The Life and Politics of Lee Atwater*. New York: Addison-Wesley, 1997.

Burnham, John. "The Influence of Psychoanalysis upon American Culture." In *American Psychoanalysis: Origins and Development*, edited by J. Quen and E. Carlson, 52–72. New York: Brunner/Mazel, 1978.

Carbine, Mary. "'The Finest Outside the Loop': Motion Picture Exhibition in Chicago's Black Metropolis, 1905–1928." *Camera Obscura* 23 (1990): 8–41.

Card, Wallace. "Is This Trap Necessary: Ann-Margret and Treat Williams Hop Aboard a TV Remake of *Streetcar*." *People Weekly* (15 August 1983): 98.

Carney, Raymond. *The Films of John Cassavetes: Pragmatism, Modernism, and the Movies*. Cambridge Film Classics. Cambridge: Cambridge University Press, 1994.

Cohan, Steven. *Masked Men: Masculinity and the Movies in the Fifties*. Bloomington: Indiana University Press, 1997.

Collins, Jim, Hilary Radner, and Ava Preacher Collins, eds. *Film Theory Goes to the Movies*. AFI Film Readers. New York: Routledge, 1993.

Corbett, John. "Ephemera Underscored: Writing Around Free Improvisation." In *Jazz Among the Discourses*, edited by Krin Gabbard, 217–240. Durham: Duke University Press, 1995.

Crouch, Stanley. "Jazz Criticism and Its Effect on the Art Form." In *New Perspec-*

tives on Jazz: Report on a National Conference Held at Wingspread, Racine, Wisconsin, edited by David N. Baker, 71–87. Washington, D.C.: Smithsonian Institution, 1990.

Davis, Miles, and Quincy Troupe. *Miles: The Autobiography*. New York: Simon and Schuster, 1989.

Doherty, Thomas. *Pre-Code Hollywood*. Film and Culture Series. New York: Columbia University Press, 1999.

Douglas, Ann. "50th Anniversary for Actors Studio and Its 'Streetcar' Ride to Renown." *New York Times*, 3 October 1997, E1, 24.

Erenberg, Lewis A. *Steppin' Out : New York Nightlife and the Transformation of American Culture, 1890–1930*. Chicago: University of Chicago Press, 1984.

Esman, A. "Jazz—A Study in Cultural Conflict." *American Imago* 8 (1951): 219–226.

Gabbard, Krin. *Jammin' at the Margins: Jazz and the American Cinema*. Chicago: University of Chicago Press, 1996.

———. "Kansas City Dreamin': Robert Altman's Jazz History Lesson." In *Music and Cinema*, edited by James Buhler, Caryl Flinn, and David Neumeyer, 142–157. Hanover: University Press of New England, 2000.

Gary, Romain. *White Dog*. New York: New American Library, 1970.

Gendron, Bernard. "Moldy Figs and Modernists: Jazz at War (1942–1946)." *Discourse* 15, no. 3 (1993): 130–157. Reprinted in *Jazz Among the Discourses*, edited by Krin Gabbard, 31–56. Durham: Duke University Press, 1995.

Goldman, Herbert G. *Jolson: The Legend Comes to Life*. New York: Oxford University Press, 1988.

Grant, Barry Keith, ed. *The Dread of Difference: Gender and the Horror Film*. Austin: University of Texas Press, 1996.

Herodotus. *The Histories*. Translated Robin A. Waterfield. Oxford: Oxford University Press, 1999.

Hirsch, Foster. *A Method to Their Madness: The History of the Actors Studio*. New York: Norton, 1984.

James, David E., and Rick Berg, eds. *The Hidden Foundation: Cinema and the Question of Class*. Minneapolis: University of Minnesota Press, 1996.

Jameson, Fredric. *The Political Unconscious: Narrative as a Socially Symbolic Act*. Ithaca: Cornell University Press, 1981.

Kelley, Robin D. G. "Miles Davis: A Jazz Genius in the Guise of a Hustler." *New York Times*, 13 May 2001, Arts and Leisure 1, 7.

Kernfeld, Barry. "Two Coltranes." *Annual Review of Jazz Studies* 2 (1983): 7–61.

Kolin, Philip C. *Williams: A Streetcar Named Desire*. Plays in Production. Cambridge: Cambridge University Press, 2000.

Lott, Eric. "All the King's Men: Elvis Impersonators and White Working Class Masculinity." *Race and the Subject of Masculinities*, edited by Harry Stecopoulos and Michael Uebel, 192–227. Durham: Duke University Press, 1997.

———. *Love and Theft: Blackface Minstrelsy and the American Working Class*. New York: Oxford University Press, 1993.

Lord, Albert Bates. *The Singer of Tales*. Cambridge, Mass.: Harvard University Press, 1960.

Manso, Peter. *Brando: The Biography*. New York: Hyperion, 1994.

Margolis, N. "A Theory of the Psychology of Jazz." *American Imago* 11 (1954): 263–290.

Martin, Henry. *Charlie Parker and Thematic Improvisation*. Studies in Jazz, No. 24. Lanham, Md.: Scarecrow, 1996.

Meltzer, David, ed. *Reading Jazz*. San Francisco: Mercury House, 1993.

Miller, Miles D. "Jazz and Aggression." *Psychiatric Communications* (1958): 7–10. Reprinted in *Keeping Time: Readings in Jazz History*, edited by Robert Walser, 234–239. New York: Oxford University Press, 1999.

Naremore, James. *Acting in the Cinema*. Berkeley and Los Angeles: University of California Press, 1988.

Parry, Milman. *The Making of Homeric Verse: The Collected Papers of Milman Parry*. Edited by Adam Parry. Oxford: Clarendon, 1971.

Pfeil, Fred. "Rock Incorporated: Plugging in to Axl and Bruce." In *White Guys: Studies in Postmodern Domination and Difference*, 71–104. New York: Verso, 1995.

Ray, Robert B. *A Certain Tendency of the Hollywood Cinema, 1930–1980*. Princeton: Princeton University Press, 1985.

Rogin, Michael. "Blackface, White Noise: The Jewish Jazz Singer Finds His Voice." *Critical Inquiry* 18 (1992): 417–453.

———. *Blackface, White Noise: Jewish Immigrants in the Hollywood Melting Pot*. Berkeley and Los Angeles: University of California Press, 1996.

Schickel, Richard. *Brando: A Life in Our Times*. New York: Atheneum, 1991.

Straw, Will. "Sizing Up Record Collections: Gender Connoisseurship in Rock Music Culture." In *Sexing the Groove: Popular Music and Gender*, edited by Sheila Whiteley, 2–16. New York: Routledge, 1997.

Szwed, John F. Personal communication. 8 August 2000.

———. "Race and the Embodiment of Culture." *Ethnicity* 2, no. 1 (1975): 19–33.

Torgovnick, Marianna. *Gone Primitive: Savage Intellects, Modern Lives*. Chicago: University of Chicago Press, 1991.

Walser, Robert. "'Out of Notes': Signification, Interpretation, and the Problem of Miles Davis." In *Jazz Among the Discourses*, edited by Krin Gabbard, 165–188. Durham: Duke University Press, 1995.

Williams, Linda. *Playing the Race Card: Melodramas of Black and White From Uncle Tom to O. J. Simpson*. Princeton: Princeton University Press, 2001.

Zabor, Rafi. *The Bear Comes Home*. New York: Norton, 1997.

MICHAEL JARRETT

Cutting Sides
Jazz Record Producers and Improvisation

Cultural historians often understand the improvisations of jazz musicians as analogous to recitations by epic poets: The jazz musician (take, for example, Louis Armstrong) is to popular music what Homer is to poetry: to create *The Iliad* and *The Odyssey*, Homer "rapped odes." He rhapsodized, which means he wove or stitched songs together. Or as Walter Ong puts it, summarizing Milman Parry's groundbreaking work on the use of formulaic elements in ancient poetry: "every distinctive feature of Homeric poetry is due to the economy enforced on it by oral methods of composition" (21). Acknowledging with Ong that the phrase "oral methods of composition" is something of an oxymoron, we might take refuge in "the fact that to this day no concepts have yet been formed for effectively, let alone gracefully, conceiving of oral art as such without reference, conscious or unconscious, to writing" (10). We might also acknowledge that the phrase pretty well defines improvisation even as it pays tribute to an imperialistic ideology ruled by textuality. Improvisation is one of the names that writing (or composition) assigns to its other.

Louis Armstrong may have "composed" music on the fly, but he didn't create music ex nihilo. "Musicians and other students of jazz know that this is simply not so," write Alan Perlman and Daniel Greenblatt. "A jazz solo, though impromptu, is constructed according to specific harmonic and melodic constraints," and "these constraints are in many ways analogous to the syntactic and semantic constraints of natural language" (169). Jazz improvisers stitch songs together; their methods recall the poetic productions of "the Lakota Sioux in North America or the Mande in West Africa or of the Homeric Greeks" (Ong, 11). Excluding "free" and atonal styles of playing (which themselves, of course, have their own lexicons and patterns of meaning), Perlman and Greenblatt note: "The basic lexicon of jazz licks is not large—there are perhaps two or three dozen that most players rely on—but, since any lick can be played over any chord, beginning with any scale/chord-tone and repeated indefinitely up and down the entire range of the instrument, the number of improvisational possibilities becomes enormous" (176).

What we know of rhapsodies created in oral cultures can help us understand jazz improvisations created in current Western culture. But as with all analogies, this one works only to a point, generating knowledge but only at a price. Jazz and jazz practices of improvisation did not arise within an ancient, oral, or "prehistoric" culture. Jazz musicians are not displaced bards, shamen, or griots. And to imagine otherwise is to flirt with primitivist myths that are romantic and racist. Jazz was made possible by electronic culture; it developed within the paradigm that Ong labels "secondary orality." As David Stowe observes in *Swing Changes*, "this sort of cultural phenomenon could occur only amid the new technologies and industrial organizations that had emerged in the early decades of the century, particularly the 1920's" (2). The radio, the phonograph and jukebox, and even the telephone (whose lines carried the signals of live-remote broadcasts) established material conditions that both enabled and sustained jazz as a music dependant upon improvisation. For example, in its need for material that listeners would hear as simultaneously familiar and new—two seemingly opposed demands—radio rewarded excellent sight readers and skilled improvisers. It's likely that Coleman Hawkins never played "Body and Soul" exactly the same way twice, and it's just as likely that his listeners never failed to recognize the tune.

Yet many of the musicians who played jazz—not to mention fans who supported it and the cultural commentators who wrote about it—regarded electronic culture, and especially recording technologies, with great ambivalence if not outright hostility. The reasons for this antipathy are many and varied, but notice that nonimprovising musicians tour in support of their recordings (and very often seek to replicate the sound of these records in performance), while improvisers typically make records to augment or to supplement income gained by live performance. Despite some notable exceptions, recordings have never been a significant or a reliable source of income for jazz musicians; in fact, recordings have been regarded as an impediment to improvisation. Early on, the rigors of cutting records forced drummers to substitute wood blocks for kits that caused styluses to jump grooves, and thus the sound of jazz groups was altered. More significant, recording media have rarely accommodated what

Jed Rasula calls "a music that legendarily thrived on the ad hoc ingenuity of self-perpetuating performances that could even outlast the stamina of individual musicians" (134). Recordings, especially 78s, required improvisers to create the musical equivalent of haiku and sonnets instead of epic poems. *Copia* surrendered to brevity; less metaphorically, the improvising skills that enabled performers to work ballrooms and clubs—to play for roughly the same audience set after set, night after night—were constrained, even curtailed, in recording studios.

"Recording," writes Rasula, "tends to reify improvisation, converting the extemporaneous into scripture" (144). And so, through the sort of sleight of hand that writing always plays (that it cannot help playing as it assimilates all things unto itself), improvisation is objectified and textualized. Recorded improvisations become texts available and suitable for study. Rasula observes: "Critics and historians have always used jazz records as primary sources, while pretending that what they are really talking about is something else, some putative essence of a 'living tradition' that cannot be 'captured' by the blatant artifice of technology" (135). This practice relies on recordings even as it conveniently ignores their status as a history already inscribed in a medium other than written language (137). Consequently, words exact a type of revenge "on a wordless but nonetheless highly articulate history, a history that threatens to preempt the written documents that adhere to it" (136). The entire history of jazz can be heard as one colossal improvisation defining what improvisation can be: jazz as one answer to the question, What is improvisation? Getting this definition into words, however, or between the covers of a book requires either trickery or violence. When we write about improvisation, what are we really writing about? And in order to write about improvisation, what must we do to it?

Writing about improvisation leads us into a bind. While no route out of this bind is wholly satisfactory, at least one route seems honest. It encourages us to go ahead and write about recordings—to treat recordings as recordings. And it enjoins us to notice how recordings have been used to conceptualize improvisation and to render jazz as history. For example, we might ask: As a system of artificial memory, a technology for writing electronically, what can the phonograph and associated recording media teach us about improvisation (its meaning and function) within secondary orality or electronic culture? Or translated into print, what does phonography already say, not about improvisation as "the putative essence of a 'living tradition' that cannot be 'captured' by the blatant artifice of technology" but about improvisation as an effect generated or maintained by technologies of mechanical reproduction? Jazz histories, as attempts to bring improvisation into written language, very often rely on a curious and contradictory stance toward recordings. They require recordings; records are a readily available trace of jazz practices, including improvisation. And, simultaneously, they disavow them; records are a technology that unsettles concepts, such as improvisation, essential to historicizing jazz.

To illustrate some of these points and to raise others, I have interviewed a number of jazz record producers and organized a montage of comments and narratives. It's a brief oral history of jazz record production, concentrating primarily on the posttape era. It's very much the paper equivalent of a cinema verité documentary or the jam session in which everybody gets a chance to solo. In this montage, the producers describe their philosophy of production, explaining their role in supervising the creation of some now-classic jazz recordings. Readers will notice that these industry workers—perhaps in sympathy to musicians but definitely in concert with what Jacques Derrida would label "a metaphysics of presence" (74)—typically employed a nonintrusive, "inaudible" style of production analogous to Hollywood's style of invisible and continuity editing. Or more accurately, these industry men (and it was almost always men) shaped jazz at its most material level by controlling its mise-en-scène. They chose the artists and they chose repertoire (A&R). They aimed the spotlights. Above all, they were mediators. They stood between artist and record company, between artist and technology, between artist and public. And thus they profoundly affected what came to count as jazz or improvised music.

With the development of magnetic tape in the 1950s, producers gained even more power to shape sound than they had had in the days of cutting acetates. In fact, tape enabled A&R men to become record producers. It converted every recording studio, at least theoretically, into a little record company. Alfred Lion founded Blue Note; Norman Granz founded Verve; Orrin Keepnews, Riverside; Ross Russell, Dial; Lester Koenig, Contemporary; and Bob Weinstock, Prestige. By making editing and, eventually, multitracking practical, tape allowed record production to catch up with film production. Once sounds could be manipulated as easily as images, record producers became the music-industry analogue to film directors. If they had the desire and the talent, producers could become auteurs, recording artists in their own right, impressing signature sounds onto records. Very few jazz producers chose this rock-identified option. For example, at the major record labels—Columbia, RCA, Decca, and ABC Paramount— producers enjoyed enormous creative freedom, but most continued to disguise any trace of their labor. They did not employ certain studio effects readily available to them (such as multitracking), and they routinely rendered technique inaudible through production. Production was typically used to efface production. Their practices reinforced the popular conception of jazz as a spontaneous music, independent of and antithetical to recording technologies.

John Coltrane simply didn't need Bob Thiele, Miles Davis didn't need George Avakian, and Charles Mingus didn't need Nat Hentoff—at least not in the way that the Ronnettes needed Phil Spector or the Beatles needed George Martin. Jazz producers generally concede that their power resides in invisibility; their art, in concealing itself. Notice that, apart from the occasional reference to John Hammond, very few histories of jazz even mention producers—much less theorize their role. And what, we might ask, is this role? What exactly does a jazz producer do? In the studio the producer has one overriding task: to efface the logic of recording—the implications of mechanical reproduction—and thereby enable musicians to emerge as real-time auteurs (or improvisers). Producers, with the aid of engineers, do not capture the sounds of musicians improvising—or rather, what we hear as improvisation is not a matter of what is recorded. Producers work hard to enable and to record sounds that, when we hear them, will give every impression of having escaped the clutches of production and the constraints of recording technologies. Wherever and whenever this effect of "having escaped" is created, it is called improvisation. Again, improvisation is one of the names that recording technologies assign to the Other.

Invisible Men

HAL WILLNER: When I started out, I basically wanted to be a staff producer because, to keep the analogy to films going, it seemed that it created some amazing things. When there were staff directors, things would happen—people would get assigned. You'd have someone like Victor Fleming, who got to direct *The Wizard of Oz* and *Gone With The Wind* in the same year. It made for some incredible combinations. Record producers, at the time I started, were well-versed. They had to be into every type of music. Generally, they were able to keep hands off directly and still go after capturing their artist. I guess I got to see the very end of that era. It's really unfortunate that it doesn't exist now; it created some amazing things, as opposed to a producer who—"this guy gets great drum tracks"—that sort of thing.

CRAIG STREET: Let's just suppose that I am lucky enough to keep doing what I'm doing for the next twenty or twenty-five years. Let's suppose that's a possibility, something that can happen. Then, I would hope that at the end of that period of time, that there's a body of work, one hundred or two hundred or whatever recordings that are done at that point in time. What I would want probably more than anything is to have it be so that, when you get to the end of a record that I worked on with somebody, that you'd have no idea that I was there. You couldn't tell.

There are some producers who have an identifiable sound that I love. I love Daniel Lanois. I think he's wonderful. But you know it's a Daniel Lanois record the minute it comes on. There're other people who have a signature sound: Babyface or Jam and Lewis. You know who the producer is before you know who the musician is. That's cool. That's one end of production. But I would rather go along and, say, end up like somebody like Glyn Johns where you don't know it's a Glyn Johns until you look over and look at the credits. And then you might say, "Okay, it makes sense. This is the kind of thing that he would probably do."

Or Tom Wilson. There's no way that you know that's a Tom Wilson record. But it is, because certain things happen. Producers or production in that way is what I would call translucent. That is, it's not transparent. It's not, *not* there. But it's not completely apparent. At the same time it could be very much like the air that you breathe. If it weren't there, you would definitely know it. If Tom Wilson weren't in the room, you know that he wasn't in the room. But if he's there, things just sort of chug along the way that they do.

ED MICHEL: Despite the fact that I say, "You shouldn't be really aware of the fact that a producer is there," I find it fascinating that the same artist will make very, very different kinds of records for different producers. The records Charlie Parker made for Norman Granz are not much like the records that he made for Dial or the records he made for Savoy. That's true of most artists as they move from place to place.

WAYNE HORVITZ: One of the myths of producing is that you have a strong image ahead of time. Production is a very improvised art. Things are really done on the fly. So many things that you can't even predict have to do with how things sound. The studio has a sound. Sure, in an ideal world, you could fly around all over the place and check out studios, but of course you pick studios for all sorts of pragmatic reasons. Things you thought might work don't. Then you have to find things that do work. Sticking too much to your plan can really work against you in a lot of ways.

TOM DOWD: The most important function for anybody who tries to contribute to the recording of jazz artists and jazz performances is not to paint the picture, but rather to capture it. It's like being a sports photographer, instead of a portrait painter. The artist is the impressionist, the artist is the creator, and you are just a damn witness. The minute you start getting in their face with "Why don't you do this or that?" it's not a good marriage, not to my way of thinking.

MILT GABLER: I wanted the record to sound like I was hearing the artist in the room. If the record didn't have the proper balance, I'd go in and change it. Don't forget, we didn't have multi-mikes. The most we had was three or four mikes, and there was only one main mike really, and a vocal mike. One you'd crack for the rhythm section. But they all had to be picked up on the main mike. Proper balance, to get it you had to move the horns back or closer. We'd use platforms. I won't get into the Guy Lombardo balance. His band was so successful, they never wanted to change their sound. We had special platforms designed for different horn sections so they would be exactly the same distance from the one microphone every time they recorded. The engineers would come out with a tape and measure the height, the distance from the wall.

MICHAEL CUSCUNA: There are just two different ways of accomplishing things. I feel very strongly that, as a producer, you should really be as invisible as possible, to the extent of working with artists and, sometimes, planting ideas in ways that let them think it's their idea. You really should be wallpaper, if you possibly can. The Leiber and Stoller and Phil Spector Schools: they're really arrangers. They're almost the artist with a hired singer. I love what Spector and what Leiber and Stoller did, not so much as producers but as arranger-architects of records. They don't make careers. They don't enhance individual artists. They are the artists.

Waxing Eloquent

MILT GABLER: She [Billie Holiday] came to me and wanted to use strings. I knew the jazz magazines would jump on me for doing that. But I did it anyway. I just used them to play like an organ background. They weren't way out, written in a jazz sense. They were used to give the record sweetness.

Billie Holiday wanted to record "Strange Fruit," but Columbia wouldn't let her, right?

That's right. She came to me almost in tears one day when I had the store on Fifty-Second Street.

I said, "Whatsa matter, Billie?" Columbia Records was a block away.

She said, "They won't let me record 'Strange Fruit,' my biggest number."

I said, "I know. I hear it in the club." I said, "You go back and tell them . . ."

I had just started to record the year before to make Commodore Records, and I always made instrumentals. I let the musicians sing the vocals, like Teagarden or Lips Page.

I said, "You go back and tell them that I'll record it. I'm only a little record label. I just make records for my store," which was true. "I'll record that thing in a second. Go up there and get permission."

I recorded it at one of Columbia's studios. I used a club band led by Frankie Newton. I picked the other tunes. I said, "We'll do a blues." Of course, she had made that great "Billie's Blues" on Vocalion. I wanted to get a blues. And we did, "I've Got a Right to Sing the Blues" and "Yesterdays," Jerome Kern. "Fine and Mellow" was the blues. I helped her get some lyrics together on that.

I would acquiesce on anything that Billie had her mind on making. She liked to do stuff for friends. Sometimes I liked the material; sometimes I didn't. But I knew that she was trying to help some songwriters. She knew it was good for them, and she'd help them by doing the song.

The writers would come to me. They would write a Billie Holiday–type song. Some of those writers were darn good. I accepted their material. Some of them were published by Decca Publishing Company; many were published by big publishers. The first ones, E. B. Marx, got a lot of the copyrights.

That never was the reason I did it or gave it to those publishers. They romanced the artists on their own. They all hung around Fifty-Second Street. You were a good publisher if you were able to get something at the source, like "Lover Man" was a Fifty-Second Street song. The songwriters came to Billie to sing the song at the club she was in.

TEO MACERO: The producer had a lot of roles when I was working—I still work—in the studio. They took care of the artist's needs and wants. They made sure his career was being taken care of with the major record company in terms of promotion and the record clubs. They made sure that he made the right kind of records, and they were always looking out for his interests.

It's not just making a record. We were really into it. We did everything. We'd do promotion. We'd go on the road. We'd do whatever we had to do to get them in the record club—make all kinds of deals, even internally, with the company. I used to have to take all these people out to lunch, wine and dine them, and say, "Look, I'm making this record. I'll make something else for you—a special track or two—if you put this record in the club."

MILT GABLER: I started to reissue records in the middle thirties and, finally, put them out on my own label, the Commodore United Hot Clubs of America label. I built up such a following on those reissues that the major companies decided that they would put the records out themselves. That's when I decided to make Commodore Records. That was in 1937.

By '38, I'd started to do my own records. I chose the musicians specifically for the sessions because of the way they played and the way they enjoyed playing and who they liked working with. But I never told them what to blow! I might tell them when I wanted them to play. "You take the first chorus after the theme is stated." They'd follow in a certain progression due to what horn they were playing and how they speak on their instruments.

I might pick some standard tune that we were going to play and, then, tell them about it on the job the night before. Sometimes I guess they would woodshed it, but there were almost never written arrangements. Sometimes there were some sketches. But I never had arrangements on those first records.

With Lester Young, we used the guys from Basie's Band. I had Lester play clarinet. Well, he played tenor on a date, too. Of course, they were working together every night. The arranger was Eddie Durham, the first guy to play electric guitar. He had written little parts.

Sometimes, if you're just doing a blues, like I named "Countless Blues," it's like a head arrangement. They work a little figure out by head, and then we set the riff, take three solos after that. Everybody knows the chords of the blues. All they do is pick a key.

I'd tell them. Buck [Clayton] would take the first chorus and Lester the second one—take it on in, come back to the riff.

Don't forget there was no tape. Records ran mostly anywhere from 2'40" to 3'15". That's the most you could get on a record before you'd run into the cut-off groove of a 78. Everything had to be laid out in front. I was the first one to make 12-inch jazz recordings. You couldn't get enough playing time to let the guy really blow on a three-minute record. I could make it four minutes on a 12-inch.

GEORGE AVAKIAN: The first jazz album anybody ever recorded—and by that I mean not a collection of 78-rpm reissue sides packaged into a 78-rpm package album—was 1939. I was a student at Yale, and I got the idea of bringing together the old white Chicago musicians, the first white group that really picked up on the New Orleans jazz guys who had moved to Chicago. They created a style of their own which didn't stay put. It was in flux. I wanted these guys to go back to the way they had been playing 10–12 years earlier, as evidenced on the group of records which had earned the name "Chicago Style." A French author named Hugues Panassié, who wrote the first good book on jazz, called it "Le Style Chicago." The name stuck, but it is forgotten now. These were people whose names you're probably familiar with: Eddie Condon, Bud Freeman, Pee Wee Russell, Dave Tough. You know, that crowd of young musicians who came up in the twenties.

So right from the beginning, a creative idea resulted in recording sessions. I set up three sessions for three different groups, reviving several of the tunes that they had played, in much the same style they had kind of dropped. I'll give you one good reason. One of these groups' characteristics was the explosive way in which they kept up the tension throughout their performances. Among the devices used was that of everybody joining in on the last two bars of each solo to create a springboard for the next soloist. Have you ever noticed that on certain records? Jelly Roll Morton used it, for example, and the Chicagoans used it fairly well. The excitement created on the few records that they made was quite terrific.

I said to Eddie Condon one day, "Eddie, how come you don't do that anymore?" He looked at me and said, "George, you mean night after night after night after night after night?" And I realized that this was fine for record sessions and occasional performances, but those guys were used to playing six nights a week from 9:00 P.M. to 4:00 A.M., except on Sunday when they had to stop at 3:00 A.M. because of the New York Blue Law, that the churches put through.

That's how a creative idea resulted in a recording rather than the recording simply being supervised by a producer.

Contexts for Creation

MILT GABLER: You know what the scale was on Fifty-Second Street for a three-hour [jam] session? Ten dollars—double for the leader and contract. They'd come every week. I'd have some jugs there in the back near Zooty's drums. Be the bartender. Boy, they used to have a ball. That's where George Wein and Norman Granz got the idea of jazz concerts: from Jimmy Ryan's on Fifty-Second Street. They were so successful. When they closed the clubs on Sunday afternoons, the Hickory Club and the other ones, they all started to run jam sessions. Then, they started to broadcast them. It grew from that. Granz came in from the coast once, I remember, on a Saturday night. He said, "Milt, this is the greatest! I'm going back to California and do the same thing." The next thing you know, you had JATP [Jazz at the Philharmonic]. Wein is still doing it.

BOB WEINSTOCK: We had a basic framework, and we'd discuss who we were going to use. I didn't try and shove people down their throat, and they didn't try and shove 'em down my throat. Same with the material. I'd have suggestions. They'd have suggestions. My knowledge of songs was tremendous. I'd say, "Hey Trane, do you know 'Russian Lullaby'?"

"Sure, man."

Boom. "Russian Lullaby," just like that. He could teach it to everybody on the session. It was all very loose. I hated charts. I hated arrangements. That's where me and Alfred [Lion] differed. Alfred would have rehearsals. I never had a rehearsal. I didn't believe in it. I believed jazz had to swing and be loose. It had to be mutual. You couldn't tell those giants—and they were greats—what to do.

MICHAEL CUSCUNA: In working with the Blue Note catalog, I put a long, long time going through the unissued material. There was such a lot of it. It ranged from abysmal and flat, unhappening performances to just some incredible stuff that you'd think, "God, I can't believe this is sitting here, just wasting away!"

The most interesting thing is, when I started to go through the outtakes of a lot of great Blue Note albums, there were very few alternate takes. And in the few cases that there were, if you listened to the alternate takes alone, without the master takes, you were listening to a major disaster. Only two or three out of the five tunes would have alternate takes and a few false starts. They'd sound horrible. Get to the master tape, and it was a master-piece. *Maiden Voyage* was that way. *Out to Lunch* was that way.

Part of it was Alfred Lion's insistence—at a time when it wasn't common as an approach to jazz recording—on planning readings and on rehearsals. He'd get the musicians to a point of comfort with the material from a rhythmic standpoint and from an ensemble standpoint. That way they could play fresh solos and everything else was perfect. It's in the pocket; everyone's playing together.

The greatness of those records, of the first take, and on such difficult material, substantiates that method of working. Some of those records are just so vital, alive, and perfect. And the way people were dealing with incredibly complex material in those days was just awesome. There was youthful enthusiasm and intellectual curiosity coupled with such great ability. Those are the things that Alfred, by encouraging people to rehearse and compose, those are the things that really helped foster and contribute to that era, especially during the sixties.

So you're telling me that, at Blue Note, there was very little cutting and splicing.

If Alfred heard a great trombone solo on one take, and it matched the tempo and could fit into another take, where everyone else was great, he would do that occasionally. That was the extent of it. Of course, if there was a fuck-up at the end, which happens a lot, you'd do an insert. But that would be it.

GEORGE AVAKIAN: What did the 12-inch LP really accomplish in terms of creativity? Already, the concept that I used in making a 10-inch LP—a pop LP—was think of it as a radio program in which the entire package has a purpose. It's programmed. You start with something that catches the attention of the listener on the outside first track. In fact, I did this deliberately on both sides. I'd try to find a real attention-grabber. Then I'd pace the program and end with something that makes the person want to turn the record over. I applied that to everything—including the reissues from the old 78-rpm albums (that's how the 10-inch LPs really began). Gradually, I created more and more new product just for that type of recording.

But the 12-inch LP opened up something else again. I realized, now we've got some real space. With jazz musicians, you can give them a chance to spread out. You don't have to have a three-minute performance on every recording. The first artist that I did this with was Erroll Garner. I deliberately told him, he was one who could do this, "Let's do some recordings where you play approximately six minutes for each track. We'll have six songs on the 12-inch LP instead of the usual 12." That worked marvelously, and then I went on with using, of course, Duke Ellington for long works and the Buck Clayton Jam Sessions, in which, for the first time, there were studio jam sessions which ran as long as, I believe, 27 minutes for one continuous performance.

That was one way of creating an LP in a way that didn't exist previously. This went on into other things like recording dance bands on location, which had never been done deliberately. It was always accidental that somebody happened to record, say, the Benny Goodman Orchestra of 1937 off the air.

HAL WILLNER: I often go the opposite route. I see it like a Venus flytrap. You invite them in, eat them, and spit them out. I often prefer to start out records kind of quiet—kind of inviting you in—and place my strongest thing at the end. I do agree with wanting to have it so people want to turn the record over. But I've found that when you grab people, especially with CDs, a lot of people won't get much past that. They'll just play that track over and over again. CDs are a one-sided thing. If you talk to a lot of people, they'll tell you they don't even get to the end of a CD.

BOB WEINSTOCK: I sensed that we were going to have LPs. I'd heard rumblings. And I did three sessions that were monumental. The first one was Miles Davis with Sonny Rollins and Jackie McLean. Art Blakey was on drums. I think it might have been Walter Bishop and Tommy Potter, but I'm not sure. Anyway, I just said, "Miles, we're going to stretch out."

He said, "You mean we're just going to play?"

I said, "As long as you want almost—within reason."

He said, "Okay, who should I use?"

I said, "You seem to love Sonny Rollins." If you look at the early ones, Sonny's on a lot of them. I said, "You love Sonny."

He said, "What about this young guy Jackie McLean? He's pretty good too, if we're going to stretch out."

I said, "Yeah, I've heard him. He's good." If you listen, that session we did "Dig," "Blueing." Now Jackie doesn't play on all the tunes. He wasn't really that great at the time. He was good.

So Miles and Sonny stretched out. That's how it went. We'd always talk about the personnel, what we're going to do. A lot of times they'd have tunes. Other times, I'd have tunes. Our main emphasis was just to play and stretch out. We accomplished that there.

The next one I did either Zoot Sims with a quartet or Gerry Mulligan's Tentet. One of those two were first. On the Gerry thing I had him stretch out. He played a long solo, and then him and Allen Egar would play. They'd look at me, if I wanted them to play more. I'd shake my head, "Yeah," "no," or whatever. Then they'd switch. I'd sort of "cut my throat." He'd know he'd be going out at the end of the chorus.

One of the best Zoot albums ever made, is called *Zoot Swings the Blues*, where he just kept going on and on and on.

On the Set

ESMOND EDWARDS: Coleman Hawkins was one of my real heros as a kid, because of "Body and Soul." At our little teenage parties we used to dance to jazz records: Basie and Duke and so forth.

When I got to record him, it was like "Wow! This is really an experience." But Coleman, you could tell him six months in advance you had a session, and he would not do anything towards preparing for it. I would learn that, and I'd show up at the date with a briefcase full of sheet music and say, "Hawk, you want to try this? You want to try that?" I have his bottle of vodka there. He didn't give a shit one way or the other. It was just music.

Surprisingly, a lot of the tunes which I considered well-known standards, he wasn't that familiar with, but the guy, you'd stick the music in front of him. He'd run it down once. And it was like he wrote it the second performance.

You learned with each individual group or groups how to best approach the session. A guy like Jack McDuff, he generally had an organized group. They'd come in with material rehearsed already.

Sometimes, you'd give the artist a direction. We want an album. Of course, when we did the groovesville and the bluesville and the ballads and swingsville, so forth, we'd say, "Okay, Hawk, we're going to do an album of ballads." Still, I'd have to come in with all the tunes for him. He would not have given any thought at all to the session prior to coming in.

The things that Mal Waldron was involved in, he always had some of the tunes that he'd written either for the occasion or just in his repertory. It would go that way. But a lot of times I was a combination of traffic cop, psychologist, and "producer/director," trying to keep things moving—waking a guy up when he was on the nod so he could start his solo. Everything. It depends.

ORRIN KEEPNEWS: I've found—and this perhaps has a good deal to do with my early training at the hands of Thelonious Monk—that I've always tended to present ideas: concept ideas or who-to-play-with ideas or repertoire ideas. I've always made it abundantly clear that I am making suggestions. I don't care to say, "Hey, this is the way it has to be," and lay down a bunch of rules. I find that the idea—if it's properly understood by the artist—the idea of making suggestions is extremely valid. A variety of things can happen. Ideas can be accepted or, hopefully, when they are rejected, it's not just a matter of somebody saying, "No." It's a matter of being spurred on to come up with a substitute or variation.

For example, a lastingly important thing about the album *Monk's Music* is the combination of Coltrane and Coleman Hawkins on the same record. Now, I didn't suggest that, but I made some instrumentation and personnel suggestions to Monk which caused him—in saying "No, I don't want to do that" or "I've already done something too much like that"—to say, "How about if instead I do . . . ?" Thereupon, came that magnificent idea.

GEORGE AVAKIAN: Newport '56 was the first time anybody recorded on location at any kind of musical festival. I asked Duke Ellington to do a special composition that we could call the "Newport Jazz Festival Suite." He did, but the biggest surprise was when Duke told the guys, "Look we've all worked very hard for this, and George has knocked himself out, but don't worry about the performance. Billy Strayhorn and George have set up a studio tomorrow morning, and we're going to go back to New York and make patches." (Which I did successfully, very few patches, but I wanted everything to be as perfect as possible on that composition.)

Then Duke said, "After we do this, let's just relax and have a good time. Let's play something that we haven't played for a long time."

He called for "Diminuendo and Crescendo in Blue." The guys kind of looked at each other. They were saying, "Yeah, I remember." "Well, I don't." Paul Gonsalves was one of the ones who said, "I don't remember that one," and Duke said, "That's just a blues. We change keys, I bring you in, and you blow until I take you out. We change keys again, and that's it."

Actually Gonsalves had played it maybe three times, but the surprise element of forgetting the tension of making the first recording ever at an outdoor festival resulted in a tremendous performance.

NAT HENTOFF: Once I decided that I wanted a particular leader, then the leader decided what sidemen he or she wanted. When possible—and I think it was always possible in our cases—the leader would choose someone to edit the final tape so that the final cut was the musician's, not mine.

In a sense I was a supervisor/producer or whatever. I don't like the kind of A&R people I used to see who would, over the PA system, say something hurtful or just nasty, thereby putting everybody down. If I had anything to say to anybody, I would come into the studio and say it to the leader. I would never interfere with the sidemen because that's the leader's job.

My main job was not much of a job at all, just to keep the atmosphere congenial when things got stuck. If there was too much paper on the date, I would do what I think is the standard thing to do. I would say, "Why don't you play the blues for awhile?" That usually would manage to calm everything down, and often we would use the blues cut because it was so relaxed after all that tension. But by and large I did not interfere much at all. I made sure there were plenty of sandwiches and beer and stuff like that, which I think is an important function for the A&R man. The main thing was knowing whom I wanted. I wouldn't dare tell Mingus or Max Roach or Booker Little or any of the people I asked to make recordings, I wouldn't tell them what to do. I would just try to smooth things out if there were any hassles, and there were very few.

Charles Mingus Presents Charles Mingus is a famous case of smoothing it out. Did you suggest that the band dim the studio lights and pretend they were playing a club?

Mingus did. This is a group that had been working for a long time. They were about ready to disband, and Mingus wanted an aura or an atmosphere very much like the club. I think it was the Showboat, that they had been working in. It was a fairly small club, and when we came into the studio, he said to the engineer or whoever was around, it wasn't quite darkness, but it was pretty close to it. I don't know why, he just thought it was a good idea, and it certainly worked out very well.

It also helps, at least it helped me, to have an engineer who knew something about music but, more to the point, would not become the dominant force in the proceedings, like Rudy Van Gelder used to do. I mean Van Gelder is very good, but he really was a tyrant. I used a guy named Bob d'Orleans, who was very hip but laid back. Again, the whole thing is atmosphere. There oughtn't to be anything to get anybody's back up. The only thing should be the music, and if you have either an A&R man or an engineer who wants to run the damn thing, then you've got a mess.

Cut 'n' Splice

GEORGE AVAKIAN: I'll tell you a secret about hiding splices. At Columbia Records we had a big stairwell, seven stories high, at 799 Seventh Avenue. There would be a speaker with a microphone in front of it up at the top floor. We'd play something into that speaker and, then, rerecord it with the echo of that whole seven-story stairway. That is a pretty extreme echo, but you could use it for certain tricks.

One of the ways that I used to hide splices was this. If there was a splice that sounded like a splice, and it was suitable to have (usually it was on the beat of a bar), it was useful to insert a soft cymbal. Bob Prince [an engineer] would go in there with a cymbal and a padded stick; the cymbal would be suspended by fairly thick cord. He'd listen for the point that was being played to him and, then, he'd hit the cymbal lightly. That would hide the splice.

I remember the one place it really was necessary was Erroll Garner's *Concert by the Sea*, which was done on a 7 1/2-inch speed Wollensack, a small German machine that weighed a ton. It was done by an army guy, with special permission from Erroll's manager, who then listened to it and said, "Gee, this is great!"

He sent it to me, and I said, "This was the best Erroll Garner yet, but the sound is awful. I'll see what I can do with it." I cleaned it up. But there was one place where Erroll hit a strong chord—"POW"—on the downbeat, and the machine went dead for an instant. So you hear this silent gap.

I covered it by this technique of echo plus the echoed cymbal stroke, and to this day, I don't know where it is. It worked perfectly. I can't find it.

There was another thing that I could never find. On the very first Buck Clayton Jam Session somebody—I think it was Urbie Green, a very good trombone player—happened to fail to get two notes during a solo. One of these things where he and the instrument just choked up together. There was no way I could splice that in. You just got this soft kind of sound for two notes, and then he continued blowing a great solo.

I couldn't possibly ask Urbie to come in and overdub it. I felt that was too embarrassing, and I mentioned it to Buck. He said, "I'll come in, and I'll blow the two right notes on the trumpet down on low register." And he did. I don't know what two notes they are, and Buck couldn't find them either. We talked about it the last time I saw him before he died. He said, "George, did you ever find those two notes?"

MICHAEL CUSCUNA: Lots of times with Mosaic—when I'm dealing with that material—I try to undo splices. I put together a Buck Clayton CBS thing where George [Avakian] did a lot of splicing. I tried to find the original takes that were the source of his take and put out both takes. At this point in time, when you've got bands of that magnitude, if there's a moderately boring or routine trombone solo in between solos by Ben Webster and Buck Clayton, you can kind of put up with it, because all of that material is so precious to us now. Because it's never going to happen again, our criteria have changed, from when they did the initial albums to when we do authoritative reissues.

On the Buck Clayton project I found tapes in three conditions. I found some where there were clean, untouched copies. And because Columbia would always do two reels—an A-reel and a B-reel—I found tapes where I had to reconstruct. Then, I found ones where all there was was the spliced master. Reconstruction requires more patience than anyone should ever have to endure. When you're compulsive and you want to get it right, you go through it. But it's absolutely maddening. Not only is it time-consuming detail work, but you're actually undoing something that someone did, and which you feel, at this point, they didn't have to do. There are lots of projects where you run into that kind of thing.

Perhaps the producers at that time felt that they were the audio equivalent of, say, auteurist filmmakers such as Alfred Hitchcock and John Ford?

I wouldn't use that analogy. You can use it to describe a whole project. The Buck Clayton Jam Sessions were George Avakian's idea; in that since he was the director. But in the sense of splicing to make "the best possible product," you're actually being a film editor. I think they approached it in the same sense that a film editor will shoot three takes of a scene from different camera angles and put the whole thing together in a way that is best. Film editors have a lot more autonomy than a lot of directors will lead you to believe. I think that's what they were trying to do, trying to make the best possible frozen moments that they could.

GEORGE AVAKIAN: At the beginning, when we were given a chance to use Ampexes on an experimental basis, we were still cutting on disks. We were told, "You cannot cut the tape because you don't know what will happen. There'll be clicks, or it will fall apart or something." I was credited with being the first person who cut. There was a bit of a flap about it, when the writers found out about it.

One prominent writer, who is now very well known in another field, a wonderful guy I don't want to embarrass, called me one day. He said, "Hey George, I hear that the new Brubeck album you put out has splices in it. How come?"

I said, "The playing wasn't always perfect, and in order to make it come out better, I did certain inserts from other tapes."

"George, how can you do that? You're messing with an artist's creation"—and so forth.

Finally, I said, "Look, I'll give you Dave's number. Why don't you call him and ask him what he thinks about it?"

Later the phone rings, and the guy is on the phone. I said, "Well, did you have a nice talk with Dave?"

He said, "Yeah, I sure did."

I said, "What did Dave say?"

He said, "George saved my fucking ass."

CRAIG STREET: There's a difference between a wrong note and something that is simply alive. I believe that you should fix things that are wrong: somebody slipped off the chair and there are four bars missing from the bass part. You go back in, and you fix that. But you don't fix maybe a note that's a quarter-tone off and then kind of resolves back into where it's supposed to go. Somebody might say, "Well, it's the wrong note." It's not the wrong note. It feels good. Why should you change it?

ESMOND EDWARDS: I did a lot of editing. As a matter of fact, I learned to edit by watching Rudy [Van Gelder]. He was so funny. When he would edit a tape, he'd hunch over the editing block so you couldn't see what he was doing, and he wouldn't answer any questions about it. How much could he hide? He wasn't editing with earphones because he certainly needed input from me if we were taking out a solo or a couple of measures. I had to be able to hear it to be able to tell him what needed to be done.

Eventually, we bought our own Ampex two-track machine, which I kept in my office in Jersey, and instead of spending the money with him editing, I started doing all the editing in my office myself. I learned to do it and became quite proficient at it. It stood me in good stead in later years when I went to Cadet/Argo in Chicago and started working with Ramsey Lewis.

Ramsey was not the most precise pianist. I would take a note from bar twelve and move it up to bar two and stuff like that. Fortunately, Eldee Young was like a machine in terms of keeping time, and I was able to do a lot of that without it being apparent.

In terms of my physically cutting tapes, when I went to Chicago and, again, dealing with Ramsey Lewis, we did "The 'In' Crowd" at the Bohemian Caverns in D.C. The performance was maybe nine to eleven minutes long. Those were the days when you had no chance of getting a record played if it was over three minutes long.

Fortunately, you could get airplay on pop and r&b stations of an instrumental. They may play it a minute before the news break or something like that. Radio wasn't nearly as tightly formatted as it is today.

I had to take this, let's say, nine-minute track and cut it down to two-minutes-and-30-odd-seconds. I did it, and it worked seamlessly. But I had to do all kinds of things, like maybe take the third chorus and put it up front. When he hit a clinker, find the same note somewhere else in the tune.

The tape, it looked like it had been through a buzz saw with all those splices in it, but it worked fine. I was able to do that myself.

A lot of producers edit in conjunction with the engineer, and the engineer does the actual physical cutting of the tape. And a lot of it is done electronically these days with digital equipment. Today, with a lot of artists being more involved in the production of their records and being their own producers, and wearing both hats, it's their function to get in there and oversee that aspect of the production of the record.

ED MICHEL: One of the first things I did, when I was a baby editor, was practice on tapes from *Chet Baker Sings*. I put together a glorious 15-minute tape of "Look for the silver . . . oh shit. Look for the . . . shit, silver lining . . . shit. God dammit, shit. Look for the . . . shit." It just went on and on and on. I can't find it any more. It broke my heart. I loved to play that tape for people. Chet required an inordinate amount of editing, especially when he sang, because he wasn't a very good singer.

He was my first junkie. I have no good memories of him at all. Whereas, by the time I knew Art [Pepper] fairly well, I was used to that shit. I didn't know that anybody could be as irresponsible as Chet was. His mystique is really lost on me. He was a dodo surfer who could play really good trumpet. He was a killer trumpet player for a minute and, apparently, got back to it again. But I was so burned that I can't listen to much Chet Baker anymore.

On the other hand, I did have a chance to hear Chet playing with Bird, or it was actually Bird playing with Chet's quartet. Chet was holding up his end just fine, and that's coming from a guy who didn't like him very much. He was okay. He could play.

The Business of Improvisation

CREED TAYLOR: My business is to make an appealing framework for the artist and not to say hands-off because he's jazz and that is pure art. . . . Weinstock, Norman Granz, Orrin Keepnews, and John Hammond—I believe they had such a high, almost hands-off regard for the freedom of jazz that if the producer put himself into restructuring what was going on, then it would lose its spontaneity. That's why they're one side of the fence, and I am on the other side of the fence.

ED MICHEL: There are directors who are complete auteurs of their films, and there are producers who are complete auteurs of their records. That's okay, but by my choice, I'll record musicians who amaze and delight me, and I'll try and give them the wherewithal to be able to do that. In fact, they're out there working in front of the public. They're playing every night. They have a chance to check out their repertoire and find out what works. I'd always rather record a working band than put together an ensemble that just met for the first time in the studio.

JOHN SNYDER: Generally, up until recently I would say my role was to take the artist and his concept and his point of view and just put it down on tape and not really fool with it too much. Now I am more particular about it. I think if somebody is choosing a piano player who is not particularly good or there are ten guys that are better, I am going to say that. "I am okay if you want to use this guy because he is in your band, but is he in your band because he will work for $300 a week? You can do better." I know the argument about loyalty, and I know the argument about closeness. I buy them. I think they're good arguments, but you can also make records with musicians that are not quite up to the job, and you are not going to sell as many of them, I don't think. The idea is to speak up and be more back-and-forth with the artist. Then again, some guys, especially jazz guys, they know what they want.

TEO MACERO: Being a musician myself, when I heard something bad, I had to cut it out. I couldn't stand to hear a bad solo. A guy plays eight bars or twelve bars that were bad, I'd just take it out.

I used to do that all the time with Miles's stuff. We took out many solos. Some of them were pretty good, in fact. But because of the length of the record and because of the fact that we were trying to sell Miles and not some guitar player or saxophone player, it became a way of doing business.

I took out all of the drum solos. You listen to my records, you don't hear any of that stuff—except maybe occasionally with Joe Morello and the Dave Brubeck Quartet and, once in a while, with Miles. By and large, they're very short solos. The bass solos are out, too. I used to think of the rhythm section as a rhythm section. If you're going to sell an artist—Charlie Byrd or whomever—you've got to sell the artist and not the bass player and the drummer. You could do that collectively, but you can't do that if the guy's going to play thirteen choruses of something.

ED MICHEL: My sense is, if you trust the musicians, it's their judgment that's important. If you don't trust the musicians, why are you recording them? What I try and do beforehand is have an understanding of what the guy's music is about, guy being a nonsexist term: how the structure of it works, and have the studio set up to handle about any set of conditions that the leader is likely to ask for. There have been circumstances where piano players have said, "Gee, it would really be nice if I had an electric piano on this," and I could say, "Turn around. There's one behind you miked and ready to go."

ORRIN KEEPNEWS: The idea of having him [McCoy Tyner] play the celeste and harpsichord came out of a conversation about an accident on a Monk session, "Pannonica," one of the numbers on *Brilliant Corners.* There was a celeste in the studio left over from a previous day, and Monk said, "Hey, set that up over here by the piano." That way he could play both simultaneously, one hand on each.

So the conversation that I had with McCoy involved satisfying his curiosity and giving him a historical fact. That, conversationally, led its way to the combination effects, piano and celeste, on *Trident.*

The idea of doing a pure trio record emerged from the fact that our last few projects had been rather complicated, involving large groups. So it was certainly a natural enough point to say, "We've been doing complicated things for awhile. Let's get back to basics, take the best available bassist and the best available drummer and go into the studio." Frequently, great ideas are simply applications of a little common sense.

BOB THIELE: Coltrane was getting a lot of bad critical comments about some of his records. A lot the critics at *Down Beat* and magazines like that, a lot of those guys didn't know what he was doing or what he was playing. They didn't understand it.

I got with John, and I said, "Why don't we surprise everybody? Let's do some familiar ballads." Then I said, "What the hell, why don't we try a vocal record? There are plenty of great singers out there." So he said, "Let me think about it."

I was really surprised. He called up one day and said, "I'd like to use Johnny Hartman."

That's how that came about. I wasn't going to say no. I knew Johnny. He was a hell of a singer. But it was John who wanted him. It was almost like putting a pop singer—say, like an Arthur Prysock or someone—with Coltrane.

CREED TAYLOR: *Jazz Samba,* it took three hours to record that in a black church in Washington. Stan and I took the shuttle down one day about noon. We got to the church at 1:00, and we got the 5:30 shuttle back to New York after we finished recording it.

We did it on a two-track, 7½-inch portable Ampex. There was a kind of a small auditorium in the church, and they set up in the pulpit. I sat outside with the guy who brought the portable Ampex by and monitored it with a headset.

My main concern going back was Keter Betts, the bass player. I told Stan, "I hope we can EQ this thing. I think we've got some boomy bass on this damn thing."

And did I think that that was going to be a hit? No. I didn't realize what we had. I really didn't. Afterwards, I started listening to the songs "Desafinado," slightly out of tune. I thought it was curiously attractive, but I didn't know it was going to do what it did.

On *Getz/Gilberto,* I'd had the experience with, the groundwork laid with *Jazz Samba.* That did so well. It was like a pop album.

I knew we had it in the bag with Jobim actually performing on this Getz/Gilberto thing. Of course, the surprise came when Astrud came in with her little voice to sing the lyric with that accent. I knew that that was going to be an absolute smash. You would have to be deaf and totally out of it not to feel that.

JOEL DORN: The first week I worked at Atlantic, Neshui [Ertegun] went to Europe. He left me a note. Eddie Harris was going to have some kind of dental work done. He wanted to come in and record twenty or thirty songs so he'd have albums in case there were problems with his teeth or his embouchure.

He did maybe twenty-one songs in two or three nights. Arif [Mardin] produced it. And there was a young engineer that had just started there named Bruce Tergeson. He was in the first generation of the engineers as artists.

My first job at Atlantic was to listen through all this Eddie Harris shit and pick out the best stuff and make a record. One tune was like a 27-minute version of "Listen Here." I listened through all the stuff, and I was like, "Oh my God, there's tons of shit here!" Bruce heard "Listen Here," and he said, "This is a hit, if we make it shorter." So more he than me, we edited it down to like seven minutes. Chopped it up. Took a chorus from here and a chorus from there. Whacked it up. It sold like a million singles and a million albums. It was a top-20 record.

Aesthetic Samurai

ED MICHEL: You can really control what goes onto tape, what comes out on record. First of all, just by the guys you sign. That really controls the overall aesthetic. The people you go out of your way to sign. What's interesting about the way I have worked is, I've never had a label. I've always worked for somebody running their label for them and, generally speaking, they signed the artists. There've been very few times when I could go out and sign the artist I wanted to, when somebody said to me, "Hey, why don't you go record three or four people you think ought to be recorded." I could count things like that on the fingers of one hand. Mostly it's somebody else's idea of who should be recorded. Okay, I don't mind that. I don't even mind being an aesthetic samurai, doing somebody's aesthetic dirty work for them because they've made decisions about it. That's the basic kind of decision that you made about music or any other art form: Who is it that you are going to give the available space?

JOHN SNYDER: I remember Sun Ra. We rehearsed for a week because I wanted to see what that would be like. I made one record with him for

A&M where I just kind of showed up. But we got along real well. On the date he just didn't know me, and so he just did his thing. It was like riding a bronco and just holding on.

The second record, though, I said, "We're going to budget for rehearsals for Sun Ra, and we're going to bring everybody in, and we are going to work everything out." Okay, okay, so we go do the rehearsals, and we've got the record date. We had three days or something. After the first night, I said, "Sonny, you didn't record any of the songs we rehearsed."

He said, "John, look at it this way. Suppose I was a football coach, and we had a big game on Sunday, but we have been practicing all day, every day for the week before that." He said, "But we never played that game we played on Sunday, on Monday or Tuesday or Wednesday. We just practiced for it."

I said, "Well, okay. But that's not quite the same thing is it?"

He said, "No, it's the same thing." He said, "We got used to playing together and playing in certain ways, in certain feelings, and I am just taking those and plugging them into another format, another structure."

That's what he did. In a sense it was the ultimate in improvisatory music, but it was as rehearsed as you could get it. They had rehearsed being ultimately improvisatory. They had never rehearsed exactly the same thing that they played. That's the difference.

ED MICHEL: Generally I'll edit because the performer, the artist, would like something changed. If it is just a question of tacking on a different ending, that's one thing. But to really change the structure of something, I'll generally say, "Why don't you just do another take and play it?" First of all, it's cost-effective, and it'll more accurately reflect what the performer wants to do.

And that decision is typically made in playback?

There are guys who want to hear playback. The artists are very different. No two are the same in any way. Some people want to hear playback of everything. Most people want to hear playback of the first tune and maybe the second tune, and from then on, they know it sounds right. They'll ask for a playback if they're not certain. Once you've worked with somebody, they'll say, "Do I need another one?" I'll say "yes" or "no." In that context I'm always ready to do another take, no matter how good it is. There've been colossal takes that I would have thought, "God, this is one of the high points of Western culture." And the guy will say, "Can I do another one?" I'll say, "Certainly." There might be a better one behind it. Why not?

For example, on a Keith Jarrett date, the *Death and the Flower* date: There's one tune that he does—it's a duo with Charlie Haden. I think "Prayer." They played it, and I thought, "Jesus, that's good."

Keith said, "Let's do another one."

I said, "Absolutely." They did another one. Keith played an even better solo, and then it broke down. It just stopped at about five minutes. And I said, "Well, we've got the first one. There's no problem. Why not do one more just for the hell of it because it's going so well?" The third one was the take. When I'm teaching a production class, sometimes I do that at schools, I'll play that as an indicator of "Don't stop just because it's good."

HELEN KEANE: With [Bill Evans'] *Symbiosis* it was sixty-five men, and it was a live date, totally live, which is unheard of nowadays. Occasionally, classical records are done this way, but not very often. In other words, all sixty-five musicians played at the same time and were recorded at the same time. Which is really amazing.

This was done for a German company. We were right between signings then, and so we were available, contractually, to do this for a man named Mr. Brunner-Schwer that had this record company called MPS. But he also liked to play with engineering. That was his hobby. He was a multimillion-aire, and he had his own studio in Germany.

So what he did, after Claus Ogermann and I spent twelve hours one night mixing the album, when it was released, Brunner-Schwer had re-mixed the whole thing himself—added echo and reverb. He ruined it.

Claus started a lawsuit. It was taken off the market and, then, reissued the real way.

But you can't do that. A record appears, disappears. When it reappears, nobody pays any attention. The one that's out now is the real one. So that's the *Symbiosis* story. Everybody was all together. We had multitracks, but nobody was isolated. It was something to see. And there were amazingly few takes for something as complex as it was.

MICHAEL CUSCUNA: A lot of the compositions were things that had been written over the ten years leading up to it—not all necessarily for big band. Basically, at Arista, we'd do a few small-group records. In those days they were selling relatively well. Then, we'd do a large-budget production of something that Anthony [Braxton] really wanted to realize. We would be very lean on the small-groups records, watch the dollars, carry those budgets—the left-over money—over into doing something big. I think *Creative Orchestra Music* certainly was the most ambitious, probably the most expensive record, that we did.

We had reached a point where we had built up the bank account in terms of stealing from one budget to give to another. In those days on Arista—a large independent—Anthony was selling very well. I don't remember the exact numbers, but it was well over ten thousand. That was certainly very good for an experimental artist in 1976.

When an artist like that is on a major label, the main long-term goal is to get a lot of those things done that you would not be able to do otherwise. Most of the time, artists have their moment in the sun on a major label at a couple of periods in their life; the rest of the time, they record for independent labels—for people who do it because they love the music. So that was all the more reason for us to really accomplish something. Up to that point, Anthony had been recording for Delmark and a few small French labels—recording for a pittance.

I guess it comes off more serious than the tone of the project itself, but we had a really great time. I hired Seldon Powell to play first tenor, because of his doubling ability and his reading ability. It was a lot of fun to watch him interacting with Roscoe Mitchell: New York versus Midwest; young generation versus old. We did the rehearsals at a place called Bill's—a big rehearsal hall in New York—and then we recorded at Generation Sound. It should've been a very pressured time. We had some wrinkles along the way. But it was a very celebratory time.

Anthony is like a journalist. There's never a project where he's not writing the last of the arrangements at four in the morning, six hours before rehearsal. So there was a mad dash to get everything arranged and copied before the beginning of the rehearsals. But once it started, it was wonderful.

Anthony has a great sense of humor. If you interview him, he goes into automated academician and theorist, but that's this other person. Really, Anthony is a very funny guy and loves to laugh all the time.

Writing with Sound

BOB BELDEN: What I found out was how much of an influence Miles had on the sessions. He was directing the band to start and stop. He was even saying to Teo, "You can put this part and edit it onto this part." He was telling Teo what to do. For some reason, this record is just a little bit, Miles has just got a little more intensity about it—his focus on it. . . . *Bitches Brew* is not just about what album was issued. It was really the crystallization of this process he was developing as a composer, as an arranger.

TEO MACERO: I rolled the tape every time we went to the studio from the beginning to end. That's why you got a lot of wonderful little vignettes here and there.

Miles later on said, "Yeah, yeah, use that piece, that shit, up front."

I said, "Yeah, I hear that."

It was well constructed. Miles approved everything.

CRAIG STREET: I tend to roll tape constantly when musicians don't even know tape is rolling. People will be in the room rehearsing, and I'll be, "Keep rehearsing. Go through it again." I might start rolling tape. You never know when something is going to happen. And tape is really cheap. You can always erase tape. It's the least expensive thing that there is on a recording project, practically. There's nothing as expensive as a take that you didn't get because you weren't at the machine. Then, you're talking expensive. If somebody is playing during a rehearsal and it's fantastic and they turn around and say, "Did you get that?" And you say, "No." You're stuck. That mood may not pass that way again. Creativity is a really elusive kind of a thing. That kind of inspiration may walk into a room once in the course of a day. You'd better have the machine rolling.

JOHN SNYDER: When we made this record with James Blood [Ulmer] for Artists House, *Tales of Captain Black,* Ornette [Coleman] rehearsed those guys—Blood, Denardo [Coleman], and Jamaaladeen [Tacuma]— every day for a month. We came to the studio, and we made the record in three hours. It was just a question of putting it down.

When I convinced him to record the old quartet—[Don] Cherry, Billy [Higgins] and Charlie [Haden]—he brought them in, kept them up for weeks and rehearsed them every day.

He came to the studio, and he said, "Okay, we are going to go through it. We are going to play these songs"—eight songs, I think it was—"and we are going to play them straight through. We are going to stop a minute between every song, but we are not going to stop more than that, and we are going to play them straight down."

He did that; took an hour. And he did them in the order they were going to be on the record. He came back into the control room, listened to the whole thing straight through one time, didn't stop, and said, "Okay, fellows, let's go do it again." Right back out to the studio, did all eight songs again, one after the other, stopped one minute between each song, and the record date was over. And he made a great record that never came out.

TEO MACERO: If you go back in the history of *In a Silent Way,* we had something like forty reels of tape that I had mixed: forty reels, two huge piles. Miles and I went through that shit, and we cut it down to eight-and-a-half minutes on each side. Miles threw out all of the garbage. I'm sure they're probably going to put all that stuff back in.

Miles left the studio. He said, "That's it"—nine minutes on one side, eight and a half minutes on the other.

I said, "Miles, we can't do that. Leave me alone for a little bit, and I'll see what the hell I can do." I built it up to make it eighteen minutes. If you listen to it very carefully—we were doing this with a razor blade, any techniques we could muster, to bring that thing back up. By itself—with the repeats—that's what really makes it a work of art.

There were a lot of things that we did with Miles, even in those days. I was recording Miles on two or three different tracks. He would wander around in the studio. Later on, we put three tracks on there of Miles. I don't recall the album, but we were doing that kind of thing. I could take what was coming direct and use that as the front, and then take another source and put a little reverb on that, and then take another one and do something else with it. We were doing a lot of experimental things in those days.

BOB BELDEN: Sometimes, when Teo eventually got to where the music was so abstract that there was no melody, he would create the melody. Teo would go in, like on "He Loved Him Madly," and loop. He did it inadvertently because the tape he was using was defective. They just joined the first half of the reel with the second half of the reel, and looped the main melody. He was working with loops in '67 and '68. His version of "Circle in the Round" has a few little loops. That was really Teo's first edit-mania piece.

TEO MACERO [on *Jack Johnson*]: Miles comes to me. He says, "Lookit, I'm going to California. I've got $3,000. I'll give you $1,500. You put together some music from the vault."

I said, "Fine, okay." He left for California, and I went to the vault, found some music. I pasted it together, edited it together, and we turned it all around. There's a lot of repeats in there. It's like the beginning of the fusion thing—the repetitive sounds that they're doing today. It repeats over and over and over and over. Jesus!

I did a concert: the Isle of Wight. It was 1973. Every major group in the world was there in England. Jimi Hendrix, he blew up the stage at the end. I was in charge of recording all those artists: Emerson, Lake and Palmer, the Who, Ten Years After.

Before they went on, I'd go into this wagon where they were sitting. I used to wear a sweater—very conservative dresser—and everybody would say, "Hey, you don't belong in here, man. Leave us alone!"

They were smoking some joints, and I don't know what-the-hell else. I'd say, "Looka here, I'm a producer for CBS."

"We don't give a shit, man. Get the fuck out of here!"

I said, "But look, I've got to record you in about twenty minutes. It would be nice if you'd give me some information so I don't make any mistakes."

The cat would say, "What do you do, man? Who are you?"

"Well, I used to work with Miles Davis."

He says, "You did? Did you produce that *Jack Johnson* record?"

I said, "Yeah."

Every rock artist in the world knew that record! So I'd walk in the door: "I'm the producer of *Jack Johnson*."

They'd say, "Hey, come on in, man. Sit down and smoke a joint."

I'd say, "No thanks. I got too much on my mind. We got three separate crews out there. We've been working twenty-four hours a day for six or seven days."

CRAIG STREET: Quite often what somebody is afraid of is where the best stuff is. Like if somebody says, "I really don't feel comfortable playing guitar and singing, but I do play guitar." You say, "Hey, what's there?"

A lot of what I learned dealing with Cassandra [Wilson] was that. I knew she played guitar. On the first record, *Blue Light 'Til Dawn*, if there were songs that she'd written or if there were songs that we'd ultimately agreed to do, I would have her invent some version of that song with her playing guitar and singing into a cassette.

I would then give that cassette to the musicians and say, "Here's the foundation that we're going to work from." So instead of letting them hear a Robert Johnson song or a Hank Williams song or hear a Joni Mitchell song, I'd let them hear her interpretation of that and, then, I would let them expound on that.

WAYNE HORVITZ: Jazz records, hopefully, what you're really trying to do is capture something that's not that far from the way the band plays live. There are some exceptions to that. I think Weather Report—I'm a pretty big fan of their early records—those are records that show a studio sensibility applied to music that we call jazz. But again, with strong pop and rock influences.

In terms of my experience, Bill Frisell is called a jazz artist. I've produced three of his records. One of them falls into one category; the other two fall into the other category. The first one I did, *Is that You?* was very much a multitrack record where hardly any musicians played on it. If they did, they often played after we'd laid down the basic tracks. In other words, we'd put down drum machine and sequence things and then have Bill do a bunch of overdubs. Then Joey Baron came in and played drums on some things at the very end. That was more like producing a songs kind of record in that we really came up with lots of the ideas in the studio or in preproduction. We'd go into a cheaper studio first and make a little mockup of the thing. That was a blast for me.

The other two records I did for Bill—the covers record, *Have a Little Faith,* and *Where in the World?*—I enjoy listening to them just as much to the first record, and I enjoyed producing them, but they weren't near as interesting to produce because essentially you get great musicians, a great engineer, a good studio, and there's still some work for you to do. But not a whole lot. The guys are playing great, and the sounds are coming off great. It's more a matter of making sure the flow happens and making sure that the people stay focused, stay having a good time. If one of those things isn't happening, you try to create a situation where it does happen. But there's not that much more to it than that.

BILL LASWELL: In the past composition was notation, and to me it's memories. To me, tape is composition. That replaces notation because it's all memory. Once it's on tape, it's no different than having it on paper.

Cage said, thirty years ago, that in the future records will be made by records. In the last ten or fifteen years, DJs have proven that in genres like hip-hop—which are made from older records.

As far as writing something down on paper and calling it a composition that can be played and repeated, to me it's not that different than recording something, memorizing it, and repeating it. Whether you memorize it by, then, notating it is one way. Or whether you do it with a computer or whether you do it with a sampler or whether you use the actual piece and reproduce it the way DJs reproduce records to create records, it's all a new way. There's always a new way to create music, and it always comes down to collage because you are always fitting things together.

The more sort of desperate and far-fetched concepts that do fit together as collage, if you can make them feel like music, then that's an achievement. All of these things didn't come in styles. They didn't come in forms. It all started with the person who had an idea, who was copied and copied and copied. Then it's preserved by people who know very well they can't do better.

Works Cited

Derrida, Jacques. *Of Grammatology*. Translated by Gayatri Chakravorty Spivak. Baltimore: Johns Hopkins University Press, 1976.

Ong, Walter J. *Orality and Literacy: The Technologizing of the Word*. New York: Methuen, 1982.

Perlman, Alan M., and Daniel Greenblatt. "Miles Davis Meets Noam Chomsky: Some Observations on Jazz Improvisation and Language Structure." In *The Sign in Music and Literature*, edited by Wendy Steiner, 167–183. Austin: University of Texas Press, 1981.

Rasula, Jed. "The Media of Memory: The Seductive Menace of Records in Jazz History." In *Jazz Among the Discourses*, edited by Krin Gabbard, 134–162. Durham: Duke University Press, 1995.

Stowe, David. *Swing Changes*. Cambridge, Mass.: Harvard University Press, 1994.

PART FOUR

COLLABORATIVE DISSONANCES

EDDIE PRÉVOST

The Discourse of a
Dysfunctional Drummer
Collaborative Dissonances, Improvisation,
and Cultural Theory

·‿

I prepared a keynote address for the 1999 Guelph Jazz Festival colloquium
with a listening audience in mind. Thereafter, upon being asked to contribute the address as a chapter to the present volume, I had thought to
convert it somewhat. This did not prove easy or satisfactory, if only because some of the lingering rhetoric and the prevailing pessimism of the
talk did not lend themselves willingly to linguistic transformation. Further, given the effect this address had upon some of its listeners, I was persuaded to leave the text pretty much as it was. For this I beg the reader's
indulgence. Changes, however, have been made largely through a welcomed editorial intervention that encouraged me to explain a few things
more fully. Immediately hereafter I have added a few additional thoughts
by way of explanation.

   The rather gauche alliteration of my title, I have to admit, was intended
to discomfort my listeners and maybe even set up a certain amount of antagonism. The title, however, addresses a real situation: most of the world
and perhaps especially most of the musical world, would find what I have
done in the name of music over the past thirty-five years incomprehensible.
(Of course, and fortunately, I am not alone in this situation.) On a simple
practical level it was even difficult for me to offer evidence that I was "properly trained and experienced" enough as a percussionist to meet Canadian
immigration requirements in order to be granted a visa to attend the
Guelph Jazz Festival. And certainly, as I listened to the preceding papers of

the 1999 colloquium (mine was the final presentation), I felt that something of a disjunction was opening up—like a chasm—between the worldview I offered and the more (rightly) analytical, scholarly, and optimistic offerings of my fellow speakers. Such was my growing apprehension as paper succeeded paper that I almost lost my nerve and actually considered completely rewriting my text. A combination of inertia, tiredness (I did not sleep for the first two nights after my arrival in Canada from England), and bloody-mindedness prevailed.

I did, and I do, feel out of joint: despite a certain amount of positive critical perception about the work with which I am involved and the long-standing support of particular individuals, this work has largely been ignored. I am not, however, particularly downcast although (naturally) I feel disappointed that the world continues to move farther and farther away from the ideals I feel make living a life important, many of which—with examples attached—are referred to in the main text. My reflections, although tinged with pessimism, may owe more to my middle-age angst than anything else. They are, however, the reflections of somebody who has been and done and has few regrets about actions and consequences. But, as ever, context is all: the world chooses.

Improvisation and Postmodernism

Making music is not enough. A musician and an audience must be aware of the procedures and the life preferences that ultimately inform the art they embrace. Improvisation in music makes specific demands upon musicians: theirs is "a music-making in the moment" aesthetic that commands their attention to materials and responses to other musicians as well as to the sense of moment that is sharper in practice than most other forms of music making. Audiences, too, need a matching listening aesthetic if they are to be able to know what is occurring and thereby judge and enter into dialogue with its value. Anything less will not only result in an impoverished experience; it will also be an act of cultural cowardice, possibly amounting to social immorality. You will note from this initial outburst that I am not of the postmodernist persuasion, according to which absence of meaning often seems to be the desired state of affairs. This stance, in my opinion, is a moral cop-out. Music is malleable; a diverse range of social signifiers measures its value. The most powerful signifiers in the current cultural climate are linked to indicators of "success" and "style," all of which are maintained by marketeers. To adhere to this, even in an unthinking way, is the moral cop-out. There are other social signifiers for music; in improvised music we do well not to lose sight of the positive social features of collaboration and problem solving that improvisation entails. In contrast, by making any statement at all I risk being wrong. And it is a willingness to embrace possible controversy that marks out the veracity in (and of) an improvisation. Risk and doubt are two crucial tools for the improvising musician.

As a naive young man I became interested in jazz. It was its otherness that attracted me: it had a form, an ethos and, I intuited, a "seriousness" that had nothing whatsoever to do with the musics prescribed by school or by the then adult-dominated media—which in the British 1950s was the very paternalistic and ever middle-aged BBC. Curiously, the moment I entered the world of jazz—and bear in mind that I was a continent away from its origins—I found that "jazzers" were forever at each others' throats. The 1940s and 1950s saw what I could only describe as a schism between the traditional revivalists and the modernists. And, within the various camps debates raged quite vociferously, even one about the validity of the saxophone in the revivalist, traditional jazz band. Apart from these quirky distinctions I could sense the mobility of the form. It let people in. You could sense that musicians were actively contributing. You could sense the playfulness and the developmental possibilities with a specific piece and thereafter in the general form itself. It was living.

I have always been fascinated by all the styles of jazz and found the debates between various camps a little hard to bear. I actually played "trad" jazz—as New Orleans revivalist jazz was called in England—before later going on to modern jazz. And, as the sixties progressed, being a typical feisty young man I looked to the experimental and the other adventures I saw in jazz. The debates raged on. Disgruntled British jazz fans walked out of John Coltrane concerts—to the jeers of his supporters—apparently disliking endless choruses on "Greensleeves." Ornette Coleman caused a complete division in those who had been previously allied in the neat modernist camp. Better and worse was to come. Crowds flocked to see Sun Ra's first U.K. concert, which I (together with other members of AMM) encouraged and helped Victor Schonfield to organize. I was also at a famous public performance that was recorded by BBC-TV of the Albert Ayler Quintet; I remember sitting near to Roland Kirk who must have been in London to play at Ronnie Scott's Club. This concert became famous in the British jazz world not so much as a groundbreaking cultural phenomenon—which it was—but as a subject of vandalism and prejudice and the overt use of corporate cultural power. A senior BBC television executive apparently ordered the tapes destroyed and the program was never screened. War had been declared on those who proposed an alternative to the prevalent officially approved modes of music. This response marked a retrenchment in a hitherto more liberal emergent cultural environment.

And, of course, the war goes on still: it is a war of values and human perspectives made sharper, I think, by the contradictions that improvisation threw up in the production of music. By definition it was less controllable; ideological sacred cows like property relations were brought into question. Who owns the music if most of it is improvised? There is of course only one answer (ethically at least): the musicians. But this scenario was beginning to shake all too many expectations in "normal" social relations.

Improvisation and Radicalism

I am, of course, nervous about the idea of using jazz (or *any* kind of music) to help fly a political banner. Some readers may be aware of my connection with British composer Cornelius Cardew, who for a number of years was a member of the improvisation group AMM. Later, in his tragically shortened life, he created music expressly to serve political occasions that were initially of a Maoist persuasion. The irony for those who stood apart from this particular activism was that the music itself turned out to be so conservative. For example, the tune for his song "We Sing for the Future" is excruciatingly reminiscent of "The Eton Boating Song," which is associated with England's most famous public (that is, "private") school: the educational bastion of the British establishment and class system. Music for Cardew had apparently by that time ceased to be important in itself and was only of use in the overall process of political propaganda. But we are all exposed by our acts. And, I suggest, the way people make music inevitably tells you something significant about their worldview, consciously and otherwise.

Perhaps I am being unfair to Cornelius. His commitment to social revolution far outweighs any temporary musical shortcomings; perhaps my point is too cheap. In improvisation, however, we assume responsibility for the music produced: there is no composer we can blame for an unsatisfactory performance. But this artistic stance can also be a cover. So often one feels that a musician is telling the audience to "like it or lump it": "take me for what I am or do not take me at all." Mostly audiences are amazingly tolerant (too much so?) toward the musicians they admire. Artists in particular do well to remember that the creative process is a communal one involving dialogue. All creations are part of the social process, part of the communicative rituals that help generate the kind of civil society in which I would prefer to live.

So, however paradoxically, I am arguing that music is always political. We are, then, drawn into a discussion of the nature as well as the content and configuration of a political life. Elsewhere, I have joined with others

to point to the (albeit simplistic) characterization of the symphony orchestra as an exemplary model of social and political organization that so
well mirrors and enforces the mores of late nineteenth-century capitalism.
The factory model in miniature: for "composition" read "product blueprint," for "managing director" read "conductor"—and there is no semantic confusion of the role and naming of the "foremen," although some of
them may be women these days. Even conductor Roger Norrington talks
of the "industrialization of classical music." This kind of analysis suggests
that the manner in which music is made inevitably portrays—and perhaps
ideologically reinforces—a social configuration. Large forces of production do need strong guidelines and disciplined movement. All musicians
who have been involved in large ensembles know that the more people in a
band the more difficult it is to control and the less individual freedom
there is inherent in such a structure. So it behooves musicians and audiences to acknowledge the manner of music making, the interrelations of
musicians, and the general attitudes that influence structures. With these
guidelines in mind, forms of music implicitly reflect a particular set of
(cherished?) social values.

In the formulation of the improvising ensemble AMM, a group of
strong-minded (not to say bloody-minded) individuals entered upon an
experiment in a nonhierarchical musical structure. There was no prescribed
form, although it soon became apparent about what was allowed and what
was not allowed. In fact, nothing was allowed that prescribed form. Whenever a compositional device was suggested or whenever there was an intuitive reference to another form of music (for example, jazz), then this allu-
sive quality was annihilated. This improvisatory project—not without its
difficulties—involved creating music as if it was being made for the first
time. Of course, it had all the arrogance that comes with youth. The form
AMM music subsequently made followed practice. And the particular
"laminal" effect, in which individual contributions were layered together as
much as combined in (say) an atomistic nature, evolved. Form was not
therefore avoided; rather, it was allowed to emerge as the framework into
which we could freely contribute the constituent parts. The resultant music
(if "music" is an acceptable term in this context) very quickly became self-
referential and was called AMM music. A BBC producer of one of the first
radio programs we made in the 1960s wrote on the tape box, to indicate the
nature of the content, "defies description."

Obviously, the individual musicians had some kind of musical or performance strategy, but the common characteristic seemed to be to define the
subject while making the music. Individuals brought specific qualities that
enriched the ensemble, but what seemed to be most important and what

seemed to work best was the collective creative activity, wherein ideas were tested in the heat of the furnace that was performance. In the early days AMM met at least twice a week, once to perform and then again to discuss the session and the implications thereof. In doing this we began to articulate our creative theory.

Freedom and Improvisation

At the heart of this experiment in music was an experiment in social discourse. Improvising means individual responsibility for the sounds produced and collective responsibility for the overall performance. Many other examples of this kind of activity, recorded and anonymous, occurred right across the industrially developed parts of the world, especially, it seems, in North America and in Western Europe; anywhere, I guess, where there were sufficient material resources for ordinary people to start thinking about things other than subsistence. For me personally the music I made was the result of Britain's postwar welfare state. But apart from this newly found resource that we converted into freedom it soon became apparent that music was itself a powerful social mechanism. There were, of course, power struggles within these musical exchanges and collaborations. The freedom to play loudly at the expense of the audibility of another's music is a common arena for dispute. Less common, but as relevant, are issues of hyper- and microactivity, of forbearance, of generosity toward others in letting certain developments occur. These are all features foreign to the making of most other musics in Western cultures. Human intercourse may indeed thrive and develop in an environment of competitive thrust, but it only survives and matures with reciprocal understanding and cooperation. These things, however, have to be much more than objectives or useful metaphors in polemic. If they are not deeply embedded within the productive mechanisms and objectives of the music, then all talk is meaningless twaddle.

I make no apologies here for going over old theoretical ground, if only because I sense that it is still not understood. I am persuaded to repeat myself even if only to court a response similar to the one I received at a symposium in San Diego where a delegate informed me that my analysis was illogical but failed to elaborate on how and why. The current movement, which I shall describe as contemporary improvisation, can define itself easiest by contrast with other forms of music making. As a means of social and cultural expression, music depends upon solving technical problems of sound production and of collaborating with other people. I make my contrasting analysis this way: most musical forms solve the technical problems of making music prior to any performance. In Western classical music the musical decisions are substantially preformed before the performance. Anything improvised must allow the musical development to be dictated by the situation. Musical problems are therefore set and solved within the context of the performance.

How far this process is allowed free rein is a measure of the confidence and trust the musicians have in each other. It is also a measure of their common musical property rights, which is important to consider given that a capitalist society is underpinned by the notion of private property. In musical improvisation, and especially that of the collective kind, it is impossible to apportion a property quota to each player. The only workable criterion is actual physical presence within the musical situation. Musicians and audiences might have their own ways of measuring the respective value of each contribution, but this is no help when it comes to the bureaucracy of music economics. Trust and generosity (if sometimes fragile) become necessary as the measures of equity. This is *not* a popular working economic principle in our present culture.

The other important convergent analytical proposition is the degree to which dialogue shapes the performance. Again, if we conceive of a standard Western classical music performance we note that the relations between the musicians are mediated through the score, whereas in a collective improvisation the mediation is unpredictably direct, one musician to the other. These very important categorical differences are what I think dictate the veracity of a collective improvisation. Of course, there are other improvising procedures that may appear to counter these analytical propositions. In particular, I refer to the notion of musicians performing individual improvisations alongside others within the same performance space and time frame. Though this may be thought of as a pejorative commentary on certain performance strategies, what I mean here is that it is evident that some musicians play without any regard to the contributions of their fellow performers. (How far this is actually possible is open to debate.) I concede that this may be a tenable artistic mode, even if it counters the important thrust of dialogue in the music and its attendant philosophy. It offers a kind of "parallelism" that in effect posits the audience as the source of compositional decisions. Either way, the performance is not "controlled" by an external agency, such as "the composition," which is a preformed dictate of how a performance should proceed and be expressed. These analytical considerations seem to me to be at the heart of any meaningful attempts at "collaborative assonance"—although, paradoxically, it appears that most of the rest of the world interprets these activities as willful acts of "dissonance."

These kinds of considerations fueled the work of AMM; subsequent to those uncertain formative moves a body of work has arisen, documented on recordings that mark more than thirty years of activity. I would not, however, claim that in those early days we had developed a coherent analysis. Our responses and initiatives were much more intuitive. And, of course, continuity is not necessarily a mark of relevance. In the case of AMM I can assure you that it is not the mark of popular or commercial support. Contrary perhaps to the perceptions of many people, AMM performs much less often than many of its contemporaries and other musicians who now occupy a similar aesthetic territory. Perhaps we have passed our "sell by" date, or, we are not sexy enough. No. According to our albeit small audience, we still have something important to offer. In a way it feels like our time has arrived, although we may be fast approaching the category of dinosaur.

Much of improvisation owes its origins to free jazz. The characteristic ensemble lineup, the practice of call and response and even the addiction to a club space are all reminiscent of jazz origins. AMM, by contrast—perhaps because of our connection to and awareness of experimental musics (Cage, Stockhausen, Wolff, Cardew, et al.)—practiced and offered a different musical agenda and experience. The AMM practice (so to speak) is now more commonplace than it used to be, while one senses that the free jazz model is receding in prevalence. There are other reasons, though, why a relative state of obscurity and marginality persists for these kinds of music.

Dissonance, Improvisation, Alienation

One musician's dissonance is another's jazz. And in the fullness of time and familiarity a dissonant form may become quietly soothing. Old men can revel in memories of turbulent times past. Is this always to be thus? What do we mean in this debate by "dissonance"? Is there a critical paradox in my own perception of much that passes as jazz? At once I find it smooth, pleasant, and anodyne while I also find it repugnant. This kind of music dissonates for me precisely because I find it treacly and without any intellectual stimulation or emotional impact. Is it not the irritation of grit that makes the pearl? I want a string of such pearls in my music. What is it that we propose when we make or appreciate music? Don't tell me there is no meaning in music other than some kind of aural massage or self-contained intellectual stimulation. What I suggest is that whether it is understood or not by the practitioner or listener, and even when it is denied, we expose our deepest feelings and thoughts when we engage with music. It is a measure of our psyche.

The creative attraction of improvisation to musicians and listeners alike is to risk a determination to conquer doubt, a desire for a musical formulation to supersede the modes with which we are dissatisfied. Conceptual as well as aural dissonance are both stock shots of the avant-garde, used to move an audience's expectations and perhaps lift them to new planes of perception. Cage's silent piece "4'33" maybe is the ultimate example of this, although I have always thought that LaMonte Young's "Piano Piece for David Tudor No. 1"—in which the piano is offered a bale of hay and a bucket of water—might run it a close second. Much of contemporary improvising music might seem to owe its development to similar alienation strategies in which musicians force change through unconventional means and approaches. Dispensing with composition. Using conventional instruments in unconventional ways. Not using conventional instruments at all. Audiences and musicians alike are fascinated or repelled by new techniques and the development of "performance" within music, both of which at times transcend even sound production.

But all alienation strategies and all avant-gardes become exhausted, just as a joke repeated ceases to be funny. The effect is weakened by repeated applications. The ultimate fragility of the alienating method is that it is inherently reactive. It exists by virtue of negating a negative. The compulsion may be to do something different. I think aspirant improvising musicians, in particular, feel compelled (understandably) to make a place for themselves. This often implies a reaction to what has gone before. Ultimately, however, I think that an improvising musician must cast aside such considerations and not worry about self-perception or audience response. Such a musician needs to abandon all ideas of whether the music made is successful or not. The focus has to be on the operation at hand: mixing self with material and blending the responses of fellow musicians and audiences.

There are, of course, varying degrees of alienation. And the alienating methods explored by the musical avant-garde of the 1960s and 1970s often reduced composition to a comical parody by offering unrealizable ultra-democratic ideals. In some sense this activity made for expansive and creative opportunities. It is interesting to note, however, how so many advocates of this "leveling" scuttled back to the protective folds of the musical establishments, leaving their unschooled associates high and dry now that experimentation is (for them) exhausted. I was one of those who was left "high and dry."

Improvisation has moved in and out of fashion. But it is not difficult to tell who the long-distance runners are. The experience of being involved was not for me simply a passing phase. It was a life-informing experience that carried me forward into my adulthood. And as our economy

and political society moved into a world of Reaganite/Thatcherite imperatives it subsequently presented me with as many problems to solve as it may
have informed and sustained my early musical life.

Race, Class, Improvisation

Jazz and even the creative stance of improvised dissonance have themselves become subject to proprietorial claims. When I was in my twenties I
felt that being a young white man born and brought up in postwar London, England, that I had less moral proprietary rights over jazz than, for example, a young black man living in New York or Chicago. Although there
were, and are, powerful white voices in the jazz world, I saw then—and still
see now—even larger "Keep Off" signs. I understand. I am sympathetic
and vocally supportive. Any beleaguered community like that of black
North America, deserves support. The cause of all oppressed minority social groups is something to which every mature adult should attend; you
don't know when you might be in a minority yourself. And, actually I do
come from such a minority group. My name is French; I am of French Hu-
guenot stock. Dissident (and probably dissonant?) French Protestants at
odds with the orthodoxy in prerevolutionary France who were repressed
had to flee the land of their birth in fear of their lives and livelihoods. It was
perhaps easier for my ancestors to fit in. But color is only an extended ex-
cuse for prejudice and discrimination, which at its heart always beats to an
economic rhythm.

Being white in certain cultural fields in this topsy-turvy world of cultural displacement and uncertainties is not necessarily an advantage. It is
certainly not true for many musicians in Europe, where there is a patroniz-
ing desire for exoticism—which has been fulfilled to a large extent by visiting non-European musicians (and note my emphasis upon the word "visiting"). This situation has infected musical criticism and plagued musical life
in Europe for generations. My and AMM's first real supporter (and for a
short idealistic time our one and only manager) Victor Schonfield, once
said to me that the problem with AMM was that no matter how creative
and innovative the group might be, it suffered from two major disabilities
in this world: it wasn't black and it wasn't American. The point I am strain-
ing to make here is that the exoticism—no matter how superficially attractive—got in the way of an appreciation of the music's inner motivations
and potential social richness. Audiences were massaged with messages of
primitivism and exotica. This is where the real racism lies. Being black was
an important ingredient in the artistic perception to the (then) largely
white middle-class European audiences. Obviously the economic impera-

tive ruled. Who could blame African-American musicians from scoring in Europe when perhaps the pickings were so lean back home? But the aesthetic point was missed. And to some extent the aesthetic point was believed to be unobtainable because it was so alien and exotic.

I am treading very dangerous waters here. But the issue is not and has never been about race, although racist behavior has muddied the waters a great deal. The issue, in my opinion, has always been about class and about the way people relate to each other. Our general culture in this late twentieth-century period is firmly entrenched in the individualist ethos: dog eat dog (which is just a neat twist on the old British imperialist "divide and conquer"). Sure, I can see white European liberals getting off on "black" culture. These egalitarian sentiments might even be sincere. But I doubt whether the capitalist ethos will actually let them do more than applaud the most commercially successful of the black artists they admire—who, one notes, themselves develop highly individualistic bourgeois tendencies and tastes. Who can blame them? But do not let these facts blind us to the underlying realities. In certain and often unfathomable respects, "black" culture sometimes sells better than its white counterpart (even though this may do little to advance the economic and social situation for African-Americans). If, therefore, collaborative dissonances in music are the distress flares of a culture in crisis, when the people begin to see the distress flares as a celebratory fireworks display, then those of us who wish to create a civil society based upon equity and freedom are in deep trouble.

The problem with the concept of dissonance is of course that it implies the existence of consonance. In the artistic endeavor we associate with jazz and its correlative contemporary improvised musical expressions, we have effects that mirror social alienation. The music to a large extent—where it has not yet allowed itself to become ameliorated by market forces into an anodyne form—is, I repeat, an attempt to negate a negative situation. It is a fight back. In musical improvisational terms it is (if only intuitively realized) an attempt to put the musician at the heart of the creative process. Hitherto, within what we refer to as classical music or within mass-produced pop, the musician has been creatively peripheral. He has been replaceable and little more than a factotum. Dissonance is both a demand and a supportive expression for the right to exist. To repeat: dissonance implies consonance. Our problem is that the battlefield for this contest for moral and social values is situated on foreign soil. The perceived high ground of privilege is paradoxically just where we don't really want to be. Fighting for a piece of the action is itself a losing scenario. I have to admit to being extremely pessimistic about the future in this respect. Cultural activity is now so completely ring-fenced by the prevailing imperative of real or perceived economic advantage that improvising musicians, as even the small audience base begins to widen, find themselves subject to the imperatives and the rigors of the market. Festival organizers are courted and pressured by agents and managers. Any idea of musical presentation as an expression of creativity within the context of developing a civil society is thus diminished.

As befits a capitalist bourgeois culture, "the art of selling" is valued above all other arts. And the world of art—ever refreshed with "novelty" even from "dissonant" quarters—is now in complete collusion with this cultural aesthetic. Examples abound: student musicians are taught as much about marketing themselves as about furthering their techniques and developing their intellectual capacities and moral resources. Just recently, for example, I read—in a so-called quality British broadsheet newspaper that allegedly serves the liberal intelligentsia—that a new chairman of Britain's Institute of Contemporary Arts has been appointed. He, proudly by his own admission, knows absolutely nothing about the arts. This is not uncommon. The devastating corollary to this particular story is how craven and uncritical the newspaper was in its report of this situation. In fact, they seemed to think that the appointment of a whiz kid financier was a good thing.

In retrospect I see that much of the avant-garde of the 1960s and 1970s was little more than an attempt by vigorous individuals to map out and objectify a space in which they could flourish. Some of these enterprising individuals became increasingly engaged in the cultural marketplace. For others it was a moment to assert power and authority, paradoxically within a milieu of anarchism or the antiestablishment. Many of these individuals subsequently looked for other places to restate and reinvent their authoritarianism within a more demanding and/or a more current forum. Because by the mid-1970s avant-gardism was passé. If you look closely, however, you will see that many of those paragons of the alternative culture have reinvented themselves and now lead the current cultural hegemony. I speak here of musicians, composers, and artists of all kinds who have moved away from forms arising from social and political aspirations. Do I need to name names? Perhaps not naming ensures that we all (myself included) review our objectives and motives from time to time, for fear of being included in such a list!

In 1998, I attended a conference organized by a left-wing magazine in England in which the effects and the legacy of the youth culture in 1960s were examined and—surprise, surprise—found wanting. I found myself discussing this phenomenon with speakers, some of whom were not even born when that so-called "progressive" decade began. I listened patiently to their descriptions. I heard them dismantle the totems of hippiedom and dowse the imploding stars in the rock firmament with derision. My fellow panelists were convinced that the 1960s phenomenon was more dressing than substance. They were all manifestly fed up with the constant reference to this period as a seminal moment in the development of an alternative culture. In brief, they did not believe that it lived up to the claims made on its behalf, in portrayals of the 1960s culture that had become publishing fodder during the 1990s. My copanelists were correct, of course, but unfortunately they revealed that they too were subject to a massive imbalance of information and the subsequent distortion of many of the ideals and objectives that people of that period attempted, albeit feebly, to develop and project. There is a parallel history of 1960s dissonance—which includes improvisation, away from exotic fashions, drugs, and "free love"—that has been entirely marginalized.

My best friend, the pianist John Tilbury, always tells me when I am ill or depressed no matter what the symptom, that the cause of my distress is "monopoly capitalism." I'm not sure why but hearing him say it always cheers me up. He has a point. Everything we hear about the dissonant times of the 1960s is of course mediated through a parasitical media industry. The excesses and successful commercial exploitation of many facets of those times has become what those times represent.

The dissonance of Pink Floyd, with whom in the early days (believe it or not) the improvising ensemble AMM shared concerts, evaporated as soon as the new markets became apparent. The emperor's new clothes were mass-produced in Carnaby Street. The new culture—as projected—was nothing more than the commercial exploitation of the group in society with the loosest change. There is little to suggest that subsequent shifts in presentation of popular culture are anything other than a new lick based on the same theme, as the story of the Sex Pistols probably confirms. Alienation has been successfully marketed. And now old punk rockers reminisce, presumably about the halcyon days when their heroes deigned to spit upon them. I have since lost count (and patience) with observing other examples. Indeed, now I think that even the ideas of alienation and dissonance themselves are no longer so necessary; clearly they were co-opted as marketing ploys for youth with money to spend. Perhaps the more violent exhortations of the black rappers were the last examples of this phenomenon. How quickly, we note, the movement was emasculated. Vicious outpourings very soon became lucrative investment portfolios.

Meanwhile, in small corners of the world, there are people who have enough confidence in their own powers of intellectual and moral discrimination to say no and that enough is enough. If we want to live in a world that values human endeavor and cherishes association and dialogue, then we have to start by examining our own motives and practices. Artists need to ensure that their musical practices are closely in tune with the avowed aesthetic imperative. And audiences too are not without their share of responsibility to demand veracity and transparency in place of cute sound bites from the artists with whom they share and celebrate their aesthetic preferences. It might be though—and I make no apologies for ending on a bleak note—that we are all too enmeshed in the capitalist trick of treating each other as commercially exploitable units to do justice to the ways in which improvised music invokes the ideals of collaborative dissonance.

NATHANIEL MACKEY

Paracritical Hinge

·⤳

When I received the invitation to speak at the colloquium on which this book is based, the theme "Collaborative Dissonances: Jazz, Discrepancy, and Cultural Theory" struck a responsive chord.[1] It seemed to be, or to propose to be, a colloquium after my own heart, a colloquium attentive to the role of improvisation in advancing collaborative/discrepant encounters and to the bearing of such encounters on the theorization of cultural agency and value. When I read, among the topics for consideration in the call for papers, of "the 'cognitive dissonance' that results when creative practitioners enter collaboration from different disciplinary and/or cultural locations," I said yes. When I read of "the extent to which the dissonances that result from collaborative practices might be seen to reduce the effects of hierarchies in the production and valuation of knowledge," I said yes. When I read of "the cultural work of *participatory discrepancies* (Charles Keil) . . . the implications of Keil's claim that 'music, to be personally involving and socially valuable, must be *out of time* and *out of tune*,'" I again said yes. When I read of "the emancipatory potential of 'discrepant engagement,' of 'practices that, in the interest of opening presumably closed orders of identity and signification, accent fissure, fracture, incongruity' (Nathaniel Mackey)," I again, of course, said yes, but the quotation from my book of essays *Discrepant Engagement* and the recourse to the coinage that gives the book its title made me fear my presence here might be redundant. I wasn't sure that simply reiterating my call for discrepant engagement was quite what was in order.

What I decided was to highlight the practice of mine out of which, more than any single other, the critical formulation I call discrepant engagement emerged. That practice is the writing of fiction, specifically that of a work called *From a Broken Bottle Traces of Perfume Still Emanate,* running through which are installments of a scribal-performative undertaking known as "The Creaking of the Word," a name borrowed from the Dogon of Mali that I see as related to—a parent or an ancestor to—discrepant engagement. In the introduction to *Discrepant Engagement* I put it this way: "Recalling the derivation of the word *discrepant* from a root meaning 'to rattle, creak,' I relate discrepant engagement to the name the Dogon of West Africa give their weaving block, the base on which the loom they weave upon sits. They call it the 'creaking of the word.' It is the noise upon which the word is based, the discrepant foundation of all coherence and articulation, of the purchase upon the world fabrication affords" (19). The writing of *From a Broken Bottle,* I emphasize, played a large part in what led me to this. I also suggest that the promise of collaborative dissonances the colloquium seeks (I assume) to advance as well as to examine might accrue to bearing that discrepant foundation in mind.

From a Broken Bottle grew out of my interest in the relationships between literature and the improvisatory music we call jazz, an interest reflected in *Discrepant Engagement*'s repeated recourse to jazz (and African-American music more generally) as an instructive model of artistic and cultural experimentation, a music whose lessons have not been lost on a number of the writers dealt with in the book nor on me in my role as writer-critic. One such lesson is a discontent with categories and the boundaries they enforce, with the impediment to social and aesthetic mobility such enforcement effects. Saxophonist Oliver Lake writes in the poem "Separation" on the jacket to his 1976 album *Ntu: Point from which Creation Begins*:

> first it's the salad
>   then the meat
>   then the vegetables. . . .
>   "WAIT"
> bring all my food at one time on the same plate!
> dixieland, be-bop, soul, rhythm & blues, cool school, swing, avant-garde, jazz, free jazz, rock, jazz-rock
>
> WHAT KINDA MUSIC U PLAY?
>
>   "GOOD KIND"
>
> Aretha franklin & Sun Ra is the same folks,
> Coltrane & the Dixie humming birds same folks
> Miles & muddy waters same. There is no . . . .
>   there is no . . . .
>
>   LABELS DIVIDE! SEPARATE
>   THE ORAL AND THE LITERARY
>
> One music—diff feelings & experience, but same. . . . the total
>
> sound—mass sound—hear all the players as one

Lake's insistence accents a history of boundary crossing that resonates throughout the music, a history that begins with the contributions made to the development of early New Orleans jazz by the closer association between the black middle class of the time—Creoles, *gens de couleur*, mulattoes—and working-class black people from whom they had held themselves apart. That history includes Charlie Parker's famous quotations from such disparate material as Woody Woodpecker cartoons and Bizet's *Carmen*, Yusef Lateef's recourse to non-Western instruments and traditions, Archie Shepp's inclusion of march music in his avant-garde classic "A Portrait of Robert Thompson (as a young man)," John Handy's collaborations with Ali Akbar Khan, Don Cherry's use of Balinese gamelan instruments on his *Eternal Rhythm* album, and so on.

Boundary crossing and its implied if not explicit critique of categorization deeply informed *Discrepant Engagement* and *From a Broken Bottle* both. I used a line from Bessie Smith's "Black Mountain Blues" as the title of the former's introduction, explaining: "I have . . . offered its fortuitous, figurative title, 'And All the Birds Sing Bass,' as a discrepant note meant to call attention to the problematics of rubric-making, a caveat meant to make the act of categorization creak. Such creaking is always present, even in the case of more customary groupings—groupings that appear unproblematic, proper, only because we agree not to hear it" (*Discrepant*, 12).

Improvisation, in its divergence from the given, frequently will not allow us not to hear noise, the creaking of categorization, the noise categorization suppresses, and the noise (not admitting doing so) it makes. The cacophonous element of the avant-garde jazz of the 1960s is an obvious example, a relativization of the very notion of noise that reflected critically upon the term's employment as an instrument of dismissal and derogation. Such relativization valorizes noise as the antidote to the derogation the term conventionally conveys, not unlike the manner in which Cuban poet Nicolás Guillén reclaims the Spanish term *algarabía* (noisy chatter) as what Vera Kutzinski calls a "master trope for cross-cultural exchange." *Algarabía*, Kutzinski points out, literally means "Arabic" and its etymological origins go back to the Moorish occupation of Spain and to associations with the oriental bazaars that came to be commonplace in medieval Spain (180–182). The equation of Arabic with "noisy chatter," of the bazaar's linguistic and cultural heterogeneity with "noisy chatter," reminds us that the notion of noise is often freighted with xenophobic predilections (some of Thelonious Monk's early detractors accused him of playing "Chinese music"), the very predilections cross-cultural dialogue and discrepant collaboration seek to overcome. Additionally, an attribution of otherness available to xenophobic recoil and cross-cultural espousal—dismissive predilection as well as discrepant embrace, noise, whether derogatorily engaged or affirmatively engaged—frequently functions as the sign and the sound of alterity.

The creaking of the word's boundary crossing, its critique of categorization, entails a critique and a complication of genre. *From a Broken Bottle*'s conversation with improvisatory music necessarily involved me in a practice of writing that, genre-wise, was multiform if not indeterminate. The work, as James Weldon Johnson said of the early ragtime songs, "jes' grew." What began as brief, prose-poetic, manifestolike letters of an ars poetica grew into longer excursions that, while for the most part maintaining the epistolary form, availed themselves of aspects of conventional as well as experimental narrative, essayistic analysis and reflection, diaristic and anecdotal elements, literary-critical techniques and a variety of influences ranging from mythology to anthropology to album liner notes. The work's multiformity, its improvisatory sampling or juggling of different discourses, genres, and forms, involved me in a practice of discrepant engagement spurred or inspired by characteristics of the music it sought, so to speak, to be in concert with. Art Lange and I, in the editors' note to our anthology *Moment's Notice: Jazz in Poetry and Prose,* discussed, among other things, "writings which blur the line between genres, bending genre in ways which are analogous to a musician bending notes" (ii).

From a Broken Bottle increasingly declared itself, early on, to be of that order. The music's origins among people policed by racial categorization suggest that it bends notes in an effort, as Ralph Ellison puts it, to hear and see around corners, outmaneuver the rigidities of a taxonomic grid. Think, in this regard, of writing that similarly bends genre while indicting racial taxonomy: such multiform, mixed-genre writing as W. E. B. Du Bois's *The Souls of Black Folk,* Jean Toomer's *Cane,* or Ishmael Reed's *Mumbo Jumbo,* and of the insistency with which it invokes African-American music.

The creaking of the word's critique of categorization also, of course, entails a critique and a complication of language, a critique and a complication of which those of genre are necessarily part and parcel, a critique and a complication of that which is nothing if not an instrument of categorization. The creaking of the word critiques and complicates the word, spurred in part by instrumental music's wordlessness, the apparent dispensability of words, and in part by the music's emulation of speech, its deployment of speechlike rhythms and inflections as if in possession of words or aspiring to be so. As Lange and I wrote:

It is particularly unsurprising that a music which so frequently and characteristically aspires to the condition of speech, reflecting critically, it seems, upon the limits of the sayable, should have provoked and proved of enormous interest to practitioners of the art of the word—writers. . . . In addition to offering tributes to and portraits of individual musicians, depictions of and meditations upon the social and cultural milieu in which the music exists, evocations of the music's import for specific audiences and so forth, writers have been moved to inspect, as artists witnessing other artists wrestling with the limits of their particular medium, the possibilities and resistances peculiar to writing. Mack Thomas once wrote, in liner notes, of Eric Dolphy confronting "the barrier that begins with what the horn will not do." Writers, tracking what John Clellon Holmes calls "the unnameable truth of music," have had to deal with a similar confrontation. Charles Lloyd, asked to comment on a piece of his music by a radio interviewer, answered, "Words don't go there." Writers influenced by jazz have been variously rising to the challenge of proving him wrong. (*Moment's Notice*, i–ii)

That challenge is also, I would add, a contagion, an infectious testing of terms and limits that wants not to hold itself apart, but rather wants to close, among other distances, conventional critical distance. It wants to be anthropologist and informant both, participant-observer.

So here, I'd like to try, in line with the colloquium's theme of collaboration, to get fiction to "sit in" with the kinds of critical and analytic discourse characteristic of colloquia, to pursue the possibility of fiction collaborating with those kinds of discourse. The fiction in question, *From a Broken Bottle*, perhaps enhances that possibility by being fiction that, as I've already stated, doesn't entirely reside within the genre of fiction. It's a type of fiction that wants to be a door or to support a door or to open a door permitting flow between disparate orders of articulation. It wants to be what I call a paracritical hinge, permitting flow between statement and meta-statement, analysis and expressivity, criticism and performance, music and literature, and so forth. It traffics in a mix—a discrepant, collaborative mix—of idioms, genres, registers, dispositions. ("Paracritical" is meant, of course, to echo and to be analogous to such terms as "paramedical" and "paralegal," its prefix indicating an auxiliary, accessory relationship to criticism, a near equation with or a close resemblance to criticism. *Webster's Ninth Collegiate Dictionary* defines a hinge as "a jointed or flexible device on which a door, lid, or other swinging part turns." I'd like to suggest a translative project or prospect in a quality so often attributed to the music: the quality known as swing—the verb, not the noun. "Hinge's" work as verb highlights contingency, haunted by tenuousness and risk, an intransitive creaking well worth bearing in mind. The coinage wants to suggest that improvisation, the pursuit of new expressivity, whether musical or literary, is an operation best characterized by the prefix "para-," an activity supplemental to more firmly established disciplines and dispositions, an activity that hinges on a near but divergent identity with given disciplines and dispositions. The given is just the beginning.) It's a work in which, while I'm not a musician, I write as a musician. Comprising letters written to an "Angel of Dust" by a composer/multi-instrumentalist who signs his letters "N.," the work began in the late seventies and consists, so far, of three volumes, *Bedouin Hornbook, Djbot Baghostus's Run,* and *Atet A.D.* I include here a selection of letters from the latter that bear on the colloquium's concerns (intermedia and interdisciplinary conversation, improvisation's utopic horizon, cultural theory's diagnostic desire—all shaded by a blue, dystopic truth), but let me first elaborate on the work's genesis.

The work began, no doubt, in the dreams I had during my late teens and early twenties of playing with some of the greats of the music. These were literal dreams in which I played alongside John Coltrane, Ornette Coleman, Thelonious Monk, and others. I repeatedly had these dreams. But that was fantasy, not yet fiction, albeit the letter that begins *Bedouin Hornbook,* the first volume in the series, grew out of a related dream I had one night in my early thirties, a dream in which, although I played alone, the presence of Eric Dolphy seemed implied by the fact that I played a bass clarinet, that of John Coltrane by the fact that the tune I intended to play was "Naima," that of Archie Shepp by the fact that what I actually played was "Cousin Mary" done the way he plays it on *Four for Trane.* The catalyst for the work, however, took place several months prior to this dream. I was living in Los Angeles at the time and had already written a couple of "Angel of Dust" letters as part of a serial poem called "Song of the Andoumboulou"; they were really short statements on poetics. What planted the idea of N. writing as a musician and prompted, eventually, the "Cousin Mary" letter I just mentioned (which is the letter that got the series going on a track of its own, apart from "Song of the Andoumboulou," the letter in which N. announces the formation of a band) was an odd concert I went to one night in 1977.

A concert series at the Century City Playhouse presented "outside" music on Sunday nights. I saw posters announcing a concert by a group called A Love Supreme, a name that piqued my interest, so I decided to go. What was odd about it was that I was the only person to show up. I got there to find that, besides the band, there were only three people there: the fellow I bought a ticket from at the ticket window, the fellow who took my ticket at the door, and me. Even so, I went in and sat down and before too long the lights lowered and the band came onstage and played—for me. It was a strange experience, as though I was there on a special assignment or by special appointment, an appointment I didn't know I had, an odd appointment of an almost mystic sort. The band played and I sat, an audience of one, listening, wondering why in a city of more than two million people and a greater metropolitan area of several more million, I was the only person to show up to hear a band called A Love Supreme.[2] I felt as though I'd been summoned, as though I was part of the band, had been inducted into the band. It started me wondering, at least, what being in such a band might be like. That one of the members of the band read poetry from a notebook at one point during the concert not only seemed intent on saying the music invited poetic support, literary assistance or accompaniment, but seemed as well to be directed at me. This experience led eventually to *From a Broken Bottle* and the fictional band in which N. plays, known first as the Deconstructive Woodwind Chorus, next as the East Bay Dread Ensemble, next as the Mystic Horn Society, most recently as the Molimo m'Atet.

I include extracts from *Atet A.D.*, a work that in a sense responded to what I felt was a call. Before doing so, I should note that the band began as a quintet, consisting of reedmen Lambert and Penguin, violinist/percussionist/bassist Aunt Nancy and keyboardist/vocalist Djamilaa in addition to reedman/trumpeter N., and that the second volume, *Djbot Baghostus's Run,* is largely taken up with the decision to add a drummer to the group and the decision that the drummer would be a woman. A search ensues, during which the three men in the band are beset by the same dream, a collective dream that seems to announce that the drummer will be named Djeannine, and the two women in the band are likewise beset by a shared dream, one that appears to announce that the drummer will be named Penny. When they find the right drummer her name turns out to be Drennette. Penguin, in the course of her first few weeks in the band, takes a liking to her and eventually makes an aborted romantic overture, out of embarrassment over which he goes into hiding. *Djbot Baghostus's Run* ends with no one in the band knowing where Penguin is. In *Atet A.D.* he returns, comes out of seclusion. Penguin's primary horn is the oboe, whose "high wood" root *(haut bois)* is construed, given his quixotic bent, as "high would." He turns out to have been in retreat in a place called Wouldly Ridge. The first letter is written a few months after his return from Wouldly Ridge, during a gig in Seattle.

•

_____ 5.VI.82

Dear Angel of Dust,

The other shoe finally dropped. We're in Seattle playing a three-night stint at a club called Soulstice. Last night, the first night of the gig, new repercussions on a number of fronts came to light. Foremost among them is that the wouldly subsidence in which Penguin and

Drennette's embryonic romance had gotten hung up seems to've given way—exacting a ledge, an atomistic ledge, from the lapse it rescinded. You've no doubt noticed that since Penguin's return from Wouldly Ridge it's been as though his embryonic courtship of Drennette had never occurred. He's not only not pursued it further, he'll neither speak nor hear talk of it. Whenever I've brought it up he's acted like he had no idea what I was talking about, staring at me with a blank, uncomprehending look on his face, as though English were a foreign language, as if I spoke some unheard-of tongue. Aunt Nancy, Lambert and Djamilaa say it's been the same with them. Drennette likewise has acted like nothing ever happened. She and Penguin have been nothing but normal in their dealings with one another.

It's hard to say what it was, why it was wouldly subsidence took this occasion to exact wouldly ledge. My guess is that the air of anticlimactic futurity pervading this town had something to do with it, the datedness of what was once thought of as "things to come." I'm referring, of course, to the Space Needle. That the future has no place in which to arrive but the present, that its arrival is thus oxymoronic, is the sort of reflection one can't help entertaining in the shadow of such a monument as that—a monument, when it was built, to the future, a future it prematurely memorialized, prematurely entombed. Today it's more properly a monument to the past, a reminder of the times in which it was built, tomb to the elapsed expectancy it all turns out to've been. I remember my aunt and uncle driving up for the World's Fair twenty years ago—hopelessly long ago it seems now.

But by no means to be ignored is the reinforcement given elapsed or outmoded future by us happening to hear "Telstar," the early sixties hit by the Tornadoes, on the jukebox in a diner we had lunch in yesterday. The tinny, strained, "futuristic" sound of it said it all, spoke to a sense of lost occasion elapsed future began infusing us with the moment we laid eyes on that Needle. I thought of every wish which had seemed to miss the mark in being fulfilled, though I corrected myself at once, admitting the case to be one of an "it" which could only be projected, never arrived at. Anticlimactic "it," I reminded myself, allotted virtual space, an ironic investiture missed opportunity couldn't help but inhabit. Disappointment, the needling sense of a missed appointment, couldn't help but be there. This we knew before "Telstar" came on. We knew it all the more once it did.

The weather played a part as well. It hasn't rained outright since we've been here but it's been overcast and drizzling, a thin mist coming down pretty much all the time. That mist, it seemed, went with us into the club last night. It adopted a low profile for the occasion, close to the floor like a carpet so intimate with our feet we'd have sworn we dragged it in. What had been of the air was now oddly underfoot. In a way it was like the world had turned upside down, the way the mist, instead of falling from the sky, came up from the floor, ever so lightly addressing the soles of our feet. The difference this would make in our music was evident at once. No sooner had we taken the stage than the low-lying mist was an atomistic ledge we stood on which made our feet feel as though they'd fallen asleep—not entirely numb but (you know the feeling I'm sure) put upon by pins, subject to a sort of pointillist embrace. Point had become a hydra, its pinpoint tactility multiply-pinned. We couldn't help knowing it was "missed" on which we stood (missed mark, missed opportunity, missed appointment), no less real, no less an actual mist even so. What it came down to was an odd, pointillist plank-walk, notwithstanding we walked in place if it can be said we walked at all. The ledge onto which we stepped calibrated a tenuous compound or compaction of low-lying spray with spreading phantasmality (phantom feet and/or the phantom ledge on which "missed" insisted we stood).

We stood on lost, oddly elevated ground, elegiac ledge. This was no mere materialization of loss even so, no glib legitimation of lack, elegy (lapsed eligibility) notwithstanding. We stood upon or perhaps had already stepped across an eccentric threshold, thrust, or so it seemed, into a post-expectant future, the anti-expectant gist of which warned us that "post-" might well turn out to've been premature. What expectant baggage did we weigh ourselves down with even now? What ingenuous out did we disingenuously harbor hopes of having secured? The needling mist which addressed our feet multiply apprised us of an inoculative boon we sought even as we disavowed all promise, all prepossessing "post-." Post-expectant futurity stood accused of harboring hope. Nonetheless we stood by it, one and all, atomistic ledge an exemplary rug allotting endless rapport, unimpeachable aplomb.

Post-expectant futurity stood its ground. It was this of which our feet grew multiply-possessed before we hit a single note. Though its multiply-pinned massage ostensibly comforted the soles of our feet, the needling mist became a goad of sorts. The quantum-qualitative lift it afforded gave an operatic lilt and leverage to the post-expectant ground on which we stood. Ground and goad rolled into one, it coaxed an abrupt, acquiescent grunt from each of our throats, an abrupt, expectorant exhalation whose fishbone urgency furthered itself once we began to play. Part seismic splint, part psychic implant exacting an auto-inscriptive lilt, it put the phrase "inasmuch as what we want is real" on the tips of our tongues, amending our attack and our intonation in ways we'd have not thought possible had it not been so palpably so. What this meant was that "want" walked arm in arm with "real" across bumptious ground. We knew it all at once, it seemed, an instantaneous jolt as though the needling mist were an electric mace.

We were several bars into our opening number before fishbone urgency let go of our throats. The ripped, expectorant permission it apprised us of abruptly left us on our own, ushered albeit we were that much farther along the pointillist plank on which we walked. Djamilaa, Penguin, Aunt Nancy, Lambert and I stood in staggered array, stumbling in place while Drennette sat as though caught in a suspended spill. She looked as if she'd fallen backwards, as if her fall had been broken by the stool on which she sat. She too, it appeared, stumbled in place.

Our collective stumble suspended us in time it seemed, notwithstanding the atomistic ledge had a decidedly glide aspect and sense of advance running thru it. This was its odd, contradictory confirmation of post-expectant premises, the odd, post-expectant way it had of rolling promise and prohibition into one. The piece we opened with was Lambert's "Prometheus." The expectorant, post-expectant permission the occasion laced it with put one in mind of Charles Davis's "Half and Half," the rash, rhythmelodic treadmill effect Elvin Jones and Jimmy Garrison's band exact on the *Illumination* album. Still, it went way beyond that in the anticlimactic refractivity, the visionary hiccup we fostered and factored in. It was this which tallied with while taking elsewhere the iterative carpet-ride on which we ran in place. Iterant weave and itinerant rug ran as one. Atomistic ledge came on as though steeped in deep-seated conveyance, *run* so deeply woven into wouldly arrest it was all we could do to keep our feet on the floor. The conveyor-belt bridge and the bedouin breach it addressed introduced a deep, irredentist quiver to the needling mist, an ever so agitant feather's touch tickling our feet.

What struck us most was how quickly we'd moved onto mixed-metaphorical ground. Where was it we stood if stand could be said to be what we did? Where was it we stumbled if stumble said it better? So many different sensations complicated one another: mixed-metaphorical conveyor-belt/carpet-ride, mixed-metaphorical mist/pointillist plank, mixed-metaphorical feather/pinpoint massage, mixed-metaphorical splint/low-lying spray . . .

The other shoe I spoke of to begin with fully partook of this dispensation, a mixed-metaphoricality which brought off being a hammer, a broken pedal and a shoe at the same time. It seemed a Cinderella fit or effect wherein hammer, broken pedal and shoe were now showcase items, encased in or even constituted of glass. Hammer had been placed under glass by the Penny dream. Broken pedal had been placed under glass by Drennette's concussive spill, shoe (slipper, to be more exact) by the presumption of fairy-tale artifice, fairy-tale fit. These three were one, a see-thru insistence upon breakage, atomization, the meaning, however chimeric, of atomistic ledge. The other shoe, the newly shod alterity onto which or into which or invested with which we now stepped, came down with a resounding report it took us a while to realize was us—a new sound which, unbeknown to ourselves, we'd come up with (or which, "unbeknown" being the case, had come up with us).

Other shoe mixed-metaphorically segued into other shore, the floor sliding away like sand when a wave retreats. Suppositious wave, I turned around and saw, was intimated, ever so exactingly meted out, by the drumroll Drennette now sustained, a roll which required all but acrobatic skill, so at odds with the suspended spill it appeared she was in. Suppositious retreat, the spasmic thumps thrown in on bass drum, tended to be consistent with suspended spill, suppositious wave rolling back upon itself so as to pull what ground one thought there was back with it. Thus it was that Drennette played out the mixed-emotional endowment her final bicycle ride with Rick had left her with, the promise and the putting aside of promise her critique of "antique emotion" so insisted on. Promise and resistance to promise rolled pregnancy and post-expectancy into one, the bass drum pedal sounding the post-expectant "floor" the broken pedal had introduced her to.

Drennette's anti-foundational patter recalled the fact—recalled while commenting upon the fact—that it was Lambert's debut of "Prometheus" which had launched us on our quest for a drummer. Whatever hope he might have had of bedrock solidity had long since been given an antithetic spin, made to comply with and to confirm or anticipate (or so it seemed in retrospect) the sense of anticlimactic futurity we've been under since getting here. The rhythmic anchor Lambert announced he wanted had turned out to be exactly that, turned out to be a *rhythmic* anchor. Rhythmicity, Drennette insisted, contends with bedrock foundation, the sense of an unequivocal floor anchorage implies.

That the atomistic ledge on which we stood entailed wouldly subsidence having been rescinded became clear the more one listened to Penguin. The piece's "love slave" thematics, the subtextual strain having to do with Epimetheus's "hots" (as Penguin put it) for Pandora, was the thread he pulled out and pursued. It took us a while to realize it, but this was largely what was new about the way we sounded. Never before had we so equated Promethean fire with Epimethean "hots." While at first it was difficult to pick out Penguin's advancement of that equation from the avalanche of sound we put forth, his needling insinuation that "Pandora" was an apter title than "Prometheus" gradually came to the fore. Gradually he blew louder, needling insinuation becoming more blunt, less innuendo than hammerlike assertion. The more assertive he became the more Drennette encouraged the equation he advanced, quickening the pace with rabbitlike rolls as though they were wheels for him to ride. Penguin, in turn, grew bolder, swifter, quickening the pace to play Epimetheus to what he took to be Drennette's Pandora (or took, it turned out, to be Djeannine's Pandora, took to be Drennette's Djeannine).

It was a blistering pace which Penguin handled without the slightest loss of articulacy. With each note he did as he wished. He clearly had something to say, something which all but leapt out of him, so Lambert and I backed away from our mikes, letting him solo first. Drennette's rabbitlike rolls continued to feed the Epimethean heat with which he blew, heat which was all the more astonishing considering the finesse with which he played, the nuanced ability to speak which, notwithstanding the frenzy it appeared he was in, he maintained. His oboe spoke. It not only spoke but did so with outrageous articulacy, so exquisitely so a balloon emerged from its bell. Lambert and I looked at one another. We traded looks with Aunt Nancy, Djamilaa and Drennette as well. It was hard to believe one's eyes but there it was, a comic-strip balloon enclosed in which one read the words Penguin's oboe spoke: *Drennette dreamt I lived on Djeannine Street. I walked from one end to the other everyday, back and forth all day. Having heard flamenco singers early on, I wanted in on duende.* Penguin took a breath and with that the balloon disappeared.

Another balloon took the first balloon's place when Penguin blew again, a balloon in which one read: *A long-toed woman, no respecter of lines, Drennette obliged me by dreaming I walked up and down Djeannine Street, stepping, just as she or Djeannine would, into literality, notwithstanding the littered sidewalk and the unkempt yards.* He took another breath and when he blew again the third balloon read: *Sprung by her long toe, Drennette (part gazelle, part tumbleweed) leapt away as I reached out to embrace Djeannine. Among the weeds in a vacant lot a half-block away, she ran a few steps and turned a cartwheel. All I wanted was to bury my head between her legs, press my nose to the reinforced crotch of her white cotton panties.* He took another breath and when he blew again the fourth balloon read: *Something I saw, thought I saw, some intangible something led me on. Something I saw not so much as in some other way sensed, an audiotactile aroma, the synaesthetic perfume Djeannine wore which was known as Whiff of What Was, a scent like none I'd otherwise have known.*

While this fourth balloon hung in the air several people in the audience stood up and came forward to get a better look, not stopping until they stood in front of Penguin, squinting to make out the last few words. I had already noticed that *a* and *scent* were written somewhat close together, so I took it they were trying to determine whether what was written was *a scent* or *ascent*. They returned to their seats when Penguin took another breath and the fourth balloon disappeared. In its place, when he blew again, was a fifth which read: *The salty-sweet, sweating remembrance of Drennette's long-toed advance animated the street with an astringent allure, a ruttish funk I fell into which was more than mere mood. Drennette's advance made the ground below the sidewalk swell, cracking the concrete to release an atomistic attar, dilating my nostrils that much more.*

This went on for some time, a new balloon appearing each time Penguin blew after taking a breath. There was a sixth, a seventh, an eighth balloon and more. How many there were in all I can't say. I lost count. In any case, I understood them as a ploy by way of which Penguin sought to gain relief, comic relief, from the erotic-elegiac affliction of which the oboe so articulately spoke. By way of the balloons he made light of and sought to get leverage on the pregnant, post-expectant ground Drennette so adamantly espoused or appeared to espouse. The leverage he sought gave all the more torque to the dream-projection he projected onto her, the "street" he later admitted to be based on the housing projects he lived in as a child. There was a regal touch to it as well, each balloon both cartoon and cartouche, this latter aspect very much in keeping with the stately tone the oboe wove into its erotic-elegiac address. Wounded kingship came thru loud and clear, an amalgam of majesty and misery, salty-sweet. Love lost was as easily loss loved it intimated, a blasé spin the blue funk it announced increasingly came to be amended by. Such grim jest or indifferent gesture increasingly infiltrated courtly ordeal, cap and bells inaugurating an alternate crown, King Pen's cartoon/cartouche. Laughing to keep from crying some would call it, but in fact it went much deeper than that.

Penguin wrapped up his solo with a round of circular breathing which introduced an unexpected wrinkle to what had by then become a pattern: blow/balloon emerge, take a breath/balloon disappear, blow/balloon emerge, take a breath/balloon disappear, blow/balloon emerge, take a breath/balloon disappear . . . The breath he now took was continuous with the one he expelled and the balloon, instead of disappearing, hung in the air above the bell of his horn growing larger the longer he blew. The steady enlargement, however, was only partly what was new about the new wrinkle he introduced. Two-dimensional up to this point, the balloon acquired a third dimension as it grew, becoming a much more literal balloon. What was also new was that there were now no words written inside it. By making it more a literal than a comic-strip balloon Penguin put aside the comic lever he'd made use of up to this point. He was now nothing if not emotionally forthright, the empty balloon all but outright insisting, the way music so often does, that when it came to the crux of the matter, the erotic-elegiac fix one was in, words were beside the point.

The admission that words fail us would normally not have been so unexpected, normally come as no surprise. Music, as I've said, does it all the time. But in this case it seemed a new and unusual twist, so persuasively had the comic-strip balloons insisted it could all be put into words. It's a measure of Penguin's genius that he could endow something so close to cliché with new life. The balloon not only swelled like a pregnant belly but, thanks to the mixed-metaphorical ground onto which we'd moved, it appeared to be a sobriety-test balloon as well. Penguin blew into it intent on proving himself sober even as he extolled the intoxicant virtues of Djeannine's audiotactile perfume. Whiff of What Was notwithstanding, the vacant balloon seemed intended to acquit him of drunken charges, the admission of words' inadequacy a sobering descent from the auto-inscriptive high to which the earlier balloons had lent themselves. Even so, this descent could easily be said to have been further flight, so deciduously winged was the winded ferocity with which Penguin blew, what falling off there was reaching beyond itself with a whistling falsetto—stratospheric screech and a crow's caw rolled into one.

So it was that sobering descent mounted higher and higher. The balloon grew bigger and bigger, a weather balloon pitting post-expectant wind against pregnant air. Penguin put a punning spin on it, wondering out loud whether it might also be the other way around, pregnant wind encountering post-expectant air. With us crescendoing behind him all the while (Lambert and I had now joined back in), he eventually answered his own question when the balloon swelled and swelled and finally burst with a loud bang, pricked by a post-expectant needle, the needling mist which was now not only on the floor. It was with this that he brought his solo to an end, whereupon the audience went crazy, loudly applauding the release he'd had them hungering for, the release he now at last let them have.

Penguin timed it exactly right. The audience couldn't have stood another beat, much less another bar, couldn't have held its collective breath a moment longer. We too, the rest of us in the band, breathed easier now, inwardly applauded the release we too had begun to be impatient for. All of us, that is, except Drennette, who quickly apprised us, with the solo she now insisted upon taking, of the fact that the ground on which we stood was, if anyone's, hers, that impatience had no place where post-expectancy ruled.

Post-expectant futurity brought one abreast of the ground, Drennette announced, annulled, in doing so, any notion of ground as not annexed by an alternate ground. This was the pregnancy, the unimpatient expectancy, she explained, Penguin, albeit put upon and perplexed, had been granted rare speech, rare fluency by. Djeannine Street, alternate ground par excellence, inflected each run of heavy bass drum thumps with ventriloquial spectres, Drennette's recourse to the sock cymbal insistent that she and Djeannine, long spoken for, had spooked (her word was "inspirited") wouldly ledge, atomistic ledge.

It was a wild, outrageous boast, but she had the chops, it turned out, to back it up. The drumset had become a wind instrument by the time she finished her solo. A gust of wind arose from each roll and with each roll the storm she brewed grew more ferocious. We felt it at our backs when we joined in again, pressing as it pestered us toward some occult articulation only Drennette, not looking ahead, saw deep enough to have inklings of. Not so much needling as pounding us now, the needling mist partook of that wind—mystical hammer rolled into one with atomistic pulse. Wouldly ledge, needling mist and Penguin's auto-inscriptive high would all, post-expectancy notwithstanding, turn out to have only been a beginning.

Suffice it to say we made some of the most ontic, unheard-of music we've ever made. Say what one will about unimpatient expectancy, I can't wait to play again tonight.

As ever,
N.

•

_____ 10.VI.82

Dear Angel of Dust,

We're back in L.A. Got back from Seattle a few days ago. The Soulstice gig, all in all, went well, though the last two nights were a little bit disappointing. It's not that we didn't play well or that the music wasn't well received. We played with characteristic fluency and fire both nights and both nights the crowd, noticeably larger than the first night, got into it, urged us on. Even so, the post-expectant ground we stepped onto the first night was nowhere to be found on nights two and three. The pointillist tread, the wouldly "one step beyond" with which we'd been blessed, pointedly avoided us the next two nights. No atomistic plank-walk lay before us, no needling mist massaged our feet. It was ground we couldn't get back to no matter how hard we tried, ground we couldn't get back to perhaps because of how hard we tried.

The most conspicuous difference was that no balloons emerged from Penguin's horn. It was this which left the audience a bit disappointed, notwithstanding the applause and the hip exhortations they repeatedly gave the music. Word of the balloons had quickly gotten around town after night number one and it was this which in large part accounted for the larger turnout the next two nights. Clearly, people came hoping to see the balloons emerge again. Though we've never thought of ourselves as crowd-pleasers, never been overly concerned with approbation, we'd have been happy to oblige them had it been up to us. But that the balloons didn't emerge amounted to an anti-expectant lesson which, while not exactly the same, was consistent with the post-expectant premises onto which we had stepped and again hoped to step. The air of anticipation the audience brought with them was so thick that before our final number the second night, the balloons not having reappeared and, clearly, to us in the band, not likely to, Aunt Nancy stepped forward and spoke into the mike. "Remember what Eric said," she admonished them. "'When you hear music, after it's over, it's gone in the air. You can never capture it again.'"

It was a lesson we ourselves have had to ponder. Post-expectant ground was clearly evaporative ground, but it was hard not to be disappointed we couldn't find it again. It had been a lapse to expect otherwise we admitted, but that's been easier to say than to accept. Lambert, in any event, said it best as we were discussing this at rehearsal the other night. "It's about digesting what you can't swallow," he said at one point. That, I think, says it all.

As ever,
N.

•

_____ 17.VII.82

Dear Angel of Dust,

The balloons are words taken out of our mouths, an eruptive critique of predication's rickety spin rewound as endowment. They subsist, if not on excision, on exhaust, abstract-extrapolative strenuousness, tenuity, technical-ecstatic duress. They advance the exponential potency of dubbed excision—plexed, parallactic articulacy, vexed elevation, vatic vacuity, giddy stilt. They speak of overblown hope, loss's learned aspiration, the eventuality of seen-said formula, filled-in equation, vocative imprint, prophylactic bluff. They raise hopes while striking an otherwise cautionary note, warnings having to do with empty authority, habitable indent, housed as well as unhoused vacuity, fecund recess.

The balloons are love's exponential debris, "high would's" atmospheric dispatch. Hyperbolic aubade (love's post-expectant farewell), they arise from the depth we invest in ordeal, chivalric trauma—depth charge and buoy rolled into one. They advance an exchange adumbrating the advent of optic utterance, seen-said exogamous mix of which the coupling of tryst and trial would bear the inaugural brunt. Like Djeannine's logarithmic flute, they obey, in the most graphic imaginable fashion, ocular deficit's oracular ricochet, seen-said remit.

The balloons are thrown-away baggage, oddly sonic survival, sound and sight rolled into one. They map even as they mourn post-appropriative precincts, chthonic or subaquatic residua come to the surface caroling world collapse. They dredge vestiges of premature post-expectancy (overblown arrival, overblown goodbye), seen-said belief's wooed risk of inflation, synaesthetic excess, erotic-elegiac behest. The balloons augur—or, put more modestly, acknowledge—the ascendancy of videotic premises (autoerotic tube, autoerotic test pattern), automatic stigmata bruited as though of the air itself.

Such, at least, was the insistence I heard coming out of Dolphy's horn. "The Madrig Speaks, the Panther Walks" was the cut. I sat down to listen to it only minutes ago and found myself writing what you've just read. Never had Eric's alto sounded so precocious and multiply-tongued, never so filled with foreboding yet buoyant all the same, walk (panther) and talk (madrig) never so disarmingly entwined.

Listening, more deeply than ever, bone-deep, I knew the balloons were evanescent essence, fleet seen-said equivalence, flighty identity, sigil, sigh. This was the horn's bone-deep indenture, wedge and decipherment rolled into one. This could only, I knew, be the very thing whose name I'd long known albeit not yet found its fit, the very thing which, long before I knew it as I now know it, I knew by name—the name of a new piece I'd write if I could.

What I wouldn't give, that is, to compose a piece I could rightly call "Dolphic Oracle." It would indeed ally song (madrig) with speech, as well as with catlike muscularity and sinew—but also with catlike, post-expectant tread, oxymoronically catlike, post-expectant prowl, post-expectant pounce, an aroused, heretofore unheard of, hopefully seen-said panther-python mix . . .

Yours,

N.

•

_____ 26.VII.82

Dear Angel of Dust,

Could be. Yes, possibly so. The balloons, for all their outward display and apparent address of popular wish (literal access, legible truth) may well, as you say, signal an inward turn. As I've said before, the last thing we want is to be a lonely hearts band, but that may in fact be what, under Penguin and Drennette's influence, we're becoming or may even have already become. Are the balloons' apparent roots in problematic romance, their repeated erotic-elegiac lament, a default on collectivist possibility, a forfeiture of possible bondings greater than two, an obsessed, compensatory return (would-be return) to pre-post-romantic ground?

I don't know. I'm not so sure, for one thing, it can all be laid at Penguin and Drennette's feet. To whatever extent the balloons embody a retreat from more properly collectivist wishes, an introspective move masquerading as wished-for romance, costume-courtly complaint, the larger social, political moment we find ourselves in would have to have had a hand in it, no? I don't much subscribe to the increasing talk, in these dreary times, of "empowerment," "subversion," "resistance" and so forth. I once quoted Bachelard's line, "Thirst proves the existence of water," to a friend, who answered, "No, *water* proves the existence of water." I find myself more and more thinking that way. I find myself—and this goes for everyone else in the band, I think—increasingly unable (albeit not totally unable) to invest in notions of dialectical inevitability, to read the absence of what's manifestly not there as the sign of its eventual presence. To whatever extent hyperbolic aubade appears to have eclipsed collective "could," the balloons' going on about love's inflated goodbye should alert us to the Reaganomic roots of that eclipse.

I drove down to Santa Ana yesterday. An old friend and I went to the store at one point and on our way we passed a neighborhood park which has more and more become a camp for the homeless. Park Avenue people now call it, irony their one defense. Anyway, as we drove past, my friend, looking out the window, sneered, "Look at them, a bunch of dialects." He meant "derelicts." So much for malaprop speech as oppositional speech, I couldn't help thinking, so much for oppositional *any*thing.

That's how I sometimes feel, how we all sometimes feel. Not all the time, but often enough to nourish what you call an inward turn. I don't altogether buy your inward/outward split, but if you're saying the balloons' erotic-elegiac lament mourns the loss of larger bonding as well, I agree.

Yours,

N.

PS: What the two occasions the balloons have emerged on have in common is the ur-foundational/anti-foundational sense and/or apprehension we had—atomistic ledge/needling mist/pointillist plank-walk in Seattle, subterranean strum/"collapsed" contour/tar pit premises at Keystone Korner. Each entailed an excavation of substrate particles or precincts, erstwhile plummet or plunge. Are the balloons mud we resurface with, mud we situate ourselves upon, heuristic precipitate, axiomatic muck, unprepossessing mire? I ask because of my acquaintance with earth-diver myths—myths in which an animal plunges into primeval waters and brings up a mouthful or a beakful of mud, mud from which the world is then made. In some the animal is a tortoise, in others a boar, in others a duck, in others a loon. Could the balloons, I'm asking, be a pseudo-Bahamian play on the latter, namesake play with B'-*Ba* overtones, the spirit or the embodied soul of namesake play going by the name B'Loon?

I say yes. B'Loon, not unrelated to Djbouche, is our murky, mired cry, a call for world reparation. It muddies our mouths with the way the world is even if only to insist it be otherwise. Such insistence notwithstanding, it implicates us (myth advancing mud, mouth proving mud) in the pit we'd have it extricate us from.

Notes

1. The fictional extracts included in this piece originally appeared in Nathaniel Mackey's *Atet A.D.* City Lights, 2001. Copyright © 2001 by Nathaniel Mackey. Used by permission of the author and City Lights Books. "Paracritical Hinge" appears in Nathaniel Mackey's *Paracritical Hinge: Essays, Talks, Notes, Interviews.* Madison: University of Wisconsin Press, 2004.

2. I later learned that the band was led by a fellow named Shamsu-'d-Din. I was told this by saxophonist Ghasem Batamuntu, who sat in with the band that night. I don't know what's become of Shamsu-'d-Din, but Ghasem later moved to the San Francisco Bay Area, where he started a band called the Nova Ghost Sect*Tet, and then on to Amsterdam, where he currently lives. They recently released a CD, *Life on Uranus,* on a Dutch label, A-Records.

Works Cited

Kutzinski, Vera M. *Against the American Grain: Myth and History in William Carlos Williams, Jay Wright, and Nicolás Guillén.* Baltimore: Johns Hopkins University Press, 1987.

Lake, Oliver. *Ntu: Point from which Creation Begins* (Arista/Freedom Records AL 1024).

Lange, Art, and Nathaniel Mackey, eds. *Moment's Notice: Jazz in Poetry and Prose.* Minneapolis: Coffee House Press, 1993.

Mackey, Nathaniel. *Discrepant Engagement: Dissonance, Cross-Culturality, and Experimental Writing.* New York: Cambridge University Press, 1993.

JOHN CORBETT

Out of Nowhere
Meditations on Deleuzian Music, Anti-Cadential Strategies, and Endpoints in Improvisation

·⁓

How to end?

To produce, somehow, a work without an introduction.[1] And more centrally, one that lacks a conclusion. Creating a piece that points outward in both directions, to something happening before it begins and something lurking after it is finished. What resolve it takes to create work without resolution. To disengage linear, hierarchical links, breaking apart the inevitable sequence of good form: introduction, exposition, development, recapitulation, conclusion. With what task is the end-moment conventionally charged? (What similar or different task is involved in the process of ending an improvisation?) What must it accomplish? In music, so often, the end entails the configuration of an amnesiac: absorbing the inconclusive openness of the work's interior regions into a cadence that makes the listener forget—not simply by reassuring (the return to tonal center, refreshed and safe at home), but by distracting (creating explosive fireworks, elaborate series of resolving chords, each one more solid and authoritative than the last, to draw the listener's attention from the text's exposed core). A finish line that seems definitive, final, the end, ba-boom.[2]

The conventional cadence could be seen as the resolving moment, the release-point of tension-and-release, the "fort" of "fort-da." But it is also a trick, a technique used to erase or evaporate any disquietude created in musical exploration by overpowering what came before it. The most compelling (compulsive) devices in Western music—dynamic extremes (fade to silence or huge crescendo into punch-chord endpoint), harmonic resolution (triumph of tonal center through "perfect cadence" [a dominant chord followed by the final tonic chord, or any "imperfect" cadences that alter or invert such chords], the "plagal" or so-called Amen cadence, wearing its religious authority on its sleeve) and rhythm cadences (ritardando, slowing down to a gradual stop, or accelerando, speeding up to a sudden stop)—are typically deployed in the attempt to corner the listener's attention and leave the volatility of the work's internal section in its conclusion's dust.

To make music consisting only of middle. Intermezzo. Interminable work. Work that always remains to be made. Nothing radical, only radial. No ends, mere means. No succession of segments. To subvert the formal and underlying ideological function of the cadence. No striation, but a smooth, mobile instrument of creative thought. This is an important part of the aesthetic (and micropolitical) agenda for some, but not all, improvising musicians.

Perhaps it is fitting that the new electronic and electroacoustic music underground—what Markus Müller has called "discourse-techno"—has found French philosopher Gilles Deleuze a suitable philosophical icon. Creation of soundworks based on fuzzy logics, nonlinearity, collisions of inorganic and organic energies in cybernetic machines of desire, small communities of autodidacts operating without institutional affiliation—such concepts jibe well with the Deleuzian (and Deleuzo-Guattarian) political-poetics of rhizomatics, minoritarianism, deterritorialism, and nomadology.[3] A return in certain youth subcultures to an ethic of experimentation—psychedelic drugs, experimental and nonconventional art forms, alternative lifestyles—reminiscent of the late sixties, when Deleuze's ideas first gained an audience, is in part responsible for this grassroots "rediscovery."[4]

The premium Deleuze and Guattari placed on creativity and invention—"There is no such thing as the social production of reality on the one hand, and a desiring-production that is mere fantasy on the other"(28)—as opposed to negative dialectics or pragmatism, has clearly made their work appealing to young experimentalists. For instance, a small German record label specializing in discourse-techno and vanguard digital music has named itself Mille Plateaux in homage to Deleuze and Guattari's book of the same title (suffice to say, no other record company has lifted its name from the work of Theodor Adorno or Jürgen Habermas). When Deleuze committed suicide in 1996, Mille Plateaux's producers assembled a collection, *In Memoriam Gilles Deleuze,* which includes a fragment, drawn from a very scratchy record, of Deleuze speaking, as well as a selection of sound works by twenty-six different individuals and groups.

The most interesting of the double disc's tracks is "You Are * Here 0.9 B," by Oval: as on Oval's other records, tiny fragments of skipping digitalia and computer noise are regurgitated and given form, presence, even texture (against the notion of complete dematerialization in virtuality). Jim O'Rourke's "As In" begins with a practically silent field recording of rustling motion, which quickly shifts into an Alvin Lucier–like resonance document. But if the homespun spirit of the collection is heartening, much of the actual work turns out to be a disappointment: a hodgepodge of neopsychedelia created on new technology that contains but a few bright moments. Even Ralf Wehowsky, who has produced some of the most challenging records of electroacoustic music in the last half-decade, contributes a droll collage, "Happy Deterritorializations," with collaborator Achim Wollscheid. Like the other recent Deleuze dedication, *Folds and Rhizomes* (and its remix companion, *Double Articulation*), on the Belgian label Sub Rosa, *In Memoriam Gilles Deleuze* leaves one to search for a more suitable remembrance.

> Nomad space is smooth, or open-ended.
> — Brian Massumi

In what way is the ending cadence usually structured? It starts with a cue, a signal that the end is near (hence there are so-called false cadences, endings that seem imminent, but never materialize); the signal allows a listener to expect a final moment, to immerse him-/herself in the exquisite wholeness of closure. To know what is coming. To prepare to forget. The awkward composer telegraphs a conclusion the way a bad boxer telegraphs a punch.

Conventional cadences are not simply the temporary termination of a flow, but complex mechanisms designed to play on memory and to shut the music machine *down,* not just shut it off. A sublation (such as a cadence) must subsume what has come before into a higher form, transforming it into something on another level, something more lofty and worthy of consideration. The cadence completes the musical piece, sealing it off and crushing down what appeared in its middle, reducing the vulnerable, inconclusive interiority to disposable filler. In Deleuzian terms, the cadence is territorial. Using highly codified emotional signifiers embedded in functional harmony and Western conventions of rhythm, it asserts a stratification, a hierarchical placement of elements that organizes how one should feel in response to a particular musical event. Earlier, tension is produced, chaos is introduced, but with the cadence it is resolved, warded off. The conclusion is effective. The acoustical field has been reterritorialized.[5] Following Deleuze-Guattari's frightened little kid singing to comfort himself in "1837: Of The Refrain," (*A Thousand Plateaus,* 311) the cadence is the *final* refrain. The return home, shield against chaos, it is this final refrain that succeeds in comforting.

To resist the final refrain. The breast-mouth assemblage is all flows and breaks. Likewise, the shit-machine continues endlessly, pumping out and chopping off pieces of feces like a frozen custard maker or Deleuze-Guattari's ham-slicing machine. "The anus and the flow of shit it cuts off, for instance; the mouth that cuts off not only the flow of milk but also the flow of air and sound" (*Anti-Oedipus*, 36).[6] To suck, you have to stop singing; to sing, you've got to stop sucking. All flows and breaks. How to produce music with that constancy, flow, and inability to forget?

Improvisers are faced with somewhat different formal, social, and technical problems to solve than composers (and performers of composed music), and such differences are heightened around the beginnings and ends of pieces. I do not wish to draw a hard line between improvisers and composers, or even between improvising and composing. One can of course viably subscribe to a view that plots these two approaches to creating music on a continuum; hence, improvising pianist (and composer) Misha Mengelberg's preferred term for improvising: Instant Composition. What I mean to suggest emphatically, however, is that there are very different practical and ideological problems that present themselves to musicians who are performing in real time and composers who are working at their temporal leisure. I think these differences are especially evident at the close (and, for that matter, at the beginning) of an improvisation. In the absence of a script, two issues arise in real-time music performance: How will a piece of improvised music begin and how will an end be decided upon? Like composition, the practice of improvisation has developed its own conventions of closure. Among the most common: the *fade-out*, where musicians diminish their volume in tandem until silent; *long-tones*, held together until the piece seems over; *simultaneous punch-sound terminus*, in which players play high-energy staccato end notes; *cadenza*, in which one musician is left to make a final solo statement and chooses to end a piece.

Bassist Torsten Müller, when asked why his pieces were generally so short, responded: "Because I like to stop." This doesn't mean he doesn't like to play, it means he likes the process of ending, the Deleuzian open question of how to conclude. This attitude is arguably what separates the idea of "jamming" from a more refined attitude toward improvising. The jam-band keeps playing past possible endpoints, assuming that some interesting music will inevitably occur but also allowing that it is necessary to slog through boring, prosaic material to get to that interesting morsel. But if one recognizes the cluster of rich philosophical conundrums that gathers around the terminus of an improvisation—How will we find a way jointly to end this piece? Will we end together or apart? Will we end in succession or stacked? *By what criteria* will we decide the piece is over?—and in turn, practically, one experiences the close, careful kind of listening that usually occurs when people are paying attention to the question of how and when and why to end a real-time piece of music, then the attractiveness of the end, "liking to stop," means something more than just an aversion to jamming. And it's not about culminating moments, it's about flows and breaks. It's modest. It can deal with short form, and doesn't require the big build-up. The piece is started and soon its creators find an end for it. Such work points at a concentration, a condensation, a rarefaction in which every single little sound is suddenly loaded with meaning and all gestures might be the last. There's no endless jamming, but there's also no sublation, no enormous build-up of tensile energies and cathartic release. No romantic consummation. Such music merely calls for attention and response, listening and playing.

Ending is the single place in an improvisation where something consensual must occur. Even if improvisers have been playing antagonistically for an entire piece, they must *in the end* decide to agree that the piece is over. Or at least decide to stop playing.[7] The nature of that consensus is not uniform; indeed, it might reflect some of that foregone antagonism. It sometimes happens that one person decides the piece "should" end. Saxophonist Peter Brötzmann has been known to end a piece that he feels has gone long enough (or too long) by offering a visual cue, leaping in the air or stomping his foot. (This is usually an attempt to impose communication on a situation that has had some kind of communication difficulties, in Brötzmann's view.) I once overheard saxophonist Evan Parker and bassist Barry Guy after a duet concert discussing the fact that at a certain moment in a piece they had started "hunting for an ending," which suggests on the other hand that the music itself might be considered a third member and that it might offer an endpoint rather than needing one foisted on it. This example emphasizes the close listening part of the process, the idea that improvising posits a performer who is not only interested in controlling the situation but also one responsive to and in dialogue with what it has to offer.

Preparing for a performance with the DKV Trio in 1997, Dutch reed player Peter van Bergen requested that his three collaborators (Hamid Drake, Kent Kessler, and Ken Vandermark) try to improvise "illogical forms." The result was that places in the music that might otherwise have served as transitions from one section to another—freely improvised sectionality being one of DKV Trio's signatures—instead were treated as endpoints. The internal, intuitive "logic" that steers a piece of improvised music was interrupted. Because the endings were therefore ambiguous and anti-cadential, the music had an intriguingly unbalanced, inorganic feeling.

Not all improvisers are particularly concerned with beginnings and endings. At a concert in Vancouver, the British group AMM began by telling the audience the approximate length of the performance—an hour, nonstop—and inviting them to come and go as they pleased. This had the effect of letting the audience members, many of whom were unfamiliar with improvised music, off the hook; a smart move, it probably kept them there longer than they would otherwise have stayed and assured them that they were not expected to remain indefinitely. Such a sustained improvisation seems to deny the significance of beginning and ending, if only by shifting the balance in favor of the middle; indeed, the sheer length of time taken by the musicians forces the listener to confront the immediacy of the resulting sounds rather than anticipating the more formal aspects of the work that cluster around its entryways and exits—the orifices of a piece. (Eliminating a concentration on the music's orifices meant in this case that the audience was less fixated on the building's orifices—entryways and exits.) Without markers foreshadowing an impending finish, the music just might *go on forever*. By announcing a finite duration, AMM allayed the fear that *it would never end*.[8] There's a relaxation inherent in being offered an ending and an anxiety attached to the hint of interminability. Between these poles stretches a profound fear of inconclusiveness, taut like a laundry line.

In his solo work, and in much of his ensemble composition and improvisation, German pianist Georg Gräwe confronts the problem of ending in a manner different from that of many of his colleagues. Rather than improvise great build-ups to climaxes or slip out gradually through slow fades, Gräwe tends to play continuously, emphasizing flow—his quite astounding facility allows him to maintain rolling momentum and establish simultaneous multidirectional rhythms—and avoiding simple repetitive patterns and sequences.

But it is his endings that are the most startling. They descend suddenly on a piece, yanking it away like a rug pulled from under your feet or a doorknob that comes off in your hand. Endings that come out of nowhere. Such endpoints are not dramatic, more evanescent; each improvisation seems as if it could continue infinitely; when it is over, a piece has not drawn to a conclusion but has simply stopped. Gräwe does this without making pieces that wander or drift aimlessly; his inconclusiveness isn't wishy-washy. And he does it without making the endpoints weird, "illogical," or misshapen. One could make endings that are simply the suspension of obvious (but unstated) endpoints; Gräwe makes plausible stops, graceful stops, elegant stops, but stops that happen most unexpectedly.

Music that lives in the middle. The seven varied solo piano pieces on *Gedächnisspuren* cessate, they don't culminate. Work that commits suicide, ending before its "natural" life is over. On "1,"for instance, the pianist ends midphrase, just as a rapidly unfurling line seems to move in a different direction.[9] That motion implies something beyond the end. Without cueing an impending finish, the stopping doesn't give a listener enough time to forget the complex music that came before. "5" ends with a single muted cluster following a dense rhythmic tangle; it is more decisive than the truncated phrase of "1," but so sudden and unexpected that it leaves the piece just as open and inconclusive: "For me, the music is going on all the time. If I play something, I have this image that it's like opening the window: you get a glimpse of what's going on all the time. My music is going on in my head all the time. When I write or play I open a window for a short time. But the stream is going on" (Gräwe). The Gräwe-Vandermark Large Band addresses both ends of the spectrum when it comes to options for ending. Co-leader Ken Vandermark composes pieces with an extremely strong sense of closure, often using powerful musical punctuation marks (sharp unison stops, dramatic recapitulation of "head" material) and traditional cadential harmonic motion from jazz and rock genres. Gräwe, on the other hand, composes open-ended pieces that avoid repetition and move from section to section without strong endpoints or obvious transition-markers, except for changes in arrangement (that is, a section change segued by a piano solo or clarinet/bass/drum trio). Indeed, at the group's first performance,[10] several audience members, ambivalent about whether to clap between sections of Gräwe's 53-cell piece "Snapshots 1–53" finally broke the silence and applauded, imposing their own sort of external cadence for that particular section. Even on Gräwe's quartet record, *Melodie und Rhythmus,* which explores tonality and metrical rhythms more directly than any of his previous ventures, conventional strategies of closure are suspended.[11]

Territorialization and deterritorialization aren't exclusive or binary opposites (Deleuze and Guattari were far too savvy Zen-o-philes for such reductivism); each contains the other, yin-yang. The point is not to dismiss or outlaw cadential strategies, which can of course be immensely satisfying and can, in many circumstances, be used in creative and unorthodox ways: "How could movements of deterritorialization and processes of reterritorialization not be relative, always connected, caught up in one another?" (*Thousand,* 10). But other strategies exist, too, such as Gräwe's endless intermezzo.

Eight minutes and forty-five seconds into the second track of a record of improvised duets between Gräwe and wind player Anthony Braxton, *duo*

(Amsterdam) 1991, the music stops completely; both musicians (and the attentive audience) recognize that the improvisation is, for some reason, not finished. Everyone sits quietly, continuing the music. It turns out that it is only halfway through. The inverse of an inconclusive ending—a conclusive non-ending.

Notes

1. A version of this essay, originally titled "Out of Nowhere: Deleuze, Gräwe, Cadence," appeared in *Discourse* 20, no. 3 (Fall 1998): 219–225.

2. Susan McClary's exposition of the ideological dimensions of the gendered terms "masculine" and "feminine" as applied to musical endings is pertinent here. The conclusion I am caricaturing is a "masculine" ending (3–17; 53–79).

3. For a glossary of these and other Deleuze-related concepts, see Brian Massumi, *A User's Guide.*

4. No other figures more precisely deserve the term "grassroots" than Deleuze and Guattari, given that grass—even configured as a manicured lawn—is a rhizome.

5. The concept of territorialization has to do with modes of organization and hierarchies (how one thing is logically and rationally related to other things as a way of avoiding what Deleuze and Guattari call "signifying rupture," which is something like a breakdown in those hierarchies and modes of organization). It also involves the question of attribution (how one decides on and ascribes authorship, asserts ownership of ideas and confirms his or her territory). The latter has obvious implications for the application of Deleuze and Guattari to the study of improvisation, in which the question of authorship is, in theory, always in the aggregate, joint, and therefore difficult to assign with any singularity. See John Corbett, "Ex Uno Plura" 74–87.

6. Cellist Fred Lonberg-Holm tells a story of playing a tape piece of his when he was a student, the subject of which was endings; it used various standard ending strategies, including a standard "perfect" V-I cadence. Composer Charles Dodge, who was in the audience, insisted on taking Lonberg-Holm aside to discuss endings, expounding a theory that the way composers end pieces has a lot to do with how they were toilet-trained.

7. In rare cases, one musician might pack up and leave before the others are finished playing, but at some point the ensemble is all no longer playing and a de facto consensus is met.

8. There is a history of very extended improvisations, including the thirteen-hour Circadian Rhythm concert at the London Musicians' Collective in 1978 (designed to be longer, but ended early). The longest concert I've attended was a four-hour-straight event at the Guelph Jazz Festival in 1998, with a rotating cast that included Michael Snow, Joe McPhee, David Prentice, and various others. It was a fascinating experience for me, and played all sorts of wicked tricks on my sense of time. I suspect that this was exacerbated by the fact that the impending duration of the piece was announced beforehand. Had it not been, surely time would have been distorted in somewhat different ways.

9. All the pieces on *Gedächnisspuren* are titled according to the track number only.

10. August 7, 1997, the Bop Shop, Chicago.

11. It should be noted that there are clearly musics in many other cultural contexts that deploy noncadential strategies and work by some version of endless intermezzo. I think, for instance, of the idea of intensities in Gamelan musics (potentially very Deleuzian, plateau-like, it seems to me) or the way that Inuit throat-game

singing always ends with the song breaking apart and eventually with laughter and the song starting again.

Works Cited

Corbett, John. "Ex Uno Plura: Milford Graves, Evan Parker, and the Schizoanalysis of Musical Performance." In his *Extended Play: Sounding Off from John Cage to Dr. Funkenstein*, 74–87. Durham: Duke University Press, 1994.

Deleuze, Gilles, and Félix Guattari. *Anti-Oedipus: Capitalism and Schizophrenia*. Translated by Robert Hurley, Mark Seem, and Helen R. Lane. Preface by Michel Foucault. Minneapolis: University of Minnesota Press, 1983.

——. *A Thousand Plateaus: Capitalism and Schizophrenia*. Translation and Foreword by Brian Massumi. Minneapolis: University of Minnesota Press, 1987.

Massumi, Brian. "Translator's Pleasures of Philosophy." In *A Thousand Plateaus: Capitalism and Schizophrenia*, by Gilles Deleuze and Félix Guattari, ix–xv. Translation and Foreword by Brian Massumi. Minneapolis: University of Minnesota Press, 1987.

——. *A User's Guide to Capitalism and Schizophrenia: Deviations from Deleuze and Guattari*. Cambridge, Mass.: MIT Press, 1992.

McClary, Susan. *Feminine Endings: Music, Gender, and Sexuality*. Minneapolis: University of Minnesota Press, 1991.

DANIEL FISCHLIN, AJAY HEBLE, AND BENJAMIN LEFEBVRE

Toward Further Dialogue
A Bibliography on Improvisation

⸜⸝

This bibliography attempts to bring together the diverse discourses and resources in which improvisation figures. In preparing it we have searched a number of different databases, both musical and not, and we have sought to include references that will allow people with a range of interests in improvisatory discourses generally to pursue further study. To that end we have included references to different ethnic and national improvisatory practices in music, dance, pedagogy, the literary arts, and so forth. It is clear that some of the most exciting areas of future research in improvisatory practices lie in intercultural and transdisciplinary studies, and we have included materials that may facilitate some of these future studies. Additionally, in the accompanying webography we have sought to make available a wide range of online resources that may be of benefit to different constituencies (performers, audiophiles, academics, arts presenters) as these constituencies go about the business of shaping the various communities of practice and discourse in which improvisation enacts a crucial mode of being. In no way do we intend this resource to be comprehensive or definitive, though to the best of our knowledge this is as extensive a list as yet exists. Finally, we thank the many people who took the trouble to extend this list as we were mapping it: Chris Blackford, Mike Chamberlain, Michael Dessen, George Lewis, Francisco Martinelli, Eddie Prévost, and Julie Dawn Smith. It came as no small surprise when we began work on this resource that there is a comparatively small corpus of work that addresses the relations between improvisation and cultural theory, and we look forward to the future contributions our readers and contributors will make to improvisatory discourse generally.

I. Book and Periodical Sources

Aaron, Tossi. "Music Improvisation and Related Arts." *Music Educators Journal* 66, no. 5 (1980): 78–83.

Abdul, Raoul. *Blacks in Classical Music*. New York: Dodd, Mead, 1977.

Abrams, Muhal Richard, and John Shenoy Jackson. "Association for the Advancement of Creative Musicians." *Black World* 23, no. 1 (1973): 72–74.

Abramson, Robert M. "Dalcroze-Based Improvisation." *Music Educators Journal* 66, no. 5 (1980): 62–68.

Addison, Richard. "A New Look at Musical Improvisation in Education." *British Journal of Music Education* 5, no. 3 (1988): 255–267.

Adorno, Theodor W. *Introduction to the Sociology of Music*. Translated by E. B. Ashton. New York: Continuum, 1989.

———. "Perennial Fashion—Jazz." In *Critical Theory and Society: A Reader*, edited by Stephen Eric Bronner and Douglas MacKay Kellner, 199–209. New York: Routledge, 1989.

Ake, David. *Jazz Cultures*. Berkeley and Los Angeles: University of California Press, 2002.

Allen, Ray. "Shouting in Church: Narrative and Vocal Improvisation in African-American Gospel Quartet Performance." *Journal of American Folklore* 104 (1991): 295–317.

Allerton, Martin. "Of Foot Concertos and Crazy Accordions." *Rubberneck* 13 (1993): 24ff.

Alperson, Philip. "On Musical Improvisation." *Journal of Aesthetics and Art Criticism* 43, no. 1 (1984): 17–29.

Amsden, Robert L. "A Correlational Study: Awareness of Self, Awareness of Environment, Mental Imagery, Communicative Competency, and Theatrical Improvisation." Ph.D. diss., Bowling Green State University, 1983.

Anderson, Doug. "Improvisation for Vocal Jazz Ensembles." *Music Educators Journal* 66, no. 5 (1980): 89–94.

Astaxova, A. M. "Improvisation in Russian Folklore." In *The Study of Russian Folklore*, edited by Felix J. Oinas and Stephen Soudakoff, 91–110. The Hague: Mouton, 1975.

Attali, Jacques. *Noise: The Political Economy of Music*. Translated by Brian Massumi. Minneapolis: University of Minnesota Press, 1985.

Bailey, Derek. *Improvisation: Its Nature and Practice in Music*. Ashbourne, Eng.: Moorland, 1980.

Baker, David N. "Improvisation: A Tool for Music Learning." *Music Educators Journal* 66, no. 5 (1980): 42–51.

———. "Jazz Improvisation—The Weak Link." *Instrumentalist* 26, no. 4 (1971): 21–24.

Baker, Houston A. *Blues, Ideology and Afro-American Literature*. Chicago: University of Chicago Press, 1984.

———. *Modernism and the Harlem Renaissance*. Chicago: University of Chicago Press, 1987.

Balliger, Robin. "Sounds of Resistance." In *Sounding Off!: Music as Subversion/Resistance/Revolution*, edited by Ron Sakolsky and Fred Wei-han Ho, 13–26. Brooklyn, N.Y.: Autonomedia, 1995.

Banham, Martin. "Freetown Workshop: Improvization [*sic*] Leads to Local Documentary." *Theatre Quarterly* (London) 3, no. 10 (1973): 38–43.

Baraka, Imamu Amiri. [LeRoi Jones]. *Black Music*. New York: William Morrow, 1968.

———. *Blues People: Negro Music in White America*. Westport, Conn.: Greenwood, 1980.

Barasch, Frances K. "The Bayeux Painting and Shakespearean Improvisation." *Shakespeare Bulletin* 11, no. 3 (1993): 33–36.

Barber, Karin. "Quotation in the Constitution of Yorùbá Oral Texts." *Research in African Literatures* 30, no. 2 (1999): 17–41.

Barkin, Elaine. "Forum: Improvisation." *Perspectives of New Music* 23, no. 2 (1985): 63.

Barrett, Robert Hawkes. "The Jazz Improvisational Style of Clarinetist Buddy De-Franco." Ph.D. Diss., University of Oklahoma, 1996.

Barricelli, Jean-Pierre. *Melopoiesis: Approaches to the Study of Literature and Music.* New York: New York University Press, 1988.

Barry, Malcolm. "Improvisation: The State of the Art." *British Journal of Music Education* 2, no. 2 (1985): 171–175.

Bastien, David T., and Todd J. Hostager. "Jazz as a Process of Organizational Innovation." *Communication Research* 15, no. 5 (1988): 582–602.

Bauer, Scott Matthew. "Structural Targets in Modern Jazz Improvisation: An Analytical Perspective." Ph.D. Diss., University of California, San Diego, 1994.

Bearden, Kenneth. "Monkeying Around: Welty's 'Powerhouse,' Blues-Jazz, and the Signifying Connection." *Southern Literary Journal* 31, no. 2 (1999): 65–79.

Beauchamp, Lincoln T., Jr., ed. *Art Ensemble of Chicago: Great Black Music—Ancient to the Future.* Chicago: Art Ensemble of Chicago, 1998.

Bechtel, Ben. "Improvisation in Early Music." *Music Educators Journal* 66, no. 5 (1980): 109–112.

Beeman, William O. "Why Do They Laugh?: An Interactional Approach to Humor in Traditional Iranian Improvisatory Theater." *Journal of American Folklore* 94, no. 374 (1981): 506–526.

Béhague, Gerard. "Improvisation in Latin American Musics." *Music Educators Journal* 66, no. 5 (1980): 118–125.

Belgrad, Daniel. *The Culture of Spontaneity: Improvisation and the Arts in Postwar America.* Chicago: University of Chicago Press, 1998.

Bell, Clive. "Personal Remarks on Improvisation." *Rubberneck* 15 (1993): 34ff.

Belt, Lynda, and Rebecca Stockley. *Acting Through Improv: Improv Through Theatresports: A Curriculum to Improve Acting Skills.* Rev. ed. Seattle: Thespis, 1995.

Benston, Kimberly W. *Performing Blackness: Enactments of African-American Modernism.* New York: Routledge, 2000.

Benward, Bruce, and Joan Wildman. *Jazz Improvisation: In Theory and Practice.* Dubuque, Iowa: Brown, 1984.

Berendt, Joachim Ernst. *Ein Fenster aus Jazz: Essays, Portraits, Reflexionen.* Frankfurt am Main: S. Fischer, 1977.

Bergen, Elizabeth F. von. "The Consort Concept: Education Through Improvisation." *Instrumentalist* 31, no. 10 (1997): 49–51.

Berliner, Paul. *Thinking in Jazz: The Infinite Art of Improvisation.* Chicago: University of Chicago Press, 1994.

Bernard, Catherine. "D. M. Thomas et le 'roman d'improvisation': Entre voix et écriture." *Recherches anglaises et nord-américaines* 21 (1988): 13–20.

Biddlecombe, G. C. "The Role of Improvisation in Performance." *Strad* 80, no. 954 (1969): 255ff.

Blackford, Chris. "Free, but not That Free." *Rubberneck* 8 (1991): 4–8.

Bley, Paul, with David Lee. *Stopping Time: Paul Bley and the Transformation of Jazz.* Montreal: Vehicule, 1999.

Blom, Lynne Anne, and L. Tarin Chaplin. *The Moment of Movement: Dance Improvisation.* Pittsburgh: University of Pittsburgh Press, 1988.

Born, Georgina, and David Hesmondhalgh, eds. *Western Music and its Others: Difference, Representation and Appropriation in Music.* Berkeley and Los Angeles: University of California Press, 2000.

Bouley, Allan. *From Freedom to Formula: The Evolution of the Eucharistic Prayer from Oral Improvisation to Written Texts.* Washington, D.C.: Catholic University of America Press, 1981.

Boulez, Pierre. *Orientations.* Cambridge, Mass.: Harvard University Press, 1986.

Bradshaw, Merrill. "Improvisation and Comprehensive Musicianship." *Music Educators Journal* 66, no. 5 (1988): 113–115.

Brathwaite, Kamau. *Roots*. Ann Arbor: University of Michigan Press, 1993.

Braxton, Anthony. *Tri-Axium Writings*. 3 vols. Dartmouth: Synthesis/Frog Peak, 1985.

Bremer, J. M. Review of *Improvisation, Typology, Culture, and "The New Orthodoxy": How "Oral" is Homer?* by D. G. Miller. *Journal of Hellenic Studies* 105 (1985): 177–178.

Broecking, Christian. *Der Marsalis-Faktor: Gespräche über afroamerikanische Kultur in der neunziger Jahre*. Waakirchen-Schaftlach, Switz.: Oreos, 1995.

Brothers, Thomas. "Solo and Cycle in African-American Jazz." *Musical Quarterly* 78, no. 3 (1994): 479–509.

Brown, Lee B. "'Feeling My Way': Jazz Improvisation and Its Vicissitudes—A Plea for Imperfection." *Journal of Aesthetics and Art Criticism* 58, no. 2 (2000): 113–123.

———. "Musical Works, Improvisation, and the Principle of Continuity." *Journal of Aesthetics and Art Criticism* 54, no. 4 (1996): 353–369.

Brown, Marion. *Recollections: Essays, Drawings, Miscellanea*. Frankfurt: Jurgen A. Schmitt , 1984.

Budds, Michael J. "The Art Ensemble of Chicago in Context." *Lenox Avenue* 3 (1997): 59–72.

Bulow, Harry T. "Impressions After an Improvisation." *Perspectives of New Music* 20 (1981–1982): 651.

Burnard, Pamela. "Examining Experiential Differences Between Improvisation and Composition in Children's Music-Making." *British Journal of Music Education* 17, no. 3 (2000): 277–345.

Burnard, Paul. "Bodily Intention in Children's Improvisation and Composition." *Psychology of Music* 27 (1999): 159–174.

Butcher, John. "Singular Pleasures: The Art of the Solo Improvisor." *Rubberneck* 27 (1998): 25–27.

Buzelin, Jean, and Françoise Buzelin. *Willem Breuker*. Paris: Editions du Limon, 1992.

Cage, John. *Silence*. Cambridge, Mass.: MIT Press, 1966.

Cantrick, Robert. "Does 'Musical Improvisation' Refer?" *Journal of Aesthetics and Art Criticism* 44, no. 2 (1985): 192–193.

Carles, Philippe, and Jean-Louis Comolli. *Free Jazz/Black Power*. 1971. Paris: Gallimard, 2000.

Carruth, Hayden. "The Opposing Concepts of Spontaneity and Expediency in Improvisation." *Virginia Quarterly Review* 61 (1985): 249–251.

Carter, Curtis L. "Improvisation in Dance." *Journal of Aesthetics and Art Criticism* 58, no. 2 (2000): 181–190.

Cartwright, Julienne. *Here-and-Now Music Therapy: Experimental Music Improvisation with Dementia Sufferers*. Bristol, Pa.: Kingsley, 1995.

Carvalho, John. "Improvisations, on Nietzsche, on Jazz." In *Nietzsche, Philosophy and the Arts*, edited by Salim Kemal, Ivan Gaskell, and Daniel W. Conway, 187–211. Cambridge: Cambridge University Press, 1998.

Catanzaro, Mary. "Song and Improvisation in *Lessness*." *Samuel Beckett Today/Aujourd'hui* 2 (1993): 213–218.

Chartrand, Pierre. "Improvisation et dance folklorique." *Canadian Folk Music Journal* 15, no. 1 (1987): 35–37.

Chevigny, Paul. *Gigs: Jazz and the Cabaret Laws in New York City*. New York: Routledge, 1991.

Chod'zko, Alexander. *Specimens of the popular poetry of Persia, as found in the ad-*

ventures and improvisations of Kurroglou, the bandit-minstrel of northern Persia and in the songs of the people inhabiting the shores of the Caspian Sea, orally collected and translated, with philological and historical notes. New York: Franklin, 1971.

Cochrane, Richard. "Playing By the Rules: A Pragmatic Characterization of Musical Performances." *Journal of Aesthetics and Art Criticism* 58, no. 2 (2000): 135–142.

Colli, Giuseppe. "Openness, Density, Mystery and Wonder . . . The Strange Case of Biota." *Rubberneck* 20 (1995): 4ff.

Comnes, Gregory. "The Law of the Excluded Muddle: The Ethics of Improvisation in William Gaddis's *A Frolic of His Own.*" *Critique: Studies in Contemporary Fiction* 39, no. 4 (1998): 353–366.

Corbett, John. "Ephemera Underscored: Writing About Free Improvisation." In Gabbard, *Jazz Among the Discourse*, 217–240.

———. *Extended Play: Sounding Off from John Cage to Dr. Funkenstein.* Durham: Duke University Press, 1994.

Couldry, Nick "Freedom and reason." *Rubberneck* 13 (1993): 40ff.

———. "Turning the Musical Table: Improvisation in Britain, 1965–1990." *Rubberneck* 19 (1995): 4–38.

Craig, Susan. "Improvisation Symposium, Eastern Michigan University." *Diapason* 90, no. 6 (1999): 7.

Crispell, Marilyn. "Elements of Improvisation." In Zorn, *Arcana*, 190–192.

Cruz, Jon. *Culture on the Margins: The Black Diaspora and the Rise of American Cultural Interpretation.* Princeton: Princeton University Press, 1999.

Dahlhaus, Carl. "Was heißt improvisation?" *Neue Zeitschrift für Musik* 133 (1972): 9–23.

Dalcroze, E. Jaques. "L'improvisation musicale." *Revue musicale* (May 1933): 344–358.

Danielou, Alain. "The Psychology of Improvisation in the Music of North India." *World of Music* 17, no. 4 (1975): 16ff.

Davies, Hugh. "My Invented Instruments and Improvisation." *Rubberneck* 22 (1996): 36ff.

Davis, Francis. *Bebop and Nothingness: Jazz and Pop at the End of the Century.* New York: Schirmer, 1996.

Day, Steve. *Two Full Ears: Listening to Improvised Music.* Chelmsford: Soundworld, 1998.

Day, William. "Knowing as Instancing: Jazz Improvisation and Moral Perfectionism." *Journal of Aesthetics and Art Criticism* 58, no. 2 (2000): 99–111.

Dean, Roger T. *New Structures in Jazz and Improvised Music Since 1960.* Philadelphia: Open University Press, 1992.

Dean-Lewis, Tim. "How Weird Can Things Get? (Maps for Pantonal Improvisation)." *Annual Review of Jazz Studies* 8 (1997): 203–226.

Deliège, Célestin. "Indétermination et improvisation." *International Review of the Aesthetics and Sociology of Music* (December 1971): 155–191.

Desmarais, Lorraine. "L'improvisation et la composition." *Compositeur canadian/ The Canadian Composer* 1, no. 2 (1990): 10–11.

———. "Jazz improvisation." *Compositeur canadien/The Canadian Composer* 1, no. 2 (1990): 20–21.

De Stefano, Reno. "Wes Montgomery's Improvisational Style, 1959–1963: The Riverside Years." Ph.D. diss., University of Montreal, 1996.

DeVeaux, Scott. *The Birth of Bebop: A Social and Musical History.* Berkeley and Los Angeles: University of California Press, 1997.

———. "Constructing the Jazz Tradition: Jazz Historiography." *Black American Literature Forum* 25, no. 3 (1991): 525–560.

———. *Jazz: Who's Listening?* National Endowment for the Arts (U.S.) Research Division Report 31. Carson, Calif.: Seven Locks, 1995.

Diamond, Lisa, and Lynn Lefkoff. "Common Goals at Play: Improvisation and Negotiation." *Theater* 23, no. 2 (1992): 21–24.

Díaz-Pimienta, Alexis. *Teoría de la improvisación: primeras páginas para el estudio del repentismo.* Havana: Ediciones Unión. 2001.

Dickstein, Morris. "Ralph Ellison, Race, and American Culture." *Raritan* 18, no. 4 (1999): 30–50.

Dobbins, Bill. "Improvisation: An Essential Element of Musical Proficiency." *Music Educators Journal* 66, no. 5 (1980): 36–41.

Donington, Robert, and George J. Buelow. "Figured Bass as Improvisation." *Acta musicologica* 40, no. 1 (1968): 178–179.

Duchartre, Pierre-Louis. *The Italian Comedy: The Improvisation, Scenarios, Lives, Attributes, Portraits and Masks of the Illustrious Characters of the Commedia Dell'arte.* Translated by Randolph T. Weaver. New York: Dover, 1966.

Durant, Alan. "Improvisation in the Political Economy of Music." In *Music and the Politics of Culture,* edited by Christopher Norris, 252–282. New York: St. Martin's, 1989.

Durrant, Phil. "Reasons for Now." *Rubberneck* 26 (1997): 34ff.

Dutton, Paul. "Twenty Years of Freedom: Jazz & Free Improvisation at the Music Gallery in Toronto." *Coda* 274 (1997): 2–5.

Du Vignal, Philippe. "Improvisation et création au Théâtre Laboratoire vicinal de Bruxelles." *La Rivista Dalmatica* 30, nos. 1–2 (1977): 211–219.

Eastley, Max. "My Development of Improvisation Through Sound Sculptures (extracts from a book in progress)." *Rubberneck* 23 (1996): 26ff.

Eckard, Paula Gallant. "The Interplay of Music, Language, and Narrative in Toni Morrison's *Jazz.*" *CLA Journal* 38 (1994): 11–19.

Eldredge, Sears A. *Mask Improvisation for Actor Training and Performance: The Compelling Image.* Evanston: Northwestern University Press, 1996.

Eloy, Jean-Claude. "Improvisation: Refuge, Utopia or Necessity?" *World of Music* 12, no. 3 (1970): 6–21.

Eshun, Kodwo. *More Brilliant than the Sun: Adventures in Sonic Fiction.* London: Quartet, 1998.

Fabre, Michel, and John A. Williams. *A Street Guide to African-Americans in Paris.* Paris: Cercle D'Etudes afro-américaines, 1996.

Fähndrich, Walter, ed. *Improvisation: 10 Beiträge.* Winterthur, Switz.: Amadeus, 1992.

———. *Improvisation II: 12 Beiträge.* Winterthur, Switz.: Amadeus, 1995.

———. *Improvisation III: 13 Beiträge.* Winterthur, Switz.: Amadeus, 1998.

Fell, Simon H. "Report on the Composition of Improvised Music No. 1." *Rubberneck* 15 (1993): 28ff.

———. "Report on the Composition of Improvised Music No. 2." *Rubberneck* 17 (1994): 30ff.

———. "Report On the Composition of Improvised Music No. 3." *Rubberneck* 24 (1997): 30ff.

———. "Report On the Composition Of Improvised Music No. 4." *Rubberneck* 28 (1998): 22ff.

Figgins, Margo A. "Mirrors, Sculptures, Machines and Masks: Theater Improvisation Games." In *Teaching Shakespeare into the Twenty-First Century,* edited by Ronald E. Salomone and James E. Davis, 65–77. Athens: Ohio University Press, 1997.

Finch, Douglas. "Improvisation and Innovation." *New Notes* (February 1998): 1.

——. "On the Process of Musical Improvisation." *Canadian Federation of Music Teachers' Association's Newsletter* (Winter 1987): 14–16.

Finkelman, Jonathan. "Charlie Parker and the Role of Formulas in Jazz Improvisation." *Jazzforschung/Jazz Research* 29 (1997): 208–209.

Floyd, Samuel A., Jr. *The Power of Black Music: Interpreting its History from Africa to the United States.* New York: Oxford University Press, 1995.

Franko, Mark. "Montaigne's Dance: A Customary Improvisation." *RLA: Romance Languages Annual* 2 (1990): 100–104.

Fraser, Wilmot A. "Jazzology: A Study of the Tradition in which Jazz Musicians Learn to Improvise." Ph.D. diss., University of Pennsylvania, 1983.

Frost, Anthony, and Ralph Yarrow. *Improvisation in Drama.* New York: St. Martin's, 1990.

Fry, C. "Computer Improvisation." *Computer Music Journal* 4, no. 3 (1980): 48–58.

Gabbard, Krin. *Jammin' at the Margins: Jazz and the American Cinema.* Chicago: University of Chicago Press, 1996.

——, ed. *Jazz Among the Discourses.* Durham: Duke University Press, 1995.

——, ed. *Representing Jazz.* Durham: Duke University Press, 1995.

——. "Writing the Other History." Introduction to Gabbard, *Representing Jazz,* 1–8.

Gagne, Cole. *Soundpieces 2: Interviews with American Composers.* Metuchen, N.J.: Scarecrow, 1993.

Gallegos, Aaron McCarroll. "Spiritual Improvisation: John Coltrane's Quest for Freedom." *Sojourners* (July–August 1999): 54ff.

Gardner, Iva. "Improvisation: The Lost Art." *American Music Teacher* 18 (1969): 24.

Gennari, John. "Jazz Criticism: Its Development and Ideologies." *Black American Literature Forum* 25, no. 3 (1991): 449–523.

Gerstin, Julian. "Interaction and Improvisation Between Dancers and Drummers in Martinican Bèlè." *Black Music Research Journal* 18, nos. 1–2 (1998): 121–165.

Gilman, Owen W., Jr. "Vietnam, Chaos, and the Dark Art of Improvisation." In *Inventing Vietnam: The War in Film and Television,* edited by Michael Anderegg, 231–250. Philadelphia: Temple University Press, 1991.

Gilroy, Paul. "'To Be Real': The Dissident Forms of Black Expressive Culture." In *Let's Get It On: The Politics of Black Performance,* edited by Catherine Ugwu, 12–33. Seattle: Bay, 1995.

Gioia, Ted. "Jazz: The Aesthetics of Imperfection." *Hudson Review* 39, no. 4 (1987): 585–600.

Goldberg, Harold. "How Can They Study Jazz Improvisation?" *Music Journal* (April 1959): 122.

Goldstaub, Paul. "Opening the Door to Classroom Improvisation." *Music Educators Journal* 82, no. 5 (1996): 45–51.

Goldstein, Malcolm. *Sounding the Full Circle: Concerning Music Improvisation and Other Related Matters.* Sheffield, Vt.: Goldstein, 1988.

Gottlieb, Marvin R. "Oral Poetic Principles, Improvisation and Fixed Text Interpretation." In *Proceedings of Seminar/Conference on Oral Tradition,* edited by Isabel W. Crouch and Gordon R. Owen, 180–186. Las Cruces: New Mexico State University, 1983.

Gould, Carol S., and Kenneth Keaton. "The Essential Role of Improvisation in Musical Performance." *Journal of Aesthetics and Art Criticism* 58, no. 2 (2000): 143–148.

Gray, Herman. "Jazz Tradition, Institutional Formation, and Cultural Practice:

The Canon and the Street as Frameworks for Oppositional Black Cultural Politics." In *From Sociology to Cultural Studies: New Perspectives,* edited by Elizabeth Long, 351–373. Malden, Mass.: Blackwell, 1997.

———. *Producing Jazz: The Experience of an Independent Record Company.* Philadelphia: Temple University Press, 1988.

Gray, John. *Fire Music: A Bibliography of the New Jazz, 1959–1990.* New York: Greenwood, 1991.

Green, Lucy. *Music, Gender, Education.* Cambridge: Cambridge University Press, 1997.

Greenblatt, Stephen J. "Improvisation and Power." In *Literature and Society,* edited by Edward W. Said, 57–99. Baltimore: Johns Hopkins University Press, 1980.

Griffin, Farah Jasmine. *If You Can't Be Free, Be a Mystery: In Search of Billie Holiday.* New York: Free, 2001.

Grigson, Lionel. "Harmony + Improvisation = Jazz." *British Journal of Music Education* 2, no. 2 (1984): 187–194.

Groesbeck, Rolf. "Cultural Constructions of Improvisation in Tayampaka, a Genre of Temple Instrumental Music in Kerala, India." *Ethnomusicology* 43, no. 1 (1999): 1–30.

Gronow, Pekka. Review of *Stability in Musical Improvisation: A Repertoire of Icelandic Epic Songs,* by Svend Nielsen. *Ethnomusicology* 28, no. 2 (1984): 342–343.

Gulda, Friedrich. "Liberation Through Improvisation." *World of Music* 13, no. 3 (1971): 42–49.

Hagberg, Garry. "Improvisation in the Arts." Foreword. *Journal of Aesthetics and Art Criticism* 58, no. 2 (2000): 95–97.

Hall, Edward T. "Improvisation as an Acquired, Multilevel Process." *Ethnomusicology* 36, no. 2 (1992): 223–35.

Halprin, Lawrence. *The RSVP Cycles: Creative Processes in the Human Environment.* New York: George Braziller, 1969.

Hamilton, Andy. "The Aesthetics of Imperfection." *Philosophy* 65, no. 253 (1990): 323–340.

———. "The Art of Improvisation and the Aesthetics of Imperfection." *British Journal of Aesthetics* 40, no. 1 (2000): 168–185.

Harbison, Patrick L. "How to Study Jazz Improvisation." *Instrumentalist* 33, no. 3 (1978): 25–27.

Harker, Brian. "'Telling a Story': Louis Armstrong and Coherence in Early Jazz." *Current Musicology* 63 (1999): 46–83.

Harriott, Joe. "The Truth About Free Form Jazz." *Rubberneck* 25 (1997): 30–31.

Harshbarger, Scott. "The Rhetoric of Improvisation: *Michael* and Quintilian's *Institutio Oratoria.*" *Wordsworth Circle* 25, no. 1 (1994): 37–40.

Hartman, Charles O. *Jazz Text: Voice and Improvisation in Poetry, Jazz, and Song.* Princeton: Princeton University Press, 1991.

Hayes-Roth, Barbara. "Getting Into the Story." *Style* 33, no. 2 (1999): 246–266.

Hebdige, Dick. "Even unto Death: Improvisation, Edging, and Enframement." *Critical Inquiry* 27, no. 2 (2001): 333–353.

Heble, Ajay. *Landing on the Wrong Note: Jazz, Dissonance, and Critical Practice.* New York: Routledge, 2000.

Heffley, Mike. *The Music of Anthony Braxton.* Westport, Conn.: Greenwood, 1996.

Herndon, Marcia. "Toward Evaluating Musical Change Through Musical Potential." *Ethnomusicology* 31, no. 3 (1987): 455–468.

Ho, Fred Wei-han. "'Jazz,' Kreolization and Revolutionary Music for the 21st Century." In *Sounding Off!: Music as Subversion/Resistance/Revolution,* edited

by Ron Sakolsky and Fred Wei-han Ho, 133–143. Brooklyn, N.Y.: Autonomedia, 1995.

Hobsbawm, Eric. *The Jazz Scene.* New York: Pantheon, 1993.

Hood, Mantle. "Improvisation as a Discipline in Javanese Music." *Music Educators Journal* (February–March 1964): 34–38.

Hood, Richard A. "Works in Progress: Improvisation and Tradition in Mountain
Music." *Popular Music and Society* 17, no. 3 (1993): 63–76.

hooks, bell. "Performance Practice as a Site of Opposition." In *Let's Get It On: The
Politics of Black Performance,* edited by Catherine Ugwu, 210–221. Seattle: Bay,
1995.

"ITG Jazz Improvisation Competition." *ITG Journal* 9, no. 3 (1985): 59.

Iver, Vijay S. "Microstructures of Feel, Macrostructures of Sound: Embodied
Cognition in West African and African-American Musics." Ph.D. diss., University of California, Berkeley, 1998.

Jackson, David. "Soundbeam, Fractal Bridge and Improvisation." *Rubberneck* 23
(1996): 36ff.

Jameson, Fredric. Foreword to Attali, *Noises,* vii–xiv.

Jencks, Charles, and Nathan Silver. *Adhocism: The Case for Improvisation.* New
York: Doubleday, 1972.

Jendyk, Margaret Faulkes. "Creative Drama, Improvisation, Theatre." In *Children
and Drama,* edited by Nellie McCaslin, 15–28. Lanham, Md.: University Press
of America, 1986.

Johnson, Corrine Sue. "Dudley Riggs' Brave New Workshop: A Model for Improvisation Pedagogy." Ph.D. diss., University of Oregon, 1989.

Johnstone, Keith. *Impro for Storytellers.* New York: Routledge/Theatre Arts, 1999.

———. *Impro: Improvisation and the Theatre.* 1979. London: Eyre Methuen, 1981.

Jost, Ekkehard. *Europas Jazz, 1960–80.* Frankfurt am Main: Fischer Taschenbuch, 1987.

———. *Free Jazz.* New York: Da Capo, 1981.

———. *Jazzmusiker: Materialne zur Soziologie der afro-amerikanischen Musik.*
Frankfurt am Main: Ullstein Materialen, 1982.

———. *Sozialgeschichte des Jazz in den USA.* Frankfurt am Main: Wolke, 1991.

Kaeppler, Adrienne L. "Spontaneous Choreography: Improvisation in Polynesian
Dance." *Yearbook for Traditional Music* 19 (1987): 13–22.

Kanellopoulos, Panagiotis A. "Children's Conception and Practice of Musical Improvisation." *Psychology of Music* 27 (1999): 175–191.

Kartomi, Margaret J. "Musical Improvisations by Children at Play." *World of
Music* 33, no. 3 (1991): 53–65.

Kassebaum, Gayathri Rajapur. "Improvisation in Alapana Performance: A Comparative View of Raga Skankarabharana." *Yearbook for Traditional Music* 19
(1987): 45–64.

Keizer, Arlene R. "*Beloved:* Ideologies in Conflict, Improvised Subjects." *American Review* 33, no. 1 (1999): 105–123.

Kelley, Robin D. G. "Dig They Freedom: Meditations on History and the Black
Avant-Garde." *Lenox Avenue* 3 (1997): 13–27.

Kennedy, Raymond F. "Jazz Style and Improvisation Codes." *Yearbook for Traditional Music* 19 (1987): 37–43.

Ketch, James. "Jazz Improvisation and the Blues Tradition." *ITG: Journal of the
International Trumpet Guild* 9 (1985): 18ff.

Keyes, Christopher. "Teaching Improvisation and 20th-Century Idioms." *Music Educators Journal* (May 2000): 17ff.

Kim, Jin Hi. "No World Conversation, No World Improvisation." *Rubberneck* 18
(1995): 18ff.

King, Bill. "Jazz Improvisation." *Canadian Musician* 18, no. 2 (1996): 27.

Kinsman, Alan. "A History of Gentle Giant." *Rubberneck* 16 (1994): 12ff.

Knauer, Wolfram. *Jazz in Deutschland.* Darmstädter Beiträge zur Jazzforsschung Band 4. Hofheim, Ger.: Wolke Verlag Hofheim, 1996.

——. *Jazz und Komposition.* Darmstädter Beiträge zur Jazzforsschung Band 2. Hofheim, Ger.: Wolke Verlag Hofheim, 1991.

——. "Simulated Improvisation in Duke Ellington's *Black, Brown, and Beige.*" *Black Perspective in Music* 18, nos. 1–2 (1990): 20–38.

Kobe, Reiner. "Jazzverwandtes, Intersität und Improvisation bei der Berlinale 1996." *Jazz Podium* 45 (1996): 42.

Kofsky, Frank. *Black Music, White Business.* New York: Pathfinder, 1998.

——. *Black Nationalism and the Revolution in Music.* New York: Pathfinder, 1970.

Konowitz, Bert. "Improvisation on Keyboard Instruments." *Music Educators Journal* 66, no. 5 (1980): 86–88.

——. *Music Improvisation as a Classroom Method: A New Approach to Teaching Music.* New York: Alfred, 1973.

Kowald, Peter. *Almanach der "365 Tage am Ort": Luisenstrabe Wuppertal.* Cologne: Walter König, 1998.

Kraft, Wayne B. "Improvisation in Hungarian Ethnic Dancing: An Analog to Oral Verse Composition." *Oral Tradition* 4, no. 3 (1989): 273–315.

Krieger, Franz. Review of *Charlie Parker and Thematic Improvisation*, by Henry Martin. *Jazzforschung/Jazz Research* 29 (1997): 208–209.

Kuharski, Allen. "Identity and Improvisation: Backstage in the Theater of Jan Kott." *Theater* 25, no. 3 (1995): 80–84.

Kuzmich, John, Jr. "Improvisation Teaching Materials." *Music Educators Journal* 66, no. 5 (1980): 51ff.

Laborde, Denis. "Des concours d'improvisation poétique chantée en Pays Basque, ou comment construire une identité culturelle." *Canadian Folklore/Folklore canadien* 18, no. 2 (1996): 19–33.

Larson, Steve. "'Integrated Music Learning' and Improvisation: Teaching Musicianship and Theory Through 'Menus, Maps, and Models.'" *College Music Symposium* 35 (1995): 76.

Lee, Byong Won. "Improvisation in Korean Musics." *Music Educators Journal* 66, no. 5 (1980): 137–145.

Levaillant, Denis. *L'improvisation musicale: Essai sur la puissance du jeu.* Paris: J.-C. Lattès, 1981.

Levy, Adam. "True Believer: John McLaughlin Reaffirms His Faith in Improvisation." *Guitar Player* (January 2001): 78ff.

Lewis, George E. "Interacting with Latter-Day Musical Automata." *Contemporary Music Review* 18, no. 3 (1999): 99–112.

——. "Teaching Improvised Music: An Ethnographic Memoir." In Zorn, *Arcana,* 78–109.

Lipiczky, Thom. "Tihai Formulas and the Fusion of 'Composition' and 'Improvisation' in North Indian Music." *Musical Quarterly* 71, no. 2 (1985): 157–171.

Lipsitz, George. *Dangerous Crossroads: Popular Music, Postmodernism and the Poetics of Place.* London: Verso, 1994.

Litweiler, John. *The Freedom Principle: Jazz After 1958.* New York: Da Capo, 1990.

Lock, Graham. *Blutopia: Visions of the Future and Revisions of the Past in the Work of Sun Ra, Duke Ellington, and Anthony Braxton.* Durham: Duke University Press, 1999.

———. *Chasing the Vibration: Meetings with Creative Musicianships.* Devon, Eng.: Stride, 1994.

Locke, David. "Improvisation in West African Musics." *Music Educators Journal* 66, no. 5 (1980): 125–133.

Lozar, Tomaz. "e. e. cummings: The Poem as Improvisation." *Acta Neophilologica* 4 (1971): 61–73.

MacAdams, Lewis. *Birth of the Cool: Beat, Bebop, and the American Avant-Garde.* New York: Free, 2001.

Mackenzie, Ian. "Improvisation, Creativity, and Formulaic Language." *Journal of Aesthetics and Art Criticism* 58, no. 2 (2000): 173–179.

Mackey, Nathaniel. *Discrepant Engagement: Dissonance, Cross-Culturality, and Experimental Writing.* Cambridge: Cambridge University Press, 1993.

Madura, Patrice Dawn. "Jazz Improvisation for the Vocal Student." *Teaching Music* (June 1997): 26–28.

———. "Relationships among Vocal Jazz Improvisation Achievement, Jazz Theory Knowledge, Imitative Ability, Musical Experience, Creativity, and Gender." *Journal of Research in Music Education* 44, no. 3 (1996): 252–267.

Makarova, Viera. "Whose Line Is It Anyway?: Or, Teaching Improvisation in Interpreting: Papers from 2nd Lang. Internat. Conf., Elsinore, Denmark, 4–6 June 1993." In *Teaching Translation and Interpreting II: Insights, Aims, Visions,* edited by Cay Dollerup and Annette Lindegaard, 207–210. Amsterdam: Benjamins, 1994.

Malcolm, Douglas. "'Jazz America': Jazz and African American Culture in Jack Kerouac's *On the Road.*" *Contemporary Literature* 40, no. 1 (1999): 85–110.

———. "Solos and Chorus: Michael Ondaatje's Jazz Politics/Poetics." *Mosaic* 32, no. 3 (1999): 131–149.

Malm, William P. "Shoden: A Study in Toyko Festival Music: When Is Variation an Improvisation?" *Yearbook of the International Folk Music Council* 17 (1975): 44–66.

Marmande, Francis. "The Laws of Improvisation, or the Nuptial Destruction of Jazz." Translated by Carol Johnson. *Yale French Studies* 89 (1996): 155–159.

Martin, György. "Improvisation and Regulation in Hungarian Folk Dances." *Acta Ethnographica Academiae Scientarum Hungaricae* 29, nos. 3–4 (1980): 391–425.

Martin, Henry. *Charlie Parker and Thematic Improvisation.* Newark: Institute of Jazz Studies, Rutgers–State University of New Jersey; Lanham, Md.: Scarecrow, 1996.

Martinelli, Francesco. *Anthony Braxton: A Discography.* Pontedera, Ital.: Bandecchi and Vivaldi, 2000.

Matteson, Rich. "Improvisation for Jazz Instrumentalists." *Music Educators Journal* 66, no. 5 (1980): 95–99.

Matthews, James H. "'Magical Improvisation': Frank O'Connor's Revolution." *Éire Ireland* 10, no. 4 (1975): 3–13.

McGill, Kathleen. "Improvisatory Competence and the Cueing of Performance: The Case of the Commedia dell'Arte." *Text and Performance Quarterly* 10, no. 2 (1990): 111–122.

———. "Women and Performance: The Development of Improvisation by the Sixteenth-Century Commedia dell'Arte." *Theatre Journal* 43, no. 1 (1991): 59–69.

McGregor, Maxine. *Chris McGregor and the Brotherhood of Breath: My Life with a South African Jazz Pioneer.* Flint, Mich.: Bamberger, 1995.

McKean, James. "Notes on Improvisation, William Carlos Williams, and Jazz." In *Conversant Essays: Contemporary Poets of Poetry,* edited by James McCorkle, 348–361. Detroit: Wayne State University Press, 1990.

McLeish, Martin. "Sun Ra and Relative Dimensions in Space." *Rubberneck* 15 (1993): 18ff.

McMillan, Ros. "'To Say Something That Was Me': Developing a Personal Voice Through Improvisation." *British Journal of Music Education* 16, no. 3 (1999): 262–273.

McMurray, Peter. "What's Become of Jazz?" *Crescendo & Jazz Music* 37, no. 3 (2000): 27–28.

Mehegan, John. *Jazz Improvisation*. New York: Watson-Guptill, 1959.

Mehldau, Brad. "Brahms, Interpretation & Improvisation." *JazzTimes* 31 (2001): 55ff.

Merod, Jim. "Jazz as a Cultural Archive." *boundary 2* 22, no. 2 (1995): 1–18.

Miller, Leta E. "C. P. E. Bach and Friedrich Ludwig Dülon: Composition and Improvisation in late 18th-century Germany." *Early Music* 23, no. 1 (1995): 65–80.

Minton, Sandra Cerny. *Choreography: A Basic Approach Using Improvisation*. Revised ed. Champaign, Ill.: Human Kinetics, 1997.

Monson, Ingrid. "Doubleness and Jazz Improvisation: Irony, Parody, and Ethnomusicology." *Critical Inquiry* 20, no. 2 (1994): 283–313.

———. *Saying Something: Jazz Improvisation and Interaction*. Chicago: University of Chicago Press, 1996.

Montgomery, Will. "Between Precision and Wildness: Rova Saxophone Quartet." *Rubberneck* 26 (1997): 12ff.

———. "Reaching for the Unattainable." *Rubberneck* 23 (1996): 16ff.

Moore, Daniel. "Conversational Improvisation." *Percussive Notes* (August 1990): 32–34.

Morgenroth, Joyce. *Dance Improvisations*. Pittsburgh: University of Pittsburgh Press, 1987.

Morris, Robert. "Compositional Spaces and Other Territories." *Perspectives of New Music* 33, nos. 1–2 (1995): 328–358.

Mosher, Barrie S. "Teaching Jazz Improvisation: A Model for an Extended Workshop." *Music Educators Journal* 62, no. 9 (1976): 52–55.

Moten, Fred. "Tragedy Elegy Improvisation: Voices of Baraka, II." In *Semiotics 1994*, edited by C. W. Spinks and John Deely, 431–449. New York: Peter Lang, 1995.

Msosa, Watson. "From Cultural Aesthetic to Performance Technique: Continuities and Contrasts in Improvisational Milieux of Vimbuza and Jazz." *Journal of Humanities* 13 (1999): 47–58.

Muro, Don. "Improvisation with Synthesizers." *Music Educators Journal* 66, no. 5 (1980): 105–108.

Murphy, John P. "Jazz Improvisation: The Joy of Influence." *Black Perspective in Music* 18 (1990): 7–19.

Myers, Mitch. "Anti-Mercenary Improvisation." *Down Beat* (November 2000): 26–30.

Nachmanovitch, Stephen. *Free Play: Improvisation in Life and Art*. Los Angeles: Tarcher; New York: St. Martin's, 1990.

Nagrin, Daniel. *Dance and the Specific Image: Improvisation*. Pittsburgh: University of Pittsburgh Press, 1994.

Nettl, Bruno. "Thoughts on Improvisation: A Comparative Approach." *Musical Quarterly* 40, no. 1 (1974): 1–19.

Nettl, Bruno, with Melinda Russell, eds. *In the Course of Performance: Studies in the World of Musical Improvisation*. Chicago: University of Chicago Press, 1998.

Neumann, Frederick. *Ornamentation and Improvisation in Mozart*. Princeton: Princeton University Press, 1986.

Nielsen, Aldon Lynn. *Black Chant: Languages of African-American Postmodernism.* Cambridge: Cambridge University Press, 1997.

Nofze, Mathias. "Improvisation—Performance—Szene." *Musik & Bildung* 28 (1996): 56–57.

Noglik, Bert. *Jazz-Werkstatt International.* Frankfurt am Main: Fischer Taschenbuch, 1982.

———. *Klangspuren: Wege improviserter Musik.* Hamburg: Rowohlt Taschenbuch, 1992.

Norris, Christopher. "Utopian Deconstruction: Ernst Bloch, Paul de Man and the Politics of Music." In *Music and the Politics of Culture,* edited by Christopher Norris, 305–347. New York: St. Martin's, 1989.

Norton, Glyn P. "Strategies of Fluency in the French Renaissance Text: Improvisation and the Art of Writing." *Journal of Medieval and Renaissance Studies* 15, no. 1 (1985): 85–99.

Novack, Cynthia J. "Contact Improvisation: A Photo Essay and Summary Movement Analysis." *Drama Review* 32, no. 4 (1988): 120–134.

———. "Looking at Movement as Culture: Contact Improvisation to Disco." *Drama Review* 32, no. 4 (1988): 102–119.

———. *Sharing the Dance: Contact Improvisation and American Culture.* Madison: University of Wisconsin Press, 1990.

Novello, John. "Blues and Blues Improvisation." *Canadian Musician* (December 1997): 24–25.

Nozati, Annick. "An Economy of Means." *Rubberneck* 24 (1997): 4ff.

Nzewi, Meki. "Philological Derivations in Melo-Rythmic Improvisation." *African Musicology* 1, no. 1 (1983): 1–13.

Ochs, Larry. "Devices and Strategies for Structured Improvisation." In Zorn, *Arcana,* 325–335.

Oliveros, Pauline. *Software for People.* Baltimore: Smith, 1984.

O'Meally, Robert G., ed. *The Jazz Cadence of American Culture.* New York: Columbia University Press, 1998.

O'Neill, Clare Cecilia. "Structure and Spontaneity: Improvisation in Theatre and Education." Ph.D. diss., University of Exeter, 1992.

Panish, Jon. *The Color of Jazz: Race and Representation in Postwar American Culture.* Jackson: University Press of Mississippi, 1997.

Pastras, Philip James. "A Clear Field: The Idea of Improvisation in Modern Poetry." Ph.D. diss., Rutgers University, 1982.

Patterson, Tom. *Ashe: Improvisation and Recycling in African-American Visionary.* Winston-Salem, N.C.: Diggs Gallery, Winston Salem State University, 1993.

Pavlicevic, Mercédès. "Improvisation in Music Therapy: Human Communication in Sound." *Journal of Music Therapy* 37, no. 4 (2000): 269–285.

Peggie, Andrew. "The Place of Improvisation in Music Education." *British Journal of Music Education* 2, no. 2 (1985): 167–169.

Perkins, Terry. "Mustafa's Jazz Clinics Teach Improvisation to High Schoolers." *Down Beat* (June 1997): 72.

Perlman, Alan M., and Daniel Greenblatt. "Miles Davis Meets Noam Chomsky: Some Observations on Jazz Improvisation and Language Structure." In *The Sign in Music and Literature,* edited by Wendy Steiner, 169–183. Austin: University of Texas Press, 1981.

Pesquinne, Blaise. "De l'improvisation dans le jazz." *Revue musicale* (September–October 1934): 177–188.

Pietra, Christopher J. Della, and Patricia Shehan Campbell. "An Ethnography of

Improvisation Training in a Music Methods Course." *Journal of Research in Music Education* 43, no. 2 (1995): 112–126.

Pietropaolo, Domenico. "Improvisation as a Stochastic Composition Process." In *The Science of Buffoonery: Theory and History of the Commedia Dell'arte,* edited by Domenico Pietropaolo, 167–175. Ottawa: Dovehouse, 1989.

Pope, David. "Avoiding the 'Wrong' Notes in Jazz Improvisation." *Saxophone Journal* (January–February 1998): 34–35.

———. "Creative Jazz Improvisation: Freeing Jazz!" *Saxophone Journal* (January–February 1996): 60–61.

———. "Critical Thinking About Jazz Improvisation." *Saxophone Journal* (September–October 1996): 54–56.

———. "The Japanese Scale for Jazz Improvisation." *Saxophone Journal* (March–Aprril 1997): 42–43.

———. "Note Sculpting in Jazz Improvisation." *Saxophone Journal* (July–August 1996): 10–13.

Porter, Eric. *What Is This Thing Called Jazz: African-American Musicians as Artists, Critics, and Activists.* Berkeley and Los Angeles: University of California Press, 2000.

Porter, Lewis. "John Coltrane's *A Love Supreme:* Jazz Improvisation as Composition." *Journal of the American Musicological Society* 38 (1985): 593–621.

Powers, Harold. "A Canonical Museum of Imagery Music." *Current Musicology* 60–61 (1996): 5–25.

Prévost, Eddie. "Improvisation: Music for an Occasion." *British Journal of Music Education* 2, no. 2 (1985): 177–186.

———. *No Sound is Innocent: AMM and the Practice of Self-Invention.* Essex: Copula, 1995.

Puri, Rajika, and Diana Hart-Johnson. "Thinking with Movement: Improvising Versus Composing?" In *Human Action Signs in Cultural Context: The Visible and the Invisible in Movement and Dance,* edited by Brenda Farnell and Drid Williams, 158–185. Metuchen, N.J.: Scarecrow, 1995.

Putschögl, Gerhard. *John Coltrane und die afroamerikanische Oraltradition.* Graz: Adeva, 1993.

Quinn, Richard. "The Creak of Categories: Nathaniel Mackey's *Strick: Song of the Andoumboulou 16–25*." *Callaloo* 23, no. 2 (2000): 608–620.

Quinn, William A., and Audley S. Hall. *Jongleur: A Modified Theory of Oral Improvisation and Its Effects on the Performance and Transmission of Middle English Romance.* Washington, D.C.: University Presses of America, 1982.

Rabinof, Sylvia. "Musicianship Through Improvisation." *Music Journal* 26, no. 8 (1968): 24–25.

Racy, Ali Jihad. "Creative and Ambience: An Ecstatic Feedback Model from Arab Music." *World of Music* 33, no. 3 (1991): 7–28.

———. "The Many Faces of Improvisation: The Arab Taqasam as a Musical Symbol." *Ethnomusicology* 44 (2000): 302–320.

Radano, Ronald. *New Musical Figurations: Anthony Braxton's Cultural Critique.* Chicago: University of Chicago Press, 1993.

Radano, Ronald, and Philip V. Bohlman, eds. *Music and the Racial Imagination.* Chicago: University of Chicago Press, 2000.

Rammel, Hal. "Invention's Perspective on Improvisation." *Rubberneck* 22 (1996): 26ff.

Ramsey, Guthrie P., Jr. "Who Matters: The New and Improved White Jazz-Literati: A Review Essay." *American Music* 17, no. 2 (1999): 205–215.

Reeves, Scott D. *Creative Jazz Improvisation.* Englewood Cliffs, N.J.: Prentice-Hall, 1989.

Riley, Howard. "The Life of Riley." *Rubberneck* 18 (1995): 9–11.

Roach, Joseph. "Kinship, Intelligence, and Memory as Improvisation: Culture and Performance in New Orleans." In *Performance and Cultural Politics,* edited by Elin Diamond, 217–236. London: Routledge, 1996.

Robinson, Nathalie Gail. "Improvisation and Composition: Agents for Synthesis." *National Association of Schools of Music, Proceedings* (August 1997): 37–42.

Rockwell John. *All American Music: Composition in the Late Twentieth Century.* New York: Da Capo, 1997.

Rodgers, Paul C., Jr. "Brown's Ormond: The Fruits of Improvisation." *American Quarterly* 26, no. 1 (1974): 4–22.

Roig-Francolí, Miguel A. "Playing in Consonances: A Spanish Renaissance Technique of Chordal Improvisation." *Early Music* 23, no. 3 (1995): 461–471.

Rose, Richard. "Eight Elements of Jazz Improvisation." *Music Educators Journal* 71, no. 9 (1985): 46–47.

Rosenfeld, Paul. "A Plea for Improvisation." *Modern Music* (November–December 1941): 10–15.

Ross, Stewart L. "A Selected Bibliography of Jazz Improvisation Books." *Instrumentalist* (November 1974): 69.

Rothenberg, David. "Sudden Music: Improvising Across the Electronic Abyss." *Contemporary Music Review* 13, no. 2 (1996): 23–46.

Rovere, Walter, and Carla Chiti. *John Zorn.* San Giovanni Valdarno, Ital.: Materiali Sonori Edizioni Musicali, 1998.

Rowe, Robert. "The Aesthetics of Interactive Music Systems." *Contemporary Music Review* 18, no. 3 (1999): 83–87.

Rupert, John. "Improvisatory Structures in Kerouac's 'October in the Railroad Earth' and *The Subterraneans.*" *Kerouac Connection* 21 (1991): 5–17.

Russo, Greg. *Cosmik Debris: The Collected History and Improvisations of Frank Zappa.* Floral Park, N.Y.: Crossfire, 1998.

Ruud, Even. *Music Therapy: Improvisation, Communication, and Culture.* Gilsum, N.H.: Barcelona, 1998.

Ryan, Judylyn S., and Estella Conwill Majózo. "Jazz . . . On 'The Site of Memory.'" *Studies in the Literary Imagination* 31, no. 2 (1998): 125–152.

Saindon, Ed. "Vertical Improvisation: Improvisational Techniques Based on Tension Resolution." *Percussive Notes* 38 (2000): 33–38.

———. "Vertical Improvisation: Tension-Release Principles." *Down Beat* (April 1999): 78.

Saint-Jacques, Diane. "Mise en action et mise en fiction: Le processus de production en improvisation." *Theatre Research in Canada/Recherches théâtrales au Canada* 19, no. 2 (1998): 125–139.

Saldaña, Johnny. *Drama of Color: Improvisation with Multiethnic Folklore.* Portsmouth, N.H.: Heinemann, 1995.

Santoro, Gene. "Jazzing Politics." *The Nation* (17 December 2001): 30–37.

Sarath, Ed. "A New Look at Improvisation." *Journal of Music Therapy* 40, no. 1 (1996): 1–38.

Sawyer, R. Keith. *Creative Conversations: Improvisation in Everyday Discourse.* Cresskill, N.J.: Hampton, 2001.

———. "Improvisation and the Creative Process: Dewey, Collingwood, and the Aesthetics of Spontaneity." *Journal of Aesthetics and Art Criticism* 58, no. 2 (2000): 149–161.

———. *Pretend Play as Improvisation: Conversation in the Preschool Classroom.* Mahwah, N.J.: Erlbaum, 1997.

———. "Responding to the Commentaries . . . Moving Forward: Issues for Future Research in Improvisation and Education." *Psychology of Music* 27 (1999): 215–216.

———. "The Semiotics of Improvisation: The Pragmatics of Musical and Verbal Performance." *Semiotica* 108, nos. 3–4 (1996): 269–306.

Sbait, Dirgham H. "Debate in the Improvised-Sung Poetry of the Palestinians." *Asian Folklore Studies* 52, no. 1 (1993): 93–117.

Scheiffele, Eberhard. "The Theatre of Truth: Psychodrama, Spontaneity and Improvisation: The Theatrical Theories and Influence of Jacob Levy Moreno." Ph.D. diss., University of California, Berkeley, 1995.

Schiaffini, Giancarlo. "Pensées éparses sur l'improvisation." *Dissonanz* (February 1998): 24–26.

Schleiner, Louise. "Providential Improvisation in *Measure for Measure*." *PMLA* 97, no. 2 (1982): 227–236.

Schlieder, Frederick William. *Lyric Composition Through Improvisation: An Exposition and Synthetic Use of the Fundamental Laws of Rhythm, Melody and Harmony as Applied to the Creation of a Basic Form of Lyric Composition.* Boston: Birchard, 1927–46.

Schuller, Gunther. *The Swing Era: The Development of Jazz, 1930–1945.* Vol. 2 of *The History of Jazz.* New York: Oxford University Press, 1989.

Scuderi, Antonio. "Framing and Improvisation in Dario Fo's Johan Padan." *Theatre Annual* 49 (1996): 76–91.

Shapiro, Michael. "Improvisational Techniques for the Literature Teacher." *Teaching Shakespeare Through Performance,* edited by Milla Cozart Riggio, 184–195. New York: MLA, 1999.

Shepherd, John, and Peter Wicke. *Music and Cultural Theory.* Cambridge: Polity, 1997.

Shew, Bobby. "Notes on Jazz Improvisation." *International Trumpet Guild Newsletter* 7, no. 1 (1980): 9–11.

Signell, Karl. "Esthetics of Improvisation in Turkish Art Music." *Asian Music* 2 (1974): 45–49.

———. "Improvisation in Near Eastern Musics." *Music Educators Journal* 66, no. 5 (1980): 133–136.

Simpkins, Cuthbert Ormond. *Coltrane: A Biography.* Baltimore: Black Classic, 1975.

Simpson, Dallas. "Improvisational Binaural Sound Art: The Foundations of Location Performance." *Rubberneck* 24 (1997): 22ff.

Siron, Jacques. "Enchevêtrement de voies : Au carrefour de la polyphonie et des musiques improvisées contemporaines." *Cahiers de musiques traditionnelles* 6 (1993): 119–138.

———. *La Partition intérieure : Jazz, musiques improvisées.* Paris: Outre mesure, 1992.

Small, Christopher. *Music of the Common Tongue: Survival and Celebration in African American Music.* Hanover: Wesleyan University Press, 1987.

———. *Music: Society: Education.* London: John Calder, 1980.

———. *Musicking: The Meanings of Performance and Listening.* Middletown, Conn.: Wesleyan University Press, 1998.

Smallwood, Richard. "Gospel and Blues Improvisation." *Music Educators Journal* 66, no. 5 (1980): 100–104.

Smith, Christopher. "A Sense of the Possible: Miles Davis and the Semiotics of Improvised Performance." *Drama Review* 39, no. 3 (1995): 41–55.

Smith, Gregory E. "In Quest of a New Perspective on Improvised Jazz: A View from the Balkans." *World of Music* 33, no. 3 (1991): 29–52.

Smith, Hazel, and Roger T. Dean. *Improvisation, Hypermedia and the Arts since 1945.* Amsterdam: Harwood Academic, 1997.

Smith, Leo. *Notes (8 Pieces); Source—A New World Music: Creative Music*. New Haven, Conn.: Kiom, 1973.

Smith, Roger. "Solo Improvising." *Rubberneck* 27 (1998): 28ff.

Smith, Stuart. "*Return and Recall* (Improvisation—The First Step) at U.M.B.C." *Perspectives of New Music* 22, nos. 1–2 (1983–1984): 286–289.

Snow, Michael. *Music/Sound: The Michael Snow Project*. Toronto: Knopf Canada, 1993.

Sobchack, Tom. "Ragtime: An Improvisation on Hollywood Style." *Literature/Film Quarterly* 13, no. 3 (1985): 148–154.

Soules, Marshall Ian. "Sam Shepard Improvises." Ph.D. diss., Rutgers University, 1994.

Stanyek, Jason. "Articulating Intercultural Free Improvisation: Evan Parker's Synergetics Project." *Resonance* 7, no. 2 (1999): 44–47.

Steinberger, Peter J. "Culture and Freedom in the Fifties: The Case of Jazz." *Virginia Quarterly Review* 74 (1998): 118–133.

Stern, Max. "Organizing Procedures Involving Indeterminacy and Improvisation." *Interface* 17 (1988): 103–114.

Sterritt, David. "Revision, Prevision, and the Aura of Improvisatory Art." *Journal of Aesthetics and Art Criticism* 58, no. 2 (2000): 163–172.

Stock, Jonathan. "Three Erhu Pieces by Abing: An Analysis of Improvisational Processes in Chinese Traditional Instrumental Music." *Asian Music* 25, nos. 1–2 (1993–1994): 145–176.

Stoloff, Bob. *Scat!: Vocal Improvisation and Techniques*. Brooklyn, N.Y.: Gerard and Sarzin, 1996.

Subotnik, Rose Rosengard. *Developing Variations: Style and Identity in Western Music*. Minneapolis: University of Minnesota Press, 1991.

Such, David G. *Avant-Garde Jazz Musicians: Performing "Out There."* Iowa City: University of Iowa Press, 1993.

Suhor, Charles. "Jazz Improvisation and Language Performance: Parallel Competencies." *Et cetera* 43, no. 2 (1986): 133–140.

Susilo, Hardja. "Improvisation in Wayang Wong Pangsung: Creativity Within Cultural Constraints." *Yearbook for Traditional Music* 19 (1987): 1–22.

Sutton, R. Anderson. "Variation and Composition in Java." *Yearbook for Traditional Music* 19 (1987): 65–95.

Sweet, Robert E. *Music Universe, Music Mind: Revisiting the Creative Music Studio, Woodstock, New York*. Ann Arbor: Arborville, 1996.

Szabo, Helga. "Improvisation Stimulates Development." *Music Journal* 30, no. 8 (1972): 30ff.

Szwed, John F. *Space Is the Place: The Lives and Times of Sun Ra*. New York: Da Capo, 1998.

Tallmadge, William H. "Teaching Improvisation." *Music Educators Journal* (November–December 1960): 58–60.

Tapscott, Horace. *Songs of the Unsung: The Musical and Social Journey of Horace Tapscott*. Edited by Steven Isoardi. Durham: Duke University Press, 2001.

Taylor, Arthur. *Notes and Tones: Musician-to-Musician Interviews*. New York: Da Capo, 1993.

Thomas, Judith. "Orff-Based Improvisation." *Music Educators Journal* 66, no. 5 (1980): 58–61.

Thomas, Pat. "Islam's Contribution to Jazz & Improvised Musics." *Rubberneck* 15 (1993): 8ff.

Thompson, Keith P. "Vocal Improvisation for Elementary Students." *Music Educators Journal* 66, no. 5 (1980): 69–71.

Thompson, Robert Farris. *Flash of the Spirit: African and Afro-American Art and Philosophy.* New York: Vintage, 1983.

Tirro, Frank. "Constructive Elements in Jazz Improvisation." *Journal of the American Musicological Society* 27, no. 2 (1974): 285–305.

Titlestad, Michael. "Improvisation: Meaning and Invention in Music and Discourse." *Scrutiny* 2 5, no. 2 (2000): 13–23.

Titon, Jeff Todd. "Every Day I Have the Blues: Improvisation and Daily Life." *Southern Folklore Quarterly* 42 (1978): 85–98.

Toop, David. *Ocean of Sound: Aether Talk, Ambient Sound and Imaginary Worlds.* London: Serpent's Tail, 1996.

———. *The Rap Attack: African Jive to New York Hip Hop.* London: Pluto, 1984.

Touma, Habib H. "Maqam, a Form of Improvisation." *World of Music* 12, no. 3 (1970): 22–31.

———. "The Maqam Phenomenon: An Improvisation Technique in the Music of the Middle East." *Ethnomusicology* 15 (1971): 38–48.

Treitler, Leo. "Medieval Improvisation." *World of Music* 33, no. 3 (1991): 66–91.

Tremblay, Danielle. "Quand les femmes se mêlent d'improvisation." *Musicworks* 54 (1992): 20–23.

Trimillos, Ricardo D. "Time-Distance and Melodic Models in Improvisation Among the Tausug of the Southern Philippines." *Yearbook for Traditional Music* 19 (1987): 23–35.

Tucker, Bruce. "Narrative, Extramusical Form, and the Metamodernism of the Art Ensemble of Chicago." *Lenox Avenue* 3 (1997): 27–41.

Tufnell, Miranda, and Chris Crickmay. *Body Space Image: Notes Towards Improvisation and Performance.* London: Virago, 1990.

Valone, James J. "Musical Improvisation as Interpretative Activity." *Journal of Aesthetics and Art Criticism* 44, no. 2 (1985): 193–194.

Van Waesberghe, Jos. Smits. "Guido of Arezzo and Musical Improvisation." *Musica disciplina* (1951): 55–63.

Velleman, Barry L. "Speaking of Jazz: Jazz Improvisation through Linguistic Methods." *Music Educators Journal* 65, no. 2 (1978): 28–31.

Vikár, László. "Improvisation dans la musique des peuples de la Moyenne Volga." *Yearbook of the International Folk Music Council* 7 (1975): 107–115.

Vuisje, Bert. *De Nieuwe Jazz: Twintig Interviews door Bert Vuisje.* Baarn, Netherlands: Bosch and Keuning, 1978.

Walker, William Franklin. "A Conversation-Based Framework for Musical Improvisation." Ph.D. diss., University of Illinois, Urbana, 1994.

Walser, Robert, ed. *Keeping Time: Readings in Jazz History.* New York: Oxford University Press, 1999.

———. "Out of Notes: Signification, Interpretation and the Problem of Miles Davis." In Gabbard, *Jazz Among the Discourses,* 165–188.

Walton, Ortiz. *Music: Black, White and Blue.* New York: William Morrow, 1972.

Warkow, Esther. "Taqasim: The Art of Improvisation in Arabic Music." *Asian Music* 15, no. 2 (1984): 162–163.

Watrous, Peter. "Lessons from a Master of Improvisation." *New York Times,* 29 January 1996, C15.

Wegman, Rob C. "From Maker to Composer: Improvisation and Musical Authorship in the Low Countries, 1450–1500." *Journal of the American Musicological Society* 49 (1996): 409–479.

Weintraub, Wiktor. "The Problem of Improvisation in Romantic Literature." *Comparative Literature* 16 (1964): 119–137.

Welch, Graham F. "Education and Musical Improvisation: In Response to Keith Sawyer." *Psychology of Music* 27 (1999): 211–214.

Welwood, Arthur. "Improvisation with Found Sounds." *Music Educators Journal* 66, no. 5 (1980): 72–77.

Werner, Craig Hansen. *Playing the Changes: From Afro-Modernism to the Jazz Impulse.* Urbana: University of Illinois Press, 1994.

Whitehead, Kevin. *New Dutch Swing.* New York: Billboard, 1984.

Whiteoak, John. *Playing Ad Lib: Improvisatory Music in Australia, 1836–1970.* Strawberry Hills, Australia: Currency, 1999.

Wickes, John. *Innovations in British Jazz.* Volume 1, 1960–1980. Chelmsford, Eng.: Soundworld, 1999.

Wigram, Tony. "Therapeutisch improviseren op de piano." *Adem* (April 1999): 200–202.

Williams, Davey. "Towards a Philosophy of Improvisation." *Improvisor* 4 (1984): 32–34.

Williams, William Carlos. *Kora in Hell: Improvisations.* San Francisco: City Lights, 1957.

Wilmer, Valerie. *As Serious As Your Life: The Story of the New Jazz.* New York: Serpent's Tail, 1992.

Wilson, Phil. "Tailoring the Teaching of Improvisation." *Instrumentalist* (May 1989): 13–15.

Wiskirchen, George C. "If We're Going to Teach Jazz, We *Must* Teach Improvisation." *Music Educators Journal* 62, no. 3 (1975): 68–74.

Wollner, Gertrude Price. *Improvisation in Music: Ways Toward Capturing Musical Ideas and Developing Them.* Garden City, N.Y.: Doubleday, 1963.

Wunsch, Ilse Gerda. "Improvisation . . . How?" *American Music Teacher* 21, no. 6 (1972): 22–23.

Yared, Nazik Saba. *Improvisations on a Missing String.* Translated by Stuart A. Hancox. Fayetteville: University of Arkansas Press, 1997.

Young, James O., and Carl Matheson. "The Metaphysics of Jazz." *Journal of Aesthetics of Art Criticism* 58, no. 2 (2000): 125–133.

Zaporah, Ruth. *Action Theater: The Improvisation of Presence.* Berkeley, Calif.: North Atlantic, 1995.

Zorn, John, ed. *Arcana: Musicians on Music.* New York: Granary, 2000.

II. Webography*

AACM: Association for the Advancement of Creative Musicians   http://www.aacmchicago.org/

Actuelle CD   http://www.actuellecd.com/

All About Jazz   http://www.allaboutjazz.com/

Asian Improv   http://www.asianimprov.com/

Avant Magazine   http://www.avantmag.com/

BBC Radio 3   http://www.bbc.co.uk/radio3

Bimhuis: Dutch Center for Improvised Music   http://www.bimhuis.nl/html_en/index.html

Anthony Braxton and the Tri-Centric Foundation   http://www.wesleyan.edu/music/braxton/

Center for Black Music Research   http://www.cbmr.org/

*As with any webography, readers are cautioned that this list compiles a selection of materials that was available at a particular juncture in the development of this book. It has not been possible to ascertain whether all of these sites remain active, or even, indeed, have maintained the same content or URL.

Center for Jazz Studies, Columbia University http://www.columbia.edu/cu/cjs/
Coastal Jazz and Blues Society http://www.jazzvancouver.com/
Creative Music Studio http://www.creativemusicstudio.org/
Effendi Records http://www.effendirecords.qc.ca/
Emanem Records http://www.emanemdisc.com/
European Free Improvisation http://www.shef.ac.uk/misc/rec/ps/efi/
Festival international de musique actuelle, Victoriaville http://www.fimav.qc.ca
La Folia Online Music Review http://www.lafolia.com/
Free Jazz Improvisation (John Voigt) http://people.ne.mediaone.net/johnvoigt/
freejazz.org: Freedom in Music http://www.freejazz.org/
Guelph Jazz Festival http://www.guelphjazzfestival.com/
Hertz-Loin http://www.hertz-lion.com/
Improvised Music from Japan http://www.japanimprov.com/
The Improvisor LaDonna Smith's Online Magazine http://www.the-improvisor.
    com/
Incus Records http://www.incusrecords.force9.co.uk/
Indiana University School of Music http://www.music.indiana.edu/music_
    resources/improv.html
International Index to Music Periodicals http://music.chadwyck.com/iimp/search
Jazz Festivals http://nfo.net/.LNX/lfest.html
Jazz Grrls: A List of Jazz Women on the Web http://www.jazzgrrls.com/
Jazz Improvisation and Jazz Education by Jim Snidero http://www.jimsnidero.
    com/
A Jazz Improvisation Primer (Mark Sabatella) http://www.outsideshore.com/
    primer/primer/
Jazz Improv Magazine http://www.jazzimprov.com/
Jazz-Institut Darmstadt http://www.darmstadt.de/kultur/musik/jazz/index-us.
    htm
Jazz Lessons: Jazz Improvisation http://www.jazclass.aust.com/im1.htm
Jazz Links: Education http://www.pk.edu.pl/~pmj/jazzlinks/education.html
Jenny's Jazz: The Jazz Improvisation Forum http://www.ohio.net/~osvaths/
The Kitchen http://www.thekitchen.org/
Knitting Factory http://www.knittingfactory.com/
London Musicians Collective http://www.l-m-c.org.uk/
Francesco Martinelli http://space.tin.it/musica/upsma/
Matchless Recordings http://www.matchlessrecordings.com/
Ottawa International Jazz Festival http://www.ottawajazzfestival.com/
Perfect Sound Forever http://www.furious.com/perfect/
The School for Improvisational Music http://www.schoolforimprovisational
    music.org/
Ishmael Wadada Leo Smith http://music.calarts.edu/~wls/
Soundlist: Experimental Music, Free Improvisation, Sound Art http://audiolab.
    uwaterloo.ca/~soundlst/
Trummerflora http://www.trummerflora.com/
Verge Music Distribution http://www.vergemusic.com/
Zucasa Network http://www.zucasa.com/zcnt/3

Contributors

·⤳

JOHN CORBETT writes about music and sound for such periodicals as *Down Beat, Pulse!* and the *Chicago Reader.* The author of *Extended Play: Sounding Off from John Cage to Dr. Funkenstein,* he has published scholarly essays in the *Drama Review, October,* and *Discourse* and is an active liner notician for a variety of record companies. Based in Chicago, where he enjoys the vibrant creative music scene, Corbett is cohost of the weekly radio program *Writer's Bloc* on WNUR-FM. He is adjunct associate professor at the School of the Art Institute of Chicago and has, over the last six years, organized a weekly concert series and six festivals of jazz and improvised music at the Empty Bottle. He was appointed artistic director of Berlin JazzFest 2002.

MICHAEL DESSEN is currently completing his Ph.D. in critical studies and experimental practices at the University of California, San Diego, where he is the recipient of a Humanities Fellowship. As a scholar, his main research area is late twentieth-century experimental and improvised musics, particularly those emanating from African-American traditions. His publications include an article on Yusef Lateef in *Musicworks* magazine (Fall 1998). He holds a B.M. in performance with highest honors from the Eastman School of Music and a M.M. in jazz composition from the University of Massachusetts, Amherst. Dessen's own compositions are documented in his work with the Cosmologic quartet and with his own ensembles. A trombonist, he collaborates with a wide range of artists and has been featured on recordings by Yusef Lateef (*Fantasia for Flute*), Anthony Davis (*Tania*), Marcelo Radulovich, and Jason Robinson, among others.

DANIEL FISCHLIN is Professor in the School of English and Theatre Studies at the University of Guelph and past Director of the Joint Ph.D. Program in Literary Studies/Theatre Studies at Wilfrid Laurier University and the

University of Guelph. He has published extensively in various areas of cultural criticism and interdisciplinary studies, including recent books on Shakespearean adaptation, the Uruguayan writer Eduardo Galeano, and early modern monarchic writing. *The Other Side of Nowhere* is his third book on a music-related topic.

KRIN GABBARD is Professor of Comparative Literature at the State University of New York–Stony Brook. He is the author of *Jammin' at the Margins: Jazz and the American Cinema* (University of Chicago Press, 1996) and the editor of *Jazz Among the Discourses* and *Representing Jazz* (both Duke University Press, 1995). He has contributed essays to the *New Grove Dictionary of Jazz* (2d ed.) and to *The Cambridge Companion to Jazz*. His most recent project is a book tentatively titled *Magical Negritude: White Hollywood and African-American Culture.*

AJAY HEBLE is Professor in the School of English and Theatre Studies at the University of Guelph. He is the author of *Landing on the Wrong Note: Jazz, Dissonance, and Critical Practice* and *The Tumble of Reason: Alice Munro's Discourse of Absence,* and the coeditor of *New Contexts of Canadian Criticism.* He is Artistic Director and Founder of The Guelph Jazz Festival. He is also a pianist, and his first CD, a live concert recording of improvised music with percussionist Jesse Stewart, has been released on the IntrepidEar label.

MICHAEL JARRETT is the author of *Sound Tracks: A Musical ABC* (Temple University Press) and *Drifting on a Read* (State University of New York Press). He teaches at Penn State University, York Campus.

BENJAMIN LEFEBVRE is a Ph.D. candidate at McMaster University in Hamilton, Ontario. His most recent academic publications have appeared in *Canadian Children's Literature/Littérature canadienne pour la jeunesse, Essays on Canadian Writing, University of Toronto Quarterly,* and *Making Avonlea: L. M. Montgomery and Popular Culture* (University of Toronto Press).

GEORGE LEWIS is Professor of Music in the Critical Studies/Experimental Practices area at the University of California, San Diego. An improvisor-trombonist, composer, and computer/installation artist, and a member of the Association for the Advancement of Creative Musicians (AACM) since 1971, Lewis's work is documented on more than one hundred recordings. His articles on music and cultural studies have appeared in journals such as *Contemporary Music Review, Black Music Research Journal, Lenox Avenue* and *Leonardo Music Journal.* His book, *Power Stronger Than Itself: The As-*

sociation for the Advancement of Creative Musicians is forthcoming from the University of Chicago Press. Lewis is a recipient of a MacArthur Genius award.

NATHANIEL MACKEY is the author of five chapbooks of poetry, *Four for Trane* (Golemics, 1978), *Septet for the End of Time* (Boneset, 1983), *Outlantish* (Chax, 1992), *Song of the Andoumboulou: 18–20* (Moving Parts, 1994) and *Four for Glenn* (Chax Press, 2002), and three books of poetry, *Eroding Witness* (University of Illinois Press, 1985), *School of Udhra* (City Lights, 1993) and *Whatsaid Serif* (City Lights, 1998). *Strick: Song of the Andoumboulou 16–25,* a compact disc recording of poems read with musical accompaniment (Royal Hartigan, percussion; Hafez Modirzadeh, reeds and flutes), was released in 1995 by Spoken Engine Company. He is the author of an ongoing prose composition, *From a Broken Bottle Traces of Perfume Still Emanate,* of which three volumes have been published: *Bedouin Hornbook* (Callaloo Fiction Series, 1986; 2d ed.: Sun & Moon, 1997), *Djbot Baghostus's Run* (Sun & Moon, 1993) and *Atet A.D.* (City Lights, 2001). He is the editor of the literary magazine *Hambone* and coeditor (with Art Lange) of the anthology *Moment's Notice: Jazz in Poetry and Prose* (Coffee House Press, 1993). The author of a book of critical essays, *Discrepant Engagement: Dissonance, Cross-Culturality, and Experimental Writing* (Cambridge University Press, 1993; paper edition: University of Alabama Press, 2000), he is a professor in the Department of Literature at the University of California, Santa Cruz.

INGRID MONSON is the Quincy Jones Professor of African American Music at Harvard University. She is the author of *Saying Something: Jazz Improvisation and Interaction,* winner of the Sonneck Society's Irving Lowens award for the best book published on American music in 1996, and the editor of *The African Diaspora: A Musical Perspective.* She is currently working on *Freedom Sounds: Jazz, Civil Rights, and Africa, 1950–1967* (forthcoming). She has published articles in *Ethnomusicology, Critical Inquiry, World of Music, Journal of the American Musicological Society, Women and Music,* and the *Black Music Research Journal.* Her research interests include jazz, the African diaspora, and cultural theory. She is also a trumpet player.

MARK ANTHONY NEAL is an assistant professor of English at the State University of New York–Albany. He is the author of *What the Music Said: Black Popular Music and Black Public Culture* (Routledge, 1998) and *Soul Babies: Black Popular Culture and the Post-Soul Aesthetic* (Routledge, 2002).

PAULINE OLIVEROS's life as a composer, performer, and humanitarian is about opening her own and others' sensibilities to the many facets of sound. Since the 1960s she has influenced American music profoundly through her work in improvisation, meditation, electronic music, myth and ritual. Many credit her with being the founder of present-day meditative music as well as being the "founder of Deep Listening." All of Oliveros's work emphasizes musicianship, attention strategies, and improvisational skills.

During the 1960s John Rockwell named Oliveros's work *Bye Bye Butterfly* as one of the most significant of that decade. In the 1970s she represented the United States at the World's Fair in Osaka, Japan; during the 1980s she was honored with a retrospective at the John F. Kennedy Center for the Performing Arts in Washington, D.C., and the 1990s began with a letter of distinction from the American Music Center presented at Lincoln Center in New York. Oliveros's work is available on numerous recordings. Her books include *Software for People: Collected Writings 1963–1980* and *The Roots of the Moment: Collected Writings, 1980–1996*.

EDDIE PRÉVOST cofounded in 1965 the seminal improvising ensemble AMM, a group that has included formally and informally trained musicians including John Tilbury, Lou Gare, Cornelius Cardew, Keith Rowe, Christian Wolff, and Rohan de Saram. AMM has performed worldwide and has an extensive discography. Prévost has also worked and recorded with numerous free jazz and improvising musicians (for example, Evan Parker, Marilyn Crispell, Paul Rutherford), with a number of younger musicians (for example, Jim O'Rourke, Tom Chant and John Edwards, who, with Prévost, comprise the Eddie Prévost Trio) as well as with musicians from other cultures (most notably Yoshikazu Iwamoto). He has also performed in the technoambient field (GOD, Main, EAR) and plays the "open-ended" compositions of Cardew, Wolff, and Cage. During 1998 he made music for the Merce Cunningham Dance Company during their London season. His first solo CD *Loci of Change* was released by Matchless Recordings (MRCD32) in 1996. His book *No Sound is Innocent* was published by Copula in 1995 and a second book is in progress. Since November 1999 Prévost has convened a weekly open improvisation workshop (administered by the London Musicians' Collective). This has led to numerous ongoing performance collaborations with younger musicians. And the workshop approach, which is called "Procession," has also been used in a number of countries.

DANA REASON is a San Diego–based pianist, composer, and improvisor originally from Montreal, Canada. She has appeared at the San Francisco

Jazz Festival, Frau Musica (Nova) Cologne, Beyond the Pink (LA), the Guelph Jazz Festival, the Banff Arts Festival, the Knitting Factory (NY), the Music Gallery (Toronto), and the Sound Symposium in Newfoundland. Her performance credits include work with Pauline Oliveros, Paula Josa Jones's Dance Works, George Lewis, Malcolm Goldstein, Cecil Taylor, Joe McPhee, and Richard Teitlebaum, among others. Her critical writings on and reviews of music have appeared in *Twentieth Century Music, The Improvisor,* and *Musicworks.* She was the coorganizer and chair of the groundbreaking 1999 "Improvising Across Borders" Symposium held at the University of California, San Diego, where in 2002 she completed her Ph.D. in the Critical Studies/Experimental Practices Program in Music. Her doctoral research focused on women improvisors of the late twentieth century.

JULIE DAWN SMITH received her Ph.D. in interdisciplinary studies from the University of British Columbia in 2001. Her current project is *Diva-dogs: Sounding Women Improvising,* an exploration of gender, sound, and improvisation. Former executive director of the Jazz Institute of Chicago and coproducer of the "Women of the New Jazz" festivals in Chicago in the 1990s, she is currently assistant producer of the Vancouver International Jazz Festival. Julie makes experimental musical instruments from found objects and uses their sounds as the source material for composition and improvisation.

MICHAEL SNOW is a musician, visual artist, and filmmaker. He has performed as a soloist and with various ensembles in Canada, the United States, Europe, and Japan. He is one of the founding members of the Toronto-based free improvisation group CCMC. Many recordings of his music have been released including *3 Phases: Snow solo piano solo Snow,* a three-CD box set on OHM éditions and *aCCoMpliCes,* which assembles performances by CCMC (Michael Snow, John Oswald and Paul Dutton).
   His films have been presented at festivals in Australia, Canada, France, Germany, Great Britain, Italy, Japan, the Netherlands, and the United States, and are in the collections of several film archives, such as Anthology Film Archives in New York City, the Royal Belgian Film Archives, Brussels, and the Oesterreichesches Film Museum, Vienna. His classic film *New York Eye and Ear Control* is a landmark in experimental jazz cinema.
   As a visual artist, Snow is represented in private and public collections worldwide including the National Gallery of Canada, the Art Gallery of Ontario (Toronto), the Museum of Modern Art (New York), Museum Ludwig (Cologne and Vienna), Centre Georges Pompidou (Paris), and

both the Musée des Beaux-Arts and Musée d'art Contemporain in Montreal. Retrospectives of his painting, sculpture, photoworks, and holography have been presented at the Hara Museum (Tokyo), of his films at the Cinémathèque Française (Paris), Anthology Film Archives (New York), and L'Institut Lumière (Lyons). A major retrospective of his work in each of these media was presented at the Power Plant and the Art Gallery of Ontario in 1994. He has received numerous awards, including a Guggenheim Fellowship (1975), the first Governor General's Award in Visual and Media Art (Film) (2000), and the Order of Canada (1982).

MARSHALL SOULES is the coordinator of media studies at Malaspina University–College on Vancouver Island, and also teaches drama and writing in the English department there. His doctorate in performance studies from Rutgers University explores improvisational practices in drama, music, writing, and other arts. As a percussionist, he owes a great musical debt to his teacher Babatunde Olatunji, the Nigerian master drummer.

JASON STANYEK is Assistant Professor of Ethnomusicology at the University of Richmond. He received his Ph.D. in Critical Studies and Experimental Practices from the University of California, San Diego, where he pursued his studies under the guidance of George E. Lewis. His major areas of research are Brazilian music, intercultural music, improvisation, music and diaspora, and African-American popular music. He is active as a guitarist, composer, and *cavaquinho* player.

SHERRIE TUCKER is assistant professor of American studies at the University of Kansas, and the author of *Swing Shift: "All-Girl" Bands of the 1940s* (Duke University Press, 2000), winner of the 2001 Emily Toth Award of the Women's Caucus of the American Culture Association/Popular Culture Association.

Index

hip hop, 36n2, 211–12, 348; cultural position of, 207–210, 213–20. *See also* bebop; rap
Hirayama, Michiko, 59
Hirsch, Shelley, 151
history, 148–49, 251–54; recuperated, 2, 6–7, 9–10, 94, 261
Ho, Fred Wei-han, 294n1
Hobbs, Christopher, 157
Hoffman, E. T. A., 77
Holbrook, Joseph, 12
Holiday, Billie, 25, 325–26
Holzaepfel, John, 167
Holmes, John Clellon, 371
Homer, 314, 319
hooks, bell, 30, 116
hope, 2, 11, 25–29, 34
Horiuchi, Glenn, 152, 175
Horvitz, Wayne, 347–48
Hughes, Bill, 50
Hughes, Langston, 135
Humanities, 21–22, 25, 27
humanity, 13, 26
human rights, 22, 153
Hutchins, Edwin, 96
Hutchinson, Brenda, 68, 69
Hutton, Ina Ray, 254
hybridity, 100–101, 118, 163, 175

Ibarra, Susie, 54, 57, 59, 61–62, 64, 65, 175
Iborra, Diego, 122n27
Ibrahim, Abdullah, 89, 94, 112. *See also* Dollar Brand
Ibsen, Henrik, 287
Ice Cube, 210
ICP Orchestra (Instant Composer's Pool), 38n9
Ielmini, Davide, 8–9
Ile Omo Olofi, 109
Illumination (Impulse!), 376
imagination, 25
imperialism, 16, 363
improvisation, 1–2, 13–14, 16, 72, 362–63; and aesthetics, 3–4, 145, 388; and agency, 30–31, 34; and audience, 71, 73, 148, 289–90; channeling through, 58–59, 66; and character, 274, 278, 284–86; and collective, 24, 30, 34, 38n7, 46, 48; and commodification, 5, 31, 39n14; and community formation, 2–6, 10, 12–13, 17, 23–25, 32–33, 95–96, 105, 125n45, 184–85,

231, 240; and composition, 47, 48, 50–53, 64, 65, 131–32, 135–37, 149, 168, 319, 390; in context, 133, 134, 148, 156; as dialogue, 2, 27, 38n8, 57, 59, 89, 269–70; and discourse, 14–15, 18, 21, 139; and empathy, 6–7, 148; as epistemological other, 142–44, 147; excludes women, xii, 57, 62–63; and freedom, 2, 5–6, 26, 153–54, 229, 271, 272, 293, 359; and gender, 11–12, 233–34, 57, 246, 250, 255, 261; and genre mobility, 50, 165–67, 168; group, 6, 53, 75–76, 91, 105, 144, 158, 178; history of, 141–42, 149, 227, 261; and identity, 268–70, 271, 272–74, 278; impossibility of, 46, 145–46; and individuality, 23–24, 38n7, 59; and intercultural connection, 94–95, 104–105, 115–18, 152, 174–79, 185, 188; as language, 376–80; marginalization of, 18, 37n6; materials of, 12–13, 20; and memory, 11, 37n5; methods of, 34, 155, 237, 290; in the moment, 30, 63–66, 69–70, 354; origins of, 18, 20, 131–32; as performance, 11, 22, 29, 294n5; and present, 9, 48–49; protocols of, 269–71; repetition in, 34, 279, 355, 361; and resistance, 2, 4, 11, 15, 22, 37n5; and responsibility, 356, 358; and risk, 75–76, 208, 354–55, 361; and scholarship, xiv, 14, 15, 18–22, 25, 27, 35, 62, 132, 168, 321; social, 36n2, 196, 203, 207–10, 212, 217, 220; and social activism, 2, 20, 79, 87, 104, 134; social context of, 31, 276; and structure, 29, 31–32, 75, 82, 154–56, 178, 181–82, 275–77, 283–84, 292, 315, 319–20, 342, 391–93; technologies of, 53–54, 56, 58, 60, 69, 71–72, 81, 82, 190n19, 320–23; theories of, 77–78, 131–33, 146, 150–52, 274–76, 283, 291, 316n12, 319; therapeutic value of, 293, 379; training for, 38n10, 59–60, 65–67, 95, 153–55, 314; transformation in, 183, 249; as transgression, 8, 13, 38n7, 39n15, 276; vocal, 7, 36n3, 60, 63, 173, 181, 213; and voice, 278–79; and women, 55, 61, 225–26, 229, 237–39, 246–47, 257, 260, 262–63; and writing, 370; written music, 21, 38n9, 64–65, 76–77
Improvisation for the Theatre (Spolin), 291

Martin, Henry, 315
Martinez, Sabu, 109
Marx, E. B., 326
Masaoka, Miya, 152, 165, 175
Masked Men (Cohan), 310–11
Massumi, Brian, 389
Matory, J. Lorand, 90
Mattes, Al, 48
Mazon, Mauricio, 205
McCarthy, Bill, 214–15
McClary, Susan, 262, 394n2
McDuff, Jack, 332
McGregor, Chris, 152
MC Hammer, 214
McKibbon, Al, 110, 122n22
McLean, Jackie, 331
McPhee, Joe, 68, 394n8
Meintjes, Louise, 93, 112
Melodie und Rhythmus (OkkaDisk), 393
Meltzer, David, 305
memory, 6–10, 113, 148, 284–85, 321, 348
Memory of Fire (Galeano), 5
Memphis Bleek, 216
Mendes, Nelson, 100, 121n17
Mengelberg, Misha, 38n9, 75–76, 151, 153, 390
"Message from Kenya," 109
Metamorphosis (Nonesuch), 120n14
metaphysics, 2, 10, 12, 287, 322
Method acting, xiii, 278, 284, 301–302, 314
Method Man, 213
Metrics, 7
Micheaux, Oscar, 299
Michel, Ed, 337–38, 339, 341, 342–43
Miley, Bubber, 46
Mille Plateaux, 388
Miller, Glenn, 256
Miller, Leaf, 68
Mingus, Charles, 4, 32, 46, 47, 323, 333–34
Minh-ha, Trinh T., 246, 249, 263
Minton, Phil, 151
Mintz, Sidney W., 101–102
Misurell-Mitchell, Janice, 260–62
Mitchell, Roscoe, 80–81, 153, 344
Moment's Notice: Jazz in Poetry and Prose (Lange and Mackey), 370–71
Mondrian, Piet, 298
Monk, Thelonious, 47, 134, 332, 339, 369, 372

Monk's Music (Riverside), 332
Monson, Ingrid, 187; on community, 24, 119n2, 197; on improvisation, 35; on modal jazz, 269–70; on musicians, 78, 178, 214, 272; on race, 206, 248
Mora, Rafael, 122n27
Morello, Joe, 339
Moreno, J. L., 293
Mori, Ikue, 72, 151
Morris, Lawrence "Butch," 29, 39n12
Morton, Jelly Roll, 47, 175, 328
Moss, David, 151
Mozart, Wolfgang Amadeus, 45–46, 48
Mozart (Hildesdeimer), 45
Müller, Markus, 388
Müller, Torsten, 390
Mulligan, Gerry, 331
multiphonics, 28
Mumbo Jumbo (Reed), 370
Muñequitos de Matanzas, Los, 190n19
Murphy, Dudley, 308
Murray, Albert, 278–79
Murray, David, 89, 98, 112, 120n14, 124n39, 150, 175
Murray, Dierdre, 68
music, 11, 17, 47, 155, 228; aesthetics of, 111, 124n39; Afrological, 133, 151, 156, 168, 261; and civic life, 25–26, 355–57; concert, 18, 53, 67; and culture, 17, 21, 39n17, 115; electronic, 53–54, 56, 388; Eurological, 133, 138, 142–45, 147–49, 153–55, 157–58, 163, 167, 168, 261; experimental, 137, 140–41, 164–67, 170, 174, 388; industry, 36n1, 79, 92, 94, 214–20, 322–23, 363–65; inequities in, 62–63, 143–44; origins of, 20, 58; and politics, 12, 356; reading, 59, 61; revolutionary potential of, 9, 28, 34–35; and rhetoric, 17, 230; and rhythm, 183–85, 190n19; rock, 304, 346–47, 365; scholarship, 92, 152, 163–69, 174, 185, 190n20; value of, 354–55; and writing, 370–71, 383–84; written, 21, 38n9, 64–65, 76–77
Musica Electronic Viva, 12, 158
music, classical, 59–60, 363; and improvisation, xi–xii, 46, 64; performance of, 71, 74, 359
Music Improvisation Company, 12
musicking, 2, 26, 29, 35–36, 87

Sertso, Ingrid, 165
sexism, xii–xiv, 52, 251
Sex Pistols, 365
sexuality, xiii, 230, 234; interracial, 306–308; lesbian, xiii, 63, 231, 234–36
Shamsu-'d-Din, 386n2
Sharp, Elliott, 151
Shelemay, Kay, 93
Shepard, Sam, 286
Shepp, Archie, 25, 72, 89, 94, 112, 153, 369, 372
Shorter, Wayne, 100, 112, 121n16, 125n43
Siddall, Gillian, 251, 255
Sigel, Beanie, 215–16
Sign and the Seal, The (BMG), 124nn35, 41, 174, 182
Signifying Monkey, The (Gates), 279–80
Silence (Cage), 137
Silloway, Ward, 256
Silvestre, Rosangela, 124n41
Simon, Paul, 31, 39n14, 93, 95, 112–13
Sims, Zoot, 331
Slatern, Niall, 279
Slave Culture: Nationalist Theory and the Foundations of Black America (Sterling/Stuckey), 121n18
slavery, 5–6, 7, 38n7, 104–105, 113, 186; and community, 101–102, 121n18
Sloane, Hans, 103
Slobin, Mark, 93–94, 112
Sloboda, John, 145–46
Small, Christopher, 26, 87; on bebop, 202, 204; on improvisation, 18, 23–24, 29, 75–76, 197
Smith, Bessie, 305, 369
Smith, Julie, xiii
Smith, LaDonna, 66
Smith, Marvin "Smitty," 188n2
Smith, Wadada Leo, 37n6, 150, 165, 175
Snead, James, 227–28
Snoop Doggy Dog, 210, 212
Snow, Michael, xiv, 10, 47, 394n8
Snyder, John, 338–39, 341–42, 345
social capital, 214–16
Sokol, Casey, 48
Solomon, Larry, 147–48
Somers, Margaret R., 143
Sompa, Titos, 120n14
son, 37n5
Songs of the Unsung (Tapscott), 3
Sonic Language of Myth, The (BMG), 183

Sonic Meditations, 55
Son para el Che (SPLASC[H]), 8–9
Sony, 36n1
Soules, Marshall, xiv
Souls of Black Folk, The (Du Bois), 370
sound, 64, 114, 124n35, 156: experiments in, 46, 53; and gender, 259, 262; production of, 45, 158, 361; symbolic, 269
Southern, Eileen, 104
Space Between, The (Sparkling Beatnik), 56
Spector, Phil, 325
Spirit! The Power of Music (Universal/Verve), 112
spirituality, xii, 176, 178–79, 182–83, 189nn4, 10, 190n18; and improvisation, 196, 220n3; and transformation, 183, 188
Spitalny, Phil, 254, 257
Splendid Master Gnawa Musicians of Morocco, The (Verve), 33–34, 113
Spolin, Viola, 291
spontaneity, 139; culture of, 271; illusion of, 285, 287, 323; and improvisation, 31, 95, 145–48, 208; and performance, 276, 281, 315; and society, 22, 202, 236; and structure, 155, 289, 291, 338
Spontaneous Music Ensemble, 12
Springsteen, Bruce, 5
Staley, Jim, 151
Stanislavsky, Konstantin, 278, 284, 287, 289, 302
Stanyek, Jason, xii, 33
Stearns, Marshall, 122n26
Stevens, John, 232
Stewart, Rex, 46
Stockhausen, Karlheinz, 136, 138, 155, 170, 360
Stomping the Blues (Murray), 278–79
Stone, Fred, 58
Stowe, David, 320
Straw, Will, 301
Street, Craig, 323–24, 336, 345, 347
Streetcar Named Desire, A (film; Kazan), 298, 300, 303–304, 310–11, 313, 315, 316n10
Strindberg, August, 285–87
Stuckey, Sterling, 121n18, 122n23
Subcultural Sounds: Micromusics of the West (Slobin), 93–94
Subotnik, Morton, 53, 157–58

MUSIC/CULTURE
A series from Wesleyan University Press
Edited by George Lipsitz, Susan McClary, and Robert Walser